JOURNAL FOR THE STUDY OF THE OLD TESTAMENT
SUPPLEMENT SERIES
184

Editors
David J.A. Clines
Philip R. Davies

Executive Editor
John Jarick

Editorial Board
Richard J. Coggins, Alan Cooper, Tamara C. Eskenazi,
J. Cheryl Exum, John Goldingay, Robert P. Gordon,
Norman K. Gottwald, Andrew D.H. Mayes, Carol Meyers,
Patrick D. Miller

Sheffield Academic Press

Pursuing the Text

**Studies in Honor of Ben Zion Wacholder
on the Occasion of his Seventieth Birthday**

edited by
John C. Reeves
& John Kampen

Journal for the Study of the Old Testament
Supplement Series 184

BS
1186
.P87
1994

Copyright © 1994 Sheffield Academic Press

Published by
Sheffield Academic Press Ltd
Mansion House
19 Kingfield Road
Sheffield, S11 9AS
England

Typeset by Sheffield Academic Press
and
Printed on acid-free paper in Great Britain
by Bookcraft
Midsomer Norton, Somerset

British Library Cataloguing in Publication Data

A catalogue record for this book is available
from the British Library

ISBN 1-85075-501-9

CONTENTS

Preface   9
Abbreviations   12

ALAN COOPER
Creation, Philosophy and Spirituality: Aspects of Jewish
Interpretation of Psalm 19   15

DAVID B. WEISBERG
'Break in the Middle of a Verse': Some Observations on a
Massoretic Feature   34

JAMES C. VANDERKAM
Putting Them in their Place: Geography as an Evaluative Tool   46

PHILIP R. DAVIES
The 'Damascus' Sect and Judaism   70

JOHN KAMPEN
The Eschatological Temple(s) of 11QT   85

MICHAEL O. WISE
Second Thoughts on דוק and the Qumran Synchronistic Calendars   98

GEORGE J. BROOKE
The Deuteronomic Character of 4Q252   121

MARTIN G. ABEGG, JR
4Q471: A Case of Mistaken Identity?   136

NIKOLAUS WALTER
Kann man als Jude auch Grieche sein? Erwägungen
zur jüdisch-hellenistischen Pseudepigraphie   148

DANIEL J. HARRINGTON
Sirach Research since 1965: Progress and Questions   164

LOUIS H. FELDMAN
Josephus's Portrait of Ehud   177

JAMES E. BOWLEY
Josephus's Use of Greek Sources for Biblical History   202

ADAM KAMESAR
Philo, *Grammatikē*, and the Narrative Aggada   216

GETZEL M. COHEN
The 'Antiochenes in Jerusalem'. Again   243

JOHN C. REEVES
An Enochic Citation in *Barnabas* 4.3 and the *Oracles of Hystaspes*   260

SHAYE J.D. COHEN
Is 'Proselyte Baptism' Mentioned in the Mishnah?
The Interpretation of *m. Pesahim* 8.8 (= *m. Eduyot* 5.2)   278

ROBERT GOLDENBERG
Did the Amoraim See Christianity as Something New?   293

JACOB NEUSNER
What 'the Rabbis' Thought: A Method and a Result.
One Statement on Prophecy in Rabbinic Judaism   303

WILLIAM ADLER
Ad Verbum or *Ad Sensum*: The Christianization of a Latin
Translation Formula in the Fourth Century   321

STEVEN BOWMAN
Dates in *Sepher Yosippon*   349

MARK WASHOFSKY
Responsa and Rhetoric: On Law, Literature and the
Rabbinic Decision   360

IDA COHEN SELAVAN AND LAUREL S. WOLFSON
Bibliography of Works by Ben Zion Wacholder   410

Index of References   413
Index of Authors   428

PREFACE

...והעמידו תלמידים הרבה
('*Abot* 1.1)

The fulfillment of this rabbinic injunction has been a dominant characteristic of the life and career of Ben Zion Wacholder. That circle of disciples has included rabbinic students preparing for ordination, doctoral students preparing for careers in academia or religious leadership, faculty colleagues who are persuaded by the logic of his arguments, and those numerous professional scholars of Jewish life and thought in late antiquity who study his published works and consider his oral observations as he engages in vigorous discussion at academic conferences. While they do not necessarily share all (or even most) of his conclusions, the number of תלמידים indebted to Ben Zion Wacholder for new insights on or valuable criticism of their work are legion. The sheer number and range of the contributions to this volume attest, in a small way, to the breadth of his influence.

The diminutive figure of Ben Zion Wacholder is a familiar one at academic gatherings such as the annual meeting of the Society of Biblical Literature. In those settings he is renowned for his phenomenal memory and his strong opinions. It is not uncommon in certain sections for a question to arise concerning the precise wording of an obscure text. Most of us have witnessed those occasions when all heads turned admiringly toward Ben Zion as he flawlessly recited the text in question. His early training in the *yeshivas* of Poland gave him a deep appreciation of the importance of the text and his natural brilliance permitted him to remember it. His subsequent education in English literature at Yeshiva University and in Greek historiography at the University of California at Los Angeles completed the process of formal matriculation, and inaugurated a scholarly career that has consistently distinguished him from his peers in the extent of his interests and competencies.

Ben Zion Wacholder has never simply accepted the status quo concerning any question which came within the purview of his interest.

Whether the problem originated from Greek historical literature, the rabbinic corpus, the Qumran fragments, or elsewhere, the scholarly community could expect that Ben Zion would produce an original assessment of the relevant texts which could result in unanticipated conclusions. His restless, probing mind would analyze the various opinions until he reached a conclusion that he felt was firmly rooted in the texts and not necessarily derivative of the reigning scholarly consensus on the problem. 'These are what are important', he frequently urges his students, 'the primary texts. Make sure that you control the textual sources and ponder well what they have to say *before* you consult the modern pundits.' Ben Zion, as one might imagine, has little patience for second-hand scholarship or for those who unreflectively continue to parrot the popular slogans of the hour.

Hence Ben Zion Wacholder is sometimes viewed as a controversial figure. Characteristic of all Ben Zion's work is a refusal to settle for the mundane or the mediocre. For those of us who were (or are) his students it is this trait which is the most enduring. Since some of us had the privilege of assisting him in his research while pursuing our own studies, we joined him in his daily struggle with the texts and whatever hypotheses he was developing at the time. All of us remember occasions when the results of his most recent research contradicted his own earlier conclusions. 'So I was wrong!' was a frequent response to queries about his own earlier judgments. This willingness to be self-critical demonstrates the manner in which he approaches each new text and question with an openness of inquiry seldom found in our field of endeavor. Such a process demands the utmost dedication and commitment from the researcher, as well as a healthy dose of humility. Anyone who has ever encountered Ben Zion Wacholder knows that he has made that responsibility the center of his life.

The present volume of essays reflects the breadth and depth of his interests as well as his impact on every area of inquiry into which he has ventured. His drive for precision naturally attracted him to questions involving chronology and chronography, where his facility with Greek, Hebrew and Aramaic texts permits him to examine and resolve chronological issues from perspectives available to only a few. This chronographic focus naturally led him to the comparative study of early universal histories in conjunction with their biblical, Graeco-Jewish and rabbinic analogues, thereby rekindling almost single-handedly scholarly interest in the so-called 'minor' Jewish Hellenistic authors (Demetrius,

Eupolemus *et al.*). Questions regarding the history of exegesis prompted his repeated forays into the study of the Dead Sea Scrolls, Second Temple era pseudepigrapha and the early rabbinic literature. An abiding interest in the varieties of Jewish messianism and forms of Jewish mysticism probably derives from his early encounters with Hasidic masters in his native Poland.

When Ben Zion in 1977 turned his attention to the newly published Qumran Temple Scroll, he followed the pattern established in his earlier research—he questioned the prevailing assumptions and proposed an alternative hypothesis. While all of his conclusions in *The Dawn of Qumran* and a subsequent series of complementary articles were not accepted by the majority of the scholarly guild, he had nevertheless raised important questions concerning the origin, development and historical significance of the Qumran literature, questions which have taken on an added relevance in recent years. Similarly, his controversial involvement in the preliminary publication of previously unavailable Qumran texts is simply one more illustration of a lifetime of scholarship dedicated to accepting neither the status quo nor easy solutions to difficult problems.

As Ben Zion approaches his seventieth birthday (with we might add no discernible sign of abatement), we wish to express publicly our admiration for and appreciation of his many significant scholarly achievements. We would moreover like to voice our gratitude for his invaluable guidance and insightful tutelage in the pursuit of our individual professional projects. The present work, a volume consisting of studies contributed by his students, faculty associates and professional colleagues, is a small but at least tangible token of our esteem. To Ben Zion Wacholder—our teacher, our model and our friend—we respectfully dedicate this volume.

John Kampen
John C. Reeves

ABBREVIATIONS

AB	Anchor Bible
ABD	D.N. Freedman (ed.), *Anchor Bible Dictionary*
AbrN	*Abr-Nahrain*
ABRL	Anchor Bible Reference Library
AcSal	Acta salmanticensia
AGJU	Arbeiten zur Geschichte des antiken Judentums und des Urchristentums
AJS Review	*Association for Jewish Studies Review*
ALGHJ	Arbeiten zur Literatur und Geschichte des hellenistischen Judentums
AnBib	Analecta biblica
ANRW	*Aufstieg und Niedergang der römischen Welt*
ASNSP.L	*Annali della Scuola Normale Superiore di Pisa: Lettere, storia e filosofia*
BA	*Biblical Archaeologist*
BBB	Bonner biblische Beiträge
BDB	F. Brown, S.R. Driver and C.A. Briggs, *Hebrew and English Lexicon of the Old Testament*
BHS	*Biblia hebraica stuttgartensia*
BibOr	Biblica et orientalia
BJS	Brown Judaic Studies
BSOAS	*Bulletin of the School of Oriental and African Studies*
BZAW	Beihefte zur ZAW
CAD	*The Assyrian Dictionary of the Oriental Institute of the University of Chicago*
CBQ	*Catholic Biblical Quarterly*
CBQMS	*Catholic Biblical Quarterly* Monograph Series
CCL	Corpus Christianorum, Series Latina
Cl.Q	*Classical Quarterly*
CQ	*Church Quarterly*
CRINT	Compendia rerum iudaicarum ad novum testamentum
CSCO	Corpus scriptorum christianorum orientalium
CSEL	Corpus scriptorum ecclesiasticorum latinorum
DJD	Discoveries in the Judaean Desert
EJ(D)	*Encyclopedia Judaica* (Berlin, 1928-34)
EncJud	*Encyclopaedia Judaica*
EPhM	Études de philosophie médiévale
EvT	*Evangelische Theologie*

FGrH	F. Jacoby, *Die Fragmente der griechischen Historiker* (Leiden, 1954-64)
GCS	Griechische christliche Schriftsteller
GKC	*Gesenius' Hebrew Grammar*, ed. E. Kautzsch, trans. A.E. Cowley
GRBS	*Greek, Roman, and Byzantine Studies*
HNT	Handbuch zum Neuen Testament
HR	*History of Religions*
HSM	Harvard Semitic Monographs
HTR	*Harvard Theological Review*
HUCA	*Hebrew Union College Annual*
ICC	International Critical Commentary
IDB	G.A. Buttrick (ed.), *Interpreter's Dictionary of the Bible*
IDBSup	*IDB*, Supplementary Volume
IEJ	*Israel Exploration Journal*
JAOS	*Journal of the American Oriental Society*
JBL	*Journal of Biblical Literature*
JJS	*Journal of Jewish Studies*
JQR	*Jewish Quarterly Review*
JRS	*Journal of Roman Studies*
JSHRZ	Jüdische Schriften aus hellenistisch-römischer Zeit
JSJ	*Journal for the Study of Judaism in the Persian, Hellenistic and Roman Period*
JSOTSup	*Journal for the Study of the Old Testament* Supplement Series
JSPSup	*Journal for the Study of the Pseudepigrapha*, Supplement Series
JTS	*Journal of Theological Studies*
KB	L. Koehler and W. Baumgartner (eds.), *Lexicon in Veteris Testamenti libros*
LCL	Loeb Classical Library
MGWJ	*Monatsschrift für Geschichte und Wissenschaft des Judentums*
MHUC	Monographs of the Hebrew Union College
MSL	Materialen zum sumerischen Lexikon
NHC	Nag Hammadi Codex
NovTSup	*Novum Testamentum* Supplements
OBO	Orbis biblicus et orientalis
OGIS	*Orientis Graeci Inscriptiones Selectae*
OTL	Old Testament Library
OTS	*Oudtestamentische Studiën*
PAAJR	*Proceedings of the American Academy of Jewish Research*
PCPS	*Proceedings of the Cambridge Philological Society*
PEQ	*Palestine Exploration Quarterly*
PG	J. Migne (ed.), *Patrologia graeca*
PhAnt	*Philosophia antiqua*
Ph.S.	Philologus. Supplementband
PL	J. Migne (ed.), *Patrologia latina*
PW	Pauly-Wissowa, *Realencyclopadie der classischen Altertumswissenschaft* (Stuttgart, 1894-1980)
RA	*Revue d'assyriologie et d'archéologie orientale*

RAC	*Reallexikon für Antike und Christentum*
RB	*Revue biblique*
RE	*Realencyklopädie für protestantische Theologie und Kirche*
REB	Revised English Bible
REJ	*Revue des études juives*
RevQ	*Revue de Qumran*
RHR	*Revue de l'histoire des religions*
SAPh	Studien zur antiken Philosophie
SBA	Schweizerische Beiträge zur Altertumswissenschaft
SBAW.PPH	*Sitzungsberichte der bayerischen Akademie der Wissenschaften: Philosophisch-philologische und historische Klasse*
SBLDS	SBL Dissertation Series
SBLMS	SBL Monograph Series
SBLPS	Society of Biblical Literature: Texts and Translations: Pseudepigrapha Series
SBLSCS	SBL Septuagint and Cognate Studies
SBLSP	SBL Seminar Papers
SCO	*Studi classici e orientali*
Sem	*Semitica*
SPAW	Sitzungsberichte der preussischen Akademie der Wissenschaften
StPhilo	*Studia Philonica*
TAPA	*Transactions of the American Philological Association*
Theoph	Theophaneia
TLZ	*Theologischer Literaturzeitung*
TSAJ	Texte und Studien zum antiken Judentum
TU	Texte und Untersuchungen
VC	*Vigiliae christianae*
VT	*Vetus Testamentum*
VTSup	*Vetus Testamentum*, Supplements
WBC	Word Biblical Commentary
WUNT	Wissenschaftliche Untersuchungen zum Neuen Testament
ZAW	*Zeitschrift für die alttestamentliche Wissenschaft*
ZDMG	*Zeitschrift der deutschen morganländischen Gesellschaft*
ZDPV	*Zeitschrift des deutschen Palästina-Vereins*

CREATION, PHILOSOPHY AND SPIRITUALITY:
ASPECTS OF JEWISH INTERPRETATION OF PSALM 19*

Alan Cooper

Why does the Bible begin with the creation of the world? We must
leave aside as unproductive the most obvious answers, namely that the
intent is either historiographical or scientific. In other words, there is no
good reason to think that the biblical author was interested in composing
a universal history (it is clearly a national history); nor can it have been
the primary concern to elucidate how the world was created (the
account is too incomplete and inconsistent). The answer to our question,
then, must be based not on the story's surface, but on meanings and
values that are encoded and implicit within it, and on its intertextual
relatedness to other accounts of and allusions to creation that pervade
biblical literature, especially its poetic portions.[1]

* This paper was commissioned for a 'Symposium on Creation' held at
McMaster University in Hamilton, Ontario on March 20-21, 1993. Excellent critical
responses were presented on that occasion by David Reimer and Ron Sweet. A
number of other friends and colleagues offered useful comments on various drafts.
Special thanks are due to James Ackerman, Daniel Frank, Herbert Marks, Hava
Tirosh-Rothschild, and Raymond Van Leeuwen. I have retained the somewhat popular tone of the original lecture, on the assumption that many readers of this volume
will not be acquainted with medieval Jewish biblical exegesis. It is a great pleasure to
honor my colleague and friend Ben Zion Wacholder with this article, despite the fact
that, as far as I know, Psalm 19 appears nowhere in the Qumran corpus.
    1.   For some recent studies of the significance of creation in biblical and post-
biblical thought, see the following: B.W. Anderson, *Creation versus Chaos*
(Philadelphia: Fortress Press, 2nd edn, 1987 [1967]); *idem* (ed.), *Creation in the Old
Testament* (Philadelphia: Fortress Press, 1984); B.S. Childs, *Biblical Theology of the
Old and New Testaments* (Minneapolis: Fortress Press, 1993), pp. 107-18;
R.J. Clifford and J.J. Collins (eds.), *Creation in the Biblical Traditions* (CBQMS,
24; Washington: Catholic Biblical Association, 1992); J.D. Levenson, *Creation and
the Persistence of Evil: The Jewish Drama of Divine Omnipotence* (San Francisco:
Harper & Row, 1988); L. Mazor (ed.), *The Creation in Science Myth and Religion*

A form of our question appears as early as the midrash *Genesis Rabba*: 'What is the sense of God's revealing to Israel what was created on the first day, and on the second and third?'[2] That rabbinic question is taken up by Rashi (Troyes, 1040–1105), the most popular of the medieval Jewish commentators.[3] The Bible, he reasons (following another version of the midrash),[4] might just as well have begun with Exod. 12.2—'This month shall mark for you the beginning of the months'—since that verse contains the first law that is addressed to the Jewish people as a collective, and it is self-evident that the giving of the Law is the Bible's primary purpose. So, then, 'what is the sense of beginning with "in the beginning"?' Because, as Ps. 111.6 puts it, '[God] recounted his mighty deeds to his people, in giving them the possession of the nations'.

The Israelite conquest of Canaan—occupied at the time by seven nations—cannot be deemed an illegitimate or criminal act. Rather, Israel asserts (in Rashi's words) that 'the whole earth belongs to the Holy One, blessed be he; he created it and he gives it to anyone he sees fit to give it to. By his will, he gave it to [the prior inhabitants], and by his will he has taken it from them and given it to us.'

By this exegetical masterstroke,[5] the creation story is conjoined to the

[Hebrew] (Jerusalem: Magnes, 1990); S. Niditch, *Chaos to Cosmos: Studies in Biblical Patterns of Creation* (Chico, CA; Scholars Press, 1985); D. Novak and N. Samuelson (eds.), *Creation and the End of Days: Judaism and Scientific Cosmology* (Lanham, MD: University Press of America, 1986).

2.   *Genesis Rabba* 1.2 (ed. J. Theodor and C. Albeck; 3 vols.; Jerusalem: Wahrmann, 2nd edn, 1965), I, pp. 4-5. All translations in this paper are my own unless otherwise indicated.

3.   *Peirushei Rashi al ha-torah* (ed. C. Chavel; Jerusalem: Mossad Harav Kook, 1982), pp. 1-2.

4.   Cf. *Midrash Tanḥuma* on Genesis (ed. S. Buber; Vilna: Romm, 1885), p. 4a.

5.   Namely, the homiletical deconstruction of Ps. 111.6. Rashi knows that the 'mighty deeds' of the first colon refer to the dispossession of the nations, not to the creation of the world. In his commentary on the psalm (in any Rabbinic Bible), he first gives the plain meaning of the verse, and only then cites the *Tanḥuma* passage that he applies to the interpretation of Gen. 1.1. The treatment of Ps. 111.6 *in situ* provides a good example of Rashi's standard operating procedure: first he gives the plain grammatical sense of the text, and then he uses the midrash to uncover a deeper level of meaning. The homily, although non-literal, is not inconsistent with the language of the text. For a detailed explanation of the method, see S. Kamin, *Rashi's Exegetical Categorization in Respect to the Distinction between Peshat and Derash* [Hebrew] (Jerusalem: Magnes, 1986).

national history as its fitting and proper introduction. The fact that Israel's god created the world gives him the right of eminent domain; as its ultimate owner, he can assign any portion of it to anyone he chooses. As simple and attractive as that solution might appear, however, it is also irritating, even bordering on triviality. Can the creation story really be nothing more than an apology for the divine prerogative of dispossession?

Annoyance with that sort of reading finds expression in the commentary of Ramban (Naḥmanides), the best-known Jewish exegete of the thirteenth century (Gerona, 1194–1274). Ramban begins his lengthy exposition of Gen. 1.1 by quoting Rashi, and then continuing in a critical vein:

> This has to be questioned. It is of the greatest necessity that the Torah [in the narrow sense of the Pentateuch] begin with 'In the beginning God created,' for it is the very root of the Jewish religion. One who does not believe in this, thinking that the world is eternal, is a heretic, utterly devoid of Torah [in the broader sense of the Jewish tradition]. The correct answer [to the question 'what is the sense of beginning with "In the beginning"?'] is that because the act of creation is a profound mystery, it cannot be comprehended from Scripture alone. It can only be understood properly by means of the [Oral] Tradition [*qabbalah*] vouchsafed by God to Moses. And those who understand it [that is, the 'profound mystery'] are obliged to conceal it.[6]

Rashi, according to Ramban, has misconstrued the rabbinic question. 'What is the sense of beginning with "In the beginning"?' does not raise the issue of how the creation story can be read exoterically in relation to the Israelite *Heilsgeschichte*. It is, rather, a more fundamental question, pertaining to the incomprehensibility of the story on its face: 'what does it *really* mean', or, 'what is its true, inner, esoteric meaning?' In raising this latter question, Ramban sets forth a bewildering paradox: creation is foundational for the Jewish faith, yet it is (and needs to be!) incomprehensible to all except for those few individuals who are in possession of the esoteric cipher required for decoding the biblical story.

Now the rabbinic question takes on an entirely new aspect. For if the 'profound mystery' of creation can be comprehended only by those who know the abstruse, orally-transmitted *qabbalah*, there seems to be little point in the rest of us having the Bible's creation story. So again, why begin the Bible with it, instead of starting right in with the recitation

---

6. *Peirushei ha-torah le-rabbeinu Moshe ben Naḥman (Ramban)* (ed. C. Chavel; 2 vols.; Jerusalem: Mossad Harav Kook, 1959/60), I, p. 9.

of the Law, which is clearly intended for everyone's benefit?

To see what is at stake, we turn to the late thirteenth-century Spanish commentator Baḥya ben Asher, who was strongly influenced by Ramban. In the introduction to his Torah commentary, Baḥya writes:

> The sense [of the rabbinic question] is that since the commandments are the root of the Torah, it would have been appropriate for the opening words of the Torah to be none other than a commandment. And why do we need the story of the creation of the world, the whole matter of which might have been transmitted by means of the *qabbalah* and not written in the Torah at all?[7]

Baḥya's answer comes from the aforementioned verse from Psalm 111, 'he recounted his mighty deeds to his people'. But that midrashic proof-text, from which he conspicuously omits the second half-verse, is all that he shares with Rashi:

> God did not wish that this great matter be transmitted solely by means of the *qabbalah*, but that the [written] Torah attest to it as well. For from the starting point of faith in the creation of the world, a person can attain knowledge of God on the basis of his ways and his deeds. And that is, indeed, the most that an individual can attain, since knowledge of God's essence and being is unattainable, hidden even from the angels.[8]

The significance of creation, in this view, abides not in any relatedness to the biblical story, but in the striving of the individual believer towards the ultimate felicity, namely knowledge of God. As Maimonides puts it in the conclusion to his *Guide of the Perplexed*, 'It is clear that the perfection of man that may truly be gloried in is the one acquired by him who has achieved, in a measure corresponding to his capacity, apprehension of Him, may He be exalted...'[9] Baḥya continues:

---

7.   *Rabbeinu Baḥya: Bei'ur al ha-torah* (ed. C. Chavel; 3 vols.; Jerusalem: Mossad Harav Kook, 1966), I, p. 12.

8.   *Bei'ur al ha-torah*, I, p. 12.

9.   Maimonides, *Guide of the Perplexed*, 3.54 (ed. Y. Qafiḥ; 3 vols.; Jerusalem: Mossad Harav Kook, 1972), III, p. 695 (cited according to the translation of S. Pines [Chicago: University of Chicago, 1963], p. 638). In his *Mishneh Torah*, Maimonides asserts, 'One loves God only through knowledge of Him. The love is in proportion to the knowledge, be it little or great. Therefore a person must strive to attain knowledge by means of those disciplines that provide knowledge of the Creator, in accordance with that person's capacity to comprehend' (*Hilkhot Teshuvah* [Laws of Repentance], 10.6). On the mystical reinterpretation of such philosophical notions concerning the knowledge and love of God, see M. Idel, *Kabbalah: New Perspectives* (New Haven: Yale University Press, 1988), pp. 35-58.

Just as a person is obliged and commanded to refrain from delving into the unattainable [that is, God's essence], so is it a commandment and an obligation to seek out and delve into that which is knowable, for by this does a servant find favor with the master [cf. 1 Samuel 20.4]. We know him on the basis of his actions, and therefore the divine wisdom made it obligatory that the Torah begin with the creation of the world, in order to recount to his people his mighty deeds...All of the great principles [of Judaism] follow logically from belief in creation, and the entire Torah is founded and built upon them, each one leading inevitably to the next: creation necessitates providence, and providence necessitates both retributive justice and prophecy; out of prophecy arises the Torah, which is why it is absolutely essential for the Torah to begin with the creation of the world.[10]

Baḥya's wonderfully circular formulation, while dependent on Ramban's, is also profoundly different from it. For Ramban, the significance of creation appears to abide in its esoteric dimension, which one may not expound at length in writing. For Baḥya however, the esoteric and the exoteric appear to co-exist in parallel planes, rendering knowledge of God—albeit limited—accessible even to those who are uninitiated in the mysteries of *qabbalah*.[11]

Any reader can observe that the stories at the beginning of Genesis document God's creation of the world, his providential care and concern for the first humans, his revealing his will to them, and his punishing them for their defection. Baḥya's insight into the basic significance of those stories is echoed in the words of a modern biblical theologian: 'creation was the starting point, because everything human beings can think and say about God and his relation to the world and humankind depends on the fact that he created all this'.[12]

Even a simpleton, then, can learn the essential tenets of the Jewish faith from the surface of the creation story. For the initiate, however, speculation about the secrets of creation—whether of the mystical or philosophical variety—is not only a possibility; it is a positive obligation.[13]

---

10. *Bei'ur al ha-torah*, I, p. 13.

11. See E.R. Wolfson, 'By Way of Truth: Aspects of Naḥmanides' Kabbalistic Hermeneutic', *AJS Review* 14 (1989), pp. 103-78, esp. 130-31.

12. R. Rendtorff, 'Some Reflections on Creation as a Topic of Old Testament Theology,' in Eugene Ulrich, *et al.* (eds.), *Priests, Prophets and Scribes* [Joseph Blenkinsopp Festschrift] (JSOTSup, 149; Sheffield; JSOT Press, 1992), pp. 204-12 (quote on 207).

13. See H.A. Davidson, 'The Study of Philosophy as a Religious Obligation,' in

One well-known admonition to this effect comes from the late eleventh-century Spanish philosopher Baḥya Ibn Paquda:

> As for the nature of contemplation [of creation], it is discerning the traces of God's wisdom within creation, and evaluating them in accordance with the observer's powers of discrimination. Although this wisdom is manifest in diverse ways among created things, it is all the same in source and origin...Contemplation of creation in order to learn God's wisdom from it is incumbent upon us on the grounds of reason, Scripture, and tradition... For the Creator arranged the world wisely, with proper order and clear divisions, in order that it might hint at and teach us concerning him—just as an artifact is to its artisan, or a house to the builder who built it.[14]

But what is the precise nature of that divine wisdom encoded in creation? And how may its traces be apprehended using the complementary tools of observation and interpretation? The answers to those questions, obviously, depend to a considerable extent on the predilections of the commentator. A good starting point, perhaps, is the remark with which Baḥya ben Asher begins the introduction to his Torah commentary: 'Know that our holy Torah is bound up with the divine wisdom, and that all wisdom is [alternatively: all of the sciences are] contained within it'.[15] This view may be related to Maimonides' opinion that the Torah provides all the means required for the attainment of ethical and intellectual perfection,[16] but Baḥya goes beyond Maimonides in his assertion of the Torah's radical self-sufficiency.

Baḥya's prooftext is Ps. 19.8, *torat adonai temimah*, 'The Torah of the Lord is perfect'—perfect in the particular sense of its requiring no supplementation (in Ramban's words apropos of Ps. 19.8,[17] 'it has neither deficiency nor superfluity'). And this prooftext naturally draws our attention to its source, one of the most remarkable literary compositions in the Bible, in itself a profound reflection on the relationship between creation and Torah. The relevant portions of the psalm may be translated as follows:

S.D. Goitein (ed.), *Religion in a Religious Age* (Cambridge, MA: Association for Jewish Studies, 1974), pp. 53-68.

14. Baḥya Ibn Paquda, *Sefer torat ḥovot ha-levavot*, 2.1-3 (ed. Y. Qafiḥ; Jerusalem, 1973), pp. 98-101.

15. *Bei'ur al ha-torah*, I, p. 8.

16. *Guide*, 3.27 (ed. Qafiḥ, 3.556-58; trans. Pines, pp. 510-12).

17. *Peirushei ha-torah*, II, p. 23 (on Lev. 4.25).

2. The heavens proclaim the glory of God,
   the sky expresses his handiwork.
3. Day to day utters speech,
   and night to night declares knowledge.
4. There is no speech,
   there are no words,
   their voice is unheard.
5. Throughout the earth their voice(?)[18] goes forth,
   to the end of the world their words.
   He placed in them a tent for the sun,
6. who is like a groom coming out from under his
   wedding canopy,
   like a hero joyfully running his course.
7. His rising-place is at one end of the heavens,
   and his circuit reaches the other end,
   nothing escaping his heat.
8. The Torah of the Lord is perfect,
   restoring the life-spirit.
   The decrees of the Lord are sure,
   making the simple wise.

---

18. The Hebrew form *qawwam* is difficult. The normal meaning of *qaw* is 'string' or 'measuring line'. Some modern scholars consider that sense of *qaw* to be appropriate here—referring, for example, to the linear 'course' that the heavenly bodies follow, or perhaps to their 'range' or area of influence. Others either emend *qawwam* to *qolam*, which means 'sound' or 'voice,' or else they find philological justification for understanding *qaw* in that sense without emendation. For a convenient summary, see L. Koehler and W. Baumgartner (eds.), *Hebräisches und Aramäisches Lexikon zum Alten Testament* (Leiden: Brill, 3rd edn, 1967–90), p. 1011.

Among medieval Jewish commentators, the most common interpretation relates the *qaw* to a builder's measuring line or plumb-line (e.g., Jonah Ibn Janaḥ, *Sefer ha-shorashim* [ed. W. Bacher; Berlin: Mekize Nirdamim, 1896], p. 443). By exhibiting traces of the creator's handiwork in the manner of its construction, the universe attests to the existence of the creator. Thus, for example, the commentary of Joseph Bekhor Shor (France, 12th century) on Ps. 19.5, self-consciously elaborating the above-cited analogy of Baḥya Ibn Paquda:

> Anyone observing [the heavens] can discern the creative activity of our God. Just as a person entering a house that has been built with wisdom and knowledge—lacking nothing and free of defect—can discern that it was built by a wise and knowing builder, although the architect is not actually visible and the house does not speak, in like manner a person observing the perfection of the heavens must know that they were created by a great, wise, and knowing creator, incomparable in wisdom.

See M. Idel, 'Peirush mizmor 19 le-R. Yosef Bekhor Shor', *Alei Sefer* 9 (1981), pp. 63-69 (quote on p. 66).

9. The precepts of the Lord are just,
    rejoicing the heart.
  The commandment of the Lord is lucid,
    making the eyes light up,
10. The fear of the Lord is pure,
    abiding forever.
  The judgments of the Lord are true,
    altogether righteous.

Since the purpose of this paper is to discuss traditional commentary on Psalm 19, I do not wish to devote much attention to modern critical scholarship on the psalm. It is important to note, however, that there has been considerable debate over its literary unity. Verses 2-7 and 8-10 are often said to belong to two originally distinct psalms, dubbed Psalms 19A and 19B respectively. The following remarks by Hans-Joachim Kraus are representative:

> It has been recognized for a long time already that Psalm 19 is composed of two psalms. Section A deals with hymnic praise of Yahweh in nature, Section B with the glory of the Torah...Tradition has welded the two together. For that reason we have the obligation in connection with an interpretation of the two parts to inquire into the reason for the combination and for its meaning.[19]

The need for such inquiry was naturally self-evident to the traditional commentators, who were just as aware as modern critical scholars of the psalm's apparent bifurcation.

Clearly the psalm juxtaposes two alternative witnesses to God's presence in the world, linking the testimony of the heavens to the precepts of Torah. But what, exactly, do these two entail? What is one supposed to learn from the soundless words of the passage of time (vv. 2-5)? And how are those 'words,' so to speak, related to the teachings of Torah (vv. 8-10)? Are they analogically linked—a single revelation encoded and represented in two distinctive ways? Or, rather, are the two teachings, while complementary up to a point, ultimately intended to be contrasted with one another?

Kraus opts for a contrastive reading. Since creation's hymn to the creator in Psalm 19A is not expressed in language (v. 4: 'there is no speech; there are no words'), he states, it 'cannot be perceived by humans'. The heavens can praise God's glory, but cannot reveal God's

---

19. H.-J. Kraus, *Psalms 1–59: A Commentary* (trans. H.C. Oswald; Minneapolis: Augsburg, 1988), pp. 268-69.

will to humanity. As Kraus puts it, 'For that reason Psalm 19B has been added...to reveal the deciphered code word. In the Torah—there God is perceivable, that is where we recognize who God is.'[20] The Torah makes perceptible that which creation never ceases to proclaim, yet is unable to communicate. The respective teachings of the two, presumably, are identical, but only that of the Torah is comprehensible.

The contrastive line of interpretation is actually a commonplace in traditional Jewish commentary. I will present two examples here, from the aforementioned Ramban and Bahya ben Asher respectively. In a sermon on the perfection of the Torah,[21] Ramban says:

> After saying 'the heavens proclaim the glory of God', the psalm continues
> in praise of Torah, which proclaims the praise of God even more than the
> aforementioned heavens, sun, moon, and stars.

The heavenly bodies attest to the divine glory by virtue of their motion. Since 'all things that move require a mover', there must, therefore, be 'an almighty God directing them by his power and divinity'. That fact, in Ramban's view, explains the use of the divine name *'el* ('God'), which signifies 'power', in Ps. 19.2.

To understand how planetary motion attests to the Prime Mover, one must have a fairly sophisticated knowledge of astronomy.[22] Ramban continues:

> The 'sky' [Ps. 19.2b], which is the uppermost sphere that moves from
> east to west in opposition to the movement of the other [spheres], 'tells of
> the work of his hands', namely the created things.[23]

---

20. *Psalms 1–59*, p. 275.

21. *Kitvei rabbeinu Moshe ben Nahman* (ed. C. Chavel; 2 vols.; Jerusalem: 1963), I, pp. 141-75.

22. Cf. Abraham Ibn Ezra (1089–1164—his commentary is in any standard Rabbinic Bible), who introduces his exposition of the psalm with the remark that those who are unversed in astrology will be unable to understand his interpretation.

23. This line of interpretation, according to which the movement of the spheres demonstrates the necessity of the Prime Mover, may be traced to Saadia Gaon (882–942). Saadia renders Ps. 19.2 in Arabic, 'The heavens demonstrate the glory of God, and the spheres attest to the handiwork of the Creator.' The reason for this demonstration is that 'the first half of this psalm serves as proof of what is in its second half...Once an intelligent person is convinced of the existence of the Creator, that person must also be convinced that His words are true, His Torah is a source of light, and so forth.' See *Tehillim im targum u-feirush haga'on rabbeinu Sa'adyah ben Yosef Fayyumi* (ed. Y. Qafih; Jerusalem, 1966), p. 83. Contrast Maimonides' opinion

This 'proof' for the existence of God (the proof from motion, in this instance)[24] has been 'brought forth by the philosophers solely by means of speculation'. The Torah's 'clear proofs of the divine glory', in contrast, are not beset by the doubts inherent in speculation. Rather, 'Torah removes all doubt from the minds of the wise, and also of those who do not comprehend planetary motion or the configurations of the stars'.

Bahya begins the first of the two articles on 'Torah' in his *Qad ha-qemah* (the first Jewish encyclopedia) by quoting Ps. 19.8-10.[25] He then notes that those encomia of the Torah follow the mention of the heavenly bodies:

> After mentioning and expounding upon the matter of the sun, and report-ing a few of its many actions and virtues, [the psalm] comes around to saying that there is a light that is greater than the sun, namely the Torah. For while the sun attests to and proclaims the divinity of God, as well as his power and exaltedness, does not the Torah attest to it even more, and is not its virtue far greater than that of the sun?

He proves his contention by a detailed comparison of the relative merits of the sun and the Torah. In every case, the sun, for all its virtue, is found wanting. For example, 'one who looks directly at the sun is blinded, whereas the Torah "makes the eyes light up"' [Ps 19.9]. Or, the sun only provides its light during the day, while the light of the Torah is perpetual. Bahya's inevitable conclusion is that

> we learn from all of this that the great virtues of the Torah exceed those of the sun...The light of the Torah and the commandments far exceeds that of the heavenly bodies. Since that is the case, the only way for a person to be rescued from the darkness of the ordinary things of this world is to fulfill the Torah and the commandments, which are above the sun.

In contrastive readings of the two parts of Psalm 19, the declaration of the heavens is deficient in comparison with the revelation of the Torah. This point is made forcefully by Menahem Meiri (Provence, 1249–1316) in his Psalms commentary:[26]

concerning the spheres, in *Guide*, 2.5 (ed. Qafih, 2:281-83; trans. Pines, pp. 259-61).

24. See H.A. Davidson, *Proofs for Eternity, Creation and the Existence of God in Medieval Islamic and Jewish Philosophy* (New York: Oxford, 1987), pp. 237-80.

25. *Kitvei rabbeinu Bahya* (ed. C. Chavel; Jerusalem: Mossad Harav Kook, 1970), pp. 421-29.

26. Menahem Meiri, *Peirush le-sefer tehillim* (ed. Y. Hakohen; Jerusalem: Mekize Nirdamim, 1936), p. 47.

Although great principles of the faith may be ascertained by means of investigation of the configurations of the planets, this is insufficient for the attainment of truly perfect faith. That is why the psalm ascribes perfection to the Torah [in Psalm 19.8a]: by belief in what it contains, one attains the requisite level of faith, whether one came to know these things through investigation or solely by means of the revelation.

Knowledge in matters of faith, according to Meiri, may come from three sources—the senses, reason, and revelation—but 'human faith cannot be perfected' except by belief in the revealed Torah.[27]

Creation is in itself a valid source of knowledge of God—it is, for example, a commonplace in Jewish thought that long before the giving of the Torah, Abraham 'discovered the true faith by meditating on nature'[28]—but creation is both an esoteric and an inadequate source of that knowledge. As such, it is exceeded and superseded by the Torah.

And perhaps preceded by it as well. The conceptual (if not temporal) priority of the Torah to creation is well established in Jewish thought, based on the understanding that Wisdom, who says 'God created me at the beginning...' in Prov. 8.22, is Torah personified. The beginning of *Genesis Rabba* even asserts that God consulted the Torah in order to create the world, the way an architect refers to a blueprint.

Bahya's adroit use of light-imagery alerts us to another exegetical possibility. Jewish writing delights in conjoining the words *torah* and *'or* ('light'), as well in the pairing of such derivatives as *hora'ah* and *he'arah* ('instruction/illumination'). The intent of the association, obviously, is to identify the Torah as the luminary *par excellence*, and it is so recurrent that it hardly requires comment. Bahya, for instance, cites the well-known liturgical phrase, *veha'er eineinu betoratekha*, 'illumine our eyes with your Torah'.

---

27. Cf. the anti-Maimonidean argument of Judah Loew (Maharal; Prague/ Moravia, c. 1525–1609), that since the human soul is of divine origin, it cannot be perfected by natural means. 'Rather, its perfection is by means of the Torah and commandments, which are above nature.' He proves this claim by referring to Ps. 19.8ff. (*Tif'eret Yisra'el* [Prague, 1593], p. 10). Maharal also gives an elaborate interpretation of those verses in the introduction to *Tif'eret Yisra'el*, pp. 4-6.

28. See L. Ginzberg, *The Legends of the Jews* (7 vols.; Philadelphia: Jewish Publication Society, 1909–38), V, p. 210 n. 16. For some later versions of the same idea, see my article, 'An Extraordinary Sixteenth-Century Biblical Commentary: Eliezer Ashkenazi on the Song of Moses', in B. Walfish (ed.), *The Frank Talmage Memorial Volume* (2 vols.; Haifa: Haifa University Press, 1993), I, pp. 129-50, esp. 134-35.

The juxtaposition of the sun (among all created things) with the Torah in Psalm 19 certainly conduces to interpretations that see the two as alternative sources of 'light', in the sense of intellectual or spiritual illumination. And the two alternatives can be read into Genesis 1 as well: the preternatural light called into existence by the divine word on the first day (1.3) may be differentiated from the light provided by the heavenly bodies on the fourth (1.15).

The nature of that first light is the subject of a beautiful homily in *Gen. R.* 3.5, which I quote here as cited and glossed by Baḥya in his Torah commentary:[29]

> Rabbi Simon said: The word 'light' occurs here [i.e., in Genesis 1.3-5] five times, corresponding to the five books of the Torah. 'Let there be light' corresponds to the book of Genesis, with which God occupied himself when he created his world. 'And there was light' refers to Exodus, in which the Israelites were redeemed and came forth out of darkness, as it is written, 'all the Israelites had light in their dwellings' [Exodus 10.23]. 'God saw the light' corresponds to the book of Leviticus, which is filled with many laws. 'God separated the light' corresponds to the book of Numbers, in which those Israelites who would enter the land were separated from those who would not. 'God called the light' refers to Deuteronomy, which is filled with many commandments. In the light [sic!] of this midrash with respect to these five lights: the first is the light of creation; the second is the light of redemption; the third is the light of repentance, for one who offers a sacrifice repents and confesses over it; the fourth is the light of the Temple; the fifth is the light of the Torah and the commandments.

In this remarkable text, the 'light' of Gen. 1.3-5 is disengaged from the light of nature. Fabricated by word—'God said, "Let there be light"'— it becomes the Word, literally the books of the Torah. But then the books themselves dissolve into metonymies for the great principles of the faith: creation, redemption, repentance, Temple, and commandments.

The books find themselves reconstituted in two midrashic interpretations of Psalm 19 that associate the psalm's heavenly utterances with the texts and teachings of the traditional Jewish curriculum:

> 'The heavens proclaim the glory of God'—that is, the Torah, which was given from heaven, proclaims the glory of God; similarly, the Torah says of itself, 'When he established the heavens, I was there' (Proverbs 8.27).

---

29. *Bei'ur al ha-torah*, I, pp. 24-25.

'The sky expresses his handiwork'—these are the tablets [of the Ten Commandments], of which it is said, 'The tablets were the work of God' (Exodus 32.16).[30]

'Day to day utters speech'—that is, Torah, Prophets, and Writings. 'And night to night declares knowledge'—that of the [interpretation of] Scripture. 'There is no speech, there are no words, their voice is unheard'—these refer to the laws [derived by such interpretation]. 'Throughout the earth, going forth in gatherings[31] of [those who study] them'—these are the academies, where people assemble to hear and debate words of Torah.[32]

In the first of the above texts, the testimony of the heavens is effectively a metaphor for that of the Torah itself. As William Braude explains, 'even as the Torah, heaven-given, declares the glory of God's ordering of creation, so the array in the firmament declares the glory of God's handiwork—the Torah'.[33]

In the second text, the heavenly teachings allude more subtly to those of the Torah. The authority of the Written Law can be seen clearly, by the light of day. That of the Oral Law may seem as obscure as the darkness of night, but its promulgations (the laws, or *halakhot*, derived by methodical interpretation of Scripture) may be discussed and even disputed in the academies. The metaphoric discourse of nature, then, symbolizes the dialectic of Jewish learning, which is the very fountainhead of rabbinic Judaism.

Now, finally, we are approaching the 'mysteries' of creation, what I referred to before as the 'meanings and values that are encoded and implicit within it'. To ascertain more precisely the nature of those mysteries, we may consider a few more analogically-oriented interpretations of Psalm 19, in other words, those that see the respective teachings of creation and Torah as parallel and complementary to one another.

---

30. *Pesiqta Rabbati* (ed. M. Ish-Shalom [Friedmann]; Vienna, 1880), p. 203 = *Midrash Bereshit Rabbati* (ed. C. Albeck; Jerusalem: Mekize Nirdamim, 1940), p. 12.

31. An ingenious reinterpretation of the problematic *qawwam*, deriving it from the root *qwh* in the sense of 'collect, gather'.

32. *Seder Eliyyahu Rabba*, ch. 2 (ed. M. Ish-Shalom [Friedmann]; Jerusalem: Bamberger & Wahrmann, 1960 [orig. Vienna, 1900–1904]), pp. 10-11. While the translation of this difficult text is my own, it depends heavily on the comments in W.G. Braude and I.J. Kapstein, *Tanna debe Eliyyahu: The Lore of the School of Elijah* (Philadelphia: Jewish Publication Society, 1981), p. 60 nn. 32-35.

33. W.G. Braude, *Pesikta Rabbati* (2 vols.; New Haven: Yale University Press, 1968), II, p. 885.

The analogical approach is typically found among those modern exegetes who consider the Psalm to be a literary unity. Peter Craigie, for example, remarks:

> Just as the sun dominates the daytime sky, so too does the *Torah* dominate human life...There could be no life on this planet with the sun; there can be no true human life without the revealed word of God in the *Torah*.[34]

Essentially the same view had already been set forth by David Qimḥi (Provence, c. 1160–1235):[35]

> By attaching the matter of the Torah to the matter of the sun, [the Psalmist] means just as the heavens and the sun and the spheres attest to and proclaim the glory of God and his wisdom, so do the Torah and its commandments with which he commanded his people Israel attest to his wisdom and uprightness....Furthermore, just as the heavens and the sun provide benefit to the world and allow it to exist, so the Torah, which is perfect and restores the soul [19.8], enables the soul to exist.[36]

A more emphatic assertion of the analogical approach comes from the later philosophical commentator Isaac Arama (Aragon, c. 1420–1494):

> These two exalted things, namely the Torah and the world, are united in virtue and praiseworthiness, the one dependent upon the other and each the image [*defus*] of the other...It is, therefore, not without significance...that human knowledge on a given topic may come from either one of them. In fact, each one serves as a proof for the other, to the extent that [the Psalmist] paired and united the two in [Psalm 19].[37]

34. P.C. Craigie, *Psalms 1–50* (WBC, 19; Waco: Word Books, 1983), pp. 183-84.

35. D. Qimḥi (Redaq), *Ha-peirush ha-shalem al tehillim* (ed. A. Darom; Jerusalem: Mossad Harav Kook, 1974), pp. 47-48.

36. For further elaboration of this analogy—that as the sun is to the world, so is the Torah to the human soul—see Profiat Duran (Spain, late 14th-early 15th cen.), *Ma'aseh Efod* (ed. J. Friedländer and J. Kohn; Vienna, 1865), pp. 1-2. The sun is deficient in comparison to the Torah, according to Duran, for while 'living things exist by virtue of the natural heat that they acquire from the sun', only the Torah makes possible eternal 'rest and quietude for the human soul...when it returns to its source'.

37. I. Arama, *Aqeidat Yiṣḥaq* (ed. H. Pollack; 6 vols.; Pressburg, 1849), p. 27a. A similar analogy appears in the Psalms commentary by Arama's son Meir, *Me'ir tehillot* (Venice, 1590), 16b-17a. Knowledge of God may be obtained in two ways, 'by investigation and speculation, and by means of the revealed Torah'. The purpose of Ps. 19 is to indicate the nature of the two, and to elucidate some 'specific differences' between them.

To Arama, the world may be a Torah write large, but only for those who have eyes to see it. Scientific, philosophical, and religious truth can be ascertained by faithful 'reading' of the evidence. As long as revealed truth is understood, as a matter of principle, to have absolute priority over human reason, the world and the book may be construed as mutually elucidating manifestations of God's will, and thus mutually illuminating sources of knowledge of God.[38]

It is, then, the task of the 'reader' to find the hermeneutic cipher for decoding word and world simultaneously. Psalm 19 is a good place to begin the process of decoding, because of the way it brings the two together. The cipher may entail an esoteric allegorization, such as can be observed in the Zohar's three substantial discussions of the psalm,[39] which are replete with that work's characteristic theosophical symbolism. Those sermons are too complex to discuss in this context.

Or the cipher may be more philosophical, as in the sixteenth-century philosopher Moses Almosnino's (Salonika, c. 1515–1580) lengthy discussion, in his treatise *Tefillah le-Moshe*, of the extent to which the psalm's depiction of the heavens is compatible with Aristotle's. Almosnino concludes with a remarkably detailed map of the relationship between the respective dominions of the heavenly spheres and the Torah, in accordance with the following principle:[40]

> Since the entire lower world is under the sway of the stars which are themselves servants of the king of the world,...the poet explains in these verses [i.e., Psalm 19.8-10] that the one who fears God and endeavors to fulfill his perfect Torah will come under his wondrous providential care.

---

38. See S.H. Wilensky, *R. Yiṣḥaq Arama u-mishnato ha-pilosofit* (Jerusalem: Mosad Bialik, 1956), pp. 58-70.

39. *Zohar* 1.8 discusses the preparations for the sacred marriage that takes place on Shavuot; *Zohar* 2.136 describes the dramatic events that occur in heaven prior to the onset of Shabbat; and *Zohar ḥadash* to *ki tissa* (p. 45a) reinterprets the testimony of the heavens as emanations of the sefirot. Both the Shabbat sermon and the *Zohar ḥadash* passage take the word *mesapperim* in Ps. 19.2 in the sense of 'sparkling/glowing [like sapphire]'. This interpretation may be linked to the popular kabbalistic etymology, first found in *Sefer ha-bahir* 125, that derives the term 'sefirot' from *mesapperim*. See G. Scholem, *Origins of the Kabbalah* (Philadelphia: Jewish Publication Society, 1987), p. 81.

40. M. Almosnino, *Tefillah le-Moshe* (Tel-Aviv: Ha-makhon le-ḥeqer yahadut Saloniqi, 1988), p. 141.

> Corresponding to the seven things that are under the influence of the seven
> planets, the Torah influences us in like form and manner for good all our
> lives.

For the pious Jew, divine providence reinforces the positive influence of
the planets, and also annuls their negative effects. Although the dominion of the heavenly bodies may be subverted by the Torah, the planets
remain essential to the divine purpose, nonetheless. In Almosnino's
words, 'their existence and motion teach [*yoreh*, from the same root as
Torah] of the existence of their creator, for on the basis of their motion
we perceive the existence of God, since nothing moves without a mover
until we arrive at the First Cause'.[41]

That statement of Almosnino's leads me, finally, to an exegetical *tour
de force* that combines elements of both the contrastive and analogical
approaches to the interpretation of Psalm 19. This interpretation appears
in a commentary on the book of Psalms by a little-known fifteenth-
century Spanish exegete, Joel Ibn Shuaib.[42]

Ibn Shuaib affirms that five principles of the Jewish faith can be
inferred from the motion of the heavenly bodies as described in Psalm
19, and that the selfsame principles are found explicitly and more
perfectly in the Torah. Before introducing those specific principles, the
Psalmist, according to Ibn Shuaib, begins with a general one, namely
that 'the Torah of the Lord is perfect' (19.8a). From the standpoint of
its capacity to perfect the human soul ('restoring the life-spirit'), he
asserts, the Torah far exceeds the heavens.

Next comes the first principle of the faith, the existence of God,
indubitably proved by planetary motion, and alluded to by Ps. 19.3, 'day
to day utters speech'. This 'utterance' (that is, the elegant perfection of
planetary motion) adequately demonstrates the existence of God—the
'great and wondrous' daily circuit of the sun providing the exemplary
proof. But the Torah manifests that perfection even more forcefully and
conclusively. Not only is the Torah's testimony absolutely 'sure'; it is
also accessible to all, 'making [even] the simple wise' (19.8b).

The second specific principle of the faith is creation *ex nihilo*. This
doctrine is encoded in the verse 'the sky expresses his handiwork'
(19.2b), which refers to the mathematical perfection of the heavens that

41. *Tefillah le-Moshe*, pp. 128-29.

42. Joel Ibn Shuaib, *Nora Tehillot* (Salonika, 1568/9), 38b-44a, summarized by
Almosnino, *Tefillah le-Moshe*, pp. 138-40. For the little that is known about Ibn
Shuaib, see *Encyclopaedia Judaica* (16 vols.; Jerusalem: Keter, 1971), VIII, p. 1201.

is ascertainable by astronomical observation. Such precision can only be ascribed to the creator (the argument from design).[43] Yet again, the Torah's witness to this doctrine is superior to that of creation itself, as is proved by 19.9a, 'the precepts of the Lord are just, rejoicing the heart.' The term 'precepts', according Ibn Shuaib, refers to the aforementioned mathematical precision.[44] The Torah's report of that precision, unlike that of the astronomers, is 'just'—that is, free from the possibility of doubt or error. Moreover, the Torah's precepts 'gladden the heart', since those who pursue knowledge of God through the Torah achieve true felicity.

The third principle is divine providence, hinted at by the influence of the heavenly bodies over the lower world. That influence is indicated by 19.5a, 'their sign shines forth on all the earth' (thus the REB's rendering of this problematic text, nicely compatible with Ibn Shuaib's interpretation, in view of the astrological connotation of the word 'sign'). When one tries to ascertain the nature of providence from the heavens by means of astrology, one is prone to failure, either due to inadequacies of perception or because of the profundity of the matter under consideration. The Torah compensates for those two deficiencies: 'the commandment of the Lord is lucid', making the object comprehensible, and, furthermore, it 'makes the eyes light up', thus providing proper and adequate direction for the believer (19.9b).

The fourth principle of the faith is exclusive devotion to God (and to no other), which is indicated by the heavens' 'proclaiming the glory of God' at the beginning of the psalm. The heavens, however, are deficient in two respects. First, they have a nasty (albeit understandable) propensity for misleading people into thinking that they, themselves, are divine.[45] They might thereby lead people into error and impurity, whereas 'the

43. See Davidson, *Proofs for Eternity*, pp. 213-36.

44. The basis for Ibn Shuaib's interpretation is the fact that the term *piqqudim* in the psalm, normally translated 'precepts' or 'commandments', may also denote 'numbers'. One of the meanings of the biblical root *pqd* is 'to enumerate'. Ibn Shuaib refers to the biblical phrase *pequdei ha-mishkan* (Exod. 38.21), which he takes to signify the precise enumeration of the ritual requirements associated with the Tabernacle. In rabbinic Hebrew, incidentally (e.g., *M. Yoma* 7.1), *pequdim* or *piqqudim* is the title of the Book of Numbers (= Greek *arithmoi*, Latin *numeri*).

45. According to Meiri (*Peirush le-sefer tehillim*, p. 47), the very reason for juxtaposing the heavens with the Torah in Ps. 19 is so that 'one will not go astray and ascribe dominion to the heavenly configurations... but will know that their motion and agency are by divine command'.

fear of the Lord is pure' (19.10a). Secondly, the tendency of the heavenly bodies to wax and wane, alternately to appear and disappear from view, is in distinct contrast to the Torah, which 'abides forever' (19.10a).

The fifth and final principle is reward and punishment, which is indicated by the motion of the heavenly bodies, especially those changes in position and aspect that induce particular effects in the world. Such effects are implied by 19.3, 'their sign shines forth on all the earth, their message to the ends of the world'. But the stars sometimes lie, since God subverts their influence for the sake of his people; 'the judgments of the Lord', on the other hand, 'are true' (19.10b). Astral influence, moreover, is amoral, while the Torah's is 'altogether righteous' (19.10b), affecting the destiny of all people in accordance with their just deserts.

The evaluation of Ibn Shuaib's commentary poses a challenge for the modern biblical scholar. Until recently, it could have been dismissed as eisegesis—as the commentator reading his religious concerns into the text instead of reading the psalm in its 'proper' historical context.[46] In the current intellectual climate, however, such a parochial standard seems invalid: the evaluative criteria of modern scholarship do not automatically take precedence over the values of traditional communities of interpretation. Biblical scholars have consequently been developing a new sensitivity to traditional commentary, seeking to appreciate it on its own terms.

There is nothing innovative about Ibn Shuaib's ideas as such. The interest of his interpretation lies, rather, in his use of the genre of commentary to yoke those ideas to, or, rather, to discover them in the psalm. His success should be determined according to the elegance and ingenuity with which he goes about his task (considerable, in my view). That success can be measured according to the density and suggestiveness of the interplay between his worldview and the language of the psalm, or, to put it another way, according to the extent to which the horizon of the interpreter appears (perhaps unexpectedly) to converge with that of the authoritative text.

Ibn Shuaib, then, brings us full circle back to Baḥya ben Asher,[47] so I

---

46. It should be noted that the historical context of Ps. 19, like that of virtually all the psalms, can only be determined *ex hypothesi*. See my article, 'The Life and Times of King David according to the Book of Psalms', in R.E. Friedman (ed.), *The Poet and the Historian: Essays in Literary and Historical Biblical Criticism* (Chico, CA: Scholars Press, 1983), pp. 117-31.

47. There is even an indirect connection between the two, since an ancestor of Joel

will conclude simply by repeating Baḥya's answer to our initial question—'Why does the Bible begin with the creation of the world?' That answer turns out to have the signal virtue of providing the best possible inducement to the interpretation of Genesis 1 and Psalm 19 alike:

> All of the great principles [of Judaism] follow logically from belief in creation, and the entire Torah is founded and built upon them, each one leading inevitably to the next: creation necessitates providence, and providence necessitates both retributive justice and prophecy; out of prophecy arises the Torah, which is why it is absolutely essential for the Torah to begin with the creation of the world.

God created both world and Torah in order to enable humankind to attain the ultimate felicity, which is knowledge of him. As for God's felicity, according to the midrash *Eliyyahu Rabba*: 'although everything is his, since everything is his handiwork, his greatest joy is in the seed of Abraham'—preoccupied with his Torah.[48]

Ibn Shuaib, the famous homilist Joshua Ibn Shuaib, was a contemporary of Baḥya ben Asher, and both Joshua and Baḥya were disciples of the redoubtable Naḥmanidean, Solomon ben Adret (Rashba).

48. *Seder Eliyyahu Rabba* (ed. Ish-Shalom [Friedmann]), p. 10. See Braude and Kapstein, *Tanna debe Eliyyahu*, pp. 59-60.

'BREAK IN THE MIDDLE OF A VERSE':
SOME OBSERVATIONS ON A MASSORETIC FEATURE*

David B. Weisberg

Professor Ben Zion Wacholder, a life-long interpreter of the form and content of texts and scrolls,[1] has brought numerous valuable insights to the study of Qumran manuscripts and the elucidation of biblical and rabbinic texts. As his neighbor on the third floor of the library for close to three decades, and as his co-author and co-teacher, I frequently have had occasion to appreciate his creative mind and imaginative approach to textual study. Thus I am aware that this article, which touches on Ben's interests and is dedicated to him, is only small recompense for the amount of knowledge I have acquired from him through the years. Nevertheless I hope he will accept it in the spirit of friendship in which it is written, as I wish him many more years of original work.

Our discussion on the 'break in the middle of a verse' is organized as follows:

1. definition of *pisqa*;
2. review of scholarly literature on *pisqa be'emṣa' pasuq* since the discoveries at the Dead Sea;
3. massoretic[2] listing of *pisqa be'emṣa' pasuq* and discussion of the term פרידגמא;
4. Pentateuchal examples;

* For their kind help I wish to thank John Kampen and John C. Reeves, editors of this Festschrift; Hendrik Gert Platt and Robert Southard, participants in the 1993 seminar in massoretic studies at Hebrew Union College; and Arnona Rudavsky and Allan Satin, of the Hebrew Union College library staff.

1. See *The Dawn of Qumran: The Sectarian Torah and the Teacher of Righteousness* (MHUC, 8; Cincinnati, 1983), p. xiii.

2. For a discussion of this term, see I. Yeivin, *Introduction to the Tiberian Masorah* (trans. and ed. E.J. Revell; Missoula, MT, 1980), pp. 34-36. See also P. Haupt, 'Masora', *JBL* 37 (1918), pp. 219-28.

5.   proposal suggesting possible analogous usage of *pisqa be'emṣa' pasuq* with the Akkadian *ḫīpu*;
6.   conclusion.

The word *pisqa* itself, as is known, signifies an 'interruption, broken line; space indicating a new section, paragraph'[3], as used in the expression *pisqa be'emṣa' pasuq* (= 'break in the middle of a verse'). This feature is indeed an old and difficult problem of biblical scribal practice, yet the subject at hand has not been one of the more heavily researched topics in the area of massoretic studies.[4] Therefore, in order to place matters in helpful perspective, the next section will present a brief review of scholarly literature on this theme since the discovery of the DSS.

In his 1952 study of the Isaiah MS from Qumran, Curt Kuhl noted passages which contained spaces within the sentence and were therefore worthy of special mention:

> besonders auffallend sind einige andere Stellen...dass sich die Zwischenräume innerhalb des Satzgebildes befinden und dass der Text in seinem grammatisch-stilistischen Aufbau irgendwelche Härten und Unebenheiten enthält.[5]

While he treated the problem of the different sorts of breaks as one (not isolating the breaks in the middle of a verse from those occurring elsewhere), he noted that these breaks appeared to occur at junctures in the text demarcating (both at beginning and end) prayers, words of the Deity, certain changes of subject, etc.[6] Thus, in his view, the cause for these breaks was literary and stylistic.

Three years later, in 1955, Avigdor Ohr surveyed the problem, correctly considering it separate from that of the other types of 'break' in the MT.[7] His suggestions for the solution to why this designation is present in the MT all basically point to 'lower critical matters' of the

3.   M. Jastrow, *Dictionary*, II (New York, 1950), p. 1201 mng. 2.

4.   An early researcher of modern times was H. Graetz, 'Ueber die Bedeutung der masoretischen Bezeichnung: "Unterbrechung in der Mitte des Verses"', *Monatschrift für Geschichte und Wissenschaft des Judenthums* 27 (1878), pp. 481-503; 36 (1887), pp. 193-200, cited in Sandler (see below, n. 9 pp. 222f.).

5.   C. Kuhl, 'Schreibereigentümlichkeiten: Bemerkungen zur Jesajarolle (DSIa)', *VT* 2 (1952), pp. 316-17.

6.   Kuhl, 'Schreibereigentümlichkeiten', pp. 314ff.

7.   See the suggestions summarized by A. Ohr, 'Pisqa be'emṣa' pasuq mahu?', in *Pirsumei ha-ḥevrah le-ḥeqar ha-miqra' be-yisra'el*, I (Jerusalem, 1955), pp. 31-42, esp. pp. 37-38.

biblical text and cover the gamut of logical possibilities, such as textual corruption, and the like.

In 1959, Peretz Sandler examined the feature in question.[8] From Sandler's presentation,[9] one realizes the difficulty of knowing in which realm we are located (aesthetic, rhetorical, lower-text-critical, etc.) as we seek explanations for the origin of this text feature.

M.Z. Segal, in the year following Sandler's publication,[10] argued that the purpose of *pisqa be'emṣa' pasuq* was to demarcate the end of one section and the beginning of another. Here I find the criticism of Talmon[11] valid. Talmon stated that since the feature which we are discussing comes *in the middle* of verses or sentences and not at the end of verses or between sections, Segal's proposal to the effect that it divided between sections would seem to be incorrect.

In an essay linking the massoretic *pisqa be'emṣa' pasuq* with the method of writing a Scroll of Psalms from Cave 11 at Qumran (11QPsᵃ), Shemaryahu Talmon added important insights to this problem of biblical scribal practice.[12] Talmon's summary of different possibilities of approach, which appears to be based upon Sandler, p. 234, is worth summarizing here:

> In the discussion of the matter on hand scholars are divided into two camps. On the one hand we have the monists who posit one key-explanation only for all instances of the *p.b.p.* On the other hand, there are the pluralists, in whose opinion the phenomenon is not of one cloth, and is assumed to fulfill diverse functions in the transmission of the MT. Another division of opinion concerns the very nature of the *p.b.p.* Some students would define it as a Massoretic note which is meant to draw attention to textual matters pure and proper. It is taken to reveal the Massoretes' doubts about passages which, assumedly, in their opinion had suffered textual corruption...
>
> As against this, other scholars insist on the integrity of the MT and reject completely the very suggestion that the *p.b.p.* was meant to indicate textual flaws...[13]

---

8.   See P. Sandler, 'Le-ḥeqer ha-pisqa be'emṣa' ha-pasuq', *Pirsumei ha-hevrah le-ḥeqar ha-miqra' be-yisra'el*, VII (Jerusalem, 1959), pp. 222-49.

9.   See especially Sandler, pp. 234-238.

10.   'הפיסקא באמצע פסוק', *Tarbiz* 29 (1960), pp. 203-206.

11.   See below, n. 12.

12.   'Pisqah Be'emṣa' Pasuq and 11 QPsᵃ', *Textus* 5 (1966), pp. 11-21.

13.   Talmon, 'Pisqah', p. 14.

Talmon argued that the *pisqa be'emṣa' pasuq* pointed to 'extraneous expansions'[14]—actually supplementary midrashic expositions, or 'poetical paraphrases'[15] as he put it—not to be considered 'as integral components of the Bible':[16] 'They were intended to remain outside the authoritative canon as some kind of appendices to the original Scriptural version.'[17] In so arguing, Talmon rejected other viewpoints on the *pisqa be'emṣa' pasuq*, such as 'evidence of textual deficiency at junctures so singled out'.[18]

Taking as his central point of focus another MT feature that could as well be described as designating 'breaks' or 'lacunae', namely the *parashiot petuchot* and *setumot*, Josef M. Oesch made them the object of a special study.[19] Oesch described various methods of division used in the DSS (1QIs^b)[20] and matched the features he had isolated with those designated by Maimonides. Important traditions and observations on why these divisions might have entered the texts were explored and medieval and Qumran manuscripts were scrutinized, yet this investigation does not bear directly on our problem. Another example of 'breaks' in the MT is *qere ve-lo kethiv*,[21] which designates 'the ten instances where...words have dropped out of the text'.

Having defined the term in question and examined some scholarly opinions on its function, we now need to inquire as to where in Scripture the feature may be found. The researcher will discover that to this question there is no uniform answer. It appears that different MSS have different traditions; some do not mark the feature in question at all.[22] For purposes of this article, I shall adopt the massoretic note preserved by C.D. Ginsburg in his monumental *Introduction*. In this work, Ginsburg examined the *pisqa be'emṣa' pasuq*, which he called a 'break'. The

---

14. Talmon, 'Pisqah', p. 21.
15. Talmon, 'Pisqah', p. 18.
16. Talmon, 'Pisqah', p. 21.
17. Talmon, 'Pisqah', p. 21.
18. Talmon, 'Pisqah', p. 17.
19. *Petucha und Setuma, Untersuchungen zu einer überlieferten Gliederung im hebräischen Text des Alten Testaments* (Orbis Biblicus et Orientalis, 27; Göttingen: Vandenhoeck & Ruprecht, 1979). See Maimonides, *Mishneh Torah, Hilkhot Sefer Torah*, ch. 8. Maimonides' list is cited in Oesch, Tabelle I, p. 1$^+$.
20. Oesch, *Petucha und Setuma*, pp. 248ff.
21. Ginsburg, *Introduction*, Index p. 1011a *s.v.* Lacunae.
22. See Ohr, pp. 35-37 and 42.

reference to the feature in question occurs in a description of one of the manuscripts studied by him:

> Another contribution which this MS. [Manuscript No. 14, (see *Introduction*, p. 543) = British Museum Library Add. 9401-9402, dated 1286 AD] makes to textual criticism is the indication of the passages where there is a hiatus in the Pentateuch. The List of these 'Breaks in the middle of the verse', as they are Massoretically called, embracing the whole Hebrew Bible, is of extreme rarity. I have found it in only one MS.[23]

The full list, according to *The Massorah* is: Gen. 4.8; 35.22; Num. 25.19; Deut. 2.8; 23.18; Judg. 20.18; 1 Sam. 4.1; 10.11; 10.22; 14.12; 14.19; 2 Sam. 19.8; 1 Sam. 16.2; 1 Sam. 16.12; 1 Kgs 13.20; Jer. 13.12; Ezek. 3.16; Hos. 1.2; 1 Chron. 17.3; 2 Chron. 29.12; 29.14; 34.26.[24] Note that in the list as published the order of verses is not strictly kept; for example, the entry for 1 Sam. 16.2 occurs *after* the one for 2 Sam. 19.8[25] and there is an incorrect number in the heading of the relevant section, 185: the list notes eighteen occurrences of this feature instead of the more complete tally as displayed in the list, twenty-two.

Further, according to Ginsburg,

> The printed Massorah of Jacob b. Chayim gives only the List of the five passages in the Pentateuch. Our MS. marks the hiatus in four out of the five instances and among these is Gen. IV 8. Against each of the four passages the Massoretic Annotator has in the Massorah Parva פריגמי = פריגמא = πρηγμα, πραγμα, *break, hiatus*...[26]

Here we are presented with a challenge, for the meaning of the term פריגמא quoted in the massorah and cited by Ginsburg is elusive and puzzling. Graetz[27] cites Eli Levita as having inquired but having been

23. *Introduction to the Massoretico-Critical Edition of the Hebrew Bible* (with prolegomenon by H.M. Orlinsky; New York, 2nd edn, 1966), p. 547.
24. C.D. Ginsburg, *The Massorah Compiled from Manuscripts* (London, 1880), p. 57a, entry 185.
25. With regard to the question of the wrong order of these verses, my colleague Alan Cooper has kindly shared with me some thoughts about errors and inaccuracies in medieval editions. He cites as an example *Nora Tehillot* by Joel Ibn Shu'eib (1568–1569) of Salonika, in which the first three or four pages of commentary on Ps. 19 have running heads that identify the Psalm as 'Psalm 20', then, midway through the same section, the running heads revert to the reading 'Psalm 19'.
26. *Introduction*, p. 547.
27. *MGWJ* 27 (1878), pp. 481-82.

unsuccessful in learning from what language the term derives: ואיני יודע מאיזה לשון הוא. Identification with πρᾶγμα 'deed, act', etc.[28] seems not to fit the required meaning. A number of colleagues to whom I have put the question have made the following suggestions regarding this term.

1. Ann Michelini, of the Department of Classics, University of Cincinnati, proposes a reading originating from Ϝρηγμα, 'trouble, difficulty, marginal marking', a word familiar in Byzantine MSS brought to Europe. This is the antecedent form of the word cited in the next proposal.[29]

2. Adam Kamesar, of Hebrew Union College, Cincinnati, notes the citation of this passage in Krauss[30] but suggests the reading ῥῆγμα, 'breakage, fracture'.[31] This assumes the annotator of the Massorah Parva did not transmit the Greek term accurately.

3. Frank Shaw, Department of Classics, University of Cincinnati, thinks of Latin *fragmentum*, 'a broken off piece'.[32]

At this point I should like to outline and present a few examples of the feature we have been discussing. My effort is in no sense intended to be exhaustive but is rather exploratory and investigative, my purpose being to illustrate more clearly the issues at hand and to give possible categories of explanation for the biblical occurrences. For this reason, I shall confine myself to the first four out of five examples from the Pentateuch (where we have available both codices and scrolls). First the data will be presented in tabular form and then a short analysis will follow. Clearly the other evidence would be important to follow up.

The reader will be interested to note that in the locations we are investigating, the marginal notation *pisqa be'emṣaʿ pasuq* has *not* been entered by the massoretes who edited B19a, the manuscript upon which are based BHS and its predecessors, BHK and BH³.[33]

28. Liddell and Scott, *A Greek-English Lexicon* (Oxford, 1958), p. 1457.

29. Liddell and Scott, p. 1568, *s.v.* ῥῆγμα.

30. S. Krauss, *Griechische und lateinische Lehnwörter im Talmud, Midrasch und Targum* (Hildesheim, 1964), II, p. 488.

31. Liddell and Scott, p. 1568b.

32. *Oxford Latin Dictionary* (Oxford, 1982), p. 739.

33. Codex Leningrad B19a (Jerusalem, Makor, 1970).

Pentateuchal Examples of the Massoretic Feature
Pisqa Be'emṣa' Pasuq (= 'Break in the Middle of a Verse')

Listing in Ginsburg, *The Massorah*:	Identification and Location of Break in Hebrew Text:	Notation in *B19a*:	Notation in Torah Scroll (=Tiqqun[34] +*Letteris*[35]):
Gen. 4.8	אל הבל אחיו Break occurs *after* quoted words.	*ethnakta*; See critical note in BHS	normal spacing *ethnakta*;
Gen. 35.22	ויהי בשכן ישראל בארץ Quoted words mark *beginning* of verse. Break occurs after וישמע ישראל	double accentuation: *ethnakta* and *sof pasuq*; פ	open space to end of line; double accentuation: *ethnakta* and *sof pasuq*;
Num. 25.19	ויהי אחרי המגפה Break occurs *after* quoted words.	*ethnakta*; פ; no marginal notation	open space to end of line; double accentuation: *ethnakta* and *sof pasuq*; פ
Deut 2.8	ונעבר מאת אחינו בני עשו Quoted words mark *beginning* of verse. Break occurs after ומעציון גבר	*ethnakta*; ס unmarked	*ethnakta*; ס
Deut 23.18	לא תהיה קדשה מבנות ישראל Quoted words mark *beginning* of verse. No break is evident.	unmarked	Note somewhat larger than normal space for ס; otherwise normal *sof pasuq*

We record the following with regard to *pisqa be'emṣa' pasuq* in the Pentateuch:

1.   There is a lack of uniformity in the MSS with regard to this tradition;
2.   There is a lack of correlation between scroll and codex;

---

34. *Tiqqun Laqore'im* (New York, Ktav, 1946).
35. For comments on the Letteris edition of the Hebrew Bible, see Ginsburg, *Introduction*, p. 195.

3.   A break in the text between Deut. 23.17 and 18 fails to appear
in the manuscripts examined. It is possible that this is either an
error or perhaps a reflection of a tradition that is unknown to
us. I shall not include this passage from Deuteronomy in our
inquiry.

1. Gen. 4.8. To be noticed is the LXX 'plus': Διέλθωμεν εἰς τὸ
πεδίον,[36] which would imply a lacuna of something like נלכה השדה,[37]
which could be the reason for the feature in the MT.[38] The RSV translates 'Let us go out to the field', noting the ancient versions that have
this reading and notifying the reader that the Hebrew lacks these words.

However, note the interpretation of my colleague, Herbert C. Brichto:[39]
'There's absolutely nothing missing. But someone [i.e., the translator of
the LXX verse here] later assumed something might have been missing.'
Brichto translates: 'Cain thought: "It's all my brother's fault"'.

2. Gen. 35.22. Ginsburg,[40] to Gen. 35.22 observes a difference between
'Westerners' and 'Easterners', the former showing only *ethnakta*, the
latter only *sof pasuq*. Note the LXX to Gen. 35.22, which has the 'plus':
καὶ πονηρὸν ἐφάνη ἐναντίον αὐτοῦ, 'and the thing appeared
grievous before him'.[41]

Brichto comments on the verse: 'Here one might assume a sort of
gap—'let's think about it'. [Jacob does not comment at this point, but
he returns to the theme in his 'blessing' at the end of Genesis, where he
excoriates Reuben; the 'break' would serve to indicate (in the case of
Joseph's dreams) 'and his father kept the matter to himself'. He knew
the brothers were involved in foul play but he could not accuse them or
he would lose them too.]'

36. A. Rahlfs, *Septuaginta* (Deutsche Bibelgesellschaft Stuttgart, 1979), Gen. 4.8.

37. *BHS*, critical note to Gen. 4.8.

38. H.B. Swete, *An Introduction to the Old Testament in Greek* (New York, Ktav,
1968), p. 243, notes: 'As a whole, the Law [in the LXX version] has escaped material
changes in either direction [i.e., containing as a rule very few 'pluses' or 'minuses'
as compared with the massoretic text]. But there are a few important exceptions [our
passage is here quoted].'

39. These and the following comments by Brichto were furnished in an oral
communication of 14 January 1994.

40. Ginsburg, *The Hebrew Bible* (London, 1908), to Gen. 35.22 notes a difference between 'Westerners' and 'Easterners', the former showing only *ethnakta*, the
latter only *sof pasuq*.

41. See E. Tov, *The Text-Critical Use of the Septuagint in Biblical Research*,
(Jerusalem Biblical Studies 3; Jerusalem: Simor, 1981), p. 134.

One might see in this feature an *aposiopesis*—a deliberate break: 'an abrupt breaking off in the middle of a sentence without the completion of the idea, often under the stress of emotion'.[42]

3. Num. 25.19. The LXX reads the words ויהי אחרי המגפה together with the opening words of the following verse (which begins ch. 26, cp. the translation of the RSV) 'After the plague the Lord said to Moses and to Eleazar'.

4. Deut. 2.8. Like Num. 25.19, this verse in the LXX reads smoothly. There is no indication of any massoretic feature such as *pisqa be'emṣaʿ pasuq*.

If the verse in the MT were read without the *pisqa be'emṣaʿ pasuq* it could be understood without any problems, such as the rendering of the RSV, which leaves a paragraph break after the words 'Ezion-geber' and before the beginning of the next section of v. 8, 'And we turned and went...'

> So we went on, away from our brethren the sons of Esau who live in Seir,
> away from the Arabah road from Elath and Ezion-geber.
> And we turned and went in the direction of the wilderness of Moab.

It would appear from our brief investigation of these four verses that there is no single explanation that covers every case. Essentially the only thing that is totally evident is that the Massorah marked these verses to contain a *pisqa be'emṣaʿ pasuq*. No generalization seems possible.

We should now like to call attention to a practice from ancient Mesopotamia, which, we suggest, might have some bearing upon our understanding of the feature under discussion in the Hebrew Bible, the *pisqa be'emṣaʿ pasuq*. Alan Millard has noted:

> Although earlier copies of any part of the Bible are denied us, neighboring cultures can show how ancient scribes worked, and such knowledge can aid evaluation of the Hebrew text and its history.[43]

In asking 'how old these practices...might be',[44] Millard noted that 'Throughout the history of cuneiform writing there was a tradition of

42. K. Beckson and A. Ganz, *A Reader's Guide to Literary Terms* (New York: Noonday Press, 1960), p. 12.

43. A. Millard, 'In Praise of Ancient Scribes', *Biblical Archeologist* 45.3 (1982), p. 143.

44. Millard, 'Praise of Ancient Scribes', p. 143.

care in copying'.[45] He commented upon the feature under discussion here:

> Certain other points illustrate the scrupulosity of the scribes in handling texts, their traditionalism, and their care as glossators attempting to elucidate texts. First, scribes copying from clay tablets might find their exemplars damaged. In some cases they may have been able to restore the damaged text and hide the fact from us. Sometimes the scribe simply recorded the damage by writing 'break' or 'recent break' in smaller script on his copy, even when the restoration seems obvious to us.[46]

A.L. Oppenheim has pointed out the element of conservatism that would make preservation of older traditions more likely:

> there is the large number of tablets that belong to what I will call the stream of tradition—that is, what can loosely be termed the corpus of literary texts maintained, controlled and carefully kept alive by a tradition served by successive generations of learned and well-trained scribes.[47]

Within the 'stream of tradition' in Mesopotamia, when a text was received which for one reason or another contained a break of a few characters or words, the scribes did not intentionally fill in the space, but took care to mark that there was a break which they consciously attempted to preserve. The Akkadian term for this was *hīpu*.[48]

Here are a few instances of the feature in question:

Examples of the 'Break on a Tablet'

Expression	Reference	Dialect of MS	Type of Text
hīpu 'break'	Nbk 403:8	Neo-Babylonian	administrative
hīpu 1 šumi 'break of one line'	Nabnitu XXII 263	CT 12 48 IV 13[49] = Standard Babylonian	lexical
hīpu labīru[50] 'old break'	ACh Supp 33:17	Standard Babylonian	astrological

45. Millard, 'Praise of Ancient Scribes', p. 146.

46. Millard, 'Praise of Ancient Scribes', p. 146.

47. A.L. Oppenheim, 'Assyriology—Why and How?', in *Ancient Mesopotamia* (Chicago: University of Chicago Press, 1977), revised edition completed by Erica Reiner, p.13. For further details, see ch. V, especially, 'The Scribes', pp. 235-49.

48. *Chicago Assyrian Dictionary* H 196 and *Akkadisches Handwörterbuch* 347b. Assyriological conventions used here are those of the *Chicago Assyrian Dictionary*.

49. See MSL 16 p. 199, 263, fn.

50. Writings are also described as 'copied from old copies', e.g., CT 38 13:104 cited in *CAD* L 29b.

hīpu eššu 'new break'	TCL 6 37 r. ii 7, 11	Neo-Babylonian	lexical
hīpā lišallim 'let him repair the breaks'	StOr 1 33 r. 9	Standard Babylonian	colophon[51]

From the perspective of the Akkadian usages there are some uncertainties the determination of which would be necessary, such as the extent of the practice of writing these scribal messages, both in time and space; the significance of some of the specific formulae, such as 'let him repair the breaks' (was it permissible in some circumstances to fill in the broken stretches?); the meaning of 'new break' (does this refer to recent breaks that were distinguishable from those that entered the texts long before the time of the scribe?); and the full range of genres in which the terms are employed. The author recognizes the crucial nature of these questions but realizes that future studies will be needed in order to carry the matter further.

Let us summarize the examples gleaned from among Akkadian texts and from the Massorah and then let us consider the possibility of comparison.

The feature noted in Akkadian texts deals with the occurrence of a break in the tablet that had been transmitted through time.

We have observed the lack of unanimity among modern scholars as to the reason for the placement of the *pisqa be'emṣa' pasuq*. The suggestions vary from a marker of textual corruption to *aposiopesis* to a supplementary midrashic exposition.

On the basis of the evidence, the two terms do not appear to be identical nor do they refer to phenomena that denote the same thing. Nevertheless we can assert that if massoretic scribes copying biblical MSS were in possession of a tradition that advised them to mark the text at points at which a 'break' occurred within a verse, then the massoretic scribes were acting in the spirit of (but not necessarily consciously imitating) a convention that was old and had its roots in the ancient Near East. This convention was based upon the concept of 'reverence for tradition'.

I think that an advantage of my approach is that I do not seek to offer an explanation of why each individual break occurred. The explanations proposed by scholars, though thought-provoking, are, at the present stage of our knowledge, unprovable, and as such must remain in the

---

51. See H. Hunger, *Babylonische und assyrische Kolophone* (AOAT 2; Neukirchen–Vluyn: Kevelaer, 1968), #498:3.

realm of speculation. In contrast, what we are proposing requires the fewest possible assumptions- in fact, only two, namely, that: (1) the breaks called *pisqa be'emṣa' pasuq* were recorded due to scribal reverence for tradition and (2) there could conceivably be a parallel between the practice as found in the Hebrew Bible and that known from Mesopotamia.

We feel that this is as far as our present knowledge can take us. Therefore, in our view, it is unnecessary to assume that the break indicates either a midrashic exposition on the one hand, or a damaged section of text on the other.

PUTTING THEM IN THEIR PLACE:
GEOGRAPHY AS AN EVALUATIVE TOOL[*]

James C. VanderKam

There is evidence that maps were made at fairly early times in the ancient Near East. Naturally, they assumed different forms and served varied purposes. Only a few have survived from the vast cuneiform literature that has been recovered in the last two centuries. 'They are impressed on small clay tablets like those generally used by the Babylonians for cuneiform inscription of documents—a medium which must have limited the cartographer's scope.'[1] One well known *mappa mundi* (BM 92687) from Babylon has intrigued students of the Enoch literature as possibly being the model on which its conception of the world is based. This proves not to be the case[2], but the map is important nevertheless. On it the earth is circular, and it is surrounded by a body of water termed the Bitter River. Beyond the river are eight regions, each shaped triangularly and each described in the text on the reverse of the tablet. At the center of the earth lies Babylon, while the few other details include the Tigris and Euphrates Rivers, eight cities marked by small circles, and three other geographical areas: Bit-Yakin, Habban, and Urartu. The map dates from the seventh or sixth centuries, but it was copied from an earlier model. In the *mappa mundi* we have an early instance of a text and accompanying schematic map which attempted to be comprehensive and clearly served a political end.

In the Greek-speaking world mapmaking also began at an early date, with Ionians playing a leading role in the development. As cartography

*   I am grateful to my colleague Jerry Neyrey for his helpful comments on an earlier draft of this paper.
    1.   L. Bagrow, *History of Cartography* (revised and enlarged by R.A. Skelton; Chicago: Precedent, 2nd edn, 1985), p. 31.
    2.   For bibliography and analysis, see VanderKam, 'I Enoch 77,3 and a Babylonian Map of the World', *RevQ* 42 (1983), pp. 271-78.

was then considered a branch of philosophy, not a practical discipline, its products could elicit guffaws from experienced travelers such as Herodotus. Bagrow reports about a sixth-century map in which the world has seven parts:

> head and face in the Peloponnesus, backbone in the Isthmus, diaphragm in Ionia, legs in the Hellespont, feet in the Thracian and Cimmerian Bosphorus, epigastrium in the Egyptian Sea, hypogastrium and rectum in the Caspian. If this anonymous natural philosopher, not content with theory, actually sketched out his map, we can draw instructive conclusions about the state of cartography in his time.[3]

The early maps supplied enough information to suggest where the author did and in this case presumably where he did not live. It was not until the early Hellenistic period that different, more scientific principles began to govern cartography, as can be seen in the work of Dicaearchus (350–290), Eratosthenes (276–195), and much later in that of Ptolemy (87–150) himself.[4]

Some examples of a more theoretical approach to mapmaking are the concern of this essay. The Hebrew Bible contains a few attempts to place the nations of the earth in some sort of systematic arrangement, a scheme that while it echoes historical and geographical facts serves a larger end. The first text to be considered is Genesis 10, with its table of the nations. It, with a few other biblical givens, served as the model for later efforts at representing the world and its inhabitants; in fact, it continued to do so well into the medieval period. There were many subsequent re-editions and revisions of the table: the editions and ancient translations of Genesis (cf. 1 Chron. 1.4-23), *Jubilees* 8–10, *Genesis Apocryphon* 12–17 (very fragmentary),[5] Josephus's *Antiquities* 1.109-39 (especially 1.122-39), and Pseudo-Philo's *Liber Antiquitatum Biblicarum* 4(–5). Here the re-reading given to Genesis 10 in *Jubilees* 8–10 will be the center of interest. *Jubilees*, which transparently uses Genesis as its base, provides opportunities to study fundamental issues of interpretation and ideological cartography as practiced by one learned writer. In the following pages, Genesis 10 and *Jubilees'* reworking of it

3.   *History of Cartography* , p. 33.
4.   For another sketch of early cartography, see A. Peters, *The New Cartography* (New York: Friendship, 1983).
5.   More material is now available; see J.C. Greenfield and E. Qimron, 'The Genesis Apocryphon Col. XII', *AbrN* Supp. 3 (1992), pp. 70-77.

will first be studied; then, implications will be drawn regarding the circumstances that *Jubilees* addresses by means of chs. 8–10.

1. *The Table of Nations in Genesis 10*

The list in Genesis 10, situated between the genealogical notice of Noah's death and the Tower of Babel story, presents itself as a genealogy[6] of the sons of Noah to whom children were born after the flood. Use of the term תולדת associates it with the larger genealogical structure of the priestly work (Gen. 2.4b; 5.1; 6.9; 11.10, 27; 25.12, 19; 36.1, 4, 9; 37.2; Num. 3.1). Although the sons' names appear in the order Shem-Ham-Japheth in 10.1, the list proceeds in reverse order from Japheth (10.2-5) to Ham (10.6-20) and last to Shem (10.21-31). Each of the sections is marked off by a formulaic, summary statement:

10.5 for Japheth: מאלה נפרדו איי הגוים בארצתם איש ללשנו למשפחתם בגויהם
10.20 for Ham: אלה בני חם למשפחתם ללשנתם בארצתם בגויהם
10.31 for Shem: אלה בני שם למשפחתם ללשנתם בארצתם לגויהם.

The entire genealogy is then concluded with a general line which employs some of the same vocabulary found in the summaries for each section: אלה משפחת בני נח לתולדתם בגויהם ומאלה נפרדו הגוים בארץ אחר המבול.

The three families multiplied and branched out as follows:[7]

1. The sons of Japheth a. Gomer
   1. Ashkenaz
   2. Riphath
   3. Togarmah
   b. Magog
   c. Madai
   d. Javan
   1. Elishah
   2. Tarshish
   3. Kittim
   4. R/Dodanim[8]
   e. Tubal

6.   It fits into the category that R.T. Hood ('The Genealogies of Jesus', in *Early Christian Origins* [ed. A. Wikgren; Chicago: Quadrangle Books, 1961], pp. 2-3) calls 'Organization', that is, 'to indicate a relationship (in the most general sense) between individuals in terms of relationship by blood' (p. 2).

7.   The spellings of names are those of the NRSV. All English quotations from the Bible are also from this version.

8.   MT begins the name with *D*, the SP, LXX and 1 Chron. 1.7 with *R*.

```
                    f. Meshech
                    g. Tiras
2. The sons of Ham  a. Cush
                        1. Seba
                        2. Havilah
                        3. Sabtah
                        4. Raamah
                                    a. Sheba
                                    b. Dedan
                        5. Sabteca
                        6. Nimrod (see vv. 8-12 for a narrative about him)
                    b. Egypt
                        1. Ludim
                        2. Anamim
                        3. Lehabim
                        4. Naphtuhim
                        5. Pathrusim
                        6. Casluhim (whence came the Philistines)
                        7. Caphtorim
                    c. Put
                    d. Canaan
                        1. Sidon
                        2. Heth
                        3. Jebusites
                        4. Amorites
                        5. Girgashites
                        6. Hivites
                        7. Arkites
                        8. Sinites
                        9. Arvadites
                        10. Zemarites
                        11. Hamathites
                        v. 18; v. 19 gives borders) ואחר נפצו משפחות הכנעני)
3. The sons of Shem  a. Elam
                     b. Asshur
                     c. Arpachshad (v. 24)
                         1.Shelah
                             a. Eber
                                 1. Peleg (כי בימיו נפלגה הארץ v. 25)
                                 2. Joktan (vv. 25-29; borders v. 30)
                                     a. Almodad
                                     b. Sheleph
                                     c. Hazarmaveth
                                     d. Jerah
                                     e. Hadoram
```

                                          f. Uzal
                                          g. Diklah
                                          h. Obal
                                          i. Abimael
                                          j. Sheba
                                          k. Ophir
                                          l. Havilah
                                          m. Jobab
          d. Lud
          e. Aram (v. 23)
             1. Uz
             2. Hul
             3. Gether
             4. Mash

The LXX offers largely the same lists but with a few changes. First, it designates Ελισα as Japheth's fifth son, thus giving him eight, not seven as in the MT. Nevertheless, it also names an Ελισα as the first son of Javan. Apart from a few predictable variations in spelling, the only other significant differences occur in Shem's genealogy. There Arpachshad begets a certain Καιναν who in turn becomes the father of Shelah; at the end of the list of Shem's sons, another Καιναν appears; and Obal, Joktan's eighth son in the MT, is not present. The resulting numbers for the versions are:

	Generations							
Versions:	*1*	*2*	*3*	*4*	*5*	*6*	*7*	*totals*
MT	3	16	36	3	2	13		73
LXX	3	18	36	3	1	2	12	75

In light of these numbers one can appreciate Westermann's remark: 'Seventy peoples are mentioned in this chapter (the number emerges with a little assistance)'.[9] To reach it one must ignore the three sons of Noah in the MT form and a few other stray descendants in the LXX.

The source critics had until recently reached something of a consensus about the way in which to distribute the verses between J and P. Skinner[10] divided in this fashion:

P   1a, 2-7, 20, 22-23, 31-32
J   1b, 8-19, 21, 25-30

    9. *Genesis 1–11: A Commentary* (Minneapolis: Augsburg, 1984), p. 529.
    10. J. Skinner, *A Critical and Exegetical Commentary on Genesis* (ICC; Edinburgh: T. & T. Clark, 2nd edn, 1930), p. 188.

Westermann differs only by making a decision about v. 24: it belongs to
J, not to the redactor of the chapter, despite the abruptness with which
Arpachshad is introduced.[11] The source critics add that the introduction
to J's table appears in Gen. 9.18-19:[12] 'The sons of Noah who went out
of the ark were Shem, Ham, and Japheth. Ham was the father of
Canaan. These three were the sons of Noah; and from these the whole
earth was peopled [נפצה].' If so, the story of Noah's drunkenness is
enveloped by the two parts of the Yahwistic table. Van Seters, however,
argues that all of v. 1 is from J, noting that the use of תולדת to introduce
a segmented genealogy would be atypical for P. He also thinks that the J
version, which did have a Japheth section, formed the basis for the table,
not P. 'P's only contribution was to make additions of names within the
Ham and Shem lines, to modify the whole of the Japheth line in his own
style, and to furnish a few summary statements.'[13]

The P sections are purely genealogical, and give no indication of
where the sundry peoples lived. They are fathers and sons, nothing
more. Mothers and daughters are absent.[14] There also seems to be no
hint by which the reader is enabled to discern which are the better
peoples and which should be avoided. One could infer that the whole
leads up to Shem who is listed last and hence best.[15] But P does not say

11. *Genesis 1–11*, pp. 499, 525.
12. *Genesis 1–11*, p. 499.
13. *Prologue to History: The Yahwist as Historian in Genesis* (Louisville:
Westminster/John Knox, 1992), p. 176 (see pp. 174-87 on the table of nations). See,
too, J. Blenkinsopp, *The Pentateuch: An Introduction to the First Five Books of the
Bible* (ABRL; New York: Doubleday, 1992), p. 88. Van Seters also points to the
parallels in the Hesiodic *Catalogue of Women* to the J material here.
14. It is interesting that the new material from the Genesis Apocryphon gives a
prominent place to the daughters of Noah's three sons. In 1QapGen 12.9 Noah says
that '[son]s were born to me [...dau]ghters after the flood'; lines 11-12 mention that
Shem was the father of five daughters, Ham of seven, and Japheth of four. The
numbers form a pattern: Shem's line has exactly as many sons as daughters so that
they could marry without going outside the immediate family for spouses. Ham,
however, has as many daughters as Japheth has sons, and Japheth has as many
daughters as Ham has sons. Hence, they could reasonably intermarry. For the text
and translation, see Greenfield and Qimron, 'The Genesis Apocryphon Col. XII',
pp. 72-73.
15. As R.B. Robinson ('Literary Functions of the Genealogies of Genesis', *CBQ*
48 [1986], pp. 602-603) points out, placing Shem at the end does locate the material
about him before the tower of Babel episode in which there seems to be a play on שם
(see Gen. 11.4: ונעשה לנו שם).

that or give any indication that in the list first, middle, or last is best. The reader is not even told how Israel might some day fit into the scheme.[16] P's list is classified as a 'segmented genealogy', that is, it traces several lines of descent from a single ancestor,[17] and serves the obvious function of showing how all humanity descended from a common ancestor after the flood.

If the source division is correct, J had no Japheth section, unless it was entirely omitted in favor of P's version.[18] The first longer section attributed to J (vv. 8-19) contains the narrative about Nimrod, Egypt's and Canaan's offspring, and notices about boundaries; the second (vv. 25-30) is largely genealogical (Arpachshad's line), but it, too, mentions boundaries and uses other language associated with J (e.g., ילד in the *qal* or *pual* conjugations rather than the *hiphil* as in P).

On the basis of his source division, Westermann disengages the differing emphases of the two documents as follows:

> The genealogies in J are also closer to narrative...accordingly, the J-texts in Gen 10 describe more an *event*—how humankind spread over the earth and became the nations that they now are. The P-texts, following the basic line of P, describe rather a *situation*—the state of being nations as a result of the spread of humankind over the earth. P puts the emphasis on what is common to all nations, J on the contrary stresses the different ways in which the different groups have developed.[19]

Many grant that P supplies the foundation for the chapter, as it does for all of Genesis 1–11, and that its comprehensive list is intended to demonstrate the fulfillment of the blessing/command to populate the

---

16.   D.E. Gowan (*Genesis 1–11: From Eden to Babel* [International Theological Commentary; Grand Rapids: Eerdmans/Edinburgh: The Handsel Press, 1988], pp. 113-14) comments on the neutral presentation even of peoples who were enemies of Israel.

17.   See R.R. Wilson, *Genealogy and History in the Biblical World* (New Haven and London: Yale University Press, 1977), p. 9.

18.   As J. Blenkinsopp notes (*The Pentateuch*, p. 88), the standard theory has held that J had no additions to the Japheth genealogy for peoples in Asia Minor, Armenia, and the Aegean area because these became known to Israel after J was supposed to have been written (in the tenth or ninth century). Blenkinsopp and others now doubt that J was as old as the standard documentary hypothesis has held.

19.   *Genesis 1–11*, p. 502. E. Speiser (*Genesis* [AB 1; Garden City: Doubleday, 1964], p. 71) writes: '*P*'s list , in particular, was conceived as a catalogue of states, as opposed to tribal units. Hence the summaries stress the term *gōy* "nation" (5, 20, 31, 32), whereas '*am* does not occur at all'.

earth. J, however, 'wishes to demonstrate how the drive for power and status exercises its corrupting influence here as previously. Hence the allusion to another false start with the creation of the first empire in the land of Shinar (10.8-12), an allusion skillfully worked out in narrative form in the account of the frustration of that attempt in the same region (11.1-9)'.[20] The J additions or supplements (however they are related to the priestly material) could serve yet another purpose: they may be an attempt to tie an objective, dispassionate list more closely to Israel and its history. This conclusion is suggested by several considerations:

1. The expansion involving Arpachshad deals with the area from which Israel's ancestors came and to which the exiles were later led.
2. The additional notices about the Philistines and the Canaanite nations would have obvious relevance. The boundaries of the Canaanites are given in a straightforward and generous manner; there seems to be no after-effect from the curse in 9.25.
3. Gen. 10.21 notes that Shem was the father of all the בני עבר, the eponymous ancestor of the Hebrews.[21]

2. *Jubilees' Re-reading of Genesis 10*

While the biblical versions or paraphrases found in the targumim often attempt to identify the scriptural names with contemporary peoples and places (see also Josephus, *Genesis Rabbah*), *Jubilees* like the LXX reproduces the Hebrew names without modernizing them. Apart from his straightforward borrowing of names, however, the author has interfered heavily with the genealogical material in Genesis 10—a sure sign that he wished to make a point that more directly suited his purposes.

20. Blenkinsopp, *The Pentateuch*, p. 88.
21. See P.S. Alexander, 'Geography and the Bible: Early Jewish Geography', *ABD*, II, p. 980. An obvious problem in connection with Gen. 10–11 is that Genesis 10 presupposes dispersal of the nations and differentiation of languages, while at the beginning of ch. 11 neither has occurred. It seems as if ch. 10 and 11.1-9 should be reversed from this point of view. Gowan (*Genesis 1–11*, p. 113) finds a theological rationale for their present placement: 'The nations in ch. 10, in their diversity and distribution throughout the earth, do not yet stand under the judgment of 11:1-9, so that a remarkably neutral attitude toward those enemies and rivals of Israel is presented'.

a. *The Witnesses to the Text*

Jubilees was written in Hebrew between about 170 and 150 BCE.[22] The
issue of its original language had largely been settled before 1947, and
the Qumran manuscripts have verified that Hebrew, not Aramaic, was
the language of composition. There are the following 14 or 15 copies
from Qumran: 1Q17-18; 2Q19-20; 3Q5; 4Q176 frags. 21-23 (two
copies?), 216, 218-23/24, 11Q12.[23] The earliest of the copies—4Q216—
can be dated paleographically to c. 125–100 BCE;[24] later proposed dates
for the book's composition can, therefore, reasonably be excluded.
Unfortunately, none of the fragmentary manuscripts retains any part of
chs. 8–10, the section in which the book re-works the material in
Genesis 10. For this section the surviving witnesses are: (a) the Ethiopic
version (complete text), (b) citations from the chapters in an anonymous
Syriac chronicle (8.2-4, 11-12, 22-27, 29-30; 10.29) and (c) citations
from the chapters in the writings of several Greek authors (Cedrenus,
Historiarum Compendium for 8.2-3; 10.15; Syncellus, *Chronographia*
for 10.1, 3, 7-9; Theodosius of Miletus, 10.29-31, 34; cf. the *Catena of
Nicephorus* for 10.21).[25]

The medieval text נח ספר reproduces much the same material as one
finds in *Jub.* 10.1-14, but this section has little direct relevance to the

22. See the analysis in VanderKam, *Textual and Historical Studies in the Book of
Jubilees* (HSM 14; Missoula, MT: Scholars Press, 1977), pp. 207-85 where a date
Between 161 and 152 is defended. More recently, G. Nickelsburg (*Jewish Literature
between the Bible and the Mishnah* [Philadelphia: Fortress Press, 1981], pp. 78-79)
and J. Goldstein ('The Date of the Book of Jubilees', *PAAJR* 50 [1983], pp. 63-86)
have argued for the period just before 167 BCE. M. Knibb ('Jubilees and the Origins
of the Qumran Community' [An Inaugural Lecture in the Department of Biblical
Studies, King's College London, 17 January 1989], pp. 16-17) also opts for a date
before 167.

23. See the list in VanderKam, 'The Jubilees Fragments from Qumran Cave 4', in
*The Madrid Congress: Proceedings of the International Congress on the Dead Sea
Scrolls, Madrid 18-21 March 1991* (2 vols.; ed. J. Trebolle Barrera and L. Vegas
Montaner; Leiden: Brill, 1992), II, pp. 635-48. 4Q217 is omitted from the list above
because, while Milik has identified it as a manuscript of *Jubilees*, it seems to be a copy
of a text which uses similar language.

24. VanderKam and Milik, 'The First *Jubilees* Manuscript from Qumran Cave 4:
A Preliminary Publication', *JBL* 110 (1991), p. 246.

25. All of the versional evidence for *Jubilees* is collected in VanderKam, *The Book
of Jubilees* (2 vols.; CSCO 510-11, Scriptores Aethiopici 87-88; Leuven: Peeters,
1989). Citations from the texts and all the translations of *Jubilees* in the paper are
from this edition.

geographical teachings of chs. 8–10. The fact that several chroniclers excerpted from *Jubilees* 8–10 illustrates their normal practice: where works such as *Jubilees* or *1 Enoch* expanded the scriptural base, chroniclers cited from them to make their histories more complete.

b. *Jubilees 8–10*
Although chs. 8–10 are the primary cartographical section, much of ch. 7 introduces the topic and sets the tone for chs. 8–10.

Jubilees 7.7-12. As in Genesis, the story of Noah's drunkenness and the response of his sons to his condition precedes the table of nations (Gen. 9.20-27). The curse which Canaan there receives appears to be of no consequence in Genesis 10, but in *Jubilees*, though it is surprisingly phrased no more vociferously than in Genesis, it manifestly sets the stage for what is to follow. The only differences of wording worth noting come in *Jub.* 7.10-11//Gen. 9.25-26. In *Jub.* 7.10 the writer adds words to the end of Gen. 9.24 which make it somewhat clearer that it is Ham's son, not Ham, who gets cursed (see 7.13, quoted below): וידע את כל אשר עשה לו בנו הקטן ויקלל את בנו. The other difference surfaces in 7.11//Gen. 9.26 where ברוך יהוה אלהי שם ויהי כנען עבד למו becomes *yetbārak 'egzi'abhēr 'amlāku la-sēm wa-yekun kanā'an gabro.* The suffix on *gabro* (עבדו) interprets the ambiguous למו[26] as singular (as in LXX, OL, Targum Pseudo-Jonathan), not plural (as in Syriac, Targum Onkelos, and Targum Neophyti). The result is that Canaan is to be the servant of Shem alone, not of Shem and Japheth (although see 7.10// Gen. 9.25). The same may be the case in 7.12 where, however, *Jubilees'* manuscript evidence is divided, with the preferred reading being the plural (agreeing with the Syriac, LXX, and all the targums). The major point is that *Jubilees'* author uncharacteristically squanders an opportunity to hit one of his favorite targets.

Jubilees 7.13-17. The next pericope, without parallel in Genesis, clarifies which segments of the family are the troublemakers and which are the better sorts.

> 7.13 When Ham realized that his father had cursed his youngest son, it was displeasing to him that he had cursed his son. He separated from his father—he and with him his sons Cush, Mizraim, Put, and Canaan.

26. See GKC §103f n.3 (p. 302).

> 7.14 He built himself a city and named it after his wife Neelatamauk. 7.15 When Japheth saw (this), he was jealous of his brother. He, too, built himself a city and named it after his wife Adataneses. 7.16 But Shem remained with his father Noah. He built a city next to his father at the mountain. He, too, named it after his wife Sedeqatelebab. 7.17 Now these three cities were near Mt. Lubar: Sedeqatelebab in front of the mountain on its east side; Neelatamauk toward its south side; and Adataneses toward the west.[27]

Note the verbs *separated* for Ham, *was jealous* for Japheth, and *remained* for Shem. In the lengthy section about the demons who mislead his offspring—a passage that is seemingly unrelated to the geographical concerns that dominate these chapters—Noah rehearses the reactions of the brothers: 'But now I am the first to see your actions—that you have not been conducting yourselves properly because you have begun to conduct yourselves in the way of destruction, to separate from one another, to be jealous of one another, and not to be together with one another, my sons' (7.26). If only the other two could be more like Shem!

Jubilees 7.18-19. The next two verses list the sons of Shem and Japheth (in that order), drawing them from Gen. 10.22 and 2 (with a supplement on Arpachshad from Gen. 11.10). Ham's sons are not listed here (though v. 19 ends with 'These were Noah's sons') because they were named already in 7.13 and perhaps to separate them more emphatically from the better lines.

The division of the earth. The author of *Jubilees* rearranged his biblical model in several places in order to achieve a more unified presentation. In general he follows the Shemite genealogy and inserts stories only at the correct points in it.

1. *Jub.* 8.1-10: He begins with the date (the beginning of the 29th jubilee [1373 *anno mundi*]) and then reproduces four generations from the line of Shem as recorded in Gen. 11.10-18 (cf. 10.22-25). Arpachshad,

---

27. The sides of Mt Lubar on which the brothers build their cities are in the same directions as their patrimonies will later be. The names of the wives/cities are worth noting: Neelatamauk seems composed of נחלת and מחוק (inheritance of what is destroyed), while Sedeqatelebab consists of צדקתהלבב. It is less clear what Adataneses (the first letter is *'alef*, not *ayin* in Ethiopic and Syriac spellings) means. For the spellings of the names in the different texts, see the chart in VanderKam, *The Book of Jubilees*, II, p. 66.

Kainan, Shelah, Eber, Peleg. Note that the additional generation known also from the LXX is present here. For each member of the genealogy he supplies not only dates for marriage and birth of the first son but also the name of the patriarch's wife. The familial connections of the wives show that intermarriage occurred even in Shem's line. The notice about Kainan (one of those who married outside Shem's line [8.5]) is expanded by a story about the inscription he discovered and in which the Watchers had recorded astrological information. The writer offers an etymology for Shelah ('I have truly been sent' [8.5]), and, following Gen. 10.25, does the same for Peleg: 'In the sixth year [1567] she [Azurad] gave birth to a son for him, and he [Eber] named him Peleg because at the time when he was born Noah's children began to divide the earth for themselves. For this reason he named him Peleg' (8.8). In other words, *Jubilees* reproduces the Shemite genealogy as far as Peleg so that it can locate the division of the earth at the etymologically appropriate juncture—something Genesis does not do. However, to engage in action so momentous as dividing the earth for all time at the *end* of a jubilee period (1567 was the sixth year of the seventh week in the 32nd jubilee; cf. 8.7) would be untoward or at least non-schematic. So, we read that there was something wrong with this division: Noah's sons began to do so for themselves (*ba-mawā'el za-tawalda 'axazu daqiqa nox yetkāfalu lomu medra*). *Jub.* 8.9 supplies more evaluative commentary: 'They divided it in a bad way among themselves and told Noah'. The phrase 'in a bad way' has elicited some debate. R.H. Charles took it to mean 'secretly' (δόλῳ), but there appears to be no evidence supporting his conjecture.[28] The writer is simply disapproving of what Noah's sons did at this point. The division was being done improperly.

Jub. 8.10 shows that the second time around it was done decently and in good order: 'At the beginning of the thirty-third jubilee [1569–1617] they divided the earth [*kafalewwā la-medr*] into three parts—for Shem, Ham, and Japheth—each in his own inheritance. (This happened) in the first year of the first week [1569] while one of us [the angels of the presence] who were sent was staying with them'. An auspicious year had been reached—the first of a jubilee period—and now there was also angelic and paternal supervision of the process. The verse does not name the subjects of the verb *kafalewwā* but the end of the verse and 8.11 make clear that the angel and Noah were the authoritative parties who lent legitimacy to this second and successful distribution. It will be recalled that in Genesis Noah dies before the table of nations is recorded. It is also perhaps not accidental that at this early juncture we are told that the three parts for the three sons were 'each in his own inheritance'. There does not seem to be room for trading or for redrawing boundaries.

2. *Jub*. 8.11-30. *Jub*. 8.11 introduces the actual division in language reminiscent of Moses' and Joshua's distribution of the promised land among the tribes: the assigned portions are called lots (!; see Num. 26 and 34; Josh. 14.2; 15.1; 17.4; 18.6, 8-9 [where a book is mentioned as in *Jub*. 8.11], 10; 19.51). Noah is the explicit subject of 'divided'. Other than the names, the entire chapter is without parallel in Genesis.

With this prelude, the earth is apportioned to the three sons in the remainder of ch. 8. Here the order is Shem, Ham, Japheth—an exact reversal of the order in Genesis 10. The change is predictable. Also the concern is very different than in the P sections of Genesis 10. *Jubilees* defines the lots of the three sons by naming their boundaries and the geographical entities found in each. The author thus leaves no question about where the inherited portions lie.

Shem: *Jub*. 8.12-21 deals with Shem and his territory. Before any indication of its whereabouts is given, the writer declares: 'In the book there emerged as Shem's lot the center of the earth which he would occupy as an inheritance for him and for his children throughout the history of eternity...' Similar words follow the detailed specification of the boundaries. 'This share emerged by lot for Shem and his children to occupy it forever, throughout his generation until eternity' (8.17; the thought is repeated in v. 21). It is obvious that the writer is concerned about violations of these boundaries. This is never acceptable; they were fixed already by Noah on the basis of the book. Shem's territory lies south of Japheth's, with the two divided by the Tina (= the Don) River (8.12). It is also said to be in the middle of the earth (8.12). The author relates Shem's good fortune to the earlier blessing that Noah had pronounced upon him in ch. 7 (8.18). The special character of his territory is underscored by the fact that it included the holiest places on earth: the Garden of Eden, Mt Sinai, and Mt Zion. 'He [Noah] knew that the Garden of Eden is the holy of holies and is the residence of the Lord; (that) Mt Sinai is in the middle of the desert; and (that) Mt Zion is the middle of the navel of the earth. The three of them—the one facing the other—were created as holy (places)' (8.20). For the location of Mt Zion the author borrows Ezekiel's colorful phrase טבור הארץ (Ezek.

38.12; cf. 5.5) but refers even to the center of it.[29] The territory is said to be 'a blessed and spacious land. Everything in it is very beautiful' (8.21).

Ham and Japheth: *Jub.* 8.22-24 describes Ham's patrimony, and 8.25-29 deals with that of Japheth. Ham's territory is to the south (v. 22) and it, too, is an eternal possession: 'This is the land which emerged for Ham as a share which he should occupy for himself and his children forever throughout their generations until eternity' (v. 24). Japheth's lot was to the north of the Tina River (vv. 25-29, and 8.12). Naturally, he and his children were to occupy it forever (v. 29). If we have missed the evaluative clues that have been dropped thus far, the conclusion informs us: 'However, it [Japheth's lot] is cold while the land of Ham is hot. Now Shem's land is neither cold nor hot but it is a mixture of cold and heat' (v. 30).[30]

3. *Jubilees 9*. The text continues to be related loosely to Genesis 10. Noah's three sons, now in the order Ham, Shem, and Japheth (that is, from south to north), decided to divide their shares among their sons. The names of the sons are those of Genesis 10 as given in the MT. Further boundaries are described. We should note here that of Ham's four sons, Canaan is given territory the farthest to the west. Beyond him was the sea (9.1, apparently the Mauk Sea which destroys all that comes its way—8.22).[31] His neighbor to the east was Put (Libya), and Egypt was still farther in that direction. Here the writer simply draws an easy inference from the order of Ham's sons in Genesis 10. Among Japheth's seven sons, Madai was assigned land farthest to the west (9.9; contrast Genesis 10 where Madai is between Magog and Javan), while Javan was given some islands toward Lud's border (9.10).

Jub. 9.14-15 rounds off the entire pericope regarding the division of the earth.

---

29. For other instances of the phrase, see Charles, *Book of Jubilees*, p. 69.

30. F. Schmidt ('Naissance d'une géographie juive', in *Moïse Géographe: Recherches sur les représentations juives et chrétiennes de l'espace* [ed. A. Desreumaux and F. Schmidt; Paris: Librairie philosophique J. Vrin, 1988], p. 22) characterizes *Jubilees'* descriptions of the territorial boundaries thus: 'Ces limites sont décrites à la façon des trois itinéraires circulaires circonscrivant les trois domaines'. In the Genesis Apocryphon Noah apparently travels around the world after the flood (Greenfield and Qimron, 'The Genesis Apocryphon Col. XII', p. 70).

31. The name of this sea may be the second element in Neelatamauk, the name of Ham's wife. See VanderKam, *Book of Jubilees*, II, pp. 54-55 for a discussion of the word.

60   *Pursuing the Text: Studies in Honor of Ben Zion Wacholder*

> 9.14 In this way Noah's sons divided (the earth) for their sons in front of
> their father Noah. He made (them) swear by oath to curse each and every
> one who wanted to occupy the share which did not emerge by his lot. 9.15
> All of them said: 'So be it'! So be it for them and their children until
> eternity during their generations until the day of judgment on which the
> Lord God will punish them with the sword and fire because of all the evil
> impurity of their errors by which they have filled the earth with wicked-
> ness, impurity, fornication, and sin.

Anyone caught infiltrating another's lot would have sealed his own fate
by this curse.

4. *Jubilees 10. Jub.* 10.1-14 seemingly has nothing to do with the
subject. In it arrangements are made for counteracting the influence of
Prince Mastema's demons, whose numbers are reduced by 90 per cent.
There is reference in the passage to the blessing of being fruitful and
filling the earth (10.4). Helpful anti-demon medicinal information was
imparted to Noah by the angels of the presence, and this he recorded in
a book (10.12-13). Before he died, Noah 'gave all the books that he had
written to his oldest son Shem [cf. Gen. 10.21] because he loved him
much more than all his sons' (10.14). A theme from later stories in
Genesis—parental favoritism toward one son—is here read back into
Noah's relations with Shem; it simply reinforces what one could have
inferred from the territory Shem had inherited. Noah's death notice then
appears (10.15-17) and a new section begins at v. 18 as the date shows.
To this point no one has actually gone to his assigned home; all continue
to loiter around Lubar. They needed some incentive to leave.[32]

Jub. 10.18-19 resumes the genealogy of Genesis 11 at the place where
it had stopped in ch. 8—with Peleg (Gen. 11.18-19). That is, the story in
Jubilees continues to follow a consistent structure according to the post-
diluvian genealogy. Stories are spliced into it where word-plays indicate
they should be. Peleg begets Reu (רעו; LXX Ραγαυ, *Rāgew* in Ethiopic
Jubilees), and once he is on the scene another narrative is inserted into
the genealogical framework. Of Ragew we learn:

> and he [Peleg] named him Ragew, for he said: 'Mankind has now become
> evil through the perverse plan to build themselves a city and tower in the
> land of Shinar'. For they had emigrated from the land of Ararat toward the
> east, to Shinar [see Gen. 11.2], because in his lifetime they built the city
> and the tower, saying: 'Let us ascend through it to heaven' (10.18-19).

---

32. Note that *Jubilees* eases the difficulty presented by Genesis 10, especially the
J sections where there is movement to different places, whereas the Tower of Babel
story assumes that all are still in one place.

The tower of Babel story is then given in vv. 20-26. As he reproduces the biblical account, the writer ties it to his concerns in these chapters. He quotes God as saying to the angels of the presence:' "The people here are one, and they have begun to work. Now nothing will elude them. Come, let us go down and confuse their tongues so that they do not understand one another and are dispersed into cities and nations and one plan no longer remains with them until the day of judgment"' (10.22). What the Lord God intended happened: 'From there they were dispersed [Gen. 11.8] into their cities, each according to their languages and their nations' (v. 25). Gen. 11.8, while noting the dispersal, does not mention 'their languages and their nations'. The summaries in Genesis 10 do.

Jub. 10.27-36 concludes the section on the division of the earth and reveals the purpose for a number of the matters which the author has been underscoring all along. Verse 27 introduces the section with the notice that they were scattered from Shinar. It turns out that only two of the three family branches were involved in the dispersion mandated by God on the evil tower-builders: Ham and Japheth and their sons. *Jub.* 10.28-34 is the critical paragraph. We learn that Ham and his sons dutifully trudged off to the south (v. 28), but one of his sons, Canaan, who had the farthest to go, must have had roving eyes as he journeyed. 'When Canaan saw that the land of Lebanon as far as the stream of Egypt was very beautiful, he did not go to his hereditary land to the west of the sea. He settled in the land of Lebanon, on the east and west, from the border of Lebanon and on the seacoast' (v. 29). He really should have known better as his family remarked with fitting indignation. He was, of course, already the recipient of one curse; now he was risking another. His father Ham and two of his brothers—Cush and Mizraim (not Put who also had a long trip ahead of him)—laid out the facts for him:

> 'You have settled in a land which was not yours and did not emerge for us by lot. Do not act this way, for if you do act this way both you and your children will fall in the land and be cursed with rebellion, because you have settled in rebellion and in rebellion your children will fall and be uprooted forever. 10.31 Do not settle in Shem's residence because it emerged by their lot for Shem and his sons. 10.32 You are cursed and will be cursed more than all of Noah's children through the curse by which we obligated ourselves with an oath before the holy judge and before our father Noah'. 10.33 But he did not listen to them. He settled in the land of Lebanon— from Hamath to the entrance of Egypt—he and his sons until the present. 10.34 For this reason that land was named the land of Canaan.

Though he was warned by his own family, Ham rejected their counsel and took upon himself the full force of a second curse.[33] In v. 34 the author explains how it is that even in the Bible one reads the misleading phrase 'the land of Canaan' (Gen. 11.31; 12.5; 13.12; 16.3; 17.8): it was not because the land belonged to Canaan; it was due to his stealing it from Shem and his descendants.

The last paragraph deals with a rearrangement in Japheth's patrimony. Rather than going to the far west, Madai, who had married into Shem's family, did not like the land near the sea and *requested* other territory 'from Elam, Asshur, and Arpachshad, his wife's brother. He has settled in the land of Medeqin near his wife's brother until the present' (v. 35). In this way Shem's patrimony was further reduced, although by consent, not theft. The result is that an explanation was found for the presence of a non-S(h)emitic people in S(h)emitic territory. The two lands farthest west are the problematic ones in *Jubilees'* scheme: they are located farthest from the east, the cardinal point toward which the map is literally oriented, and nearest the destructive Mauk Sea.

3. *Jubilees' World Map*

Jubilees' ideological attempt to put the nations in their places has been the subject of a number of studies. The first detailed geographical and historical analysis was made by G. Hölscher who treated it after studying Gen. 2.10-14 (the four rivers of paradise) and Genesis 10.[34] Hölscher found that *Jubilees'* views about the form and lands of the earth were similar to those that prevailed in the Hellenistic-Roman world. More specifically, they were like the old Ionian conception of the world:

> Es nimmt nicht Wunder, dass auch ein jüdischer Gelehrter um 100 v. Chr.
> ganz in den einstigen ionischen Vorstellung lebt; die Erdkarte, die er

---

33. Hood ('The Genealogies of Jesus', pp. 3-5) describes 'magnification' or its opposite as one function of genealogies. With reference to *Rhetoric to Alexander* xxxv (a pseudo-Aristotelian work), he indicates that 'if the speaker's purpose is the denunciation of his subject, he should make advantageous use of bad ancestry' (p. 4; cf. his remarks on 'characterization' [pp. 5-6]) The author of *Jubilees* clearly pursues this strategy for Canaan's descendants.

34. *Drei Erdkarten: Ein Beitrag zur Erdkenntnis des hebräischen Altertums* (Sitzungsberichte der Heidelberger Akademie der Wissenschaften, philosophisch-historische Klasse 1944/48, 3; Heidelberg: Carl Winter, Universitätsverlag, 1949). The section on *Jub.* 8–9 is pp. 57-73.

zeichnet, ist bis auf allerlei eingefügte jüngere Namen den alten ionischen Karten recht ähnlich.[35]

P.S. Alexander has also defended a connection between *Jubilees'* map and the 'so-called Ionian world map'.[36] As Alexander, following Hölscher, sketches the evidence, he notes the following traits of the Ionian maps: (1) the earth is disc-shaped, with water (Ocean) surrounding it; (2) the *omphalos* of the world was Delphi; (3) the earth consisted of three parts or continents, usually divided by rivers (the Tanais=the Don and the Nile); (4) the surrounding Ocean invaded the land mass at the Caspian, Erythrean (Indian Ocean), and Mediterranean Seas.[37] He also indicates that there are strong affinities between *Jubilees'* arrangement and the later Macrobius or zone maps, that is, maps which divide the earth into parallel zones distinguished by their temperatures.[38]

The parallels that Hölscher and Alexander have found are impressive: division of three world zones by two parallel rivers which are the same in the Ionian maps and in *Jubilees*. Alexander finds this a significant 'harmonisation of the Bible and "science": the author of Jubilees interpreted the Bible in the light of the non-Jewish "scientific" knowledge of his day. He was, it seems, open and receptive to such alien knowledge and envisaged no fundamental clash between it and the truth of the Bible'.[39]

Several authors have provided sketches of *Jubilees'* map: (1) Hölscher;[40] (2) M. Testuz;[41] (3-4) Alexander;[42] and (5) F. Schmidt.[43] Only the last two are correctly rather than conventionally oriented.

---

35. *Drei Erdkarten* , p. 57.

36. 'Notes on the "Imago Mundi" of the Book of Jubilees', *JJS* 33 (1982), p. 197.

37. 'Notes', pp. 198-99.

38. 'Notes', pp. 202-203.

39. 'Notes', pp. 210-11.

40. *Drei Erdkarten*, p. 58.

41. *Les idées religieuses du livre des Jubilés* (Geneva: Librairie E. Droz/Paris: Librairie Minard, 1960), p. 58.

42. The first map is from his 'Notes on the "Imago Mundi"', p. 213; the second appears in his 'Geography and the Bible', p. 982.

43. 'Naissance d'une géographie', p. 23.

1.

2.

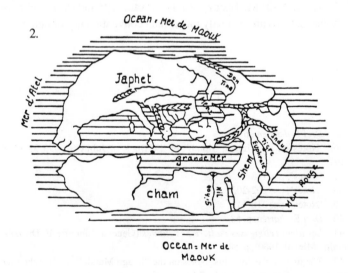

3.

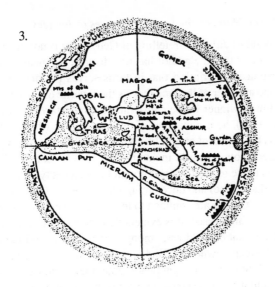

4. 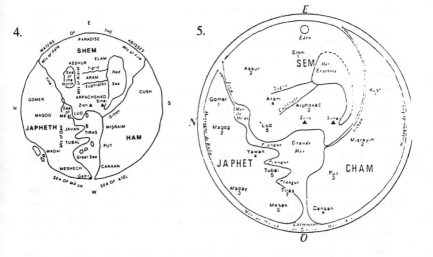 5.

4. *The Map and the Larger Purposes of Jubilees*

The general point of *Jubilees'* retelling of Genesis 10 is not difficult to perceive. It is clear that the author has transformed a genealogical list into a geographical description that in turns serves politico-religious ends. Shem, the ancestor of the Israelites, is the favorite of his father and the overwhelming winner in the cartographic sweepstakes. Indeed (as emerges elsewhere), he is a member of the priestly line which will culminate in Levi himself. Not only is he holy; his inheritance encompasses the most sacred spots on earth, including the 'holy of holies'. Shem's patrimony was twice reduced: once through the generosity of several of his sons (the Madai case) and once through thievery (the Canaan affair). Interestingly, the Greeks are confined to their islands and not given land in Asia Minor or farther east. It is evident that the writer has decided to make the table of nations address, among other concerns, primarily the problem of who really owned the land of Canaan. Was it the Canaanites, whose name might incline the ignorant to grant them land rights, or was it Israel who held it for some centuries after Joshua's conquests?

In confronting the question of who owned the land, the writer of *Jubilees* resorted to a tactic which he often used: moving later realities into earlier times. The procedure can be documented for various areas: legal concerns, holidays, circumcision, and the like. To give an example only from the first category, the stipulations in Lev. 12.2-5 about a woman's times of purification after bearing a male or female child are traced back to the different dates when Adam and Eve were introduced into the garden (3.8-14). In the present case, the author does something similar. The territories of the nations were not, on his view, the casual acquisitions or conquests of history; they had been assigned by Noah with the guidance of an angel of the presence who may have brought Noah a book detailing the national boundaries. The favorable location of Shem's lot corresponded with the blessing that Noah had earlier pronounced on him ('"may the Lord live in the place where Shem resides"' [7.12]). The fate of Canaan was consonant with the curse which Noah had visited upon him (7.11-12). Canaan, as Genesis 10 indicates, was the father of a number of the nations which the Israelites met and defeated in Canaan. In Genesis we read about the boundaries of the promised land first in ch. 15 (by which time Canaan's descendants were already in the land; cf. Gen. 12.6); *Jubilees* improves on Genesis by moving the territorial allottments back into ch. 10, before the Bible has made reference to any Canaanite in the land.

The way in which *Jubilees* formulates the Canaanite usurpation makes one believe that when the book was written the issue of who owned Canaan was debated.[44] There are no contemporary sources which evidence such discussions, but much later texts give some reason for thinking that the Jewish people had been branded as robbers for taking Canaan from its original, rightful owners. Written evidence for such disputes does not appear until the classical rabbinic texts and the writings of Procopius (sixth century CE).

1. *Gen. R.* 61.6: The dispute in the passage picks up at least one of the points raised in *Jubilees*. It appears in a series of debates before Alexander the Great, with Gebiah b. Qosem representing the Jewish side.

> The Canaanites said, 'We lay claim, and we bring our evidence from their own Torah. Throughout their Torah it is written, "the land of Canaan." So let them give us back our land.' Said to him Gebiah b. Qosem, 'My royal lord, does a man not do whatever he likes with his slave?' He said to him, 'Indeed so.' He said to him, 'And lo, it is written, "A slave of slaves shall Canaan be to his brothers" (Gen 9:25). So they are really our slaves.' They abandoned the field in shame.[45]

2. *b. Sanh.* 91a: The story here takes a similar form, but the litigants are the Africans who present themselves as the descendants of Canaan and cite Num. 34.2 in support of their claim on the land (see also *Meg. Ta'an.* 3.5 where some manuscripts read 'Canaanite' not 'Africans').

3. Procopius, *de bello vandalico* 4.10, 13-22: The context is an aside; Procopius breaks off his account of the wars to explain how it was that the Moors settled in Libya.

> When the Hebrews had withdrawn from Egypt and had come near the boundaries of Palestine, Moses, a wise man, who was their leader on the journey, died, and the leadership was passed on to Joshua, the son of Nun, who led this people into Palestine, and, by displaying a valour in war greater than that natural to man, gained possession of the land. And after overthrowing all the nations he easily won the cities, and he seemed to be altogether invincible. Now at that time the whole country along the sea from Sidon as far as the boundaries of Egypt was called Phoenicia. And one king in ancient times held sway over it, as is agreed by all who have

44. So Charles, *Book of Jubilees*, p. 68.

45. The translation is that of J. Neusner, *Genesis Rabbah: The Judaic Commentary to the Book of Genesis. A New American Translation.* II. *Parashiyyot Thirty-Four through Sixty-Seven* (BJS 105; Atlanta, GA: Scholars Press, 1985).

written the earliest accounts of the Phoenicians. In that country there dwelt very populous tribes, the Gergesites and the Jebusites and some others with other names by which they are called in the history of the Hebrews. Now when these nations saw that the invading general was an irresistible prodigy, they emigrated from their ancestral homes and made their way to Egypt, which adjoined their country. And finding there no place sufficient for them to dwell in, since there has been a great population in Aegypt from ancient times, they proceeded to Libya. And they established numerous cities and took possession of the whole of Libya as far as the pillars of Heracles, and there they have lived even up to my time, using the Phoenician tongue. They also built a fortress in Numidia, where now is the city called Tigisis. In that place are two columns made of white stone near by the great spring, having Phoenician letters cut in them which say in the Phoenician tongue: 'We are they who fled from before the face of Joshua, the robber ['Ιησοῦ τοῦ λῃστοῦ], the son of Nun.[46]

4. Rashi, too, uses this tradition, but he adduces it as he comments on Gen. 1.1. The question he asks is why the Scriptures begin with an account of creation. He quotes Ps. 111.6 and writes:

For should the peoples of the world say to Israel, 'You are robbers [לסטים], because you took by force the lands of the seven nations of *Canaan*', Israel may reply to them, 'All the earth belongs to the Holy One,

---

46. Translation of H.B. Dewing, *Procopius*, II (LCL; Cambridge: Harvard/ London: Heinemann, 1953). The rabbinic references and Procopius's story are surveyed in H.Z. (J.W.) Hirschberg, *A History of the Jews in North Africa*. I. *From Antiquity to the Sixteenth Century* (Leiden: Brill, 1974), pp. 40-48. He also refers to the older analyses of these accounts by A. Aptowitzer ('Les premiers possesseurs de Canaan: légendes apologétiques et exégétiques', *REJ* 82 [1926], pp. 275-86) and J. Lewy. Lewy thought that the stories in the rabbinic texts were to be viewed against the backdrop of Hasmonean expansion which led to displacement of non-Jewish peoples. He also brought *Jub.* 8–10 into the discussion. Hirschberg thinks the story of Joshua the robber 'is a product of the propaganda of Greeks and Hellenized *Poeni* in Africa, who sought to defame the Jews when these began to arrive there in increasing numbers' (p. 46). For the Procopius material in relation to *Jubilees*, see also Alexander, 'Retelling the Old Testament', in *It is Written: Scripture Citing Scripture: Essays in Honour of Barnabas Lindars, SSF* (ed. D.A. Carson and H.G.M. Williamson; Cambridge: Cambridge University Press, 1988), p. 118, n. 3. A. Büchler ('Traces des idées hellénistiques dans le livre des Jubilés', *REJ* 89 [1930], pp. 326-29) mentions the idea of the dispute but adduces no passages. Cf. also W. Bacher, 'The Supposed Inscription upon "Joshua the Robber"', *JQR* 3 (1891), pp. 354-57; J. Lewy, 'Ein Rechtsstreit um Boden Palästinas im Altertum', *MGWJ* 77 (1933), pp. 84-99, 172-80.

blessed be He; He created it and gave it to whom he pleased. When He willed He gave it to them, and when He willed He took it from them and gave it to us'.[47]

The late date of all these sources forces one to be cautious in using them to clarify second-century BCE debates, but they do at least show that the issues addressed in *Jubilees* 8–10 reappear in later polemical literature. It is unproven but not unlikely that such disputes were the occasion for the way in which the writer shaped his account. In distinction from these treatments, however, *Jubilees* asserts Israel's ancestral right to the promised land by means of an elaborate presentation of the division of the world among the three sons of Noah. Shem's patrimony was the center, it was holy, there God dwells and is worshiped, and there no outsider such as Canaan, so horribly condemned by two curses, should venture. It was only right that Israel, Shem's descendants, later drove the children of Canaan from the land they had stolen from its legitimate owners.

47. Translation of M. Rosenbaum and A.M. Silbermann, *Pentateuch with Targum Onkelos, Haphtaroth and Rashi's Commentary*. I. *Genesis* (New York: Hebrew Publishing, 1935), p. 2. See also *Gen. R.* 1.11, 1.

THE 'DAMASCUS' SECT AND JUDAISM

Philip R. Davies

The thesis I wish to dedicate to Ben Zion Wacholder is that we may learn much about Second Temple Judaism by analysing one of its sects. Accordingly, I intend (a) to define the contents of the *Damascus Document* as emanating from a Jewish sect, (b) to ask about the social and ideological structure of that sect and (c) to ask about the social and political structures of Second Temple Judaism in Palestine that this structure implies. The history of scholarship has tended to focus on the identity of the sect and the reasons for its formation. But before either of these questions should be asked, we must try to understand as far as possible the *character* of the sect. So I shall not discuss here whether we are dealing with Essenes, Sadducees, or any other known group, nor shall I offer a theory as to what events prompted this sect to come into existence. I am rather interested, to use the fashionable jargon, in the conditions of possibility of Jewish sects in general, and this one in particular.

Sect: A Definition

I am defining a *sect* in this paper as an entity of a *social* kind, and therefore characterized not by what it *believes* but by its *constitution as a particular kind of social unit*, comprising a *socially dissenting* part of some larger society. Where a social group separates itself, not as a distinct member of a wider society, in which it plays a part and interacts with other such groups, but as a complete and autonomous society within itself, be that understood as an alternative to the society in which it is physically located, or as an expression of that society's ideal, then this social group constitutes, in my definition, a sect. That wider society from which it secedes could be a nation, state, ethnos, or an even smaller group—for instance, some sects arise within other sects, as I think was the case with the *yahad* of 1QS.[1] So my investigation relates concretely not to the nature of the ideas that the sect has, but to the social expression of those ideas.

The value of such a study of sects extends beyond an understanding of the sect itself. For the nature of a sect derives necessarily from that body of which it *is* a sect. A sect will share to some extent the premises upon which the society of which it is a sect operates. Thus, the study of sects can be an important part of the analysis of the societies from which they are generated, and an examination of Jewish sects can give an insight into the nature of Jewish society. Indeed, we might propose that there cannot be Jewish sects until there is a sufficiently coherent definition of what a 'Judaism' might be; a sect must articulate itself in terms of a fairly developed norm, or what it can see as a norm, whether that norm is concretely expressed in society or merely maintained by the society as an ideal construct.[2] So the study of sects is a kind of pathology, and just as Freud used pathology to illuminate the nature of the non-pathological, so we can use sects to illuminate the non-sectarian.[3]

The importance of the Qumran scrolls in this context is not so much that they articulate hitherto unfamiliar or even unexpected Jewish religious beliefs such as astrology or dualism, but that they describe

1. As I argued in *The Damascus Covenant* (JSOTSup, 25; Sheffield: JSOT Press, 1983).

2. I cannot here debate the question of what kind of an entity 'Judaism' was in the late Second Temple period. It was not necessarily a single religious system; perhaps it is better defined as a 'genus', with G. Boccaccini, *Middle Judaism: Jewish Thought 300 BCE to 200 CE* (Minneapolis: Augsburg Fortress, 1991). On the other hand, if Judaism is not necessarily a single system, it may have comprised a largely homogeneous set of public practices, as Sanders has argued (*Judaism, Practice and Belief 63 BCE-66 CE* [London: SCM Press/Philadelphia: Trinity Press International, 1992]). It seems to me that at the level of the history of ideas or of intellectual systems, the notion of 'Judaisms' is preferable, while at the level of religion as a public activity, Sanders' account works better. Both forms of description could be applied with equal validity to twentieth-century European or North American Christianity: Catholicism, Calvinism, fundamentalism are different intellectual (I use the term 'intellectual' of fundamentalism loosely) systems, while as a public religion, Christianity in all of these forms exhibits a certain homogeneity. At all events, my postulation of a Jewish sect requires some assent to Sanders' proposition of a 'common Judaism'.

3. A more recent dramatic example of this technique is given in Oliver Sacks's *The Man Who Mistook His Wife For a Hat* (London: Duckworth, 1985).

communities in which religious dissent assumed concrete social forms, which in turn gave rise to the development of more or less complete ideological systems.[4] I am concerned in this paper with one such community, which I understand to have been a sect, and whose beliefs and practices are articulated in the *Damascus Document*. We know that Judah in the late Second Temple period contained numerous social groups: the Essenes of Josephus, Pliny and Philo (if they are the same), Pharisees, Sadducees, the Fourth Philosophy, Samaritans (perhaps), the numerous baptising groups that are attested in the texts of early Church Fathers, Dositheans, Boethusians and so on. In some cases we can define them—in the sense I have just given—as sects, in some cases not. But in hardly any case do we know much about their social or ideological structures or mechanisms. The *Damascus Document* may be our very best testimony. If we want to understand the pluralism of Second Temple Judaism, it is important to analyse in as much detail as we can one of its sects.

The 'Damascus' Sect

I believe the 'Damascus' community as defined in the *Damascus Document* was a sect, because (a) it draws ideological boundaries between itself and the rest of 'Israel', (b) it realizes those boundaries socially and even geographically in a segregated lifestyle and (c) it claims exclusively to be the true 'Israel'. In fact, it displays nearly all of the characteristics of the 'ideal type' *Christian* sect delineated by Bryan Wilson[5]—exclusivity, monopoly of truth, essentially lay membership, religious equality, accession by merit, voluntarism, the expulsion of dissidents, total allegiance and protest. I am not going to examine all of these features (those scholars familiar with CD can try this themselves), but concentrate essentially on the question of boundaries, the areas at

---

4.   How far the descriptions are accurate, or literal, accounts of existing communities, or edited accounts, or idealized accounts is an important question, which I have raised elsewhere ('Redaction and Sectarianism in the Qumran Scrolls', in F. García Martínez, A. Hilhorst and C.J. Labuschagne [eds.], *The Scriptures and the Scrolls* [Leiden: Brill, 1992], pp. 152-63). For the present purposes, it may be enough to say that I take the 'Damascus' community to have been a real one, but that in any event even imagined or 'edited' sects can be used to analyse the society in which they are projected.

5.   B.R. Wilson, *Religion in Sociological Perspective* (Oxford: Oxford University Press, 1982), pp. 91-93.

which sectarian identity is affirmed and sustained against the outside. From this focus the ideology and structure of the sect also unfold for our inspection.

Boundaries of the Sect
It is well recognized that many Palestinian Jewish texts express—if not always, or consistently, or thoroughly—certain characteristics of exclusivity. These characteristics appear, for instance, in the legends of Ezra, Nehemiah, in the Abraham cycle (though only to a limited extent), the Sinai covenant, the conquest accounts of Joshua, and the idealized anti-Canaanite society drawn by Deuteronomy. Each of these cases reflects a basic dichotomy between Israel and other nations. While a similar chauvinistic attitude might be found in many societies, and indeed is not necessarily a prominent feature of every manifestation of Judaism, yet in Judaism the distinction between Jews and non-Jews is perhaps unique in its definitive power. It is important that we recognize this matrix in analysing a Jewish sect which, of course, we should expect to draw a perhaps even sharper boundary between itself and the outside than Jews did with respect to non-Jews.

In the *Damascus Document* we indeed encounter boundaries between the sect and non-Jews and between the sect and other Jews. The distinction between the two 'outside' categories, other Jews and non-Jews, does not always appear to be of importance, or at least not clearly drawn. We twice find the expression בני השחת (6.15; 13.14), perhaps the clearest expression of a basic dualism in the sect's world-view. But whether this phrase means non-Jews, other Jews or both is unclear.[6] In 2.1ff., where we have a predestinarian and dualistic account of human origins, with humanity divided between the 'chosen' and the 'wicked', it is also on the surface unclear where the sect draws its boundaries. However, this account lies between two others which detail the sins of Israel and compare the salvation of the righteous with the sin and future punishment of the righteous remnant. The juxtaposition suggests that at least this part of the document seeks to oppose the true with the false *Israel*, the rejected with the chosen *Israel*, and that there is no direct confrontation with non-Jews, the world beyond Israel being functionally

6. Rabin (*The Zadokite Documents* [Oxford: Clarendon Press, 2nd edn, 1958], pp. 24, 67), assumes Jews, but without argumentation. The phrase appears also in 1QS 9.16; 10.19 and 1QH 2.21; in *Jub.* 10.3 it refers to those drowned in the Flood (and thus not only Jews); in 15.26 the referent is unclear.

neutral and/or irrelevant. It may seem an obvious or trivial point, but at least it distinguishes this sect from the more successful Pauline sect of slightly later times.

There are, in any case, several points at which non-Jews enter the regulations of sectarian life, and we shall need to investigate the terminology that may apply to them, starting with CD 11.14-15:

אל ישבית [א]יש [ב]מקום קרוב לגוים בשבת

let no one spend the sabbath in a place close to non-Jews

which distinguishes between other Jews and non-Jews (the sectarian is allowed to spend the sabbath near Jewish non-members) and also implies that on other days communication with non-Jews was allowed. Indeed, dealings with non-Jews are also implied in the ban on selling them clean beasts or birds for sacrifice, or any cereal or wine (12.8-10).

Together with these texts we may take 12.6-7, where again גוים denotes a non-Jew:

אל ישלח את ידו לשפוך דם לאיש מן <u>הגוים</u> בעבור
הון ובצע וגם אל ישא מהונם כל בעבור אשר לא ינדפו
כי אם בעצת חבור ישראל

let no one commit bloodshed against any non-Jewish person for reason of gain or profit; let no one take away any of their property, so that they should not blaspheme—except on instruction from the 'commonwealth of Israel'

We might in passing also note the allusion in 9.1 to execution by the חוקי הגוים. In 11.2, though, we encounter a different term:

אל ישלח את <u>בן הנכר</u> לעשות את חפצו ביום השבת

no-one may send a *ben ha-nekar* to do something for him on the sabbath day

Rabin offers both 'proselyte' and 'gentile' as translations of בן הנכר. I think 'non-Jew/Gentile' is certainly to be preferred. It is inherently improbable that a member of the sect would encourage a proselyte to bypass sabbath rules. Here we may even have the oldest reference to the *shabbas goy*! Thus, גוי and בן נכר both denote non-Jews.

To find 'proselytes', which are obviously an important topic, we should probably look to 14.3ff.:

(3) וסרך מושב כל המחנות יפקדו כלם בשמותיהם הכ[הני]ם לראשונה
(4) והלוים שנים ובני ישראל שלשתם <u>והגר</u> רביע ויכתבו בש[מות]יהם
(5) איש אחר אחיהו הכהנים לראשונה והלוים שנים ובני ישראל
(6) שלושתם <u>והגר</u> רביע

The four categories of member in the sect are here given as priest, levite, Israelite and גר. This last word could, without consideration of its context, mean either 'proselyte' or 'non-Jew'.[7] 'Proselyte' is surely meant, though a proselyte to the sect, and thus one in the process of initiation into it, who does not yet have a full place in 'Israel' or 'Aaron'. In Ezekiel (cf. CD 3.21-4.4, based on Ezek. 44.15) a גר is a non-Israelite living among Israelites who is nevertheless treated as more or less an 'honorary Israelite'.[8] Thus, new entrants to the sect, Jews living within the sect, are regarded analogously to Ezekiel's non-Jews living among Israel, which would be consistent with the sect regarding itself as the true Israel (on which see later). The rabbinic meaning of the term might be similarly explained.

The boundary between Jew and non-Jew is not crossable, it seems, from the sect's point of view. But this is not an important boundary. What about the *really* important boundary between sectarian and non-sectarian Jew, between the false and the true Israel? This is a boundary signified in CD by two main symbols. One is a wall: at 4.12 CD quotes Micah 7.11: 'the wall is built', but the real wall-building is attributed to outsiders, the 'builders of the wall', the phrase perhaps derived from Ezek. 13.10[9] and who first appear in 4.19 but recur in 19.24-25 and 8.18 (= 19.31). The other image is that of 'straying away', and becoming lost. From CD's perspective, it is the outsiders, the false Israel which has strayed away from the true Israel, just as Ephraim departed from Judah (8.11ff; MS A only). We encounter this theme of straying throughout the *Admonition* (e.g. 1.13; 2.13; 4.1).

Crossing the boundary *into* the sect is possible in several ways. We have encountered the case of the גר, one who enters the sect by voluntary admission and presumably passes through a stage prior to full membership (but we do not have information about this, and so caution is required. Cf. 15.5ff.). Unfortunately, or perhaps interestingly, CD gives little or no detail about the status and admission of such persons, and the idea that the 'Qumran sect' had an intricate admission system is derived

7. The first three terms appear in 4.1ff., in the midrash on Ezek. 44.15, where 'Israelites' appear as בחירי ישראל; however, in this midrash the terms come from the cited text, which the midrash then converts into other categories.

8. See especially Ezek. 14.7; 47.32 (cp. 22.7, 29)

9. 'Because, yea, because they have misled my people, saying, "Peace", when there is no peace; and because, when the people build a wall, these prophets daub it with whitewash...'

from 1QS and from the writings of Josephus on the Essenes. We have to infer such a process, but cannot know as yet how stringent it was.

But since the sect lives, at least partly, in communities of households, there are other forms of admission. Let us consider the sequel to 12.6-8a quoted earlier, which was evidently dealing with non-Jews:

(8b) אל ימכר איש בהמה

(9) ועוף טהורים לגוים בעבור אשר לא יזבחום ומגורנו

(10) ומגתו אל ימכר להם בכל מאדו ואת עבדו ואת אמתו אל ימכור

(11) להם אשר באו עמו בברית אברהם

no-one should sell clean animals or birds to non-Jews, so that they may not sacrifice them. One must strenuously avoid selling them anything from one's threshing floor or wine-press. Nor may one sell one's male or female slave to them, since they have come, together with one, into the covenant of Abraham.

Like its context, this concerns dealings with non-Jews, גוים, but what about the עבד and the אמה? Why must *they* not be sold to non-Jews? Because, says CD, they too are reckoned among those belonging to the 'covenant of Abraham'. They are in it along with their owner. Now, the position of slaves within the comunity is worth close consideration, since they constitute a kind of boundary; they are a marginal group. Jer. 34.8-9 proposes that 'no one should enslave a Jew, his brother'; perhaps the Damascus covenant members invoked Deut. 15.12, which commanded the release of all Hebrew slaves after six years. But if such slaves were 'Hebrew' or 'Jewish', were they also members of the 'Damascus covenant'? The term used in this connection is 'covenant of Abraham', not 'new covenant' or 'covenant of Damascus', which elsewhere in CD designates the sect.

Slaves, then, do not seem to have been full members of the sect. Its rigid boundaries were permeable at this point. Unlike proselytes, who also represented a point of transition on the boundary, slaves were not ideologically committed, were never about to become members of the sect. At any rate, this is the implication I draw. In the light of this conclusion we can now proceed to interpret 7.6b (I cite the text as in ms A):

ואם מחנות ישבו כסרך ארץ ולקחו נשים והולידו בנים והתהלכו

על פי התורה...כאשר אמר בין איש לאשתו ובין אב לבנו

And if they live in camps, following the 'rule of the land' and take wives and have children, these (also) shall follow the torah...as it says, 'between a man and his wife and between a man and his child/son'.

As I have argued before,[10] we can only make sense of this statement in its context by taking the *wives and children* as the subject of והתהלכו, and not the male sectarian, who would obviously obey the rules if he were married and with children, as he would otherwise. Wives and children, like slaves, belong to the household. But not being slaves, they are, I would suggest, members of the 'new covenant of Damascus' and subject to its laws, since I take 'torah' to refer to the sect's own definition of the 'law of Moses'.

Socially, then, the sect functions as a society based on the *household*. All members of the household are deemed to belong to the sect, except the slaves, who must nevertheless be Jewish. At least, this applies to life in 'camps'. CD 7.6b implies, of course, that not all members of the sect married or lived in such 'camps', and the *Laws* mention 'city' as well as 'camp' life (cf. 12.19, סרך מושב ערי ישראל; 10.21, חוץ לעירו). Note also 20.13: ולא יה[יה] להם משפחותיהם חלק בבית תור[ה] But of the distinctions between the two lifestyles we are insufficiently informed, though we might guess that in the cities the סרך ארץ was not the rule.

The Sect as 'Israel'
Did the sect regard itself as the true Israel? The answer is clearly 'yes', though the language of CD does not place a radical stress on this. In 1.5 the sect is the 'remnant that remained of Israel'; in 3.19 it is a 'sure house in Israel'; in 4.3-4 the 'elect of Israel'. In several places the term 'Israel' retains its wider connotation: 1.4 'hid his face from Israel'; 3.14 'the hidden things (נסתרות) in which all Israel had erred'; 4.13 Belial let loose on 'Israel'; 5.20 'Israel' led astray; 20.15-16 the anger of God kindled against 'Israel'. The name 'Israel' can thus be used not only of the nation of the past, but also the nation of the present. But we also find 'Israel' applying to the sect: 'cities of Israel' in 12.19, clearly referring to its dwellings (cf. the 'seed of Israel' in 12.22), and in 12.8 the חבור ישראל (cf חבר in 14.16). In 3.13, too, the 'covenant with Israel' is that made with the sect. One should not make much of this ambiguity of terminology ('Israel' is also used to refer to non-priests). The sect is the real Israel, and is therefore Israel; but there is also a wider Israel, a false Israel, but still an Israel that cannot easily be called anything else. The wider Israel, according to CD, is misled by Belial and stumbles towards its punishment on the day of divine visitation. It is to this Israel

10. *Damascus Covenant*, p. 142.

that the sect of CD basically opposes itself, rather than the wider world that includes non-Jews.

The Damascus sect also claims the identity of Israel by means of its story of its own origins. It traces its foundation to the aftermath of the exile, when either God's covenant with Israel was renewed (6.2) or a new one made (3.13), and the divine will was revealed through the law (6.2ff.). CD even makes room for a list of those original members of the sect (4.6, cf. Ezra 2; Neh. 12). It has a founder who revealed the divine will (the דורש התורה, 6.7; 7.18). Here again is a counterpart to Nehemiah and Ezra. Indeed, we even have an emphasis on the interpretation of the law (CD 6.4ff.; Neh. 8.7-8). The sect thus claims to be as old as the wider society of 'Israel', claiming continuity with the righteous ones of the pre-exilic time, and branding the rest of Israel as the successors of the wicked pre-exilic ones who were destroyed for their sins (2.14ff.).

Ideology of the Sect
Having considered the social organization and the boundaries, ideological and social, of the sect, we can now turn to its internal ideological structures.

The expressed aim of the members of the sect is to 'return to the Law (*torah*) of Moses', to which end that *torah* was revealed to every member (15.12f.; 16.5 etc.), and they will live according to it through 'all the age of wickedness' until the day of reckoning (see 6.10f.; 3.15-16). The laws in CD are based upon scripture in the great majority of cases, reinforcing the impression gained by the impregnation of the entire *Admonition* by scriptural language that the writers are steeped in it. This sect is perhaps the earliest Jewish society explicitly to set itself to live entirely by the Mosaic law as it understands it to have been revealed.[11]

According to CD's rhetoric, scripture is also accepted by outsiders, and so functions as a common denominator between insiders and outsiders. Otherwise the polemic of appealing to scriptural texts, or to written laws not obeyed would not work. It explains the divergence

11. A question to be considered (briefly) is whether the laws of CD remain strictly within the practical, or stray into the theoretical; e.g., regulations about 'simpletons and lunatics' (15.15) or those taken captive by foreigners (14.15). Even in the material from Cave 4, I have not come across any legislation that strikes me *prima facie* as purely theoretical, elaborated for the sake of legal theory and not for practical purposes. But see further below, pp. 83-84 for an elaboration on this issue.

between itself and outsiders, both sharing the same scriptures, as the result of the mischief of Belial (4.12-13) from which each member is delivered upon admission to the sect (16.4-5). The sect therefore arises within the context of what might be called a 'scriptural Judaism', which recognizes the authority of the written 'law of Moses' and also of prophetic writings. For this reason, I doubt that the origin of the sect *as a sect* can be pushed back to the Persian or even the Ptolemaic period: claims to exilic origin are a common theme in Jewish literature. This is one illustration of my contention that a Jewish sect is not possible until a certain coherence within Judaism is possible. Scripture, or perhaps better, torah, is perhaps, a common denominator, difference over which makes sectarian division meaningful.

Another important element of CD's Judaism is relations with the Temple. Again, the Temple may be seen as a common denominator which gives meaning to sectarian division. CD 6.12-13 seems to refer to a 'covenant' regarding this matter:

וכל אשר הובאו בברית לבלתי בוא אל המקדש להאיר
מזבחו חנם ויהיו מסגירי הדלת

all who have been entered into a covenant not to come into the sanctuary to light its altar in vain, who shall be 'closers of the door'

I have elsewhere[12] examined the ideology of the Temple in CD and concluded that the members of the Damascus sect had not abandoned it entirely, but used it to a limited extent, believing that only they, in possession of the true divine will and law, were not defiling it by, for example, sending offerings to it (11.17ff.). There is mention of a sectarian place of worship (11.22: בית השתחות) and the midrash on Amos 9.11 (7.14-20) argues that the books of the law and of the prophets have been exiled from the tent (Temple) to Damascus, which is the place to which the 'Interpreter of the Law' came. In other words, there are two centres of holiness: the Temple and the law, and both should be together. But when the Temple is not administered according to the law, but defiled, and the law, on the sect's view, lies with them alone, then the Temple itself plays a role in the life of the sect circumscribed by the law, and thus limited. Certain of the Temple's functions, such as worship, will be devolved to other institutions, and the sect's priesthood will attend to the holiness of the sect itself. Thus the ideology of holiness

12. 'The Ideology of the Temple in the Damascus Document', *JJS* 33 (1982): *Essays in Honour of Yigael Yadin*, pp. 287-301.

which underlies the life of the sect is in some measure the result of sectarian separation from the Temple as the single Jewish seat of holiness.

Formation of the Sect

It has to be acknowledged that we have little clear evidence in CD itself as to what it was that prompted the sect to form. The account it gives of being the remnant preserved after the exile is primarily an ideological one, and in any case gives no explanation in terms of historical processes. The issues that CD claims separate the sect from the rest of Israel surface in the polemical *Admonition* rather than the *Laws*. As I see them, they relate to the correct separation of times, places and of sexual relations. The disputes in legal interpretation actually concern two basic issues: calendar and purity. CD 3.13 reads: 'but with those that adhered to the commandments of God, who survived of them, God established his covenant with Israel...revealing to them the hidden things (נסתרות) in which all Israel had erred; his holy sabbaths and his glorious festivals...' The 'nets of Belial' (4.15ff.) concern purity, specifically sexual purity: marriage and fornication, sexual intercourse close to menstruation, and incest. There is also a list of stipulations in 6.14bff. which comprise keeping apart from outsiders, abstaining from unclean wealth (profit from Temple property), robbery and murder, separating clean and unclean, holy and profane, observing sabbath and the Festival of Atonement, setting aside holy offerings, refraining from illicit sex, avoiding impurity. (We might add 'eating blood' from 3.6.)

The ideological framework of the *Damascus Document* is thus basically one of 'distinguishing' (6.17: להבדיל בין הטמא לטהור ולהודיע בין הקודש לחול. Such concerns are found also in, say, Leviticus and the Mishnah. They do not represent a unique set of sectarian preoccupations, but a structure shared among several Judaisms that start from premises central to the Judean cult and its priesthood. The sect arises from a sector of Jewish society in which Temple, scriptural law and purity are agreed bases. Those who formed the sect therefore probably already had views regarding the sacredness of objects and times. We can, then, at least propose that CD's sect arose within the context of a priestly Judaism. There is no fundamental ideological difference in its character.

This observation is consistent with the character and probable setting of *Jubilees* and parts of *1 Enoch*, each dated to the Maccabean/ Hasmonean period, and perhaps reflecting the overt priestly rivalry that led to the flight of one high priest and the murder of another. Even the account of history that the *Apocalypse of Weeks* (*1 En.* 93.1-10; 91.11-17) and *Jubilees* contain[13] is basically identical to that in CD—a chosen root emerging after the exile—and there is no reference to the building of the Second Temple (though its existence is certainly to be inferred); we find accusations of calendrical error in *Jubilees*, and concern with calendrical differences is an established feature of *1 Enoch*. All three texts refer to revealed teaching; the *Apocalypse of Weeks* refers also to the emergence of an 'elect of righteousness' after the rise of an 'apostate generation'. *Jubilees*, like CD, lays claim to a set of divinely revealed laws that validate the calendrical and other views of the writers, in a manner that anticipates the projection of the 'oral law' in rabbinic literature. There is abundant evidence to link CD, *Jubilees* and the Enoch tradition into a history which culminates in the formation of the Damascus sect. But there are still important missing links which stand in the way of a theory.

For instance, CD, despite its criticism of the priestly establishment, directs itself against Israel as a whole. Its criticism of *leaders* is not central. Indeed, it identifies the 'people' rather than the rulers as those from whom it is segregated and whom it regards as in error. Thus, in 8.8, the criticism is that the 'princes of Judah' did not 'withdraw (reading נזרו, √זור, *niphal*) from the people (עם)'; in 8.16, again, the members of the sect סרו מדרך העם. The sect sees itself as separated from the *people*.[14] The separation from all other Jews (if that is what 'people' means) is what makes the sect a sect and not just an opposition party.

'Separation from the people' is echoed in 4QMMT, and prompts us to look at this text for other possible clues. This text is apparently addressed to a ruler of Israel (presumably the high priest) indicating issues of legal disagreement between the writer and the recipient. Earlier in the text (C7) comes the statement that 'we (have) separated (פרשנו) from the majority (רוב) of the people'. Here again we find separation

---

13. I have analysed these in *Beyond the Essenes* (Atlanta: Scholars Press, 1987), pp. 107-34.

14. I am ignoring most of the interesting material in CD 20 because of my conviction that it reflects the formation of the *yahad* and not the Damascus community, even though this includes a further reference to the 'people' in 20.24, where the 'house of Peleg' are said to have 'returned to the way of the people in some respects'—in any case, the reading is uncertain. See the discussion in *Damascus Covenant*, pp. 192-94.

from the *people*. The issues in the text about which the writers dispute revolve mainly around matters of purity that affect the Temple and related cultic behaviour. The writers apparently no longer participate in certain cultic activities together with the rest of the people of Israel because they deem them to be improperly done, and to fail to remove impurity. The writers do not condemn the addressee in this text, but apparently hope to bring about a change of heart. The text does not suggest that a sect, or even a community, either exists or is contemplated. A certain number of people, probably a defined group, simply do not participate in certain kinds of cultic behaviour together with their fellow Judeans. This presumably means either abstinence from certain aspects of the Temple cult or, more probably, conducting these separately, and it encourages me to associate 4QMMT with CD, since the attitude towards the Temple in CD is the expected outcome of a failure to resolve the demands in 4QMMT. Like *Jubilees,* then, 4QMMT may help us to clarify the evolution of the laws in CD. Perhaps it reveals something of the early stages in the formation of the Damascus sect. But how, precisely, does it help explain sectarian formation? That it expresses disagreement on points of order is not necessarily significant. Different schools of interpretation regarding the administration of the Temple cult existed other than as sects; Pharisees and Sadducees had their own traditions. And as far as complaints about impurity and priestly misbehaviour go, we find in both Ezra and Nehemiah, whose accounts I take to be retrojections of later situations, reference to such practices that are reformed: in Nehemiah 7 priests with foreign wives are expelled from the priesthood; in Nehemiah 13 Ammonites and Moabites are expelled; Eliashib the priest removes tithes for levites and other temple officials to another room; the levites do not get their portion; there is trading on the sabbath; intermarriage is again forbidden (and the example of Solomon's sin is cited, much as MMT cites previous kings); Neh. 13.30-31 concludes 'Remember them, O my God, because they have defiled the priesthood and the covenant of the priesthood and the Levites. Thus I cleansed them from everything foreign…I provided for the wood-offering, at appointed times, and for the first-fruits…'. In Ezra 9–10 we also find separation from the people, and priests with foreign wives are specifically mentioned (10.18ff.). It seems, then, that the theme of uncleanness, priestly defilement and greed are common. Is the context of MMT so different from that of Nehemiah or Ezra?

The important difference between Ezra–Nehemiah and 4QMMT is

presumably that Ezra and Nehemiah are presented as effecting the reforms, supported by their community, because they are national leaders, or presented as such. The writers of 4QMMT are not. They cannot make the reform. Thus Ezra and Nehemiah, and the groups they represented, became part of the accepted system, while the writers of 4QMMT perhaps became a sect.

And yet I feel that it is premature to try and integrate 4QMMT, *Jubilees*, *1 Enoch* and CD into a single theory. Indeed, it still seems to me unwise to press the question of origins in our present state of understanding. It is tempting to conclude that the circles from which the sect emerged had already a tradition of torah which differed from that of other Jews; indeed, that conclusion seems reasonable. But such differences clearly do not explain the formation of a sect, since they must have existed before the sect was formed. What was it that made it necessary for such differences to be expressed in *social isolation*?

But if we cannot answer that question of *causes*, we can nevertheless explore the *effects* of sectarian formation.

'Torah' and 'Testament'

Some of the laws we find in CD, relating to holiness, the sabbath and the calendar, seem to have existed before the sect, while laws about sectarian organization and discipline follow upon its establishment. But what about the remaining laws? If we accept that the material from Cave 4 now assigned to the 'D' corpus pertains to the Damascus community[15] we have a remarkable range of legislation, involving issues such as sacrificial slaughter, skin diseases, tithing, and fraud. These, and the existence of 11QT and other legal texts consistent with it, may perhaps attest a tradition of legal theory and/or practice predating the sect, but equally it may represent *the outcome of a sectarian exercise in extending its own laws and practices to encompass a wider definition of the 'Israel' it held itself to be.*

For an explanation of this second alternative I refer to a recent article by Wayne McCready applying Neusner's distinction of what he calls 'testament' and 'torah'[16] to 11QT. In Neusner's analysis, 'testament'

---

15. See the convenient survey of the 4QD material by J. Baumgarten in *The Damacus Document Reconsidered* (ed. M. Broshi; Jerusalem: Israel Exploration Society, 1982), pp. 51-62.

16. *Testament to Torah* (Englewood Cliffs: Prentice-Hall, 1988).

refers to a religious system, text or set of texts, that does not have a potential for engendering a total religious system, whereas 'torah' does. Neusner traces the evolution from 'testament' to 'torah' in the case of the scriptures over the period 500 BCE–700 CE. A similar kind of distinction might be made on a more limited scale between a 'testament' that belongs with a certain group, and operates only within a restricted social and temporal boundary, and a body of texts that is given the status of a national symbol, and thus acquires the possibility of becoming the nucleus of a religious system that embraces 'Israel' in a fuller sense—thus a 'torah'. McCready has argued that 11QT represents an attempt at creating the 'Jewish world-view' for which many looked to them. He argues that while the Hasmoneans created the matrix for a 'Jewish world-view' through their establishment of a politically united and independent 'Israel', they did not in fact fulfil this potential, and it was left to 'sectarian' groups to articulate that vision, and inscribe the 'torah'.

McCready may be correct to see in a 'sectarian' circle the earliest attempts to define a torah, albeit for a group that consciously set itself against the political and religious authorities of its time. The Temple Scroll itself, and the attempt which is evident in the *Damascus Document* to organize a community around the laws of 'scripture', suggest the production of a system, a fully-fledged Judaism, a 'torah' in Neusner's sense.

Such a conclusion adds considerably to our understanding of the dynamics of the genus 'Judaism'; the 'Israel' which CD defines follows a pattern which is reflected in other Jewish documents, and which anticipates in many ways the Judaism of the rabbis. Just as it was the loss of certain central symbols that cleared the way for the development of that complete and articulate Judaism, so the constitution of a sect, the provision of a segregated but Jewish lifestyle for a self-defined 'Israel' provided the conditions for the creation of an earlier systematic 'Judaism'.

THE ESCHATOLOGICAL TEMPLE(S) OF 11QT

John Kampen

Studies of 11QT continue to proceed with the assumption that there are two future temples envisioned in that document. These temples most frequently are described as a utopian version to be built by human beings and an eschatological structure to be erected by God. Such a viewpoint, delineated in the introduction and commentary to the *editio princeps* of this important text,[1] continues to be espoused by the vast majority of Qumran scholars.

In his work on this Qumran scroll Ben Zion Wacholder challenged the reading of 11QT 29 which formed the foundation for this viewpoint.[2] When we examine the case in 11QT we see that it rests primarily on the utilization of the term עד in 29.9. Does the use of this term in this one phrase provide sufficient evidence to justify such a major hypothesis? Does the term even support the interpretation ascribed to it by the vast majority of Qumran scholars? This article will investigate the use of the term עד throughout the Qumran corpus and then reexamine the interpretation of 11QT 29.8-10, with a view to understanding its consequences for our perceptions of the future temple in 11QT.

This essay is dedicated to Ben Zion Wacholder as an expression of thanks for the many hours over the course of a number of years which he devoted to the raising up of this disciple. Since my introduction to Qumran studies came through the hours spent in his study on

---

1. Y. Yadin, מגילת המקדש (3 vols. and sup.; Jerusalem: Israel Exploration Society, 1977), I, pp. 140-44; II, pp. 91-92. This viewpoint is repeated in his English translation, *The Temple Scroll* (3 vols. and sup.; Jerusalem: Israel Exploration Society, 1983), I, pp. 182-87; II, pp. 128-29. Subsequent references in this essay are to the English edition.

2. B.Z. Wacholder, *The Dawn of Qumran: The Sectarian Torah and the Teacher of Righteousness* (Cincinnati: Hebrew Union College Press, 1983), pp. 21-30.

מגילת המקדש and the publication of *The Dawn of Qumran*, I could think
of no better subject for this volume. Since his agile and active mind is
continuously involved in the reevaluation of texts and their interpretation
I cannot guarantee that he any longer supports the interpretation of
11QT 29 ascribed to him in this work.

One or Two Temples in 11QT?

Since the description of the temple in this Qumran document appears to
follow so closely its Pentateuchal model, Yadin answers the question he
poses:

> to which Temple was the author referring?…It seems unnecessary to elab-
> orate upon the question, as the answer becomes eminently clear; the
> Temple laws presented in the scroll are those conveyed by the Lord to
> Moses—as are the laws of the Tabernacle—as an eternal command to the
> Children of Israel.[3]

Citing 11QT 29.8-10 in support of his claim that the temple described in
this composition was 'the Temple to be built one day by the Children of
Israel, and not the eschatological Temple', Yadin believes that the latter
is alluded to in other texts such as *1 En.* 90.29 and *Jub.* 1.15-17, 26-29.[4]
This edifice, to be erected on יום הבריה ('the day of creation'),[5] would be
the fulfillment of the promise of the Lord to Jacob at Bethel. The parallels cited for the latter edifice are, of course, problematic. There is no
necessary reason to connect the gilded temple containing elaborate fur-
nishings described in 11QT with any of the historical structures
mentioned earlier in the historical recital found in *1 Enoch* 89 or 90.
Nowhere in 11QT do we find it referred to as the structure erected by
Solomon, alluded to in *1 En.* 89.50.[6] It would be very surprising to find
the polluted structure of *1 En.* 89.73-74 to be the edifice described in
11QT. If the temple in this Qumran composition represents an implicit
criticism of these earlier temples, then the actual structure described in

---

3.   Yadin, *Temple Scroll*, I, p. 182.

4.   Yadin, *Temple Scroll*, I, pp. 183-84.

5.   This is the reading proposed by E. Qimron, 'מן העבודה במילון ההיסטורי',
Leshonenu 42 (1978), pp. 136-45, see p. 142; but note Wacholder, *Dawn of Qumran*,
p. 238 n. 127. I prefer to read הבריה because of the apparent parallels with *Jub* 1.29
(see nn. 56 and 57 below).

6.   Since it is a future structure it cannot be equated with the wilderness tabernacle of *1 En.* 89.36 either.

11QT is not represented in *1 Enoch* and the analogy between the two works breaks down.[7] It is very hard to equate the temple described throughout 11QT to any edifice in the book of *Enoch* other than the one referred to as 'a new house, greater and loftier than the first one' in *1 En.* 90.29.[8] While *Jubilees* 1 refers to a future sanctuary at least three times,[9] there is no necessary reason to connect any of the references with the second future temple projected in Yadin's hypothesis. Since *Jub.* 1.26-29 raises problems of interpretation similar to those found in 11QT 29, it will receive further discussion below. Most interpreters have followed Yadin's interpretation of this text fairly closely or proposed some minor variations of it.

Producing one of the first translations of 11QT, Johann Maier argued that this text described a utopian temple for the period after the conquest, thereby providing a model for what the Second Temple should have been like, hence an implicit critique.[10] An attempt to suggest that it actually did influence the Herodian reconstruction of the temple is found in the work of M. Delcor.[11] While following Yadin in distinguishing between the two temples, Jacob Milgrom did note 'apparently, the cult will remain unchanged', that is, in the messianic temple.[12] In her recent work, Devorah Dimant continues to read this column in the same manner.[13] While the novel effort of Michael Wise represents a valiant attempt to resolve the contradictions between Yadin's and Wacholder's

7.   J. Maier, *The Temple Scroll: An Introduction, Translation & Commentary* (trans. R.T. White; JSOTSup, 34; Sheffield: JSOT Press, 1985 [German original 1978]), pp. 58-59, 86.

8.   The argument for relating the temple in 11QT with any of those earlier structures in *1 Enoch* is even more difficult to sustain if one accepts some of the connections between Qumran and *1 Enoch* proposed by G.W.E. Nickelsburg ('*1 Enoch* and Qumran Origins: The State of the Question and Some Prospects for Answers', *SBLSP* 25 [1986], pp. 341-60).

9.   *Jub.* 1.17, 26, 29.

10.   Maier, *The Temple Scroll*, pp. 58-59, 86.

11.   M. Delcor, 'Is the Temple Scroll a Source of the Herodian Temple?', in *Temple Scroll Studies: Papers Presented at the International Symposium on the Temple Scroll; Manchester, December 1987* (ed. G.J. Brooke; JSPSup, 7; Sheffield: JSOT Press, 1989), pp. 66-89, see p. 85 on col. 29.

12.   J. Milgrom, 'The Temple Scroll', *BA* 41 (1978), pp. 105-20, see p. 114.

13.   D. Dimant, '*4QFlorilegium* and the Idea of the Community as Temple', in *Hellenica et Judaica: Hommage à Valentin Nikiprowetzky ל׳ז* (ed. A. Caquot, M. Hadas-Lebel and J. Riaud; Leuven/Paris: Éditions Peeters, 1986), pp. 165-89, see p. 189.

views by differentiating between God's promise of an eternal presence to Jacob and its visible manifestations in ephemeral temples, I do not find the work convincing.[14] The contrasting portrayals and critiques of the temple which characterize the literature of the Second Temple era suggest that the temple as *the* dwelling place for God was much more significant than presumed by Wise.

Wacholder's primary challenge to this reading of 11QT 29 was based on the claims advanced rather consistently throughout the document for the *eternal* validity of its laws and prescriptions.[15] Agreeing with Wacholder with regard to the hypothesis that there is only one future temple envisioned in the scroll was Phillip Callaway.[16] While Callaway maintained, along with Wacholder, that the meaning of the term עד in 11QT 29.9 was 'while' (in German, '*während*'), he took a very different view of the source question in 11QT 29. Both of these subjects require further discussion. I will begin with an examination of the source question.

A survey of source critical studies suggests that at least 11QT 29.3-10 is to be regarded as a redactional composition.[17] In their early essay on this subject Wilson and Wills did not include col. 29 among the sources utilized by the author of the scroll, thereby recognizing that this portion of the text was a redactional composition.[18] Callaway made a similar observation.[19] For our purposes the most important observation is made by Michael Wise: 'here the redactor of the scroll reveals his own hand'.[20] When we discuss this column it is clear that we are attempting

14. M.O. Wise, 'The Covenant of Temple Scroll XXIX, 3-10', *RevQ* 14 (1989), pp. 49-60. The term which is at the center of this paper is the only evidence in all of 11QT for the 'two-stage' eschaton cited on p. 60 n. 37.

15. *Dawn of Qumran*, p. 23.

16. P. Callaway, 'Exegetische Erwägungen zur Tempelrolle XXIX, 7-10', *RevQ* 12 (1985), pp. 95-104. My reservations expressed above concerning the approach of Wise to the topic also apply to his critique of Callaway ('Covenant Scroll', pp. 53-54).

17. On the subject of source criticism and 11QT note the cautions of S.A. Kaufman, 'The Temple Scroll and Higher Criticism', *HUCA* 53 (1982), pp. 29-43. For a listing of studies concerning sources see Wise, 'Covenant', p. 49 n. 2.

18. A.M. Wilson and L. Wills, 'Literary Sources of the Temple Scroll', *HTR* 75 (1982), pp. 275-88.

19. P. Callaway, 'Source Criticism of the Temple Scroll: The Purity Laws', *RevQ* 12 (1985–87), pp. 213-22.

20. Wise, 'Covenant', p. 49. Note his more extensive work, *A Critical Study of*

to assess the ideology of the scroll, not one of the sources which went into its composition. While disagreeing about the meaning of these lines concerning the nature of the temple, Wise is correct in pointing to their significance for understanding the purpose of the composition. Wacholder had suggested that the distribution of statements concerning the eternal nature of the temple and its rites throughout the scroll means that they were not simply adapted from a Mosaic exemplar, and by implication, from any one source.[21] Wise registers no difficulties with such a stress on the eternal nature of the promise in col. 29, but states that it only applies to the covenant with Jacob and not the temple.[22] While Wacholder's neglect of source analysis may prove inadequate for a comprehensive analysis of the significance of 11QT 29 in the context of the rest of the composition, Wise must account for the stress on the eternal nature of its architectural, ritual and purity legislation. I am unaware of any work from a source critical standpoint which would contradict the argument for the centrality of 11QT 29 as a key to the ideology of the composition as a whole. Now let us examine the use of the preposition.

In addition to the passage which is the central subject of this paper, 11QT 42.16 is significant: ויושבים שמה עד העלוֹת[23] את עולת המועד אשר לחג הסוכות ('and they shall sit there during the burnt offerings, the burnt offering of the festival [which is specified] for the feast of booths'). While Yadin and Vermes have employed the translation 'until' in this sentence,[24] the term 'during' utilized by Maier is clearly preferable.[25] If we followed Yadin and Vermes, the assembled dignitaries would remain seated only until the time of the sacrifice, a doubtful interpretation, since the sacrifice would have constituted the central activity of the event. Utilizing the common definition of the term, Schiffman can only make sense of the phrase by suggesting that they remained seated 'until the

---

the *Temple Scroll from Qumran Cave 11* (Studies in Ancient Oriental Civilization, 49; Chicago: Oriental Institute, 1990), pp. 23, 133, 157-61.

21. Wacholder, *Dawn of Qumran*, p. 23 and p. 239 n. 135.

22. Wise, 'Covenant', pp. 54-60.

23. While the ע has been erased and then suspended above the line there is no reason to question the term in this line. See Yadin, *Temple Scroll*, II, p. 180.

24. Yadin, *Temple Scroll*, II, p. 180; G. Vermes, *The Dead Sea Scrolls in English* (London: Penguin, 3rd edn, 1987), p. 142.

25. Maier, *The Temple Scroll*, p. 39.

burnt offering of the festival has been offered'.[26] However, the perfect tense is not employed in the text at this point. The rendering of the term proposed in this paper makes its addition to the translation unnecessary. Other passages in 11QT also require reexamination.

An emphasis on the duration of the specified time period can be found in 11QT 63.14-15: ולוא תגע לכה בטהרה עד שבע שנים ('she shall not touch your purity for seven years').[27] The emphasis in the phrase is on the seven year interval and upon what is not to occur within that period. The translation of 11QT 43.6-9 poses problems similar to those found in column 29.

יהיו אוכלים את הדגן עד השנה השנית עד יום חג הבכורים והיין מיום מועד התירוש
עד השנה השנית עד יום מועד התירוש...

...they shall eat the grain until the second year during the feast of first fruits; and the wine from the feast of new wine until the second year during the feast of new wine...

In this column the specification of the feast day occurs within the context of the future period, that is, the second year, stipulated in the text. The second use of עד in each phrase serves to designate the future date more precisely; it does not propose a second future era beyond the first one.

Determining the temporal significance of the preposition in 11QT 59.9 is more difficult: אשר הפרו בריתי ואת תורתי נעלה נפשמה עד יאשמו כול אשמה ('because they violated my covenant and even loathed my law while [or 'until'] they incurred all [manner of] guilt'). It does appear that the incurring of guilt is something that happens at the same time as they have 'violated my covenant and even loathed my law'.[28] The imperfect tense of יאשמו could find explanation as a continuation of the tense of ואסתיר ('and I will hide') in line 7. The future beyond the projected period of apostasy, then, begins with אחר ('afterwards'), the following word in line 9. Such an interpretation saves the reader from having to project a 'two-stage' period of apostasy. Failing any evidence to support the latter viewpoint and since biblical parallels for this usage are

---

26. L.H. Schiffman, 'The Sacrificial System of the *Temple Scroll* and the Book of Jubilees', *SBLSP* (1985), pp. 217-33 (231).

27. The proposed translation is not contradicted by the wording of the following phrase: וזבח שלמים לוא תואכל עד יעבורו שבע שנים ('and she shall not eat a sacrifice of the peace offering while [or 'until'] seven years pass').

28. See Wacholder, *Dawn of Qumran*, p. 20.

unavailable,[29] the translation of עד as 'while' in this column becomes the most acceptable alternative. Before returning to column 29 let us examine the usage of the term in other compositions from Qumran.

The Preposition עד *in other Qumran Literature*

It is quite clear that the foremost portion of evidence in support of the hypothesis that two future temples are envisioned in 11QT is the presence of the term עד in 11QT 29.9. All of these studies assume that the only correct translation of this Hebrew term is 'until'. The adequacy of this limitation is what must be tested. While an examination of this term throughout Hebrew and related ancient Near Eastern literature could prove instructive, this essay concentrates on its appearances in Qumran literature. While such a limitation could appear arbitrary I would argue that these are the primary documents which reflect the influence of 11QT.[30] It is of course possible that 11QT was authored after some of the other Qumran documents discussed in this section, a prospect which I consider doubtful.[31] In that case it would reflect the influence of the other works. Major indicators of the possible meanings of a term must first of all come from the literature most closely related to the material in which it is found.

A brief survey of the term's use in the biblical materials helps to establish the setting for this examination. We do not have to spend time on its substantive use, which is primarily to designate the meaning of 'perpetuity', conveying a sense of duration or of the future.[32] When we turn to its usage as a preposition, we see that it most commonly means 'as far as', 'up to' or 'even to' with reference to space, 'even to' or 'until' in temporal contexts. In BDB we also find 'during' listed as a possible definition. While it is described as rare, it is said to designate '*as*

---

29. Yadin, *Temple Scroll*, II, p. 268.

30. Contra H. Stegemann, 'The Literary Composition of the Temple Scroll and its Status at Qumran', in Brooke (ed.), *Temple Scroll Studies*, pp. 123-48.

31. The relatively early dating of this document was already proposed by Yadin, *Temple Scroll*, II, pp. 386-90. His stance is to be preferred over that advanced by M. Hengel, J.H. Charlesworth and D. Mendels, 'The Polemical Character of "On Kingship" in the Temple Scroll: An Attempt at Dating 11QTemple', *JJS* 37 (1986), pp. 28-38. Attention must be paid to those arguments for earlier dating: Wacholder, *Dawn of Qumran*, pp. 33-140, 202-12; Stegemann, 'Literary Composition of the Temple Scroll', pp. 126-43.

32. See BDB, p. 723 and KB (3rd edn), III, pp. 742-43.

far as the limit indicated, including the time previous', and to be more frequent in Aramaic.[33] KB includes the following list of texts with the definition of *während*: 2 Kgs 9.22, Job 20.5, Judg. 3.26, Jon. 4.2.[34] We do find Aramaic references of this type in Dan. 6.8, 13; 7.12, 25. As a conjunction the term also can carry a similar temporal sense, for example, 1 Sam. 14.19, Ps. 141.10, Job 1.18[35] and Song 1.12.[36] From the biblical evidence it is clear that the preposition עד is employed, not only to designate some future time, but also to convey a sense of duration with regard to a certain point in time.

Since connections between 11QT and CD are well documented, this text proves a good starting point for the examination of Qumran texts.[37] As expected, there is ample evidence throughout the composition for the utilization of the preposition to designate 'until'.[38] But this definition does not encompass the totality of the word's semantic range within its folios. In CD 12.5 the term is used to convey a sense of duration: ושמרוהו עד שבע שנים ('and they shall keep it for seven years').[39] A similar sense is found in CD 15.15: ויל[מד] עד שנה תמימה ('and he shall study for an entire year'). In CD 12.15 a concurrent temporal sense is the only possible meaning: ...וכל החגבים במיניהם יבאו באש או במים עד הם חיים ('All the locusts according to their kinds shall be put into fire or water while they

33. BDB, p. 724, but note the Aramaic references on p. 1105. Note Wacholder, *Dawn of Qumran*, p. 239 n. 137.

34. KB, III, p. 743. The additional references cited in BDB, p. 724, may be questionable with regard to this definition: Exod. 33.22; Job 7.19.

35. Many manuscripts read עוד rather than עד in this verse.

36. BDB, p. 725; KB, III, p. 744.

37. For example, note the following: Yadin, *Temple Scroll*, I, pp. 394-96; Wacholder, *Dawn of Qumran*, pp. 99-135; P.R. Davies, *Behind the Essenes* (BJS, 94; Atlanta: Scholars Press, 1987), pp. 107-34; *idem*, 'The Temple Scroll and the Damascus Document', in Brooke (ed.), *Temple Scroll Studies*, pp. 201-10; but note L.H. Schiffman, 'The Temple Scroll and the Systems of Jewish Law in the Second Temple Period', in Brooke, *Temple Scroll Studies*, pp. 239-55, see pp. 243-44.

38. CD 2.9 (text corrupt), 17; 3.13, 19; 4.8; 5.5; 6.10; 9.18; 10.3, 7, 10; 12.12, 23; 14.7, 9; 15.11; 16.8, 9; 20.1, 5, 14. CD 20.23 reads עוד in the recent text of E. Qimron, *The Damascus Document Reconsidered* (Jerusalem: Israel Exploration Society/Shrine of the Book, 1992), p. 47.

39. Note the parallel passage in 4Q271 (4QD^f) 3 i 20 (see B.Z. Wacholder and M.G. Abegg, *A Preliminary Edition of the Unpublished Dead Sea Scrolls: The Hebrew and Aramaic Texts from Cave Four* [Washington: Biblical Archaeology Society, 1991], I, p. 26, where the MS is listed as 4QD^c).

are alive...').[40] The same case can be made for CD 2.10: ונהייה[41] עד יבוא
בקציהם לכל שני עולם ('and what will be, what will come in their epochs
during all the years of eternity'). The context of this phrase already
indicates a discussion of eternity, עד indicates the continuation of that
time period.[42] The word is used in the same manner in an almost
identical phrase in 4Q268(4QD^c) 1.8.[43] The inclusive nature of the
term, but not in a temporal context, is seen in CD 10.4: וזה סרך לשפטי
העדה עד עשרה אנשים... ('This is the rule for the judges of the congregation,
comprised of ten men...').[44] A similar usage is in evidence in CD 13.1.[45]
We do find confirmation in this composition, closely related to 11QT,
for the use of the term to designate a concurrent period of time,

---

40. Fragments of this text are also found in 4Q266 (4QD^a) 18 i 1 (see Wacholder
and Abegg, *Preliminary Edition*, I, p. 18, where following the older listing of MSS, it
is specified as 4QD^b). The temporal implications of CD 2.21 are more difficult to
determine since the term's primary meaning here is causative: ולא שמרו את מצות
עשיהם עד אשר חרה אפו בם ('they did not keep the commandments of the One who
made them so that His anger was kindled against them'). This translation follows
A. Dupont-Sommer, *The Essene Writings from Qumran* (trans. G. Vermes; Oxford:
Basil Blackwell, 1961), p. 125. But note C. Rabin, *The Zadokite Documents* (Oxford:
Clarendon Press, 2nd edn, 1958), p. 8.

41. This word should read נהיות (Qimron, *Damascus Document Reconsidered*,
p. 13).

42. In CD 2.10 it is listed as a substantive by K.G. Kuhn, *Konkordanz zu den
Qumrantexten* (Göttingen: Vandenhoeck & Ruprecht, 1960), p. 156.

43. See Wacholder and Abegg, *Preliminary Edition*, I, p. 1, where following the
older listing of MSS, it is listed as 4QD^a. They have probably correctly reconstructed
the same line in 4Q266 (4QD^a) 2 i 6 (older list is 4QD^b).

44. Note the parallel passage in 4Q270 (4QD^e) 10 iv 16 (see Wacholder and
Abegg, *Preliminary Edition*, I, p. 44). The connection of this phrase with CD 12.5,
13.1 and 15.15 is noted by Rabin, *Zadokite Documents*, p. 49.

45. More difficult to interpret is the temporal meaning of CD 20.20: עד יגלה
ישע וצדקה ליראי אל ('while [or until] justice and righteousness are revealed to those
who fear God'). The interpretation of the term in this context depends upon one's
understanding of the chronology of the events described in the column. Does the era
when justice and righteousness will be revealed coincide with the time of those who in
20.17 turn from the 'transgression of Jacob'? Note the following studies: J. Murphy-
O'Connor, 'A Literary Analysis of Damascus Document XIX, 33–XX, 34', *RB* 79
(1972), pp. 543-64, see pp. 550-52; Wacholder, *Dawn of Qumran*, pp. 101-102, 108-
109, but note also, *idem*, 'The Date of the Eschaton in the Book of Jubilees: A
Commentary on Jub. 49.22–50.5, CD 1.1-10 and 16.2-3', *HUCA* 56 (1985), pp. 87-
101, see pp. 97-99; P.R. Davies, *The Damascus Covenant: An Interpretation of the
'Damascus Document'* (JSOTSup, 25; Sheffield: JSOT Press, 1983), pp. 186-90.

especially when the context indicates a sense of duration. A similar meaning for the term can be found in 1QS.

This preposition appears a number of times in 1QS 6.16-21. All of these references cannot designate movement toward a point in time; there are not a multiplicity of futures implied in the text. Let us look at 1QS 6.16-17 as an example: לוא יגע בטהרת הרבים עד אשר ידרשוהו לרוחו ומעשו עד מילאת לו שנה תמימה ('he shall not touch the purity of the many until they have examined his spirit and his deeds [while-?] he completes one entire year').[46] In this phrase the completion of the period of one year does not follow the examination of his spirit and his deeds; such an examination occurs during that period of one year. The presence of עד in this sentence is to designate the duration of the period of time already specified in the prior phrase. 1QS 6.21 then has a similar meaning: אל יגע במשקה הרבים עד מילאת לו שנה שנית ('he shall not touch the drink of the congregation while he completes a second year').[47] The duration of the two year period during which the daily activity of the person who שגג ('sinned inadvertently') is monitored, and during which he (she?) is separated from the purity and the council, is conveyed through the use of עד in 1QS 8.26. Following 1QS 6.17, these examples of a particular usage demonstrate the manner in which the term can be used to indicate the duration of time rather than some future point in time. Incidental examples of similar usages can be found scattered throughout other compositions from Qumran.

While the precise meaning of 1QH 8.30 is the matter of some dispute there is little doubt that עד ימימה ('daily' or 'annually') indicates duration rather than some future point in time.[48] In 1QM 8.7 the priests blow their trumpets a second time 'while' the three formations are approaching the enemy line. When we turn to 4Q507 1.3 we find the phrase ועד היותנו..., which is translated with the sense of duration in the DJD publication, 'et aussi longtemps que nous sommes...'[49] Note also 4Q514 1 i 8: וגם אל יאכל עד בטמאתו ('and he also shall not eat during his unclean-

---

46. Some translators convey the import of simultaneous activity through the use of the conjunction: A. Dupont-Sommer, *The Essene Writings from Qumran* (trans. G. Vermes; Oxford: Basil Blackwell, 1961), p. 86.

47. The duration of two years of time is also indicated in 1QS 7.19-20, even though עד does not appear in those lines.

48. Concerning the time period indicated see the note of J. Licht, מגילת ההודיות: ממגילת מדבר יהודה (Jerusalem: Bialik, 1957), p. 138.

49. DJD 7:176.

ness').[50] The citation of these occurrences in CD, 1QS and other Qumran texts by no means contradicts the fact that the predominant meaning of עד when used as a preposition is 'until'. It does point to the presence of another use for the term to convey a sense of simultaneous activity, a meaning which finds a basis in those phrases where it is utilized to signify duration. Since evidence of this usage has been attested in both 11QT and other Qumran writings we can return our attention to 11QT 29.

Column 29

In Yigael Yadin's response in the introduction to his outstanding commentary on 11QT to Bertil Gärtner's attempt to spiritualize the temple at Qumran,[51] he describes the relationship between the future temple to be built by the children of Israel and the messianic temple: 'there is not the slightest hint that the character of the Temple will differ in any way...or that its ritual will be different...The only difference is that the Lord Himself will build it.'[52] I already mentioned Milgrom's view concerning the continuity between the future temple described in the scroll and the messianic temple.[53] The entire body of evidence for two temples similar in character and ritual, one to last up to the messianic period and another one to be built at its advent, rests on the interpretation of the preposition עד in 11QT 29.9. Such an analysis cannot be permitted to stand. The unrealistic nature of the temple itself, for example, its gilding and the perfection implied in its architecture, as well as the elaborate legislation for the protection of its sanctity all attest to an idealized future life to be lived in the context of a messianic temple. These emphases receive particular importance when we recall the argument of Wacholder already mentioned above concerning the eternal nature of the legislation found throughout the document.[54] Permit me to add one important qualification which I think has been the source of some confusion. I am attempting to describe what I think is the viewpoint reflected within the scroll on this matter. This argument makes no claims concerning the

50. DJD 7:296.
51. B. Gärtner, *The Temple and the Community in Qumran and the New Testament* (Cambridge: Cambridge University Press, 1965).
52. Yadin, *Temple Scroll*, I, p. 187.
53. Milgrom, 'Temple Scroll', p. 114.
54. Wacholder, *Dawn of Qumran*, pp. 23 and 239 n. 135.

manner in which readers of this document used the information contained within it and perhaps appropriated different portions of the legislation for their own lives. That is the subject for a different paper. This essay concerns the nature of the temple(s) envisioned within the text as we find it in 11QT.

The examples cited in the previous sections of this essay negate any argument which could propose that עד in 11QT 29.9 could only mean 'until':

[ו]שכנתי אתמה לעולם ועד ואקדשה [את מ]קדשי בכבודי אשר אשכין עליו את
כבודי עד יום הבריה אשר אברא אני את מקדשי להכינו לי כול הימים כבריה אשר
כרתי עם יעקוב בבית אל

> [and] I shall dwell with them forever. I shall sanctify my [san]ctuary with my glory when I make my glory dwell upon it during the day of creation[55] when I shall create my sanctuary to establish it for myself for all time, in accordance with the covenant which I made with Jacob at Bethel.

Such a reading of these lines makes the sanctuary prescribed throughout 11QT to be the sacred edifice to be constructed on the day of creation. One related text must yet receive consideration.

A text with intepretative problems similar to the one discussed in this essay is found in *Jub.* 1.29. As translated by Wintermute the text reads as follows:

> from [the day of creation until] the day of the new creation when the heaven and earth and all of their creatures shall be renewed according to the powers of heaven and according to the whole nature of earth, until the sanctuary of the Lord is created upon Mount Zion.[56]

As noted already in the work of Wacholder, this translation of the equivalent term for עד in the Ethiopic text (*'eska*) cannot mean 'until'.[57] In the case of this text we are already in the era of the new creation. *Jub.* 1.27 uses the same term to distinguish between the day of creation and the time when the new sanctuary will be built. In this text it is clearly stated that it is during the era of this new creation when 'the

---

55. See n. 5 above.

56. O.S. Wintermute, 'Jubilees', in *The Old Testament Pseudepigrapha* (ed. J.H. Charlesworth; Garden City: Doubleday, 1985), I, p. 54.

57. Wacholder, *Dawn of Qumran*, p. 24. See the note concerning this term in J.C. VanderKam, *The Book of Jubilees* (CSCO 510-511; Scriptores Aethiopici 87-88; Louvain: Peeters, 1989), II, p. 54. I thank him for promptly sending me a copy of this note.

sanctuary of the Lord is [to be] created upon Mount Zion'. The connection between *Jubilees* and 11QT has been argued previously and in various locations.[58] A 'two-stage' eschatology which envisions an idealized temple for each period is not part of the book of *Jubilees*. There is no reason to find such a view in the use of the same terminology in 11QT.

While this essay appears to center on a very minor point, its implications are rather extensive. Of particular importance is the need to reexamine 4Q174 (Florilegium). Recent studies of this work have been based on the assumption that two temples are projected in 11QT.[59] The latter document has been the source of much of the debate on issues such as the 'spiritualization' of the temple or the 'temple as community' in Second Temple Judaism.[60] It is to be hoped that this and other compositions from Qumran concerning the temple can receive more extensive analysis.

---

58. Note the essays on this subject in *SBLSP* 24 (1985): J.H. Charlesworth, 'The Date of Jubilees and of the Temple Scroll', pp. 193-204; B.Z. Wacholder, 'The Relationship between 11Q Torah (The Temple Scroll) and the Book of Jubilees: One Single or Two Independent Compositions', pp. 205-16; L.H. Schiffman, 'The Sacrificial System of the *Temple Scroll* and the Book of Jubilees', pp. 217-33. The significance of the book of *Jubilees* at Qumran was established by J.C. VanderKam, *Textual and Historical Studies in the Book of Jubilees* (HSM, 14; Missoula, MT: Scholars Press, 1977). Also arguing that *Jubilees* and 11QT were one composition was M. Smith, 'Helios in Palestine', *Eretz Israel* 16 (1982), pp. 199*-206*, see pp. 206*-207*. Note the comprehensive review of the subject by J.C. VanderKam, 'The Temple Scroll and the Book of Jubilees', in Brooke (ed.), *Temple Scroll Studies*, pp. 211-36.

59. Dimant, '*4QFlorilegium*', *Hellenica et Judaica*, pp. 187-89; M. Wise, '*4QFlorilegium* and the Temple of Adam', *RevQ* 15 (1991), pp. 104-32.

60. The previous discussion of this fragment receives extensive analysis in G.J. Brooke, *Exegesis at Qumran: 4QFlorilegium in its Jewish Context* (JSOTSup, 29; Sheffield: JSOT Press, 1985).

SECOND THOUGHTS ON דוק AND THE QUMRAN SYNCHRONISTIC CALENDARS*

Michael O. Wise

FAUSTUS: How many heavens or spheres are there?
MEPHISTO: Nine, the seven planets, the Firmament, and the Empyrean Heaven.
FAUSTUS: But is there not *Coelum Igneum and Christalinum?*
MEPHISTO: No, Faustus, they be but fables.
—*Doctor Faustus*

Introduction: The Qumran Synchronistic Calendars, אותות *and the Problem of* דוק

Among the calendrical texts newly available from Qumran Cave 4 are several that have been known as synchronistic calendars (4Q320, 4Q321 and 4Q321a).[1] Although some students of these texts question their designation as calendars, all agree that they concord lunar movements with the 364-day solar calendar long familiar from *Jubilees* and *1 Enoch*. Further, these synchronistic calendars distribute the service of

* It is a great pleasure to dedicate this study to Professor Ben Zion Wacholder, from whose writings on many topics involving the Second Temple period—particularly those concerning the Temple Scroll and matters of calendar and chronology—I have learned so much. I wish to thank my Egyptological colleague, Professor Janet Johnson, for discussing Egyptian calendrical matters with me and for reading an earlier draft of this paper. I also thank Professors James Vanderkam and Marty Abegg, who discussed the paper with me in some detail. The views expressed are, of course, my own, as are any errors or infelicities.

1. The first published preliminary editions were B.Z. Wacholder and M. Abegg, *A Preliminary Edition of the Unpublished Dead Sea Scrolls, Fascicle One* (Washington, DC: Biblical Archaeology Society, 1991), pp. 61-76. For photographs, see R. Eisenman and J.M. Robinson, *A Facsimile Edition of the Dead Sea Scrolls* (Washington, DC: Biblical Archaeology Society, 1991), photographs 1355-59. The DJD edition is being prepared by S. Talmon and I. Knohl.

the twenty-four priestly families by date, so construing a six-year cycle
of priestly rotation into service at the Jerusalem temple. Six years are
required for a given priestly family to return to serve once again on the
same day of the same month. For example, in the first year of the cycle,
Jedaiah begins to serve on the 25th day of the first month. Though
Jedaiah will serve repeatedly in the intervening years, six years must
pass before this division again enters service on this day.

It is this rotation of the twenty-four priestly families that necessitates a
sexennial cycle. Concording the solar and lunar calendars requires just
three years, provided a month is intercalated into the lunar version
$(354 \times 3 + 30 = 364 \times 3)$. Consequently, within the six-year priestly
cycle, the calendar concordance of year one equates to year four, year
two to year five, and year three to year six. Each year is distinguishable
from its analog only by the name of the priestly rotation serving at any
given time.[2]

Years one and four in the calendar concordance are designated in
another calendrical text, 4Q319, as אות ('sign') years.[3] This term, deriving from Gen. 1.14, identifies a particular astronomical configuration.
Just what that configuration may be is disputed, but it obviously
involves the sun and the moon. The phenomenon occurs at the beginning of years one and four, but not the other years. For the inventors of
these calenders, these two years of the cycle—and particularly year
one—reprised the heavenly situation at the time of creation. The term
אות, then, signifies the astronomical relation of the sun and moon when
the sexennial priestly cycle begins, and therefore presumably relates to
the other phenomena of the concordances in some schematically consistent way. These other phenomena have themselves spawned divergent
interpretations, in particular the term דוק.

דוק is a recurring term in 4Q321 and 4Q321a, attaching to the sixteenth day of twenty-nine-day months and the seventeenth day of thirty-
day months. What does it mean? The word is apparently a masculine

2.   An additional minor difference does exist between years three and six. A
month of twenty-nine days is intercalated after year three, whereas the month intercalated after year six numbers thirty days. By this device the regular alternation
between twenty-nine and thirty day lunisolar months can continue indefinitely.

3.   The first preliminary edition was once again Wacholder and Abegg, *Dead Sea
Scrolls*, pp. 96-101. A small portion had been published by J.T. Milik, *The Books of
Enoch: Aramaic Fragments of Qumrân Cave 4* (Oxford: Clarendon Press, 1976),
pp. 62-64. The DJD edition is to be prepared by U. Glessmer.

noun derived from the verbal root דוק, which itself connotes observation.[4] In theory the noun דוק could refer either to the act of observation itself, or to the thing observed in that process. The context of the calendrical texts shows that it refers to the thing observed—logically, the moon.[5] The question is therefore what lunar phenomenon one might want to observe on the sixteenth or seventeenth day of the month.

Milik, the first scholar to work on these texts, thought that the lunar months in question began with the full moon.[6] Consequently, he argued that דוק attached to that day (cycling regularly sixteen or seventeen days after the moon is first full) on which the new moon was observed. Albani, Glessmer, VanderKam, and Wacholder and Abegg have concurred with Milik's position.[7] Talmon and Knohl have argued for a

---

4. For a discussion of the term's etymology and meaning see my 'Observations on New Calendrical Texts from Qumran', in *Thunder in Gemini* (Sheffield: JSOT Press, 1994), pp. 222-32. That the absolute form was דוק and not דוקה emerges from 4Q321a 4 1, where one reads דוקי, i.e., a masculine noun (or unmarked feminine) with 3ms suffix (note: Wacholder and Abegg, *Dead Sea Scrolls*, p. 76 read דוקי on the basis of the concordance, a mistaken reading). I propose to understand the word as a *qatl* noun with medial glide, on the pattern of מָוֶת. I base this suggestion on the vocalization patterns of cognates, Syriac *dwq'* and Babylonian Talmudic Aramaic דוקא. Both of these vocalized forms point to an underlying *qatl*. Thus the absolute form of our word would presumably be דָּוֶק. With suffixes, the diphthong would resolve as usual in Hebrew, yielding דוֹקוֹ, דוֹקָה.

5. The typical pattern of 4Q321 and 4Q321a counterposes דוק with a 3fs suffix (דוקה), and בוא, 'in it', a reference to the month (חודש or ירח—both masculine) accounting for the 3ms suffix. Thus the suffix on דוק cannot have for its referent a word for month, ruling out the understanding 'its (the month's) (appointed act of) observation' (the subjective genitive option). The 3fs suffix on דוק has as its referent לבנה, the moon. Accordingly the recurring דוקה means 'its (the moon's) observation'. The suffix is an objective genitive.

6. J.T. Milik, *Ten Years of Discovery in the Wilderness of Judaea* (London: SCM Press, 1959), p. 152 n. 5.

7. M. Albani, 'Die lunaren Zyklen im 364-Tage-Festkalender von 4QMischmerot/ 4QSe', *Forschungsstelle Judentum 'Mitteilungen und Beiträge'* 4 (1992), p. 24; U. Glessmer, 'Antike und moderne Auslegungen des Sintflutberichtes Gen 6-8 und der Qumran-Pesher 4Q252', *Theologische Fakultät Leipzig Forschungsstelle Judentum Mitteilungen und Beiträge* 6 (1993), p. 46; J. VanderKam, 'Calendrical Texts and the Origin of the Dead Sea Scroll Community', in M.O. Wise *et al.* (eds.), *Methods of Investigation of the Dead Sea Scrolls and the Khirbet Qumran Site* (New York: New York Academy of Sciences, 1994), pp. 371-86, and Wacholder and Abegg, *Dead Sea Scrolls*, pp. 60 and 104 (month 1 year 1 sets the pattern). I thank Professor VanderKam for permission to use his manuscript while in press.

different view, closer to my own. For them דוק referred to the day following the night on which the moon began to wane.[8] The recording of moonless nights—unlucky as they were thought to be—was the real purpose of these Qumran texts. They were not true calendars, but mere timetables of lunar and solar movement. In Talmon and Knohl's understanding, the month begins with the visible new moon.

Yet the emerging consensus favors a full-moon month. Does the evidence really compel that conclusion? Failing such, should we not seek to understand these texts in terms of a month beginning with a new moon or related elements? Surely that is the natural place to begin in view of the biblical evidence—חודש is, after all, overwhelmingly the most common biblical Hebrew word for 'month'—and in view of what is known about the calendars of the ancient Semitic and non-Semitic peoples who were the neighbors of the Israelites and, later, the Jews.[9] I have elsewhere[10] tried to show that the evidence of the synchronistic calendars can indeed fit neatly into a scheme wherein the months begin more or less with the new moon—actually, with the conjunction. In this approach, דוק denotes the observation not of the new moon, but of the full. Such a system would be similar to that of the Egyptian lunar calendar, whose months began on the morning when the old crescent became invisible.[11] That parallel would seem particularly telling because the Egyptians ascribed priority to a solar calendar, just as do these Qumran writings. Further, I proposed, an understanding in which the month began with conjunction roughly accords with the descriptions of lunar movement contained in other Qumran works, notably the astronomical portions of Aramaic Enoch,[12] 4Q503[13] ('Daily Prayers') and 4Q317.

---

8.   S. Talmon and I. Knohl, 'A Calendrical Scroll from Qumran Cave IV—Mish Ba (4Q321)', *Tarbiz* 60 (1991), pp. 505-22 (Hebrew). In the understanding of these co-authors, דוק does not derive from the hollow root, but rather from דקק. The substantive means then 'denigration'. I think this etymon and meaning unlikely, but I have already expressed my views and the matter need not be reargued here (see note 4 above).

9.   R. de Vaux, *Ancient Israel* (London: Darton, Longman & Todd, 1961; New York: McGraw-Hill, 1965), II, pp. 178-94 remains a very useful overview.

10.   Note 4, above.

11.   R.A. Parker, *The Calendars of Ancient Egypt* (Chicago: University of Chicago Press, 1950), pp. 9-23.

12.   Milik, *Books of Enoch,* pp. 273-97. These four copies of Aramaic Enoch prove that the astronomical portions of Ethiopic *1 Enoch* are greatly abbreviated.

13.   M. Baillet, DJD VII, pp. 105-36. Note also J. Baumgarten, '4Q503 (Daily

For the emerging consensus to be correct, we must be prepared to recognize two fundamentally different lunar systems within the corpus of the Dead Sea Scrolls.

Perhaps two clashing systems is indeed what we should see. The arguments adduced by the experts noted above certainly must be weighed. Their arguments are of two sorts: the first approach argues for the full moon on the basis of a passage in 4Q320;[14] the other attempts to read the mind of ancient biblical exegetes and imagine how they would have understood portions such as Gen. 1.16-17.[15] To my mind these

Prayers) and the Lunar Calendar', *RevQ* 12 (1985–87), pp. 399-408.

14. The only textual statement thus far adduced for the understanding of a month beginning with a full moon is 4Q320 1 i 1-5. Although the portion is damaged, the readings and restorations proposed by Wacholder and Abegg, *Dead Sea Scrolls,* p. 60 are reasonable and can serve as the basis of a discussion—provided we remember that, because of the text's condition, any understanding is tentative. The lines can be translated: (1) 'to show it forth from the east, (2) [and] to illuminate it [in the] midst of the heavens, in the foundation (3) [of the firmamen]t, from evening until morning, on the fourth (day) of the week (4) [of the sons of G]amul, in the first month of [the fir]st (5) year'. Some who see here a full moon have focused their attention on line 2, 'in the midst of the heavens', thinking that this language requires a full moon. Others have been impressed by the passage's description of the moon as illuminated. Illumination is, of course, associated with most of the lunar cycle. Line 1 may describe the moon's rise in the east, which, again, is a regular phenomenon associated with much of the lunar cycle, not just the full moon. Line 3 contains the phrase 'from evening until morning', apparently affirming the general function of the 'lesser light' as set forth in Genesis: to rule over the night. In any case the full moon is not set 'in the midst of the heavens' from evening until morning. It moves across the sky from horizon to horizon. We should not construe 'in the midst of the heavens' while ignoring 'from evening until morning'. Any understanding of these lines must seek to explain their function in the text, for they are far removed from the lines that follow stylistically. To my mind, they are a poetic incipit to the lunar and solar tabulations that follow. The purpose of the poem (whose length is uncertain but that must have begun at least one column earlier than its first preserved line) was twofold: (1) to describe, in general and biblical terms, the respective functions of the sun and moon; and (2) to assert the supremacy of the sun. The sun appears to be the implicit subject of the suffixed infinitives in lines 1 and 2 (להראותה, לאירה [*si vera lectio*]). The poem put exegesis at the behest of polemics. The language is sufficiently general and imprecise to allow either view of the month's beginning, and does not reveal the author's concept of the moon's situation at the time of its creation.

15. The argument is that the moon must have been full at the time of its creation in order to qualify as a 'light'. This is certainly a logical position and seems to be a straightforward reading of the biblical portion. Yet the ancients might have read things

arguments do not compel assent, but research on these texts is only just beginning. Prudence would dictate considerable flexibility in any present understanding of them. In just such a frame of mind, I propose here to return to the question of the meaning of דוק, looking at the term from two new vantage points.

First, I want to ask which (if either) proposed understanding of דוק would arise more naturally from actual observation of the Judaean heavens. Since we are uncertain what the term meant, we cannot, of course, test directly for the phenomenon designated by דוק. Besides, either proposed meaning involves events so common as to be trivial. But we can test for the concomitant phenomena of the אות years. If it can be determined whether אות involved lunar conjunction with the sun, or rather a full moon, the meaning of דוק falls into place. Would sky watchers in Jerusalem more often observe a full moon or lunar conjunction at the time of the vernal equinox, when the solar calendar's year began? Presumably the Qumran texts are somehow connected—even if only schematically and at several removes—to actual observation of the sun and moon.

Secondly, I want to ask what light 4Q317 may shed on the problem of דוק. Heretofore this largely unpublished text involving lunar movement, written in cryptic alphabet A, has figured in the discussion only generally. Perhaps a more detailed consideration of the largest portion of this scroll can help decide which understanding of 4Q320, 4Q321 and 4Q321a better commends itself.

Sun and Moon in Second Temple Palestine

'As always,' said Nilsson, 'the concrete phenomenon is the starting point'.[16] Nilsson was describing the way in which primitive peoples begin to construct a lunar calendar, but the statement is equally valid for more developed cultures such as Second Temple Palestine. Behind abstract systems one ought to detect at least minimal observational data. In trying to understand the synchronistic calendars, then, it may be useful to investigate the concrete phenomena.

We can start by selecting a nineteen-year period, for, with a discrepancy of mere hours, the relevant lunar phenomena cycle every nineteen

---

rather differently; indeed, I think they did. See further note 35 below.

16. M.P. Nilsson, *Primitive Time-Reckoning* (Lund: C.W.K. Gleerup, 1920), p. 150.

years. For example, the astronomical new moon of 379 BCE occurred at
18.52 (= 18 January 12 hours 29 minutes), the second at 16.94, and the
third at 18.30.[17] Nineteen years later, in 360 BCE, the first full moon
occurred at 18.33, the second at 16.87, and the third at 18.30.[18] This
parallelism means that, for our purposes, a detailed investigation of nineteen years will suffice. I propose to begin with the year 145 BCE, since
that is a year in which the astronomical new moon at Jerusalem roughly
coincided with Nisan 1 of a solar calendar (or, put another way, with the
vernal equinox). 145 BCE also falls within a period that has significance
for certain reconstructions of the history behind the Scrolls. How often
would the conjunction of 145 recur in nineteen years? Or, if one should
begin with a year in which a full moon coincided with Nisan 1, such as
138 BCE, how often would that situation be repeated? For the years
145–127 BCE, the answers to these questions are tabulated below
(Table 1).[19]

Table 1: *Sun And Moon At The Vernal Equinox, 145–127 BCE*

Year[a]	Equinox[b]	Date Observed[c]	Moon[d]
145	3/23 9:44 PM	3/24	waxing crescent
144	3/24 3:32 AM	3/24	waxing gibbous
143	3/24 8:38 AM	3/24	waning gibbous
142	3/24 2:36 PM	3/24	conjunction
141	3/23 8:59 PM	3/24	waxing gibbous
140	3/24 2:37 AM	3/24	waning crescent
139	3/24 5:53 AM	3/24	waxing crescent
138	3/24 1:56 PM	3/24	full

17.   As is the convention, times are given in terms of the Julian calendar and
Greenwich mean time, and by decimal rather than sexagesimal reckoning for hours
and minutes.
18.   Figures cited according to F.K. Grinzel, *Handbuch der mathematischen und
technischen Chronologie* (Leipzig: Hinrichs, 1911), II, p. 561.
19.   My data were obtained using the computer program 'Sky Travel', which uses
a cursor that can be placed on a world map. After entering a date and time, one can see
the sky as an observer at that point in space and time would see it. I thank
E.W. Faulstich,who markets this program, for making it available to me at no cost.
For the equinoxes, note also B. Tuckerman, *Planetary, Lunar and Solar Positions
601 B.C. to A.D. 1 at Five-Day and Ten-Day Intervals* (Philadelphia: American
Philosophical Society, 1962). For data on new and full moons, complete coverage for
the centuries before and after the turn of the eras can be had by combining Grinzel,
Handbuch, II, pp. 544-575 with the more easily available E.J. Bickerman, *Chronology
of the Ancient World* (Ithaca, NY: Cornell University Press, 1968), pp. 110-42.

137	3/23 8:22 PM	3/24	waning crescent
136	3/24 1:45 AM	3/24	first
135	3/24 6:00 AM	3/24	waning gibbous
134	3/24 1:05 PM	3/24	conjunction
133	3/23 5:56 PM	3/23	waxing gibbous
132	3/24 12:55 AM	3/24	last
131	3/24 6:03 AM	3/24	waxing crescent
130	3/24 12:39 PM	3/24	waxing gibbous
129	3/23 6:00 PM	3/23	waning crescent
128	3/23 11:40 PM	3/24	waxing crescent
127	3/24 6:03 AM	3/24	full

[a]Dating by the Julian calendar. Dates for this period can be converted into the Gregorian calendar by subtracting three days.

[b]Jerusalem local time. Jerusalem is located at 30 degrees 51 minutes N latitude, 35 degrees 30 minutes E longitude.

[c]At 6:00 AM, the approximate time of sunrise (except for 133 BCE).

[d]At 6:00 PM on 3/23, generally the evening preceding the day of the vernal equinox.

When considering the data of Table 1, one must bear in mind that ancient astronomers had to rely on such instruments as the gnomon, the Jacob's staff, the quadrant and the armillary sphere. Accuracy never exceeded 2 minutes of arc, and was often considerably worse. Accordingly, whether observers in Jerusalem would be able to identify the time of the equinox (when the sun, moving on the celestial equator, reached 1 Aries) is dubious. Error might easily lead to the identification of any of five days as the equinox: the actual day and two days on either side of it. Indeed, the error might have been greater still.[20] (On the other hand, contemporary Greek astronomers determined the time of the equinox very accurately.)[21] Beyond the problem of accuracy, whether the equinox was actually observed, or merely calculated, perhaps on the basis of the more easily observed summer solstice, remains an open question.

Allowing, then, for these uncertainties, can we detect any patterns in the evidence that might explain the development of the Qumran

20. Cf. O. Neugebauer, 'The Alleged Babylonian Discovery of the Precession of the Equinoxes', *JAOS* 70 (1950), p. 5: 'a possible error of at least two days was considered as irrelevant'.

21. See the discussion by R. Newton, *Ancient Planetary Observations and the Validity of Ephemeris Time* (Baltimore: Johns Hopkins Press, 1976), pp. 154-66, and especially the table of equinox observations by Hipparchus (c. 190–after 126 BCE) on p. 158.

synchronistic calendars? What we ought to find is a recurrence, every three years, of one pattern or the other: either lunar conjunction roughly at the time of the equinox, or a full moon at that time. Beginning in 145 BCE, the pattern of conjunction seems to hold for a few years. The actual day of the equinox (3/23) was also the last day when the moon was visible at sunset. 3/24 was perhaps the last day of visibility at sunrise, though the moon might not have been visible even then. 3/25 was the day of conjunction. When we recall the observational difficulties, either 3/24 or 3/25 could have been identified as the vernal equinox as well as the day of conjunction. In 142 BCE, 3/24 was the day of the equinox and also the day of lunar conjunction. In 139 BCE a lunar conjunction occurred on 3/20, which, within the limits set out, would perhaps accord with the equinox. Thereafter, however, the pattern breaks down. For 136 BCE, the last day of lunar invisibility was 3/17, and by 133 BCE we are nearing full moon at the time of the equinox—it was full on 3/26. Apparently, then, only a six-year period exists when observation might support the interpretive option for the calendars that I earlier proposed. True, the years 137–134–131 BCE also support that option, but that group of years is mutually exclusive with the group that begins in 145 BCE.

Yet, for the full-moon option the data are hardly more comforting. The years 141-138-135 BCE might work, although in 135 BCE the moon was full on 3/19, probably outside the range of observational error. The group 133–130–127 BCE is promising. In 133 BCE, as noted, the full moon was on 3/26. In 130 BCE, it was full on 3/25, and in 127 BCE, on 3/22. Any of these dates could easily have been identified as the vernal equinox. By 124 BCE, however, the pattern begins to break down (full moon on 3/18), and by 121 BCE it has collapsed altogether. In that year the moon was in conjunction at the time of the equinox. Further, even granting the marginal years, the two groups of years are once again mutually exclusive.

For either option, then, reality appears to comply with ideology for no more than six years. Surely that period is much too short to inspire anyone to develop the Qumran concordant calendars. Even if one were to imagine them developing virtually overnight—spurred on, perhaps, by some crisis-driven fervor—observed reality would badly and immediately diverge. Observation does not seem to lie behind the Qumran calendars. Perhaps they express an entirely theological concept derived from ruminations on Genesis: something that never really existed. Have we to do with Marlowe's *Coelum igneum?*

Not necessarily. Inherent in the dates of Table 1 is the presupposition of frequent interpolation. That is, the dates are tabulated according to the Julian calendar, which follows a 365¼-day year. Presumably the Qumran calendar of 364 days was intercalated more or less regularly so that lunations would at least roughly coincide with the seasons. The Scrolls themselves, however, nowhere tell us how—or indeed, whether—the 364-day year was intercalated. What if one takes the 364-day year seriously; how will that affect concordance of solar and lunar phenomena? Will either option for the meaning of דוק, and the system thus implied, emerge from the data?

If one begins with the year 145 BCE and designates that year as an אות year, with 3/24 as Nisan 1 and the day of the moon's conjunction with the sun, and begins calculating 364-day years, the results are as follows. Nisan 1 of 142 BCE will fall on 3/21 of the Julian calendar. Is the moon in conjunction with the sun on that date? The answer is yes. For 139 BCE, Nisan 1 is 3/18, again a day of lunar conjunction. For 136 BCE, the date will be 3/15, once again a day of conjunction. For the following years, the projected dates will be: 133, 3/12; 130, 3/9; 127, 3/6; 124, 3/3; 121, 2/29; and 118, 2/26. In every case, a Jerusalem observer would find the moon in conjunction with the sun. Every three years, in other words, the astronomical situation of 145 BCE would recur, and each such year could fairly be designated an אות year. Further, we have already moved some thirty years from the beginning point, and the pattern has yet to break. This pattern probably holds long enough to have given rise to the system of the synchronistic calendars. Yet there is an obvious problem: Nisan 1 is receding further and further towards the beginning of the Julian year. Within another thirty years that date would back into the previous Julian December. Since the Jewish festivals by their nature tie Nisan 1 to the agricultural year, this problem could not have been ignored for very long. In other words, despite what we noted above, some system of intercalation must have been used, or the calendars could not have really worked.

Any system of intercalation must relate to the lunar cycle because of the requirements imposed by the אות years. An intercalary period should also be a multiple of seven because of the Qumran calendar's origins in Genesis and its consequent ties to the week of creation. For this mindset the week, culminating in the sabbath, was the invariable element: the irreducible and indivisible constant for all time reckoning.[22] How could a year *not* be an exact multiple of seven, since it was made up of weeks? How could the whole be anything more or less than the sum of its parts? Such reasoning was the logical foundation behind the attacks on 360 and 365-day years that appear, for example, in *1 Enoch*. What I suspect, therefore, is that the proponents of these synchronistic calendars intercalated a full lunar cycle—four weeks, twenty-eight days—somewhere between years twenty-seven and thirty of the pattern we are investigating. The pattern dissolves if one intercalates fewer days over shorter periods. To illustrate, based on our exemplary period: adding seven days in 138 BCE does not work, since it results in Nisan 1 at 3/22 in 136 BCE, when, however, sky watchers would see a new moon, not a conjunction. Similarly, adding fourteen days after fourteen years results in a waxing gibbous moon at Nisan 1 of 130 BCE. Adding twenty-one days after twenty-one years results in a waning gibbous moon at the concomitant Nisan 1 of 124 BCE. No, the only way to intercalate the pattern we are observing without disrupting it is to add a full lunar cycle, twenty-eight days.

Intercalating twenty-eight days in 117 BCE would result in a Nisan 1 of 3/24 in 115 BCE. The moon was then in conjunction for a Jerusalem observer. For the years that follow Nisan 1 would be: 3/21 in 112 BCE, 3/18 in 109, 3/15 in 106, 3/12 in 103, 3/9 in 100, 3/6 in 97, 3/3 in 94, 2/28 in 91, and 2/25 in 88. In each case, the moon was in conjunction as the pattern of אות years requires. After 88 BCE, twenty-eight days would once more be intercalated, resulting in a Nisan 1 of 3/23 for 85 BCE. Sixty years from our starting point, the pattern still holds rather well. But it is now beginning to be slightly inaccurate.

In 85 BCE the actual conjunction was on 3/22, and on 3/23 the new moon was first visible in the evening. Observed phenomena are beginning to slip with respect to the dates predicted by the system, and it only gets worse. By 61 BCE, the predicted Nisan 1 would be 2/29, but the actual date of lunar conjunction in Jerusalem would be 2/27. By 55 BCE, after a third intercalation of twenty-eight days, the system is off by fully four days. What solution the calendar's proponents would offer for this problem I do not know. Perhaps further research will suggest possible

---

22. Also, if one did not intercalate whole weeks, the basic halakhic advantage of the 364-day calendar—the recurrence of each calendar date on the same day of the week every year, which avoids festival and sabbath offerings being required on the same day—would be compromised.

approaches. Ancient analogies testify, however, that quite possibly people would be content to do nothing. One notes, for example, that at the time of the adoption of the Julian year in 46 BCE, the equinox of the Roman calendar had slipped to a point fully three months too early.[23] The problems thus raised would seem to us acute, but no action was taken for many years.

The Julian equivalent of Nisan 1 would vary in the period investigated between 2/25 and 3/24, about a month. This variation is no greater than in the traditional Jewish calendar of the rabbis, or the Babylonian lunisolar calendar. In the years 538-520 BCE, for example, Nisan 1 varied between 12 March and 18 April in the Babylonian version.[24] If some version of the proposed system did function, the variation of Nisan 1 highlights a provocative basic fact about the Qumran synchronistic calendars: despite its users' emphasis on the sun, it was instead the moon that actually controlled the system. Ideology had to defer here to what anyone who looked at the sky could see was true. Solar regularity must acquiesce to lunar foibles, or no אות system was possible.

What has emerged from this investigation of the observed phenomena is potentially significant. Presupposing years of 364 days, and that אות years were times of lunar conjunction on Nisan 1, the concordant calendars tie in very well with observed reality for over sixty years. They retain a certain accuracy for nearly ninety. That figure compares favorably with other ancient lunar calendars. For example, the Egyptian version referred to above was reasonably accurate for about one hundred and fifty years. Afterwards, it, too, began to slip, such that it seemed to early researchers to predict new moons rather than conjunctions—a slippage of two to three days, just as in our Qumran texts.[25] The fact that the Qumran timetables work thus well would seem to support my earlier proposal: דוק designates the day of observing the full moon. Actually, however, matters are not so simple.

We have seen that my proposal for the meaning of דוק can work, but we have yet to see that the other option *cannot* work. And here one encounters a problem in the effort to decide which proposal is preferable, for in fact the full-moon option works just as well as the

---

23. A perusal of Bickerman, *Chronology*, pp. 13-61, will supply the dubious reader with example after example of the ancients' frequently casual attitude toward precise agreement of the conventional calendar with astronomical realities.

24. Bickerman, *Chronology*, p. 24.

25. Parker, *Calendars*, p. 15.

conjunction option. Thus (returning to Table 1), if one designates 138
BCE an אות year, calls 3/24 Nisan 1, and begins to reckon by 364-day
years, then 135, 132, 129, etc. reprise the configuration of 138 BCE. The
full-moon option works as well as my proposal for the simple reason
that the underlying lunar cycle is one and the same. The two options
simply begin at different points in that cycle. Both options hold for sixty
to ninety years. After a period of years watching the heavenlies,
observers in Jerusalem could equally well have devised either system.

Both systems work provided only that the cycle begins in a year
when the heavenly phenomena are correct. In other words, the moon
must be in conjunction or full. Thereafter, the calendars will accord with
observed reality as indicated. Consequently, the conjunction option could
begin in 145 BCE, but it could as well begin in 164 BCE, or 183 BCE,
etc., working forward or backward at nineteen-year increments. The full-
moon option could begin in 138 BCE, or in 157, or 119, or 100, or 81
BCE. Unfortunately for those interested in possible historical implications,
it is not possible to deduce a single year in which the synchronistic
system—whichever it was—must have begun. The astronomical situation is therefore quite different than it is, for example, with the Sothic
cycle of the Egyptian solar calendar. The facts so far permit no deductions about when the Qumran calendar system may have been devised.
But one potentially significant deduction does seem to emerge.

If the proposed system of intercalation—which, of course, could work
equally well with either understanding of 4Q320, 4Q321 and 4Q321a—
is correct, it probably follows that the groups behind the synchronistic
calendars knew the Metonic Cycle. That method of intercalating the
lunisolar calendar seven times in nineteen years was known in Babylon
by 380 BCE,[26] so it would be surprising if it were unknown among the
Jews two centuries later. Yet there has heretofore been no direct evidence that it was known. On the contrary, it is a commonplace that the
lunisolar calendar among the Jews was based on observation, not calculation.[27] If that be true, then the Jews lagged well behind their neighbors
in their understanding of astronomy, since both the Greeks and the

---

26. O. Neugebauer, *The Exact Sciences in Antiquity* (New York: Dover, 2nd edn,
corrected, 1969), p. 140.

27. For example, see the discussion of the Jewish calendar in the standard work
by E. Schürer, *The History of the Jewish People in the Age of Jesus Christ* (*175 BC–
AD 135*) (ed. G. Vermes, F. Millar, M. Black and M. Goodman; Edinburgh: T. & T.
Clark, rev. edn, 1973–87), II, pp. 587-601.

Babylonians used the cycle. In this connection it is intriguing to observe that, given the proposed intercalation, over a fifty-seven year period the number of intercalations required by the Qumran calendars would equal the number required by the Metonic system. Intercalating seven times in nineteen years, the Metonic system would, of course, intercalate twenty-one times in fifty-seven years. The sexennial system of the Qumran synchronistic calendars intercalates once every three years, twice in six years. That works out to eighteen intercalations in fifty-four years. If, however, an additional month (twenty-eight days) were added every twenty-eight years, then the result is twenty intercalations in fifty-six years. Since year three of the Qumran calendars—corresponding to the fifty-seventh year—was intercalated at its end, the total finally becomes twenty-one intercalations, just as in the Metonic cycle. True, the total number of days in the two systems differs slightly, but the ideology of 4Q320, 4Q321 and 4Q321a would not allow a closer match than we get.

To this point one cannot say which understanding of רוק commends itself. We now know that observational phenomena would support either proposal. That is more than we knew before, and it is useful to find that the Qumran system could actually have worked about as well as ancient analogs did. That, too, is more than we knew before. To answer the question before us, however, we must take another tack, and thus I propose to consider 4Q317 and what it might contribute to the discussion.

4Q317 and the Meaning of רוק

4Q317 is a Hebrew text extant in seventy-six fragments, most quite small.[28] It describes the variable appearance of the moon in terms of the illuminated area, measured from one to fourteen parts. Day after day, the writer sets out what portion of the moon is visible or covered up. This method is essentially that of the truncated portions surviving in *1 En.* 73.4-8,[29] and is the same used in 4QEnastr[a-d] (Aramaic Enoch) and in 4Q503. As noted above, the scribe has encrypted the text by

28. The latest photographs of this text in the PAM series are 43.375-43.380. See Eisenman and Robinson, *Facsimile Edition,* photographs 1369-1374. The DJD edition is to be prepared by U. Glessmer and S. Pfann.

29. See the comments of O. Neugebauer, *The 'Astronomical' Chapters of the Ethiopic Book of Enoch (72 to 82)* (Copenhagen: Royal Danish Academy of Sciences and Letters, 1981), pp. 13-16.

using a cipher known to modern researchers as cryptic A (to differentiate it from systems known as cryptic B and cryptic C). 4Q317 is one of at least six Qumran scrolls known to make use of cryptic A.[30] Milik published thirteen lines from one fragment of the scroll (fragment 1 ii 2-14) in 1976.[31] To that portion I here join an additional twenty lines, the whole comprising two large fragments contained on PAM 43.375. Together these fragments make up a nearly complete column, missing perhaps no more than a single line.

Milik wrote of 4Q317 that it described the phases of the moon 'for the successive days of the solar year of 364 days', and that his lines concerned 'the fifth to tenth days of an unspecified month'.[32] In my view, however, the text does more than tabulate the phases of the moon for one 364-day year. 4Q317 explicates the system for at least three, and possibly six, years. Milik did not recognize this fact, owing, perhaps, to his belief that the Qumran concordances describe months that begin with the full moon. I propose that the portion below concerns the sixth month of year three (or year six; recall that they are the same except for the priestly courses in service) in the sexennial system. If I am correct, 4Q317 is a powerful argument in favor of understanding דוק in the sense I have proposed. The column reads as follows:

4Q317 Frgs. 1 ii 1-22 + 2 ii 1-10

1　[ערש]א [וכן תבוא ליום]
2　[33][בח]משה בו [תכסה שתים]
3　[ע]שרא ולן [תבוא ליום בששה בו]
4　תכסה שלוש [עשרא וכן תבוא ליום]
5　[34]בש<ב>עה בו תכס]ה ארבע עשרא וכן]
6　תבוא ליום　　*vacat*　[　　　　　]

30. Texts written in cryptic A, in addition to 4Q317, are 4Q249 'Midrash Sepher Moshe'; 4Q298 'Words of a Sage to the Sons of Dawn'; 4Q313, 'Diverse fragments' (*non vidi;* no photograph of this text is included in the PAM series) and 4Q324c, 'Mishmarot C^f'. In addition, although the rest of the text is in the familiar square script, several significant phrases of one of the 4Q copies of the Community Rule, 4Q259, are written in this alphabet. Texts in the undeciphered cryptic B are 4Q362 and 4Q363. The only text in the undeciphered cryptic C system has yet to receive a 4Q number, but it can be studied on PAM 43.387.

31. Milik, *Books of Enoch,* pp. 68-69.

32. Both quotations are from Milik, *Books of Enoch,* p. 68.

33. Letter forms corrected from בארבעה.

34. Corrected from בששה by means of changing the letter forms and insertion of a superlinear *beth.*

7 [בתוך היום כול משול]הֹ[35] בו בשמנֹה[36]

8 [יכלה השמש ובבוא <וחצי עשרא ארבע> ממעֹל הרקיע[37]

9 [להגלות יחל וכן] להכסוֹת אורה

10 [תגלה בו בתשעה] *vacat* לשבת באחד[38]

11 [ללילה תבוא וכן] אחֹ[ת מחלוכת[39]

35. This restoration is based on another fragment, which we can call fragment 3 (top of PAM 43.376). Line 7 of that fragment contains the phrase היוֹת [כול] התמשל [בֹ[תוך. This line of fragment 3 and those immediately preceding clearly describe a waning moon, as here in our portion. The reading receives further confirmation from another fragment, fragment 4, lines 4-9 (bottom of 43.376). Thus the reading is certain, although at first blush one might expect rather a *Niphal*, i.e. תֹמשׁל, 'it is ruled'. Perhaps the statement about the moon 'ruling' when in conjunction is a declaration that its essential nature is darkness (cf. *1 En.* 73.4, 'its whole disk is empty without light'). Certainly the text operates on the premise that the moon's true source of illumination is the sun, whose essential nature is, of course, light. In any case, this clear reading is a salutary warning that we do not understand everything about this text and its *confrères*. Neither can we necessarily imagine all the possible ancient exegeses of Gen. 1.14-19, or indeed, of Gen. 1.3-5. One could easily argue for the moon's special connection in certain scrolls to the Sons of Darkness, who followed the wrong (i.e., a lunarsolar) calendar. Cf., for example, 1QS 1.10-15 and its implications. Accordingly, this reading argues against the full-moon month for the synchronistic calendars, since the moon 'rules' when it is dark, not light.

36. Letter forms corrected from בשבעה.

37. The restoration of this line derives from fragment 3, line 8, which reads in part [יכלה השמש ובבוא <וחצי עשֹרא [א]רֹבע> עֹ[הרקי. Milik's reconstruction and translation of fragment 2 line 8, and indeed of lines 7-9, are somewhat different and entirely unconvincing, both logically and grammatically (though he stipulates they are tentative [*Books of Enoch*, p. 68 n. 1.]). In particular, his reconstruction has a problem of gender concord between subject and verb (אור is masculine in 4Q317), and does not know the reading [יֹ[כלה.

38. That lines 7-10 refer to the same day of the month—in other words, that the eighth day of the solar month is equivalent to the first day of the week—is clear in the light of other fragments, taken together with the clear reading of line 11, אחֹ[ת מחלוכת (signaling the beginning of the next cycle). Fragment 3 of PAM 43.376 demonstrates the necessary shifts and focus. In its line 6, the word תכסה is preserved; in its line 10, the word תֹגלה. Therefore the shift from waning to waxing takes place in its lines 7-9. While the date is lost, line 9 does preserve the phrase יֹ[וֹחל להגלות בארבֹעֹה לשבת. That phrase demonstrates the recurrent focus: the text paid special attention to the dates on which the shifts from one lunar phase to another occurred. To describe that shift the author used stock phrases, modified only slightly according to whether the shift was from waxing to waning, or the opposite. In each case these phrases occupied three lines or slightly more.

39. Read מחלוקת.

12 בעשׂרה בו ת[נ]גלה שתים וכן תבוא]

13 ללילה *vacat* בעש[ת]י עשר בו תגלה שלוש]

14 וכן תבוא ללילה] *vacat*   [

15 בשנים עשר בו[תגלה ארבע וכן]40

16 תבוא ללילה בש[לושה עשר בו] *vacat*

17 תגלה חמש וכן תב[ו]א ללילה]

18 בשלושה עשר בו תג[ל]ה שש וכן תבוא ללילה]41

19 [בח]מ[ש]ה עשר [בו תגלה שבע וכן תבוא]

20 ללילה *vacat* בש[ש]ה עשר בו תגלה]

21 שמונה וכן [תבוא ללילה   *vacat*]

22 [בש]<בב>[עה] עשר [בו תגלה תשע וכן תבוא ללילה]

23 [בשמונה עשר בו תגלה עשר וכן תבוא ללילה]

24 בתש[ע]ה ע[ש]ר בו תגלה עשתי עשרא וכן תבוא ללילה]

25 בתשעה עשר [בו תגלה שתים וכן תבוא ללילה]42

26 בעשרים בו [תגלה שלוש עשרא וכן תבוא ללילה]43

27 בׄאׄחד ועשרי[ם בו המשל כול הלילה בתוך הרקיע]44 45

28 ממעל <ארבע ע[ש]רא וחצי> ובבוא [השמש יכלה אורה להגלות]

29 וׄכן יחל לה[כסות]46 בׄאׄחד לשבת   *vacat*   [

30 בׄשׄלוש<ה> ועׄשׄרים בו תכסה מחלוקת אחת וכן]47

31 תׄ[ב]וׄא ליום]   *vacat*   [

32 בשלושה ועשרי[ם בו תכסה שתים וכן תבוא ליום]48

33 בחמשׄה ועשׄרׄי[ם בו תכסה שלוש וכן תבוא ליום]

40. Letter forms corrected from בעשתי עשר.

41. *Sic;* correct would be בארבעה עשר.

42. *Sic;* correct would be בעשרים.

43. Using a superlinear cipher for 'one', the scribe has corrected בעשרים to באחד ועשרים.

44. The restoration המשל כול הלילה (*Niphal* 3fs imperfect) is not confirmed by other fragments and is therefore only conjectural. The movement of the text leads one to think that the moon is most emphatically subject to the power of the greater light, the sun, when it is itself shining most brightly. See note 35 above.

45. Using a superlinear cipher for 'two', the scribe has corrected באחד ועשרים to בשנים ועשרים.

46. This reconstruction is required if the scribe continues to be off in his counting. If he were correct here, or if he later corrected the word, the reconstruction would be בשנים.

47. The scribe first wrote בשנׄים, then corrected the letter forms (and added a superlinear *heh*) to read בשלושה.

48. Using a superlinear cipher for 'four', the scribe has corrected בשלושה ועשרים to בארבעה ועשרים.

Translation[49]

1 elev]en (parts, מחלוקות), [and thus it (i.e., the moon, לבנה) enters the day.]

2 [On the fi]fth (corrected from 'fourth') day (lit., 'in it', i.e., the month) [twe]lve (parts) [are obscured,]

3 and thus [it enters the day. On the sixth day,]

4 thir[teen] (parts) are obscured, [and thus it enters the day.]

5 On the seventh (corrected from 'sixth') day, [fourteen (parts)] are obscur[ed, and thus]

6 it enters the day. *vacat* [   ]

7 On the eighth (corrected from 'seventh') day, it ru[les all day in the midst]

8 of the firmament abo[ve, fourteen and one-half parts. With the setting of the sun] its light

9 [ceases] to be obscured, [and thus begins to be revealed]

10 on the first day of the week. *vacat* [On the ninth day]

11 on[e] part [is revealed, and thus it enters the night.]

12 On the tenth day [two (parts) are] re[vealed, [and thus it enters]

13 the night. *vacat* On the elev[enth day three (parts) are revealed,]

14 and thus it enters the night. *vacat* [   ]

15 On the twelfth (corrected from 'eleventh') day [four (parts) are revealed, and thus]

16 it enters the night. *vacat* On the thir[teenth day]

17 five (parts) are revealed, and thus it enter[s the night.]

18 On the fourteenth day (corrected from 'thirteenth') [six (parts)] are reve[aled, and thus it enters the night.]

19 [On the fif]teenth [day seven (parts) are revealed, and thus it enters]

20 the night. *vacat* On the six[teenth day] eight (parts) [are revealed,]

21 and thus [it enters the night. *vacat*]

22 [On the sev]enteenth [day nine (parts) are revealed, and thus it enters the night.]

23 [On the eighteenth day ten (parts) are revealed, and thus it enters the night.]

24 On the ninete[enth day eleven (parts) are revealed, and thus it enters the night.]

25 On the twentieth [day (corrected from 'nineteenth') twelve (parts) are revealed, and thus it enters the night.]

26 On the twenty-first day (corrected from 'twentieth') [thirteen (parts) are revealed, and thus it enters the night.]

27 On the twen[ty]-second [day (corrected from 'twenty-first') it is ruled all night in the midst of the firmament]

28 above, fourt[een and one-half (parts).] With the setting of [the sun, its light ceases to be revealed]

29 and thus it begins to be ob[scured on the first (or perhaps, 'second') day of the week.]

49. So far as possible, I have tried to align the English translation's line numbers with the line numbers on which the equivalent Hebrew occurs. Word order differing in the two languages, however, English idiom has sometimes required that I depart from this procedure.

30 On the tw[enty]-third [day one part is obscured, and thus]
31 it e[n]ters the day. *vacat* [   ]
32 On the twen[ty]-fourth [day (corrected from 'twenty-third') two (parts) are
   obscured, and thus it enters the day.]
33 On the twen[ty]-fifth [day three (parts) are obscured, and thus it enters the day.]

These portions of 4Q317 raise many questions and pose difficult problems. This is not the place for a full scale study, but for our purposes that
is not required, since in general the movement of the text is clear.
Indeed, the language is so formulaic that virtually complete restoration is
possible (especially with the help of other fragments not published here).
As the moon is waning, it is 'obscured' (תכסה); as it is waxing, it is
'revealed' (תגלה). When either process has culminated, fourteen and one-
half parts of the moon's light—which only has fourteen parts—are
declared visible or invisible, as appropriate. The mathematical impossibility of this latter aspect of the text is clear testimony to the primitiveness
of the system, and suggests a naïve reworking of an original twenty-
eight day lunar cycle for use with twenty-nine and thirty day lunisolar
months. (The mathematical naïveté also warns against seeking more
than a rough-and-ready precision in correlations between observation
and predicted lunar-solar phenomena in the synchronistic calendars.)

Having completed one half of the cycle, the moon begins the other.
Correlated with this flip-flop is the description of the moon's entry 'into
the day' or 'into the night'. As the moon wanes, it enters the day; as it
waxes, it enters the night. Apparently this terminology reflects actual
observation. Between first crescent and full moon, the moon is best
observed in the west at the time of sunset. When it begins to wane, the
opposite is the case and it is best observed in the east at sunrise. The
new moon appears on the western horizon at sunset, and last visibility
occurs on the eastern horizon at sunrise. To generalize in another way,
one observes the moon waxing during evenings and waning during
mornings. So understood, the references in 4Q317 to entering 'day' and
'night' make sense (though other understandings may be possible). The
author aligns every step of the moon's cycle with succeeding days of the
364-day solar calendar. The entries pattern very regularly: first, the
author records the date in the solar calendar month; next, he stipulates
what portion of the moon is visible or obscured; last, he states that with
thus-and-so a proportion of light visible, the moon enters the day or the
night. Essentially, we have before us an ancient exemplar of triple-entry
bookkeeping, belonging to the genre 'list'.

WISE דוק *and the Qumran Synchronistic Calendars* 117

Two aspects of the text require particular comment in connection with our search for the meaning of דוק. First, lines 7-10 equate the eighth day of the solar calendar to the first day of the week, that is, Sunday. That equation is a crucial clue to the identity of the month in question. In the 364-day system, a particular date of any given month falls on the same day of the week every year. Accordingly, the month here explicated must be a month three, six, nine or twelve, for only in those months does a Sunday ever fall on the eighth day of the month.

Secondly, these lines of 4Q317 are replete with scribal errors. Such mistakes are unsurprising in a formulaic text, so much of which involves numbers. These errors reveal important information about the mind and working habits of the scribe. Those of lines 2, 5 and 7 he corrected by slight erasures and modifying letter forms. The number '10' in line 12 is uncorrected, showing that the scribe must have been double-checking his work at regular intervals as he went along, rather than revising after he had completed the whole. Otherwise, this number should have been a correction of '9'. Realizing that he was off by one unit in the day of the month, the scribe made the necessary changes in the first dozen lines before proceeding farther.

Almost immediately, however, he blundered again, and had to correct the '11' that he had first written in line 15 so that it read '12'. Then, in line 18, he wrote the wrong number, '13', repeating the number that he had just written in line 16. He did not try to correct this mistake per se, but compensated by skipping to the proper number, '15', at the beginning of line 19. Lines 20, 22, and 24 appear to be correct, but the poor preservation of the relevant portions of the manuscript precludes certainty. Line 25 is once again in error. Once more the scribe repeated a number from the previous line. This error begat another, the '20' of line 26 standing where it should read '21'. Like toppling dominoes, lines 27, 30 and 32 followed that original error of line 25. Before penning line 33, however, the writer realized his mistake, and added superlinear ciphers to correct each of the problem numbers. These continual mistakes testify not only to the scribe's method of working, but to his confusion as he went about his work. Doubtless that confusion explains the fact that one very significant *lapsus calami* escaped his attention entirely.

Given the scribe's method and the remains that can actually be read, little doubt clouds the contents of any given line. Thus the one ultimately uncorrected blunder in these lines fairly leaps out. Line 26 has assigned thirteen-fourteenths of waxing illumination to the twenty-first day of the solar month in question. The next line goes immediately to fourteen and one-half portions of light. (The number is only partially reconstructed, and virtually certain). The scribe has passed over the number fourteen that ought to have stood on this line, as the pattern in lines 4-5, for example, demonstrates.[50] The significance of this observation is that the full moon described in lines 27-30 ought to stand, not on the twenty-second, but on the twenty-third. And that date points to my original proposal for the meaning of the term דוק.

We have already established that the solar month in question is either month three, six, nine or twelve. Now we must ask whether the synchronistic calendars align the term דוק with the twenty-third day of the solar calendar for any of those months within the sexennial cycle. The answer to this question is, of course, yes. The alignment occurs in the sixth month of years three and six. The alignment occurs only then. In the sixth month of year three, 4Q321 specifies that דוקה occurs 'on the second of Hakkoz, on the twenty-third' of that month.[51] In the same month of year six, that same text assigns דוקה to 'the second of Pethahiah, on the twenty-third of it'.[52]

In sum, 4Q317, like the synchronistic calendars, aligns lunar phenomena with the 364-day solar calendar over a period of several years. And this text explicitly places a full moon on the twenty-third day of the month it describes. Based on the text's clear statement in line 10, that month must be a month three, six, nine or twelve. 4Q321 locates the disputed term precisely in agreement with these stipulations. The equation is hard to avoid: דוק refers to the full moon. The texts themselves say so.

---

50. Another way of interpreting the evidence is to suggest that the scribe did not notice the mistake in line 28 because there wasn't one—fourteen-fourteenths was what it implied, and that was just what the scribe intended. Subsequently, a corrector (whose hand is, however, suspiciously like that of the primary scribe) wrote in 'fourteen and one-half' above the line, thereby altering the text's entire system. One cannot help noticing that all the notations for 'fourteen and one-half' in this text were written in above the line. This peculiarity may indicate an *ad hoc* reworking not just of an earlier text, but of an earlier system. Whether that be so or not, 4Q317 as it stands ties in with the system of the synchronistic calendars.

51. 4Q321 1 iii 3.

52. 4Q321 2 i 2.

Conclusion

I have argued that actual observations would allow, and that 4Q317 seems to require, the connection of the term דוק with the full moon. The underlying system of the synchronistic calendars would then follow: the month begins at or near the conjunction, and special attention is paid to the day of the full moon and to the final day of visibility. Indeed, interest in the final day of visibility is the *sine qua non* for a calendar whose months begin at lunar conjunction. Final visibility is what determines the time of conjunction, since by its very nature conjunction defies observation. If my proposed understanding of the system is right, the fact that 4Q320 tabulates the last day of each lunar month is just what we should expect.

Apart from the suggestive parallels with Egyptian practice, further evidence for this approach to the synchronistic calendars may perhaps be found in the Samaritan calendrical system. Early on in research on the Scrolls, Massingberd Ford drew attention to the primacy of the solar calendar for the Samaritans.[53] In her view, this shared ideology was of great significance for understanding the historical origins and perspectives of the Qumran finds. Necessarily ignorant of the synchronistic calendars, she had no opportunity to point out a second, equally striking parallel practice: beginning the lunisolar month at the conjunction.[54] This oddity of the Samaritan lunisolar calendar has never been explained. Further, according to a Samaritan tradition that specialists have doubted, the time of the conjunction was always based on calculation, not observation. If I am right, however, the Qumran synchronistic calendars may shed light on both these problems. It appears that the Samaritan-Qumran traditions are mutually illuminating.

These calendrical parallels require no theory of a direct connection between Samaritan groups and those behind the Qumran caches. A shared common heritage could account for the evidence. A significant and perhaps sizeable proportion of Second Temple Jews evidently embraced a calendrical system opposed to what eventually would

---

53. J. Massingberd Ford (*sic*), 'Can We Exclude Samaritan Influence from Qumran?', *RevQ* 6 (1967–69), p. 123: 'Perhaps the most concrete connection between the Qumran community and the Samaritans is their common use of the solar calendar'. The author's name also appears as Massingberg Ford in this same article.

54. S. Powels, 'The Samaritan Calendar and the Roots of Samaritan Chronology', in *The Samaritans* (ed. A. Crown; Tübingen: Mohr, 1989), esp. pp. 723-24.

become 'the Jewish calendar'. The system they affirmed dated at least as far back as the third century BCE and focused on the sun. When it came to lunisolar practice, the month was begun at the conjunction. Of course, the groups that embraced this system would disagree among themselves on many of the fine points, as is clear already from the discrepancies contained in *Astronomical Enoch*.[55] We should expect to find substantial reworking and disagreement manifested in corpora of calendrical writings deriving from these circles. And so we do: 4Q317, for example, appears decidedly less sophisticated than the synchronistic calendars.

In the end the authors of all these writings were concerned to find and explicate the truth. That truth could begin nowhere but in God's revelations to Moses and the prophets and proceeded from there. Observation must agree with what exegesis of the Bible declared to be true. Such correlation between observation and biblical exegesis was the foundation of the Qumran synchronistic calendars. Eventually, as we have seen, their system would begin to depart from observation. Perhaps there existed some further method of fine-tuning, another punctiliar inter-calation activated by the observations these texts list in so tireless and repetitive a fashion. Or perhaps, as Beckwith once suggested in another connection,[56] the deviations would be attributed to rebellion in the heavens, the leaven of angelic sin. The more and more evident failure of the heavenlies to complete their movements as required presumably caused some tension in the circles using the synchronistic calendars. Nevertheless, the copying and recopying of these works shows that their implied claims were not thereby abandoned. Observation aside, here was calibrated a higher truth. The writers spoke of the Firmament (הרקיע), but Marlowe might have said that they actually described the Empyrean Heaven.

---

55. The words of Neugebauer, *'Astronomical' Chapters,* p. 3, speak to this point and bear repetition: 'What we have is not the work of one author (or 'redactor') but a conglomerate of closely related versions made by generations of scribes who assembled, to the best of their knowledge, the teaching current in their community about the structure and the laws of the cosmos.' Elsewhere Neugebauer speaks of the 'communities' that produced the Enochic cosmologies. We must factor into our attempts to understand the Qumran calendrical materials both geography and chronology.

56. R. Beckwith, 'The Modern Attempt to Reconcile the Qumran Calendar with the True Solar Year', *RevQ* 7 (1969-71), pp. 392-93, citing *1 En.* 80.2-8.

The Deuteronomic Character of 4Q252

George J. Brooke

Although the photographic plates of 4Q252 had been generally available for several months, and although the *Preliminary Concordance* which includes it analytically had been available on a more restricted basis for several years,[1] it was the publication of two works in close succession towards the end of 1992 which immediately provoked a flurry of interest in 4Q252. The first of these two publications was a preliminary transcription and translation with notes of the largest fragment of 4Q252 by T.H. Lim.[2] The second was the publication of the complete text, reconstructed from the *Preliminary Concordance*, with reference to the photographic plates, by Ben Zion Wacholder and Martin Abegg.[3]

---

1. *A Preliminary Concordance to the Hebrew and Aramaic Fragments from Qumrân Caves II-X* printed from a card index prepared by R.E. Brown, J.A. Fitzmyer, W.G. Oxtoby and J. Teixidor; prepared and arranged for printing by H.-P. Richter (Göttingen, 1988).

2. T.H. Lim, 'The Chronology of the Flood Story in a Qumran Text (4Q252)', *JJS* 43 (1992), pp. 288-98.

3. Thus the Hebrew text is available on the basis of the work of J.T. Milik and others in B.Z. Wacholder and M. Abegg, *A Preliminary Edition of the Unpublished Dead Sea Scrolls* (Washington, 1992), II, pp. 212-15; in R.H. Eisenman and M.O. Wise, *The Dead Sea Scrolls Uncovered* (Shaftesbury, 1992), pp. 86-87; column 5 was published by J.M. Allegro in 'Further Messianic References in Qumran Literature', *JBL* 75 (1956), pp. 174-75 + plate I. Columns 1.1–2.5 together with related biblical passages are printed in parallel Hebrew columns in U. Glessmer, 'Antike und moderne Auslegungen des Sintflutberichtes Gen 6-8 und der Qumran-Pesher 4Q252' (Theologische Fakultät Leipzig, Forschungstelle Judentum, Mitteilungen und Beiträge 6; Leipzig, 1993), pp. 30-39. A diplomatic transcription, a kind of preliminary edition, is available in my study 'The Thematic Content of 4Q252', in *Papers of the Annenberg Research Institute 1992–1993* (ed. D. Goldenberg; Philadelphia, forthcoming). Further comments on readings can be found in H. Jacobson, '4Q252: Addenda', *JJS* 44 (1993), pp. 118-20; T.H. Lim, 'Notes on 4Q252 fr. 1, cols i-ii', *JJS* 44 (1993), pp. 121-26; M. Kister, 'Notes on Some New

Are the six fragments assigned to 4Q252 all part of this same Herodian manuscript? H. Stegemann has recently proposed that two different manuscripts are involved.[4] His argument is based in large measure on the forms which the exegesis of Genesis takes in the various pericopae of 4Q252. Because he assumes that within any one text like this, the commentator is likely to have followed a single pattern, Stegemann separates the handling of the chronological material concerning the flood and Abram's entry into the land, all of which is largely paraphrastic, from the more formal exegesis of Gen. 36.12 and 49.3-27 which is extant in other fragments. He fails to notice, however, that the technical formula כאשר כתוב occurs in frag. 1 at the start of column 3 and thus indicates in one and the same fragment a different handling of scripture than the merely paraphrastic which predominates in the handling of the chronological items in columns 1 and 2. Moreover, the material remains strongly suggest that all six fragments assigned to 4Q252 do indeed belong together. Most especially there is no reason to doubt that all were written by the same hand. In addition, the phrasing which survives in column 3 on the far left-hand edge of frags. 1 and 3 and on the right-hand edge of frag. 5 can be suitably juxtaposed, not only in relation to the context of Gen. 18.31-32 and especially Gen. 22.10-12, but also in the precise way in which such matching phrases feature in the correct lines when counting from the top margin which is extant in both frags. 1 and 5.

The purpose of this short study is to add some further confirmation to the proposal that all six fragments of 4Q252 should be taken together. The basic thesis of this study is that, amongst other things, there is a thoroughgoing use of Deuteronomy lying behind the various pericopae. In two places this is quite explicit (4Q252 3.2-6; 4.1-3), but in other places as well the theology and purpose of Deuteronomy are apparent.

1. *4Q252 3.2-6*[5]

In 4Q252 3.2-6 there is an exegetical discussion of part of the Sodom and Gomorrah story of Genesis 18. The surviving text reads as follows:

Texts from Qumran', *JJS* 44 (1993), pp. 287-89; H. Jacobson, '4Q252 fr. 1: Further Comments', *JJS* 44 (1993), pp. 291-93; M. Bernstein, '4Q252: From Re-Written Bible to Biblical Commentary', *JJS* 45 (1994), pp. 1-27.

4.   H. Stegemann, *Die Essener, Qumran, Johannes der Täufer und Jesus* (Freiburg, 1993), pp. 170-72.

5.   All references to 4Q252 are to column and line number.

2. עמו]רה וגם	
3. [צדיקים	העיר הזואת]
4. [ים לבדם יחרמו	אנוכ]י לא]
5. [הנמצא בה ושלליה	ואם לוא ימצא שם]
6.	] ומפיה ושאר

2.	Gomo]rrah and also
3. this city[	] righteous
4. I [will] not [	] only they shall utterly destroy,
5. and unless there are found there[	]which is found in it and its booty
6. and its little children, and the rest [	

Lines 1-2 of this column seem to be citing a secondary scriptural text which mentions the number twelve. Since the only text between Gen. 15.17 and 18.20ff. where the number twelve is found is Gen. 17.20, it is possible that the bottom of 4Q252 column 2 contained some kind of interpretation of it which was then supported with a secondary scriptural citation at the top of column 3. The next section of the Genesis commentary concerns Gomorrah and 'this city', a reference to Sodom which is the principal subject of the debate between Abraham and God concerning the number of righteous required to fend off divine destruction. That debate seems to be summarized in little more than one line of text. The rest of lines 4-6 concern the character of the complete destruction which is the fate of Sodom and Gomorrah.

M. Kister has noted that this section of 4Q252 may refer to the law of *herem* of Deut. 13.14-18,[6] but M. Bernstein has pointed out more closely that the destruction described uses two terms which must clearly recall the Deuteronomic law of the sacrificial ban for the idolatrous city. חרם occurs nowhere in Genesis itself but is the hallmark of Deut. 13.16-18 (מן החרם; החרם אתה). It also occurs in Deut. 7.2 and 7.26, in which those to be driven out of the land are listed, a passage which is recalled in Deut. 20.17 where the term is forcefully repeated (החרם תחרימם). The second term which features in 4Q252 and Deuteronomy 13 is שלל with a third person suffix. The town that comes under the ban is to be utterly destroyed with all its inhabitants, livestock and spoil. It appears that the compiler of the commentary in 4Q252 understood the total destruction of Sodom and Gomorrah as evidence that these two towns had come under the ban as that is legislated in Deuteronomy 13. As with the term חרם, so with שלל the laws for war of Deuteronomy 20 also may have influenced the precise terminology of 4Q252 3.5-6. Thus the phrase

6. Kister, 'New Texts from Qumran', p. 288.

הנמצא בה (4Q252 3.5) seems to reflect Deut. 20.11 (כל העם הנמצא בה)
more than the corresponding phrasing in Deut. 13.16 (ואת כל אשר בה)
and of these two legal passages the little children of 4Q252 3.6 are
mentioned only in Deut. 20.14 but in the context of spoil which can be
taken and enjoyed by the capturing Israelite army. Thus it seems that the
legal commentary on the destruction of Sodom and Gomorrah in
4Q252 is a justification for the total annihilation of the two towns on the
basis of the law of the sacrificial ban; combined with that is some terminology from the laws for waging war of Deuteronomy 20.

Now the commentator is not simply providing a suitable legitimization
for the divine action against Sodom and Gomorrah. He is also implying
two other matters. In the first place for the justification to be worth
making explicit, the commentator is showing that he understands that
Deuteronomy can be read backwards, that is, it can be seen to apply to
situations and times before Moses is described as uttering it on the eve
of Israel's entry into the land. Thus, ahead of any straightforward historical reading of the Pentateuchal books comes the assumption that there
is an overall consistency between the various sections of the Law. This
consistency can be made plain in the kind of exegesis to be found in
4Q252, but it is also present in a variety of other contemporary texts.
So, for example, in the book of *Jubilees* laws which are only formally
promulgated later in the Mosaic period are seen to apply in earlier
periods: for instance, the patriarchs variously keep particular festivals
and make appropriate sacrifices. In other texts a similar presupposition is
also evident. In the Temple Scroll laws from various parts of the
Pentateuch are harmonized with one another to iron out variations
which remain in the Pentateuch as it stands. These marks of inner consistency lie behind many of the variants in particular scriptural
manuscripts, such as 4QpaleoExod[m] (and the Samaritan tradition generally), which fill out various pericopae so that each event that happens
is predicted and conversely each prophecy is explicitly fulfilled.[7]

A second implication of the fragmentary exegesis of the Sodom and
Gomorrah material in 4Q252 needs to be made explicit. Deut. 12.1
states clearly that 'these are the statutes and ordinances that you must
diligently observe in the land that the Lord, the God of your ancestors,
has given you to occupy all the days that you live on the earth'. By

---

7.   See J.E. Sanderson, *An Exodus Scroll from Qumran: 4QpaleoExod[m] and the
Samaritan Tradition* (Harvard Semitic Studies 30; Atlanta, 1986), pp. 271-73, 299-
306.

applying the law of the sacrificial ban to Sodom and Gomorrah, the exegete implies that the law for living in the land applies to those two towns. This is not a claim based on the necessary internal consistency of the Pentateuch, but rather on a particular view of the extent of the land. Gen. 10.19 provides a geographical description of the extent of the land of the Canaanites: 'And the territory of the Canaanites extended from Sidon, in the direction of Gerar, as far as Gaza, and in the direction of Sodom, Gomorrah, Admah, and Zeboiim, as far as Lasha'.[8] The logical way of understanding the text is that the land of the Canaanites which was the gift to Israel extended as far as Sodom and Gomorrah, but did not include them. So, after a careful appraisal of the idioms in Gen. 10.19 and 25.18, J.A. Loader has recently concluded that 'Sodom, Gomorrah, Admah and Zeboim fall outside the territory of Canaan'.[9]

However, if in the text of Gen. 10.19 the location of Sodom and Gomorrah outside the land has to be argued for, in light of the same set of towns being repeated in Deut. 29.22 it is possible to argue that from the perspective of Deuteronomy they were considered to be included within the land. As divine destruction has fallen on the idolatrous Sodom and Gomorrah in the past, so it can fall on any other part of the land, on any idolatrous individual, family or tribe.[10] The application of the law of ḥerem of Deut. 13.12-18 to Sodom and Gomorrah in 4Q252 is thus the use of a Deuteronomic concern deliberately to clarify the extent of the borders of the land. For Deuteronomy and the compiler of 4Q252 the cities of Sodom and Gomorrah fall within the land which is subject to the laws promulgated in Deut. 12.1-26.15. One may justifiably wonder whether an actual political reality was being hinted at here since under the later Hasmoneans and especially under Herod the Great, the land was certainly extensive enough to have included Sodom and Gomorrah.

8.   The Samaritan Pentateuch reads here: מנהר מצרים עד הנהר הגדול נהר פרת ועד הים האחרון.

9.   J.A. Loader, *A Tale of Two Cities: Sodom and Gomorrah in the Old Testament, Early Jewish and Early Christian Traditions* (Contributions to Biblical Exegesis and Theology 1; Kampen, 1990), p. 49.

10.   Several commentators note that Deut. 29.22 needs to be read in association with Deut. 13.12-18; see, e.g., M. Weinfeld, *Deuteronomy and the Deuteronomic School* (Oxford, 1972), pp. 109-10.

2. *4Q252 4.1-3*

The second explicit use of Deuteronomy occurs in the short pericope which is concerned with Amalek. The text reads:

1.	תמנע היתה פילגש לאליפז בן עשיו ותלד לו את עמלק הוא אשר הכ[הו]
2.	שאול [ ] כאשר דבר למושה באחרית הימים תמחה את זכר עמלק
3.	מתחת השמים

1. Timna was the concubine of Eliphaz, the son of Esau. And she bore him Amalek, he whom
2. Saul destroyed. *vacat* As he spoke to Moses, 'In the latter days you will wipe out the memory of Amalek
3. from under the heavens.'

Both Eisenman and Wise in their comments on this pericope and Stegemann identify the supporting quotation as from Exod. 17.14: מחה את זכר עמלק מתחת השמים.[11] However, there is even greater overlap between the text of 4Q252 4.2-3 and Deut. 25.19: תמחה את זכר עמלק מתחת השמים. The saying in Deuteronomy naturally recalls the incident in Exod. 17.8-17 but the text of Exodus offers no explanation as to why Amalek should be completely annihilated. In Deut. 25.17-18 an explanation is offered: Amalek had attacked cruelly from behind, he did not fear God. In order to underline the difference between Exodus and Deuteronomy, M. Weinfeld comments that 'the passage in Deut. 25.17-19 is a genuine deuteronomic one and actually revises the ancient traditions of the war with Amalek in accordance with the deuteronomic concept'.[12] For the purposes of this study it is thus important to note that the immediate scriptural context of Deut. 25.19 is a neat reflection of Deuteronomic concerns.

That Deuteronomy is in the mind of the compiler of 4Q252 is confirmed from two other points. First, the context in Deuteronomy is striking. In a fashion quite different from that of the description of Amalek in Exodus, in Deuteronomy both before and after this saying there is mention of the gift of the land: 'Therefore when the Lord your God has given you rest from all your enemies on every hand, in the land that the Lord your God is giving you as an inheritance to possess, you shall blot out the remembrance of Amalek from under heaven; do not forget. When you have come into the land that the Lord your God is

---

11. *Dead Sea Scrolls Uncovered*, p. 82; *Die Essener*, p. 171.
12. *Deuteronomy*, p. 275.

giving you as an inheritance to possess, and you possess it, and settle in it, you shall take...' I have elsewhere argued at length that the gift of the land is one of the principal themes of the whole commentary in 4Q252.[13]

Secondly the phrasing of Deut. 25.19, 'when the Lord your God has given you rest from your enemies on every hand', allows for a quasi-eschatological interpretation of the saying. This is made plain in 4Q252 4.2 through the addition of באחרית הימים at the opening of the saying. Apart from Gen. 49.1[14] and Num. 24.14,[15] the phrase באחרית הימים occurs in the Pentateuch only in the book of Deuteronomy. In Deut. 4.30 it is used in a context which, as with the Sodom and Gomorrah material in Deut. 29.22, refers to the future idolatry of Israel (Deut. 4.25) and the divine mercy which will attend those who return to God, mercy which is available because God will not forget the covenant with Israel's ancestors (Deut. 4.31). In Deut. 31.29 Moses describes the future provocation of God by Israel. These deuteronomic uses of באחרית הימים may be sufficient to justify the adaptation of the saying of Moses in Deut. 25.19, but two other points support such an adjustment. On the one hand the phrase is widely used of the eschatological age in the so-called sectarian texts from Qumran,[16] of which 4Q252 in its final form may well be one. On the other hand the immediate context of the saying of Moses in Deut. 25.19 concerning the rest that God will give from 'your enemies on every side' is echoed in the eschatological handling of the oracle of Nathan[17] in 4Q174 whose principal extant column interprets 2 Sam. 7.11, 'and I will give you rest from all your enemies', of the rest that

13. 'Thematic Content of 4Q252', forthcoming.

14. Gen. 49.3ff. forms the subject of the next pericope of 4Q252, but intriguingly the pericope is introduced, not with the repetition of Gen. 49.1 which contains the phrase באחרית הימים, but rather with the brief title: ברכות יעקוב.

15. Num. 24.15-17 is part of the oracle of Balaam which is used eschatologically in 4QTest 9-13 and CD 7.18-20.

16. E.g., 1QpHab 2.5; 9.6; 1QSa 1.1; 4Q174 1.2, 12, 15, 19; CD 4.4; 6.11.

17. It is just possible that Nathan featured explicitly in 4Q252 5.7. This part of the text was made known by J.M. Allegro in 1956. In light of the sequence of thought in this part of 4Q252, D.R. Schwartz has proposed restoring the lines as 'For [(the house of?) "Judah"] is the assembly of the men of [the community and "scepter" is the Interpreter of the Law], as Nathan [said: "I will chasten him with the scepter of men"] (2 Sam 7.14, perhaps only alluded to without citation)': 'The Messianic Departure from Judah (4QPatriarchal Blessings)', *Theologische Zeitschrift* 37 (1981), p. 266.

will be given to the sons of light from all the sons of Belial.

The use of Deuteronomy at this juncture in 4Q252 is not just to underline the gift of the land which seems to be particularly relevant for the commentator. Rather, the commentator is able to use the law for the land in Deuteronomy 12–26 for his own eschatological purposes. Clearly he understood Deuteronomy to have applied as the law of the land after the conquest as the former prophets tell it, especially since in this very context he recalls the way in which Saul faced the Amalekites (but was unable to carry out this command entirely).[18] But he also recognized that the legislation of Deuteronomy could be fulfilled in a suitable way only in the eschatological period, his own time, since all previous generations had fallen short in obedience to the covenant. Thus, as in using the law of the sacrificial ban in relation to Sodom and Gomorrah the commentator shows how the laws of Deuteronomy apply to preceding material which describes earlier times, so in using the Amalek saying from Deut. 25.19 he is able to show how the laws of Deuteronomy apply to all subsequent events, both in a negative way of all later generations who may have aspired to keep the covenant, but did not (with a few notable exceptions, of course), and in a positive way of the eschatological age which is dawning in his own experiences.

In the Temple Scroll, a text roughly contemporary with 4Q252, Deuteronomy is also made to look forward to the present eschatological age in anticipation of the age when God himself will create his sanctuary. Several scholars have argued for the eschatological intent of the Temple Scroll.[19] In relation to the Amalekites, Ben Zion Wacholder himself has noted how the author of the scroll in his use of Deuteronomy consciously seems to avoid mentioning them, as also the Ammonites and Moabites.[20] Wacholder portrays the Moses of the Temple Scroll as 'the lawgiver of the future'. In the future the land will be perfectly governed in anticipation of the final creative act of God. As 4Q174 makes explicit that the גר and foreigner would be excluded from the eschatological

---

18.   M. Bernstein notes that the commentator's awareness of the existence of Amalekites after Saul's time is the basic factor motivating him to adapt Moses' saying in Deut. 25.19 through the addition of באחרית הימים.

19.   Most thoroughly and recently, M.O. Wise, *A Critical Study of the Temple Scroll from Qumran Cave 11* (Studies in Ancient Oriental Civilization, 49; Chicago, 1990), esp. pp. 200-201.

20.   B.Z. Wacholder, *The Dawn of Qumran: The Sectarian Torah and the Teacher of Righteousness* (MHUC, 8; Cincinnati, 1983), pp. 28-29.

sanctuary, so 4Q252 makes it plain that the Amalekite will ultimately be annihilated. None of these categories need feature in the eschatological law of the Temple Scroll, since they would not be present in the land at that time. 4Q174 and 4Q252 provide a bridge between the book of Deuteronomy itself and the Temple Scroll by explaining that all non-Israelites who are indeed mentioned in Deuteronomy would be excluded from the land, life in which is legislated for in the Temple Scroll.

3. *4Q252 5.1-2*

This third example concerns Deuteronomy only indirectly. At the start of column 5 Gen. 49.10a is interpreted. The opening words of the interpretation are an adaptation of Jer. 33.17:

4Q252:	לישראל ממשל [לוא י]כרת יושב כסא לדויד
Jer. 33.17:	לא יכרת לדויד איש ישב על כסא בית ישראל

There is widespread agreement that this section of Jeremiah is a passage which displays more of the flavour of Deuteronomy than almost any other in the book. The concern in the discussion of Jacob's blessing of Judah is with the covenant of kingship, but in Jeremiah 33 the phraseology in relation to David is matched with a parallel phrase concerning the levitical priests: 'and the levitical priests shall never lack a man in my presence...' The reference to 'levitical priests' (לכהנים הלוים)[21] in Jer. 33.18 is unique in Jeremiah, but is commonly compared with the same phrase in Deut. 18.1 (לכהנים הלוים).[22] Deut. 18.1-8 outlines the rights of the levitical priests and is significant for its statement that Levites from anywhere in Israel have the right to participate in the Jerusalem cult and to have equal portions with other Levites there. For Deuteronomy itself it seems as if there was a concern not to distinguish priests from Levites; quite the reverse is more likely, namely, that Deut. 18.1-8 is an attempt to demonstrate that the whole landless tribe of Levi shared a particular inheritance.[23] However, it is not unlikely that the phrase כהנים הלוים[24]

---

21. LXX, Syr and Vulg. insert 'and' between priests and Levites.

22. Syr. reads *lkhn' wllwj'*.

23. See the thorough analysis of the pericope by J.G. McConville, *Law and Theology in Deuteronomy* (JSOTSup, 33; Sheffield: JSOT Press, 1984), pp. 124-53, esp. pp. 142-47.

24. The phrase occurs in Deut. 17.9, 18; 18.1; 24.8; 27.9; Josh. 3.3; 8.33; Jer. 33.18; Ezek. 43.19; 44.15; Ezra 10.5; Neh. 10.29, 35; 11.20; 1 Chron. 9.2; 2 Chron. 5.5; 23.18; 30.27. In many instances there is versional evidence for a conjunction

would have been read by the compiler of 4Q252 in both Jer. 33.18 and Deut. 18.1 in the form הכהנים והלוים for which there is much versional evidence. The same phrase in Ezek. 44.15 is explicitly interpreted in CD 3.21–4.4 of two groups, the priests who went out from the land of Judah and the Levites who joined them. The concern to identify the Levites separately may well have been reflected in the commentator's mind, had he proceeded to discuss Jer. 33.18. Elsewhere in the texts that more closely display the ideology of the community and its associated movement, Levi and the Levites are frequently singled out as having particular responsibilities.[25] Most especially for the purposes of this study are they given the role in 1QS 1–2 of reciting the iniquities of Israel and cursing those who belong to Belial. This association with cursing derives directly from Deut. 27.14-26. The overall interest in blessings and curses lies behind much of 4Q252. The point of this somewhat lengthy digression is to suggest that the broader context of Jer. 33.17 leads us towards the kind of people who may have been responsible for the interpretative traditions of 4Q252: they may well have been Levites who now considered themselves part of the 'men of the community' (4Q252 5.5), disenfranchised cultic personnel.

The broader context of Jer. 33.17 concerning the covenant may also be significant for the better understanding of the scriptural background of 4Q252. It is noteworthy that in recalling the covenant ceremony in Jer. 34.17-20 reference is made to the ritual of passing between the parts of the calf. Only here in Jeremiah and in Gen. 15.9-19 is this ceremony mentioned in the whole Bible. In Gen. 15.9-19 the covenant that is established with Abram is the gift of the land. It is this covenant and its accompanying ritual which seems to be referred to in 4Q252 2.11-14 whose fragmentary text contains paraphrastic renderings of Gen. 15.9a and 15.17b. Thus it is the Deuteronomic material and the wider context of Jeremiah 33–34 which may be especially significant for the compiler of 4Q252, rather than the covenant made with Moses himself.

---

coming between the two nouns. This is reflected in the Syr. for Deut. 18.1, in the LXX, Syr. and Vulg. for Jer. 33.18, and in the Syr. and Vulg. for Ezek. 44.15.

25. See my study, 'Levi and the Levites in the Dead Sea Scrolls and the New Testament', in *Mogilany 1989. Papers on the Dead Sea Scrolls offered in memory of Jean Carmignac: Part I* (ed. Z.J. Kapera; Qumranica Mogilanensia, 2; Kraków, 1993), pp. 105-29.

4. *4Q252 2.7*

A fourth connection with Deuteronomy may rest implicitly in the adjustment of Gen. 9.27 in 4Q252 2.7. Gen. 9.27 ('May God make space for Japheth, and let him live in the tents of Shem; and let Canaan be his slave' NRSV) is nearly always understood to mean that part of the descendants of Japheth may dwell with those of Shem. In 4Q252 (and *Jub.* 7.12), however, the abbreviated and adjusted text makes God the subject of שכן so that in effect Japheth is excluded from the tents of Shem and the dwelling of God himself is proposed.

Though the uses of the *qal* of שכן are many and widespread, the root in the *pi'el* is almost entirely restricted[26] to a particular Deuteronomic usage which speaks of the dwelling of the name of God. This is explicit in Deut. 12.5 (*qal*), 11; 14.23; 16.2, 6, 11; 26.2; Jer. 7.3, 7; Neh. 1.9.[27] G. von Rad has described the phrase 'to make his name dwell there' (Deut. 12.5, 11, 14) as 'the real centralizing formula'[28] in Deuteronomy; perhaps of all the commentators on Deuteronomy von Rad has made it most plain that 'the ordinances for standardizing the cult and establishing only one sanctuary were and still are considered the most important and strikingly distinctive feature in all the new Deuteronomic arrangements for ordering Israel's life before its God'.[29]

Given the other direct and indirect connections between Deuteronomy and 4Q252, the possibility should be allowed that the change to Gen. 9.27 is not motivated solely negatively to ensure the exclusion of Japheth from the land, but also positively by this central theological motif in Deuteronomy. Since it may be that the following phrase, 'the land He gave to Abraham his friend' (4Q252 2.8), defines the 'tents of Shem',[30] it is not a case of arguing that the compiler of 4Q252 was concerned with the centralization of worship in the place where God makes his name dwell. Rather his concern seems to reflect the exclusivist tendency of Deuteronomy, whether it is Jerusalem alone or the whole land that is involved.

26. The exception is Num. 14.30.

27. Ps. 78.60 and Jer. 7.12 use the *pi'el* of שכן of God's earlier dwelling at Shiloh.

28. G. von Rad, *Deuteronomy: A Commentary* (OTL; London, 1966), p. 89.

29. *Deuteronomy*, pp. 88-89.

30. As argued by Bernstein, '4Q252: From Re-Written Bible to Biblical Commentary', *JJS* 45 (1994), pp. 11-12.

Once again, it is the Temple Scroll which may help clarify the situation. The Temple Scroll uses שכן more than any other Qumran text. In the redactional section of column 29, God says 'I will dwell (שכנתי) with them for ever and ever', while the Deuteronomic formula is most obvious in 60.13 in rehearsing and adapting Deut. 18.6: 'And if a Levite comes from any of your towns out of all Israel, where he lives—and he may come when he desires—to the place which I shall choose to settle (לשכן) my name upon, then he may minister like all his fellow-Levites who stand there before me'.[31] Ben Zion Wacholder has seen the frequent repetition of the term שכן in the Temple Scroll as a clue to the proper understanding of the whole scroll. For him all of its contents refer to the eschatological age, when Israel will finally turn to God and God will keep his promises given to the patriarchs that he will dwell with his people forever.[32] However, Wacholder has played down the significance of Deuteronomy in the Temple Scroll as a whole: the author of the scroll 'apparently found the Book of Deuteronomy the least interesting of the five Mosaic books'.[33] More suitably, many scholars agree with Wacholder's insistence that the Temple Scroll is eschatological law but see Deuteronomy as playing a controlling role in the final form of the scroll, from the harmonization of Exod. 34.10-16 and Deut 7.25-26 in the opening remains of the scroll right through the final Deuteronomic section, the rehearsal of the law for the land (Deut. 12–26) from which has been excluded everything that would not apply in the eschatological age.[34]

In light of these understandings of the Deuteronomic material in the Temple Scroll, the adaptation of Gen. 9.27 in 4Q252 2.7 may become clearer. In the eschatological age, when the divine promises to the patriarchs, especially Abraham, would be realized, God himself would dwell in the tents of Shem. The appeal to the patriarchs is suggested in

---

31. Y. Yadin, *The Temple Scroll* (Jerusalem, 1983), II, p. 274. Cf. 11QTª 45.12, 13, 14; 46.4, 12; 47.4, 11, 18; 51.7; 53.9; 56.5.

32. *The Dawn of Qumran*, pp. 21-30. Whether there are two eschatological temples, that defined in the scroll, and that which God himself will create (11QT 29.7-10), or just one (thus combining the information in the scroll with God's own creative act, as Wacholder prefers), remains a matter of debate.

33. *The Dawn of Qumran*, p. 15.

34. As Wacholder himself has implied (*The Dawn of Qumran*, pp. 28-29), but which has been thoroughly and convincingly worked out in relation to Deut. 12–26 by M. Wise (*Critical Study of the Temple Scroll*, esp. pp. 161-75).

Deuteronomy itself. Apart from Deut. 29.12, in which Moses talks of the covenant which establishes the people as God's people, every mention of the patriarchs by name in Deuteronomy (1.8; 6.10; 9.5, 27; 30.20; 34.4) concerns the promise of the gift of the land. It is not surprising, therefore, that after 'in the tents of Shem He (God) will dwell', the next sentence in 4Q252 2.8 is 'the land He gave to Abraham his friend'. To focus on the Deuteronomic usage of שכן is not to be concerned with the central sanctuary alone but with the whole land.

5. *Blessings and Curses*

The fifth way in which the ethos of Deuteronomy permeates the fragmentary text of 4Q252 concerns the use of blessings and curses. M. Kister has described the link between most of the various passages in 4Q252 as follows:

> this text emphasizes promises and blessings to the fathers of the Jewish people, and discusses the legitimacy of dispossessing or destroying other peoples: Canaan, Sodom, Amalek. This theme probably had concrete political significance for the author. It reflects conflicts with other nations, and expresses his hope for absolute dominion over the Land of Israel.[35]

As far as blessings are concerned, it is perhaps not insignificant that of the 128 occurrences of the verb ברך in the Pentateuch, 70 are in Genesis and 36 in Deuteronomy; there are only 22 uses in Exodus, Leviticus and Numbers taken together.[36] Deuteronomy is concerned with the ongoing recognition of the blessing of Israel as the holy people, as the promises to the patriarchs are realized in the conquests of the peoples encountered in the wilderness and in the imminent law-abiding occupation of the God-given land. The covenantal character of the whole book is ratified through the declaration of blessings and curses. In its few pericopae 4Q252 recalls the blessing of Noah's sons (2.7), the blessing of Abraham which Isaac passes on to Jacob (3.12-13), and the blessings of Jacob (4.3–6.3).

However, the ethos of Deuteronomy is more apparent in the way 4Q252 describes those accursed. This is clear, firstly, in as much as both

---

35. 'New Texts from Qumran', p. 288.

36. Similar proportions are reflected for the noun ברכה: 30 occurrences in the Pentateuch as a whole, 16 in Genesis, 12 in Deuteronomy, but only 2 in Exodus–Numbers.

the pericopae concerning Sodom and Gomorrah and also Amalek contain material which derives from Deuteronomy. Deuteronomy also repeats the traditional lists of the peoples who are to be expelled from the land which has been given to the Israelites (Deut. 1.7; 7.1; 20.17); these include the Canaanites. Secondly, in Deuteronomy 27, a chapter which interrupts the flow of Moses' speech, the Shechem ceremony is described in which it is the Levites who declare in a loud voice to all Israel a series of curses. Moses continues his speech in ch. 28 and announces how obedience leads to blessings, disobedience to curses. This way of ratifying the covenant is echoed in the opening columns of 1QS: as in Deuteronomy 27, it is the Levites who are associated explicitly with the curses.

There is also a less tangible way in which the Deuteronomic curses and displaced and annihilated peoples are reflected in 4Q252. This Deuteronomic vehemence makes for what von Rad, for one, has noted about the whole of the book of Deuteronomy: it 'is marked by a pronounced warlike spirit which pervades the hortatory part (chs. 6–11) as much as the legal part (chs. 12–26)'.[37] For von Rad this militant piety is to be associated with Levitical circles, especially since according to the law of warfare in Deut. 20.2 the priest must make a speech before the battle commences. Whatever the reasons may be for the belligerent stance of Deuteronomy itself, it is noteworthy that in other Qumran texts the confusion and destruction of Japheth, implied in the revised form of Gen. 9.27 in 4Q252 2.7, features only in the War Rule (1QM 1.6; 18.2), in which, of course, both priests and Levites have very well demarcated roles. Like Deuteronomy, the War Rule is a text of militant piety, and like Deuteronomy 'we ought also to raise the question whether it cannot, after all, be explained, just by reason of its characteristically warlike stamp, as arising out of a particular political situation in Israel'.[38] The actual political situation which is provoking the Deuteronomic exegesis of Genesis visible in 4Q252 may well be similar to that of the War Rule. The oppression of foreign nations is understood to be an indication that the eschatological age has dawned. It is time for Israel to live up to its calling in the divine gift of the land. All foreign nations are to be removed or annihilated. There is to be no chance of idolatry. The curse of Amalek will be fulfilled. God will dwell with his people.

37. *Deuteronomy*, p. 24.
38. Von Rad, *Deuteronomy*, p. 24.

Conclusion

Although the chronicling of the flood narrative according to the solar calendar in 4Q252 1.1–2.5 shows no trace of Deuteronomic influence, there is both an explicit and an implicit use of Deuteronomy in several other parts of this Genesis commentary. The Deuteronomic ethos is apparent, firstly, in the way the exegete assumes the consistency of the Pentateuch in applying laws to the patriarchal period which supposedly were only promulgated later. This ethos is suggested, secondly, in the way that Deuteronomy is conceived as normative both for the immediate subsequent history of Israel in the land (explicitly the time of Saul) and for the eschatological age, when unfulfilled blessings and curses will be fulfilled. Perhaps, thirdly, the Deuteronomic character of the commentary's use of Jeremiah 33 together with the belligerent curses may help to identify the author or compiler within Levitical circles as a Levite. Fourthly, the concern with the dwelling of God may subtly reflect the same Deuteronomic concern. Lastly, the interweaving of blessings and curses in 4Q252 is a narrative expression of the ratification of the covenant. The Deuteronomic character of 4Q252 is not all there is to appreciating the remarkable variety of exegesis in 4Q252, but the motifs highlighted in this short study show that for the most part, for all that there is a variety of exegetical forms, there is an overall consistency of approach. In addition the way Deuteronomy and matters Deuteronomic may lie behind much of 4Q252 may help to explain something of the text's relationship to the ideology of other texts found at Qumran in which Deuteronomy also plays a significant role, such as the Manual of Discipline (at least in its 1QS form), the Damascus Document, and the Temple Scroll.

4Q471: A CASE OF MISTAKEN IDENTITY?

Martin G. Abegg, Jr

It is with great pleasure that I participate in a festschrift in honor of my teacher and friend, Ben Zion Wacholder. My relationship with him began at Hebrew Union College-Jewish Institute of Religion in the fall of 1987, when with knocking knees I successfully convinced him that I had sufficient background to join his 'team' of graduate research assistants. I thus became one of a continuing line of fortunate pupils, several of whom are included in this collection, who have become a part of Ben Zion's family, and for a time his eyes. It seems appropriate to publish the results of my research on 4Q471 in Professor Wacholder's honor as it was one of the first of the 'new' Qumran texts that we read together.

4Q471, earlier referenced by its preliminary designation Sl 86 (Strugnell 86) and included in the allotment of John Strugnell, has recently been reassigned to Esther Eshel.[1] She, lately with Menahem Kister and earlier with Chanan Eshel, has published two of the eight fragments of this manuscript.[2] This article examines that which she has labeled 4Q471 fragment 1.[3]

---

1. Eshel was kind enough to show me her preliminary transcriptions of this group of fragments at the SBL annual meeting in New Orleans (1990). Their importance for my dissertation, *A Critical Edition of the War Scroll*, at that time in progress, was immediately apparent.

2. E. Eshel and H. Eshel, '4Q471 Fragment 1 and Ma'amadot in the War Scroll', in *Proceedings of the International Congress on the Dead Sea Scrolls—Madrid, 18-21 March 1991* (ed. J. Trebolle Barrera and L. Vegas Montaner; Leiden: Brill, 1992), pp. 611-20, and E. Eshel and M. Kister, 'A Polemical Qumran Fragment', *JJS* 43 (1992), pp. 277-81.

3. In the transcriptions of John Strugnell this fragment was assigned the number

4. For this and additional fragments see B.Z. Wacholder and M.G. Abegg (eds.), *A Preliminary Edition of the Unpublished Dead Sea Scrolls: The Hebrew and Aramaic Texts from Cave Four. Fascicle Two* (Washington, DC: Biblical Archaeology Society, 1992), pp. 294-96, and R. Eisenman and M. Wise, *The Dead Sea Scrolls Uncovered* (Rockport, MA: Element, 1992), pp. 30-33.

Both the original title of Eshel's Madrid Congress paper, '4QM^g: Unpublished Fragments on the War Scroll from Cave 4, and Some Observations on the Recension of this Composition',[4] as well as the more conservative current designation, '4Q471 Fragment 1 and Ma'amadot in the War Scroll', suggest that a brief review of the materials from Cave 4 that have been suggested as having affinity with the Cave 1 manuscript of the War Scroll (1QM) is in order.

4Q491-496 (4QM^{a-f})

In 1982, building on the preliminary work of C.-H. Hunzinger, Maurice Baillet published six manuscripts bearing the title War Scroll and successive superscript letters, a-f, in DJD VII. These are known otherwise by their Q numbers: 4Q491-496.[5] Upon examination, these manuscripts can be categorized in accord with two general characteristics. The first group, which contains the extant remains of 4Q491a, 4Q492, 4Q494 and 4Q495, bears a close resemblance to the work from Cave 1, offering a few variants and preserving some text which was lost in the time-ravaged columns of 1QM.[6]

The manuscripts of the second group, 4Q491b, 4Q493 and 4Q496, attest to the existence of two or more editions or recensions of the War Scroll. These contain additional lines or phrasings and also vary dramatically in the order and presentation of the material.

4Q491c (4Q491 f11i), the so-called 'Song of Michael', which I prefer to call the 'Hymn of Exaltation', should in my judgment, not be classified as a War Text.[7] An examination of genre based on vocabulary

---

4. S.A. Reed, *Qumran Cave 4 (4Q364-4Q481) Strugnell*, Fascicle 9 of the *Dead Sea Scroll Inventory Project* (Claremont: Ancient Biblical Manuscript Center, 1992), p. 21. Note also that M^g is the name given this fragment in the *Companion Volume* of *The Dead Sea Scrolls on Microfiche* (ed. E. Tov with the collaboration of S.J. Pfann; Leiden: Brill, 1993), p. 45.

5. M. Baillet, *Discoveries in the Judean Desert VII: Qumrân Grotte 4 III (4Q 482-4Q520)* (Oxford: Clarendon Press, 1982), pp. 12-68.

6. 4Q491 appears to be three separate manuscripts originally grouped together because of similar paleography and/or subject matter. See my forthcoming study, '4Q491 (4QMilhama^a)—An "Ensemble" of Manuscripts?' In my estimation 4Q491a consists of Baillet's fragments 8-10, 11 ii, 12-15, 18, 24-28, 31-33, 35; 4Q491b: 1, 2, 3, 4, 5, 6, 7, 16, 17, 19, 20, 21, 23; and 4Q491c: 11i, 12.

7. M. Smith, 'Ascent to the Heavens and Deification in 4QM^a', in *Archaeology and History in the Dead Sea Scrolls: The New York University Conference in*

points to a close relationship to Hodayot, and indeed Eileen Schuller has recently published a study of 4Q427 7 i t ii (4QHod[a]) which reveals a clear though complex relationship to 4Q491[c].[8] Its claim of inclusion with the rest of 4Q491 was based on paleographic criteria only. Baillet himself admitted that the supposed join with fragment 11 ii 'est seulement probable'.[9]

Three additional manuscripts must be reviewed before we turn our attention to 4Q471 1. 4Q285 and 4Q497 have at one time or another been mentioned in the literature as being related in some way to the War Scroll. To this list we must now add 11Q14 due to its coincidence with 4Q285.

4Q285 (Serek ha-Milḥamah)

4Q285, introduced by J.T. Milik in his seminal 1972 article: 'Milkî-ṣedeq et Milkî-reša', has gained recent notoriety for its supposed 'Pierced Messiah' passage.[10] This manuscript was initially called *Berakot* (*sic*) *Milḥamah* (*BM*), and later renamed *Serek ha-Milḥamah* by J.T. Milik. Milik concluded that the fragments of this document conserved the last scenes of the War Scroll which had been entirely lost in the Cave 1 exemplar. Although no coincident text can be offered to make a certain connection with 1QM, my own studies suggest that Milik's proposition is quite plausible if not likely.[11]

4Q497 (Texte ayant quelque rapport avec la Règle de la Guerre?)

4Q497, the original honoree of the siglum 4QM[g], or seventh manuscript of the War Scroll, is found on the back of a badly fragmented papyrus

Memory of Yigael Yadin (ed. L.H. Schiffman; Sheffield: JSOT Press, 1990), pp. 181-88.

8.   E. Schuller, 'A Hymn from a Cave 4 Hodayot Manuscript: 4Q427 7 i + ii', *JBL* 112 (1993), pp. 605-28.

9.   Baillet, *DJD VII*, p. 27.

10.   J.T. Milik, 'Milkî-ṣedeq et Milkî-reša' dans les anciens écrits juifs et chrétiens', *JJS* 23 (1972), p. 143. Devorah Dimant's comment that this text was known in several copies now appears to have been made in error. See her 'Qumran Sectarian Literature', in *Jewish Writings of the Second Temple Period* (ed. M.E. Stone; Philadelphia: Fortress Press, 1984), p. 516 n. 155.

11.   See my 'Messianic Hope and 4Q285: A Reassessment', *JBL* 113 (1994), pp. 81-91.

manuscript, the recto of which contains 4Q499, a work classified as a hymn or prayer.[12] According to Maurice Baillet, the manuscript is extant in 54 fragments of which he transcribes 49. Only seven fragments bear recognizable words which in total add but 16 entries to the concordance. As to the lexical relationship with the War Scroll, the correspondence is high with 15 of the 16 extant words. However, an examination shows the same lexical correspondence with the Covenant of Damascus, while 4Q511 (Songs of the Sage), and 1QH account for 14. I have concluded, given Baillet's failure to reconstruct any of the fragments as certainly coincident with 1QM, that the special relationship suggested between 4Q497 and the War Scroll must be rejected.

11Q14 (Berakot)

11Q14, published by A.S. van der Woude as 11Q Berakot,[13] must now be considered a War Scroll text on the strength of its coincidence with 4Q285 1.[14] The introductory formula וענה ואמר, 'and he answered and said', partially preserved at 11Q14 1-2 ii 2, occurs introducing a liturgical address by an individual only in 1QM 15:7; 16:15; 4Q491 10 ii 14; 11 ii 12; 15 5. The last line (11) of 4Q285 1 preserves the word ובקרבכם (and when you draw near), which perished in 11Q14. This one word most certainly ushers us into the context of Deut. 20.2, והיה כקרבכם אל המלחמה ונגש הכהן ודבר אל העם, 'And when you draw near to battle, the priest shall come and speak with the people'. This verse is also quoted in the War Scroll at the beginning of the Ritual Serek series (1QM 10.2), the first address of the High Priest before the assembled troops.[15]

An unpublished fragment (5) of 11Q14 appears to suggest a further relationship with the War Scroll:[16]

---

12. Baillet, *DJD VII*, pp. 69-72. For his original and bolder assessment see, 'Les manuscrits de la règle de la guerre de la grotte 4 de Qumran', *RB* 79 (1972), pp. 224-25. Baillet excludes fragments 49, 50, 51, 53 and 54 for lack of any significant traces.

13. A.S. van der Woude, 'Ein neuer Segensspruch aus Qumran (11QBer)', in *Bibel und Qumran: Beiträge zur Erforschung der Beziehungen zwischen Bibel und Qumranwissenschaft: Hans Bardtke zum 22.8.1966* (ed. S. Wagner; Leipzig: Evangelische Haupt-Bibelgesellschaft zu Berlin, 1968), pp. 253-58.

14. Abegg, '4Q285', and Wacholder and Abegg, *Fascicle Two*, p. 223.

15. Y. Yadin, *The Scroll of the War of the Sons of Light against the Sons of Darkness* (trans. C. Rabin; London: Oxford University Press, 1962), p. 14.

16. See PAM 44.006, the lower center of the plate. Fragment 2 was joined to fragment 1 ii by van der Woude, 'Segensspruch', pp. 253-58. Fragments 1 i, 3, and 4

Upper Margin?

משפ[טי הגוי הנב]א	1 commandm]ents of Hagûy, prophe[sy thou
קומה ג[בור שבה פֿן]	2 Arise O h]ero. Take thou captive ?[
[בֿינים]	3]foot soldiers[

Line 1 of this fragment preserves a reference to the Book of Hagûy, whose identification remains a puzzle.[17] The possibility that the word should be read *hagôy*, 'the nation', is doubtful as the singular form with the definite article occurs in extant Qumran literature only at 1QpHab 2.11, a quotation of Hab. 1.6. The last word in the line, הנבא, 'prophesy thou', seems the most likely reconstruction in light of the imperative of line 2. Less likely, but possible is הנב]יא, 'the prophe[t'. The articular form, lacking a preceding name, occurs elsewhere in Qumran literature only in contexts related to Deuteronomy 13 and 18.[18]

Lines 2 and 3 suggest a possible association with the War Scroll. The first two words of line 2 are extant elsewhere only in the 'Hero's Hymn' at 1QM 12.10 and reconstructed with certainty when the hymn is repeated in column 19 (1QM 19.2-3). The coincident letters of 11Q14 5 2 are underlined in the following transcription.

קומה גבור	Rise up, O H<u>ero</u>
<u>שבה</u> שביכה איש כבוד	<u>Take away</u> your captives (spoil?), O man of glory
(1QM 12.10b-11a)	

The cave 11 fragment offers a variant object of the taking, perhaps an unattested nominal form of the root פשט, which means 'to strip the slain' in the *piel* (2 Sam. 23.10; 1 Chron. 10.8; 11.13).

Line 3 preserves the suggestive בינים, 'foot-soldiers/skirmishers', although the reconstructions נבונים, 'discerning ones', and מבינים, 'understanding ones', are also possible. As בינים does not occur in conjunction with either 1QM 12.10 or 19.2-3, the fragment may be positioned after 1QM 19 in the vicinity of 11Q14 1-2ii (4Q285 1).

Thus the suggestive remains of 11Q14 5, in addition to the coincidence of fragments 1-2 ii with 4Q285 1, augments Milik's proposal that portions of the lost final columns of 1QM (War Scroll) have been preserved.

---

preserve a total of 8 letters which can be read with certainty.

17.   CD 10.6 (= 4Q266 f17iii:4; 4Q270 f10iv:17), 13.2; 1QSa 1.7; 4Q417 f2i.16, 17; and 4Q491 f11i.21. See Wacholder and Abegg, *Fascicle Two*, pp. xii-xiv.

18.   1Q29 f1.5; 4Q375 f1i.1, f1i.4; 11QT 54.11, 54.15, 61.2, 61.3, and 61.4.

4Q471 (4QMᵍ ?)

Initial observations of the text of this manuscript revealed serious doubts as to the integrity of Strugnell's eight fragments. I eventually settled on four groups of fragments, an arrangement that I felt was vindicated when the photographs became available. Eshel, working independently, has divided the original classification into three parts, as is evidenced by the entries in the official catalog.[19]

The first of my four groups contains what were originally designated fragments 1 and 2.[20] Esther Eshel and Menahem Kister have published the larger of these fragments and cataloged it as 4Q471ᵃ.[21] This manuscript warns against making a war not blessed by God (1.1-3). The text admonishes the readers not to exalt themselves (1.7) and make choices in concert with evil (1.8; 2.7) but to keep the requirements of the covenant (2.2). Although the subject of the published fragment concerns war (1.3), a relationship with the War Scroll is almost certainly not to be suggested. Eshel and Kister have reached the same conclusion.[22]

Fragment 3 is a scrap of a hymnic or possibly liturgical document praising God for life (3.3), righteous judgment (3.3-4) and forgiveness for sins committed (3.5). Again, any certain connection with the War Scroll is lacking.

Fragments 6 and 7 are very likely an additional manuscript of 4Q491c. Baillet used these fragments in *DJD VII* (p. 29) to suggest reconstructions in his edition of 4Q491. As discussed above, this hymn should be considered a work independent of the War Scroll. If my conclusions are correct, the most certain link of 4Q471 to the War Scroll may no longer be maintained.

The fourth and last manuscript to be extracted from 4Q471 consists of the original fragments 4 and 5. The larger of these has been published by the Eshels as 4Q471 Fragment 1.[23] For the following transcription, see PAM plates 41.583, 41.849, 42.914, and 43.551.

---

19. Tov, *Companion*, p. 45.

20. In this portion of the paper, fragment numbers for 4Q471 refer to Strugnell's original transcription. See Wacholder and Abegg, *Fascicle Two*, pp. 294-96.

21. Eshel and Kister, 'Polemical', pp. 277-81.

22. 'Examination of the fragment's contents suggest that it does not belong to the War Scroll', Eshel and Kister, 'Polemical', p. 277.

23. Eshel and Eshel, '4Q471 Fragment 1', pp. 611-20.

Transcription and Reconstruction

]ה מכול אש[ר [	1
ומן הכהונים שנים עשר]כול איש מאחיו מבנ[י [	2
]ה והיו עמו תמיד וש[מרו]	3
[אהרון	
]אותו מכול דבר חטא? ונשיאים שנים עשר]כול שבט ושב[ט] איש	4
[אחד לבית אבותיו והיו עמו תמיד אנשים ברו]רים ומ[ן] ה]לוים שנים	5
והי]ו יושבים עמ]ו תמיד ע]ל	6
[עשר	
ל]מען יהיו מלמדים] אותו[	7
[המשפט והתורה	
א]ת מחלקו]ת	8
]מח[	9

Translation

1.   ] from all tha[t
2.   And from the priests, twelve,] each man from his brothers from the sons of
3. [Aaron.   ] and they shall be with him continually, and k[eep]
4. [him from all matter of sin. And twelve commanders from] each tribe, a man
5. [per household. They shall be with him continually, men who are pu]re. And from [the] Levites twelve
6.   and they shall b]e sit[ting with hi]m continually for
7. [judgment and Torah   in] order that they might be teaching[him
8.   ] division[s
9.   ] [

The Eshels have made a good case for a relationship between this fragment and the top of column 2 of 1QM, text which details the various groups which served in the temple or its precincts during the sabbatical year. In synopsis, the Eshels' reconstruction catalogs three of these groups: lines 2-4 details a group of twelve priests termed ראשי הכוהנים (heads of the priests, 1QM 2.1), the 26 heads of the temple courses, ראשי המשמרות, follow in line 5 (1QM 2.2), and the third an assemblage of 12 Levites, lines 5-6 (1QM 2.2).

My questions concerning this interpretation are two. First, given the fact that the reconstruction of the lines offered by the Eshels suggests that the fragment preserves approximately 40 per cent of the original line length, it appears telling that nearly all of the technical terminology of 1QM 2 is found in the reconstructed portions rather than the extant text. For example, the term ראש (head or chief) occurs 8 times in the first 4 lines of 1QM, but not at all in 4Q471 f1. משמרת (course) appears 4 times in 1QM but not at all in 4Q471. Nor are the words עדה (congregation), אב (leader), מעמד (station?), מקדש (sanctuary), and להתיצב

(to attend) present; terms which form the very core of the discussion in
1QM. The technical terminology in common can be reduced to תמיד
(continually), לויים (Levites), שבט (tribe), and שנים (two, as in twelve).
Although this is certainly not insignificant vocabulary, it may not be
determinative of conjunction with 1QM 2.

The second question pertains to the word עמו (with him) of 4Q471
f1.3 and partially reconstructed at line 6. With whom do the priests serve
continually? The Eshels do not speculate. Although the preposition is not
found in 1QM 2, one might surmise that he is the high priest, mentioned
in 1QM 2.1, but lacking in both the extant text and reconstruction of
4Q471.

There is, however, an additional locus which satisfies the common
terminology examined in discussion of the first question. These terms
(exchanging שבט, 'tribe', for the nearly synonymous מטה, 'tribe') also
form the basis for the discussion found in the Temple Scroll (11QTS)
57.5-14. This section, coming after a lengthy quote from Deut. 17.14-20
regarding the appointment and requirements of the king (11QTS 56.12-
21) and the king's obligation to muster an army (11QTS 57.1-5), deals
with the organization and duties of the royal guard (11QTS 57.5-11) and
the makeup of the king's council (11QTS 57.11-15). These ten lines, in
addition to satisfying the significant technical terminology of 4Q471, also
suggest a solution for the mysterious personage represented by עמו in
line 3. As we read in 11QTS 57.11-12 ושנים עשר נשיי עמו עמו, 'and the twelve
captains of his people are with him', that is the king, named at the beginning of this section, 11QTS 56.13: אשימה עלי מלך ככול הגואים אשר סביבותי, a
quote from Deut. 17.14, 'I will appoint a king over me, as all the nations
which are around me'. This same form is found in 11QTS 57.6 and 9
detailing the continual presence of the 12,000 royal guardsmen, אשר
לוא יעוזבוהו, 'which never leave him alone', so that on one hand he might
not be seized by the foreigners, a fact mentioned in both 57.7 and 11,
and on the other, be kept from all matter of sin. I will now undertake a
line per line evaluation of 4Q471 1.

The context of line 1 is lacking. If the text does detail a thirty-six
member council along the lines of 11QTS 57.11f, line 1 would then
close the previous discussion. Clauses introduced by מכול אשר, 'from all
that', are not common in Qumran literature, with but three additional
examples. 11QTS 58.3 is suggestive as it also concerns the king's
responsibility when he hears of anyone who is seeking to rob *anything*

that belongs to Israel. This is too speculative, however, to be at all sure.[24]

At the beginning of line 2 the Eshels do not suggest any reconstruction preceding the initial word כול, 'every, each'. I have determined that the line may well refer to the choosing of the 12 priests. My reasons are two.

First, the last word in the line, מבני, 'from the sons of', is very likely followed by אהרון (Aaron), a point with which the Eshels agree. Although the biblical solution for this construction is most usually ישראל (Israel) with some 17 instances, the pattern is not followed in the Qumran literature. The phrase *'from* the sons of Israel' never occurs in the known texts. Of the 18 instances of מבני where context can be determined, אהרון, the most frequent resolution, follows in 4.[25]

Secondly, as lines 4 and 5 clearly describe the selection of two additional 12 member groups, the captains (likely) and the Levites (certainly), a selection of twelve priests is to be expected, as detailed in 11QTS 56.12. And so I posit: ומן הכוהנים שנים עשר כול איש מאחיו בני אהרון, 'And from the priests, 12, each man from his brothers, from the sons of Aaron.'

It is conceivable that the pronominal suffix of the form מאחיו, 'from his brothers', refers to a party other than that of איש (man, each). If this is true, the person designated here, and that referred to by עמו (with him) in lines 3 and 6 would likely be the same. If the suggested reconstruction, מבנ[י אהרון] (from the sons of Aaron), is correct, the high priest rather than the king might be at the center of the text. However, the expression is more easily explained by similarities to the structurally similar 'the one—the other' expressions such as Gen. 13.11, ויפרדו איש מעל אחיו, 'they separated one from the other'. By this interpretation איש would be in the *casus pendens* (nominative absolute) and the suffix of מאחיו would be a retrospective (resumptive) pronoun in reference to it.[26]

In line 3 we find disagreement over the first and last words of the line. The Eshels suggest a reconstruction based on the text of 1QM: ואת ראשי הכהנים יסרוכ]ו, 'and the chiefs of the priests, and they shall dispose (or order)', with the final *waw* of יסרוכו visible at the right of the fragment. I am not able to offer a sure replacement for this proposal, but I point out that the evidence for this letter better fits a *he* than a *waw*.

---

24. See also 1QH 15.11 and 4Q418 f81.2.

25. 1QM 7.10; 4Q266 f6ii.5 (= 4Q267 f4iii.8), f6ii.8; 4Q513 f10ii.8.

26. See P. Joüon, *A Grammar of Biblical Hebrew* (trans. and rev. T. Muraoka; Rome: Pontifical Biblical Institute, 1991), §§147c, 156.

The leftward extension of the upper bar of the *he* in this hand is extreme, matching the trace found here.

At the left of the line, Esther and Chanan have suggested ישרתו, 'they shall serve', a verb used four times to describe the function of the groups detailed in 1QM 2.1-4. I have preferred ושמרו, 'and they shall guard', on the basis of 11QTS 57.10, in the context of describing the function of the royal guard:

ויהיו עמו תמיד יומם ולילה אשר יהיה שומרים אותו מכול דבר חט

And they shall be with him continually, day and night, guarding him from every evil thing.

Line 4 details the choice of a second group. At this point the Eshels and I differ only on the makeup of the committee, or perhaps better, their title. They have suggested, on the model of the War Scroll, ראשים, 'the leaders', while I have reconstructed as per 11QTS 57.12, נשיאים, 'captains'.

At line 5, the Eshels reconstruct the relatively sure רים[with 1QM 2.2 and read ששה ועשרים, 'twenty-six', the number of משמרות or priestly courses. It is now clear from the available copies of the sectarian calendar, that elsewhere this number is consistently twenty-four as recorded at 1 Chron. 24.7-18. The War Scroll clearly stands isolated at this point. I have preferred to read ברורים, 'pure' or 'approved', from 11QTS 57.8, again describing the character of the royal guard.

The end of line 5 then introduces a description of the third and final group of councilors, the twelve Levites. In this the Eshels agree.

The first word of line 6, I have reconstructed as יושבים, 'sitting', as is the action ascribed to the Levites at 11QTS 57.13. The Eshels prefer וישרתו, 'and they shall serve'. Paleography would appear to rule out this possibility, however. Our scribe rather consistently distinguished between *waw* and *yod*. The head of the *yod* is formed with two short strokes; first up and left and then up and right, forming a distinct triangular 'flag' before finishing the letter with a down stroke. The *waw* simply moves up and right, forming a 'hook', before the downward stroke. Here then, the order is *yod-waw*, as in יושבים, suggesting a continued relationship with 11QTS 57.13. The rest of the line appears to follow the pattern established in line 3 of our fragment. The most immediate subject of this 'sitting' is the Levitical consort. Although the proposed reconstruction is patterned after the description of the responsibilities of the combined thirty-six member council at 11QTS 57.13, the consistently fuller characterization of each component of the council in 4Q471 argues that the end of line 6 continues to discuss the Levitical component. The Eshels have reconstructed לפניו תמיד כול הימים, 'before continually him all the days', a phrase which does not occur in the War Scroll. Again, neither they nor the War Scroll provide the antecedent for 'him', while clearly, according to 11QTS 56 and 57, 'he' is the king.

Line 7 reveals the last point of disagreement in the transcription of the fragment. The Eshels follow John Strugnell, who read מלמדי ח[, 'teachers of...?' The Eshels solve the *heth* with חרב, 'sword', suggesting that a new group has now come into view, the sword trainers. An examination of the plate reveals clearly that the *heth* is rather the top of a final *mem*. Thus I read מלמדים, in a periphrastic construction with והיו, 'and they shall be teaching.'

At this point it is likely that the fragment has moved to a statement of the purpose (למען) of the whole council of 36-12 priests, 12 captains and 12 Levites. There are a number of electives that might complete the verb and suggest the object of the teaching. 1QS 3.13 is concerned with the discernment of spirits, 1QSa 1.7 suggests the book of *Hagûy*, בינה, 'understanding', is a candidate from 1QH 2.17, while המשפטים, 'judgments', from 4Q158 and תורת מושה at 4Q266 complete the catalog.

I fully agree with the Eshels that מחלק[ות, 'divisions', is fairly certain at line 8. We need not, however, follow them to 1QM 2.10 which refers to a 'war of divisions'. More commonly the word signifies the division of time, perhaps here in reference to the eschatological nature of this king and his council. The Hebrew name for the book of *Jubilees*, ספר מחלקות העתים, the book of the Divisions of the Times (CD 16.3), would make an interesting proposal providing a possible object for teaching (l. 7). However, traces of the last letter of the previous word allow a *taw*, with a *beth* or *'ayin* being suitable alternates. At 11QTS 15.5 and elsewhere the word retains its biblical usage of priestly division or course (as Neh. 11.36).

Another possibility is to read מחלקים (1QpHab 6.6), 'dividing', a *piel* participle in parallel with the 'teaching' in line 7. However, the expected periphrastic construction with והיו, 'they will be', is not allowed by the preceding traces.

The final line of the fragment, line 9, contains two letters, a certain *mem*, followed by either a *heth* or a *he*. The Eshels continue in the context of the War Scroll with מלחמה, 'war'. There are far too many possibilities to be at all sure.

Conclusion

Based on several paleographic considerations, conjunction of technical terminology, and antecedent for the third person pronominal suffixes, I have suggested that 4Q471 fragment 1 is related to the text of 11QTS 57.11-15 rather than 1QM 2.1-4. The practical results of this conclusion are two.

First, the special connection between the War Scroll and 4Q471 which has been suggested by the Eshels and the preliminary conclusions of John Strugnell must be held in doubt.

Secondly, it is suggestive that both 11QTS 57 and 1QM 2 themselves share such suggestive and technical vocabulary as תמיד, 'continually', לויים, 'Levites', שנים, 'two', and שבט or מטה, 'tribe'. Ben Zion Wacholder proposed a connection between 1QM 2 and 11QTS 57 in his provocative work, *The Dawn of Qumran,* without the benefit of 4Q471.[27] As a point in his argument that the War Scroll is indebted to the Temple Scroll, Wacholder wrote: 'The royal charter in 11QTorah 56-59 which prescribes a council of 36 members, shows a remarkable similarity to the structure of service in the War Rule [1QM 2]'. It may be that 4Q471 forms a link in this connection. One must ask, however, if this relationship is not more apparent than actual, relying on the similarity in the mechanics of choosing, natural divisions available to choose from, and logical preference of the number 12 for equitable representation.

The proposed reconstruction of 4Q471 1 puts us on the horns of the familiar dilemma. Was the Cave 4 manuscript the remains of a *Serek*, describing the make-up of this and other organizational matters which the author of 11QTS then condensed for his purposes? Or did the author of 4Q471 find the brief description of the king's council in 11QTS too imprecise for his larger design? Just as likely, of course, is that the two manuscripts and their copyists never came in contact but yet reflect a third text or tradition that has been lost. We can speculate, but we will likely never know.[28]

27. B.Z. Wacholder, *The Dawn of Qumran* (Cincinnati: Hebrew Union College Press, 1983), p. 80.

28. An earlier version of this article was presented to the Qumran Group of the Society of Biblical Literature, Washington, DC, November 1993. I am especially indebted to the responses of Moshe Bernstein and Joseph Baumgarten.

KANN MAN ALS JUDE AUCH GRIECHE SEIN?
ERWÄGUNGEN ZUR JÜDISCH-HELLENISTISCHEN PSEUDEPIGRAPHIE

Nikolaus Walter

Im Schlußteil seiner bahnbrechenden Untersuchungen zu den Fragmenten jüdisch-hellenistischer Historiker schrieb Jacob Freudenthal vor 120 Jahren:

> Die meisten anderen Hellenisten [neben bzw. vor Philon von Alexandrien—(N.W.)]—alle, deren Fragmente Alexander [Polyhistor—(N.W.)] gerettet hat—haben eine wahre Muttersprache nicht gekannt und mit ihr des reinsten, ursprünglichsten, unentbehrlichsten Quelles aller dichterischen Begabung und Darstellung entbehrt, den keine mühsam erlernte und keine Mischsprache zu ersetzen vermag. Der Muttersprache aber entbehrten sie, weil sie keine wahre Heimath besaßen. Palästina war auch den Hellenisten keine Heimath, die auf seinem Boden lebten, selbst einem Eupolemos nicht, der die glorreiche, aber bald gehemmte Tätigkeit Juda Makkabi's...hatte aufsteigen und niedergehen sehen...So war seine [Eupolemos'—(N. W.)] Heimath weder bei dem Volke, mit dem Hoffnung und Erinnerung und religiöse Ueberzeugung ihn verband, noch und gewiss viel weniger bei dem, dessen Schriftthum er studirte, und dessen Sprache er schrieb. Sein Geschichtswerk wollte griechisch und judäisch zugleich sein, und weil es beides sein wollte, ist es keines von beiden.[1]

Wenn ein so hervorragender Kenner sowohl des griechischen und römischen Altertums als auch der jüdischen Tradition zu einem solchen Urteil kommt, dann ist dies von hohem Gewicht und muß sehr ernst genommen werden. Nicht umsonst wird ja auch in der Philon-Forschung immer wieder diese Frage gestellt: Wer oder was wollte Philon sein—ein jüdischer Ausleger der Thora mit hoher griechischer Bildung, oder ein hellenistischer Philosoph mit jüdischen Wurzeln? Denn

---

1. J. Freudenthal, *Alexander Polyhistor und die von ihm erhaltenen Reste jüdischer und samaritanischer Geschichtswerke* I-II (= *Hellenistische Studien* I-II), (Jahresberichte des jüdisch-theologischen Seminars 'Fraenkel'scher Stiftung', Breslau 1874 und 1875), II, p. 196.

es geht—auch in dem zitierten Votum Freudenthals—ja nicht einfach
um die Sprache, sondern überhaupt um das Verhältnis der hellenistisch-
jüdischen Autoren zu griechischer Bildung. War es nur ein unter den
gegebenen Umständen der 'Diaspora'[2] unvermeidlicher, aber eigentlich
ungeliebter Wechsel der Alltagssprache? Oder konnte nicht auch aus
solcher Gewöhnung ein echter Versuch hervorgehen, sich mit der
griechischen Kultur und Bildung nicht nur im abweisenden Sinne (in
Anknüpfung an die Bekämpfung der heidnischen Götzen, vgl. Sap.Sal.
13-15), sondern auch mit der Absicht einer ernsthaften Kenntnisnahme
und Teilhabe an dieser Kultur ergeben, ohne daß dabei die jüdische
Identität aufgegeben werden müßte? Gewiß: Diese Frage ist nicht in
einem Sinne für die gesamte Diaspora-Judenschaft zu beantworten.
Freilich dürfte auch dies von vornherein wahrscheinlich sein: Bei den
hellenistischen Juden, die sich bewußt auf ein solches Wagnis einließen,
ist damit zu rechnen, daß sich in Bezug auf tradierte Vorurteile gegen
alles griechisch-heidnische Wesen ihre Vorstellungen und Meinungen
ändern würden—bis dahin, daß etwa Philon nicht nur die Klassiker
griechischer Philosophie und Dichtung sehr gut kannte, sondern auch
griechische Theatervorstellungen oder gar Ringkämpfe besuchte und
davon spricht, ohne sich zu einer Rechtfertigung veranlaßt zu sehen.[3]

Die Frage unseres Aufsatz-Titels mag zugespitzt sein. Aber wenn man
sieht, wie frühe hellenistisch-jüdische Autoren wie Eupolemos oder
Artapanos, von denen der erstgenannte ja in Palästina lebte, Mose zum
Urvater der griechischen (oder auch der ägyptischen) Kultur erhoben,[4]

---

2. Zur Wortbedeutung von διασπορά vgl. jetzt die postum veröffentlichte
Abhandlung von W.C. van Unnik, *Das Selbstverständnis der jüdischen Diaspora in
der hellenistisch-römischen Zeit*, hrsg. von P. W. van der Horst (AGJU, 17; Leiden,
1993). Van Unnik weist auf die negativen Nebentöne des Begriffes 'Diaspora' in den
frühjüdischen Quellen hin. Freilich bin ich nicht überzeugt, daß man nur von dem
(gar nicht häufigen) Gebrauch dieses Wortes her schon das Selbstverständnis des
hellenistischen Judentums insgesamt in den Blick bekommt (vgl. meine Rezension in:
TLZ 118 [1993], Sp. 1039-1041). Vgl. im übrigen etwa die schöne, postum
erschienene Abhandlung von G. Delling, *Die Bewältigung der Diasporasituation
durch das hellenistische Judentum* (Berlin und Göttingen, 1987).

3. Philon, *Omn.Prob.* 141 und 23. Daß Philon sogar in seinen Äußerungen zur
Kritik griechischer Kultur z. T. in den Spuren griechischer Vorgänger wandelt, hat
bereits Isaak Heinemann gezeigt: I. Heinemann, *Philons griechische und jüdische
Bildung* (Breslau 1932, Nachdruck Hildesheim 1962), pp. 433-46.

4. Vgl. B.Z. Wacholder, *Eupolemus. A Study of Judaeo-Greek Literature*
(Cincinnati usw. 1974), pp. 72-73, 76-77, 80-81; N. Walter, *Der Thoraausleger*

dann darf man das wohl so verstehen, daß mit dieser These die griechische Kultur nicht verächtlich gemacht, sondern eher aufgewertet und als mit der jüdischen Tradition vereinbar dargestellt werden sollte. Diese Auffassung steht offensichtlich auch hinter der Meinung des Aristobulos, daß Mose als 'Philosoph' vor oder mitten unter den griechischen Philosophen anzusehen sei.[5] Wer so urteilt, der hat nicht nur keine Berührungsängste gegenüber der griechischen Bildung, sondern ist bereit, die Schwellen zwischen jüdischer Tradition und griechischer Kultur abzubauen—durchaus im Gegensatz zu der tradierten Polemik gegen alles 'Heidnische', das als widergöttlich zu meiden sei.

Im Folgenden soll nur ein kleiner Ausschnitt aus der jüdisch-hellenistischen Literatur daraufhin befragt werden, wie in ihr die jüdisch-griechischen Beziehungen (bzw. der Wunsch nach solchen) zum Ausdruck kommen. Es soll um pseudepigraphische Texte gehen, aber nicht um solche, die—wie es sonst in der nachbiblischen Pseudepigraphie geläufig ist—unter einen Namen aus der eigenen, biblischen Tradition (z. B. Henoch, Mose, Salomo, Esra oder andere) gestellt wurden, sondern um solche Texte, die unter den Namen von *griechischen* Autoren verfaßt wurden.[6] Es geht also um literarische Produkte wie den sogenannten Pseudo-Aristeas-Brief (also einen Prosatext) oder das Gnomologion, eine Sammlung von kurzen Gedichten unter Namen der bedeutendsten griechischen Tragiker und Komödiendichter (Aischylos, Sophokles und Euripides sowie Menander, Diphilos und Philemon), um das dem Phokylides untergeschobene Mahngedicht und etwa noch um die unter dem Namen des Hekataios überlieferten Fragmente. Wenn hier jüdisch-hellenistische Schriftsteller mit der Wahl ihrer vorgeblichen Autoren nicht im Bereich der eigenen biblischen Tradition verbleiben

---

Aristobulos (TU, 86; Berlin 1964), pp. 43-51.

5.   Aristobulos F 3 (Euseb. Praep.Ev. XIII 12,1-2) und F 5 (Euseb.Praep.Ev. XIII 12,9-11). Siehe N. Walter, *Thoraausleger,* pp.41-43.

6.   Vgl. zur Pseudepigraphie in der Antike bzw. Spätantike das Standardwerk von W. Speyer, *Die literarische Fälschung im heidnischen und christlichen Altertum* (Handbuch der Altertumswissenschaft, I/1; München, 1971) und den Überblick über die Diskussion um die Bedeutung der antiken Pseudepigraphie: N. Brox (Hrsg.), *Pseudepigraphie in der heidnischen und jüdisch-christlichen Antike* (Wege der Forschung, 484; Darmstadt 1977), sowie den Sammelband der Vorträge eines Symposions zur Sache: K. von Fritz (Hrsg.), *Pseudepigrapha I* (Vandœuvres - Genève 1972) mit Beiträgen zu den Pseudopythagorica, den pseudepigraphischen Platon-Briefen sowie zur israelitischen und jüdisch-hellenistischen Pseudepigraphie (Beitrag von M. Hengel, s. unten Anm. 9).

(wie es der Fall ist, wenn Texte unter dem Namen Henochs, Abrahams oder Moses geschrieben werden), sondern in einen anderen Kulturbereich hinübergreifen und griechische Personen als angebliche Autoren wählen, dann drückt sich schon darin aus, daß die jüdischen Schreiber hier um interkulturellen Austausch bemüht sind.[7] Die von ihnen gewählten griechischen Autoren sind für sie nicht verächtliche Personen, mit denen man möglichst nichts zu tun haben möchte, sondern in ihrer Art doch Autoritäten, denen man jüdische Gedanken unterschiebt, um sie so auch in der jüdisch-hellenistischen Gemeinschaft sozusagen 'hoffähig' zu machen.

Die philologische Kritik des 19. Jahrhunderts hatte diese Fälschungen— wie man sie meist nannte (und noch nennt), früher oft noch mit herabsetzenden Beiworten wie 'frech' verziert—entlarvt und sie dann irgendwo am Rande der Literaturgeschichte registriert, sich aber sonst kaum weiter um sie gekümmert. Den Gräzisten ging es ja in erster Linie darum, die Werke der Klassiker wie Sophokles, Euripides, Menandros oder anderer und vor allem auch den Ur-Poeten Homer von derartigen *'spuria'* oder 'Wechselbälgern' zu reinigen; die Erforscher des spätantiken Judentums dagegen rubrizierten sie unter Stichworten wie Propaganda- oder Missionsliteratur oder auch—noch undeutlicher— unter Apologetik,[8] ohne freilich lange zu überlegen, wie und an welche

---

7.   Zur Begegnung des Judentums mit der griechischen Kultur verweise ich auf folgende Arbeiten: B.Z. Wacholder, *Eupolemus* (s. oben Anm. 4); M. Hengel, *Judentum und Hellenismus. Studien zu ihrer Begegnung unter besonderer Berücksichtigung Palästinas bis zur Mitte des 2. Jh. v. Chr.* (Wiss.Unters.zum NT, 10; Tübingen, 1969, 3.Aufl. 1988); M. Hengel, *Juden, Griechen und Barbaren. Aspekte der Hellenisierung des Judentums in vorchristlicher Zeit* (Stuttgarter Bibelstudien, 76; Tübingen, 1976); A. Momigliano, *Hochkulturen im Hellenismus. Die Begegnung der Griechen mit Kelten, Römern, Juden und Persern* (München 1979); H. Conzelmann, *Heiden—Juden—Christen. Auseinandersetzungen in der Literatur der hellenistisch-römischen Zeit* (BHT, 62; Tübingen, 1981); D. Rokeah, *Jews, Pagans, and Christians in Conflict* (Studia Post-Biblica, 33; Leiden, 1982); J.J. Collins, *Between Athens and Jerusalem. Jewish Identity in the Hellenistic Diaspora* (New York, 1983); G. Delling, 'Die Begegnung zwischen Hellenismus und Judentum' (*Aufstieg und Niedergang der Römischen Welt* , II. Reihe Bd. 20/1; Berlin, 1987), pp. 3-39, sowie ders., *Bewältigung* (s. oben Anm. 2); E.J. Bickerman, *The Jews in the Greek Age* (Cambridge, MA/London, 1988).

8.   So etwa bei E. Schürer, *Geschichte des jüdischen Volkes im Zeitalter Jesu Christi* vol. 3 (Leipzig, 4th edn,1909), pp. 553-629 (mit ausführlichen Informationen über die hier zu besprechenden Pseudepigrapha; zur Charakterisierung als 'Propagandaliteratur', pp. 553-54); W. Bousset und H. Greßmann, *Die Religion des*

152 *Pursuing the Text: Studies in Honor of Ben Zion Wacholder*

Leserschaft gerichtet man mit solchen Fälschungen Apologie, Propaganda oder Mission betreiben konnte.

Genau diese Frage zu klären bemühte sich vor fast 40 Jahren Victor A. Tcherikover, und er kam zu dem Ergebnis, daß die angeblich propagandistisch orientierte jüdisch-hellenistische Literatur überhaupt und insbesondere ihre Pseudepigrapha gar keine echte Chance hatten, auf nichtjüdische, griechisch-sprachige Leser einzuwirken.[9] Er begründete diese seine Ansicht (die mir durchaus richtig zu sein scheint) unter anderem mit den Gegebenheiten des spätantiken Buchmarkts, der den hellenistischen Juden kaum Gelegenheit zur Verbreitung ihrer Literatur geboten haben dürfte. Und was etwa die unter den Namen bekannter griechischer Dichter gefälschten Verse angeht, so dürfte kaum eine Chance bestanden haben, sie in die Klassiker-Werkausgaben der alexandrinischen Philologen einzuschmuggeln. Literaturkenner hätten sich wohl kaum täuschen lassen, wenn ihnen etwa unter dem Namen des Sophokles plötzlich ein bisher unbekanntes Gedicht vor Augen gekommen wäre, das die Einzigkeit Gottes in keineswegs altgriechischer, aber auch kaum in hellenistisch-philosophisch 'aufgeklärter', sondern eben doch in deutlich jüdischer Weise besingt,[10] oder wenn ihnen ein 230 Hexameter langes Poem unter dem Namen des Spruchdichters Phokylides entgegengetreten wäre, das weitgehend harmlose moralische Sentenzen darbot (und sich schon insoweit deutlich von den geistreich-

Judentums im späthellenistischen Zeitalter (HNT, 21; Tübingen, 3rd edn, 1926), pp. 24-30 und 72-73—In der englischen Neubearbeitung des Werks von E. Schürer durch G. Vermes und andere *The History of the Jewish People in the Age of Jesus Christ* III/1 (Edinburgh, 1986), pp. 617-18, wird die Charakteristik dieser Pseudepigrapha mit Recht stärker differenziert und dabei betont, daß sie nur zum Teil für heidnische, zumeist aber für jüdische Leser gedacht waren.

9. V.A. Tcherikover, 'Jewish Apologetic Literature Reconsidered', *Eos* 48,3 (1956), pp.169-93 (= *Symbolae Raphaeli Taubenschlag dedicatae* III; Wroclaw, 1957, pp. 169-93). Zur jüdisch-hellenistischen Pseudepigraphie vgl. ferner M. Hengel, 'Anonymität, Pseudepigraphie und "Literarische Fälschung" in der jüdisch-hellenistischen Literatur', in: *Pseudepigrapha I* (s. oben Anm. 6), pp. 229-329; N. Walter, 'Pseudepigraphische jüdisch-hellenistische Dichtung', in: *Jüdische Schriften aus hellenistisch-römischer Zeit (= JSHRZ)* IV/3 (Gütersloh 1983), pp. 173-276, vor allem die 'Allgemeine Einführung', pp. 175-81.

10. Zum Unterschied des jüdischen vom griechisch-philosophischen Monotheismus vgl. Y. Amir, 'Die Begegnung des biblischen und des philosophischen Monotheismus als Grundthema des jüdischen Hellenismus', *EvT* 38 (1978), pp. 2-19.

pointierten Sprüchen des echten Phokylides von Milet unterschied)—
Sentenzen, die für den Bibelkenner zwar deutlich an bestimmten Partien
aus dem 3. und 5. Buch der Thora orientiert sind, es aber geradezu
vermeiden, charakteristisch jüdische Sonderbräuche und -normen zu
nennen, so daß für den Leser die Absicht einer Werbung für das
Judentum gar nicht zu erkennen ist. Und welches nichtjüdische Publikum
sollte sich etwa von dem sogenannten Aristeas-Brief angesprochen
fühlen? In diesem Text geht es ja unter anderem um eine in Erzählform
dargebotene Erörterung über den verborgenen, aber dennoch höchst
vernünftigen Sinn mancher, vor allem kultisch-ritueller Gebote des
Mosaischen Gesetzes, die einem Griechen eher sonderbar vorkommen
mußten, sodann um eine sehr langatmige Darstellung einer Serie von
sieben Symposien an der Tafel des Ptolemaios (II.) Philadelphos,
während welcher an sieben Abenden nacheinander alle 72 aus Jerusalem
eingeladenen Gelehrten zu Wort kommen und dem König einen langen
Regentenspiegel mit vernünftiger, jeweils durch Anfügung eines
frommen jüdischen Spruches erweiterter Morallehre vortragen; all dies
ist gerahmt von der Erzählung der Übersetzung der Thora ins
Griechische, die dem regierenden Ptolemäer so wichtig ist, daß er sie auf
seine Kosten anfertigen läßt. Wen wollte ein Autor solcher Literatur
eigentlich anreden? Und was sollten ihre Texte den Lesern vermitteln?

Gehen wir von einem noch nicht erwähnten Beispiel aus: von den
jüdischen Sibyllinen, also jenen in Hexametern abgefaßten Orakeln
verschiedener Herkunft, deren älteste jüdischen Ursprungs, etwa aus der
Mitte des 2. Jh. BCE stammend, im Buch III des umfangreichen Corpus
der 'Oracula Sibyllina' enthalten sind.[11] Hier wird ein finsteres Gemälde
von der moralischen und religiösen Verkommenheit der 'Hellenen'
entworfen und auf den herannahenden, ersehnten 'Tag' geblickt, an
dem ein König 'von der Sonne' ein neues, friedliches Reich mit dem
(Jerusalemer) Tempel als Zentrum der Menschheit errichten wird.
Solche Weissagungen, in den folgenden Jahrhunderten immer wieder
ausgebaut und aktualisiert (Zusätze im Buch III sowie die Bücher IV, V
und XI zu großen Teilen), wurden schließlich, vermutlich von

---

11. Hier setze ich etwa die Analyse und Einordnung der jüdischen Sibyllinen
durch J.J. Collins voraus; vgl. seine Kurzdarstellung: The Sibylline Oracles, in:
M.E. Stone (ed.), *Jewish Writings of the Second Temple Period* (Compendia Rerum
Iudaicarum ad Novum Testamentum II/2; Assen and Philadelphia, 1984), pp. 357-81,
und seine Neuübersetzung in: J.H. Charlesworth (ed.), *The Old Testament
Pseudepigrapha,* I (= *OTP* I) (Garden City, NY, 1983), pp. 317-472.

christlichen Redaktoren, mit Sibyllen-Sprüchen anderer Herkunft zu jener umfangreichen Sammlung der Oracula Sibyllina zusammengefaßt, die dann weiterüberliefert wurde. Aber ob ein nichtjüdischer Zeitgenosse der jeweiligen Autoren die einzelnen Teilgedichte überhaupt zur Kenntnis genommen hat? Wenn, dann allenfalls mit Kopfschütteln oder gar mit Widerwillen; missionarisch werbend konnten sie wohl kaum wirken. Der bzw. die Autoren, die offenbar an eine geläufige Form geheimnisumwitterter Dichtung anknüpften, dachten wohl am ehesten an jüdische Leser, und zwar an solche Kreise im Diaspora-Judentum, die sich in ihrer jetzigen Umwelt als Fremde fühlten und gewiß auch von außen her als solche behandelt wurden—ohne daß immer sogleich an aggressive Verfolgungen gedacht werden müßte (um die Mitte des 2. Jh. BCE, in der Regierungszeit des Ptolemaios Philometor, ist davon jedenfalls nicht auszugehen). Auch die Kreise um diese jüdischen Sibyllinen sind in einem bestimmten Maße 'hellenisiert'; sie beherrschen die griechische Sprache bis hin zur Serienproduktion von Hexametern; sie sind auch von stoisch-kosmologischen Gedanken beeinflußt, können sich aber auch in die Rolle der alten heidnischen Wahrsagerin hineinversetzen. Aber dennoch sind diese jüdischen Sibyllen-Sprüche kein Zeugnis eines positiven interkulturellen Austauschs, sondern eher das Selbstzeugnis einer jüdischen Gruppe in der ägyptischen Diaspora, die auf deutliche Abgrenzung von ihrer kulturellen Umwelt bedacht war und sich die Gründe für solche Abgrenzung in den Sibyllinen selbst bestätigte. Insoweit könnte man von einer 'Hellenisierung wider Willen' sprechen.

Anders steht es dagegen um die anderen Pseudepigrapha unter griechischer Maske. Auch hier ist freilich in erster Linie mit jüdischen Lesern als Zielgruppe dieser Produkte zu rechnen. Nun werden aber dem Sophokles oder Aischylos, dem Euripides oder Menandros Aussagen angedichtet, die zusammengenommen geradezu ein kleines Kompendium wichtiger jüdischer religiöser Anschauungen ergeben; ich habe andernorts die Auffassung begründet, daß zumindest der größte Teil dieser Gedichte unter griechischen Dichternamen nicht einzeln entstand, sondern von Anfang an als ein (vorgebliches) 'Gnomologion' aus Versen, die von drei großen klassischen Tragikern und drei bekannten Komikern zu stammen vorgeben, in einem Akt 'gedichtet' und komponiert wurde.[12] Dazu kommt dann noch die Serie von

---

12. N. Walter, *Thoraausleger* (s. Anm. 4), pp. 150-201; vgl. auch: ders., in *JSHRZ* IV/3 (s. oben Anm. 9), pp. 244-54, die Texte in deutscher Übersetzung:

(echten, veränderten oder ganz neu geschaffenen) Homer-Versen und Versen, die auf andere 'uralte' Dichter (Linos und Hesiod) zurückgeführt werden, die schon Aristobulos (Fragment 5, bei Eusebios, Praep.Ev. XIII 12,13-16) um 150 BCE als Beleg für die Anerkennung zitiert, die der Sabbat auch bei Heiden genießt.[13] Jüdischen Lesern wollte der jeweilige Autor offenbar zeigen: Ihr seid mit eurem von den Vätern ererbten Judentum in eurem jetzigen Lebensraum, also in der Diaspora, durchaus nicht in absoluter Fremde, sondern befindet euch—etwa mit der Feier des Sabbats—in guter, respektabler Gesellschaft.

Und auch die dem Spruchdichter Phokylides von Milet unter-geschobenen moralischen Sentenzen in 230 Hexametern,[14] in denen biblische und hellenistisch-popularethische Traditionen miteinander verquickt wurden, sollten wohl jüdischen Lesern zeigen, wie gut biblisch-jüdische und griechische Moral zusammenpaßten und daß es nicht nötig sei, um der griechischen Kultur willen das eigene Judentum geringzuachten oder gar aufzugeben. Ja noch mehr: es bestehe kein Grund, sich der griechischen Kultur zu verweigern.

Sicher: Eine solche Annäherung an griechisches Wesen dürfte innerhalb der jüdischen Diaspora-Gemeinschaft keineswegs unumstritten gewesen sei—wenn man nur z.B. an die auch in der jüdisch-hellenistischen Literatur durchaus begegnende Ablehnung der Heiden und ihrer 'Götzen' denkt. Aber dennoch zeigen die genannten poetischen Produkte mindestens den eigenen Willen bestimmter jüdischer Gruppen (oder Schichten) in der Diaspora, sich gegenüber der sie umgebenden griechischen Kultur zu öffnen, sich positiv auf sie einzulassen, ohne aber dabei die eigene jüdische Identität aufzugeben. Und es ist anzunehmen, daß solcher Haltung auch auf der anderen, der griechischen Seite ein gewisses Wohlwollen entgegengekommen ist, wie es ja auch aus bestimmten Kreisen und für bestimmte Perioden belegt ist.

pp. 261-70; ferner H. Attridge, in J.H. Charlesworth (ed.), *The Old Testament Pseudepigrapha,* II (= *OTP* II) (Garden City, NY, 1985), pp. 821-30.

13. Auch dazu vgl. Walter, *Thoraausleger* (s. Anm. 4), 150-171, bzw. *JSHRZ* IV/3, pp. 255-56 und 271-73.

14. P.W. van der Horst, *The Sentences of Pseudo-Phocylides.* With Introduction and Commentary (Studia ad Veteris Testamenti Pseudepigrapha, 4; Leiden, 1978), und ders., Pseudo-Phocylides, in J.H. Charlesworth (ed.), *OTP* II (s. Anm. 12), pp. 565-83; eine deutsche Übersetzung auch bei: N. Walter, *JSHRZ* IV/3, pp. 182-216.

In ganz ähnlichem Sinne will auch der jüdische Autor des Pseudo-Aristeas-Briefes[15] seinen (ich meine auch hier: jüdischen) Lesern wohl das Bewußtsein vermitteln, daß die eigene, also die jüdische religiös-kulturelle Tradition Werte enthält, die sich vor dem Forum griechischer Bildung keineswegs verstecken müssen. Der angeblich griechische Erzähler, vorgestellt als ein Beamter am Hofe des Ptolemaios Philadelphos, spricht ja mit großem Respekt von den tiefsinnigen allegorischen Erläuterungen, die der jüdische Hohepriester Eleazaros in Jerusalem dem von Philadelphos dorthin entsandten Aristeas zu solchen Vorschriften des jüdischen Gesetzes gibt, die einem gebildeten Griechen auf Anhieb wenig plausibel erscheinen mochten. In Wahrheit will der Autor auf diese Weise und ebenso mit dem Bericht von dem (schon oben erwähnten) Sieben-Abende-Symposion in Alexandrien seinen Lesern zeigen, daß jüdische Gelehrte oder 'Philosophen' mit griechischer Weisheit voll und ganz mithalten können, so daß sie eben auch für ihre religiös-moralischen Sentenzen großen Beifall seitens des Ptolemäerkönigs und seiner auserlesenen griechischen Tischgäste einheimsen. Auch hinter diesem Pseudepigraphon steht also jedenfalls die Anschauung von einer möglichen kulturellen Gemeinsamkeit griechischer und jüdischer Bevölkerungsgruppen im ptolemäischen Alexandrien des 2. oder 1. Jh. BCE, sogar ein gewisser Stolz auf die eigene Tradition, mit der man auch der griechischen Seite Eindruck zu machen hofft, und zwar gerade dann, wenn man sein Jude-Sein nicht verleugnet, sondern es den nichtjüdischen Nachbarn in der rechten Weise zugänglich und verständlich macht. (Tatsächlich ist aber selbst in wohlwollenden Zeugnissen von griechischer Seite, soweit wir sie kennen, das Verständnis für die jüdische Religion und Kultur recht oberflächlich geblieben.)

Auch in den beiden voneinander zu trennenden jüdischen Schriften unter dem Namen des griechischen Historikers Hekataios (von Abdera)[16] scheint es den beiden jüdischen Autoren darum zu gehen,

---

15. Neue englische Übersetzung: R.J.H. Schutt, in J.H. Charlesworth (ed.), *OTP* II, pp. 3-34; deutsche Übersetzung: N. Meisner, *Aristeasbrief, JSHRZ* II/1 (Gütersloh, 1973), pp. 35-85.

16. Die von mir vorausgesetzte Existenz zweier jüdischer Autoren, die jeweil sehr verschiedene Schriften unter dem Namen des Hekataios verfaßt hätten (vgl. N. Walter, *JSHRZ* I/2 [Gütersloh, 1976], pp. 144-60), ist in der Forschung nicht allgemein anerkannt. Vor allem zu Pseudo-Hekataios I (Fragmente aus Josephus, c.Ap. I 183b-205a und 213b-214a sowie c.Ap. II 43) wird vielfach die Meinung

einerseits (in Pseudo-Hekataios I) eine Art 'Waffenbrüderschaft' von griechischen und jüdischen Soldaten im Heer Alexanders des Großen und der Ptolemäer (ausgehend von der Tatsache, daß jüdische Söldner in den Heeren mehrerer ptolemäischer Könige dienten) und andererseits (in Pseudo-Hekataios II) die 'philosophischen' Erkenntnisse des Abraham und ihre Übernahme durch ägyptische Priester darzustellen. Dazu kommt dann (in Pseudo-Hekataios I) noch die Anekdote vom jüdischen Soldaten Mosollamos, der vor seinen Kameraden einen für ein Orakeltier gehaltenen Vogel erschießt, ohne selbst Schaden davonzutragen, und so den heidnischen Vorzeichen-Glauben lächerlich macht.

Was verbirgt sich hinter literarischen Bemühungen solcher Art, die hier natürlich nur sehr knapp skizziert werden konnten? Man darf sich die Verunsicherung einer ethnischen Minderheit, die in der Weltstadt Alexandrien[17] mit dem Reichtum an differenzierter griechischer Kultur konfrontiert wird und in dieser Umgebung dennoch heimisch werden will, nicht zu gering denken und muß sich auch bewußt machen, daß manche andere ethnische Gruppe in vergleichbarer Lage auf die Dauer meist ununterscheidbar im kulturellen Meer des Hellenismus aufgegangen ist. Die Versuchung, das Judentum preiszugeben und sich anzupassen, war nicht gering, wie wir denn auch von einzelnen Juden wissen, die ihr erlegen sind.[18] Die von uns besprochenen Pseudepigrapha wollten wohl unter anderem jüdischen Lesern, die in ihrer Diaspora-Existenz verunsichert waren, Hilfe bringen, und zwar in diesem Falle nicht auf dem Wege der Selbstabgrenzung,[19] sondern in der Weise, daß

---

vertreten, es handele sich um Fragmente aus einem echten Werk des Hekataios, wobei einige Autoren dann doch wieder mit kleineren Zusätzen eines jüdischen Tradenten rechnen (so z. B.M. Stern, *Greek and Latin Authors on Jews and Judaism*, I [Jerusalem, 1974], pp. 22-24 und 35-44). Übrigens begegnet unter den von Alexander Polyhistor aufbewahrten Historiker-Fragmenten auch ein 'Pseudo-Eupolemos'; doch handelt es sich in diesem Falle nicht um ein Pseudepigraphon, das dem Eupolemos zugeschrieben worden wäre; vielmehr liegt ein Versehen vor: Alexander (oder Eusebios) vergaß beim Exzerpieren, den richtigen Autornamen zu nennen. Für uns ist das Fragment also eigentlich anonym, doch es hat die einmal eingebürgerte Benennung behalten.

   17. Vgl. umfassend: P. M. Fraser, *Ptolemaic Alexandria* I-III (Oxford, 1972).

   18. Als besonders prominenter 'Überläufer' ist Tiberius Alexandros, der Neffe Philons, bekannt, der als römischer Kurator von Judäa auch ausgesprochen antijüdische Maßnahmen durchführte (über ihn vgl. V. Burr, *Tiberius Julius Alexander* [Bonn 1955]).

   19. Vgl. dazu G. Delling, *Bewältigung* (s. oben Anm. 2), pp. 9-26.

man ein Gefühl für die Ebenbürtigkeit der eigenen mit der umgebenden Kultur zu erwecken suchte—unter anderem auch dadurch, daß man das höhere Alter der 'Mosaischen Philosophie' gegenüber der griechischen hervorhob und behauptete, Platon, Pythagoras und andere berühmte Griechen seien bei Mose in die Lehre gegangen.[20] Es bleibt freilich die Frage offen, ob und inwieweit dieser Position auch eine entsprechende Haltung von der anderen, der griechischen Seite her entgegenkam.[21] Das ist jedenfalls nicht immer und nicht gleichmäßig, von allen Bevölkerungskreisen her, der Fall gewesen. Eine Reihe von frühen Äußerungen nichtjüdischer Autoren über die Juden belegt immerhin, daß man zum Teil durchaus bereit war, die Weisheit der Juden anzuerkennen,[22] wie denn auch in späterer, etwa urchristlicher Zeit das Faktum der sogenannten 'Gottesfürchtigen', also solcher Nichtjuden, die für die Lehren des Judentums deutliches Interesse zeigten und wohl quasi als Gäste auch die Synagoge besuchten, ohne aber sich dem

---

20. Dieses Motiv kommt in den Pseudepigrapha besonders klar im sogenannten 'Testament des Orpheus' (bei Pseudo-Justin, De monarchia 2, u. a.) zum Ausdruck (vgl. dazu N. Walter, *JSHRZ* IV/3, p. 217-243). Nach diesem, dem mythischen Sänger angedichteten, hexametrischen 'Testament' soll Orpheus auf seinem Sterbebett seinen bisherigen Glauben an viele (nämlich 360 !) Götter zugunsten eines biblischen Monotheismus widerrufen haben, wobei er—jedenfalls nach den erweiterten Fassungen des Gedichts—auf Abraham bzw. Mose als die 'klassischen' Garanten dieses Gottesglaubens anspielt.—Ausdrücklich wird die Auffassung von der Priorität der jüdischen vor der griechischen Philosophie schon in der Mitte des 2. Jh. BCE von Aristobulos geäußert. Zu diesem Motiv vgl. N. Walter, *Thoraausleger* (s. oben Anm. 4), pp. 43-51, sowie jetzt vor allem P. Pilhofer, *PRESBYTERON KREITTON. Der Altersbeweis der jüdischen und christlichen Apologeten* (WUNT II/39; Tübingen, 1990).

21. An sich war den hellenistischen Griechen der Gedanke durchaus nicht fremd, daß sie bzw. ihre Vorfahren für ihre Kultur manches bei orientalischen Weisen gelernt hätten, so daß auch die von den Juden vorgetragene Fiktion nicht unbedingt und überall nur mit Verachtung zur Kenntnis genommen worden sein muß (vgl. dazu Pilhofer [s. vorige Anm.], Kap. I und II); vielmehr übernahmen die jüdischen Autoren eine in gewisser Hinsicht durchaus 'moderne' Anschauung und übertrugen sie auf ihre eigene literarische Tradition.

22. Vgl. dazu etwa A. Momigliano, *Hochkulturen* (s. oben Anm. 7), pp. 102-107; M. Stern, 'The Jews in Greek and Latin Literature', in S. Safrai und M. Stern (edd.), *The Jewish People in the First Century*, II (CRINT I/2; Assen, 1976), p. 1101-1159, bes. 1103-1111. Die griechischen Texte (mit englischer Übersetzung) sind zusammengestellt in M. Stern, *Greek and Latin Authors on Jews and Judaism*, I-III, Jerusalem 1974/80/84.

Judentum als 'Proselyten' völlig anzuschließen,[23] Sympathien für die Juden in bestimmten, griechisch gebildeten Kreisen erkennen läßt. Dennoch darf man—wie eingangs schon gesagt[24]—sich die Wirkung der hier besprochenen pseudepigraphischen Literatur keineswegs allzu groß vorstellen, zumal nicht nach außen; erhalten blieb sie uns jedenfalls ausschließlich durch die christlichen Nachfolger des hellenistischen Judentums, die frühkirchlichen Apologeten, die solche Stücke gern— und anscheinend gutgläubig—in ihren Schriften verwendeten.[25]

Freilich bleibt für die hellenistisch-römische Zeit schwer abzuschätzen, welche reale Basis der kulturelle Optimismus, der auf ein ebenbürtiges Neben- bzw. Miteinander jüdischer und griechischer Kultur hoffte, unter den tatsächlichen Bedingungen des Umgangs beider Bevölkerungsgruppen miteinander in Alexandrien und anderen hellenistischen Städten wenigstens zeitweilig hatte. Denn in vielen anderen Zeugnissen der hellenistisch-römischen Umwelt des Judentums herrscht eben doch Abneigung, zum Teil sogar ausgesprochene Feindschaft gegenüber den Juden vor.[26] Auf die Dauer hat die Hoffnung der zu echter Hellenisierung bereiten Gruppen des spätantiken hellenistischen Judentums jedenfalls getrogen. Unter den mancherlei

23. Vgl. K.-G. Kuhn und H. Stegemann, 'Proselyten', in Pauly-Wissowa, *Real-Enzyclopädie der classischen Altertumswissenschaft,* Suppl. IX (Stuttgart 1962), pp. 1248-1283; F. Siegert, 'Gottesfürchtige und Sympathisanten', *JSJ* 4 (1973), pp. 109-64. Die Existenz solcher 'Gottesfürchtigen' ist zwar in jüngster Zeit auch bestritten worden (z. B. durch Th. A. Kraabel, 'The Disappearance of the 'God-Fearers'', *Numen* 28 [1981], pp. 113-26), doch m. E. nicht mit zureichenden Gründen.

24. Siehe oben bei Anm. 9.

25. Vor allem Clemens von Alexandrien und Eusebios von Cäsarea, aber auch andere Kirchenväter.—Bemerkenswert scheint mir zu sein, daß Josephus, der den Pseudo-Aristeas-Brief ausführlich exzerpiert (Ant. XII 11-119), nirgends hervorhebt (wie er es sonst gern tut), daß er aus der Schrift eines *griechischen* Autors zitiert (zwar erwähnt Josephus in Ant. XII 17ff. den Aristeas—bzw., wie er schreibt: Aristaios—mehrfach, jedoch nicht als einen Autor, auf den er sich beruft; in XII 100 erwähnt er die Schrift, verzichtet aber darauf, zu betonen, daß es ein griechischer Autor sei, der die Juden so lobt); Josephus scheint die Fiktion nicht recht geglaubt zu haben.

26. Zum sog. 'Antisemitismus' (eigentlich wäre von 'Antijudaismus' zu sprechen) in der Antike vgl. immer noch I. Heinemann, in: *Real-Encyclopädie* (s. oben Anm. 23) Suppl. 5 (Stuttgart 1931), pp. 3-14, aus neuerer Zeit etwa J.N. Sevenster, *The Roots of Pagan Anti-Semitism in the Ancient World* (Suppl. to Novum Testamentum, 41; Leiden, 1975); H. Conzelmann, *Heiden* (s. oben Anm. 7), pp. 43-120, und manche weitere Literatur.

heftigen Auseinandersetzungen der griechischen mit der jüdischen Bevölkerung in Alexandrien und vollends mit dem schlimmen Ausgang des jüdischen Aufstands von 115–117 CE in Ägypten (und in weiten Teilen der Diaspora auch anderwärts) ist diese Hoffnung in der Zeit Trajans schließlich zusammengebrochen.

Blicken wir noch kurz auf die Anfänge der jüdischen Präsenz in Alexandrien zurück, so ist es in der Forschung umstritten, ob die Septuaginta—also die in ptolemäischer Zeit nach und nach erfolgte Übersetzung der hebräischen Thora (und allmählich auch der anderen Schriften der hebräischen Bibel sowie einiger weiterer Schriften) ins Griechische—ihrer eigenen Intention nach eine bewußte Hellenisierung des Glaubensgutes Israels oder aber die unter den gegebenen Bedingungen geringste mögliche Form einer solchen Hellenisierung darstellt.[27] Natürlich ging die Absicht dieses Übersetzungswerks in erster Linie dahin, den im kulturell-religiösen Ausland lebenden, immer größer werdenden jüdischen Diaspora-Gemeinden die eigene Schrifttradition in neuem, griechischem Gewande möglichst getreu zu erhalten, zumal in diesen Gemeinden je länger je mehr das Aramäische und erst recht das Hebräische außer Gebrauch kamen.[28] Die Differenz der Auffassungen reduziert sich wohl auf die Frage, wie tiefgehend, und vor allem: wie bewußt dabei die Tendenz einer gewissen Hellenisierung der biblischen Anschauungen—etwa die Vermeidung krasser Anthropomorphismen in den Gottesaussagen—mitspielte. Das kann hier nicht weiter verhandelt werden. Aber so viel ist doch sicher, daß diese großartige Übersetzungsleistung, die in der Antike ohne vergleichbare Vorgänger war und schon insofern einen interkulturellen Vorgang von nicht zu überschätzender Bedeutung für die 'abendländische' Menschheit darstellt, mindestens bei einem Teil des griechischsprachigen Judentums

27. Die an zweiter Stelle genannte Auffassung hat namentlich der Göttinger Septuaginta-Forscher R. Hanhart in mehreren Arbeiten vertreten, von denen hier genannt sei: 'Zum Wesen der makedonisch-hellenistischen Zeit Israels', in: *Wort, Lied und Gottesspruch* (Festschrift für J. Ziegler [Forschung zur Bibel 1], Würzburg, 1972), p. 49-58, sowie: ders., 'Das Neue Testament und die griechische Überlieferung des Judentums', in F. Paschke (Hrsg.), *Überlieferungsgeschichtliche Untersuchungen* (TU, 125; Berlin, 1981), pp. 293-303.

28. Vgl. dazu K. Treu, 'Die Bedeutung des Griechischen für die Juden im Römischen Reich', in: *Kairos* 15 (1973), pp. 123-44.

einen Prozeß aktiver, bewußter, willentlicher Hellenisierung in Gang gesetzt hat.[29] Die hier kurz vorgestellten hellenistisch-jüdischen Pseudepigraphen sind gewiß bescheidene, aber doch m. E. deutliche Zeugnisse für diesen Prozeß bewußten Hellenisierens in der jüdischen Diapora der Spätantike. Es ist wohl deutlich, daß ich mit dem Begriff 'Hellenisierung' einen ganz anderen Vorgang meine als jenen des *passiven* Hellenisiert-Werdens, der im ganzen Bereich des Römischen Reichs, gerade auch im Osten und damit auch im jüdischen Mutterland vor sich ging und dem sich im Grunde niemand völlig entziehen konnte,[30] nicht einmal durch Abkapselung in einer mönchartigen Gemeinschaft wie der von Qumran. Versuch und Erfolg bzw. Mißerfolg hellenistischer Juden, sich mit griechischer Kultur positiv auseinanderzusetzen, können natürlich nicht allein an Hand des schmalen Textbestandes der jüdisch-hellenistischen Pseudepigraphen unter Namen griechischer Autoren ermessen werden, sondern müßten auch an Hand der anderen literarischen Zeugnisse aus der gleichen Zeit dargestellt werden; die vorgetragenen Erwägungen können zum Gesamtthema nur einen partiellen Beitrag leisten. Aber es scheint mir doch, daß schon das bloße Vorhandensein solcher Pseudepigraphen in sich einen gewissen Aussagewert hat. Daß sich dieser Aussagewert möglicherweise nur auf eine geringe intellektuelle Oberschicht unter den jüdischen Bewohnern etwa Alexandriens bezieht, war eingangs betont worden. Es liegt auf der Hand, daß die innere Fremdheit der Mehrheit der Diasporajuden gegenüber der sie umgebenden hellenistischen Kultur durch die literarischen Bemühungen

---

29. In der Forschung ist nach wie vor strittig, ob die Initiative zu dieser Übersetzungsarbeit wenigstens zum Teil auch von den ptolemäischen Königen, insbesondere von Ptolemaios II. Philadelphos (bzw. ihren Hofbeamten) ausgegangen sei, wie das schon Aristobulos (F 3, bei Eusebios, Praep.Ev. XIII 12,1-2) und dann in großer Ausführlichkeit der Pseudo-Aristeas-Brief behaupten. Vor allem E. Bickerman ('The Septuagint as a Translation' [1959], in ders., *Studies in Jewish and Christian History*, I [AGJU, 9,1; Leiden, 1976], pp. 167-200, bes. 171-175) hat dafür plädiert, diese Überlieferung ernster zu nehmen, als es in der Forschung sonst üblich war. Ihm haben sich Gelehrte wie Y. Gutman *(The Beginnings of Jewish Hellenistic Literature*, I-II [hebr.], Jerusalem 1958/63, I, pp. 115-31) oder K. Schubert, *Die Kultur der Juden, I: Israel im Altertum* (Handbuch der Kulturgeschichte, 2. Abt.; Wiesbaden, 1970, pp. 120 und 141-43) angeschlossen; vgl. auch E. Tov, 'Die griechischen Bibelübersetzungen', in: *ANRW* II 20/1 (Berlin, 1987), pp. 121-89: p. 129.

30. Vgl. dazu M. Hengel, *The 'Hellenization' of Judaea in the First Century after Christ* (London and Philadelphia, 1989).

weniger Autoren nicht insgesamt abgebaut werden konnte;[31] der erwähnte Aufstand weiter Teile der Diaspora-Judenschaft unter Trajan läßt erkennen, daß aufs Ganze gesehen eine wirkliche gegenseitige Annäherung nicht erreicht werden konnte. Die Katastrophe, in die dieser Aufstand die Diasporajuden hineinführte (und die sich in Judäa mit der Unterwerfung der Aufständischen um Simon bar-Koseba 132–135 CE noch vergrößerte), brachte wohl alle jüdischen Bemühungen um die griechische Kultur zum Erliegen. Und die sich im 2./3. Jh. CE festigende Sammlung der Juden um die pharisäisch-rabbinischen Gelehrten hatte zur Folge, daß das Griechen- und Römertum wieder nachdrücklich als 'heidnisch' und damit für engere Kontakte als unerlaubt galt, so wie es auch in den Jahrhunderten davor, durchaus auch in der Diaspora, bei vielen Juden stets angesehen wurde. Doch nahm sich die inzwischen entstehende christliche Kirche des Erbes des zum Hellenismus hin aufgeschlossenen Judentums an.[32] Nur durch Vermittlung der Kirchenväter und durch christliche Abschreiber ist uns das meiste dessen, was wir von der jüdisch-hellenistischen Kultur noch kennen, erhalten geblieben; sie führten die Bemühungen um eine Umsetzung der israelitisch-jüdischen Tradition in eine auch für hellenistische Menschen brauchbare Form fort. Für die christliche Kirche war die Anknüpfung an die Traditionen des hellenistischen Judentums naheliegend, ja sogar innerlich notwendig, sofern die Kirche zum einen ihrer Verwurzelung in der Glaubenstradition Israels und zum anderen ihrem Gesandtsein an 'alle (Heiden-)Völker' (Mt 28,19) entsprechen wollte. Aus der Frage 'Kann man als Jude auch Grieche sein?' war nun die andere geworden,

---

31. In den von Lukas in der 'Apostelgeschichte' kurz gestreiften heftigen Auseinandersetzungen zwischen Stephanus (und seiner Gruppe hellenistisch-jüdischer Christen) einerseits und anderen hellenistischen Juden andererseits (Apg. 6,9) dürfte sich zeigen, daß auch unter den (heimgekehrten) Diasporajuden ein breites Spektrum möglicher Stellungnahmen zu grundsätzlichen Fragen des Judentums (es ging wohl um die Stellung zur Thora oder zum Tempel) zu vermuten ist.

32. Schon Lukas begann damit, wie die von ihm dem Paulus in den Mund gelegte 'Areopagrede' (Apg. 17,22-31) zeigt, die deutlich Motive aus dem jüdischen Hellenismus aufnimmt; es ist z. B. denkbar, daß Lukas das griechische Dichterzitat aus Aratos von Soloi in Apg. 17,28 von Aristobulos übernommen hat, der es etwa 200 Jahre vor ihm schon zitiert hatte (Fragment 4, bei Eusebios, Praep.Ev. XIII 12,6). Die Linie setzt sich dann bekanntlich bei den christlichen Apologeten des 2. Jh. fort; dazu sei noch einmal auf die Arbeit von P. Pilhofer, *PRESBYTERON KREITTON* (s. oben Anm. 20), hingewiesen.

in welcher Form die von manchen hellenistischen Juden begangenen Wege zu einer Begegnung von biblischem Glauben und hellenistischer Kultur nun weitergeführt werden konnten und sollten.

SIRACH RESEARCH SINCE 1965: PROGRESS AND QUESTIONS

Daniel J. Harrington, S.J.

The year 1965 can be taken as a watershed in study on the book of
Sirach, for it saw the publication of two major fragments from the Dead
Sea Scrolls and of a truly critical edition of the Greek text. This report
on Sirach research since 1965 covers the major editions and mono-
graphs; it does not treat articles, parts of books, or contributions to
handbooks. The material is divided into three sections (text, life-setting
and sources, themes), and is discussed mainly in chronological order of
publication. Each section concludes with a reflection on methodological
issues.

The book of Sirach is huge (51 chapters) and full of textual and interpretive problems. It offers a window onto Judaism around 190–175 BCE
when Ben Sira, the wisdom teacher of Jerusalem, put together his book.
It shows how important ideas and institutions in the Jewish tradition
were integrated with currents from the international wisdom movement
and (some say) Hellenism. The book is canonical for Catholics and
Orthodox Christians, and Jews and Protestants also find much that is
edifying (and some that is irritating) in it.

Text

Substantial fragments of the Hebrew texts of Sir. 39.27–44.17 were discovered at Masada in 1964 and published in 1965 by Yigael Yadin.[1] The
texts are arranged stichometrically, with each unit placed on a separate
line and divided into bicola. The orthography is relatively defective,
leaving open some readings previously regarded as settled. The script of
the manuscript can be assigned to the late second or early first century
BCE (Hasmonean), thus making this manuscript contemporary with or

---

1. *The Ben Sira Scroll from Masada with Introduction, Emendations and
Commentary* (Jerusalem: Israel Exploration Society, 1965).

slightly later than the Greek translation by Ben Sira's grandson in Egypt (c. 117 BCE). The Masada fragments agree sometimes with the text of the Cairo Geniza MS B and sometimes with its marginal notations. On the whole, however, the Masada text is basically identical with that of the Cairo Geniza manuscript and close to the Hebrew manuscript used by the grandson. It confirms that the manuscripts discovered in the Cairo Geniza represent the original Hebrew version, and are not retro-versions (on the whole) from Syriac, Greek, or Persian. It also reveals recensional activity in the Hebrew textual tradition in the period shortly after the book's composition.

The great Psalms Scroll from Qumran Cave 11 contains parts of the Hebrew text of Sir. 51.13-30—the autobiographical poem about the search for wisdom and the invitation to come to the author's school. James A. Sanders published this text first in the DJD volume in 1965[2] and then in a more popular edition in 1967.[3] On the basis of extant fragments (col. 21.11-17 = Sir. 51.13-20b; col. 22.1 = Sir. 51.30b) Sanders was able to show what earlier scholars had suspected—that Sir. 51.13-30 is an alphabetical acrostic in Hebrew and that the Cairo Geniza text was a retranslation from the Syriac version. Less convincing were Sanders's erotic translation and interpretation of the text, and his con-tention that the poem was independent of the book of Sirach. It is true that Sirach 51 is a kind of appendix consisting of two (or three) different pieces. But Sir. 51.13-30 fits what we know about Ben Sira—so much so that one can rightly say that if he did not write it, he should have.

An important milestone in scholarship on Sirach was the 1965 critical edition of the Greek text prepared by Joseph Ziegler in the so-called Göttingen Septuagint project.[4] Ziegler, who prepared many editions for this series, said that among all the books of the Septuagint Sirach pro-vides the textual critic with the most numerous and difficult puzzles. His edition of the Greek Sirach is all that a critical text should be. His critical apparatus takes account not only of the Greek manuscripts but also of the dependent versions and even occasionally the Hebrew and Syriac. In his introduction Ziegler admits the substantial authenticity and originality

---

2. *The Psalms Scroll of Qumrân Cave 11 (11QPs^a)* (DJD, 4; Oxford: Clarendon Press, 1965), pp. 79-85.

3. *The Dead Sea Psalms Scroll* (Ithaca, NY: Cornell University Press, 1967), pp. 112-17.

4. *Sapientia Iesu Filii Sirach* (Septuaginta XII, 2; Göttingen: Vandenhoeck & Ruprecht, 1965).

of the Hebrew texts, and suggests that the Hebrew MS B was the *Vorlage* for the Greek I (short) and MS A was the *Vorlage* for the Greek II (long) recensions. The presentation of the Greek text distinguishes the additional matter in the long recension by the use of small type. The numbering system of chapters and verses—a major cause of confusion when reading the older Sirach studies—that Ziegler introduced has been followed in the Anchor Bible and the New Revised Standard Version, and should be adopted in all discussions of this text.

Roughly contemporary with the publication of the Masada and Qumran fragments of Sirach came Alexander A. Di Lella's systematic defense of the substantial antiquity and authenticity of the Cairo Geniza fragments.[5] Against those who argued that the Hebrew texts were retroversions from Syriac, Greek, or Persian, he demonstrated that at some points (7.20; 7.25; 10.19; 15.19; etc.) the Hebrew manuscripts represent the original text from which the Greek and Syriac derive. He also suggested that the medieval Hebrew texts came ultimately from the Qumran community, only to be rediscovered in the late eighth century CE. Finally he allowed for textual corruptions in the medieval manuscripts and gave seven examples of what seem to be retranslations from Syriac (5.4-6; 10.31; 15.14, 15, 20; 16.3; 32.16).

Some very useful tools for studying the texts of Sirach have appeared. Francesco Vattioni has produced a synopsis with the Greek (Ziegler edition) and Latin texts on the left-hand page, and the Hebrew and Syriac texts on the right-hand page.[6] The Hebrew section includes a critical apparatus listing variants where more than one manuscript exists. Thus one can compare at a glance the four principal versions. The main part of the concordance prepared by Dominique Barthélemy and Otto Rickenbacher[7] presents the various forms of the Hebrew word in context along with their Syriac and Greek equivalents. A 78-page appendix lists the Hebrew equivalent(s) of each word in the Syriac version. The concordance of the Hebrew text prepared in connection with the Historical Dictionary of the Hebrew Language project[8] first presents the

5. *The Hebrew Text of Sirach. A Text-Critical and Historical Study* (Studies in Classical Literature, 1; The Hague: Mouton, 1966).
6. *Ecclesiastico. Testo ebraico con apparato critico e versioni greca, latina e siriaca* (Testi, 1; Naples: Instituto Orientale di Napoli, 1968).
7. *Konkordanz zum hebräischen Sirach mit syrisch-hebräischem Index* (Göttingen: Vandenhoeck & Ruprecht, 1973).
8. *The Book of Ben Sira. Text, Concordance and an Analysis of the Vocabulary*

extant Hebrew texts, then offers a concordance with each occurrence of the Hebrew word in context, and concludes with twelve lexical lists.

In his study of the Hebrew manuscripts for chs. 3–16, Hans Peter Rüger has shown the complexity and clarified the textual situation of Sirach.[9] From analysis of doublets in manuscript A, parallels or overlaps in A and C and in A and B, and select readings of A, Rüger discovered two forms of the Hebrew textual tradition—the older usually represented by Hebrew B and C and Greek I, and the younger usually represented by Hebrew A and the Syriac (and often Greek II). The younger version (produced between 50 and 150 CE) was influenced by Jewish Aramaic, and manifests targumizing tendencies. In some cases the Old Greek is the best witness for the original text (where Hebrew B or C is lacking or corrupt). Rüger preferred to explain the alleged retroversions from Syriac (Di Lella) and Greek (Ziegler) as actually reflecting different recensions of the Hebrew tradition.

Tadeusz Penar's philological notes on Hebrew texts in Sirach[10] follow the methods of his mentor Mitchell Dahood, and employ parallels from the Hebrew Bible as well as Ugaritic and Phoenician texts to illumine problems in translation and interpretation. Though the Ugaritic parallels are far removed in time from Sirach, it is not impossible that they can shed light on lexical and grammatical survivals in the Hebrew of Ben Sira.

Some of Rüger's points were confirmed and sharpened by Friedrich Vincent Reiterer's comparative text-critical and literary analysis of Sir. 44.16–45.26 (from Enoch to Phinehas) in the Hebrew, Greek, Syriac, and Latin versions.[11] While at times the Hebrew MS B preserves the original text, often it does not; on the whole, Greek I follows a different *Vorlage* that was closer than B to the original Hebrew text; the Syriac followed a Hebrew *Vorlage* different from B; Greek II sought to make Greek I conform more to the Septuagint tradition; and some differences

---

(Jerusalem: Academy of the Hebrew Language and the Shrine of the Book, 1973).

9. *Text und Textform im hebräischen Sirach. Untersuchungen zu Textgeschichte und Textkritik der hebräischen Sirachfragmente aus der Kairoer Geniza* (BZAW, 112; Berlin: de Gruyter, 1970).

10. *Northwest Semitic Philology and the Hebrew Fragments of Ben Sira* (BibOr, 28; Rome: Biblical Institute Press, 1975).

11. *'Urtext' und Übersetzungen. Sprachstudie über Sir 44,16–45,26 als Beitrag zur Siraforschung* (Arbeiten zu Text und Sprache im Alten Testament, 12; St Ottilien: EOS-Verlag, 1980).

between the Latin and Greek may be due to changes made on the basis of MS B.

The most important contribution to understanding the book of Sirach over the past thirty years is the 1987 Anchor Bible commentary authored jointly by Patrick W. Skehan and Alexander A. Di Lella.[12] Before his death in 1980 Skehan had completed the translation and textual notes on 1.1–38.23; 39.12-35; and 44.1–51.12. Di Lella finished off the translation and textual notes, wrote a 92-page introduction, provided a 35-page bibliography, and prepared a substantive commentary on each section. While taking the Greek as the base text, the translation is at least something of a composite arrived at by sifting the Hebrew, Syriac, and Latin evidence. Skehan was a master philologian and textual critic, and he leads the reader through the complexities of this notoriously difficult text in a concise and steady way. The comments by Di Lella concern issues of literary structure, rhetorical devices, biblical roots and parallels, and theology. On the whole, the commentary is a great success, saying much in short spaces, taking account of other scholarly views, and showing good judgment. I have questions about how Di Lella joins some pericopes together, his occasional forced attempts at finding historical allusions in some of Ben Sira's generic language, and his comparative lack of interest in Greek and Egyptian parallels. His introduction deals with the title and content of Sirach, historical setting, place in the canon, literary genres, relation to other works, original Hebrew text and ancient versions, poetry, and teaching. He states the problems, sifts the evidence and related scholarship, and arrives at sensible and convincing positions. The bibliography is comprehensive through the mid-1980s. This is surely one of the best and most successful volumes in the Anchor Bible series.

The Syriac version of Sirach had been the subject of a dissertation by Milward D. Nelson.[13] After sketching the history of discoveries and studies on the text of Sirach, he considers the place of Sirach in the Syriac versions, manuscripts, and editions of the Old Testament. Then focusing on Sir. 39.27–44.17 (the material corresponding to the Masada manuscript), he compares the Greek, Hebrew, and Syriac texts for the absence and presence of verses, and provides a comparative English translation of these texts. Nelson concludes that the Syriac version was

---

12. *The Wisdom of Ben Sira* (AB, 39; New York: Doubleday, 1987).
13. *The Syriac Version of the Wisdom of Ben Sira Compared to the Greek and Hebrew Materials* (SBLDS, 107; Atlanta: Scholars Press, 1988).

translated directly from a Hebrew version with affinities to both the
Masada and Cairo Geniza MS B texts, that it was nevertheless
influenced by the Greek versions, and that the first Syriac version was
produced by Jewish scholars for Syriac-speaking Jews in the third or
fourth century CE and revised by Christians before the mid-fifth century.

Using the computer databank and technical resources of the
Computer Assisted Tools for Septuagint Studies Project (CATSS) at the
University of Pennsylvania, Benjamin G. Wright[14] tested out the grandson's claim in the prologue that there is 'no small difference' between
the Hebrew original and his Greek translation. Wright first compares the
Greek Sirach with other Old Greek biblical texts regarding their fidelity
to Hebrew word-order, segmentation of Hebrew words, quantitative
representation of the Hebrew parent text, and consistency of lexical
representation. He concludes that the grandson was not concerned to
give a close formal representation of Ben Sira's Hebrew, and that there
is little or no evidence that the grandson used the Old Greek texts in
rendering the 'biblical' expressions in the Hebrew text. Since the grandson sought to give a real translation rather than a mechanical representation, attempts at reconstructing the original Hebrew on the basis of the
Greek version are unlikely to meet much success.

The various editions and analyses over the past thirty years have
vindicated the antiquity and substantial authenticity of the Hebrew text
of Sirach. But they have also shown that one cannot simply equate any
extant Hebrew manuscript with Ben Sira's text, since even in the
Masada fragments there is evidence of textual development. While
directly dependent on the Hebrew, the Syriac version seems to rely on a
later textual strand and so must be used with caution. In some cases the
grandson's Greek (Greek I) version contains the best reading. Yet by the
grandson's own admission there is 'no small difference' between the
Hebrew and the Greek. The Old Latin generally follows the Greek.

The relatively clear picture of the texts of Sirach that has emerged in
recent years raises some interesting methodological questions. What does
an editor or translator put on the page as the text of Sirach? Should it
be an eclectic text derived from text-critical reasoning on the basis of the
extant versions? Or should it be merely a synoptic presentation of the
Hebrew (and Syriac) and Greek (and Latin) traditions? For those in the
Catholic and Orthodox traditions the Greek (and Latin) version has been

14. *No Small Difference. Sirach's Relationship to its Hebrew Parent Text*
(SBLSCS, 26; Atlanta: Scholars Press, 1989).

the canonical text. But which Greek recension—short or long—should be regarded as Sacred Scripture? In fact, the claim of canonicity applies not to specific manuscripts or recensions but rather to books. Since that is so, should we not use the methods of textual criticism to determine as far as we can what the original author of the book was saying? And that process demands the rational sifting of the Hebrew and Greek textual traditions. And to what extent can we use the Syriac version to reconstruct the Hebrew text where it is lacking?

Setting in Life and Sources

In a controversial book Theophil Middendorp argued that Ben Sira sought to build a bridge between Greek culture and Jewish tradition.[15] On the one hand, Middendorp finds a wide-ranging and extensive use of Greek sources (perhaps borrowed from anthologies) and describes Ben Sira's book as an anthology according to the Greek model. On the other hand, he contends that Ben Sira freely and sometimes erroneously (by memory lapses) used words and ideas from practically every biblical book. He sees evidence in the Masada fragments for lively recensional activity, and regards passages about eschatology and the chosen people as later additions. He concludes that in Ben Sira's time the influence of Greek culture was already strong in Judea, that Ben Sira was neither pro-Ptolemaic nor pro-Seleucid, that he supported the high priest Simon against the Tobiads, and that he subordinated all foreign learning to the authority of the priests and the Torah.

Where did Ben Sira fit in Jewish society c. 190–175 BCE? Helga Stadelmann identifies Ben Sira as a priest who ran a school in Jerusalem that featured Scripture study and traditional wisdom.[16] She first establishes his positive attitude toward the worship conducted in the Jerusalem Temple (see 7.29-31; 34.21–35.20; 38.9-11; 45.23-26) and the priesthood, which is appropriately balanced by his prophetic concern for integrity and social justice. Then she considers the 'prophetic' aspects of his identity: prophetic self-consciousness (24.33), use of prophetic literary

---

15. *Die Stellung Jesu Ben Siras zwischen Judentum und Hellenismus* (Leiden: Brill, 1973).

16. *Ben Sira als Schriftgelehrter. Eine Untersuchung zum Berufsbild des vormakkabäischen Sofer unter Berücksichtugung seines Verhältnisses zu Priester-Propheten- und Weisheitslehrertum* (WUNT, 2.6; Tübingen: Mohr [Paul Siebeck], 1980).

forms, interest in the biblical prophets (46–49), and ideal of the scribe (see 24.23-34; 38.34–39.8). She suggests that the emphasis on the priestly privileges of Aaron (45.6-22) and Simon (50.1-21) indicates that scriptural learning and wisdom instruction remained the prerogatives of the priests. Although Stadelmann may not have proven that Ben Sira was a priest, she at least has demonstrated the 'priestly' aspect of his outlook and his successful fusion of the roles of priest, Scripture scholar, prophet, and sage. By her analysis of texts she has breathed life into the figure of Ben Sira and made him an attractive person.

Ben Sira's use of the Hebrew Bible has been studied by Pancratius C. Beentjes.[17] After illustrating the need for developing an adequate methodology, he insists that there be parallels not only in words but also in context. When this criterion is applied, it appears that there are fewer direct uses of Scripture in Sirach than most scholars contend. Even where there are introductory formulas, Ben Sira never simply reproduces the text but uses it for his own purposes. In 46.19c he deliberately reversed the biblical word order of 1 Sam. 12.3. The strongest evidence for his structural (rather than anthological) use of the Bible comes in chs. 42–50 (especially 45.6-26).

There is more in Jack T. Sanders's *Ben Sira and Demotic Wisdom* than its title suggests.[18] Sanders first establishes Ben Sira's extensive use of the book of Proverbs as well as other Jewish wisdom books (Job, Qoheleth) and the tradition of Torah righteousness in Deuteronomy. Then after sifting through the various scholarly proposals regarding Ben Sira's use of Greek sources, he concludes that Theogonis is the only Greek author that Ben Sira may have used (though he was not averse to Greek ideas when they supported Judaism). Finally Sanders examines the alleged parallels in Demotic wisdom instructions, and concludes that Ben Sira made extensive use of the work now preserved in Papyrus Insinger and which he calls *Phibis*: 'Ben Sira has read *Phibis*, has been much impressed by it, and has taken over not only individual proverbs from it, but much of its format as well and, indeed, its basic orientation toward life—namely, that one must be cautious and shamefast in order to secure for oneself an everlasting good name' (p. 105). The parallels

---

17. *Jesu Sirach en Tenach. Een onderzoek naar en een classificatie van parallelen, met bijzondere aandacht voor hun functie in Sirach 45.6-26* (Nieuwegein: Privately published, 1981).

18. *Ben Sira and Demotic Wisdom* (SBLMS, 28; Chico, CA: Scholars Press, 1983).

are striking. And Ben Sira claims to have travelled extensively and studied widely (see 33.16-19; 34.9-13), and it is conceivable that he read Demotic Egyptian. But Miriam Lichtheim[19] prefers to explain the coincidences as due to the participation of Ben Sira and the Demotic author in the international wisdom movement, and suggests that the Demotic work may have even used Sirach.

A systematic analysis and critique of Middendorp's approach to Ben Sira's use of Greek writings was undertaken by Volker Kieweler.[20] The book has two major parts: a presentation of the social setting of Ben Sira, and an examination of the Greek writings in which the alleged borrowings occur. Middendorp is criticized especially for his insensitivity to the diversity within both Judaism and Hellenism, and for his failure to recognize that some of the 'parallels' were already part of the native Jewish tradition. Rather than making Ben Sira a bridge between Judaism and Hellenism as Middendorp does, Kieweler situates him within the Judaism of a time forced to confront the phenomenon of Hellenism.

Middendorp's maximalist approach to Ben Sira's use of biblical and Greek sources has elicited the more restrictive and methodologically refined treatments by Beentjes, Sanders, and Kieweler. What emerges from these scholarly debates are some interesting methodological questions. How wide may one legitimately cast one's net in searching for sources or even enlightening parallels? What are the adequate criteria for deciding whether Ben Sira used Scripture anthologically or structurally in a given text? In the case of the very impressive parallels with Papyrus Insinger, how can we determine in which direction the influence is moving? Was Ben Sira strongly influenced by Hellenism, or did he reject it, or did he ignore it? Is it possible to discover behind the general language of Sirach allusions to historical events or movements between 190 and 175 BCE?

19. *Late Egyptian Wisdom Literature in the International Context. A Study of Demotic Instructions* (OBO, 52; Freiburg: Universitätsverlag; Göttingen: Vandenhoeck & Ruprecht, 1983).

20. *Ben Sira zwischen Judentum und Hellenismus. Eine Auseinandersetzung mit Th. Middendorp* (Beiträge zur Erforschung des Alten Testaments und des antiken Judentums, 30; Frankfurt: Peter Lang, 1992).

Themes

Josef Haspecker argues that 'fear of the Lord' is the basic theme of the book.[21] Though Ben Sira was not the first to use the term, he gave the clearest and most extensive presentation. Haspecker first establishes its quantitative importance by commenting on all the uses of the term in Sirach. He highlights its prominence in the author's epilogue (50.27-29) and in the first two chapters of the book, and its climactic place in lists of good things (25.7-11; 40.18-27). Next he shows how the motif occurs throughout the book, giving it theological and structural coherence. Then he explores what Ben Sira meant by 'fear of the Lord': a religious stance involving wholehearted dedication to God, trust in God, observance of the Torah, love of God, humility, and abandonment to God's will. Whether Haspecker established 'fear of the Lord' as *the* basic theme (the most explicit treatment appears only in chs. 1–2) and as structurally significant (can it be used to establish the extent of pericopes and redactional units?), is open to debate. But at least he has called attention to a major element in Ben Sira's theological outlook and demonstrated the soundness of his piety.

The theme of the 'inclination' (*yēṣer*) and free will has been explored by Jean Hadot.[22] The chief passage is Sir. 15.11-20, especially vv. 14-17. He contends that Ben Sira did not share the rabbinic distinction between the good *yēṣer* and the evil *yēṣer*. Rather, Ben Sira insists that people can avoid sin by choosing to keep the commandments, and that *yēṣer* for Ben Sira was a positive concept. This emphasis on good will or voluntarism in turn is the key to navigating the moral dualism that the sage meets in everyday life. Hadot concludes that *yēṣer* as referring to the 'evil inclination' does not occur in Sirach, and that with his affirmation of free will Ben Sira was something of a pioneer in the development of personal religion.

Johann Marböck's investigation of the 'wisdom' texts[23] views Ben Sira as a theologian in the Deuteronomistic tradition who used the concept of wisdom to help Jews to preserve and adapt their identity in

21. *Gottesfurcht bei Jesus Sirach. Ihre religiöse Struktur und ihre literarische und doktrinäre Bedeutung* (AnBib, 30; Rome: Biblical Institute Press, 1967).

22. *Penchant mauvais et volonté libre dans la Sagesse de Ben Sira (L'Ecclésiastique)* (Brussels: Presses Universitaires de Bruxelles, 1970).

23. *Weisheit im Wandel. Untersuchungen zur Weisheitstheologie bei Ben Sira* (BBB, 37; Bonn: Peter Hanstein, 1971).

the face of Hellenistic philosophical universalism. In explicating the programmatic wisdom texts (1.1-10; 24.1-34) and the texts about human encounters with wisdom (4.11-19; 6.18-37; 14.20–15.10; 38.24–39.11; 51.13-30) Marböck highlights the decisive role of wisdom in providing a basic orientation to life and linking creation, Israel's history, and individuals. He finds evidence for Ben Sira's familiarity with Greek philosophy and Stoicism in particular in the creation poems (16.24–17.14; 39.14-35; 42.15–43.33), in the passage about physicians (38.1-15), and in his comments about travel and allusions to Greek philosophy.

The 'wisdom' pericopes in Sirach (1.1-27; 4.11-19; 6.18-37; 14.20–15.10; 19.20-24; 20.27-31; 21.12-28; 24.1-34; 37.16-26; 38.24–39.14; 51.13-30) have also been studied by Otto Rickenbacher.[24] For each text he provides a 'Hebraizing' German translation, a textual analysis (form, structure, verse-by-verse textual and philological discussion), and a thematic-theological discussion (word studies, parallels in Sirach). These studies highlight the primacy of the Hebrew manuscripts and the value of the Syriac and Greek versions for establishing what Ben Sira was saying. They also show that the chief themes of the wisdom pericopes run through the whole book, thus indicating both Ben Sira's redactional activity and the theological coherence of the book.

The contours or framework of Ben Sira's approach to the problem of theodicy have been investigated by Gian Luigi Prato.[25] The method is analysis of the pertinent texts: the binary composition of creation (33.7-15), the bivalent functioning of creation (39.12-35), the place of creatures in the sapiential celebration of creation (42.15–43.33), the antinomy of responsible existence and the appeal to origins (15.11–18.14), suffering (40.1-17), death (41.1-13), and the schema of theodicy and the principle of the 'double aspect' (4.20–6.17; 9.17–11.28). Prato shows that Ben Sira's famous doctrine of 'the pairs' (33.14-15) provides a general orientation rather than an answer, and that Ben Sira regarded theodicy not as a problem about God but rather a question of human freedom and will.

About seven percent of the material in Sirach concerns women (see especially 9.1-9; 23.22-26; 25.13–26.27; 36.26-31; 42.9-14). In his systematic analysis of these texts Warren C. Trenchard contends that Ben

24. *Weisheits Perikopen bei Ben Sira* (OBO, 1; Fribourg: Universitätsverlag; Göttingen: Vandenhoeck & Ruprecht, 1973).

25. *Il problema della teodicea in Ben Sira* (AnBib, 65; Rome: Biblical Institute Press, 1975).

Sira exhibits a personal negative bias toward women.[26] He divides his treatment according to the five categories of the good wife, mother (and widow), bad wife, adulteress and prostitute, and daughter. Though some of Ben Sira's comments can be explained by the shared assumptions of a patriarchal society, Trenchard argues that by going out of his way to criticize the bad wife and the daughter he thus shows his misogynist tendency.

The literary form, structure, and theological perspective of Sirach 44–50 ('Now let us praise famous men...') have been the subject of two full-scale studies. Burton Mack argues that Ben Sira's hymn in praise of the 'fathers' was a charter text, or mythic etiology, for Second Temple Judaism.[27] His investigation proceeds in three steps: literary analysis (heroes and history), rhetorical considerations (reading and writing), and hermeneutics (text and cultural contexts). He attends to the offices and their common characteristics, the response of praise and glory, Ben Sira's place in the wisdom tradition, and his use of Hebrew and Hellenistic models. Thomas Lee contends that in chs. 44–50 Ben Sira was inspired by the encomium genre.[28] He argues that the entire text should be interpreted as an encomium of the high priest Simon II, situates the text in the framework of Greek rhetorical theory, and speculates on whether Sirach would have employed a Greek rhetorical form as his literary model.

By its position immediately after Ben Sira's reflections on wisdom and fear of the Lord in chs. 1–2, the instruction about honoring one's parents in 3.1-16[29] carries a structural prominence. Reinhold Bohlen's monograph on Sir. 3.1-16 provides an eclectic text (based on the Hebrew, Greek, and Syriac version), surveys treatments of honoring parents in various sources (the 'unwritten laws,' the Greek gnomologies, Demotic instructions, pseudo-Phocylides and Josephus's *Against Apion*

26. *Ben Sira's View of Women: A Literary Analysis* (BJS, 38; Chico, CA: Scholars Press, 1982).

27. *Wisdom and the Hebrew Epic. Ben Sira's Hymn in Praise of the Fathers* (Chicago Studies in the History of Judaism; Chicago/London: University of Chicago Press, 1985).

28. *Studies in the Form of Sirach 44–50* (SBLDS, 75; Atlanta: Scholars Press, 1986).

29. *Die Ehrung der Eltern bei Ben Sira. Studien zur Motivation und Interpretation eines familienethischen Grundwertes in frühhellenistischer Zeit* (Trierer Theologische Studien, 51; Trier: Paulinus-Verlag, 1991).

2.190-219), and provides a detailed exegesis with particular attention to other texts in Sirach (see 7.27-28) and the parallels. He concludes that Ben Sira's instruction about honoring parents was a self-conscious presentation of the biblical precept (Exod 20.12; Deut 5.16) in the context of early Hellenistic 'modernity'. His wide-ranging search for parallels again raises the question of 'parallelomania' encountered in situating Ben Sira's teaching in its context.

Since thematic studies of Ben Sira focus on specific texts, they naturally confront the textual and literary-historical problems outlined in the first two sections of this article: What is the text to be interpreted? What parallels are significant? But such studies also raise some further questions about Sirach as a book and Ben Sira as an author. How much redactional unity should one assume? Can one gather all the texts about a theme (fear of the Lord, wisdom, and so on) and present the result as Ben Sira's own view on the topic? Can one use a theme like fear of the Lord as a means for determining literary structures and divisions as Haspecker did? Is there a central theme or master concept that dominates the whole book? How can one determine where one textual-literary unit ends and another begins? Are there objective criteria for determining the literary structure of a unit? How can one decide whether a unit consists of discrete sayings or forms a logical argument? And finally how can one distinguish between cultural assumptions and personal bias as the source of Ben Sira's views on specific topics such as women?

Sirach research since 1965 has featured new editions of texts and text-critical studies, explorations of Ben Sira's life-setting and use of sources, and the chief literary features and theological themes. Much progress has been made. Yet this research has also raised some fundamental questions of methodology, some unique to Sirach and others applicable to the study of many biblical and extrabiblical texts from antiquity. Almost every scholar who writes on Sirach either begins or ends with a quotation from Sir. 18.7 that is also a fitting ending to this report: 'When human beings have finished, they are just beginning; and when they stop, they are still perplexed'.

Louis H. Feldman

1. *Introduction*

Josephus seems to have had two audiences in mind in undertaking his *magnum opus*, the *Jewish Antiquities*, which embraces nothing less than the entire history of the Jewish people from creation to the outbreak of the war against the Romans. On the one hand, his primary audience consisted of non-Jews, as is clear from his statement (*Ant.* 1.5) that he undertook his work in the belief that the whole Greek-speaking world, the great majority of which, of course, was not Jewish, would find it worthy of attention. This would appear to be confirmed by the fact that Josephus was prompted (*Ant.* 1.8) to undertake the work at the urging of his patron, Epaphroditus, clearly a non-Jew, who was 'specially inter-ested in the experiences of history'.[1] The fact that Josephus (*Ant.* 1.9) pondered 'whether our ancestors, on the one hand, were willing to communicate such information [presumably to non-Jews], and whether any of the Greeks, on the other, had been curious to learn our history', and his positive reply on both counts is a clear indication that his history was, indeed, intended for non-Jews. This is confirmed (*Ant.* 1.10-12) by the precedent for his work, namely the Septuagint, which was under-taken at the instance of King Ptolemy Philadelphus; and Josephus (*Ant.* 1.12) is quite clearly convinced that there were still in his own day 'many lovers of learning like the king'. Furthermore, at the very end of his work, Josephus (*Ant.* 20.262) boasts that no one would have been equal to the task of writing so accurate a treatise for the Greeks (εἰς "Ελληνας). Clearly, the term 'Greeks' is here used in contrast to the

---

1.   This Epaphroditus, as H.StJ. Thackeray (ed.), *Josephus* (LCL; London: Heinemann, 1930), IV, pp. x-xi, points out, is either the freedman and secretary of the Emperor Nero (Dio Cassius 67.14), or, more likely, Marcus Mettius Epaphroditus, a grammarian mentioned by Suidas who amassed a huge library.

term 'Jews' and thus confirms that it was written primarily for non-Jews.

Why was Josephus not content merely to recommend to non-Jews that they read the Septuagint, and why did he devote so many years to producing what is, in effect, a 'rewritten' Bible? A clue to the answer may be found in the introduction to his treatise *Against Apion* (1.1), which is dedicated to the same Epaphroditus, in which he declares that he has established in the *Antiquities* the extreme antiquity of the Jews, the same apologetic theme which he further pursues in *Against Apion*. Moreover, a major concern of Josephus in the *Antiquities*, as it is in *Against Apion*, is to answer the charges of intellectuals, such as the extremely influential rhetorician Apollonius Molon (*Against Apion* 2.148) in the first century BCE, that the Jews were atheists, misanthropes, cowards, reckless madmen, who had contributed no useful invention to civilization.[2] Josephus's reply to these serious charges may be seen particularly in his reshaping of biblical personalities.[3] An

2.   Similarly, the rhetorician Apion (*Against Apion* 2.135) states that the Jews had failed to produce any inventors in arts and crafts or eminent sages.

3.   See my 'Josephus' Portrait of Noah and its Parallels in Philo, Pseudo-Philo's *Biblical Antiquities*, and Rabbinic Midrashim', *PAAJR* 55 (1988), pp. 31-57; 'Abraham the Greek Philosopher in Josephus', *TAPA* 99 (1968), pp. 143-56; 'Abraham the General in Josephus', in F.E. Greenspahn *et al.* (eds.), *Nourished with Peace: Studies in Hellenistic Judaism in Memory of Samuel Sandmel* (Chico, 1984), pp. 43-49; 'Josephus as a Biblical Interpreter: the *'Aqedah'*, *JQR* 75 (1984–85), pp. 212-52; 'Josephus' Portrait of Jacob', *JQR* 79 (1988–89), pp. 101-51; 'Josephus' Portrait of Joseph', *RB* 99 (1992), pp. 379-417, 504-28; 'Josephus' Portrait of Moses', *JQR* 82 (1991–92), pp. 285-328; 83 (1992–93), pp. 7-50; 'Josephus' Portrait of Joshua', *HTR* 82 (1989), pp. 351-76; 'Josephus' Portrait of Deborah', in A. Caquot *et al.*, *Hellenica et Judaica: Hommage à Valentin Nikiprowetzky* (Leuven-Paris, 1986), pp. 115-28; 'Josephus' Version of Samson', *JSJ* 19 (1988), pp. 171-214; 'Josephus' Portrait of Samuel', *Abr-N* 30 (1992), pp. 103-45; 'Josephus' Portrait of Saul', *HUCA* 53 (1982), pp. 45-99; 'Josephus' Portrait of David', *HUCA* 60 (1989), pp. 129-74; 'Josephus as an Apologist to the Greco-Roman World: His Portrait of Solomon', in E.S. Fiorenza (ed.), *Aspects of Religious Propaganda in Judaism and Early Christianity* (Notre Dame, 1976), pp. 69-98; 'Josephus' Portrait of Hezekiah', *JBL* 111 (1992), pp. 597-610; 'Josephus' Interpretation of Jonah', *Association for Jewish Studies Review* 17 (1992), pp. 1-29; 'Josephus' Portrait of Daniel', *Henoch* 14 (1992), pp. 37-96; 'Josephus' Portrait of Nehemiah', *JJS* 43 (1992), pp. 187-202; 'Hellenizations in Josephus' Version of Esther', *TAPA* 101 (1970), pp. 143-70; and, for an overall survey, 'Use, Authority, and Exegesis of Mikra in the Writings of Josephus', in M.J. Mulder and H. Sysling (eds.), *Mikra:*

additional motive, we may suggest, was to present the biblical narrative in a more pleasing and more dramatic style and to remove obscurities and apparent contradictions and to make the narrative more credible.

But that Josephus's narrative is directed not only to a non-Jewish but also to a Jewish audience seems likely in view of the fact that a high percentage of the Jews in the world of his time knew Greek and could presumably read and profit from his account. Moreover, the very fact that Josephus (*Ant.* 1.14) says that 'the main lesson to be learnt from this history by those who care to peruse it' is that those who do not venture to trangress the laws of the Pentateuch 'prosper in all things beyond belief' indicates that he is addressing a Jewish audience, inasmuch as non-Jews are not obligated to obey the laws of the Pentateuch, with the exception of the seven Noachian commandments. Indeed, he is clearly addressing Jews in his strong condemnation of the Israelites' sin with the Midianite women (Num. 25.1-9; *Ant.* 4.131-55) and of Samson's relations with alien women (Judg. 14.1-16; *Ant.* 5.286-317).

Josephus's treatment of the brief episode of Ehud is a good illustration of his motives in his rewriting of the Bible both in its modifications and in its omissions. In particular, Josephus is careful not to offend his non-Jewish audience while, at the same time, instilling a sense of pride in his Jewish readers. Moreover, Josephus, the critical historian, is concerned to make the story more credible by omitting obscurities and other difficulties.

That this episode is of great interest to Josephus may be seen from the sheer amount of space that he devotes to it as compared with the attention which he gives to other episodes.[4] Thus, there is a ratio of 2.70 for Josephus as compared with the Hebrew text for the account of Saul, 2.21 for Balaam, 2.16 for Jeroboam, 2.01 for Jehu, 2.00 for Joseph (5.45 for the episode of Joseph and Potiphar's wife and 3.28 for the narrative dealing with Joseph's dreams and subsequent enslavement), 1.98 for Ahab, 1.95 for David, 1.93 for Jehoram of Israel, 1.87 for Samuel, 1.83

Text, Translation, Reading and Interpretation of the Hebrew Bible in Ancient Judaism and Early Christianity (CRINT, 2.1; Assen: van Gorcum, 1988), pp. 455-518.

4.   For the Hebrew I have used the standard edition of the biblical text with the commentary of Meir Loeb Malbim (New York: Friedman, s.a.); for the Septuagint I have used the text of A. Rahlfs, vol. 1 (Stuttgart: Priviligierte Württembergische Bibelanstalt, 1935). For Josephus I have used the Loeb Classical Library text.

for Absalom, 1.54 for Samson, 1.52 for Elijah, 1.32 for Daniel, 1.15 for Jonah, 1.11 for Elisha, .97 for Hezekiah, .91 for Manasseh, 1.20 for Ezra (.72 compared with the Septuagint), and .24 for Nehemiah (.18 compared with the Septuagint). For the episode of Eglon and Ehud (Judg. 3.12-30), which comprises 29 lines in the Hebrew text and 71 lines in Josephus (*Ant.* 5.185-97), the ratio is 2.45 (the ratio of Josephus to the Septuagint version A is 1.54 and to version B 1.37). Here we can see that this pericope was of very great interest to Josephus, presumably because the figure of Ehud supplied an excellent role model of bravery and ingenuity and a compelling answer to the charges of the anti-Semites, as did the episodes pertaining to Joseph, and also because the pericope itself was of great dramatic interest in a long work where there were many more drab than there were exciting episodes.

2. *The Portrayal of Ehud in Pseudo-Philo's Biblical Antiquities, in the Talmud, and in Samaritan Literature*

Inasmuch as Pseudo-Philo, in his *Biblical Antiquities*, places such an emphasis on the period of the judges (there are more references, 163, in it to the book of Judges than to any other single book of the Bible), we should not be surprised to find references to Ehud, whom he calls Zebul.[5] In view of the great, midrashic-like, liberties which he takes with

---

5.   There is a question, in view of the considerable difference in spelling, as to whether Zebul (*Biblical Antiquities* 29) is Ehud (*Ioudes* in Josephus). However, as L. Ginzberg, *The Legends of the Jews* (Philadelphia: Jewish Publication Society, 1928), VI, p. 184 n. 21, points out, there is a parallel to such an interchange of Z and I in *Biblical Antiquities* 47.1, where most manuscripts read Iambri and where the reference is clearly to Zambri. As to the interchange of D and L, there is likewise a parallel in *Biblical Antiquities* 44.2, where the manuscripts read Dedila and where the reference is clearly to Delila. Moreover, we may add, Pseudo-Philo's reference to Zebul comes immediately after his pericope on Cenez (Kenaz), just as in the Bible the reference to Ehud (Judg. 3.15) comes immediately after Othniel the son of Kenaz (Judg. 3.11) and just as in Josephus the reference to the story of Eglon (*Ant.* 5.186) comes immediately after the reference to Kenaz (*Ant.* 5.184), who in Josephus takes the place of Othniel. C. Perrot and P.-M. Bogaert (eds.), Pseudo-Philon, *Les Antiquités Bibliques* (Paris: Cerf, 1976), II, p. 165, conclude that the name must correspond to that of Ehud. To be sure, Pseudo-Philo (34.1) does mention a certain Aod, the spelling of whose name is closer to that of Ehud; but Aod is a magician who bears no resemblance to Ehud. Perrot and Bogaert suggest that it was necessary to distinguish the judge Ehud with the help of his well-known characteristic, his left-handedness; but the Hebrew word *semal*, 'left', also designates Satan-Sammael, whence finally the Latin

the events of this book, we should not be surprised to find that, on the one hand, Pseudo-Philo does not mention the incident of Ehud's assassination of Eglon, and, on the other hand, mentions several other details not found in the book of Judges. In the first place, Ehud in Pseudo-Philo (29.1) is the direct successor to Cenez, the foremost hero in all of the *Biblical Antiquities*. Indeed, his first act as successor to Cenez (*Biblical Antiquities* 29.1) is to gather the Israelites together and to acknowledge the labor with which Cenez worked for the benefit of the people throughout his life. His second act (*ibid.*) is to grant to Cenez's daughters, inasmuch as Cenez had no sons, a greater portion of the national inheritance than was received by other Israelites. His third act (*Biblical Antiquities* 29.3) is to set up a treasury for the Lord, with the instruction that the Israelites not contribute material belonging to idols. Finally, we are told that Zebul judged the people for twenty-five years (in contrast to the biblical text in the Hebrew, which says nothing about his rulership, and in contrast to the Septuagint [Judg. 3.30], which asserts that he judged the Israelites until he died, implying, but not directly stating, through the statement that the land had rest for eighty years, that he ruled the Israelites during this period, and in contrast to Josephus [*Ant.* 5.197], who states directly that Ehud ruled the Israelites for eighty years), and we are given his farewell address to the people in which he exhorts them to obey the law. What is striking is that Pseudo-Philo has none of the ingredients of the account in the Bible at all; but, in view of the tremendous liberties that he takes with the narrative of Cenez, who is not even a judge in the Bible (it is his son Othniel who is there a judge [Judg. 3.9]), it should not be surprising that he presents a totally new picture of Ehud. We should point out, however, that his portrait, though at variance with that in the Bible, is completely positive, as is that of Josephus.

As to the rabbinic tradition, there are two major points to be made. In the first place, the one remark (*Gen. R.* 99.3) about Ehud is clearly positive. There we are told that when Jacob blessed his son Benjamin, comparing him to a wolf that devours, he was alluding to the judge, Ehud, descended from Benjamin, who seized King Eglon's heart, that is, deceived him. That this is not critical of Ehud may be seen from the high regard that this midrash has generally for Benjamin and, in

---

Zebul (Zabulus, the devil, Beelzebul). We may add that when Zebul is mentioned in *Biblical Antiquities* 30.5 the *editio princeps* spells his name Iebul, which removes one of the problems of transcriptional probability.

particular, from the fact that it quotes the tradition cited by Rabbi Berekiah that after Ehud assassinated Eglon he went forth into the place where the ministering angels sat in ordered fashion, presumably in approval of his deed.

However, what is especially remarkable is the respect in which the rabbinic tradition held Eglon, who, though he is identified (*Yalqut* 665) as the grandson of the wicked King Balak, who had hired the soothsayer Balaam to curse the Jews, yet is praised (*Sanhedrin* 60a) for showing respect to God through rising from his throne (Judg. 3.20) when Ehud tells him that he has a message from the Lord; indeed, as a reward, Ruth is identified as his granddaughter (*Nazir* 24b); and her descendant, King David, is described as sitting on the throne of the Lord (*Ruth R.* 2.9). In fact, the Talmud (*Sanhedrin* 60a), citing the precedent of Eglon, argues *a fortiori* that if that king, who was only a heathen and who knew but an attribute of God's name, nevertheless arose, how much more so should an Israelite rise when he hears God's name. Such respect for Eglon, we may surmise, arises from the attitude which the rabbis generally had of respect for rulers,[6] simply because they are rulers.

We may remark that a similar respect for Ehud *qua* ruler may be seen in the statement of the *Second Samaritan Chronicle*[7] that when Ehud (here called King Yehud) heard of Eglon's defeat of Israel, he took the initiative (dangerous as it clearly was) to go to Eglon with his dramatic scheme of assassinating him and managed to escape after accomplishing his mission.

3. *The Virtues of Ehud*

A *sine qua non* for a biblical hero, as Josephus depicts him,[8] is that he be handsome, just as it would be to his pagan audience, who would think of Plato's remark (*Republic* 7.535A11-12) that the guardians of

---

6.   Cf., e.g., the statement of Rabbi Ḥananiah, prefect of the priests, in *Aboth* 3.2: 'Pray for the welfare of the government, for if it were not for fear of it, one man would swallow his fellow alive'.

7.   See J. Macdonald, *The Samaritan Chronicle II (or Sepher Ha-Yamim) from Joshua to Nebuchadnezzar* (Berlin: de Gruyter, 1969), p. 102. This work states that Yehud ruled over Israel for eighteen years, in contrast to Josephus's statement that he ruled for eighty years.

8.   See my 'Josephus' Portrait of Joseph', pp. 388-90; 'Josephus' Portrait of Moses', pp. 307-10; and my 'Use, Authority and Exegesis of Mikra', pp. 486-88.

the state should be 'the sturdiest, the bravest, and, so far as possible, the handsomest persons', in the belief that a leader will command more respect if he is handsome. Indeed, Socrates' closing prayer to Pan in the *Phaedrus* (279) is that his outward and inner beauty be as one. The philosopher Pythagoras as a child (Apollonius-Iamblichus 10, p. 11, lines 6-7; cf. Apuleius, *Florida* 15), Evagoras the king of Salamis in Cyprus as a youth (Isocrates, *Evagoras* 22-23), and the twins Romulus and Remus as young men (Dionysius of Halicarnassus, *Roman Antiquities* 1.79.10) all are represented as outstanding in physical appearance. Jews, and Josephus in particular, were particularly sensitive to the canard, as circulated by Manetho, for example (*ap.* Josephus, *Against Apion* 1.279), that Moses' appearance was marred by leprosy and that he was, in fact, expelled from Egypt because of this.

From this point of view, the biblical statement (Judg. 3.15), with which Ehud is introduced, namely that he had a shriveled ('obstructed') right hand,[9] would certainly not enhance the reader's regard for him but would simply confirm the impression given by the unfounded tale about Moses' appearance. Josephus might have solved this problem by adopting here, as he generally does elsewhere for this part of the *Antiquities*, the Septuagint version (in both of the major recensions), which reads ἀμφοτεροδέξιον, that is, that Ehud was ambidextrous; but he is quite clearly aware here, as he generally is elsewhere, of the Hebrew version, and moreover must have been influenced by the fact that when Ehud embarks upon his mission of assassinating Eglon he girds his sword on his right thigh (Judg. 3.16) presumably because he was left-handed. Josephus (*Ant.* 5.188) has a very neat solution to this problem; he says that Ehud was superior (ἀμείνων, 'better') with his left hand and derived all his strength from it, but he says nothing about his right hand being shriveled.[10] Moreover, whereas the Bible (Judg. 3.21) says that

9. The RSV translates 'a left-handed man'; but the Hebrew reads '*ish 'iter yad-yemino*, which the Targum Jonathan renders as 'a man with a shriveled right hand'. On the key word, *'iter*, Rashi cites its use in Ps. 69.16, where the meaning is 'closed'. C. Cohen, 'Right and Left', *EncJud*, XIV, p. 178, notes that the word *'iter* is of 'the nominal construction that is usually utilized for physical defects—e.g., "blind", "dumb", and "deaf".'

10. The fact that he derived all his strength from his left hand might imply that his right hand was useless, but the Latin version, significantly, reads *in laeva manu maximam fortitudinem habens*, that is, that he had the *greatest* strength in his left hand but without indicating that he had no strength at all in his right hand.

Ehud assassinated Eglon by snatching out his left hand and taking his sword from his right thigh and thrusting it into Eglon's belly, Josephus (*Ant.* 5.193), aware of the negative attitude of the ancients toward left-handed people,[11] omits all mention of Ehud's use of his left hand and says merely that he smote him in his heart. The Roman reader will consequently think of the parallel with the great Roman hero, Gaius Mucius Scaevola (Livy 2.12), who, in a similarly daring exploit, killed the scribe of the Etruscan king Porsinna and then, to show his disdain for suffering, thrust his right hand in the fire into which he was about to be flung.[12]

Josephus is at every point eager to underline the leadership qualities of such figures as the judges and the kings of Israel, especially since the race of mankind, according to Josephus (*Ant.* 3.23), is by nature morose and censorious, and since the great Greek historian Thucydides had stressed, through his portrait of Pericles, that only great and foresighted leadership can overcome the defects of the masses.

In fact, according to the Hebrew Bible (Judg. 3.30), there is no indication that Ehud was a judge, since we are told merely that the land had rest for eighty years. The Septuagint (both versions, Judg. 3.30) adds that he judged the Israelites until he died. Josephus (*Ant.* 5.197) combines the two statements and declares that Ehud held the office of governor (ἡγεμονία) for eighty years. This would make Ehud the longest ruler in the entire period of the judges. For Josephus, who attached such great importance to the rule of law and order, this achievement by Ehud was all the greater, inasmuch as the period of the judges was marked, as he says over and over again (*Ant*. 5.132, 179) by disregard of the order (κόσμου) of the constitution (πολιτείας) and contempt for the laws (νόμων). Josephus has encomia for only a select few of his biblical heroes;[13] yet he sees fit to praise Ehud by remarking

11. See C.J. Fordyce (ed.), *Catullus* (Oxford: Clarendon Press, 1961), pp. 205-206, commenting on Catullus 45.

12. That Josephus may have been acquainted with Livy's history would seem to be indicated by the fact that he (*Ant.* 14.68) cites Livy in his account of Pompey's capture of Jerusalem. On Josephus's knowledge of Latin see H.StJ. Thackeray, *Josephus the Man and the Historian* (New York: Jewish Institute of Religion, 1929), pp. 119-20; B. Nadel, 'Józef Flaawiusz a terminologia rzymskiej inwektywy politycznej' [Polish—'Josephus Flavius and the Terminology of Roman Political Invective'], *Eos* 56 (1966), pp. 256-72; and D. Daube, 'Three Legal Notes on Josephus after His Surrender', *Law Quarterly Review* 93 (1977), pp. 191-94.

13. We may note that Josephus presents encomia at the conclusion of his

that even apart from his extraordinary exploit in killing the king of the enemy, he was deserving of praise, presumably because he restored respect for law and order.

In the case of Ehud we see this quality of leadership in his success (*Ant.* 5.194) in exhorting his fellow Israelites to assert (ἀντιλαμβάνεσθαι, 'grasp for', 'seize', 'attain') their liberty (ἐλευθερίας). This is to be contrasted with the biblical statement (Judg. 3.28), according to which Ehud merely told his fellow Israelites to follow quickly, 'for the Lord has given your enemies, the Moabites, into your hands.' Here it is God who gets all the credit, there is no exhortation, and there is no mention of the key theme of 'liberty'. On the other hand, Ehud's success in exhorting his fellow Israelites may be seen in what follows, according to Josephus (*Ant.* 5.194), for we are told that they, welcoming his news, rush to arms and send heralds throughout the country to give the signal by sounding rams' horns. Ehud's achievement in arousing his fellow Israelites is seen particularly in the added detail (*Ant.* 5.195) that before the garrison of the Moabites could be mustered the host of the Israelites was upon them. All this is in contrast to the Bible's brief statement, 'And they went down after him'.

One might almost say that liberty is the leitmotif of the history of the Jewish people as Josephus sees it. In particular, it is Moses (*Ant.* 2.290) who devotes all his efforts to procuring his people's liberty (ἐλευθερίαν) from the oppressive Egyptians. When the Israelites complain against him because of their lack of food and water in the desert, Moses (*Ant.* 3.19) answers them by declaring that it is not from negligence that God has thus tarried in helping them but rather to test their manhood and their delight in liberty (ἐλευθερίαν). Indeed, when Moses addresses his people on the borders of Canaan, just before the spies are sent into Palestine to scout the land, he reminds the people (*Ant.* 3.300; cf. 4.2) that God had resolved to grant them two blessings, liberty (ἐλευθερίαν) and the possession of a favored land. Indeed, it is significant that when the conspirators plot to assassinate the Emperor Gaius Caligula, Josephus (*Ant.* 19.54) makes a point of noting that the password that they choose is 'liberty' (ἐλευθερίαν).

A major problem that concerned Josephus or any other reader or

discussions of a limited number of other biblical figures, namely Abraham (*Ant.* 1.256), Isaac (1.346), Jacob (2.196), Joseph (2.198), Moses (4.328-331), Joshua (5.118), Samson (5.317), Samuel (6.292-294), Saul (6.343-350), David (7.390-391), Solomon (8.211), Asa (8.315), Elisha (9.182), and Hezekiah (10.36).

interpreter of the Bible was how to justify the obvious trickery employed by Ehud in assassinating Eglon the king of Moab. In this connection, we should recall how strongly the Romans, Josephus's primary audience, felt about deceit, as we see, for example, in Livy's disdain (1.27-28) for the Alban leader Mettius Fufetius, who broke the treaty with Rome, and for the Carthaginians, who were known for their faithlessness (*fides Punica*). We can see Josephus's uneasiness on this matter in his treatment of Jacob's deceitfulness in obtaining the blessing from his father Isaac; in that case Josephus (*Ant.* 1.269) resolves the problem by transferring the blame completely to Rebecca and by having God himself (*Ant.* 2.173) justify the theft of the blessing on the ground that it was he who had given the princedom to Jacob rather than to Esau. Likewise, for similar apologetic reasons, Josephus totally omits Jacob's trickery with the speckled and spotted lambs and goats (Gen. 30.32-43) and stresses the fact that Simeon and Levi, in their trickery in massacring the Shechemites, acted without their father Jacob's permission.[14] In the case of Ehud, however, the fact that his action was needed in order for the Israelites to assert their liberty puts his deed on a different plane.

A quality of major importance for a hero is ingenuity. In view of the fact that the Jews had been accused by such of their opponents as Apion (*ap. Against Apion* 2.135) of not producing any illustrious men distinguished in wisdom, who were comparable to Socrates, the Stoics Zeno and Cleanthes, or Apion himself, Josephus felt a special obligation to stress that such biblical figures as Abraham, Joseph, Moses, Joshua, Samson, David, and Solomon were outstanding in precisely this virtue.[15] To be sure, Ehud does not possess wisdom in the same sense as these other biblical personalities, but he is certainly clever, in an extra-biblical addition, in that whereas the Hebrew text (Judg. 3.15) states simply that the children of Israel sent through him to Eglon, the king of Moab, a present (or presents, according to the Septuagint, in both major

---

14. See my 'Josephus' Portrait of Jacob', pp. 114-18.

15. See especially my 'Abraham the Greek Philosopher in Josephus', pp. 150-56; 'Josephus' Portrait of Jacob', pp. 109-10; 'Josephus' Portrait of Joseph'; 'Josephus' Portrait of Moses', pp. 7-13; 'Josephus' Portrait of Joshua', pp. 355-57; 'Josephus' Version of Samson', pp. 177-78; 'Josephus' Portrait of Saul', pp. 64-66; 'Josephus' Portrait of David', pp. 139-40; 'Josephus as an Apologist to the Greco-Roman World', pp. 85-89; and my 'Use, Authority and Exegesis of Mikra', pp. 488-90.

versions[16]), Josephus (*Ant.* 5.189) has Ehud (whom he calls Judes) very cleverly plan his exploit to kill Eglon by becoming familiar with him, courting (θεραπεύων, 'paying respect', 'rendering homage', 'flattering', 'being obsequious') and cajoling (ὑπερχόμενος, 'approaching someone subserviently or flatteringly') him with presents, whereby he managed to endear himself to those attending the king. Again, in cleverness reminiscent of Odysseus in the episode with Polyphemus the Cyclops, Ehud (*Ant.* 5.191), in an extra-biblical touch, arranges to fall into conversation[17] with the king and even gets the king to order his henchmen to depart so that they may be alone. One is reminded of the similar tactics successfully employed by Antipater (*War* 1.126), who through many cajoling presents (δώροις ὑπελθών) managed to induce King Aretas of Arabia to furnish an army to reinstate Hyrcanus. The most outstanding example of the successful use of such tactics is to be seen in Agrippa I (*Ant.* 18.167), who spent money in paying court to Gaius Caligula, with whom he consequently rose to higher favor. Furthermore, the fact that Ehud is able (*Ant.* 5.191) to engage Eglon in conversation (ὁμιλία—the word implies confidential discussion or personal talk) and thus to divert the king's attention is a clear indication of mental acuity.

The virtue of courage and skill in battle is stressed by Josephus in a number of additions to the biblical narrative,[18] especially since the Jews

16. See S. Jellicoe, *The Septuagint and Modern Study* (Oxford: Clarendon Press, 1968), pp. 280-83. From the fact that Josephus here uses the plural for 'gifts' one may infer that he employed the Septuagint text in his paraphrase of the book of Judges. However, in his paraphrase of the very same verse of Judges Josephus (*Ant.* 5.188) says that Ehud was superior with his left hand and therefrom derived all his strength, which would seem to accord with the Hebrew text (Judg. 3.15), which states that Ehud had a shriveled right hand, whereas the Septuagint, in both major versions, says that he used both hands alike (ἀμφοτεροδέξιον).

17. To be sure, the Latin version reads for the phrase 'fell into conversation' that Eglon sought his solitude (retreat, secrecy, retirement) (*eius secretum*); but the Greek ὁμιλίαν, 'conversation', is definitely the *lectio difficilior* and is to be preferred here.

18. See my 'Abraham the General in Josephus'; Isaac (*Ant.* 1.232); 'Josephus' Portrait of Jacob', pp. 110-12; 'Josephus' Portrait of Joseph', pp. 400-401; 'Josephus' Portrait of Moses', pp. 13-28; Phineas (*Ant.* 4.152-53); 'Josephus' Portrait of Joshua', pp. 358-61; Gideon (*Ant.* 5.217-18); 'Josephus' Version of Samson', pp. 179-89; 'Josephus' Portrait of Samuel', pp. 122-24; 'Josephus' Portrait of Saul', pp. 66-79; 'Josephus' Portrait of David', pp. 141-47; Joab (*Ant.* 7.13, 16, 126, 129); Asa (*Ant.* 8.315); Jehu (*Ant.* 9.118); Josiah (*Ant.* 10.76-77); and 'Use, Authority and Exegesis of Mikra', pp. 490-91.

had been reproached with cowardice by such of their critics as Apollonius Molon (*ap. Against Apion* 2.148). Josephus himself was especially sensitive on this point because he himself had been subjected to such a charge (*War* 3.358). Moreover, as a military general himself in the great Jewish war against the Romans, Josephus was particularly interested in military details and consequently often adds data not found in the Bible.

Hence it is significant that whereas the Bible (Judg. 3.15) introduces Ehud in general terms as a 'deliverer' (*moshia'*), Josephus (*Ant.* 5.188) refers to him as most brave (ἀνδρειότατος) in daring (τολμῆσαι) and most able (δυνατώτατος, 'most mighty') to use his body for the accomplishment of deeds (ἔργα). We may note that though, as we have remarked, many of the biblical heroes are, in extra-biblical additions, referred to as brave, only four others—Joshua (*Ant.* 3.49), Abimelech the son of Gideon (*Ant.* 7.142), Sibbechai the Hushathite (*Ant.* 7.301), and Elhanan the son of Jaare-oregim (*Ant.* 7.302)—are referred to in the superlative as 'most brave'.

As to daring, the verb τολμάω, 'to dare', which is used in both a positive and a negative sense, is used approvingly of Abraham (*Ant.* 1.155), Samson (*Ant.* 5.298), Jonathan the son of King Saul (*Ant.* 6.111), and David (*Ant.* 6.210 and, by implication, 6.177), Daniel (*Ant.* 10.256). It is also used of a certain Eleazar, who is described (*War* 7.196) as a youth of daring enterprise who stimulated his comrades by frequently making fearful havoc of the Romans at Machaerus, one of the last fortresses to fall to the Romans after the destruction of the Temple. In reading this passage about Ehud's daring exploit Josephus's Roman audience might well have thought of a similar exploit by the youths Nisus and Euryalus (Virgil, *Aeneid* 9.176-502), who boldly entered the enemy lines in their search for their leader Aeneas; but their exploit is solely military in nature, and moreover they receive advance permission from the Trojan chiefs before setting out, whereas Ehud's mission involves clever planning and, so far as we can tell, is undertaken without prior consultation.

As for the description of Ehud as δυνατώτατος, 'most mighty', this epithet is found in Josephus of only one other biblical figure, Jephthah (*Ant.* 5.257), who is described as a mighty man by reason of the valor of his forefathers (διὰ τὴν πρῴαν ἀρετήν) as also of his own troop of mercenaries which he maintained himself. Jephthah, we may add, is, like Ehud, a judge of the Israelites; and, in a number of additions to the

Bible, Josephus (e.g., *Ant.* 5.258, 260, 261) stresses his qualities of leadership.

One might perhaps fault Ehud as less than brave for the detail, added by Josephus (*Ant.* 5.192) that at the crucial point when he is just about to plunge his dagger into Ehud he is beset by fear; but a closer examination of Josephus's text reveals that it is not cowardice that is the source of Ehud's fear. He certainly is determined to go through with the attempt to assassinate Eglon; his only fear is that he may miss inflicting a mortal blow.[19]

4. *The Rehabilitation of Eglon*

Ehud's assassination of Eglon presented Josephus with at least two problems of major importance. In the first place, Josephus is very sensitive to the charge, found not only in writers such as Lysimachus (*ap.* Josephus, *Against Apion* 1.309), Tacitus (*Histories* 5.5.1), and Juvenal (14.103-104) that Jews hate non-Jews, but even in sympathetic writers such as Hecataeus of Abdera (*ap.* Diodorus 40.3.4), who describes the Jewish way of life as 'somewhat unsocial' (ἀπάνθρωπόν τινα) and hostile to foreigners (μισόξενον). In his response Josephus points with pride to the fact that two of Abraham's sons fought alongside Heracles and that the daughter of one of them actually married Heracles himself (*Ant.* 1.241), that Abraham felt compassion for the Sodomites (*Ant.* 1.176), that Joseph sold grain not only to Egyptians but to all people (*Ant.* 2.94), that Solomon, in dedicating the Temple, asked that God grant the prayers not only of Jews but also of foreigners, and that, indeed, Jews are forbidden by the Torah itself to speak ill of the gods of others out of respect for the very word 'god' (*Ant.* 4.207, *Against Apion* 2.237, following the Septuagint version of Exod. 22.28).

But Josephus goes further in his rehabilitation of non-Jewish leaders. Thus, by shifting the focus from Balaam's personality to the historical, military, and political confrontation between Israel and her enemies, he gives a relatively unbiased portrait of Balaam (see, for example, *Ant.* 4.105, 106, 112), the pagan prophet who sought to curse Israel, especially when we compare his version with that of Philo, the rabbinic tradition, the New Testament, and the book of Numbers itself. Even

---

19. In the Latin version (*Ant.* 5.192) Ehud is beset with fear lest he not be able to strike Eglon 'most bravely' (*fortissime*), but this seems most likely to be a paraphrase, rather than a translation, of the Greek.

Nebuchadnezzar, who was responsible for the destruction of the First Temple, emerges more favorably, inasmuch as Josephus omits the cruel decree which Nebuchadnezzar issued (Dan. 3.29) in which he declared that anyone who spoke a word against the Jewish God should be torn limb from limb and considerably tones down (*Ant.* 10.217) the gruesome picture of Nebuchadnezzar behaving like an animal. Likewise, one might well be critical of Darius for signing his name to an edict arbitrarily forbidding any petition directed toward any god or man for thirty days (Dan. 6.7, 9); but Josephus (*Ant.* 10.254) protects Darius's reputation by explaining that Darius had approved of the decree only because he had been misled by his advisers. Likewise, Josephus (*Ant.* 1.165) comes to the defense of the Pharaoh who took Sarai into his house (Gen. 12.15) by remarking (*Ant.* 1.165) that once he discovered her identity he apologized to Abram, stressing that he had wished to contract a legitimate marriage alliance with her and not to outrage her in a transport of passion. Moreover, we admire Joseph's Pharaoh much more, inasmuch as he expresses his appreciation to Joseph with much greater enthusiasm (*Ant.* 2.89). Even the Pharaoh of the Exodus emerges more favorably, since, in Josephus's version (*Ant.* 2.201), the blame is placed not on Pharaoh but rather on the Egyptians, who are described as a voluptuous and lazy people.

   It is, therefore, significant that in mentioning King Eglon's subjugation of the Israelites Josephus not only castigates the Israelites for doing what was evil in the sight of the Lord (Judg. 3.12) but also blames them for their lack of government (ἀναρχίας) and for their failure to obey the laws (*Ant.* 5.185), a theme that is mentioned in Josephus's description (*Ant.* 5.179) of the state of the Israelites just before the judgeship of Keniaz, Ehud's predecessor, and repeated in Josephus's account (*Ant.* 5.198) of the behavior of the Israelites shortly after the death of Ehud. Josephus then adds that it is in his contempt (καταφρονήσαντα) for their disorder (ἀκοσμίας) that Eglon makes war upon them.[20] Significantly, in the Bible (Judg. 3.12) Eglon is depicted as the means by

---

20. The Latin version of the *Antiquities* (5.186) speaks of Eglon as *despiciens inhonestam conversationem*, that is, having contempt for the shameful (dishonorable, disgraceful) intercourse of the Israelites, but it seems unlikely that Eglon would despise the Israelites for their intercourse with foreign women. Likewise, the Latin version states that Eglon *praesumeret*, that is, took the initiative, in attacking the Israelites; but it seems more likely that he was reacting to the chaos of the Israelites rather than that he made a preemptive strike.

which God punishes the Israelites for their neglect of him, whereas in Josephus (*Ant.* 5.186) Eglon acts on his own, with no mention of God's role, in taking advantage of the Israelites' anarchy.[21]

If, then, Eglon inflicts bodily injury (κακώσεως)[22] upon the Israelites, it is occasioned, according to Josephus, in an extra-biblical comment, by the anarchy (ἀναρχία, *Ant.* 6.84) which prevailed after Joshua's death and which represents the very opposite of the aristocratic rule that prevailed under Moses and Joshua and that was restored after the eighteen years of anarchy. Josephus equates such anarchy with disorder (ἀκοσμίαν) and contempt (ὕβριν) of God and the laws, as we see in his remark (*Ant.* 5.255) that after the judgeship of Jair the Israelites degenerated to such a state before the appearance of another true leader, Jephthah.

The theme of the dreadful consequences of anarchy and civil strife pervades much of Josephus's paraphrase of the *Antiquities*, as we see particularly in his editorial remarks about the builders of the Tower of Babel (*Ant.* 1.117), the rebellion of Korah (*Ant.* 4.12), the seduction of the Hebrew youth by the Midianite women (*Ant.* 4.140), and the disaster brought on by Jeroboam's secession (*Ant.* 8.205). Indeed, it is this lawlessness (παρανομίας) which, according to Josephus (*Ant.* 8.314) in an editorial comment, brought about the destruction of the kings of Israel within a short space of time. This theme would have struck a responsive chord in many of Josephus's readers, who might well be acquainted with the terrible consequences of the lawlessness (ἀνομία) brought on by the plague in Athens (Thucydides 2.53.1). Moreover, the Romans, who themselves had experienced a century of constantly recurring civil strife from the struggle of the Senate against the Gracchi through the strife of Sulla against Marius, of Caesar against Pompey, of Brutus against Antony, and of Antony against Octavian, and who had a great tradition of respect for law going back at least to the Twelve Tables, would surely have appreciated such an emphasis on the dire consequences of civil strife.

21. For other examples of the diminution of the role of God in Josephus's paraphrase of the Bible see my 'Use, Authority and Exegesis of Mikra', pp. 503-507.

22. Thackeray, *Josephus*, p. 85, translates οὐδὲν τῆς εἰς τὸ πλῆθος κακώσεως παρέλιπεν as 'he ruthlessly molested the people', but this would be at variance with Josephus's care to avoid downgrading non-Jews and especially rulers. The more literal—and more likely—translation would seem to be that 'he omitted nothing of bodily injury (κακώσεως, 'devastation', 'ruin') against the multitude'.

Furthermore, one might almost say that the theme of the dreadful effects of anarchy and civil strife is the central motif of the *Jewish War*. Thus we may note, for example, the striking coincidence that the phrase which Josephus uses to describe Jeroboam's sedition, namely that he was 'ambitious of great things' (μεγάλων ἐπιθυμητὴς πραγμάτων, *Ant.* 8.209) is similar to that which he uses to describe the arch-revolutionary, John of Gischala (ἐπιθυμήσας μεγάλων, *War* 2.587), and his literary arch-rival, Justus of Tiberias, who was 'ambitious for newer things' (νεωτέρων...ἐπεθύμει πραγμάτων, *Life* 36).

Moreover, Josephus is particularly concerned to emphasize the importance of showing respect for the legitimate ruler of a nation, even if that ruler may be guilty of performing reprehensible acts. One may readily understand why Josephus adopts this position, inasmuch as he was recipient of a multitude of favors from Roman autocrats. We may see this tendency particularly in his portraits of two arch-rogues, Ahab and Manasseh. In the former case, Ahab is at least partly exculpated in the incident with Naboth because he had used mild words with Naboth and yet had been insulted (*Ant.* 8.356). Moreover, the fact that the Jews, and Josephus in particular, had been accused of being cowards makes all the more meaningful the presentation of Ahab as a great tactician and a brave leader who is, above all, concerned for his people (*Ant.* 8.370, 415). Finally, in an editorial comment, Josephus goes out of his way to absolve Ahab of blame for listening to a false prophet; rather it is inexorable and inevitable Fate that is blamed (*Ant.* 8.409). Likewise, in his portrayal of Manasseh, we are told, in details that go beyond the biblical account, of Manasseh's major achievements in improving the city of Jerusalem (*Ant.* 10.44); again, in an extra-biblical addition, we hear that the degree of Manasseh's repentance was such that he was accounted a blessed and enviable man (*Ant.* 10.45). Hence, we have parallels for the omission in Josephus's account of derogatory elements found in the biblical narrative.

In the case of Eglon, we may note that the Bible (Judg. 3.13) remarks that he formed an alliance with Ammon and Amalek; this would surely diminish, at least for Josephus's Jewish readers, their regard for Eglon, inasmuch as the Ammonites were almost constantly at war with the Israelites and inasmuch as especially the Amalekites were the people who, though unprovoked, had attacked the Israelites during the latter's sojourn in the desert after the Exodus. Josephus, realizing that mention of such an alliance would demean the status of Eglon, very carefully omits all mention of it.

Alter[23] suggests that the Bible is actually poking fun at Eglon's stupidity, but Josephus has too much regard for legitimate rulers, as we have noted, to give such an impression. We may note that Josephus totally omits reference to the fact, which might well be a source of ridicule, that Eglon was very fat (Judg. 3.17), as well as to the fact that when Ehud kills him the fat closes upon the blade (Judg. 3.22).[24] Moreover, whereas the Bible (Judg. 3.22) mentions the gruesome detail that when Ehud thrust his sword into Eglon's belly his excrement came out, Josephus (*Ant.* 5.193) omits this indelicate remark. In particular, we may note that whereas the biblical pericope mentions that Eglon was defecating (Judg. 3.24),[25] and therefore was not interrupted by his servants, Josephus (*Ant.* 5.193), finding such a detail unseemly for a monarch, explains the failure of the servants to come to his aid sooner by remarking that they thought that he had fallen asleep.

5. *'Improvements' in the Story: Clarifications, Increased Suspense and Drama*

One basic reason for Josephus's writing of a paraphrase of the Scripture was that he sought to clear up obscurities in the text.[26] Thus, it is not

23. R. Alter, 'Sacred History and Prose Fiction', in R.E. Friedman (ed.), *The Creation of Sacred Literature: Composition and Redaction of the Biblical Text* (Berkeley: University of California Press, 1981), pp. 19-20.

24. To be sure, in the former passage (Judg. 3.17), the Septuagint, in both major versions, reads that Eglon was ἀστεῖος (that is, 'elegant', 'charming', 'refined', 'handsome'); but in the latter passage (Judg. 3.22), it is clear that Eglon is very fat, since the Greek, again in both versions, reads that when Ehud plunged his weapon into him, the fat (στέαρ) closed in upon the blade.

25. The Hebrew text reads *mesikh hu' eth ragelav* ('he is covering his feet'), but the Targum Jonathan, basing itself on *b. Yevamoth* 103a, understands this as a euphemism for moving one's bowels. The Septuagint (version B) reads: ἀποκενοῖ τοὺς πόδας, that is, 'he is draining [exhausting] his feet', clearly a euphemism for evacuating. Version A reads: ἀποχωρήσει τοῦ κοιτῶνος, that is, 'he is sitting in the retreat of the bed-chamber'; but the word ἀποχωρήσει also means 'voidance' and is used especially of excretions.

26. Thus it is by no means clear what God means when he says (Gen. 1.6), 'Let there be a firmament in the midst of the waters, and let it divide the waters from the waters'. Josephus (*Ant.* 1.30) clarifies the matter by noting that what God did was to set the heaven above the universe and to congeal ice around it, thus explaining, as the

194   *Pursuing the Text: Studies in Honor of Ben Zion Wacholder*

clear from the biblical text (Judg. 3.16) whether Ehud had previously
not consulted the Israelites before undertaking his plan to assassinate
Eglon or whether he acted in consultation with the Israelites, inasmuch
as the text simply states that the Israelites sent tribute through him and
then declares, without explaining the connection, that Ehud made a
sword for himself. Josephus clarifies this matter by stating (*Ant.* 5.194)
that after assassinating Eglon Ehud reported the matter secretly to the
Israelites at Jericho and exhorted them to assert their liberty. The fact
that they welcomed the news would make it likely that they were
previously unaware of Ehud's plan.

As the story stands in the Bible there are a number of additional
difficulties; indeed, as Halpern[27] has noted, crowded into the space of a
few verses is the highest concentration of rare and unique vocabulary in
the literature of ancient Israel. Moreover, there are a number of apparent
implausibilities.[28] In the first place, one wonders why the biblical narrator (Judg. 3.19) states that after presenting the tribute Ehud turned back
from the sculptured stones (*pesilim*, 'quarries') near Gilgal. This would
seem to be a long and useless journey, proceeding from Eglon's capital,
perhaps Medeba, and then back over the Jordan to Gilgal, and then
returning to the capital again. So considerable is this problem that
Wiese[29] adopts the radical solution of no less than surgery in postulating
that the first half of this verse is an addition by a learned scribe.
Kraeling, followed by Rösel,[30] defends the text by asserting that since at
the time that he presented the tribute the king was likely to be attended

Bible does not, the origin of rain. Another obscurity which Josephus clarifies is the
'strange' fire (Lev. 10.1) which Nadab and Abihu, the sons of Aaron, offered and on
account of which they suffered death. The rabbis (*Lev. R.* 20.8-9), noting the juxtaposition in the Bible of the warning to priests not to partake of wine and strong drink
before entering the sanctuary (Lev. 10.9), suggest that they were intoxicated when
they offered the fire. Josephus is unique in presenting the rationalization that they
brought on the altar not the incense which Moses had commanded but what they had
used previously.

27. B. Halpern, *The First Historians: The Hebrew Bible and History* (San
Francisco: Harper, 1988), p. 40.
28. See E.G. Kraeling, 'Difficulties in the Story of Ehud', *JBL* 54 (1935),
pp. 205-10; H.N. Rösel, 'Zur Ehud-Erzählung', *ZAW* 89 (1977), pp. 270-72.
29. K.M. Wiese, *Zur Literarkritik des Buches der Richter* (Stuttgart, 1926),
pp. 4-5.
30. Kraeling, 'Difficulties', pp. 206-207; Rösel, 'Zur Ehud-Erzählung', pp. 270-
71.

by enough armed guards to impress the Israelite delegation with his power, Ehud could not possibly hope to see the king in private. The trip to Gilgal was necessary in order to receive a divine message from the *pesilim*, and the king, in his eagerness to hear what he had learned there, readily admitted him to a private interview. But, we may remark, the text says not that Ehud went to Gilgal but merely that he went from Gilgal, nor is there any indication that this was the site of an oracle or that the *pesilim* were oracular stones.

A second difficulty is to be found in the fact that Ehud (Judg. 3.19), after returning from Gilgal tells the king that he has a secret errand, whereupon those that stood near the king left; but immediately there-after (Judg. 3.20) we read that Ehud came to him and again told the king that he had a message for him. In verse 19 Eglon is in a large audience-chamber, but in the next verse he is in a private room. One solution is to say that Eglon dismissed his retinue and then received Ehud alone; another is to say that the first statement was spoken by an attendant; but, as Moore[31] points out, neither of these solutions is exegetically plausible and he resolves the problem by suggesting that we have two separate sources here. Kraeling[32] resolves the problem by assuming that the storyteller is here somewhat sloppy and has left a few things to the imagination of his readers, notably that the king retired to his private chambers and that Ehud was conducted there by the king's servants.

A third and truly major difficulty is to explain how Ehud managed to escape. Glaser[33] postulates that there was a small chamber (Judg. 3.24) within the upper chamber and that this small chamber was a privy, and that Ehud made his escape by sliding down through the toilet. But why should Eglon be imagined as having locked the door upon leaving the room to go to the alleged privy? Indeed, the fact that Ehud managed to get out unsuspected would seem to indicate that he came down the stairs normally.[34] So puzzling is this question of how Ehud managed to escape that in the most recent treatment of this problem Halpern[35]

31. G.F. Moore, *A Critical and Exegetical Commentary on Judges* (New York: Charles Scribner's Sons, 1910), pp. 95-96.

32. Kraeling, 'Difficulties', p. 207.

33. O. Glaser, 'Zur Erzählung von Ehud und Eglon', *ZDPV* 55 (1932), pp. 81-82.

34. So Rösel, 'Zur Ehud-Erzählung', pp. 271-72.

35. Halpern, *First Historians*, pp. 43-60.

devotes no fewer than eighteen pages to solving the mystery.

Fourthly, why, as Halpern[36] appositely remarks, did the king's courtiers fetch a key and unlock the doors that the key had locked (Judg. 3.25)? Why did they not check the unlocked access that Ehud had used?

What is most remarkable about these four difficulties is that all of them are resolved by Josephus by simply omitting these details: there is no mention of the trip to Gilgal; there is no second address of Ehud to the king; there is no indication that the small chamber was a privy; and there is no suggestion as to how Ehud escaped other than that he locked the door as he left.

We may also wonder how Ehud was able to hide a two-edged sword (*ḥerev*, Judg. 3.16) a cubit (about eighteen inches) in length under his clothing.[37] The Septuagint, in both major versions, to be sure, reduces the sword to a large knife (μάχαιρα) a span (σπιθαμή, about nine inches) long; but Josephus (*Ant.* 5.190) resolves the problem of credibility by reducing it to a dagger (ξιφίδιον) and without indicating its length at all.

If we wonder why Eglon should have been so foolish as to trust a member of a subdued tribute-paying nation in private conference with no one else present, Josephus (*Ant.* 5.191) explains that he had won his confidence with frequent gifts, he had come back with an allegedly divine interpretation of a dream, and he had managed to engage the king in a conversation.

Still, we may suppose that Eglon must have shrieked so that his many attendants should have heard him when he was being assailed, especially since, according to the biblical text (Judg. 3.21) Ehud's thrust was into his fat belly. In such a case death would have been delayed considerably. In Josephus's version (*Ant.* 5.193) the death blow is inflicted not in the belly but in his heart, which certainly would have hastened his end.

Moreover, if we wonder why the guards (Judg. 3.24) would have supposed that Eglon was defecating for so long, Josephus (*Ant.* 5.193)

---

36. Halpern, *First Historians*, p. 44.

37. This problem is cited by Rösel, 'Zur Ehud-Erzählung', p. 270, who concludes that it was a pointed weapon (which works more rapidly and leaves fewer traces), not perhaps a sickle-shaped sword; but neither the Hebrew *ḥerev* nor the Greek μάχαιρα lends itself to such an interpretation, whereas Josephus's ξιφίδιον seems much more likely.

has a much more reasonable answer, namely that they supposed that he had fallen asleep.

One means by which Josephus seeks to 'improve' upon the biblical narrative is through providing better motivation and through increasing the plausibility of events.[38] Thus we may wonder how Ehud had come to be so familiar with King Eglon as to be trusted by him. Josephus (*Ant.* 5.188) adds to the biblical narrative in noting that he lived in Jericho,[39] the capital of Eglon's kingdom, and that (*Ant.* 5.189) he had become familiar with the king prior to the assassination attempt. As to why the guards did not suspect that something was wrong when they did not hear from the king, Josephus (*Ant.* 5.190) explains that it was summer-time and that the guards were relaxed both because of the heat and because they were gone to lunch.

Josephus also tries to increase the dramatic interest of the biblical narrative. In the instance of our pericope, the Bible (Judg. 3.20) very

38. Thus, whereas Manoah's desire in the Bible (Judg. 13.8) to recall the angel is not well motivated, Josephus's elaboration (*Ant.* 5.280) makes it more plausible, for he has Manoah's wife entreat God to send the angel again so that her husband may see him and thus allay the suspicions arising from his jealousy of the angel. Similarly, in order to remove the implausibility of the narrative, Delilah in Josephus (*Ant.* 5.310), full of feminine wiles, uses Samson's love for her as a weapon against him; thus she keeps saying to him that she takes it ill that he has so little confidence in her affection for him as to withhold from her what she desired to know, 'as though', she adds with typical strategy, 'she would not conceal what she knew must in his interests not be divulged'. Likewise, whereas in the Bible (2 Kgs 10.1-3) we are not told why Jehu sent letters to the rulers of Samaria, and we must conjecture as to the motive from the result, Josephus (*Ant.* 9.126) spells out the motive, telling us that Jehu sent these letters because he wished to test the feelings of the Samarians toward himself—a wise move, indeed, inasmuch as if they had not been well disposed toward him he would have had to plan a military campaign against them. Again, the reader of the biblical narrative might well ask how Mordecai was able to discover the conspiracy of Bigthan and Teresh against King Ahasuerus (Esth. 2.22). Josephus (*Ant.* 11.207) has a plausible explanation which is found in no other source, namely, that the plot was discovered by a certain Jew, Barnabazos, the servant of one of the eunuchs, who, in turn, revealed it to Mordecai. Furthermore, the reader might well ask how Harbonah was able to learn (Esth. 7.9) about the gallows which Haman had prepared for Mordecai. Josephus (*Ant.* 11.261 and 266) explains this by noting that he had learned this from one of Haman's servants when Harbonah had gone to summon him to Esther's second banquet.

39. In the Latin version (*Ant.* 5.188) it is Eglon, and not Ehud, who is residing in Jericho.

prosaically has Ehud tell Eglon that he has a message from God to him. Aside from the fact that it would seem implausible that a pagan king would be so gullible as to allow himself to be deceived thus, there is nothing very original or exciting in such a device. In Josephus's version (*Ant.* 5.193) the device is much more exciting; there, as in the Bible, he has a message from God, but Ehud tells Eglon that he has a dream to disclose to him by commandment of God. At this point, excited with joy at news of this dream, Eglon, obese though he is, actually leaps up from his throne, whereupon Ehud has the opportunity that he sought to stab him with his dagger. We may note Josephus's interest in dreams in that he records no fewer than thirty-five dreams (and their truth and fulfillment in every case). We may further remark that in addition to this dream mentioned by Ehud he adds to the biblical narrative that of Amram (*Ant.* 2.212-216) exhorting him not to despair of the future and predicting the birth of Moses and that of Nathan (*Ant.* 7.147), in which God found fault with David for his treatment of Uriah and his marriage with Bathsheba.[40] In view of the fact that there is ample evidence of protest against oneiromancy, as we see, for example, in Ben Sira (31.1ff.) and the Letter of Aristeas (213-216), both of which denounce the belief in dreams, we may explain this extraordinary emphasis on dreams in Josephus as arising from the fact that, as Gnuse[41] has suggested, Josephus was addressing a pagan Roman audience, to whom dreams were very important. Josephus's expansiveness in his accounts of dreams may well have arisen from his desire to demonstrate his virtuosity as an interpreter of dreams (like his namesake he had attained renown in this field [*Life* 208-10; *War* 3.351-54]).

There is also increased drama in Josephus's portrayal (*Ant.* 5.195) of the reaction of Eglon's courtiers to the discovery of his corpse. In the Bible (Judg. 3.25) we read only that they opened the doors of the upper room and found that the king had fallen down to the earth dead. Josephus (*Ant.* 5.195) adds to the drama by stating that when they found the corpse they stood in helpless perplexity (ἀμηχανίᾳ, 'want of resources').

There is a further increase of drama in Josephus's description (*Ant.* 5.196) of the rout of the Moabites that followed. Whereas the Bible

40.   Among post-biblical figures Josephus adds the dreams of Jaddus, Theopompus, Hyrcanus, Herod, Matthias, Archelaus, Glaphyra, Monobazus, and Stratonice.

41.   R. Gnuse, 'Dream Reports in the Writings of Flavius Josephus', *RB* 96 (1980), p. 360. See my discussion in 'Josephus' Portrait of Joseph', pp. 394-400.

(Judg. 3.29) says merely that the Israelites killed ten thousand strong, able-bodied Moabites and that none escaped, Josephus (*Ant.* 5.196) adds poignant details: some were massacred on the spot; the rest took flight to seek safety in Moab, whereupon the Israelites pursued them and at the ford of the Jordan massacred multitudes of them.[42]

One of the ways in which Josephus heightens interest in his narrative is by increasing suspense. In particular, there are several instances of added suspense in Josephus's versions of the Joseph,[43] Esther[44] and Daniel narratives.[45] In the narrative of the assassination of Eglon

42. Cf. similar dramatic details added by Josephus in his account of Abraham's rout of the Assyrians (*Ant.* 1.177) and in his version of David's surprise attack upon the Amalekites. See my 'Abraham the General in Josephus', pp. 46-47; and 'Josephus' Portrait of David', pp. 166-67.

43. In the case of Joseph, for example, whereas in the Bible (Gen. 37.11) we learn merely that the brothers envied Joseph, Josephus (*Ant.* 2.12) says that the brothers understood that Joseph's dreams predicted that Joseph would exercise power and majesty and supremacy over them; however, the brothers revealed nothing of this to Joseph, pretending that the dreams were unintelligible to them. There is likewise considerable build-up of suspense in Josephus's version of the search for Joseph's cup in the sacks of his brothers. In the Bible (Gen. 44.11-12) each of the brothers, we are told, opened his sack, and the search proceeded from the oldest to the youngest; Josephus (*Ant.* 2.133) adds to this narrative by describing the feeling of relief that each felt when the cup was not found in his sack.

44. There is a heightening of dramatic suspense in Josephus's introduction of Harbonah at an earlier point than he appears in the biblical narrative. In the Bible it is not until Haman has been pointed out by Esther as the one who sought to destroy her people that Harbonah remarks (Esth. 7.9) that Haman had also built gallows for Mordecai; and the king thereupon orders Haman to be hanged thereon. In Josephus (*Ant.* 11.261) Harbonah, one of Esther's eunuchs sent to hasten Haman's coming to the banquet, notices the gallows, learns that they ironically have been prepared for the queen's uncle Mordecai, and for the time being holds his peace. As an instrument of storytelling such a detail builds up suspense, and Harbonah's later revelation is therefore all the more effective. See my 'Hellenizations in Josephus' Version of Esther', p. 153.

45. Thus there is added drama in Josephus's version of Daniel's request that the execution of the wise men be delayed. In the Bible (Dan. 2.16) Daniel asks the king to give him 'time'. In Josephus's version (*Ant.* 10.198) the drama is increased in that he asks merely for one night and, furthermore, in that Nebuchadnezzar, we are told, actually orders the execution to be postponed until he learns what Daniel has promised to disclose. One is reminded of Medea's request to Creon (Euripides, *Medea* 340-41) to allow her to remain in Corinth for just one day so that she might consider where to live in her exile and where to seek support for her children. Another

Josephus has added to the suspense, as well as enhanced the reader's admiration for Ehud's ingenuity by building up more effectively to the assassination itself. In particular, we have the added detail, noted above, that Ehud (*Ant.* 5.189) won the confidence of Eglon by courting and cajoling him with presents. The suspense is built up by the added ironic fact (*Ant.* 5.190) that it was while he was actually bringing these gifts to Eglon that he secretly girt a dagger about his right thigh. There is further added suspense in that Ehud and the king now fall into conversation. Lastly, we have the point, unmentioned in the biblical version, which adds a final touch of suspense and which also gives a more human flavor to the story, namely (*Ant.* 5.192) that fear entered into Ehud lest he strike amiss and not deal a mortal blow. It is at this point that Ehud conceives the brilliant device by which he gets the obese king to rise, namely by telling him that he has a dream to disclose to him by commandment of God. There is further suspense in the fact that, according to Josephus, in an extra-biblical comment (*Ant.* 5.195), Eglon's courtiers remained ignorant of his fate for a long time before they discovered his body.[46]

6. *Summary*

The fact that Josephus devotes so much space to the episode of Eglon and Ehud indicates how significant this was to him. Because he realized how important physical appearance was for a hero he omits the statement that Ehud had a shriveled right hand and instead states that he

case where Josephus builds up suspense is the scene where Belshazzar seeks to find the interpretation of the handwriting on the wall. In the biblical version (Dan. 5.7, 9) the king calls upon his wise men, but they fail to understand the writing. In Josephus (*Ant.* 10.236), as we have noted, there are two stages, the first when the Magi are called in and the second when he offers a third of his realm to the successful interpreter. In the second stage, as Josephus reports it, the Magi come in ever greater numbers and make ever greater efforts, all without success. There is further suspense when Belshazzar's queen begs him to send for Daniel and so condemn the ignorance of those who cannot read the writing on the wall. Josephus (*Ant.* 10.238) helps build up the suspense of dire foreboding with an unscriptural detail, namely that the queen asks her husband to call for Daniel even though 'a dark (σκυθρωπόν, 'somber', 'distressing', 'depressing', 'calamitous', 'catastrophic') outlook may be indicated by God.

46. I am grateful to my student, H.M. Sragow, for several fine insights in connection with this essay.

was superior with his left hand. He adds considerably to Ehud's stature by asserting that he held the office of governor for eighty years, longer than any other judge. We see Ehud's quality of leadership in his success in exhorting his fellow Israelites to assert their liberty—a leitmotif in the history of the Jewish people as Josephus sees it. Josephus was definitely sensitive to the charge of trickery that might have been made against Ehud, but inasmuch as the latter acts in the name of liberty this is seen in a different light. On the contrary, his cleverness in courting Eglon and in engaging him in conversation would be admired. Because the Jews had been reproached with cowardice it is particularly effective that Josephus, in an extra-biblical addition, describes Ehud as most brave in daring and most mighty in the use of his body for the accomplishment of deeds.

Josephus is eager not to cast aspersions on non-Jews, especially their leaders. Hence, instead of blaming Eglon for subjugating the Israelites he places the onus upon the Israelites themselves for their anarchy and for their failure to obey the laws—another common theme in Josephus. For the same reason he also omits such disparaging elements as Eglon's obesity and his defecating.

Josephus clarifies a number of obscurities in the biblical text. Thus he makes it clear that the Israelites were previously unaware of Ehud's plan to assassinate Eglon. Moreover, there are a number of difficulties and improbabilities in the biblical text, notably Ehud's apparently useless trip to the sculptured stones near Gilgal, the redundancy in having Ehud come twice to the king, the lack of a plausible explanation as to how Ehud managed to escape, and the failure of the king's courtiers to check the unlocked access that Ehud had used. In all of these cases Josephus resolves the problems by simply omitting these details. On the other hand, he satisfactorily explains how Eglon came to trust Ehud, namely because the latter had won his confidence with frequent gifts and because he had come to him with an allegedly divine interpretation of a dream—a detail which also increases the dramatic interest of the narrative. He plausibly explains that the reason why the king's guards did not suspect foul play was that they were relaxed on account of the summer heat and were away for lunch. Finally, Josephus has added to the suspense of the pericope by building up more effectively to the assassination itself, especially by noting that Ehud felt fear lest he strike amiss and not deal Eglon a mortal blow.

JOSEPHUS'S USE OF GREEK SOURCES FOR
BIBLICAL HISTORY

James E. Bowley

The sources used by Josephus for his magnum opus *Jewish Antiquities*
have occasioned a significant modern literature.[1] It is my goal in these
pages to begin to elucidate one aspect of this field, namely, Josephus's
explicit use of non-biblical sources for his retelling of biblical history in
the first 11 books of his *Antiquities*.

Benedictus Niese, the nineteenth-century editor of Josephus's works,
counted no less than fifty-five different authors of Greek writings mentioned by Josephus throughout his entire preserved literary output, most
of whom were not Jewish.[2] Modern scholars have deduced that a hand-
ful of these were in fact Greco-Jewish (or Samaritan) writers.[3] However,
for the purposes of this investigation it is unnecessary to separate these
from the pagan citations since the Jewish (or Samaritan) identity of these
few went unrecognized by Josephus himself, a point which has been
made by Ben Zion Wacholder, my esteemed and beloved teacher, in
whose honor I am privileged to write.[4]

---

1. Bibliographies on the subject can be found in L.H. Feldman, *Josephus and
Modern Scholarship (1937–1980)* (New York: de Gruyter, 1984), pp. 392-419 and
P. Bilde, *Josefus som historieskriver* (Copenhagen, 1984).
2. B. Niese, *Flavii Josephi Opera* (Berolini: Weidmannos, 1895), VII, p. 87.
3. *Sibylline Oracles* (*Ant.* 1.118). (Pseudo-)Hecataeus (*Ant.* 1.159; *Apion*
1.183). Demetrius, Philo the Elder, Eupolemus (*Apion* 1.218). Cleodemus Malchus
(*Ant.* 1.240-41) has been identified as Jewish (N. Walter, 'Fragmente jüdisch-
hellenistischer Historiker', in *Jüdische Schriften aus hellenistisch-römischer Zeit*, 1.2
[Gütersloh: Mohn, 1976], p. 116; A. Momigliano, *Alien Wisdom* [Cambridge, MA:
Harvard University Press, 1975], p. 93), Samaritan (J. Freudenthal, *Alexander
Polyhistor* [Breslau: Druck, 1874], pp. 132-33), and perhaps pagan (B.Z. Wacholder,
'Cleodemus-Malchus', *EncJud* 5 [1971], p. 603). For discussion of the identity of
these authors and bibliography see C. Holladay, *Fragments from Hellenistic Jewish
Authors* 1 (Chico, CA: Scholars Press, 1983).
4. B.Z. Wacholder, *Eupolemus* (Cincinnati: Hebrew Union College, 1974), p. 57.

Twenty-one different authors are acknowledged in Josephus's account of biblical history, contained in books 1–11 of *Jewish Antiquities*. While most (14) of these sources are cited only once, some are called upon more frequently so that the total number of citations is 36.[5]

Beyond these twenty-one authors, there were certainly sources which Josephus used which he did not name or credit in any way. The focus here, however, is restricted to those authors explicitly credited in Josephus's biblical history. Josephus's explicit use of pagan sources for his biblical history raises some interesting questions. How extensive are the pagan sources which bear on biblical history? What evidential weight does Josephus give the pagan texts vis-à-vis his biblical source? How does Josephus employ these authors and what can be inferred regarding his purposes in doing so? How did Josephus envision the effect these citations of Greek authors would have on the reception of biblical history among Greek readers? These questions can begin to be answered only by a careful analysis of the variety of ways in which Josephus employs pagan sources.

Most scholars who have discussed Josephus's citations of non-biblical sources in his biblical narrative have commented on the historian's apparent motives by saying that Greek authors are cited to 'confirm', 'reinforce',[6] 'supplement',[7] or 'bolster'[8] the biblical source. Such descriptions are not wrong; they are, however, imprecise generalizations which require a more precise description of Josephus's methods in bringing foreign texts to bear on his subject.[9]

---

5.   Acusilaus, 1.107. Alexander Polyhistor, 1.240. Berossus (six citations), 1.93-94; 1.107; 1.158-9; 10.18-20; 10.34; 10.219-26. Cleodemus-Malchus, 1.240. Diocles, 10.228. Dius, 8.144-49. Ephorus, 1.107. Hecataeus (two citations), 1.107; 1.158-59. Hellanicus, 1.107. Herodotus (three citations), 8.157; 8.253-62; 10.18-20. Hesiod 1.107. Hieronymus of Egypt (two citations), 1.93-4; 1.107. Hestiaeus (two citations), 1.107; 1.119. Manetho, 1.107. Megasthenes, 10.227. Menander (three citations), 8.144-9; 8.324; 9.283. Mnaseas, 1.93-94. Mochus, 1.107. Nicolaus of Damascus (four citations), 1.93-4; 1.107; 1.158-59; 7.101. Philostratus, 10.219 (227-28). The Sibyl, 1.118.

6.   T. Rajak, 'Josephus and the "Archaeology" of the Jews', *JJS* 33 (1982), p. 471.

7.   E. Schürer, *The History of the Jewish People in the Age of Jesus Christ* (rev. G. Vermes and F. Millar; Edinburgh: T. & T. Clark, 1973), I, p. 49.

8.   H. Attridge, in *Jewish Writings of the Second Temple Period* (Philadelphia: Fortress Press, 1984), p. 212.

9.   Without giving details or examples S. Cohen writes that the extra-biblical

Tessa Rajak, in attempting to determine whether the biblical section of *Jewish Antiquities* conforms to the Greco-Roman conception of *archaiologia*, is more forceful in her generalization that Josephus sees his biblical source as divinely inspired and consequently always consistent, harmonious, and impervious to criticism. Hence, extra-biblical authors are used 'not to check but only to reinforce' the biblical tradition. She concludes that, 'Josephus ransacked the obscure corners of Greek literature' but only because he thought 'the accumulation of author's names confirmed the infallibility of the Bible'.[10] I believe this generalization of Josephus's pagan citations to be a mischaracterization of the historian's methods and motives and I hope to show as much by a more detailed analysis of several of the texts in question.

My goal, then, is to articulate more precisely the manner in which Josephus employs his acknowledged extra-biblical sources for his narrative of biblical history, in order to get beyond the simple and obvious generalization that Josephus supplements his history with them. Upon a closer reading of these citations one will observe a more complex role.

Form

I shall first classify the 36 pagan citations which appear in Josephus's biblical history according to their form. Of the 36 citations, 15, or about 42 per cent, are represented by Josephus as direct *quotations* from the work of the cited author.[11] In a few of these cases the title and book number of the quoted author's work are actually given. In five of the 36 citations (14%) Josephus *paraphrases* or summarizes the content of a particular author's statement.[12] 16 (44%) are what I have termed *testimonia*.[13] That is, Josephus, after narrating a certain event, simply

sources are cited for support, explication and dramatization: *Josephus in Galilee and Rome* (Leiden: Brill, 1979), p. 37.

10. Rajak, 'Josephus', pp. 470-71.

11. Berossus, *Ant.* 1.93; 1.158; 10.20; 10.219-26. Dius, *Ant.* 8.144. Alexander Polyhistor and Cleodemus Malchus, *Ant.* 1.240. Hestiaeus, *Ant.* 1.119. Menander, *Ant.* 8.144; 8.324; 9.283. Nicolaus of Damascus, *Ant.* 1.94; 1.159; 7.101. The Sibyl, *Ant.* 1.118. S. Cohen distinguishes such direct quotations as 'citations' as distinct from other 'utilization' (*Josephus in Galilee*, p. 31).

12. Herodotus, *Ant.* 8.157; 8.253, 260; 10.18. Megasthenes, *Ant.* 10.227. Philostratus, *Ant.* 10.228.

13. Berossus, *Ant.* 1.107; 10.34. Hieronymus the Egyptian, *Ant.* 1.93; 1.107; Mnaseas, *Ant.* 1.93. Nicolaus, *Ant.* 1.107. Manetho, *Ant.* 1.107. Mochus, *Ant.* 1.107.

asserts that a named author has also written concerning the same event, or that a particular author concurs with Josephus's, and hence the Bible's, statements. In these cases we are supplied with only an author's name and, aside from Josephus's statement of agreement, we lack a meaningful report of the content of their writing as it relates to the topic at hand.

Content

The 36 citations in books 1-11 of *Jewish Antiquities* do not refer to many different aspects of Josephus's narrative. In fact, there are only 13 subjects in the course of the 11 books of Josephus's biblical history to which external sources are explicitly brought to bear. These subjects are delineated in the following chart:

Subject	*Antiquities* Reference	Cited Author(s)
1. The Flood	1.93-94	Berossus, Hieronymus, Mnaseas, Nicolaus
2. Longevity of Ancients	1.107-108	Nicolaus, Hieronymus, Berossus, Manetho, Mochus, Hestiaeus, Hesiod, Hecataeus, Hellanicus, Acusilaus, Ephorus
3. Tower of Babel	1.118-119	Sibylline Oracle, Hestiaeus
4. Abraham	1.158-160; 240	Berossus, Hecataeus, Nicolaus, Cleodemus-Malchus *apud* Alexander Polyhistor
5. Adados, king of Damascus	7.101	Nicolaus
6. Riddles of Solomon and Hiram	8.144-149	Menander, Dius
7. Egyptian kings	8.157	Herodotus
8. Isokos (Shishak)	8.253; 260	Herodotus
9. Levantine Drought	8.324	Menander
10. Shalmaneser's Invasion of Phoenicia	9.283-287	Menander
11. Sennacherib's Invasion of Egypt	10.18-20	Herodotus, Berossus
12. Baladas, King of Babylon	10.34	Berossus
13. Nebuchadnezzar	10.219-228	Berossus, Megasthenes, Diocles, Philostratus

Hestiaeus, *Ant.* 1.107. Hesiod, *Ant.* 1.107. Hecataeus, *Ant.* 1.107. Hellanicus, *Ant.* 1.107. Acusilaus, *Ant.* 1.107. Ephorus, *Ant.* 1.107. Diocles, *Ant.* 10.228. Hecataeus, *Ant.* 1.158.

A closer look at the contents will reveal that in only eight of the 36 citations does the non-biblical source, according to Josephus, refer to Jewish persons or the Jewish people.[14] In all remaining cases, the reference is only to neighboring peoples or their kings.

An obvious question must be raised: Do these citations referring to foreign peoples and kings have any real connection to Israelite affairs, which, after all, is the subject of Josephus's narrative? Except for the eight cases listed above, each citation's relevance to Jewish history is supplied by the historiographic acumen of Josephus.

This is illustrated by *Antiquities* 8.324 where Josephus quotes Menander, a Greek historian of Tyre, as follows:

> There was a drought in Ithobalos' reign, which lasted from the month of Hyperberetaios until the month of Hyperberetaios in the following year. But he made supplication to the gods, whereupon a heavy thunderstorm broke out. He it was who founded the city of Botrys in Phoenicia, and Auza in Libya. Thus these things Menander wrote, referring to the drought occurring in Ahab's reign, for it was in his time that Ithobalos was king of Tyre.

It is apparent that the second century BCE historian Menander did not actually refer to Israel, nor to king Ahab. Rather, Josephus (or an unnamed intermediate source) has identified the drought during the reign of Ahab in 1 Kings 17–18 with the drought in neighboring Phoenicia, as recorded by Menander. Regardless of the correctness of this identification, one can now understand more about how Josephus employs his sources and how he manages to include as many as he does. The Jewish historian was able to integrate external sources to his history by determining parallel chronologies of, in this case, Phoenician and Hebrew records even though the records themselves made no such connections.

Beyond showing the mutual content of disparate records, it also seems clear that Josephus was interested in giving his readers another point of view regarding the drought on which he was reporting. He certainly did not record the Phoenician polytheistic point of view because it, in Rajak's words, 'confirms the infallibility of the Bible'.[15] Josephus did not hesitate to cite his sources without censuring or criticizing the material

14.   Berossus, *Ant.* 1.58-59. Nicolaus, *Ant.* 1.94-95; 1.159-60; 7.101. Hecataeus, *Ant.* 1.159. Cleodemus Malchus (*apud* Alexander Polyhistor), *Ant.* 1.240. Menander and Dius, *Ant.* 8.144-49.

15.   Rajak, 'Josephus', p. 471.

that contradicted his own account or his main source, the Hebrew records. According to Menander, it was the Tyrian king's supplication to the Phoenician gods which brought an end to the drought, a fact surely hostile to the biblical account, but nevertheless recorded by Josephus without comment. The irony of the narrative's contradictions should not be missed, for even as the God of 1 Kings is punishing his people with drought for their worship of Baal and Asherah, the gods of Phoenicia— among whom were both Baal and Asherah—were receiving supplications to end the drought. Though it may be said that this citation supports the biblical record it must likewise be admitted that it contradicts it and in a distinctly pagan manner.

While one may be disappointed at the meager number of pagan sources cited by Josephus which deal directly with Jewish history, it can be appreciated that Josephus was not merely interested in, or limited by, specific mentions by pagans of Israel or of Jewish figures. Rather, he was able to make connections based on his own historical deductions which, while giving his narrative more credibility, also offers a broader perspective which included alien religious viewpoints and information regarding foreign nations unavailable in the biblical account.

It should finally be observed that the Greek sources which did make reference to the Jews had the potential for significant impact on the reception of Josephus's work among Greek readers, for whom *Jewish Antiquities* was explicitly intended. The two volumes entitled *Concerning the Antiquity of the Jews*, now usually called by the title *Against Apion*, were written in response to critics of the earlier work *Jewish Antiquities*. In the introduction of this follow-up work, Josephus makes it clear that the Greek readers of *Jewish Antiquities* were not indifferent to the use of Greek authors. It is equally clear that they were not impressed by the eight citations which actually mention the Jews. Josephus records their criticism with these words:

> Since I observe that a considerable number of persons, influenced by the calumnies of some, discredit the statements in my history concerning our antiquity, and adduce as proof of our relative modernity as a race the fact that it has *not been mentioned by the best known Greek historians* (τὸ μηδεμιᾶς παρὰ τοῖς ἐπιφανέσι τῶν Ἑλληνικῶν ἱστοριογράφων μνήμης ἠξιῶσθαι), I consider it my duty to devote a brief treatise to all of these points' (*Apion* 1.2-3).

Josephus then proceeds to present counter arguments, one of which is to produce even more Greek authors whose work he considered relevant to Jewish history. This exercise encompasses 25 per cent of the entire text of *Against Apion* (1.69-218), and contains references to 22 Greek authors, 15 of whom were not cited in the *Jewish Antiquities*.[16]

The object here is not to begin an analysis of these citations. Rather, I wish only to make the point that the success or failure of Josephus's *magnum opus*, the *Jewish Antiquities*, as far as the original audience was concerned (assuming Josephus's representation of their criticism is accurate), was in a large measure dependent upon what use the Jewish historian could make of Greek sources.

Function

Another method of analysis is to separate the citations according to their function in the text. That is, to what use does Josephus put his sources? The function of these citations has obvious implication for Josephus's intentions.

In the above discussion of citation form, 16 *testimonia* were distinguished from the categories of quotation and paraphrase. These 16 occasions where Josephus merely records an author as a witness to some point in his narrative serve the general function of supporting Josephus's credibility.

In some instances Josephus states that an author is in agreement with some aspect of his own history. For example, after stating that Noah lived to the age of 950, Josephus (*Ant.* 1.107-108) records a list of witnesses who testify to Josephus's veracity concerning the longevity of the ancients (μαρτυροῦσι δέ μου τῷ λόγῳ πάντες οἱ παρ᾽ Ἕλλησι καὶ βαρβάροις συγγραψάμενοι τὰς ἀρχαιολογίας). Josephus then names Manetho, Berossus, Mochus, Hestiaeus, and Hieronymus. To further substantiate the incredible ages attributed to the patriarchs, Josephus then lists six authors 'who report that the ancients lived for 1000 years', namely Hesiod, Hecataeus, Hellanicus, Acusilaus, Ephorus and Nicolaus (*Ant.* 1.108). Clearly the Jewish historian intended to demonstrate for his Greek readers that Greek and non-Greek historians, whether well-known or obscure, support the veracity of the Hebrew records. But this support is not for a specific historical event, but rather

16.   Manetho, Dius, Menander, Berossus, Pythagoras, Theophrastus, Herodotus, Choerilus, Aristotle, Hecataeus, Agatharchides, Theophilus, Theodotus, Mnaseas, Aristophanes, Hermogenes, Euhemerus, Conon, Zopyrion, Demetrius, Philo (the elder), Eupolemus.

for a theoretical matter of credibility of the marvelous in ancient sources. These *testimonia* give no additional information or commentary for Josephus's narrative. By using them, Josephus simply makes the explicit claim that a particular Greek author agrees with the statements of Josephus's biblical source. In these cases Josephus is clearly claiming the support of other authors and seeking to bolster his own credibility, as several modern scholars have described the function of Josephus's extra-biblical quotations.

In passing it is worthwhile to observe Josephus's attitude regarding the truly miraculous longevity credited to the patriarchs in his Hebrew records. Following a long tradition in such matters among Greek histori-ans Josephus writes, after listing his pagan corroborators, 'Concerning these matters, may each one decide according to his own pleasure' (περὶ μὲν τούτων, ὡς ἂν ἑκάστοις ᾖ φίλον, οὕτω σκοπείτωσαν *Ant.* 1.108). This caveat occurs here despite the eleven supporting Greek witnesses which Josephus had just produced. The formula appears throughout Josephus's work and reveals at least a formal Greek skepti-cism of the miraculous.[17] Such an attitude at least calls into question Rajak's contention that Josephus saw the Jewish tradition 'as one which may not, and at the same time need not be, questioned'.[18]

As one would expect, the 20 cases where Josephus quotes his source, or at least provides a paraphrase of its content, exhibit a more complex usage than do the 16 *testimonia*. A majority of these 20 citations contain material which I have labeled *supplementary*. That is, Josephus supple-ments the biblical history with actual historical data which are not con-tained in the biblical record. In these supplementary cases, Josephus is certainly supplying evidence which he feels supports the biblical narra-tive by showing that Greek authors also had something to say about a given historical incident. But that 'supporting role' should not obscure the genuine historiographic interests of the Jewish historian. For example, in *Antiquities* 1.95 Josephus writes as follows:

> Nicolaus of Damascus in his ninety-sixth book relates these matters [of the flood] as follows: 'There is above the country of Minyas in Armenia a great mountain called Baris, where the word is that many refugees found safety at the time of the flood, and a certain man, transported upon an ark,

---

17. See examples at *Ant.* 2.348; 3.81; 4.158; 8.262. Herodotus, 2.123; Thucydides, 6.2.1. S. Cohen observes that Josephus does not restrict his use of this disclaimer to mythology (*Josephus in Galilee*, p. 39 n. 61).

18. Rajak, 'Josephus', p. 471.

grounded upon the summit, and relics of the timber were for long
preserved; this may well be the same man of whom Moses, the Jewish
legislator, wrote.'

This passage is instructive in several ways. It lies in a section of
Josephus's narrative where he is obviously hoping to convince his
readers of the reliability of the flood narrative from Genesis by providing additional evidence from Greek writings. However, Josephus goes
well beyond any apologetic interest by providing numerous details not
available in, nor consistent with, the biblical account. In this example one
discovers the interesting tidbit that relics of the ark were long preserved.
More significantly, the name of the particular mountain, not known in
the biblical account, is given as 'Baris' (βάρις). One also learns that on
this mountain a great many refugees found safety from the flood. This
assertion is obviously at odds with the biblical narrative, Hebrew and
Greek, which affirms unequivocally that all mountains were covered and
no one, except those in the ark, escaped death (Gen. 7.19-24).

How does Josephus resolve these difficulties? Did he even notice
them? First of all it must be said that Josephus never explicitly corrects
the biblical narrative by means of an outside source. Such an action
would certainly compromise his overall goal of convincing Greek
readers that the ancient Hebrew records were credible. Having said that,
one must immediately add that Josephus seems to accept as actual fact
some of the details provided by Nicolaus.

First, in his own narrative of the flood, before external sources are
cited, Josephus says that relics of the ark are shown by Armenians to
this day (*Ant.* 1.92). This seemingly minor aside about relics is in fact
presented by Josephus as modern-day, concrete, observable evidence for
the veracity of the otherwise incredible story of the gigantic ark.[19] Here
Josephus is following the account of Nicolaus. Secondly, it is likely that
Josephus accepted Baris as the name of the particular mountain in
Armenia (Ararat) upon which the ark rested.

On two other counts, the extent of the flood and the number of
survivors, Josephus clearly sides with scripture, explicitly declaring in his
own account of the deluge that the water covered the entire surface of
the earth and that no one except Noah's family escaped (*Ant.* 1.89).
Thus we see evidence for a mixed usage of pagan citations, even in this
one quotation. Josephus's intention of supporting his native history is

19. One other citation, that of Berossus (*Ant.* 1.93), had the purpose of giving
similar modern evidence concerning the flood.

clear, as is his acceptance of certain details of Nicolaus's account. However, his rejection of some of Nicolaus's details is also clear, though he did not hesitate to quote the contradictory report without emendation. A detailed examination of other citations reveals a similar variety of purpose and usage even within one citation.

There are also citations of pagan sources which have a more *historiographic* function. On two occasions (*Ant.* 8.253-62; 10.19-20) Josephus cites Herodotus not as a supporting witness but rather as a foil. That is, Josephus only mentions something recorded by Herodotus in order to point out an error by the respected historian. In *Antiquities* 8.253 Josephus writes, almost in passing, that Herodotus had erroneously attributed the acts of the Egyptian king Shishak to Sesostris (= Ramses II, ruled c. 1287–20 BCE), who ruled nearly 400 years earlier. On a third occasion Josephus mentions Herodotus's account of Egyptian kings not to criticize it but rather to offer an explanation for something which Herodotus's readers may have found perplexing; that is, why the renowned historian does not mention the Egyptian kings after Minaias by name (*Ant.* 8.157).

These cases are interesting for several reasons. The citations of Herodotus in no way supplement Josephus's narrative by contributing historical data, nor do they use Herodotus as a witness to the veracity of the biblical text. Furthermore, even the corrections are not the kind that could have been motivated by a desire to refute detractors of Judaism or anything of the like. Rather, these corrections and explanations are of historiographic interest, though one might well suspect that Josephus as a historian took a certain pleasure in correcting the father of history.

In fact, Josephus undoubtedly saw himself in good company with many Greek historians. Criticism of Herodotus was common. Already in the late fifth century BCE, Ctesias composed a work on Persia about which the Byzantine scholar Photius said 'on practically every matter he presents a history opposed to that of Herodotus. In many places he convicts Herodotus of being a liar.'[20] F.W. Walbank's study of Polybius's polemical method concluded that he usually attacked early and famous historians by name but contemporary authors anonymously.[21]

---

20. F. Jacoby, *Die Fragmente der griechischen Historiker* 687a T2. R. Drews, *The Greek Accounts of Eastern History* (Cambridge, MA: Harvard University Press, 1973), p. 104.

21. F.W. Walbank, 'Polemic in Polybius', *JRS* 52 (1962), p. 4.

Josephus himself certainly recognized that criticism of Herodotus was popular among historians. Josephus writes in *Apion* 1.16:

> It is common knowledge what discrepancies there are between Hellanicus and Acusilaus on the genealogies, how often Acusilaus corrects Hesiod, how the mendacity of Hellanicus in most of his statements is exposed by Ephorus, that of Ephorus is exposed by Timaeus, that of Timaeus by later writers, and *that of Herodotus by everybody*.

One can almost imagine that the stature of a Hellenistic historian was measured by the number of errors he could discover in Herodotus. Whatever his motives, Josephus had now joined the ranks of Herodotean fault-finders.

In the case of the Egyptian kings lacking names in Herodotean account (*Ant.* 8.157), the Jewish historian's explanation (that the kings all had the same throne name, Pharaothai) sounds more like an apology in defense of Herodotus than a critique (νομίζω δὲ καὶ ʽΗρόδοτον τὸν ʽΑλικαρνασέα διὰ τοῦτο μὴ δηλῶσαι αὐτῶν τὰ ὀνόματα...). Regardless of the accuracy of Josephus's explanation, such a generous attitude indicates that he was not just interested in criticizing Herodotus. Taken together with his mild-mannered criticisms, these texts clearly underscore the historiographic interest of the author.

Conclusion

By using various criteria to categorize the 36 citations by the 21 Greek authors appealed to in the biblical history of Josephus's *Jewish Antiquities*, I have attempted to illuminate the variety of ways in which Josephus used his sources. The apologetic value of some citations, especially the *testimonia*, has been recognized. The 36 citations are very unevenly distributed and, in the majority of instances (28), the pagan authors are not in fact dealing with Jewish history. The other references depend entirely on Josephus's ability to relate foreign history to that of the Jews. It is clear that the usual description of these citations as supportive, while not wrong, does not do justice to the variety of ways in which Josephus employs his sources. The full measure of the Jewish historian's method and procedure will not be known until a full philological and literary investigation is made of each of these citations in their Josephan context.

As indicated by Josephus's report in *Apion* 1.2-5, his first-century Greek audience was not so interested in how Josephus used his biblical source, a subject which has occupied many modern scholars in many fruitful studies. The original readers, in contrast to the emphasis of modern scholarship, were supremely interested in how Josephus was able to incorporate their historians, that is Greek historians, into his Jewish history. If we are to read Josephus in his original historical context, and to discover the *interpretatio Graeca* of his work, modern scholarship must consider more carefully the historical and literary details of Josephus's use of pagan sources.

Final consideration must be given to Rajak's contention that Josephus's use of extra-biblical sources actually demonstrates how far afield his work stands from the methods and ideals of Greek historiography. While Josephus usually cites sources which in some manner support his narrative, 'Greek and Roman historians', writes Rajak, 'tend to do exactly the opposite, not naming their predecessors or citing their points of view except where they disagree with them or want to indicate that there is a dispute between them'.[22]

Rajak is correct in noting the tendency of Greek and Roman historians,[23] but the tendency does not define the limits of acceptable historiographic practice. The exceptions to the tendency to leave other writers unnamed, whether supportive or critical, are numerous enough that Josephus cannot be considered unique. Dionysius of Halicarnassus (1.13.1-4), of whom Josephus was certainly aware, calls on the early historian Pherecydes of Athens as his 'witness' because the genealogist's general description of Oenotrian origins was harmonious with his own. Strabo, in *Geography* 3.4.4-5, cites Artemidorus both in agreement and disagreement and in 12.8.5 he notes the accord of Herodotus. Diodorus Siculus occasionally notes the agreement of Ctesias in his Assyrian history (2.6.7; 2.8.5; 2.17.1; 2.21.8).

I should not care to deny the distinct characteristics of Josephus's historiographic task as a foreigner writing his own nation's history in order to inform Greeks. Certainly in the nature of his task, Josephus stands more with Manetho and Berossus than with Greeks writing for Greeks. And indeed the manner in which he cites Greek sources and his motives in doing so are affected by his status. But his usage of Greek

---

22. Rajak, 'Josephus', p. 471.

23. Cf. the broader statement of Walbank: 'When ancient historians wanted to take cognizance of what their predecessors had written, they seem usually, though not always, to have preferred an anonymous reference to one by name' ('Polemic in Polybius', p. 1).

authors does not put his work beyond the pale of Greek historiography. In fact, his use of Greek authors indicates that Josephus understood what was expected of him as a foreigner writing his national history. As mentioned above, one major criticism Josephus received from his readership for his *Jewish Antiquities* was essentially that he had not mentioned enough Greek historians (*Apion* 1.1-6).

It is worth asking whether Josephus, in his use of Greek authors as additional material for his native history, was following the lead of Manetho or Berossus, the two previous non-Greeks who wrote native histories for the sake of the Greeks and whose third century BCE works on Babylon and Egypt were known to Josephus. These authors, like Josephus, wrote works translated from or based on the sacred records of their nations.[24] Unfortunately, unlike Josephus's *Jewish Antiquities*, their works did not survive intact but only in fragmentary form through citations and summaries by later authors, although, when compared to other Hellenistic writers, the fragments of Berossus and Manetho are quite extensive.[25]

Since these authors, like Josephus, took upon themselves the task of explaining their native traditions and history to Greek readers, did they provide a model for Josephus's use of Greek citations? In so far as the fragmentary nature of their writings allows any answer at all, it must be no. Indeed, Berossus's interaction with Greek authors is attested only by one testimonium of Josephus (*Apion* 1.142) who says that 'in the third book of his *History of Chaldaea*, Berossus censures the Greek historians for their deluded belief that Babylon was founded by the Assyrian Semiramis and their erroneous statement that its marvellous buildings were her creation'. Josephus also testifies (*Apion* 1.74) that Manetho 'convicts Herodotus of being misled through ignorance on many points of Egyptian history'. Thus, we have Josephus's testimony that both Berossus and Manetho had criticized earlier Greek historians. For Manetho, we also have two fragments in which he, after giving the name of an Egyptian king, then gives the name as known by Herodotus in one case[26] and by Homer in another.[27] In these last two texts we have

---

24. For Manetho see *Apion* 1.73 and for Berossus see *Apion* 1.130.

25. Manetho, F. Jacoby, *Die Fragmente* 609; W.G. Waddell, *Manetho* (LCL; Cambridge, MA: Harvard University Press, 1940). Berossus, *Die Fragmente* 680; S.M. Burstein, *The Babyloniaca of Berossus* (Malibu: Undena Publications, 1978).

26. Jacoby, *Die Fragmente* 609 F2, p. 22; Waddell, frag. 15.

27. Jacoby, *Die Fragmente* 609 F3a, p. 42; Waddell, frag. 56.

the only known positive uses of Greek sources by either Berossus or Manetho.

The fragmentary evidence would thus suggest that neither Berossus nor Manetho made large-scale use of Greek sources to supplement their native histories. In regard to both of these authors, modern scholars, especially Elias Bickerman, Arnaldo Momigliano and Robert Drews, have noted that the native histories of Berossus and Manetho failed to make any noticeable impact on Greek historical writings dealing with their native lands.[28] One could speculate that Josephus also had noticed this lack of influence and considered his many positive citations of Greek authors as a methodological improvement over his predecessors.

Whatever his reasons, Josephus's employment of Greek authors to supplement and support his biblical narrative indicates not his distance from Greek historiographic practice but rather his understanding of what a foreigner writing for a Greek audience ought to do in order to receive a positive hearing. In hindsight his only regret may have been, considering the criticism of his readers, that he had not cited even more.

28. E.J. Bickerman, 'Origines gentium', *Classical Philology* 47 (1952), pp. 65-81; A. Momigliano, *Alien Wisdom* (Cambridge, MA: Harvard University Press, 1975), p. 121; Drews, *Greek Accounts*, p. 131.

PHILO, *GRAMMATIKĒ* AND THE NARRATIVE AGGADA

Adam Kamesar

Much discussion has taken place over the past century concerning the question of Philo's relationship to aggada. There are those who have claimed that he was dependent on Palestinian aggada, and those who have disputed such dependence.[1] The debate has generally focused on alleged aggadic parallels within the Philonic corpus. Some scholars have collected such parallels, for the most part with the object of demonstrating that Philo made use of, in one way or another, Palestinian aggadic traditions or methods.[2] Others have denied the validity of such parallels, claiming that they are too vague and general to prove significant links between Philo and the aggada.[3] Nevertheless, most of those who have attempted to trace the parallels have acknowledged either that there are

---

1. See, for recent surveys of the question, B.L. Mack, 'Philo Judaeus and Exegetical Traditions in Alexandria', *ANRW* 2.21.1 (1984), pp. 237-38; D. Instone Brewer, *Techniques and Assumptions in Jewish Exegesis before 70 CE* (TSAJ, 30; Tübingen, 1992), pp. 203-204. Cf. also P. Borgen, 'Philo of Alexandria: A Critical and Synthetical Survey of Research since World War II', *ANRW* 2.21.1 (1984), pp. 124-26.

2. C. Siegfried, *Philo von Alexandria als Ausleger des Alten Testaments* (Jena, 1875), pp. 145-56; L. Treitel, 'Agada bei Philo', *MGWJ* 53 (1909), pp. 28-45, 159-73, 286-91 (cf. *idem, Gesamte Theologie und Philosophie Philo's von Alexandria* [Berlin, 1923], pp. 69-78; E. Stein, *Philo und der Midrasch* (BZAW, 57; Giessen, 1931); P. Borgen, *Bread from Heaven* (NovTSup, 10; Leiden, 1965), pp. 1-20, 28-58; B.J. Bamberger, 'Philo and the Aggadah', *HUCA* 48 (1977), pp. 153-85. For the works of S. Belkin, too numerous to be listed here, see Mack, 'Philo Judaeus', p. 268 (to which references add now *Midreshei Filon*, I [New York, 1989]). The many parallels collected by L. Ginzberg in *The Legends of the Jews*, I–VII (Philadelphia, 1909–1938), may be located via the references in vol. VII, pp. 541-46.

3. S. Sandmel, *Philo's Place in Judaism* (New York, 2nd edn, 1971), esp. pp. 203-11 (see also his 'Parallelomania', *JBL* 81 [1962], pp. 2-3, 5, 8); L.L. Grabbe, 'Philo and Aggada: A Response to B.J. Bamberger', *The Studia Philonica Annual* 3 (1991) = *Heirs of the Septuagint: FS* E. Hilgert, pp. 153-66.

fundamental differences between the Philonic approach to Scripture and aggada, or that the parallels indicate only a moderate knowledge of aggada on the part of Philo.[4] In short, the question is probably less controversial than it might seem to be at first glance.

Concerning the narrative aggada specifically, that is, the elaboration of the biblical text in narrative form,[5] the controversy is even less pronounced. The extent to which this form of aggada is present in the Philonic corpus has been best delineated by S. Sandmel: extensive narrative embellishment, such as we find it in rabbinic literature or in some early Jewish Hellenistic writers, is missing from Philo, and 'whatever overlap exists between Philo and the Rabbis is strictly limited to brief motifs'.[6] In other words, according to Sandmel, one may find in Philo allusions to narrative aggadic material found in other sources, but not a narrative aggada which is comparable to that found in rabbinic literature or in early Jewish Hellenistic texts. And, despite appearances to the contrary, it is in fact this same conclusion that emerges from the studies of those who have attempted to demonstrate links between Philo and the aggada. For the parallels which one finds in these studies, in so far as they concern the narrative aggada, are of the type noted by Sandmel.[7] Thus, a balanced evaluation of the scholarship of the past century allows one to conclude that Sandmel's view is not, in this case, controversial.[8] Rather, it simply constitutes the most accurate formulation of what is more or less a consensus.[9]

---

4. Treitel, 'Agada', esp. pp. 35-36; Stein, *Philo und der Midrasch*, esp. pp. 50-51; Bamberger, 'Philo and the Aggadah', esp. pp. 154, 185.

5. For more on the meaning of the expression 'narrative aggada', see my article, 'The Evaluation of the Narrative Aggada in Greek and Latin Patristic Literature', *JTS* 45 (1994), p. 38. See also J. Fraenkel, *Darkhei ha-aggada ve-ha-midrash* ([Givatayim], 1991), II, p. 464 (cf. I, p. 287), who uses the words האגדה הסיפורית in a similar fashion.

6. *Philo of Alexandria: An Introduction* (New York, 1979), p. 133. Cf. *idem*, 'Philo Judaeus: An Introduction to the Man, his Writings, and his Significance', *ANRW* 2.21.1 (1984), pp. 34-35.

7. See the works cited above, n. 2.

8. Mack, 'Philo Judaeus', p. 238, states that 'the studies by Stein and Sandmel are in some respects contradictory in conclusion'. If the phrase 'in some respects' also refers to the issue of the extent of Philo's use of narrative aggada or narrative aggadic method, I cannot accept this statement.

9. See now Fraenkel, *Darkhei ha-aggada*, II, p. 473, who acknowledges that there is no narrative aggada of the 'classic' rabbinic variety in Philo. On the other

But while Sandmel was able to assess accurately the extent to which narrative aggada is present in Philo, a question remains as to whether he was able to account for that assessment in a completely satisfactory manner. He suggested that Philo probably had knowledge of narrative aggadic traditions, almost certainly those found in early Jewish Hellenistic texts, and perhaps some of those attested in later rabbinic literature, but because of his rationalism and elitism, he generally declined to use them.[10] Sandmel did not spell out in detail what he means by 'rationalism' or 'elitism', but others who have taken a similar position have expressed the view that the mythical character of some Hellenistic and/or rabbinic aggada, which suggests a syncretistic or popular religiosity, made it distasteful to Philo.[11] And Sandmel himself is fond of stressing the uniqueness of Philo's 'religiosity' as compared with that of the Rabbis and the minor Judaeo-Hellenistic writers.[12] But is it really the 'religiosity' of the narrative aggada that led Philo to neglect it, or are

hand, Fraenkel does quote a passage from Philo's *De Abrahamo* in a discussion of the narrative aggada as found in the parabiblical books of the intertestamental period, which he regards as different from the narrative aggada of the Rabbis (see *Darkhei ha-aggada*, II, pp. 464-70). Thus, he may accept the view which is voiced by some scholars, that Philo's 'Exposition of the Law', especially the biographies of Abraham, Joseph, and Moses, is to be associated with the genre sometimes called the 're-written Bible' (see P. Borgen, 'Philo of Alexandria', in *Jewish Writings of the Second Temple Period* [CRINT, 2.2; ed. M.E. Stone; Assen, 1984], p. 234; cf. Mack, 'Philo Judaeus', p. 258). The similarity, however, is very superficial, and may not extend significantly beyond the narrative form. Especially relevant in the present context is the fact that the expansions which we find in the Philonic biographies are often of a rhetorical and moral character (see H. Lewy's characterization of the nature of the embellishments found in Philo's formal commentaries in the introduction to his volume, Philo, *Philosophical Writings: Selections* [Oxford, 1946], p. 12 [cf. p. 18]; these remarks are just as valid in the case of the biographies). They are not the extensive 'historical' additions of the type we find in *Jubilees*, the *Liber antiquitatum biblicarum*, or in the Greek works of the minor Jewish Hellenistic historians and Josephus. Said after the Thucydidean fashion, the major Philonic embellishments are often 'in the realm of' λόγοι, even when not formally presented as such, whereas the embellishments of the 're-written Bible' include, in addition to λόγοι, a much stronger component of ἔργα.

10. See *locc. citt.* (n. 6); cf. *Philo's Place*, p. 211; 'Philo's Knowledge of Hebrew', *StPhilo* 5 (1978), p. 111; Bamberger, 'Philo and the Aggadah', p. 156.

11. See Instone Brewer, *loc. cit.* (n. 1); cf. E. Bréhier, *Les idées philosophiques et religieuses de Philon d'Alexandrie* (EPhM, 8; Paris, 3rd edn, 1950), pp. 62-66.

12. See *Philo of Alexandria*, pp. 83, 147.

there more clearly discernible 'literary' reasons for the relative scarcity of narrative aggada in the Philonic corpus? It is this question that shall be addressed in the present article. That is, there will be no concern here with 'parallels', but rather with Philo's attitude towards narrative aggada, and the role which he was willing to bestow upon it in his exegetical system.

In the first place, the sparseness of narrative aggada of the rabbinic or 're-written biblical' type in Philo may simply have been predetermined by the genres which were employed in the literary tradition of which he considered himself an heir, and the manner in which those genres were understood in the same tradition. For if one considers the narrative additions to the biblical text found in early Jewish Hellenistic literature, one notes that these do not have the same character in all of the authors. Specifically, the narrative additions of Demetrius 'the Chronographer' stand out from those of the other so-called minor Judaeo-Hellenistic authors in three important respects. In the first place, they are often occasioned by problems in the biblical text which are explicitly mentioned by Demetrius and introduced by him with language which contemporary pagan exegetes employ in introducing similar problems, called προβλήματα or ἀπορίαι in the technical vocabulary of Greek exegesis.[13] Secondly, Demetrius sometimes proposes his narrative

---

13. See Demetrius, *apud* Eusebium, *Praep. ev.* 9.21.14-15; 9.29.16. (R. Doran, 'The Jewish Hellenistic Historians before Josephus', *ANRW* 2.20.1 [1987], pp. 249-50, has disputed the standard view that in 9.21.14 an ἀπορία is being raised, and thinks that the verb διαπορεῖσθαι could refer to the 'amazement expressed by the brothers of Joseph' as related in Gen. 43.33. He fails, however, to recognize the technical terminology of ζητήματα literature. For the phrase μὴ δυναμένου αὐτοῦ τοσαῦτα καταναλῶσαι κρέα clearly indicates that what has been noted in the biblical text is an ἀδύνατον or 'impossibility', a standard type of 'problem'. See A. Gudeman, 'Λύσεις', *PW* 1.13.2 (1927), cols. 2515-17.) Cf. also *Praep. ev.* 9.21.13, 9.29.1, where narrative supplements appear to constitute solutions to problems which are not explicitly presented as such, but are clearly identifiable as προβλήματα. On these two passages, see N. Walter, 'Fragmente jüdisch-hellenistischer Exegeten: Aristobulos, Demetrios, Aristeas', *JSHRZ* 3.2 (1975), p. 281 (for 9.21.13), and Y.(J.) Gutman(n), *Ha-sifrut ha-yehudit ha-hellenistit*, [I] (Jerusalem, 1958), pp. 136-37 (for a fuller explanation of 9.29.1). In these cases, either the formal raising of the question has been omitted by Alexander Polyhistor, the *epitomator* from whom Eusebius derived his material (cf. Walter, *ibid.*, and P.W. van der Horst, 'The Interpretation of the Bible by the Minor Hellenistic Jewish Authors', in *Mikra* [CRINT, 2.1; ed. M.J. Mulder; Assen and Maastricht, 1988], pp. 529-30), or we have

additions with expressions which openly indicate their conjectural character, such as ὅσα στοχάζεσθαι and φαίνεται.[14] Finally, if one compares the narrative additions of Demetrius with those found in other early Judaeo-Hellenistic writers and in the best known examples of originally Semitic forms of the 're-written Bible', one will find that they are not particularly extensive in scope.[15] Indeed, scholars have often noted the 'sober' character of the work of Demetrius.[16]

Now, it just so happens that near contemporary Greek exegetes were also wont to provide conjectural 'supplements' to the narrative of the Homeric poems when they thought something had been implied but not explicitly mentioned by the poet. Such conjectural supplements are distinguished by features similar to those which characterize the supplements of Demetrius. They seem to have originated as λύσεις to specific προβλήματα which had been discovered in the Homeric narrative.[17] They are usually introduced by a special formula, κατὰ τὸ σιωπώμενον,[18] but also by more general formulae (such as ἴσως) which are equivalent to those employed by Demetrius.[19] Finally, they tend to be quite limited in scope.[20] Of course, I would not claim that the procedure of Demetrius corresponds exactly to that which we find in

what Gudeman has called 'versteckte ζητήματα' (see 'Λύσεις', cols. 2514-15, 2522).

14. *Apud* Eusebium, *Praep. ev.* 9.29.1, 16. See also J. Freudenthal, *Hellenistische Studien*, I (Breslau, 1874), p. 42 (cf. pp. 43, 46), who suggests that other instances of such formulae may have been omitted by Alexander Polyhistor.

15. Cf. M. Hadas, *Hellenistic Culture: Fusion and Diffusion* (New York, 1959), p. 94: 'there are touches of midrashic exegesis but no such fanciful additions of romantic details as we find in later authors'.

16. See Freudenthal, *Hellenistische Studien*, I, pp. 36-39; P.M. Fraser, *Ptolemaic Alexandria* (Oxford, 1972), I, p. 693; Walter, 'Fragmente', p. 282; C.R. Holladay, *Fragments from Hellenistic Jewish Authors*. I. *Historians* (SBLPS, 10; Chico, CA, 1983), p. 52.

17. See Kamesar, 'The Narrative Aggada as Seen from the Graeco-Latin Perspective', *JJS* 45 (1994), pp. 58-59.

18. See Kamesar, *loc. cit.* (n. 17).

19. See Porphyry, *Quaestiones Homericae ad Iliadem* (ed. H. Schrader; Leipzig, 1880–82) E.265, H.9 (p. 107 ll. 9-10), K.339, 447 (p. 159 ll. 6-7), Λ.846 (note the use of ἴσως together with the formula κατὰ τὸ σιωπώμενον on p. 170 ll. 20-21). See also Chr. Schäublin, *Untersuchungen zu Methode und Herkunft der antiochenischen Exegese* (Theoph 23; Cologne, 1974), p. 63, with my comments in 'Evaluation', p. 57 n. 68.

20. See Kamesar, 'Narrative Aggada', pp. 60-61.

the Homeric scholia. However, it bears considerably more resemblance
to this Alexandrian exegetical technique than it does to the practice of
other early Judaeo-Hellenistic writers and the authors of 're-written'
biblical material as concerns narrative additions.[21]

This circumstance would appear to add a large measure of support to
the view recently advocated by N. Walter, that Demetrius, in contrast to
the majority of the minor Judaeo-Hellenistic prose writers, is to be
classified as an exegete rather than as a historian.[22] This is not to say
that the work of Demetrius is without any connection to historiographical genres, and the state in which it has been preserved may
render fruitless attempts to assign it to a specific genre with any measure
of certainty. However, the fact that his narrative aggadic additions to the
biblical text have more in common with contemporary Alexandrian
exegetical procedure than with the narrative aggada found in other early
Judaeo-Hellenistic literature and in the originally Semitic examples of the
're-written Bible' would lead one to believe that his work had some firm
connection with Greek exegetical genres.

If this is the case, one may surmise that in Judaeo-Hellenistic circles,
more extensive narrative embellishment of the biblical text, such as that
found in the 're-written biblical' material, was felt to go beyond what
was tolerable in 'scientific' exegetical works based on Alexandrian
models.[23] It was therefore incorporated into various other genres:

21. This point has not been sufficiently appreciated in the scholarship on
Demetrius, because the comparative material in the scholia has not been examined
with sufficient depth. At least with regard to the non-chronological προβλήματα,
attention has been focused more on the terminology with which they are raised than
on the manner in which they are solved. Indeed, it may be for this reason that some
scholars, such as Wacholder (*Eupolemus: A Study of Judaeo-Greek Literature*
[MHUC, 3; Cincinnati, 1974], pp. 280-82), T. Rajak ('The Sense of History in
Jewish Intertestamental Writing', *OTS* 24 [1986], pp. 134-36, 144 n. 45), and Doran
(loc. cit. [n. 13]) have attempted to minimize the connection between Demetrius and
Alexandrian philological scholarship (cf. also I. Heinemann, *Darkhei ha-aggada*
[Jerusalem, 2nd edn, 1953/4], pp. 173-74). If the analysis offered here has anything
to it, however, such a connection will be even firmer than Gutman (*Ha-sifrut,* [I], pp.
138-39) or Walter (*Der Thoraausleger Aristobulos* [TU, 86; Berlin, 1964], p. 42, and
'Fragmente', p. 259) have believed.

22. See 'Jüdisch-hellenistische Literatur vor Philon von Alexandrien', *ANRW*
2.20.1 (1987), pp. 77-78, and 'Fragmente', pp. 259, 280-82.

23. For more recent appreciations of the 'scientific' character of the contributions
of Demetrius, see Fraser, *Ptolemaic Alexandria,* I, pp. 690-94, and C.R. Holladay,
'Demetrius the Chronographer', *Anchor Bible Dictionary* (New York, 1992), II,

'historiography' of one form or another, poetic compositions such as the *Exagoge* of Ezekiel, and 'non-scientific' exegetical works such as the ps.-Philonic homilies *De Jona* and *De Sampsone*.[24]

Now, when we turn to the narrative aggadic supplements which are found in Philo's works, we see that they have more in common with those in Demetrius than with those in other minor Judaeo-Hellenistic works, in originally Semitic compositions of the 're-written Bible', and in rabbinic literature. In the first place, we have already noted above that the extent of the narrative aggadic supplements in Philo tends to be rather limited.[25] Secondly, we also find that Philo often 'marks' these supplements with words which denote their conjectural character, or with formulae such as φασί which indicate that he regarded them as part of a tradition which was separate from the biblical text.[26] Finally, he connects narrative aggadic supplements to what he calls 'literal' interpretation,[27] and he seems to have thought that one of the key roles of such 'literal' interpretation was the furnishing of λύσεις to exegetical προβλήματα.[28] In short, we find in Philo remnants of the narrative aggadic procedure which is present in Demetrius.

It would appear therefore that as far as literal exegesis is concerned, Philo was an heir of the tradition which ultimately goes back to Demetrius. And in that tradition of 'scientific' exegesis, the narrative aggada was of a sort different from that employed in other genres. Thus,

p. 138, although both of these authors treat Demetrius primarily as a historian.

24. Concerning the 'non-scientific' character of the ps.-Philonic sermons, see F. Siegert's commentary, *Drei hellenistisch-jüdische Predigten*, II (WUNT, 61; Tübingen, 1992), pp. 30, 35-36, 293-94, and my review of the work, to appear in *JBL* 113 (1994).

25. See above, p. 217.

26. See *Opif.* 136 (μοι δοκεῖ), 137 (ἔοικεν; for the aggada, cf. Stein, *Philo und der Midrasch*, p. 4); *Jos.* 99 (ἴσως; cf. Siegfried, *Philo von Alexandria*, p. 146, Stein, *Philo und der Midrasch*, pp. 40-41); 176-77 (ἴσως, μοι δοκεῖ; cf. Siegfried, *ibid.*); *Quaest. in Gen.* 1.32. For supplements introduced with φασί, see, e.g., *Abr.* 253 (οἱ σαφέστατα διηγούμενοί φασιν; cf. Treitel, 'Agada', p. 160); *Vit. Mos.* 1.13 (φασί). Philo probably viewed supplements of this nature not only as conjectures of other exegetes (cf. Freudenthal, *Hellenistische Studien*, I, p. 42), but also as remnants of a non-biblical, oral historical tradition. That he sharply distinguished between the two, however, is improbable. Cf. *Vit. Mos.* 1.4 (cited and discussed below, pp. 231-34). On this issue in later Greek and Latin sources, see Kamesar, 'Evaluation', pp. 58-68.

27. See esp. *Quaest. in Gen.* 4(6).196.

28. See *Imm.* 133; *Sobr.* 32-33; *Conf.* 14; cf. *Quaest. in Gen.* 2.79.

most of the narrative aggadic traditions which reached Philo probably came to him through the filter of some 'Demetrian-like' Alexandrian Jewish tradition. In other words, the character of the Philonic narrative aggada, as distinguished from that found in other ancient Jewish sources, is to be explained in the first place by the exegetical genres which he chose, and the manner in which those genres were employed in the tradition of which he saw himself to be a part. In fact, Philo was so thoroughly an 'exegete', dependent on a specific tradition of exegesis, that even when he turned to ostensibly different genres, such as the βίοι, he did not stray to the form of narrative aggada which was employed in Judaeo-Hellenistic 'historical' works.[29]

Nevertheless, it may be readily acknowledged that Philo does not practise an exegesis of the 'classical' Alexandrian variety, even if he may have inherited a tradition which had links with that form of interpretation. Rather, Philo's exegetical method is fundamentally different from that of Demetrius, and therefore the explanation of the character of Philo's narrative aggada which has been given above does not fully illuminate his approach. Indeed, it is natural to assume that some more 'contemporary' and deliberate view of narrative aggada must have been held by Philo. Now, as I have indicated elsewhere, to reconstruct Jewish Hellenistic views of the narrative aggada is not an easy task.[30] However, there does seem to be sufficient evidence to allow an attempt. Specifically, there are some indications that Philo viewed the narrative aggada from the Greek perspective, and was influenced by late Hellenistic/early imperial Greek conceptions of γραμματική in determining its role. Before turning to this evidence, however, it is necessary to say something about such Greek conceptions, and Philo's familiarity with them.

In Hellenistic and early imperial times, the discipline indicated by the

---

29. Cf. V. Nikiprowetzky, *Le commentaire de l'Ecriture chez Philon d'Alexandrie* (ALGHJ, 11; Leiden, 1977), pp. 200-202, who argues that the 'Exposition of the Law', including the βίοι, despite appearances, is also basically a commentary. On the other hand, it may be acknowledged that in the *Hypothetica* Philo does provide a rather free reconstruction of certain events in early Israelite history, while explicitly noting that the reconstruction is based on conjecture and probability (*apud* Eusebium, *Praep. ev.* 8.6.5). However, this passage should not be seen as midrashic technique, as M. Petit, 'A propos d'une traversée exemplaire du désert du Sinaï selon Philon', *Sem* 26 (1976), pp. 137-42 (esp. 141-42), believes, but rather as an exceptional case, necessitated by the fact that Philo is arguing on the basis of the presuppositions of his opponents. See I. Heinemann, 'Moses', *PW* 1.16.1 (1933), cols. 369-70.

30. 'Narrative Aggada', p. 54.

term γραμματική was broader than what we mean by the word 'grammar'. It was defined not only as knowledge of 'letters' or of 'writing and reading', but also as interpretation of literary texts. The former was termed 'grammar in the general sense', 'lower grammar', or γραμματιστική, and the latter (perceived, according to the definition of Dionysius Thrax, as ἐμπειρία τῶν παρὰ ποιηταῖς τε καὶ συγγραφεῦσιν ὡς ἐπὶ τὸ πολὺ λεγομένων) was called 'grammar in the specific sense' or 'higher grammar'.[31] In fact, Philo himself is one of the primary sources for this distinction, calling the 'lower' form of grammar ἀτελεστέρα or παιδική, and the 'higher' τελειοτέρα.[32]

The 'higher' grammar was thought to consist of different parts. Yet these parts were defined in various ways. Perhaps the best known division is that of Dionysius Thrax, according to which γραμματική is made up of six parts: (1) ἀνάγνωσις ἐντριβὴς κατὰ προσῳδίαν (that is, the correct reading of the text, with regard to breathings, accents, pauses, word division, etc.); (2) ἐξήγησις κατὰ τοὺς ἐνυπάρχοντας ποιητικοὺς τρόπους (the explanation of poetical modes of expression); (3) γλωσσῶν τε καὶ ἱστοριῶν πρόχειρος ἀπόδοσις (the elucidation of rare words and subject-matter or realia);[33] (4) ἐτυμολογίας εὕρεσις (the discovery of primary meanings or etymologies of words); (5) ἀναλογίας ἐκλογισμός (the setting out of normal patterns of

31. See K. Barwick, *Remmius Palaemon und die römische Ars grammatica* (Ph.S, 15.2; Leipzig, 1922), pp. 215-17. As Barwick points out, Dionysius' definition of γραμματική refers to the interpretation of literary texts (i.e. 'higher' grammar), and what might be called the 'linguistic' translation of the definition (still influential today, see, e.g., A. Kemp, 'The *Tekhnē grammatikē* of Dionysius Thrax', in *The History of Linguistics in the Classical Period* [Studies in the History of the Language Sciences, 46; ed. D.J. Taylor; Amsterdam, 1987], p. 172), is 'vollkommen verfehlt'. This may be confirmed by the manner in which the definition is reflected in later texts. See, in addition to the scholia cited by Barwick, Philo, *Som.* 1.205 (ἐμπειρία is part of the 'higher' grammar); Sextus Empiricus, *Adv. math.* 1.57-58 (the term ἐμπειρία is paraphrased by ἑρμηνεύειν in a manner similar to that of the scholia)

32. See *Congr.* 148 (cited incorrectly as § 139 in Barwick, *loc. cit.* [n. 31]), where Philo also refers to the designation γραμματιστική for the 'lower' grammar, and *Som.* 1.205. Cf. *Agr.* 18; *Congr.* 74.

33. For further explanation of the term ἱστορία as used by classical grammarians, see W.G. Rutherford, *A Chapter in the History of Annotation, being Scholia Aristophanica*, III (London, 1905), pp. 381-82.

declension); (6) κρίσις ποιημάτων (the evaluation of the aesthetic and moral qualities of the text).[34]

Another division is that found in the scholia on Dionysius Thrax and in Varro, the origin of which has been attributed by H. Usener to Tyrannion. This is sometimes called the 'old', sometimes the 'Varronian' scheme.[35] This system was of greater practical application than that of Dionysius, and seems to have been particularly influential in early imperial times.[36] According to this scheme, γραμματική includes four μέρη or parts: (1) τὸ ἀναγνωστικόν (cf. above, ἀνάγνωσις); (2) τὸ ἐξηγητικόν (the exegetical treatment of the text); (3) τὸ διορθωτικόν (the establishment of the correct text, i.e. textual criticism); (4) τὸ κριτικόν (cf. above, κρίσις ποιημάτων). In this system, there are also four ὄργανα, or 'tools' of γραμματική: (1) τὸ γλωσσηματικόν (cf. above, γλωσσῶν...ἀπόδοσις); (2) τὸ ἱστορικόν (cf. above, ἱστοριῶν ...ἀπόδοσις); (3) τὸ μετρικόν (treatment of meter); (4) τὸ τεχνικόν (grammatical and rhetorical exegesis).[37] In all probability, these ὄργανα were seen as the components of τὸ ἐξηγητικόν, the most comprehensive of the 'parts' of grammar.[38]

---

34. Dionysius Thrax, *Ars grammatica* 1. Since, as stated above, n. 31, Dionysius' definition of grammar clearly relates to 'higher' grammar, the six parts of grammar must all be considered as parts of 'higher' grammar. Cf. E. Siebenborn, *Die Lehre von der Sprachrichtigkeit und ihren Kriterien* (SAPh, 5; Amsterdam, 1976), p. 32; B. Neuschäfer, *Origenes als Philologe* (SBA ,18.1-2; Basle, 1987), p. 35. On what basis, if any, A. Gudeman ('Grammatik', *PW* 1.7.2 [1912], col. 1809; cf. *Grundriss der Geschichte der klassischen Philologie* [Leipzig, 2nd edn, 1909, p. 5]), has ascribed the first five parts to 'lower' grammar, is unclear to me (he may have in mind passages in the scholia on the *Ars*, where the first five parts are seen as propaedeutic to κρίσις [see the edition of A. Hilgard, Leipzig 1901 (= Grammatici Graeci, 1.3), p. 15 ll. 30-31; p. 170 ll. 9-10]). Cf., however, below, p. 229.

35. See H. Usener, 'Ein altes Lehrgebäude der Philologie', *SBAW.PPH* 1892.4, pp. 582-648 (reprinted, with additions, in *Kleine Schriften*, II [Leipzig, 1913], pp. 265-314; my references follow the reprint); Barwick, *Remmius Palaemon*, pp. 223-27. C. Wendel, 'Tyrannion', *PW* 2.7.2.1 (1943), col. 1818, has challenged Usener's attribution of the system to Tyrannion, but this is a problem which need not concern us here.

36. See Schäublin, *Untersuchungen*, pp. 34-35; Neuschäfer, *Origenes als Philologe*, pp. 35-36. Cf. H.-I. Marrou, *Histoire de l'éducation dans l'antiquité* (Paris, 6th edn, 1965), pp. 250-56.

37. See Usener, 'Ein altes Lehrgebäude', pp. 269-72.

38. See Usener, 'Ein altes Lehrgebäude', p. 282 (cf. pp. 266-67); Neuschäfer, *Origenes als Philologe*, pp. 139-40, 399 n. 11. Cf. Marrou, *Histoire de l'éducation*,

The final system which is relevant in the present context is that ascribed to Asclepiades of Myrleia by Sextus Empiricus and also employed by the latter in his discussions.[39] This entails a tripartite division of grammar into τὸ τεχνικόν, τὸ ἱστορικόν, and τὸ γραμματικόν (Asclepiades; Sextus calls this third part ἰδιαίτερον). The 'technical' part corresponds to what we would call grammar, that is, the systematic treatment of language, the 'historical' part is equivalent to that same department in the Dionysian and Varronian systems, and the 'grammatical' or 'special' part is the exegetical treatment of literary texts.[40] This classification differs from the two other systems which we have mentioned in some important respects. In the first place, we find that a separate place is accorded to the science of language or what we would call grammar. Secondly, τὸ ἱστορικόν, which is just one exegetical 'tool' in the Varronian system, is also given special prominence. Indeed, 'historical' material is further subdivided by Asclepiades according to its degree of truth into 'history', 'myth', and 'fiction', and according to type of subject matter into *personae* (i.e. πρόσωπα θεῶν καὶ ἡρώων καὶ ἀνδρῶν ἐπιφανῶν or πρόσωπα θεῖά τε καὶ ἀνθρώπινα καὶ ἡρωικά), places and dates (τόποι καὶ χρόνοι), and actions (πράξεις). This second division has a parallel in the Varronian system, in which 'historical' subject matter is classified as γενεαλογ-

pp. 252-55. (A. Kaminka, 'Bibelexegese', *EJ*[D] 4 [1929], cols. 622-23, has expressed the view that the μέρη of the 'old' system are reflected in the comment on Neh. 8.8 found in *y. Meg.* 4.1 [74d] [cf. also the parallels in *b. Ned.* 37b, *b. Meg.* 3a, and *Gen. Rab.* 36.8]. It is difficult to accept this view, however, for the corrections of the scribes cannot be seen as a legitimate parallel to Alexandrian διόρθωσις, and it is most improbable that the word הכריעים indicates anything resembling κρίσις ποιημάτων. See W. Bacher, *Die exegetische Terminologie der jüdischen Traditionsliteratur*. I. *Die bibelexegetische Terminologie der Tannaiten* [Leipzig, 1899], p. 87 with n. 4).

39. See *Adv. math.* 1.252; 1.91, 96 and 97ff., 247 and 248ff., 269 and 270ff. That the Asclepiades mentioned by Sextus is to be identified with the grammarian from Myrleia is generally assumed in scholarship of the twentieth century. Doubts have again been raised by W.J. Slater, 'Asklepiades and *Historia*', *GRBS* 13 (1972), pp. 331-32, but these do not appear to be widely shared. See Neuschäfer, *Origenes als Philologe*, pp. 155, 202-203, 398-99 n. 10, 410-11 n. 122; S. Fortuna, 'Sesto Empirico: ἐγκύκλια μαθήματα e arti utili alla vita', *SCO* 36 (1986), p. 125 with n. 10; G.[M.] Rispoli, *Lo spazio del verisimile* (Naples, 1988), pp. 183-84 with n. 33; V. Di Benedetto, 'At the Origins of Greek Grammar', *Glotta* 68 (1990), pp. 36-38.

40. See Sextus, *Adv. math.* 1.92-93. A more detailed discussion of the 'special' part of grammar will be provided below, pp. 236-39.

ικόν, τοπικόν, χρονικόν, and πραγματικόν.[41]

The tripartite system of Asclepiades was particularly influential among Latin writers of the first century of the common era. As K. Barwick has noted, it is clearly visible in Seneca (*Ep.* 88.3), and is probably the basis of the bipartite system attested in Quintilian (*Inst.* 1.4.2), according to which 'grammar' is divided into *recte loquendi scientia*, and *poetarum enarratio*.[42] For if we leave out the ἱστορικόν of Asclepiades, Quintilian's categories correspond exactly to τὸ τεχνικόν and τὸ γραμματικόν. Moreover, Quintilian refers to the exegetical part of grammar not only as *poetarum enarratio*, but also as *historice* (*Inst.* 1.9.1). In all likelihood, then, since the 'historical' part of grammar was essentially exegetical, it was classed together with *enarratio* by Quintilian or his source.[43] However, Quintilian uses both names interchangeably to designate the composite whole formed by both, probably because of the fact that in the system of Asclepiades τὸ ἱστορικόν was a separate division.

We may now turn our attention to Philo. Is it possible to find the influence of any one of these systems in what he has to say about γραμματική? F.H. Colson, who translated many of the works of Philo for the Loeb Classical Library, and who was also an expert in these matters, apparently did not believe so. On the one hand, he does not see in Philo's specific discussions of the subject very much more than a general reflection of the definition of γραμματική such as we find it in Dionysius Thrax.[44] On the other hand, he does not think that Philo identifies a distinct 'technical' subdivision of the discipline, that is, our

41. On these subdivisions, see Usener, 'Ein altes Lehrgebäude', pp. 272, 286-87; Neuschäfer, *Origenes als Philologe*, pp. 155-56; and esp. Slater, 'Asklepiades', pp. 319-26.

42. See Barwick, *Remmius Palaemon*, pp. 219-23. Cf. S.F. Bonner, *Education in Ancient Rome* (Berkeley, 1977), pp. 55, 239, who points out that the tripartite system is also perceptible in Juvenal, *Sat.* 7.230-31.

43. Cf. Barwick, *Remmius Palaemon*, pp. 222-23. In general, to the extent that they differ, Barwick's explanation of the relationship between Asclepiades and Quintilian is to be preferred to that of F.H. Colson as given in his commentary on book one of the *Institutio oratoria* (Cambridge, 1924), pp. 28, 115-16 (on 1.2.14 and 1.9.1).

44. See esp. his note on *Cher.* 105 in vol. II of Philo's works published in LCL (Cambridge, MA, 1929), p. 485. The implications of this note and other notes are spelled out immediately below.

'grammar', and the τεχνικόν of Asclepiades.[45] M. Alexandre, who discusses some of Philo's grammatical terminology, does not seem prepared to go very much further than Colson as far as these matters are
concerned.[46] However, a new examination of the material reveals that
one of the systems mentioned above did indeed influence Philo, namely,
the tripartite scheme of Asclepiades. Of particular importance are two
passages, *Cher.* 105 and *Som.* 1.205. In the former passage, Philo
describes γραμματική as ποιητικὴν ἐρευνῶσα καὶ παλαιῶν
πράξεων ἱστορίαν μεταδιώκουσα, and in the latter passage, after
describing the 'lower' grammar as knowledge of writing and reading, he
goes on to describe the 'higher' as ἥ τε παρὰ ποιηταῖς ἐμπειρία
καὶ ἡ ἀρχαίας ἱστορίας ἀνάληψις. In his notes on these passages,
Colson appears to interpret the references to poetry and history as
rough equivalents of the objects of grammatical study mentioned by
Dionysius Thrax, *viz.* ποιηταί and συγγραφεῖς, probably on the basis
of the fact that in *Congr.* 148 Philo describes ('higher') γραμματική as
ἀνάπτυξις τῶν παρὰ ποιηταῖς τε καὶ συγγραφεῦσιν, a definition
which resembles that of Dionysius.[47] Yet in *De cherubim* and *De somniis*
Philo distinguishes not only between two separate *corpora*, but between
two separate activities, a point which had in fact been recognized by
H. Steinthal.[48] And these two activities are clearly identical to those
which are implied by the terms γραμματικόν and ἱστορικόν as used
by Asclepiades.

Now it is true that in his other definitions of ('higher') γραμματική,
Philo does not distinguish the two parts. However, in these cases, he not

45. See 'Philo on Education', *JTS* 18 (1917), p. 154 n. 4; 'The Grammatical
Chapters in Quintilian I. 4-8', *Cl.Q* 8 (1914), pp. 33-34.

46. See her edition of *De congressu* (Paris, 1967 = Les oeuvres de Philon
d'Alexandrie, 16), pp. 41-42, and her article, 'La culture profane chez Philon', in
Philon d'Alexandrie (Paris, 1967), pp. 108-13. More specific references are provided
below.

47. See *loc. cit.* (n. 44), and vol. V of Philo's works in the LCL edition (1934),
p. 406. In this latter note, Colson simply refers to his note on *Congr.* 148 (in vol. IV
of the LCL edition [1932], p. 580), which he understands as an echo of the Dionysian
definition. He therefore apparently regards *Som.* 1.205 as parallel to *Congr.* 148.
Alexandre, in her edition of *Congr.*, p. 209 n. 4, would seem to be essentially
following Colson.

48. See *Geschichte der Sprachwissenschaft bei den Griechen und Römern*, II
(Berlin, 2nd edn, 1891), p. 183. Steinthal's insight has been neglected by modern
annotators of Philo's works.

only describes it in a manner reminiscent of the definition of Dionysius Thrax, as he does in *Congr.* 148 (note the parallel description in *Agr.* 18: ἡ τῶν παρὰ σοφοῖς ποιηταῖς ἀκριβὴς ἔρευνα), but also simply as ἡ ἱστορία τῶν παρὰ ποιηταῖς (*Congr.* 74; cf. 15). That is, in these latter passages, he mentions only the 'historical' component of γραμματική. For this reason, and in view of the references to two distinct parts of the discipline in *De cherubim* and *De somniis*, we should understand passages such as *Congr.* 148 and *Agr.* 18 not as echoes of a general Dionysian definition, but as allusions to the γραμματικόν of Asclepiades, which naturally was described in very similar terminology (see Sextus, *Adv. math.* 1.91, 93, 270). In short, Philo, in the exact same manner as Quintilian (see immediately above), classes the exegetical and 'historical' divisions of Asclepiades together, and sometimes refers to the complex formed by the two by either name.[49]

We may now return to the other point made by Colson, namely, that Philo fails to speak of a specifically 'technical' division of grammar, that is, the τεχνικόν of Asclepiades. In the first instance, one might be tempted to explain this by appealing to Philo's mention of 'lower' grammar.[50] For since the τεχνικόν of Asclepiades also involved or at any rate came to involve not only theoretical treatment of language but also the laying down of norms,[51] it will have become difficult to distinguish the τεχνικόν from the 'lower' grammar. Indeed, some scholars have gone so far as to practically identify the two,[52] so one might claim that Philo did the same. This, however, is improbable. In the first place, in the original tripartite system of Asclepiades, there seems to have been

49. Alexandre, in her edition of *Congr.,* p. 114 n. 2, and in 'La culture profane', p. 108, apparently sees in *Congr.* 15 and 74 references only to the 'historical' part of grammar as understood in the restricted sense (she cites Marrou, *Histoire de l'éducation,* pp. 253-55). In *Congr.* 74, however, the term ἱστορία is used with an objective genitive, and thus is equivalent to the words ἀνάπτυξις and ἔρευνα as used in *Congr.* 148 and *Agr.* 18, rather than to ἱστορία as employed in *Cher.* 105 and *Som.* 1.205 (cf. also *Sacr.* 78). It may be acknowledged that in *Congr.* 15 the usage of ἱστορία is similar to that in the latter passages, but this may simply be a result of slight confusion between the two usages of the term.

50. See above, p. 224 with n. 32.

51. Cf. Quintilian's phrase cited above, *recte loquendi scientia,* and Barwick, *loc. cit.* (n. 42).

52. Slater, 'Asklepiades', pp. 317-18 (he equates the distinction in Quintilian, *Inst.* 1.4.2, with the distinction between 'lower' and 'higher' grammar); Neuschäfer, *Origenes als Philologe,* p. 202.

230   *Pursuing the Text: Studies in Honor of Ben Zion Wacholder*

a clear differentiation between 'lower' grammar and τὸ τεχνικόν. For as Barwick has indicated, while Asclepiades probably distinguished between 'lower' and 'higher' grammar, he also appears to have classified all of his three parts of grammar, including the 'technical', as subdivisions of the 'higher' grammar.[53] This view finds confirmation in Sextus Empiricus, *Adv. math.* 1.49, where 'lower' and 'higher' grammar are distinguished, and the latter is defined via what is essentially its 'technical' component.[54] Secondly, concerning Philo specifically, there is evidence that he made a similar distinction. In *Congr.* 148-50, after mentioning 'lower' grammar and exegesis (the latter to be understood as the combination of the γραμματικόν and ἱστορικόν of Asclepiades), he goes on to list certain grammatical topics and claim that they properly belong to philosophy rather than to grammar. The implication is therefore that in this regard these topics are separate from 'lower' grammar and exegesis. Now these topics, such as the parts of speech, and the study of the 'elements' (i.e. phonology), were classed as part of the τεχνικόν in the system of Asclepiades.[55] Therefore, even though Philo does not use this term, he seems to have regarded the main components of τὸ τεχνικόν as distinct from the exegetical subdivisions of γραμματική.[56] Consequently, rather than interpret this passage as a vague mention of topics of a not yet independent τεχνικόν, similar to that which we find in the enumeration of the 'parts' of grammar in Dionysius Thrax, as Colson appears to do,[57] I would view it as a

53. See *Remmius Palaemon*, pp. 254-55. Cf. B.A. Müller, *De Asclepiade Myrleano* (Leipzig, 1903), p. 34; M. Frede, 'The Origins of Traditional Grammar', in *Historical and Philosophical Dimensions of Logic, Methodology and Philosophy of Science* (The University of Western Ontario Series in Philosophy of Science, 12; ed. R.E. Butts and J. Hintikka; Dordrecht, 1977), p. 52; and with regard to Quintilian, the remarks of Colson, Comm. on *Inst.*, pp. xxix-xxx.
54. Cf. also the scholia on the *Ars grammatica* of Dionysius (ed. Hilgard), p. 164, where it is said that Ἑλληνισμός, which was a subdivision of the 'technical' component of γραμματική (see Sextus, *Adv. math.* 1.92, 175 and 176ff.), is a concern of the 'younger' grammar (i.e. 'higher' grammar, see Barwick, *Remmius Palaemon*, pp. 215-16).
55. See Sextus, *Adv. math.* 1.92; cf. 1.97-99, 131-32.
56. Cf. Siebenborn, *Die Lehre von der Sprachrichtigkeit*, p. 131.
57. See 'The Grammatical Chapters', *loc. cit.* (n. 45). Whether Alexandre takes a similar view is difficult to determine. In her edition of *Congr.*, pp. 42, 209 n. 5, and in 'La culture profane', p. 112, she notes that topics of the 'technical' part of grammar are discussed by Philo, but whether she thinks that Philo himself distinguished a

reflection of the 'Quintilianic' or 'Roman' version of the system of Asclepiades.

In short, it is the tripartite division of γραμματική or some close variation of it that we find in Philo. This will not be surprising, since that same division is also employed by other writers of early imperial times, in particular, Seneca, Quintilian (after a fashion), and Sextus Empiricus. To the implications of this tripartite scheme for Philo's attitude towards narrative aggada we shall return in due course.

At present, however, it is necessary to consider the evidence that Philo did indeed view the narrative aggada from the perspective of γραμματική. Naturally, one must start with the passage where Philo makes specific mention of what in all probability are narrative aggadic sources. This passage is found in the introduction to *De vita Mosis,* where Philo speaks of the sources on which he will base his account of the Jewish lawgiver:

τὰ περὶ τὸν ἄνδρα μηνύσω μαθὼν αὐτὰ κἀκ βίβλων τῶν ἱερῶν, ἃς θαυμάσια μνημεῖα τῆς αὑτοῦ σοφίας ἀπολέλοιπε, καὶ παρά τινων ἀπὸ τοῦ ἔθνους πρεσβυτέρων· τὰ γὰρ λεγόμενα τοῖς ἀναγινωσκομένοις ἀεὶ συνύφαινον καὶ διὰ τοῦτ' ἔδοξα μᾶλλον ἑτέρων τὰ περὶ τὸν βίον ἀκριβῶσαι (*Vit. Mos.* 1.4).

Here Philo gives the impression that he has employed oral sources as a supplement to the written biblical record in order to present a historical account of the life of Moses. And indeed, there is material in that account which corresponds to transmitted narrative aggada.[58] Thus, one can accept the general view that in *Vit. Mos.* 1.4 Philo is referring to (primarily narrative) aggadic material of one form or another.[59]

This text, however, is further illuminated by a passage in *De sacrificiis,* in which Philo discusses the value of traditional sources in a general fashion. This second passage allows us to conclude that he viewed narrative aggadic material in a manner similar to that in which he viewed the 'historical' component of γραμματική. In *Sacr.* 77-79, in the course of a discussion about the offering of 'new' firstfruits, Philo comments on the value of traditional sources of knowledge as compared

separate τεχνικόν is not clear. The fact that she refers only to Dionysius Thrax and a 'codification' of his system gives the impression that she has not adequately considered the matter.

58. See Siegfried, *Philo von Alexandria,* pp. 146-47 (cf. pp. 145-46); Stein, *Philo und der Midrasch,* pp. 43-46.

59. For more on this, see Kamesar, 'Narrative Aggada', p. 68.

232 Pursuing the Text: Studies in Honor of Ben Zion Wacholder

with 'new' wisdom, which is not taught. As he sees it, while one must acknowledge the significance of the former, this significance pales substantially in the face of 'new', 'self-taught' wisdom, the development of which is inspired by God. It is, however, his comments on the traditional sources that interest us here. He introduces these comments via citations of Lev. 19.32 and Num. 11.16, exploring the connotations of the term πρεσβύτερος which appears in both verses. He refers to the manner in which πρεσβύτεροι are appointed, and cites God's words to Moses in Num. 11.16 in the following form: οὓς γὰρ σὺ οἶδας, οὗτοί εἰσι πρεσβύτεροι. Philo then goes on to speak of the value of traditional sources of knowledge:

> ὠφέλιμον μὲν οὖν, εἰ καὶ μὴ πρὸς ἀρετῆς κτῆσιν τελείας, ἀλλά τοι
> πρὸς πολιτείαν, καὶ τὸ παλαιαῖς καὶ ὠγυγίοις ἐντρέφεσθαι δόξαις
> καὶ ἀρχαίαν ἀκοὴν ἔργων καλῶν μεταδιώκειν, ἅπερ ἱστορικοὶ καὶ
> σύμπαν τὸ ποιητικὸν γένος τοῖς τε καθ᾽ αὑτοὺς καὶ τοῖς ἔπειτα
> μνήμῃ παραδεδώκασιν (*Sacr.* 78).

As Colson has noted, Philo here describes the study of traditional sources of knowledge in a manner which corresponds to his description of the discipline of γραμματική in other passages.[60] Indeed, the term γραμματεῖς, although it is not given in Philo's citation, does occur in Num. 11.16, and may have led him to portray the study of traditional material in this fashion.[61] In addition, it would appear that Philo's description is even more specific than Colson intimates. For when Philo speaks of the object of the study of old teachings as the 'ancient record of great deeds', he probably has in mind not just γραμματική, but its historical component, i.e. τὸ ἱστορικόν.[62]

Philo continues to develop the idea of the secondary position of traditional sources as compared with 'new' wisdom by citing Lev. 26.10:

---

60. See his note on this passage in his translation of the text (1929 = LCL Philo, II), p. 153. He is followed by A. Méasson in her French translation (Paris, 1966 = Les oeuvres de Philon d'Alexandrie, 4), p. 139 n. 2, and A. Mendelson, *Secular Education in Philo of Alexandria* (MHUC, 7; Cincinnati, 1982), p. 45.

61. It may be acknowledged, of course, that the term γραμματεύς is not the equivalent of γραμματικός, and does not mean 'scholar of literature' (see E.J. Bickerman, *The Jews in the Greek Age* [Cambridge, MA, 1988], p. 163; cf. A. Deissmann, *Bible Studies* [Edinburgh, 1901], pp. 110-12). However, Philo's interpretation is based, as often, on the broader connotations of the root, and is not dependent on the precise meaning of the word γραμματεύς.

62. See above, pp. 226-27. The word δόξαι, on the other hand, could be an allusion to the third, i.e. 'exegetical' part of grammar. See below, pp. 237-39.

φάγεσθε παλαιὰ καὶ παλαιὰ παλαιῶν, ἀλλὰ καὶ παλαιὰ ἐκ προσώπου νέων ἐξοίσετε. According to Philo, the first half of this verse teaches us

> πολιὸν...μάθημα χρόνῳ μηδὲν ἀρνεῖσθαι πειρωμένους καὶ γράμμασι σοφῶν ἀνδρῶν ἐντυγχάνειν καὶ γνώμαις καὶ διηγήσεσιν ἀρχαιολογούντων παρεῖναι καὶ φιλοπευστεῖν ἀεὶ περὶ τῶν προτέρων καὶ ἀνθρώπων καὶ πραγμάτων, τοῦ μηδὲν ἀγνοεῖν ὄντος ἡδίστου (*Sacr.* 79).

It is this paragraph that allows us to establish a connection between the present passage and *Vit. Mos.* 1.4. For the bipartite differentiation of the γράμματα σοφῶν ἀνδρῶν, which are 'read', and the γνῶμαι καὶ διηγήσεις ἀρχαιολογούντων, which are communicated orally,[63] resembles the distinction between the written biblical record and the orally transmitted information of the 'elders' in that passage. And again in this paragraph, in an even more explicit fashion than in § 78, Philo refers to the object of the study of traditional sources in terminology which is associated with the grammarian's ἱστορικόν. In what is clearly a generalized description of that study, he uses the phrase φιλοπευστεῖν περὶ τῶν προτέρων καὶ ἀνθρώπων καὶ πραγμάτων, and as we have seen above, ἄνθρωποι and πράγματα constitute some of the defined objects of τὸ ἱστορικόν.[64] It would seem natural, therefore, to conclude that he viewed the narrative aggadic material, to which he refers in *Vit. Mos.* 1.4, in a similar fashion.

But what does Philo actually have in mind in *Sacr.* 79? Most scholars have simply assumed that since he is obviously speaking of Greek sources in § 78, such sources still constitute the principal object of attention in the following paragraph.[65] In this case, the γράμματα σοφῶν ἀνδρῶν would presumably denote the writings of the classical authors,

---

63. Colson, *ad loc.* (LCL Philo, II, p. 155), translates παρεῖναι with 'listen', a more accurate rendering than that found in other modern-language translations of Philo's works.

64. See above, pp. 226-27.

65. See Siegfried, *Philo von Alexandria*, p. 139; H.A. Wolfson, *Philo* (Cambridge, MA, 4th edn, 1968), I, p. 36; D.T. Runia, *Philo of Alexandria and the 'Timaeus' of Plato* (PhAnt, 44; Leiden, 1986), pp. 75-76 with n. 3; cf. Colson, LCL Philo, IV (1932), p. 577 (the passage is cited as '78f.'); M.(E.) Stein, *Filon ha-aleksandroni* (Warsaw, 1936/7), p. 54; Y. Amir, 'Authority and Interpretation of Scripture in the Writings of Philo', in Mulder (ed.), *Mikra*, pp. 428-29 (the reference in n. 40 should read *Sac.* 78-79).

234   *Pursuing the Text: Studies in Honor of Ben Zion Wacholder*

and the γνῶμαι καὶ διηγήσεις ἀρχαιολογούντων would refer to the interpretations of their writings. The term ἀρχαιολογία, or at least its Latin equivalent, is used of the 'historical' concerns of the grammarian.[66] However, it seems more probable that Philo is speaking of traditional sources generally, including Jewish sources, as E.R. Goodenough apparently thinks,[67] or indeed that he has shifted his primary focus to the latter.[68] In favor of this possibility is the fact that the term πρεσβύτεροι, with which Philo introduces his discussion of the value of traditional sources via Lev. 19.32 and Num. 11.16, is also used of Jewish interpreters in *Vit. Mos.* 1.4. Indeed, it is tempting to suggest that his apparent reference to pagan γραμματική in *Sacr.* 78 was inspired, as stated, by the presence of the term γραμματεῖς in Num. 11.16, and that the allusion to traditional Jewish sources in *Sacr.* 79 was inspired by the word πρεσβύτερος in that same verse. Moreover, the specifically Philonic usage of the term ἀρχαιολογέω must be considered. This term, not particularly common in Philo, is used to describe traditional Jewish (oral) interpretation in *Spec. leg.* 1.8.

Now, if Philo is speaking of Greek sources in § 78 of *De sacrificiis*, but of Jewish sources in § 79, he clearly regarded what we call narrative aggadic sources as something similar to the historical component of γραμματική. For in § 79 he describes such sources in a manner which recalls the ἱστορικόν, and his description is given in close connection to what is generally acknowledged as a reference to γραμματική [and especially its 'historical' component, A.K.] in § 78. However, even if Philo has primarily Greek sources in mind in § 79 of *De sacrificiis*, this does not affect the validity of the parallel between this passage and *Vit. Mos.* 1.4. For the similarity between these two passages would allow us to conclude that he viewed the Jewish sources of *Vit. Mos.* 1.4 in a light similar to that in which he viewed the Greek sources of *Sacr.* 79. Therefore, we may employ the latter passage to understand the former, and conclude that he viewed the narrative aggada as something similar to the ἱστορικόν.

66. See Suetonius, *De gramm. et rhet.* 20.
67. See *By Light, Light: The Mystic Gospel of Hellenistic Judaism* (New Haven, 1935), p. 93.
68. This may be the view of A. Mendelson (compare *loc. cit.* [n. 60] with his *Philo's Jewish Identity* [BJS, 161; Atlanta, 1988], p. 21), but he does not make such a view explicit.

Thus far, I have argued that Philo was under the influence of the (originally) Asclepiadean system of γραμματική, and that he viewed the narrative aggada as belonging to the 'historical' department of that discipline. We must now turn to the implications of Philo's acceptance of the Asclepiadean system for his view of the narrative aggada and the role he was willing to accord to it in his exegesis.

It has been noted above that a chief feature of the system of Asclepiades was the fact that the 'historical' part of grammar was separated from the other tasks of exegesis. One result of such a separation seems to have been that this part was given special prominence. In fact, S.F. Bonner has concluded that the tripartite system had an effect on actual instruction, and that the 'historical' study of literature will have constituted a separate course in the schools.[69] In any case, however, this emphasis on τὸ ἱστορικόν apparently led to a reaction, in that it came to be perceived as an area in which time was wasted on minutiae and irrelevant detail.[70] Indeed, it is noteworthy that criticism of this part of γραμματική is best attested in those writers who were under the influence of the tripartite system of Asclepiades, namely, Seneca, Quintilian, Juvenal and Sextus Empiricus. Seneca, for example, while he speaks against the art of grammar as a whole because it does not lead one to virtue, nevertheless appears to pour most of his scorn on the 'historical' part.[71] The same is true of Juvenal.[72] Quintilian, for his part, differs from these authors in that he was in the business of formulating actual recommendations. And while he recognizes the necessity of explaining *historiae,* he advises against wasting too much effort on this activity (*Inst.* 1.8.18-21). As a matter of fact, as Colson has suggested, this attitude may explain why Quintilian changes the normal sequence of the three parts of grammar in the system of Asclepiades, and treats the 'historical' part after the 'special' (i.e. exegetical) part. That is, this could be his way of de-emphasizing its importance.[73] In short, the separation

69. *Education in Ancient Rome,* pp. 238, 239. Cf. Colson, 'The Grammatical Chapters', pp. 45-46.

70. See Kamesar, 'Evaluation', pp. 42-43.

71. See *Ep.* 88. 2-8 (esp. 6-8), 37-40; *De brevitate vitae* 13 (esp. 13.9: 'dubitare se interim Fabianus noster aiebat, an satius esset nullis studiis admoveri quam his inplicari').

72. See *Sat.* 6.450-56, but esp. 7.230-36, where of the three activities of the grammarian, the 'historical' explanations are singled out for ridicule.

73. See Colson, 'The Grammatical Chapters', pp. 45-46; Comm. on *Inst.,* p. 114.

of the ἱστορικόν from the other components of exegesis, whatever its origin, seems to have led to an emphasis on 'historical' matters which came to be regarded as excessive.

However, those who had more extreme views than Quintilian may have taken more stringent measures than he suggests. In particular, it will have been possible not only to restrict greatly the 'historical' study of literature, but simply, because τὸ ἱστορικόν was a separate branch of γραμματική in the system of Asclepiades, to 'departmentalize' it away. And this is, I submit, what we have in Philo. For he describes the Essenes as doing the exact same thing with regard to another discipline of which he accepted a tripartite structure, namely, philosophy. In his essay *Quod omnis probus liber sit* 80, Philo says that the Essenes dismiss the logical and most of the physical part of philosophy, the former because it is full of irrelevancies and does not lead to virtue (cf. the preceding paragraph), and the latter because it is concerned with matters beyond the knowable. Instead, they concentrate their efforts on the ethical branch of philosophy, employing their ancestral laws as guides. And Philo's description of the procedure of the Essenes reflects no doubt his own inclinations.[74] Indeed, the very fact that he expresses their choices in terms of the Stoic tripartite division of philosophy would appear to confirm this assumption.[75] Accordingly, it may be that he undertook similar measures of 'departmentalization' with regard to γραμματική.

The basis for this suggestion is the very nature of Philonic exegesis, especially as viewed from the Graeco-Latin grammatical perspective. For the focus of Philonic interpretation is more or less the same as that of the exegetical part of grammar (i.e. the γραμματικόν or ἰδιαίτερον) in the Asclepiadean system. I refer here, however, not so much to the γραμματικόν of Asclepiades himself as to the character which that component of the discipline had acquired by early imperial times, especially as it is discernible in Sextus Empiricus, *Adv. math.* 1.

The exegetical part of grammar in the system of Asclepiades, that is,

---

74. See *Congr.* 53; *Som.* 1.53-54; Sandmel, *Philo's Place*, p. 193. Cf. O. Betz, *Offenbarung und Schriftforschung in der Qumransekte* (WUNT, 6; Tübingen, 1960), pp. 70-72.

75. Cf. W. Völker, *Fortschritt und Vollendung bei Philo von Alexandrien* (TU, 49.1; Leipzig, 1938), pp. 175, 272 n. 2; M. Petit in her edition of *Quod omnis probus liber sit* (Paris, 1974 = Les oeuvres de Philon d'Alexandrie, 28), pp. 108-109 (with p. 77).

τὸ γραμματικόν, or τὸ ἰδιαίτερον, is described as that in which τὰ ἀσαφῶς λεγόμενα ἐξηγοῦνται, τά τε ὑγιῆ καὶ τὰ μὴ τοιαῦτα κρίνουσι, τά τε γνήσια ἀπὸ τῶν νόθων διορίζουσιν (Sextus, *Adv. math.* 1.93). The first phrase obviously describes the explanation of obscure words and usages. The third phrase, on the other hand, refers to the task of determining the authenticity of the works of an author. However, it is possible, as A. Gudeman apparently believed, that textual criticism, that is, the διορθωτικόν of the Varronian system, is also included under this rubric.[76] For while it may be that Sextus is referring primarily to the determination of the authenticity of complete works, he could also be thinking of the same activity as regards sections of works, especially lines of poetry. Quintilian, simply describing the text-critical activity of [Alexandrian] grammarians, speaks of these two forms of criticism in the same breath (*Inst.* 1.4.3). And in fact, the terms γνήσιος and νόθος are used of single lines in the scholia on the *Iliad*.[77]

The second phrase, finally, according to which grammarians τὰ ὑγιῆ καὶ τὰ μὴ τοιαῦτα κρίνουσι, calls for even more discussion. Most would agree with the assessment of Gudeman, that the reference is to the κρίσις ποιημάτων of Dionysius Thrax or the κριτικόν of the Varronian system.[78] Yet there has not been general agreement on what is meant by κρίσις in this context. Some have thought that it has what is probably the 'Alexandrian' sense of the term, that is, aesthetic evaluation of a literary text, or literary criticism.[79] Others believe that it is this phrase, rather than (or together with) the third one, that describes textual criticism.[80] In favor of this latter view is the fact that in early imperial times, the word κρίσις or its equivalent sometimes includes both literary and textual criticism (i.e. both the κριτικόν and the διορθωτικόν of the Varronian system).[81] However, already Colson

76. See *Outlines of the History of Classical Philology* (Boston, 3rd edn, 1897), p. 2. Why Gudeman omits this interpretation in the later German version of this work (*Grundriss*, p. 5) I cannot say.

77. See *Schol. in Il.* O.610-14a, Y.269-72a; Θ.185b, I.395a.

78. See *Outlines*, p. 2.

79. Steinthal, *Geschichte der Sprachwissenschaft*, II, p. 185. Cf. A. Gräfenhan, *Geschichte der klassischen Philologie im Alterthum*, III (Bonn, 1846), p. 7; R. Nicolai, *La storiografia nell'educazione antica* (Biblioteca di 'Materiali e discussioni per l'analisi dei testi classici' 10; Pisa, 1992), pp. 281 n. 92, 283.

80. Müller, *De Asclepiade Myrleano*, pp. 33-35; Di Benedetto, 'Origins of Greek Grammar', p. 37 n. 32. Cf. Rutherford, *Chapter in the History*, p. 400 n. 2.

81. See V. Di Benedetto, 'La *Techne* spuria', *ASNSP.L* III.3 (1973), p. 807 n. 1;

expressed a doubt that the term ὑγιής could mean 'sound' (text), and suggested the translation 'morally sound'.[82] Colson's view is probably the correct one, although it requires some refinement. On the one hand, it must be acknowledged that in the scholia on the *Iliad* the word ὑγιής is often employed in text-critical contexts, although it is generally used of correct word division, accentuation, punctuation, spelling, etc., and therefore might be better translated in these cases as 'grammatically correct'.[83] This category is narrower than 'textually sound', and perhaps does not perfectly fit the broader implications of the statement in *Adv. math.* 1.93. However, this consideration will hardly justify Colson's interpretation, and one must turn to other arguments. In the first place, the usage of the term ὑγιής in the writings of Sextus Empiricus himself suggests that while the translation 'morally sound' may not be quite accurate, the slightly broader rendering 'philosophically sound' would be.[84] And indeed, the validity of this translation in the present passage is confirmed by the actual treatment of 'criticism' which is given in the section of *Adv. math.* 1 devoted to τὸ ἰδιαίτερον (§§ 270-320). For although Sextus does not follow closely in this section the rubrics of §93, the only form of 'evaluation' or 'criticism' which is discussed is of a philosophical and moral nature, and it is indicated by the term διακρίνω.[85]

The nature of the discussion of 'criticism' in *Adv. math.* 1.270ff. of course also excludes the view that the phrase τὰ ὑγιῆ καὶ τὰ μὴ τοιαῦτα κρίνουσι could be a reference to aesthetic evaluation of

---

Neuschäfer, *Origenes als Philologe*, p. 248. Cf. Bonner, *Education in Ancient Rome*, p. 249.

82. 'The Grammatical Chapters', p. 46 n. 1.

83. This may be determined on the basis of an examination of the examples cited in the index of H. Erbse in vol. VI of his edition of *Scholia Graeca in Homeri Iliadem* (Berlin, 1983). Cf. V. Bécares Botas, *Diccionario de terminología gramatical griega* (AcSal.Artes dicendi: Fuentes para la linguistica retorica y poetica clasicas, 3; Salamanca, 1985), p. 387.

84. See *Pyrr. hyp.* 1.34, 116; 2.42, 101, 105, 113, 124; *Adv. math.* 1.206, 310; 7.78, 109, 316, 397; 8.62, 112, 118, 122, 139; 9.41; 10.111; 11.15. (In *Adv. math.* 1.218 the adverbial form is used of speaking Greek 'correctly'; cf. directly above and the preceding note.)

85. *Adv. math.* 1.280 (cf. § 310). Note that the verb ἀθετέω does not have any text-critical connotations here, but is used as it usually is in Sextus Empiricus, and means to reject or disallow theses, arguments, the validity of the senses, etc. See *Adv. math.* 3.64; 5.49, 73; 7.62, 260; 8.56, 99; 9.2; cf. 8.142.

literature. Those who have taken this view seem to have been influenced by a conception of κρίσις which was dominant in the Hellenistic period, and especially in 'classical' Alexandrian exegesis. While this form of criticism continued, there was an increased tendency towards philosophical and moralistic evaluation of literature in early imperial times, probably as a result of Stoic influence.[86] The view of κρίσις which we find in Sextus Empiricus is in perfect accord with this trend.[87]

More than the nature of 'criticism', however, one must consider the entire character of the ἰδιαίτερον as it emerges from *Adv. math.* 1.270-320. For one would conclude from reading this section that at least in some circles this 'exegetical' part of grammar was dominated by two of the three parts mentioned in § 93, *viz.* the interpretation of obscure words and poetic usages (= the γλωσσηματικόν and τεχνικόν of the Varronian system),[88] and 'criticism' as understood in the manner described. In this section Sextus is concerned with the claim of the grammarians to understand the meaning of the words of literary texts, and to determine their philosophical (and moral[89]) value. Aesthetic criticism, textual criticism, and issues concerning the authenticity of works are neglected. When one turns to Philo, one finds a similar phenomenon. For the leading elements of Philonic exegesis are the careful explanation of words and expressions (i.e. the γλωσσηματικόν and τεχνικόν of the Varronian system), and κρίσις as understood in the moral and philosophical sense.[90]

86. Such a trend is clearly visible in books such as the *Quaestiones Homericae* of Heraclitus, the *De audiendis poetis* of Plutarch, and the *De Homero* of Ps.-Plutarch. Cf. Schäublin, *Untersuchungen,* pp. 162-63; Marrou, *Histoire de l'éducation,* pp. 249-50, 255-56 (his remarks here in fact refer to early imperial times, cf. p. 152).

87. Neuschäfer, *Origenes als Philologe,* pp. 250-53, has expressed doubts that the moral evaluation of literature was actually placed under the rubric of κρίσις ποιημάτων. His doubts will be unjustified, however, if the interpretation of the evidence from Sextus Empiricus given above is correct.

88. It would seem from Sextus, *Adv. math.* 1.253, that in the original system of Asclepiades, the treatment of glosses was included within τὸ ἱστορικόν, as in the scheme of Dionysius Thrax (see above, p. 224). However, as the system developed, the γλωσσηματικόν found a more natural position within the ἰδιαίτερον. For it appears under this rubric in the presentation of Sextus (*Adv. math.* 1.313).

89. Cf. Rutherford, *Chapter in the History,* p. 391 n. 1.

90. The fact that Philo may engage in 'criticism' without widely employing the technical term κρίσις does not detract from this argument, for this phenomenon is attested in the exegetical literature of the period. See Neuschäfer, *Origenes als*

In short, the early imperial form of the Asclepiadean γραμματικόν or ἰδιαίτερον, in which we find a shift towards moral and philosophical exegesis, appears to be reflected in Philonic interpretation. Moreover, as we have seen above, the Asclepiadean tripartite division of the entire discipline of γραμματική is also present in Philo.[91] Thus, when one removes τὸ ἱστορικόν from consideration, one will find a rough correspondence between Philo's view of γραμματική as a whole and of its principal component and the imperial form of the Asclepiadean system. It is therefore natural to suggest that Philo's obsessive concern with the γραμματικόν led him to reduce to an absolute minimum the role of the ἱστορικόν, and consequently, of narrative aggadic material in his exegetical endeavors. The very structure of the Asclepiadean system, in which τὸ ἱστορικόν is separate from the other components of exegesis, will have greatly facilitated and perhaps even encouraged this tendency.

In conclusion, Philo's procedure with regard to narrative aggada appears to have been determined by two factors. On the one hand, more extensive narrative aggadic embellishment seems to have been reduced in a certain type of Alexandrian Jewish exegesis, specifically, that type associated with Demetrius. It is this form of exegesis that has links with classical Alexandrian interpretation, and the narrative aggadic material was elaborated and/or adapted according to standards which were employed by Alexandrian Homeric exegetes. In other words, there was, as Sandmel intuitively perceived, a 'rationalist' critique and adaptation of narrative aggada. However, this operation was probably motivated more by literary than by religious considerations, and it had already been carried out by Philo's predecessors in what might be termed a 'scientific' exegetical school. In fact, it is likely that Philo had access to the narrative aggada primarily via a tradition which had passed through the 'scientific' or 'rationalist' filter.[92] Thus, the 'rationalist' component of Philo's view of narrative aggada was practically predetermined.

On the other hand, the more specifically Philonic attitude towards narrative aggada is not so much 'rationalist' or 'religious' as it is moralist. This may seem strange, since it is widely acknowledged that a chief feature of the development of narrative aggada was the tendency of the aggadists to rearrange and alter the biblical tradition on the basis of

Philologe, pp. 247, 248; cf. pp. 250-53, and above, n. 87.

91. See above, pp. 227-31.

92. I prefer the term 'scientific', often used by I. Heinemann (see, e.g., *Darkhei ha-aggada*, p. 186), to 'rationalist', employed by Sandmel, *Philo of Alexandria*, p. 133.

didactic/moralistic considerations. However, such a tendency was probably considerably less pronounced in a 'Demetrian-like' tradition of literal exegesis than in other forms of narrative aggada which are known to us. And if this is the tradition via which Philo had access to narrative aggadic sources, a 'moralistic' reaction on his part is quite comprehensible. What this means of course is that developments in Judaeo-Hellenistic interpretation run parallel to those of the Greek world as a whole. For there was a general movement in late Hellenistic and early imperial times away from the aesthetic and 'historical' criticism of classical Alexandrian interpretation towards the moral and philosophical exegesis of the Stoics. The moralistic and philosophical approach to literature of course goes back to the classical period and was always present in some measure,[93] but it is in early imperial times that it becomes particularly well incorporated into 'scientific' systems of γραμματική. Indeed, so much is clear from the treatment of τὸ ἰδιαίτερον in Sextus, *Adv. math.* 1.270-320. The same approach is also visible in Philo, and probably explains why he tends in his exegesis to minimize the role of narrative aggada, which is viewed by him as an element of τὸ ἱστορικόν.[94] The fact that he appears to have been under the influence of the Asclepiadean tripartite division of γραμματική, in which τὸ ἱστορικόν is separate from the other parts of the exegetical task, will have allowed him to perform such an operation in a most natural and thorough fashion.

93. See W. Kroll, *Studien zum Verständnis der römischen Literatur* (Stuttgart, 1924), pp. 64-86.

94. Thus, although Philo's approach to the narrative aggada involves both a greater respect for Jewish tradition and a more positive 'middle Stoic' attitude towards γραμματική (cf. E. Norden, *Die antike Kunstprosa* [Leipzig, 1898], II, pp. 673-74; A. Stückelberger, *Senecas 88. Brief* [Heidelberg, 1965], pp. 60-68) and its 'historical' component, as a whole it would not be unlike the position attributed to the author of the Pastoral Epistles by F.H. Colson, '"Myths and Genealogies"—A Note on the Polemic of the Pastoral Epistles', *JTS* 19 (1918), pp. 265-69. Colson suggests that there was a Judaeo-Hellenistic 'historical' exegesis of the Bible, which has not been preserved, similar to that of pagan grammarians, and that this form of interpretation is the target of [an essentially moralistic, A.K.] criticism in the Epistles. As we have seen above, however, this variety of exegesis has indeed been preserved in Demetrius (cf. Walter, 'Jüdisch-hellenistische Literatur', p. 78), and apparently survived in some form into Philo's time. Nevertheless, that such a Judaeo-Hellenistic form of interpretation is the object of concern in the Epistles seems to be less definitively demonstrable than that it was part of the tradition inherited by Philo. Cf. Kamesar, 'Evaluation', p. 49 n. 41.

Finally, it should be pointed out that in later Greek and Latin patristic critique of the narrative aggada these same two elements, one 'rationalist' and one 'moralist', are also present. The difference between the patristic and the Philonic attitudes is that while in the latter the 'moralist' element is dominant, in the former the 'rationalist' element seems to have been determinative.[95] In this sense, there is in the later critique of the narrative aggada a return to the 'rationalist' approach which is implicit in the fragments of Demetrius. This should not be entirely surprising, since 'scientific' Greek and Latin patristic exegesis, as it developed in the period from Origen to Cyril and Theodoret, did involve a certain revival of the spirit of classical Alexandrian interpretation.

95.　See Kamesar, 'Evaluation', pp. 42-70.

THE 'ANTIOCHENES IN JERUSALEM'. AGAIN[*]

Getzel M. Cohen

'A riddle wrapped in a mystery inside an enigma.' This is how
Winston Churchill described Russia in 1939. The same might be said of
2 Macc. 4.9.

One of the crucial events leading up to the Hasmonean Revolution was
the well-known request that Jason, the high priest in Jerusalem, made to
Antiochos IV Epiphanes. According to the author of 2 Maccabees Jason,
having bought the high priesthood, promised Antiochos an additional
150 talents if the king would grant him permission to build a gymnasium
and an *ephebeion* and to register 'the Antiochenes in Jerusalem'
(2 Macc. 4.9, τοὺς ἐν Ἱεροσολύμοις Ἀντιοχεῖς ἀναγράψαι). This
last phrase has been the subject of much debate. Three major schools of
thought are represented by the expositions of Eduard Meyer, Elias
Bickerman and Victor Tcherikover. Meyer thought the phrase meant the
Jerusalemites were given the same rights as the citizens of Antioch on
the Orontes.[1] Bickerman suggested that it indicated the existence of a
corporate entity, a *politeuma*, named after Antiochos.[2] Tcherikover,
following Bevan and Niese, argued that it demonstrated 'Jason received

---

* I am most grateful to Adam Kamesar for reading an earlier draft of this paper.

1. E. Meyer, *Ursprung und Anfänge des Christentums*, II (Stuttgart and Berlin, 1925), p. 145.

2. E. Bickerman(n), *Der Gott der Makkabäer* (Berlin, 1937), pp. 59-65; followed by M. Hengel, *Judaism and Hellenism* (London, 1974), I, pp. 277-79 who interpreted the actions of Jason and his followers as 'preparations to found the new *polis* "Antioch in Jerusalem"' (p. 277) and commented that 'we should not reject out of hand Bickermann's suggestion that the citizens of the "Antioch" formed themselves into a kind of association preparatory to the foundation of the city proper' (p. 278). Curiously in *Jews, Greeks and Barbarians* Hengel took a position apparently closer to Tcherikover: 'there were Jewish "Hellenists" from Jerusalem who were given permission by the new king Antiochus IV Epiphanes to disregard the "royal favour" (i.e. of Antiochos III) and to give Jerusalem a new constitution, namely that of a Greek city called Antiocheia' (*Jews, Greeks and Barbarians* [Philadelphia, 1980], p. 43).

from Antiochus permission to convert Jerusalem into a Greek *polis* called Antioch'.[3] Tcherikover's interpretation has been accepted, for example, by Vermes and Millar in the new edition of Schürer's *History of the Jewish People in the Age of Jesus Christ* as well as Abel and Starcky.[4] Among other things Starcky pointed to the colonizing activity of Antiochos Epiphanes and claimed that Antioch Jerusalem was, along with Antioch in Mygdonia, Antioch on the Kallirhoe, Antioch on the Saros and Antioch Ptolemais, a foundation of the king. In fact Mørkholm has demonstrated that Epiphanes' colonizing work was far more modest than generally believed and that none of the above cities can be firmly attributed to him.[5] And Bickerman objected that

> The often repeated hypothesis that Epiphanes made Jerusalem a polis named Antioch and that the inhabitants were called Antiochenes is philo-logically unsound and directly refuted by documents of 2 Macc. 11.27, 34 addressed to the *gerousia* and the *demos* of the Jews respectively and not to the Antiochenes. Likewise the letter of Antiochos IV (2 Macc. 11.22-26) speaks of the Jews and their temple.[6]

Nevertheless these objections are not, in themselves, compelling reasons for denying that Jason founded the *polis* of Antioch Jerusalem. They are, after all, *ex silentio*.

A major part of Tcherikover's discussion of 2 Macc. 4.9 is concerned with the verb ἀναγράφω. Tcherikover is uncomfortable with the definition 'to register' for ἀναγράφω. He readily admits that this definition is found on inscriptions and papyri but objects that

> [1] the list is invariably drawn up by officials...and minor civil servants and not by ministers of government... and [2] In all the above examples existent objects are counted and listed—yokes of cattle, priests, members of colonies, etc. It follows therefore that 'Antiochenes' existed in Jerusalem before Jason decided to register them. This, of course, is impossible: *Antiocheus* means a member of a certain organized community who does not exist independent of that community. This alleged registration of

3.   *Hellenistic Civilization and the Jews* (Philadelphia, 1959), p. 161; E.R. Bevan, *The House of Seleucus*, II (London, 1902), p. 168; and B. Niese, *Geschichte der griechischen und makedonischen Staaten seit der Schlacht bei Chaeronea*, III (Gotha, 1903), p. 228. See also M. Stern, *Zion* 57 (1991–92), pp. 233-43 (Hebrew).

4.   E. Schürer, *History of the Jewish People in the Age of Jesus Christ*, I (rev. G. Vermes and F. Millar; Edinburgh, 1973), p. 148; F.M. Abel and J. Starcky, *Les livres des Maccabées* (Paris, 1961), pp. 54-55.

5.   O. Mørkholm, *Antiochus IV of Syria* (Copenhagen, 1966), pp. 116-18.

6.   *The God of the Maccabees* (trans. H.R. Moehring; Leiden, 1979), p. 112.

individual existent Antiochenes, without connection with an existent community could only have taken place provided we were to interpret 'Antiochenes' as people 'holding citizen rights of the Syrian city of Antioch'; but Bickermann rightly rejects this supposition, which is in principle opposed to the basic elements of Hellenistic law.[7]

As to the first point: whether Jason personally drew up the list or whether—as is more likely—he delegated someone to do it is unclear. Tcherikover's second point is more significant. He admits that the verb can mean to register persons but objects that the persons have to be registered in an organization or community that already exists and how can this be? According to Tcherikover there was no such organization or community in Jerusalem at the time: the *polis* (so Tcherikover) or the *politeuma* (so Bickerman) did not yet exist. The third possibility, that he was registering people who were holding citizen rights in Antioch on the Orontes, was rightly dismissed by Bickerman. Since, in Tcherikover's view, there was no pre-existent community from which the 'Antiochenes' might be registered he dismissed the possibility that the verb could mean 'to register'. This difficulty prompted him to suggest that at 2 Macc. 4.9 ἀναγράφω means 'to recognize or proclaim'. In short, according to Tcherikover, 'Jason received permission from the King "to register the people of Jerusalem as Antiochenes", that is, to proclaim them as "Antiochenes". Henceforward they are not to be called "Jerusalemites" but "Antiochenes".'[8] Part of Tcherikover's thesis regarding 2 Macc. 4.9 depends on the assumption that at the time of Jason's actions there was no community of Antiochenes in Jerusalem. This assumption, however, may not be correct. In what follows I will (a) attempt to demonstrate that there may already have been Antiochenes in Jerusalem when Jason founded the gymnasium and (b) offer a tentative suggestion as to who these Antiochenes might have been. If my discussion does not convince perhaps it will at least amuse Ben Zion Wacholder, a scholar for whom I have the highest regard and a friend for whom I have the greatest affection.

The Antiochenes in Jerusalem are mentioned twice in 2 Maccabees: in the first instance they are called οἱ ἐν Ἰεροσολύμοις Ἀντιοχεῖς (4.9); in the second, ἀπὸ Ἰεροσολύμων Ἀντιοχεῖς (4.19).[9] The titulature is

---

7. *Hellenistic Civilization and the Jews*, p. 406.
8. *Hellenistic Civilization and the Jews*, p. 407.
9. The text of 2 Macc. 4.19 is corrupt. MS readings include Ἀντιοχέας, Ἀντιοχίας.

246   *Pursuing the Text: Studies in Honor of Ben Zion Wacholder*

strongly reminiscent of that found for other cities and colonies in the Hellenistic world. For example, in an important study Georges Le Rider investigated the phrase οἱ ἐν Ἱεροσολύμοις Ἀντιοχεῖς and compared it with the toponyms of various Near Eastern cities. He pointed out correctly that for cities such as Antioch in Mygdonia (Nisibis), Antioch on the Saros (Adana) and Antioch on the Kallirrhoe (Edessa) the addition of ἐν Μυγδονίᾳ, πρὸς τῶι Σάρῳ as well as ἐπὶ Καλλιρόῃ clearly have 'une valeur geographique et sont destinées à faire savoir de quels Antiochéens il s'agit'.[10] He noted similarly that in the legend Ἀντιοχέων τῶν ἐν Πτολεμαΐδι, the reference to Ptolemais has a 'valeur geographique' and hence that the toponym was Ἀντιόχεια ἡ ἐν Πτολεμαΐδι. Le Rider then suggested that the name Antioch Jerusalem was a similar phenomenon and that Bickerman's hypothesis that the phrase τοὺς ἐν Ἱεροσολύμοις Ἀντιοχεῖς ἀναγράψαι indicates the establishment of a *politeuma* must be rejected.

It is interesting to note, incidentally, that in much of the Hellenistic Near East the renamed city usually took the name of a local river, mountain or region as a way of distinguishing it from other like-named cities. Occasionally, however, the new name was simply combined with the old toponym. We know of at least two examples from Coele Syria: there are extant coins from Gaza with the legend ΣΕΛ(ΕΥΚΕΩΝ) ΤΩΝ ΕΝ ΓΑΖΗ and ΣΕΛ(ΕΥΚΕΩΝ) ΓΑΖΑΙΤΩΝ.[11] and coins from Antioch Ptolemais (Akko) with the legend ΑΝΤΙΟΧΕΩΝ ΤΩΝ ΕΝ ΠΤΟΛΕΜΑΙΔΙ.[12] If the titulature for the Antiochenes in Jerusalem is similar to that for *poleis* in Coele Syria it is also similar to that found (a) among the numerous Macedonian colonies that are attested in western Asia Minor and (b) the Phoenician settlements in Hellenistic Palestine. From western Asia Minor, for example, we have inscriptions

10. G. Le Rider, *Suse sous les Séleucides et les Parthes* (Paris, 1965), pp. 410-11.
11. *British Museum Catalogue Palestine*, p. 143 nos. 4-5; *Sylloge Nummorum Graecorum* (Copenhagen) *Palestine* no. 49; L. de Saulcy, *Numismatique de la terre sainte* (Paris, 1874), p. 211 no. 8. Cf., for example, coins of Apameia Myrleia (Bithynia) beginning in the first century BCE with the ethnic ΑΠΑΜΕΩΝ ΜΥΡΛΕΑΝΩΝ (*BMC Pontus*, p. 110 no. 15) and coinage of Hierapolis Castabala (Cilicia) of the Imperial period with the legend ΙΕΡΟΠΟΛΙΤΩΝΚΑΣΤΑΒΑΛΕΩΝ (*BMC Cilicia*, p. 84 no. 13).
12. *British Museum Catalogue Phoenicia*, pp. 128-29 nos. 1-10; *Sylloge Nummorum Graecorum* (Copenhagen) *Phoenicia* 177 and L. Kadman, *The Coins of Akko Ptolemais* (Jerusalem, 1961), pp. 92-108 nos. 1-63 and H. Seyrig, *Revue numismatique* (1962), pp. 26-32.

from Thyateira that record a dedication made to Seleukos by τῶν 'εν Θυατείροις Μακεδόνων οἱ ἡγεμόνες καὶ οἱ στρατιῶται (Orientis Graeci Inscriptiones Selectae 211) and a dedication set up by [οἱ π]ερὶ Θυάτειρ[α Μ]ακεδόνες (Tituli Asiae Minoris V.2 1166). In the second century BCE we have evidence for οἱ ἐκ Δοιδύης Μακεδόν[ες] (OGIS 314), [οἱ περὶ "Α]κρασον Μακεδόνες (OGIS 290), οἱ ἐξ Ἀγαθείρων Μακεδ[ό]νες (TAM V.2 1307), οἱ 'εκ Κοβηδύλης Μακεδόνες (TAM V.1 221), a Μακεδὼν Ὑρκάνιος (W. Vollgraff, Bulletin du Correspondance Hellénique 25 [1901], pp. 234-35) and ο[ἱ 'εκ -]εσπούρων Μακεδόνες (TAM V.2 1190).[13] These settlements of Macedonians, it should be noted, were not poleis.

I turn now to the Phoenician settlements in Palestine. When one discusses colonization during the Hellenistic period one thinks immediately of the Graeco-Macedonian settlements throughout the Near East. This was an immense undertaking. In fact its very immensity has tended to obscure other colonizing movements. One such phenomenon was the spread of Phoenician colonies throughout Palestine and the adjacent regions.[14] Evidence for Phoenicians in Palestine is extensive. For example, Tyrians may have founded a colony at Rabbath Ammon (Philadelpheia). It has also been suggested that they were settled in Gadara.[15] There were also Sidonian (i.e., Phoenician) colonies. From

13. In the Imperial period the coinage of many cities in Lydia and Phrygia bore double ethnics; see, for example, Blaundos (ΒΛΑΥΝΔΕΩΝ ΜΑΚΕΔΟΝΩΝ, BMC Lydia, pp. 47ff. nos. 45-48, 55-58, etc.) and Dokimeion (ΔΟΚΙΜΕΩΝ ΜΑΚΕΔΟΝΩΝ, BMC Phrygia, pp. 188ff. nos. 1-3, 19, 21-22, 25-33).

14. See M. Rostovtzeff, the first edition of the Cambridge Ancient History, VII (Cambridge, 1928), pp. 190-92; F.G. Millar, Proceedings of the Cambridge Philological Society (1983), pp. 58-59 and J.D. Grainger, Hellenistic Phoenicia (Oxford, 1991), pp. 112ff.

15. The evidence for Philadelpheia having a Tyrian colony is the following: Stephanos (s.v. 'Philadelpheia') says it was called Astarte. This may be a confusion with Asteria, a goddess who appears on coins of Philadelpheia and was worshipped there. Now Asteria was the mother of the Tyrian Herakles (Melkart) who was also worshipped in Philadelpheia; Cicero, De Natura Deorum 3.42; see also the commentary of A.S. Pease, M. Tulli Ciceronis De Natura Deorum, II (Cambridge, 1958) and Athenaeus 9.392d. The fact that Tyre and Philadelpheia were linked by religious ties has prompted the reasonable suggestion that Tyrians settled in Philadelpheia. See also G.F. Hill, British Museum Catalogue Arabia, pp. xxxix-xl, 40-41; Tcherikover, Hellenistic Civilization, p. 100; Hengel, Judaism and Hellenism, I, p. 43; A. Kasher, Jews and Hellenistic Cities in Eretz Israel (Tübingen, 1990), p. 25.

The evidence for Tyrians at Gadara is more tenuous. Kasher (Jews and Hellenistic

Shechem we have references to οἱ ἐν Σικίμοις Σιδώνιοι (Josephus, *Ant.* 11.344, 12.258). We do not know how many of these were actually Sidonians rather than local Samaritans claiming to be Sidonians. At the very least, the discovery of epigraphic evidence for Sidonian colonies at Marisa and Jamnia-on-the-Sea suggests that at Samaria the core of οἱ ἐν Σικίμοις Σιδώνιοι were Sidonians or their descendants.[16] At Marisa we have evidence for two Sidonians, Philotion and Eikonion, as well as for Apollophanes who was archon of οἱ ἐν Μαρίσηι Σιδώνιοι (*OGIS* 593); at Jamnia-on-the-Sea a recently published inscription has revealed the existence of a community of Sidonians in the time of Antiochos V Eupator ([οἱ ἐν τῶι τῆς Ἰαμνίας λιμ]ενι Σιδώνιοι).[17] Rostovtzeff

Cities) called attention to Meleager of Gadara who took particular pride in his birth-place and in Tyre where he was educated (*Greek Anthology* 7.417, 419) and sug-gested that this might indicate there was a Phoenician colony at Gadara; see also Hengel, *Judaism and Hellenism*, I, pp. 43, 62; *Jews, Greeks and Barbarians*, pp. 69, 118-19.

16.   On the Sidonians at Shechem see M. Delcor, *ZDPV* 78 (1962), pp. 34-38; cf., for example, A. Momigliano, *Alien Wisdom* (Cambridge, 1975), p. 108 who believed the Sidonians were really Samaritans and Hengel, who commented that 'during the period of persecution under Antiochus IV Epiphanes, the Samaritans described them-selves in a letter to the king as "Sidonians", presumably because there was a Phoenician trading colony in Shechem similar to those in Marisa and Philadelphia' (*Judaism and Hellenism*, I, pp. 90-91). In fact the epigraphic attestation for Sidonians at Marisa and Jamnia renders it likely that at Shechem the term actually referred to a group of Sidonians or their descendents; whether or not they were joined by local people is not known (see Tcherikover, *Hellenistic Civilization and the Jews*, p. 453).

I would also mention *Catalogue général des antiquités égyptiennes* (ed. C.C. Edgar; Cairo, 1911–16) 59003 (abbrev. *PCZ*) = V.A. Tcherikover and A. Fuks (ed.), *Corpus Papyrorum Judaicarum* (Cambridge, 1957) (abbrev. *CPJ*), a papyrus dated to 259 BCE which records a deed of sale drawn in Ammanitis of a slave girl, Sphragis, who was apparently a Sidonian (the text is partly restored). In Hellenistic Palestine Phoenicians were often called either Sidonians or Canaanites. See further Tcherikover's commentary to *CPJ* 1 and F.M. Abel, *Géographie de la Palestine*, I (Paris, 1933), pp. 254-58. On the tendency of cities near Judaea to identify them-selves as Phoenician or Sidonian see F. Millar, *Journal of Jewish Studies* 29 (1978), pp. 4-5.

17.   For the grave stone of Philotion, a 'Sidonia' at Marisa see J.P. Peters and H. Thiersch, *Painted Tombs in the Necropolis of Marissa* (London, 1905), p. 66 no. 7; for Eikonion, likewise a 'Sidonia', see F.M. Abel, *RB* 34 (1925), p. 275 no. 12.

On the extent of Hellenization in Marisa see G. Horowitz, 'Town Planning of Hellenistic Marisa', *PEQ* 112 (1980), pp. 93-111. Horowitz concludes that 'the town planning and architecture of Marisa in the Hellenistic period, while showing a few

suggested that the Sidonians at Marisa were organized as a *politeuma*[18] while Bar Kochva (quoted by Isaac, p. 139) suggested the same for the Sidonians at Jamnia-on-the-Sea. We may expect this was also true for the Sidonians at Shechem. Furthermore at Sidon itself there were a number of *politeumata* of Caunians (Caria), Termessians (Pisidia), Pinaereans (Lycia) and a fourth which cannot be identified.[19] The *stelae*, which probably date to the second half of the third century BCE, portray figures of mercenary soldiers with accompanying inscriptions. It is not clear, incidentally, whether the *politeumata* consisted only of soldiers or of civilian foreigners who were joined by soldiers from the respective cities. What about Jerusalem? Were there Phoenicians or other foreigners residing there? The paucity of the evidence prevents us from giving an unequivocal answer to that question. Nevertheless it may be useful to review the evidence in order to consider whether we can better understand who the Antiochenes in Jerusalem might have been.

As early as the time of the prophet Nehemiah there was a colony of Tyrian merchants there.[20] Interestingly Nehemiah was upset by the fact that the Tyrian merchants as well as Jews were conducting business in the streets of Jerusalem on the Sabbath. He was also bothered because Jews had intermarried with women of Ashdod, Ammon and Moab (Neh. 13.23-29). The problem of intermarriage was acute. Among others, a grandson of the high priest Eliashib had married the daughter

Hellenic influences, demonstrates the continuation of eastern tradition in many aspects'.

On the Sidonians at Jamnia see B. Isaac, 'Transactions of the American Philological Association', *IEJ* 41 (1991), pp. 132-44. Cf. the colony of Babylonian Jews settled in Batanaea by Herod the Great: οἱ ἐν Ἐκβατάνοις Βαβυλώνιοι Ἰουδαῖοι (Josephus, *Life* 54; cf. 56. See also G. Cohen, 'Revue archéologique', *TAPA* 103 [1972], pp. 83-95).

18. *Social and Economic History of the Hellenistic World* (Oxford, 1941), p. 520.

19. Caunians: P. Perdrizet, *RA* (1899) 42; Termessians: G. Mendel, *Catalogue des sculptures grecques, romaines et byzantines* I (Constantinople, 1912), p. 262 no. 103; Pinaereans, Mendel, *Catalogue*, I, pp. 266-67 no. 106; the unidentified *politeuma*: [-ndeans], L. Jalabert, *RA* (1904), pp. 5-6 no. 2. See also Bickerman, *Institutions des Seléucides* (Paris, 1938), pp. 88-90; Rostovtzeff, *Social and Economic History of the Hellenistic World*, p. 1401. On (primarily military) *politeumata* in the Hellenistic world see M. Launey, *Recherches sur les armées hellénistiques*, II (Paris, 1950), pp. 1064-85; for references to earlier works see p. 1064 no. 4.

20. Neh. 13.16-21; see also J. Jeremias, *Jerusalem in the Time of Jesus* (Philadelphia, 1975), p. 36.

of the Samaritan Sanballat.[21] Of course intermarriage with the surrounding non-Jewish population was a perennial problem against which the
Hebrew prophets constantly railed.

In the ancient Near East the populations of most major cities were
mixed. This was the case, for example, for Antioch on the Orontes,
Alexandreia and Memphis.[22] And according to Josephus, the population
of Seleukeia on the Tigris consisted of Greeks, Macedonians and Syrians
(*Ant.* 18.372; cf. *Ant.* 12.119). I have already mentioned the presence of
Phoenicians in many cities in the interior of Palestine in the Hellenistic
period. One thinks, too, of Meleager of Gadara who wrote, in the style
of an epitaph, 'Heaven born Tyre and Gadara's holy soil reared him to
manhood and beloved Cos of the Meropes tended his old age. If you are
Syrian, "Salaam", if you are Phoenician, "Naidius", if you are Greek,
"Chaire" and say the same yourself' (*Gr. Anth.* 7, 419, 5ff., trans.
W.R. Paton). Marisa had a strongly heterogeneous population. Tomb
inscriptions of Marisa dating from the end of the third century BCE
show a clear mix of Phoenician, Idumaean and especially Greek names.
For example, Apollophanes, the archon of the Sidonian *politeuma* at
Shechem was the son of Sesmaios (a Semitic name), the brother of Sabo
(an Idumaean name) and Ammonios (Egyptian-Hellenistic). The latter
had a son, Kosnatanos (an Idumaean name). Kosnatanos, in turn, named
his sons Babas and Babatas (Jewish-Nabataean) and his daughter,
Sabo.[23] The proximity of Marisa to Jerusalem prompted Hengel to
suggest that 'Conditions in the capital of Idumaea are certainly to be
understood as a parallel phenomenon to the Hellenizing tendency in
Jerusalem at the beginning of the second century BCE as it was a bare
twenty five miles away'. Furthermore Millar called attention to the fact
that Phoenician is the closest Semitic language to Hebrew and that the
Tyrian shekel was the currency in which the Temple dues were paid.[24]

21. Neh. 13.28; see also Josephus, *Ant.* 11.306-309.
22. Antioch: Libanius *Or.* 11.91-92; Malalas 201.12-202.6; Josephus, *Apion*
2.39, *Ant.* 12.119, *War* 7.43; and G. Downey, *A History of Antioch on the Orontes*
(Princeton, 1961), pp. 79-80. Alexandreia: Polybius 34 frg. 14 = Strabo 17.1.12.
Memphis: Strabo 17.1.32. See also Strabo, quoted by Josephus, *Ant.* 14.115, who
remarks that the population of Cyrene was divided into four groups: Greek citizens,
Libyans, metics and Jews.
23. Peters and Thiersch, *Painted Tombs in the Necropolis of Marissa*, p. 38 no. 1
(= *OGIS* 593), p. 40 no. 2; p. 44 no. 9; p. 45 nos. 10, 11; see further, Hengel,
Judaism and Hellenism, I, p. 62.
24. Hengel, *Judaism and Hellenism*, I, p. 62 and Millar, *PCPS* (1983), p. 59; see

The likelihood that there was a non-Jewish population in Hellenistic Jerusalem is certainly great. We know of prohibitions, including one issued by Antiochos III, against Gentiles entering various precincts of the temple.[25] Presumably these prohibitions were necessary because there were Gentiles in Jerusalem. However, whether they were living in Jerusalem or just visiting is not clear. In any event a non-Jewish community in Hellenistic Jerusalem might have presented a threat to traditional Jewish life that was not dissimilar to what the prophets had faced two centuries earlier.

Now one of the southernmost Phoenician cities was Akko. Under Ptolemy II Philadelphos it was renamed Ptolemais and then under the Seleucids it was renamed once again, Antioch. I have already noted that on coins its inhabitants now styled themselves ΑΝΤΙΟΧΕΩΝ ΤΩΝ ΕΝ ΠΤΟΛΕΜΑΙΔΙ. It was an important city. Its frequent appearance in the third century BCE in the Zenon papyri attests to that.[26] In fact Stern has suggested that it was the capital of Seleucid Coele Syria.[27] And just as Tyrians and Sidonians were present in Hellenistic Trans-Jordan, Samaria, Judaea and Idumaea as colonists, we may expect the same of people from Ἀντιόχεια ἡ ’εν Πτολεμαΐδι. Furthermore, if any of its citizens had been living in Jerusalem in the 170s BCE they probably would have been known as 'the Antiochenes' or 'the Antiochenes in Jerusalem'.[28] Not surprisingly the titulature attested for the Antiochenes in Jerusalem

also A. Ben-David, *Jerusalem und Tyros* (Tübingen, 1969), pp. 5-9.

25. Josephus, *Ant.* 12.145; cf. Philo, *Legatio ad Gaium* 212; *OGIS* 598, Josephus, *Ant.* 15.417 and *War* 5.194; *m. Kelim* 1.8. See also Bickerman, *Syria* 25 (1946/48), pp. 67ff. and Tcherikover, *Hellenistic Civilization and the Jews*, p. 439 n. 124 and articles cited there; Jeremias, *Jerusalem in the Time of Jesus*, p. 36 and Hengel, *Jews, Greeks and Barbarians*, p. 43.

26. See for example, *PCZ* 59004, 59008; *Pubblicazioni della società italiana per la ricerca dei papiri greci e latini in Egitto: Papiri greci e latini* (Florence, 1912–), pp. 406, 495, 616 (abbrev. *PSI*). See also Schürer, *History of the Jewish People*, II, p. 122 and n. 196; Tcherikover, 'Palestine under the Ptolemies', *Mizraim* IV-V (1937).

27. M. Stern, *History of Eretz Israel* (Tel Aviv, 1981), p. 75 (Hebrew); see also V. Tcherikover, *The Jews in the Graeco-Roman World* (Tel Aviv, 1961), pp. 41, 79-80, 104 (Hebrew) and Kasher, *Jews and Hellenistic Cities in Eretz Israel*, p. 56 n. 4; p. 69 and n. 43.

28. On the island of Delos, for example, the guild of Tyrian businessmen was known as 'the Tyrian Herakleistai, merchants and shippers', *Corpus Inscriptionum Graecarum* 2271.35; see also W.A. Laidlaw, *A History of Delos* (Oxford, 1933), p. 212.

is similar to that used by the Sidonian *politeumata* and suggests that they, too, were constituted as a *politeuma*. Of course one may well object that the same titulature could apply equally well to a group of people from some other Antioch, for example, Antioch on the Orontes. Nevertheless, given the regional importance and proximity of the Phoenician Antioch, I would opt for it rather than the larger—but more distant—city on the Orontes.

The fact that the Antiochenes in Jerusalem may have originated in Antioch Ptolemais may also explain another curious incident that the author of 2 Maccabees relates. At 4.19-20 he describes how, when the quinquennial games were being held at Tyre, Jason sent a religious embassy representing the Jerusalem Antiochenes (θεωροὺς ὡς ἀπὸ Ἱεροσολύμων Ἀντιοχεῖς ὄντας). These religious envoys, the *theoroi*, were charged with bringing 300 *drachmai* to pay for a sacrifice to Herakles-Melkart, the great god of Tyre. The envoys were bothered by the thought of using the money for a sacrifice to Herakles.[29] Instead they arranged for the money to be used for the equipping of triremes. Scholars generally assume that the envoys were Jewish and that their decision to avoid paying out the money for the sacrifice to Herakles reflects their concern about Jewish religious sensitivities.[30] But this is perhaps assuming more than is necessary. The text says nothing about the religion or ethnic background of the sacred envoys. The term used to describe the delegates is *theoros*. This word refers specifically to an envoy sent to consult an oracle or to bring an offering. We should consider the possibility that a delegation of Gentiles, coming from a city which was demonstrably in ferment over religious reforms, would have been equally sensitive to the concerns of the Jews in Judaea. Finally it is well to note where these particular games were being held. Tyre was the most important city of Phoenicia. Another Phoenician colony, the

---

29.   Alexander the Great had earlier offered sacrifices at the temple of Herakles; Arrian, *Anab.* 2.24.6; 3.6.1; Diod. 17.46.6. See also C. Bonnet, *Melqart. Cultes et mythes de l'Héraclès Tyrien en Méditerraneé* (Studia Phoenicia 8; Leuven, 1988), pp. 51-58. For Carthaginian *theoroi* who were present at Tyre during Alexander's siege of the city see Arr. 2.24.5 (Καρχηδονίων τινὲς θεωροὶ ἐς τιμὴν τοῦ Ἡρακλέους κατὰ δή τι[να] νόμιμον παλαιὸν εἰς τὴν μητρόπολιν ἀφικόμενοι) and Curtius 4.2.10 (*legati ad celebrandum sacrum anniversarium*). Cf., later on, thirty *legati* at Tyre (Curtius 4.3.19) and a Carthaginian embassy to Herakles in 310 BCE (Diodorus 20.14.1).

30.   See Bickerman(n), *Der Gott der Makkabäer*, p. 64 and Starcky, *Les livres des Maccabées*, p. 55.

Sidonian community at Shechem, was very proud of its connection with the mother city. In their correspondence with Antiochos Epiphanes the Sidonians laid great stress on this descent (Josephus, *Ant.* 12.260). If the Antiochenes in Jerusalem were themselves of Phoenician ancestry it would make perfectly good sense that Jason would want to send them and that they would want to go as a sacred delegation to Tyre.[31]

I would therefore suggest that the logical sequence in 2 Macc. 4.7-9 is as follows: Jason secured the high priesthood by paying a bribe to Epiphanes (4.8). He gave the king an additional payment in order to get permission to establish a gymnasium and *ephebeion* in Jerusalem and enroll the Antiochenes in Jerusalem in these institutions (4.9). The author of 2 Maccabees then says (4.10): ἐπινεύσαντος δὲ τοῦ βασιλέως καὶ τῆς 'ἀρχῆς κρατήσας εὐθέως ἐπὶ τὸν Ἑλληνικὸν χαρακτῆρα τοὺς 'ὁμοφύλους μετέστησεν. If one follows Tcherikover's thesis then one could understand the verse to mean that Jason immediately begin implementing the creation of the new city of Antioch Jerusalem. On the other hand, if my interpretation of 2 Macc. 4.9 is correct then we can understand this verse and those that follow in another light.

I have suggested that at the time of Jason's reforms there already existed a community of Antiochenes from Ptolemais Akko in Jerusalem. As was the case, for example, with the Sidonians in various Palestinian cities, these Antiochenes were probably organized as a *politeuma*. Jason now proposed to found a gymnasium and an *ephebeion* and to enroll these Antiochenes in both. The shock to the conservative Jewish population in Jerusalem must have been overwhelming. Jason's act was both a recognition of the community of the Antiochenes and, more importantly, a repudiation of Jewish tradition. It effectively removed the recognition that Antiochos III had earlier granted the Jews and their ancestral laws (Josephus, *Ant.* 12.142). This repudiation was particularly galling to the author of 2 Maccabees. Five times in the following verses he refers to it: εὐθέως ἐπὶ τὸν Ἑλληνικὸν χαρακτῆρα τοὺς 'ὁμοφύλους μετέστησεν (4.10); καὶ τὰ κείμενα τοῖς 'Ιουδαίοις φιλάνθρωπα βασιλικὰ διὰ Ιωάννου...παρώσας καὶ τὰς μὲν νομίμους καταλύων πολιτείας παρανόμους 'ἐθισμοὺς 'ἐκαίνιζεν (4.11); ἦν δ' οὕτως ἀκμή τις Ἑλληνισμοῦ καὶ πρόσβασις ἀλλοφυλισμοῦ (4.13); ἔσπευδον μετέχειν τῆς 'ἐν παλαίστρῃ παρανόμου χορηγίας (4.14); καὶ τὰς

---

31. On Tyre see Kasher, *Jews and Hellenistic Cities*, pp. 68-70 and Eissfeldt, *PW* s.v. 'Tyros', pp. 1876-1908.

μὲν πατρῴους τιμὰς 'εν οὐδενὶ τιθέμενοι (4.15). And this rejection of Jewish tradition, as the author of 2 Maccabees emphasizes (4.13), was the work of the high priest himself! Interestingly, the author of 2 Maccabees uses the same word, παρανόμος, to describe the 'εθισμούς Jason was introducing and the χορηγίας in the palaestra to which the priests were rushing. The contrast, of course, was with τὰς μὲν νομίμους...πολιτείας (4.11) that 2 Maccabees also refers to as τὰς μέν πατρῴους τιμάς (4.15) and τοὺς θείους νόμους (4.17), 'the divine laws' or the Torah. This was the basis of Jewish life and one violated them, as the author of 2 Maccabees warns, at one's peril! In contrast to 'the divine laws' the author of 2 Maccabees mentioned the Greek customs and attitudes that Jason was trying to introduce: τὸν Ἑλληνικὸν χαρακτῆρα (4.10), παρανόμους 'εθισμούς (4.11), 'ασμένως γὰρ ὑπ' αὐτὴν τὴν ἀκρόπολιν γυμνάσιον καθίδρυσεν, καὶ τοὺς κρατίστους τῶν 'εφήβων 'υποτάσσων 'υπὸ πέτασον ἤγαγεν (4.12), ἀκμή τις Ἑλληνισμοῦ (4.13), παρανόμου χορηγίας (4.14) and τὰς δὲ Ἑλληνικὰς δόξας (4.15). The sensitivity of the Jews in Jerusalem to Gentile influences on their way of life is a *topos* that surfaces over and over again in antiquity. In that context we can understand that the more conservative Jews in Jerusalem perceived Jason's reforms as a direct threat to their way of life, that is, the way of life prescribed by 'the divine laws'. In fact this is precisely what the author of 2 Maccabees says. For if Jason could give recognition to a Gentile community and could build a gymnasium for their use how long would it be before the blandishments of the gymnasium would attract the Jews? Not long indeed! According to the author of 2 Maccabees, the attraction of 'Hellenism' was so strong that soon after the gymnasium was built the priests were to be seen running from the Temple service to the gymnasium (4.13-14)! This, I suggest, is what the author of 2 Maccabees meant when he said εὐθέως ἐπὶ τὸν Ἑλληνικὸν χαρακτῆρα τοὺς ὁμοφύλους μετέστησεν.

Finally, we should note that the author of 2 Maccabees says nothing about the creation of a *polis*. For him the result of Jason's reforms was to introduce Greek culture and thought to Jerusalem. Tcherikover has commented that 'the setting up of the *gymnasion* and *ephebeion* at Jerusalem is not to be regarded as a cultural project and nothing more; their building is to be evaluated as a political and juridical precondition essential to the city's Hellenistic constitution'.[32] I would argue, on the

---

32. *Hellenistic Civilization and the Jews*, p. 163.

other hand, that the setting up of the gymnasium and the *ephebeion was* a cultural project. Its aim was to introduce Greek culture into Jerusalem and thereby undercut the influence of the ancestral Jewish customs and laws. Its presence brought 'Hellenism' as well as 'Greek thought and practice' to a peak in Jerusalem. And this, it would appear, was Jason's primary—if not his sole—objective.

1 Maccabees and Josephus give accounts that are similar in many details to the description of the Hellenistic reform in 2 Maccabees. 1 Maccabees, for example, stresses the desire of the Hellenizers to break down the social barriers between themselves and the Gentiles around them (1.11). According to 1 Maccabees the Hellenizers asked for and received permission ποιῆσαι τὰ δικαιώματα τῶν ἐθνῶν (1.13), they built a gymnasium in Jerusalem according to τὰ νόμιμα τῶν ἐθνῶν (1.14) and, as a result, they ἀπέστησαν ἀπὸ διαθήκης ἁγίας καὶ ἐζεύχθησαν τοῖς ἔθνεσι (1.15).

Josephus's account (*Ant.* 12.240-41) of these events ascribes the reforms to Menelaus. Josephus says the Hellenizers wanted τοὺς πατρίους νόμους (cf. *Ant.* 12.142) καταλιπόντες καὶ τὴν κατ' αὐτοὺς πολιτείαν ἔπεσθαι τοῖς βασιλικοῖς καὶ τὴν Ἑλληνικὴν πολιτείαν ἔχειν...τά τε ἄλλα πάνθ' ὅσα ἦν αὐτοῖς πάτρια παρέντες ἐμιμοῦντο τὰ τῶν ἀλλοεθνῶν ἔργα (240-41).[33] The Hellenizers, according to Josephus, wanted to repudiate the ancestral Jewish laws that were based on the Torah and that controlled their daily lives. In its place they wanted to conduct their lives by the customs and practices of the Gentiles (τὰ νόμιμα τῶν ἐθνῶν and τὰ τῶν ἀλλοεθνῶν ἔργα). For Josephus and 1 Maccabees as well as for the high priest Jason, the key point was the desire of the Hellenizing Jews to conduct their lives like Gentiles. If this desire also translated itself or was intended to translate itself into the creation of a *polis* neither Josephus nor 1 or 2 Maccabees says so explicitly.

In fact I can find only one incident that might be construed as evidence for a *polis* and even this is questionable: Jason's sending a religious delegation of Antiochenes in Jerusalem to Tyre at the time of the quinquennial games.[34] Invitations to participate in religious festivals and games were normally issued only to *poleis*. This was undoubtedly

33. On *politeia* in Josephus see A. Kasher, *The Jews in Hellenistic and Roman Egypt* (Tübingen, 1985), pp. 361-63.

34. C. Habicht, *2 Makkabäerbuch* (Gütersloh, 1976), p. 218 and Bonnet, *Melqart*, pp. 57-58. See also Grainger, *Hellenistic Phoenicia*, pp. 118-19.

the case, for example, for the cities listed in the famous Delphic *theorodokoi* list.[35] Tyre, however, was not Delphi. We may well question, therefore, whether the same conditions that applied to a festival in mainland Greece would have also applied to the games of an old native city in second-century Phoenicia. 2 Maccabees says only that when the games were being held Jason sent the *theoroi* to Tyre in order to bring 300 *drachmai* for the sacrifice to Herakles. The text, however, does add one significant detail: Epiphanes was present at the games (4.18). Undoubtedly that was the real reason Jason sent the delegation. The motivation, in short, was not so much to participate in the games as to curry favor with the king.

The *polis* epitomized Greek political and cultural life. However, it is important to recall that Hellenic life could flourish outside the *polis*. The many Graeco-Macedonian colonists living in settlements throughout Asia Minor, Asia and Egypt clearly attest to that. What one needed for continuing Hellenic vitality even more than the *polis* was the gymnasium. What was true for the rest of the Near East was also true for Jerusalem. The *polis* was not the *sine qua non* for Greek cultural survival; the gymnasium was. This was why Jason agitated for permission to build one. He may have hoped that eventually Jerusalem would develop into a *polis*. And he was undoubtedly aware that a gymnasium was a necessary component part of a *polis*.[36] One is reminded of Pausanias's

35. A. Plassart, *Bulletin du Correspondance Hellénique* 45 (1921), pp. 1-85 and L. Robert, *Bulletin du Correspondance Hellénique* 70 (1946), pp. 505-23. On the dating of the list to 230–220 BCE see C. Habicht in *Praestant Interna. Festschrift Ulrich Hausmann* (Tübingen, 1982), p. 381; Ph. Gauthier, *Nouvelles Inscriptions de Sardes*, II (Genève, 1989), p. 381 and M.B. Hatzopoulos, *Bulletin du Correspondance Hellénique* 115 (1991), pp. 345-47.

36. For the link between a gymnasium education and admission into the citizen body of a *polis* see, for example, *Supplementum Epigraphicum Graecum* VIII. 641, 104 BCE, apparently from Ptolemais in Upper Egypt. For other epigraphic evidence from Hellenistic Ptolemais see P.M. Fraser, *Berytus* 13 (1960), pp. 123-61 (p. 147 no. 11 records a dedication of the late second/first century BCE of a *politeuma* of soldiers stationed in Alexandreia).

The presence, incidentally, of a gymnasium and an *ephebeion* does not mean that there had to have been a *polis* at Jerusalem. As far as we know, both institutions could function outside a *polis*. In Ptolemaic Egypt, for example, there is abundant evidence for gymnasia in the *chora* (see Rostovtzeff, *Social and Economic History of the Hellenistic World*, pp. 324, 1395; and J. Delorme, *Gymnasion* [Paris, 1960], pp. 139-40, 199-201, 220). Evidence for ephebes in the *chora* while less prevalent does exist; see, for example, M.L. Strack, *Die Dynastie der Ptolemäer* (Berlin, 1897) nos. 142,

observation when talking about Panopeas (10.4.1). He refers to Panopeas as 'city of the Phocians' and then remarks somewhat sarcastically, 'if one can give the title "city" to those who have no magistracies, no gymnasium, no theater, no agora, no water descending to a fountain'. Nevertheless it is important to distinguish one of the components from the end-product. When Alexander's settlers in the upper satrapies were agitating for Hellenic ἀγωγὴ καὶ δίαιτα (Diod. 18.7.1) they were not demanding the establishment of *poleis*. What they wanted included at least some of the institutions to which Pausanias alluded. The presence of these would provide them with τὸν Ἑλληνικὸν χαραχτῆρα (2 Macc. 4.10) that so offended the author of 2 Maccabees.

Modern historians of the Maccabean period have been particularly concerned with the precise nature of the political organization that Jason was apparently establishing. For the author of 2 Maccabees the major issue was quite different: the gymnasium and the potential it had for undermining traditional Jewish life. He was quite struck by the enthusiasm with which the young priests and the other Jews in Jerusalem flocked to the gymnasium (2 Macc. 4.11-15). The rush to imitate things Greek reached such a pitch that, we are told, Jews who exercised in the gymnasium tried to undo their circumcision (1 Macc. 1.15). In the gymnasium the Jews were not just exercising and conducting themselves in the Greek mode. They were also interacting with non-Jews. Here we may begin to understand the distress of the author of 2 Maccabees with the activities of Jason and the Hellenizers. Jason was not just encouraging τὸν Ἑλληνικὸν χαραχτῆρα among his own people; he was facilitating and actively encouraging the mixing of Jew and non-Jew. For a critical element in the make-up of the membership of the gymnasium was to be the Antiochenes in Jerusalem. And these Antiochenes may well have been Gentiles who were from or were descended from the inhabitants of a city which was infamous for its antagonism toward the Jews.[37] Tcherikover has noted that at Philadelpheia and at Shechem 'the

143 (two inscriptions from the Fayum). See also M. Launey, *Recherches sur les armées hellénistiques*, II (Paris, 1950), pp. 857-58; P. Jouguet, *Revue de Philologie* (1910), pp. 43-44; and M. Nilsson, *Die hellenistische Schule* (Munich, 1955), p. 91.

37. 2 Macc. 5.15; 12.48. On the problem of 2 Macc. 6.8 see Hengel, *Judaism and Hellenism*, II, p. 192 no. 200; J. Goldstein, *II Maccabees* (New York, 1983), pp. 276-78 and Kasher, *Jews and Hellenistic Cities*, p. 56. The antagonism of Ptolemais may be contrasted with the apparent friendliness of Tyre. The latter city had

Hellenized Sidonians were the bearers of Greek culture in the new "Greek" towns'.[38] The same may have been true of the Antiochenes at Jerusalem. Their presence on the rolls of the gymnasium was essential if the gymnasium was to have a 'Greek' character. At the same time their presence would have made even more invidious the cultural revolution that Jason was fomenting.

I have noted earlier Bickerman's suggestion that in his reform Jason was establishing a *politeuma*, Antioch, of Jerusalemites in Jerusalem. Bickerman was correct in pointing to the likely existence of a *politeuma* in Jerusalem. I would suggest, however, that the members of the *politeuma* were foreigners, not Jerusalemites. Bickerman also suggested that Seleukeia Gaza and Antioch Ptolemais were *politeumata* and as such minted bronze coins. However, scholars have criticized his theory, noting, among other things, that (a) Seleukeia Gaza and Antioch Ptolemais were certainly *poleis*, not *politeumata* and (b) that an ethnic such as Ἀντιοχεύς normally signified the bearer belonged to a *polis*, rather than to a *politeuma*.[39] Despite the fact that both of these objections are *ex silentio* they are strong. As to the first point: the criticism of Bickerman is well taken and needs no further elaboration. With regard to the second point, I would suggest that the Antiochenes *did* belong to a *polis*: Antioch Ptolemais. And, like foreigners who resided in cities elsewhere in Coele Syria, the Antiochenes in Jerusalem may in fact have organized themselves as a *politeuma*.

In the preface to his reconstruction of Jason's activities Tcherikover remarked 'The sources furnish only a few allusions on this reform by Jason and each one has to be interpreted if we wish to understand the main lines of the project'.[40] He then proceeded to give an impressive—if highly speculative—account of the events surrounding Jason's reform. Bickerman's reconstruction was equally speculative and, I must add,

staged a great funeral for three members of the Jerusalem *Gerousia* who had been unjustly condemned to death by Antiochos (2 Macc. 4.49). But Kasher correctly notes that the Tyrians acted more from anti-Seleucid sentiment than from a desire to show themselves sympathetic to Jerusalem (p. 69).

38.   *Hellenistic Civilization and the Jews*, p. 453.

39.   See especially the criticism of Tcherikover in *Hellenistic Civilization and the Jews*, pp. 404-409, in A. Schalit (ed.) *World History of the Jewish People. The Hellenistic Age* (New Brunswick, 1972), p. 125; also Habicht, *2 Makkabäerbuch*, pp. 216-17. For Jerusalem under Roman rule see Tcherikover, 'Was Jerusalem a "Polis"?', *IEJ* 14 (1964), pp. 61-78.

40.   *Hellenistic Civilization and the Jews*, p. 161.

so is mine. For any connection of the Antiochenes in Jerusalem with Antioch Ptolemais, based on the available evidence, can only be considered to be highly theoretical. Far less speculative, on the other hand, is the assumption that Jerusalem was not isolated and did not exist in a vacuum. The mixing of population groups that was so prevelant in cities throughout the Hellenistic Near East must have been present in Jerusalem. We know it existed before the Hasmonean revolution; we know it existed afterwards. We also know that cities in regions neighboring on Judaea had heterogeneous populations. Was there a Gentile community in Jerusalem at the time of the Hasmonean revolution? Historical probability, if not concrete evidence, tells us that there was. How did it interact with the Jewish population? We do not know. What role, if any, did it play in the events surrounding Jason's reform? This, too, we do not know. The answers to all these questions would add an important new dimension to our understanding of a singular event in Jewish history.

AN ENOCHIC CITATION IN *BARNABAS* 4.3 AND
THE *ORACLES OF HYSTASPES*

John C. Reeves

The ancient 'Enochic library'—works attributed to the seventh ante-
diluvian forefather—must have been a magnificently profuse collection
of literature. Judging from the number of alleged citations and allusions
to 'books' or 'apocalypses' of Enoch, a multitude of such compositions
apparently circulated in learned circles among Jewish and later Christian
(and even Muslim) groups during the Hellenistic, Roman, and Byzantine
eras. Surviving assessments of the size of the Enochic corpus range
from the implicit 'three' or 'four' books of *Jubilees*[1] to the inherently
plausible 'thirty scrolls' of al-Ṭabarī[2] up to the assuredly fantastic '360'
of Slavonic *Enoch*.[3] Yet despite these testimonies to Enoch's loquacity,
only two indubitably Enochic books have been recovered to date—
those conventionally designated Ethiopic (1) and Slavonic (2) *Enoch*.[4]

Following the discovery and publication of these works by Western
scholars (in 1821 and 1880 respectively),[5] some applied themselves to

1. These discussions focus upon the number of separate Enochic compositions
presupposed by *Jub*. 4.17-24. See R.H. Charles, 'The Book of Jubilees', in
R.H. Charles (ed.), *The Apocrypha and Pseudepigrapha of the Old Testament*
(Oxford: Clarendon Press, 1913), II, pp. 18-19; P. Grelot, 'Hénoch et ses écritures',
RB 82 (1975), pp. 481-88; J.C. VanderKam, 'Enoch Traditions in Jubilees and Other
Second-Century Sources', *SBLSP* (1978), I, pp. 229-51; *idem, Enoch and the
Growth of an Apocalyptic Tradition* (Washington: Catholic Biblical Association of
America, 1984), pp. 179-80.
2. al-Ṭabarī, *Ta'rīkh ar-rasul wa-l-mulūk* (cf. *Annales quos scripsit Abu Djafar
Mohammed ibn Djarir at-Tabari* [ed. M.J. De Goeje; repr. Leiden: Brill, 1964], I,
p. 173 l. 3, 174 ll. 6, 8-9).
3. *2 En.* 10.7 (short version). A variant tradition records this number as '366'.
4. The so-called '3 Enoch' is a modern misnomer.
5. Regarding *1 Enoch*, the first modern European translation is R. Laurence, *The
Book of Enoch the Prophet: An Apocryphal Production...Now First Translated from*

the task of correlating the numerous citations of Enochic books found in ancient and medieval literature with the contents of the newly available texts. While some success was achieved, it must be stated that on the whole the results were disappointing. Many of the alleged citations simply did not correspond to anything contained in either Enochic work. As one scholar observed, 'the present text [of Enoch] varies considerably from that which was current in the first two or three centuries of our era...'[6] In light of the testimony of our textual witnesses, and the continuing recovery of ancient literary manuscripts, it might be more accurate to say that the texts of *1 Enoch* and *2 Enoch* represent only a portion of the Enochic literature that once circulated throughout the Near East, and we might opine that much of the 'Enochic agrapha', as we might term the numerous alleged quotations, once possessed contextual moorings within the lost corpus of the Enochic library.

The present study will devote itself to the elucidation of one of these alleged Enochic citations—one that is found within the fourth chapter of the early Christian tract known as the *Epistle of Barnabas*. *Barnabas* is a virulently anti-Judaic diatribe that nevertheless provides some valuable testimony regarding the evaluation and interpretation of scripture among certain circles in the early church during the first decades of the second century CE. While *Barnabas* largely confines itself to the exegesis of select biblical passages, in certain eschatological discussions it also quotes Enoch as 'scripture', although it identifies this author only once by name, at *Barn.* 4.3.[7] For the purposes of evaluation and discussion, let us examine this Enochic citation within its narrative context. The English rendering of Kirsopp Lake reads:

> 1. We ought, then, to enquire earnestly into the things which now are, and to seek out those which are able to save us. Let us then utterly flee from all the works of lawlessness, lest the works of lawlessness overcome us, and let us hate the error of this present time, that we may be loved in that which is to come. 2. Let us give no freedom to our souls to have power to walk

an Ethiopic MS in the Bodleian Library (Oxford, 1821). For the publication history of *2 Enoch*, consult the introductory remarks of W.R. Morfill and R.H. Charles, *The Book of the Secrets of Enoch* (Oxford: Clarendon Press, 1896); A. Vaillant, *Le livre des secrets d'Hénoch: texte slave et traduction française* (Paris: Institut d'études slaves, 1952).

6.   H.J. Lawlor, 'Early Citations from the Book of Enoch', *Journal of Philology* 25 (1897), p. 164.

7.   *Barn.* 16.5 (= *1 En.* 89.56); *Barn.* 16.6 (= *1 En.* 91.13). Both of these quotations are cited as 'scripture'.

with sinners and wicked men, lest we be made like to them. 3. *The final stumbling block is at hand of which it was written, as Enoch says, For to this end the Lord has cut short the times and the days, that his beloved should make haste and come to his inheritance.* 4. And the Prophet also says thus: 'Ten kingdoms shall reign upon the earth and there shall rise up after them a little king, who shall subdue three of the kings under one.' 5. Daniel says likewise concerning the same: 'And I beheld the fourth Beast, wicked and powerful and fiercer than all the beasts of the sea, and that ten horns sprang from it, and out of them a little excrescent horn, and that it subdued under one three of the great horns.' 6. You ought then to understand (*Barn.* 4.1-6a).[8]

This short passage features three alleged citations, all of which are problematic. The last, attributed to Daniel, would appear to reflect the contents of Dan. 7.7-8, but most commentators admit that it is at best a very liberal rendition of those biblical verses. The middle one, attributed to 'the prophet', has also been connected with the book of Daniel, since it seems to repeat the oneirocritical message of Dan. 7.24. However, if this is the case, it is somewhat strange that Barnabas does not introduce that citation with the name of 'Daniel', as it does the following one. As some have observed, the present wording of the text of Barnabas gives the misleading impression that 4.4 stems from a different source than does 4.5, which is expressly Danielic.[9] Be that as it may, let us first

8. Δεῖ οὖν ἡμᾶς περὶ τῶν ἐνεστώτων ἐπιπολὺ ἐραυνῶντας ἐκζητεῖν τὰ δυνάμενα ἡμᾶς σῴζειν. φύγωμεν οὖν τελείως ἀπὸ πάντων τῶν ἔργων τῆς ἀνομίας, μήποτε καταλάβῃ ἡμᾶς τὰ ἔργα τῆς ἀνομίας· καὶ μισήσωμεν τὴν πλάνην τοῦ νῦν καιροῦ, ἵνα εἰς τὸν μέλλοντα ἀγαπηθῶμεν. μὴ δῶμεν τῇ ἑαυτῶν ψυχῇ ἄνεσιν, ὥστε ἔχειν αὐτὴν ἐξουσίαν μετὰ ἁμαρτωλῶν καὶ πονηρῶν συντρέχειν, μήποτε ὁμοιωθῶμεν αὐτοῖς. τὸ τέλειον σκάνδαλον ἤγγικεν, περὶ οὗ γέγραπται, ὡς Ἐνὼχ λέγει. Εἰς τοῦτο γὰρ ὁ δεσπότης συντέτμηκεν τοὺς καιροὺς καὶ τὰς ἡμέρας, ἵνα ταχύνῃ ὁ ἠγαπημένος αὐτοῦ καὶ ἐπὶ τὴν κληρονομίαν ἥξῃ. λέγει δὲ οὕτως καὶ ὁ προφήτης. Βασιλεῖαι δέκα ἐπὶ τῆς γῆς βασιλεύσουσιν, καὶ ἐξαναστήσεται ὄπισθεν μικρὸς βασιλεύς, ὃς ταπεινώσει τρεῖς ὑφ' ἓν τῶν βασιλέων. ὁμοίως περὶ τοῦ αὐτοῦ λέγει Δανιήλ. Καὶ εἶδον τὸ τέταρτον θηρίον τὸ πονηρὸν καὶ ἰσχυρὸν καὶ χαλεπώτερον παρὰ πάντα τὰ θηρία τῆς θαλάσσης, καὶ ὡς ἐξ αὐτοῦ ἀνέτειλεν δέκα κέρατα, καὶ ἐξ αὐτῶν μικρὸν κέρας παραφυάδιον, καὶ ὡς ἐταπείνωσεν ὑφ' ἓν τρία τῶν μεγάλων κεράτων. συνιέναι οὖν ὀφείλετε. Text and translation cited from K. Lake (ed.), *The Apostolic Fathers* (LCL; repr. Cambridge, MA: Harvard University Press, 1959), I, pp. 348-51.

9. *Epître de Barnabé: introduction, traduction et notes* (ed. P. Prigent and R.A. Kraft; SC, 172; Paris: Cerf, 1971), p. 95.

examine the alleged Enochic quotation in 4.3 before attempting to resolve the problem of 4.4.

The first difficulty is to determine which portion of v. 3 relates the alleged Enochic citation. Is it 4.3a ('The final stumbling block is at hand...'), 4.3b ('For to this end the Lord has cut short the times and the days, that his beloved should make haste and come to his inheritance'), or both? If we compare the structure of the wording of v. 3 with the structure of the other eighty-six direct citations from sources found in *Barnabas*, we discover that the actual citation always follows the named authority. This of course follows the general pattern of proof-texting practiced in Jewish and early Christian literature.[10] Assuming that the author has not violated the pattern, the Enochic citation should be found after the incipit 'as Enoch says'. Yet this formal consideration has not impressed the editors of what is probably the most authoritative edition of Barnabas, that published in the *Sources chrétiennes* series. They suggest that 4.3a represents the Enochic quote (despite their own admission that it has no textual correspondent in any work), and that 4.3b represents an idiosyncratic 'commentary' by the author of *Barnabas* which was perhaps inspired by the general thrust of certain Enochic passages, as opposed to a precise verbatim citation.[11] While this author has profound respect for the judgment of these editors, he is going to operate under the assumption that 4.3b reproduces, in one form or another, the purported Enochic citation.

The next problem is more difficult. Does 4.3b reproduce, correspond to, or even remotely echo textual material found in our extant Enochic works? K. Lake suggested certain passages from the 'Animal Apocalypse' of *1 Enoch*; namely, *1 En.* 89.61-64; 90.17.[12] These same passages have been faithfully echoed in subsequent scholarly discussions of this verse. However, upon examination, one quickly discovers that there is little if any correlation between these passages and the alleged Enochic citation of 4.3b,[13] aside from the rather obvious shared context

10. See, for example, J.A. Fitzmyer, 'The Use of Explicit Old Testament Quotations in Qumran Literature and in the New Testament', in *idem*, *Essays on the Semitic Background of the New Testament* (repr. n.p.: Scholars Press, 1974), pp. 7-16.

11. Prigent and Kraft, *Epître*, pp. 93-94.

12. Lake, *Apostolic Fathers*, p. 348.

13. These Enochic passages refer to the recording of the misdeeds of the angelic shepherds granted dominion over humankind during the Second Temple period. I discern no specific connections with the language of *Barn.* 4.3.

of a concern with events expected to transpire at the eschaton. If this indeed is the basis of this oft-cited correlation, one could easily compile equally suitable eschatological portions from the remainder of *1 Enoch*, but such a procedure hardly advances the discussion. Surely *Barnabas* has a specific citation or cluster of citations in mind, and presumably its readers did as well.

H.J. Lawlor opined almost a century ago that *Barn.* 4.3 was not even a 'free quotation' of anything in *1 Enoch*,[14] but his assessment is actually too harsh. As a matter of fact, there is one passage in *1 Enoch* that does feature the motif of what we might term 'time-compression'— the acceleration of time as the eschaton draws near. J.T. Milik[15] has pointed to *1 En.* 80.2 as a possible correlate for *Barn.* 4.3: 'But in the days of the sinners the years will become shorter, and their seed will be late on their land and on their fields, and all things on the earth will change, and will not appear at their proper time.'[16] This proposed correlation with a passage of our present texts of *Enoch* is probably the best advanced of this type to date, but it is not without its problems. The alleged Enochic citation of 4.3 also refers to a 'beloved' who is hastening to claim 'his inheritance', motifs which are absent from the text of *1 Enoch* as we know it. From whence then do these other features stem? Does *Barnabas* use a book of Enoch that we no longer have? Or is it mistaken in its attribution of this quote to Enoch? When 4.4 cites 'the prophet also says', is it shifting to a different literary source? Is it Danielic? Or is 'Enoch' being quoted here as well?

A possibility that must be considered is that Barnabas is mistaken in its attribution of this quotation to Enoch, and that it in fact stems from a formally non-Enochic source. A very illuminating study of this interpretive option has lately been published by M. Kister.[17] Kister has conclusively demonstrated that an unattributed and heretofore unattested prophetic text quoted in *Barn.* 12.1 stems from a recently published Qumran apocryphon designated '4Q Second Ezekiel'.[18] Kister also

14.   Lawlor, 'Early Citations', p. 172.

15.   J.T. Milik, *The Books of Enoch: Aramaic Fragments of Qumrân Cave 4* (Oxford: Clarendon Press, 1976), pp. 73-74.

16.   Translation cited from M.A. Knibb, '1 Enoch', in H.F.D. Sparks (ed.), *The Apocryphal Old Testament* (Oxford: Clarendon Press, 1984), p. 269.

17.   M. Kister, 'Barnabas 12.1, 4.3 and 4Q Second Ezekiel', *RB* 97 (1990), p. 63-67.

18.   For the published text of 4Q Second Ezekiel, see J. Strugnell and D. Dimant, '4Q Second Ezekiel', *RevQ* 13 (1988), pp. 45-58, esp. 50-51; *idem*, 'The Merkabah

suggests that another portion of this same 'Second Ezekiel' recounts a message that is very similar to the Enochic citation of 4.3b. While the published portion of this part of 'Second Ezekiel' still requires some restoration, enough survives to provide some support for his suggestion. Therein we read: 'and the days will quickly hasten until humanity says, Are not the days hastening so that the children of Israel will inherit? And the Lord said to me, I will not refuse you, Ezekiel: Behold, I will cut short the days and the years...'[19] Compare again the language of 4.3b: 'as Enoch says, For to this end the Lord has cut short the times and the days, that his beloved should make haste and come to his inheritance'. Here we observe an important correlation with two components of the alleged Enochic quote of 4.3b: the phenomenon of 'time-compression', and its purpose, eschatological inheritance.

While Kister's correlation is admittedly attractive, there nevertheless remain certain problems with his proposed identification, chief among which are the Enochic ascription and the thematic complex of motifs linking *Barn.* 4.3 and 4.4. I would like to propose for consideration a complementary reading of the Barnabas pericope that draws upon traditions not normally cited in the interpretation of this passage and that may shed some light on the linkage of ideas found therein. It appears that *Barn.* 4.3-4 exhibits several points of correspondence with the contents of and traditions about the so-called *Oracles of Hystaspes*, a Parthian apocalypse akin to the *Sibylline Oracles*. This work survives only in translated Greek and Latin fragments quoted by various Christian apologetes, the most copious of which appear in the seventh book of the *Divine Institutes* of Lactantius.[20] There are four points of

Vision in Second Ezekiel (4Q385 4)', *RevQ* 14 (1990), pp. 331-48.

19. See Strugnell and Dimant, '4Q Second Ezekiel', p. 51 ll. 2-5; Kister, 'Barnabas 12.1, 4.3', p. 67 n. 14; M. Kister and E. Qimron, 'Observations on 4QSecond Ezekiel (4Q385 2-3)', *RevQ* 15 (1992), p. 598: ויתבהלו הימים מהר עד אשר יאמרו האדם הלא ממהרים הימים למען יירש בני ישראל ויאמר יהוה אלי לא אש[י]ב פניך יחזקאל ה[נני] גודד את הימים ואת השני[ם...].

20. Fundamental for the study of the *Oracles* are the following works: H. Windisch, *Die Orakel des Hystaspes* (Amsterdam: Koninklijke Akademie van Wetenschappen, 1929); F. Cumont, 'La fin du monde selon les mages occidentaux', *RHR* 103 (1931), pp. 29-96, esp. 64-96; J. Bidez and F. Cumont, *Les mages hellénisés* (Paris: Société d'éditions 'Les belles lettres', 1938), I, pp. 215-22, II, pp. 359-76; G. Widengren, *Die Religionen Irans* (Stuttgart: W. Kohlhammer, 1965), pp. 199-207; J.R. Hinnells, 'The Zoroastrian Doctrine of Salvation in the Roman World', in E.J. Sharpe and J.R. Hinnells (eds.), *Man and his Salvation: Studies in*

potential correspondence to which attention should be directed: (1) the motif of time-compression; (2) the motif of the eschatological 'ten rulers' or 'ten kingdoms'; (3) the motif of 'the beloved'; and (4) the Enochic ascription. Each of these motifs requires brief development.

(1) The motif of time-compression. As previously stated, the phrase 'time-compression' is used to describe a perception that time accelerates its passage as the eschaton approaches. In other words, years, months, and days are progressively shortened, with the result that the natural processes of organic growth and ageing are no longer synchronous with the accustomed advance of the seasons. Examples of passages featuring this motif have already been quoted from *Barnabas*, *1 Enoch*, and 'Second Ezekiel'; these could easily be supplemented by further examples from both Jewish and Christian texts.[21]

Interestingly, the *Oracles of Hystaspes*, insofar as we can reliably reconstruct this work, also contains a passage that features eschatological time-compression. Therein we read: 'then [i.e., after various woes] the year will be shortened, the month diminished, the day compressed to a brief moment...'[22] Given this parallel, some have wished to argue that the motif of time-compression has been borrowed by Jewish apocalyptists from Iranian eschatological traditions,[23] but this need not necessarily be the case. Study and reflection upon the 'historical' traditions contained in the Tanakh can lead one to conclude that from the period of Adam to the present age life-spans have progressively diminished, and

Memory of S.G.F. Brandon (Manchester: Manchester University Press, 1973), pp. 125-48; H.G. Kippenberg, 'Die Geschichte der mittelpersischen apokalyptischen Traditionen', *Studia Iranica* 7 (1978), pp. 49-80, esp. 70-75; D. Flusser, 'Hystaspes and John of Patmos', in S. Shaked (ed.), *Irano-Judaica: Studies Relating to Jewish Contacts with Persian Culture throughout the Ages* (Jerusalem: Ben Zvi Institute, 1982), pp. 12-75; M. Boyce, *A History of Zoroastrianism* (Leiden: Brill, 1975–), III, pp. 371-83.

21. *t. Sota* 14.10; *b. Sota* 47b; *2 Apoc. Bar.* 20.1; 54.1; 83.1; *4 Ezra* 4.26 (cf. v. 33); 6.21; Mk 13.20; Mt. 24.22.

22. *Tunc annus breviabitur et mensis minuetur et dies in angustum coartabitur* (Lactantius, *Div. Inst.* 7.16.10). Text cited from Bidez and Cumont, *Les mages hellénisés*, II, p. 368; translation cited from B. McGinn, *Apocalyptic Spirituality* (New York: Paulist, 1979), pp. 60-61. Note Cumont, 'La fin du monde', p. 78 n. 1.

23. See D. Winston, 'The Iranian Component in the Bible, Apocrypha, and Qumran: A Review of the Evidence', *HR* 5 (1966), p. 191. A Babylonian pedigree is suggested by W. Bousset and H. Gressmann, *Die Religion des Judentums im späthellenistischen Zeitalter* (Tübingen: Mohr, 3rd edn, 1926), p. 246.

will continue to diminish, until the End. A shortening of life-span could be interpreted to reflect an acceleration in time's motion and thus the maturity process. Hence the phenomenon of premature ageing is a common feature in texts that contain this motif, as in *Jubilees* where as the eschaton approaches 'the heads of children will be white with grey hair, and a child three weeks old will look like a man who is a hundred...'[24]

Does this passage of the *Oracles* shed any light on *Barnabas*? All that we can observe at this stage is that the *Oracles* and *Barnabas* share the motif of time-compression, hardly grounds for concluding interdependence.

(2) The eschatological 'ten rulers' or 'ten kingdoms'. *Barn.* 4.4 states: 'And the prophet also says thus: Ten kingdoms shall reign upon the earth and there shall rise up after them a little king, who shall subdue three of the kings under one' (Lake). Here we confront a motif that enjoys wide popularity in apocalyptic literature. The final years before the eschaton are periodized in accordance with a predetermined number of secular governments or rulers. These governments as a rule become progressively worse as the eschaton nears, and the military actions associated with these rulers form part of the series of 'woes' that precede the direct intervention of the deity. Their enumeration as 'ten' also assumes importance in apocalyptic tradition, presumably due to the impact of the vision of the fourth beast with the ten horns 'who are kings', as described in Daniel 7, but perhaps ultimately based on an early form of the later tradition concerning the governments of 'ten universal kings'.[25]

At first glance, *Barn.* 4.4 would seem to be Danielic. But when one compares the wording of 4.4 with the extant text(s) of Daniel, one discovers significant differences between the text of *Barnabas* and the biblical versions.[26] It is certainly not a verbatim citation, but general

24. *Jub* 23.25. Translation cited from R.H. Charles and C. Rabin, 'Jubilees', in *Apocryphal Old Testament*, p. 76. See also *Orig. World* (NHC II.5), p. 121 ll. 25-27.

25. See *PRE* 11; *Targ. Sheni* 1.1 for examples of this latter motif. Note that the seventh-century *Sefer Zerubbabel* also features the 'ten eschatological rulers' in addition to the figure of Armilus. Cf. Y. Even-Shemuel, *Midrashey ge'ullah* (Jerusalem and Tel Aviv: Bialik, 1953), pp. 79-80.

26. LXX: καὶ τὰ δέκα κέρατα τῆς βασιλείας, δέκα βασιλεῖς στήσονται, καὶ ὁ ἄλλος βασιλεὺς μετὰ τούτους στήσεται, καὶ αὐτὸς διοίσει κακοῖς ὑπὲρ τοὺς πρώτους καὶ τρεῖς βασιλεῖς ταπεινώσει. Theodotion: καὶ τὰ δέκα κέρατα αὐτοῦ, δέκα βασιλεῖς ἀναστήσονται, καὶ ὀπίσω αὐτῶν ἀναστήσεται ἕτερος, ὃς ὑπεροίσει κακοῖς πάντας τοὺς ἔμπροσθεν, καὶ τρεῖς βασιλεῖς ταπεινώσει.

similarities in content can be observed. Dan. 7.8 reports that while Daniel observed the fourth beast with its ten horns 'another *small* horn sprouted among them and uprooted *three* of the former horns...', and 7.24 interprets this same event as '*ten kings* shall arise, but *another* shall arise after them, distinct from the former, and he will subdue *three* of (the former) kings'. Here the same progression of action is featured that we find in *Barnabas*: ten kings/kingdoms among whom an eleventh appears, and who subjugates three of the original ten. Yet perhaps most tellingly, despite this obvious similarity, the author of *Barnabas* does not identify this quotation as a citation from Daniel, but rather ascribes the quotation to an unnamed 'prophet'. As others have noted, the way that *Barnabas* specifically attributes 4.5 to Daniel permits the supposition that 4.4 actually stems from elsewhere,[27] and one could add, perhaps even from the same Enochic source quoted in 4.3.

Interestingly, a tradition associated with the *Oracles of Hystaspes* also apparently attests an eschatological 'ten ruler' scheme among the roster of natural 'woes' in that work.[28] This passage states:

> civic quarrels will continually spread abroad and there will be no end of deadly wars until ten kings will emerge simultaneously. They will divide the world to destroy and not to govern it. They will greatly expand their armies and devastate the farmlands...then a mighty enemy from the far North will suddenly rise up against them. When he has destroyed the three who control Asia he will be taken into alliance with the others and will be made their chief.[29]

27. See n. 9 *supra*.

28. Not everyone agrees that Lactantius, *Div. Inst.* 7.16.1-3 stems from the *Oracles*. For example, Bidez and Cumont do not include this material within their collection of the fragments of Hystaspes. However, D. Flusser ('Hystaspes and John of Patmos') has argued compellingly that 7.16.1-3 does in fact derive from the *Oracles*, and Flusser's perspective will be adopted in the present paper.

29.   ...*tum discordiae ciuiles in perpetuum serentur nec ulla requies bellis exitialibus erit, donec reges decem pariter existant, qui orbem terrae non ad regendum, sed ad consumendum partiantur. Hi exercitibus in inmensum auctis et agrorum cultibus destitutis...tum repente aduersus eos hostis potentissimus ab extremis finibus plagae septentrionalis orientur, qui tribus ex eo numero deletis qui tunc Asiam obtinebunt, adsumetur in societatem a ceteris ac princeps omnium constituetur* (Lactantius, *Div. Inst.* 7.16.1-3). Text cited from L. Caeli Firmiani Lactanti, *Opera omnia...* (CSEL XIX; ed. S. Brandt; Prague: F. Tempsky, 1890), I, p. 635; translation cited from McGinn, *Apocalyptic Spirituality*, pp. 59-60. The motif of the 'enemy from the north' need not be biblically derived. Cumont thinks that it stems from the *Oracles*; see 'La fin du monde', p. 75 n. 2. The Jāmāsp-nāmag (§ 95ff.) also features

The same eschatological pattern manifests here that we have seen previously in Daniel and in *Barnabas*.

Among all the texts we have examined so far, it is surely intriguing to note that it is only within two—the *Oracles* and *Barnabas*—that the motifs of time-compression and the ten eschatological rulers are contextually intertwined. Are there further hints pointing to a closer connection between *Barnabas* and the *Oracles* than has heretofore been recognized?

(3) The 'beloved'. The expression 'his beloved' (ὁ ἠγαπημένος αὐτοῦ) represents an intriguing crux. Naturally, this is a christological epithet (it always possesses this sense in *Barnabas*), but, unlike most others, it occurs in a rather limited repertoire of early Christian texts, viz., *Barnabas*, the *Odes of Solomon*, and the Christian portions of the *Ascension of Isaiah*.[30] The latter two texts are normally associated with a Syrian or Palestinian provenance, and are indeed often mined by scholars seeking nuggets of information about the conceptual world of so-called 'Jewish Christianity'.[31] However, whence stems the epithet 'his beloved' in our alleged Enochic citation? Was it already present in 'Second Ezekiel' (assuming that Kister has correctly identified this source), perhaps modifying בני ישראל? Was it added by a Christian adaptor (*Barnabas*?) to replace the reference to the בני ישראל, as Kister has suggested?[32] Or is there another possible explanation?

Given the emerging connection that seems to exist between the *Oracles* and *Barnabas*, it would seem logical to search for any evidence that might point to the use of a title like 'the beloved' within the Parthian apocalypse. Interestingly, such evidence does in fact exist, but it has been seldom noticed. According to the summation of the chapter headings contained in Mani's *Book of Mysteries* that is supplied by the tenth-century Muslim encyclopaedist Ibn al-Nadīm, the second chapter

---

three rulers who are destroyed by an adversary from the north. See É. Benveniste, 'Une apocalypse pehlevie: le Žāmāsp-Nāmak', *RHR* 106 (1932), p. 375. It seems possible that Elchasai's prediction about 'war raging among the impious angels (read: kings?) of the north' (*apud* Hippolytus, *Refutatio* 9.16.4) presumes a similar textual basis.

30. *Barn.* 3.6; 4.8; *Odes Sol.* 3.5, 7; 7.1; 8.21; 38.11; *Asc. Isa.* 1.4, 5, 7, 13; 3.13, 17, 18, 28; 4.3, 6, 9, 18, 21; 5.15; 7.17, 23; 8.18, 26; 9.12. See R.H. Charles, *The Ascension of Isaiah* (London: A. & C. Black, 1900), pp. 3-4.

31. The employment of this epithet is instructive for those seeking to identify the provenance of *Barnabas*.

32. Kister, 'Barnabas 12.1, 4.3', pp. 66-67.

(*bāb*) of this Manichaean text was devoted to 'the testimony of Vištaspa (i.e., Hystaspes) about the Beloved (*al-ḥabīb*).'[33] This information raises at least two intriguing questions. Is 'the testimony of Vištaspa' that is interpreted by Mani the same work that Western writers know as the *Oracles of Hystaspes*? To whom does the epithet 'the Beloved' refer?

First, it can be demonstrated that Mani knew and utilized the conceptual framework and even the terminology of the *Oracles of Hystaspes*. The important manuscript discoveries of the present century have provided us with a sizeable sampling of authentic Manichaean apocalyptic texts,[34] and these texts display numerous points of correspondence with the traditions found in our surviving fragmentary *Oracles*.[35] As an example of such dependence, one might call attention to the 'Great Fire' (*'dwr wzrg*) which, according to Mani, will consume the created order at the eschaton. This feature looks very much like the world conflagration

33. See G. Flügel, *Mani: seine Lehre und seine Schriften* (reprinted, Osnabrück: Biblio Verlag, 1969), p. 72 l. 12; A. Adam, *Texte zum Manichäismus* (Berlin: de Gruyter, 2nd edn, 1969), p. 115. Against most interpretations, Arabic '*ly* here should be translated 'concerning, about' and not 'against' ('gegen', 'wider', 'contre', etc.). Cf. Flügel, *Mani*, p. 72 ll. 14-15; 'testimony of Jesus *about* himself in Judaea'; p. 73 l. 1: 'Adam *about* Jesus'. See especially Flügel, *Mani*, p. 360 n.

34. The most important extant Manichaean apocalyptic texts survive in Coptic and Middle Persian. See *Manichäische handschriften der Sammlung A. Chester Beatty, Band I: Manichäische Homilien* (ed. H.J. Polotsky; Stuttgart: Kohlhammer, 1934), pp. 7-42; D.N. MacKenzie, 'Mani's Šāburhragān', *BSOAS* 42 (1979), pp. 500-34; 43 (1980), pp. 288-310. An excellent introduction to Manichaean apocalypticism is G.G. Stroumsa, 'Aspects de l'eschatologie manichéenne', *RHR* 198 (1981), pp. 163-81.

35. G. Widengren, *Mani and Manichaeism* (New York: Holt, Rinehart & Winston, 1965), p. 67; *idem*, 'Manichaeism and its Iranian Background', in *The Cambridge History of Iran, Volume 3(2): The Seleucid, Parthian and Sasanian Periods* (ed. E. Yarshater; Cambridge: Cambridge University Press, 1983), pp. 981-82; M. Tardieu, *Le manichéisme* (Paris: Presses Universitaires de France, 1981), p. 42; L. Koenen, 'Manichaean Apocalypticism at the Crossroads of Iranian, Egyptian, Jewish and Christian Thought', in *Codex Manichaicus Coloniensis: Atti del Simposio Internazionale (Rende-Amantea 3-7 settembre 1984* (ed. L. Cirillo and A. Roselli; Cosenza: Marra Editore, 1986), pp. 297-314. It is certainly clear that Mani was acquainted with King Vištaspa (i.e., Hystaspes) and certain traditions surrounding him. Note M 291a 1.9: *wy]št'sp š'h*; T ii D 58 1.3: *š'h wyšt'sp*. Both of these texts are provided by W.B. Henning, 'The Book of the Giants', *BSOAS* 11 (1943–46), p. 73; see also *idem*, 'Neue Materialen zur Geschichte des Manichäismus', *ZDMG* 90 (1936), pp. 4-5.

reportedly found in the *Oracles of Hystaspes*.[36]

Therefore it would seem that Mani knew and used the *Oracles*. However, as al-Nadīm's testimony suggests and common sense dictates, the form and/or content of the *Oracles* used by Mani in third-century Mesopotamia was superior to the disconnected fragments that have been haphazardly preserved for us in Christian literature. It seems certain that within the text of the *Oracles* used by Mani there was reference made to an actor designated 'the Beloved'—either explicitly in the *Oracles* themselves, or implicitly; that is to say, a species of *derash* that interpreted a certain entity (e.g., the Great King) as being equivalent to a revered 'Beloved'.

But who is 'the Beloved'? As previously mentioned, the expression 'the Beloved' functions as a favorite christological epithet in literature that stems from certain Jewish Christian circles. Thanks to the important information recovered from the recently published *Cologne Mani Codex*, we now know that Mani is rooted in the same soil.[37] Hence it should not surprise us when we observe that both Mani and the later Manichaean community frequently use this identical epithet—'the beloved'—to refer to the same entity—Jesus.[38]

Obviously a Parthian apocalypse authored in the pre-Christian era among Zoroastrian circles would feature no blatant christological concepts or language.[39] If the expression 'the Beloved' was indigenous

36. See Justin Martyr, *Apol.* 1.20 (*apud* Bidez and Cumont, *Les mages hellénisés*, II, p. 361); M. Boyce, *A Reader in Manichaean Middle Persian and Parthian* (Leiden: Brill, 1975), pp. 80-83; ibn al-Nadīm, *Fihrist* (*apud* Flügel, *Mani*, p. 58 ll. 1-10, 235-37); al-Shahrastānī, *Kitāb al-milal wa-al-niḥal* (ed. M.S. Kilani; repr. Beirut: Dar el-Marefah, n.d.), I, p. 248 ll. 1-4.

37. L. Koenen and C. Römer, *Der Kölner Mani-Kodex: Kritische Edition* (Opladen: Westdeutscher Verlag, 1988). There are some discernible connections linking Mani's Mesopotamian heritage and Palestinian traditions; see J.C. Reeves, 'The Elchasaite Sanhedrin of the Cologne Mani Codex in Light of Second Temple Jewish Sectarian Sources', *JJS* 42 (1991), pp. 68-91.

38. The divine entity termed 'Jesus the Luminous' (*Yišō' ziwā*) is also called 'the Beloved (*ḥbyb'* = Al-Nadīm's *al-habīb*; cf. Theodore bar Konai, *Liber Scholiorum* [ed. A. Scher; Paris: Carolus Poussielgue, 1912], II, p. 317 l. 20; *Acta Archelai* 12.7-11: ὅτε δὲ εἶδεν ὁ πατὴρ ὁ ζῶν θλιβομένην τὴν ψυχὴν ἐν τῷ σώματι...ἔπεμψε τὸν υἱὸν αὐτοῦ τὸν ἠγαπημένον εἰς σωτηρίαν τῆς ψυχῆς...) and 'Jesus the Friend' (*Yišō' aryaman*). See F.C. Andreas and W.B. Henning, 'Mitteliranische Manichaica aus Chinesisch-Turkestan II', *SPAW* (1933), p. 325 ll. 9-10.

39. Most scholars date the *Oracles* around 100 BCE, and some would place it considerably earlier.

to the *Oracles*, it must necessarily refer to someone or something else, perhaps Aryaman, an Iranian *yazad* whose name signifies 'Friend' and who functions as a divine healer.[40] However, if it is true, as has been recently and brilliantly argued, that the *Oracles* underwent a series of revisions and adaptations by both Jewish and Christian groups,[41] it is then highly likely that this epithet was reinterpreted or even inserted into the *Oracles* by one of these latter groups. Presumably it was such a 'revised' version of the *Oracles* that Mani used, since we are informed that he devoted a portion of his interpretive energies to the elucidation of the *Oracles'* witness to 'the Beloved'.

Barnabas quotes a text, allegedly Enochic, that features the advent of 'the Beloved' at the eschaton. Either the original or a revised version of the *Oracles of Hystaspes* apparently incorporated the same figure. The textual complex displayed in *Barn*. 4.3-4 features time-compression and the tribulations associated with ten rulers. As we have seen, the *Oracles of Hystaspes* also include these same motifs within the same temporal context. Can these correspondences be coincidental?

(4) The Enochic ascription. This is perhaps the most interesting problem. If Kister is correct, and *Barn*. 4.3b is in fact 'Ezekielian', why does *Barnabas* expressly identify it as a quotation from Enoch? Several possibilities suggest themselves. Perhaps *Barnabas* was simply mistaken; analogous slips in source citation are not unheard of.[42] Perhaps what we know today fragmentarily as 'Second Ezekiel' was in its original context a portion of a larger work ascribed to Enoch—say, a broad vision of Jewish history stretching from creation to the eschaton that incorporated within it a selection of the future oracles or pronouncements of named prophets. Perhaps the autograph of *Barnabas* originally said 'Ezekiel', but for one reason or another a later copyist altered this name to 'Enoch', and all subsequent versions have followed this archetype without question. Finally, an intriguing possibility is that either *Barnabas* or its source has effected an esoteric identification or assimilation between the figures of Enoch and Ezekiel—both, after all, view the *kavod ha-shem*; both exhort their contemporaries to refrain from evil and pursue righteousness; and both utter prophecies focused upon eschatological

---

40. M. Boyce, 'The Manichaean Middle Persian Writings', in *The Cambridge History of Iran, Volume 3(2)*, pp. 1198-99.

41. Flusser, 'Hystaspes and John of Patmos', *passim*. Note also Windisch, *Orakel des Hystaspes*, pp. 6-9, 45-46.

42. Cf., e.g., Mk 1.2-3.

events.[43] Conceivably, when viewed in this way, Ezekiel could be labelled a type of latter-day Enoch.

This sort of interpretive assimilation should not be dismissed out of hand. Remaining within the bounds of Jewish tradition, one thinks of similar identifications proffered, like those of Phineas and Elijah,[44] or of Shem and Melchisedek.[45] If we expand those boundaries to incorporate figures from alien national or religious traditions, we are bound to notice that cross-cultural assimilation or identification of prominent culture-heroes is extremely popular in Hellenistic and even later historiography. The production of the so-called 'universal histories' stimulates this process. When different national or religious figures of like antiquity are depicted similarly in their native traditions, the tendency is to equate the two. For example, the Samaritan antiquarian Pseudo-Eupolemus states 'the Greeks say that Atlas discovered astrology, but Atlas is the same (person) as Enoch'.[46] Now, while it is conceivable that someone may have argued, on the basis of the parallels cited above, that the figures of Enoch and Ezekiel are similar, it seems inconceivable (apart from some early 'true prophet' cyclical pattern)[47] that anyone familiar with biblical

43. For medieval Jewish exercises of this sort, see G. Scholem, 'Gilgul: The Transmigration of Souls', in *On the Mystical Shape of the Godhead: Basic Concepts in the Kabbalah* (New York: Schocken, 1991), pp. 212-15.

44. Pseudo-Philo, *Bib. Ant.* 48.1; *Targ. Ps.-J.* Num. 25.12; *PRE* 8 and 47. Additional references are supplied by L. Ginzberg, *The Legends of the Jews* (Philadelphia: Jewish Publication Society, 1913–38), VI, pp. 316-17. See also R. Hayward, 'Phineas—the Same is Elijah: The Origins of a Rabbinic Tradition', *JJS* 29 (1978), pp. 22-34.

45. *Gen. R.* 26.3; *b. Ned.* 32b; *Targ. Yer. I* and *Targ. Ps.-J.* Gen. 14.18, along with traditional commentaries *ad loc.*; *PRE* 27. Additional references in Ginzberg, *Legends*, V, pp. 225-26.

46. Pseudo-Eupolemus *apud* Eusebius, *Praep.Ev.* 9.17.9: Ἕλληνας δὲ λέγειν τὸν Ἄτλαντα εὑρηκέναι ἀστρολογίαν, εἶναι δὲ τὸν Ἄτλαντα τὸν αὐτὸν καὶ Ἐνώχ. Text cited from Eusebius, *Die Praeparatio Evangelica* (ed. K. Mras; Berlin: Akademie-Verlag, 1954), I, p. 504 ll. 7-8. With specific regard to Irano-Judaic assimilations, see G. Widengren, 'Quelques rapports entre juifs et iraniens à l'époque des Parthes', in *Volume du Congrès: Strasbourg 1956* (VTSup, 4; Leiden: Brill, 1957), pp. 220-21. For a possible early Christian assimilation of Seth and Zoroaster, see W. Bousset, *Hauptprobleme der Gnosis* (repr. Göttingen: Vandenhoeck & Ruprecht, 1973), pp. 378-82.

47. From the Manichaean perspective, Enoch and Zoroaster are in fact the same figure, since each is a human manifestation of the same heavenly entity, the 'Apostle of Light'. See H.-C. Puech, *Le manichéisme: son fondateur—sa doctrine* (Paris:

material would suggest that Enoch and Ezekiel were one and the same. This interpretation can be safely dismissed given the present state of our knowledge.

I would like to suggest, based on the course of this paper's argument, that an assimilation (at some point in the exegetical process) of two culture-heroes has in fact transpired; namely, between Enoch and Zoroaster. I suggest this despite my realization that nowhere in the extant literary traditions is such an identification explicitly given.[48] The reasons for offering this correlation are based by and large upon the popular Hellenistic image of the Persian prophet, facets of which do not cohere with authentic Iranian traditions.[49] First, one of Zoroaster's primary accomplishments (according to Western interpreters) was his discovery and development of astrology.[50] Certain Jewish circles

Civilisations du Sud, 1949), pp. 61-62 and esp. p. 144 n. 241; Tardieu, *Le manichéisme*, pp. 20-24; J.C. Reeves, *Jewish Lore in Manichaean Cosmogony: Studies in the Book of Giants Traditions* (Cincinnati: Hebrew Union College Press, 1992), p. 4 n. 3, pp. 47-48 n. 132.

48. Zoroaster was identified with Nimrod (Pseudo-Clementine *Homilies* 9.3-6; Syriac *Cave of Treasures*; perhaps *Gen. R.* 38.13), Balaam (Origen, *Contra Celsum* 1.60), Ezekiel (!) (Alexander Polyhistor *apud* Clement of Alexandria, *Strom.* 1.15), and Baruch (Syriac *Book of the Bee*). See Bidez and Cumont, *Les mages hellénisés*, I, pp. 41-49; Winston, 'Iranian Component', pp. 213-16; R.J.H. Gottheil, 'References to Zoroaster in Syriac and Arabic Literature', in *Classical Studies in Honour of Henry Drisler* (New York: Macmillan, 1894), pp. 24-51; Bousset, *Hauptprobleme*, pp. 369-78. Theodore bar Konai reports a tradition that Zoroaster was originally a Samaritan priest named Azazel; see his *Liber Scholiorum*, II, p. 295 ll. 21-23. We draw closer to Enoch in the tradition recounted by the *Chronicles of Yerahmeel* (35.4; cf. M. Gaster, *The Chronicles of Yerahmeel* [repr. New York: Ktav, 1971], p. 78) that Abraham instructed Zoroaster in astrological mysteries. Compare Artapanus *apud* Eusebius, *Praep. Ev.* 9.18.1; Josephus, *Ant.* 1.167-68. Note especially Pseudo-Eupolemus *apud* Eusebius, *Praep. Ev.* 9.17.8 and J.A. Fitzmyer's plausible restoration of 1QapGen 19.25 (*The Genesis Apocryphon of Qumran Cave I* [Rome: Biblical Institute Press, 2nd rev. edn, 1971], p. 118), both of which underscore Enoch's role in Abraham's educational mission.

49. See Porphyry, *Vita Plotini* 16.15-20; Windisch, *Orakel des Hystaspes*, pp. 14-25. An exemplary discussion of Hellenistic interpretations of Zoroaster is provided by R. Beck, 'Thus Spake Not Zarathuštra: Zoroastrian Pseudepigrapha of the Greco-Roman World', in Boyce, *History of Zoroastrianism*, III, pp. 491-565. See also A. Momigliano, *Alien Wisdom: The Limits of Hellenization* (Cambridge: Cambridge University Press, 1975), pp. 141-49.

50. Passages remarking Zoroaster's association with astrology are conveniently gathered in Appendix V of A.V.W. Jackson, *Zoroaster: The Prophet of Ancient Iran*

attributed the same discovery to Enoch.[51] Secondly, Zoroaster partici-
pated in tours of the supernal and nether worlds; Enoch of course shares
these ascension experiences.[52] Thirdly, there are persistent traditions that
Zoroaster was temporarily or periodically sequestered from mortal
company.[53] One might compare the similarly mysterious occultation of
Enoch related in Gen. 5.24 and its dependent traditions.[54]

(repr. New York: AMS Press, 1965), pp. 226-59. Note also Beck, 'Zoroastrian
Pseudepigrapha', pp. 522-28.

51. Regarding Enoch's association with astrology, see the end of n. 48 *supra* and
B.Z. Wacholder, 'Pseudo-Eupolemus' Two Greek Fragments on the Life of Abraham',
HUCA 34 (1963), pp. 96-97. Note also Theodore bar Konai, *Liber Scholiorum*, II,
p. 286 ll. 5-6: 'The Chaldaean (heresy) preceded the other heresies in origin, for
Bardaiṣan says that Enoch was the name of its originator'. *kldywt'* refers to
'astrology'.

52. For such traditions relating to Zoroaster, which are often implied in the Avesta,
see especially *Dēnkard* 7.3.51-62, 8.14.2-9; *Zātspram* 21.2ff., 22.1-13; A. Hultgård,
'Forms and Origins of Iranian Apocalypticism', in *Apocalypticism in the
Mediterranean World and Near East* (ed. D. Hellholm; Tübingen: Mohr, 1983),
pp. 400-405. See also the following note. The Coptic *Zostrianos* (NHC VIII.1)
recounts a heavenly tour undertaken by the title character. According to this work's
colophon, Zostrianos is Zoroaster. Parallels between *Zostrianos* and Enochic literature have been identified by M. Scopello, 'The Apocalypse of Zostrianos (Nag
Hammadi VIII.1) and the Book of the Secrets of Enoch', *VC* 34 (1980), pp. 376-85.
Note too that the Zoroastrian pseudepigraphon *Peri phuseōs* borrows the narrative
setting of Plato's famous 'myth of Er' (*Republic* 614b-621d), substituting the name
'Zoroaster' for that of 'Er' (cf. Windisch, *Orakel des Hystaspes*, pp. 15-16). With
regard to Enoch, see *1 En.* 1.2; 14.8–19.3, 21-36, 71; *2 En.* 3–12 (short version); *Jub.*
4.21; *Cologne Mani Codex* 58.6–60.12. Neither of these lists purports to be an
exhaustive listing of the sources.

53. *Vičirkart i Dēnik* 16–17: 'Avec l'aide de Vahuman et la force de la justice et
de la vérité, il alla dans la meilleure existence pour rester dix ans parmi les *yazdat* et
les Amahraspand en s'entretenant avec Ohrmazd le Créateur omniscient. Mais au
bout de dix ans le juste Zoroastre le Spitamide, entouré d'éclat et de *xvarrah* de la
prophétie, descendit du monde spirituel dans ce monde matériel le jour de Hordat du
mois de Fravartin.' Translation cited from M. Molé, *La legende de Zoroastre selon
les textes pehlevis* (Paris: Librairie C. Klincksieck, 1967), p. 131. See also Pliny, *Nat.
Hist.* 11.97; Dio Chrysostom, *Oratio* 36.40-41; Arnobius, *Adv. gentes* 1.52;
Porphyry, *De Antro Nymph.* 6; al-Nadīm, *Fihrist* (cf. *Kitāb al-Fihrist* [ed. G. Flügel;
Leipzig: F.C.W. Vogel, 1871–72], I, p. 345); and the references cited by Bousset,
Hauptprobleme, p. 149 n. 3. Compare *Jub.* 4.23-25 and the sources cited in the
following note.

54. *1 En.* 12.1-2; 87.3-4; 106.7; *2 En.* 11.36-38, 13.77-78; 18.1-3 (all short
version); *Jub.* 4.23; *Targ. Ps.-J.* Gen. 5.24; *Sefer Hayashar (apud* A. Jellinek, *Bet*

According to Iranian tradition, a crucial step in the progress of the Zoroastrian religion was taken when Zoroaster succeeded in winning over King Vištaspa to his cause.[55] Following his conversion, Vištaspa becomes a fervent champion of the new teachings. Some traditions go further and consider Vištaspa a trusted disciple to whom Zoroaster continued to impart subsequent revelations and oracles.[56] It seems possible then that a work thought to derive from Vištaspa and his circle, such as the *Oracles*, could have been considered authentically Zoroastrian. If the 'child' who interprets the dream of Hystaspes is Zoroaster, as is sometimes argued,[57] we behold a direct connection of the resultant

ha-Midrasch [Jerusalem: Bamberger & Wahrmann, 2nd edn, 1938], IV, pp. 129-32).

55. Presumably not the same figure as the father of Darius I (Herodotus 1.209-10). On Vištaspa, see Windisch, *Orakel des Hystaspes*, pp. 10-13; Jackson, *Zoroaster*, pp. 56-79; Bidez and Cumont, *Les mages hellénisés*, I, pp. 215-17.

56. 'Vištaspa galt nicht nur als vorbildlicher Gläubiger und Beschirmer der Religion, sondern als Empfänger und Mittler von Glaubensoffenbarungen' (Windisch, *Orakel des Hystaspes*, p. 12). Iranian tradition reports that Vištaspa himself was transported to heaven in order to demonstrate the verity of Zoroaster's proclamations; cf. *Dēnkard* 7.4.84-86; Pahlavi *Rivāyat* 47.27-32 (both *apud* Molé, *Zoroastre*, pp. 59, 121); Hultgård, 'Forms and Origins', pp. 401-402. Presumably he could thus speak authoritatively about supernal matters. Moreover, there is one curious context in early Christian tradition (which is in turn dependent upon Iranian traditions) wherein Vištaspa is included among an inner circle of Zoroaster's disciples to whom esoteric oracles are revealed of 'messianic' significance. For example, Theodore bar Konai preserves a so-called 'Prophecy of Zaradusht' that treats of the future appearance of the 'star over Bethlehem' and its significance, and Vištaspa is one of the privileged hearers of this 'oracle' (*Liber Scholiorum* [ed. Scher], II, pp. 74ff.). For a full discussion, see especially Bousset, *Hauptprobleme*, pp. 378-82.

57. Lactantius, *Div. Inst.* 7.15.9: *Hystaspes quoque, qui fuit Medorum rex antiquissimus...admirabile somnium sub interpretatione vaticinantis pueri ad memoriam posteris tradidit: sublatum iri ex orbe imperium nomenque Romanum multo ante praefatus est quam illa Troiana gens conderetur.* 'Hystaspes also, a very ancient king of the Medes...handed on to posterity a wonderful dream concerning the meaning of a boy who uttered prophecies. Long before the Trojan race was founded he announced that the Roman Empire and name would be taken from the world.' Text cited from Bidez and Cumont, *Les mages hellénisés*, II, p. 366; translation from McGinn, *Apocalyptic Spirituality*, p. 59. For the proper understanding of this enigmatic passage, see especially Windisch, *Orakel des Hystaspes*, pp. 45-59. The chronological setting implied for Hystaspes would seem to be dependent upon the traditions attributed to Hermodorus and Xanthos by Diogenes Laertius, *Lives* prologue 2; cf. also Plutarch, *De Isid. et Osir.* 46. For the identification of the *vaticinans puer* as Zoroaster, see Benveniste, 'Une apocalypse pehlevie', *RHR* 106

Oracles to the prophetic gifts of the Persian sage.

If the *Oracles of Hystaspes* were thought to be dependent in some sense upon Zoroaster, and if Zoroaster and Enoch were identified by some ancient assimilationist, then it seems plausible to refer to the *Oracles* as if they were an Enochic work. This is how Barnabas or its source may have reasoned, if in fact one or the other were dependent upon the *Oracles of Hystaspes* for their content or thematic structure.

The course of the present investigation has gradually advanced the possibility that there may be a relationship between *Barn.* 4.3-4 and the *Oracles of Hystaspes*. While much of what has been said is highly speculative and reconstructive, the complexity of the interpretive task does not lend itself to simple solutions, and hence these musings are offered as a contribution to the elucidation of this enigmatic portion of *Barnabas*.

(1932), pp. 378-79; Bidez and Cumont, *Les mages hellénisés*, II, p. 367; Boyce, *History of Zoroastrianism*, III, p. 378. Hultgård ('Forms and Origins', p. 401) suggests Jāmāspa, the successor of Zoroaster. Flusser ('Hystaspes and John', p. 16) suggests that the child is in fact Hystaspes. Windisch labels this episode simply a *topos* of ancient divinatory scenes, and directs attention to other stories wherein children display mantic gifts.

IS 'PROSELYTE BAPTISM' MENTIONED IN THE MISHNAH? THE INTERPRETATION OF *M. PESAHIM* 8.8 (= *M. EDUYOT* 5.2)

Shaye J.D. Cohen

In classical rabbinic law conversion to Judaism is marked by circumcision (for men) and immersion in water (for men and women). Circumcision and immersion (or, in Christian terminology, 'baptism') are the ritual markers separating gentiles from converts. In spite of the numerous studies of these conversion rituals, an important question that remains unresolved is the date at which immersion became part of the ritual. One text frequently cited as evidence is *m. Pes.* 8.8. In this essay I hope to demonstrate that this Mishnah does not refer to 'proselyte baptism' and that, if it has any bearing at all on the question, at most it provides some of the background out of which the ritual grew.[1]

M. Pesahim 8.8 (= *M. Eduyot* 5.2)

A. A bereaved person [that is, someone who has just learned of the death of a close relative but has not yet buried the corpse] immerses and eats his Paschal sacrifice in the evening, but not [other] sacrificial meats.

B. One who learns of the death [of a close relative that had occurred some time before], and one who gathers for himself the bones [of a close relative for secondary burial]—[each of these] immerses and eats of sacrificial meats.

C. A convert who converted on the eve of the Paschal sacrifice—

D. The House of Shammai say, he immerses and eats his Paschal sacrifice in the evening.

---

1. I am expanding here on a point I first made in 'The Rabbinic Conversion Ceremony', *JJS* 41 (1990), pp. 177-203, at p. 194 n. 46. This essay draws on material to be included in my *Converts and Conversion to Judaism in Rabbinic Judaism* (forthcoming). All translations are mine. In a forthcoming study Paul Flesher reaches conclusions similar to mine, but his study differs from mine in both method and conception.

E. The House of Hillel say, he who separates himself from [his] foreskin is like one who separates himself from the grave.

Notes: A, B: 'sacrificial meats': literally, 'sacred things'.

M. Pes. 8.5-6 establishes the principle that a person prevented by impurity (or some other legal obstacle) from slaughtering the Paschal lamb on the 14th of Nisan, may nevertheless be included as a member of a group that will share the Paschal lamb, if the impurity (or other obstacle) will disappear by nightfall, when the Paschal lamb is eaten. *M. Pes.* 8.8 applies this principle to the bereaved person, whether the bereavement occured just now (paragraph A, referring to the *onen*) or long since (B), and the convert (C-E). Paragraphs C-E are cited at *m. Ed.* 5.2 as part of a collection assembled by R. Yosi of 'six matters in which the House of Hillel is more stringent than the House of Shammai'. The six cases are redacted in different forms and styles, showing that they were collected from elsewhere and placed in R. Yosi's list. The primary text is in Pesahim. I shall return below to the bereaved person and paragraphs A-B; I shall discuss first the interpretation of paragraphs C-E.

The statements of the two Houses in the Mishnah are not symmetrical. The Shammaites offer a ruling ('he immerses and eats his Paschal sacrifice in the evening') without a reason, the Hillelites a reason ('he who separates himself from [his] foreskin is like one who separates himself from the grave') without a ruling. The reason of the Hillelites implies what their ruling would be. Converts (the phrase 'he who separates himself from his foreskin' refers, of course, to circumcision, the central ritual of conversion[2]) are as impure as those who have touched a corpse. Immersion is not adequate to remove such a severe impurity, because corpse impurity can only be removed in a seven day process, on the third and seventh days of which the person being purified would be sprinkled with 'waters of purification' prepared from the ashes of a burnt red heifer (Num. 19). Thus, according to the House of Hillel, a gentile could not convert on the 14th of Nisan and eat the Paschal sacrifice in the evening. At least one week and two sprinklings would have to intervene between the two events. This is the ruling that is implied by the Hillelites' reason.

---

2. 'Foreskin' may also be a metaphor for 'the gentile state', as I shall discuss below in connection with the Tosefta, but for the moment I assume that the primary reference is to the male member and that the Mishnah is speaking of male converts.

The Yerushalmi on our Mishnah explains (*y. Pes.* 8.8 36b ed. Venice, 63a-b ed. Vilna):

> A. What is the reason [for the ruling] of the house of Shammai?
>
> B. [Scripture says] *Everyone among you or among your captives (who has slain a person or touched a corpse shall cleanse himself on the third and seventh days)* (Num. 31.19)—just as you did not become impure until you had entered the covenant, so too your captives become impure only after they have entered the covenant.
>
> C. What is the reason [for the ruling] of the house of Hillel?
>
> D. [Scripture says] *Everyone among you or among your captives (who has slain a person or touched a corpse shall cleanse himself on the third and seventh days)* (Num. 31.19)—just as you need sprinkling [with the waters of purification] on the third and seventh [days], so too your captives need sprinkling [with the waters of purification] on the third and seventh [days].

The Yerushalmi, as usual, tries to find scriptural warrant for a mishnaic debate. The Hillelite position (C-D) is clear. Numbers 31 describes the war of the Israelites against the Midianites. Since both captives and warriors can be presumed to have come into contact with corpses, Num. 31.19 ordains that both captives and warriors must be purified with the waters of purification on the third and seventh days. Since virtually all converts, not just war captives, can be presumed to have come into contact with a corpse at some point, the Hillelites require all converts to undergo purification from corpse impurity immediately after conversion (or, as in the scriptural case, enslavement, which the Yerushalmi at least understands to be a form of conversion). This explanation is not fully in accord with the Mishnah's ('he who separates himself from [his] foreskin is like one who separates himself from the grave'), because the Mishnah's implies that gentiles are impure by their very nature while the Yerushalmi's implies that they are impure only because they are presumed to have contacted a corpse at some point in their lives.[3] On the fundamental point, however, the Yerushalmi has well explained the Mishnah: the Hillelites believe that a convert immediately upon

---

3.   See S. Lieberman, *Tosefta Ki-Fshutah IV: Mo'ed* (New York: Jewish Theological Seminary, 1962), pp. 613-14. An important aspect of the Hillelite position is ambiguous in this Yerushalmi. Is the impurity of gentiles legally meaningful only at the moment of their conversion or even before? The scriptural exegesis attributed to the Hillelites in D implies that the impurity of gentiles becomes legally significant only at the moment of conversion, and that gentiles in their gentile state can neither confer impurity nor be purified, but the point is not clear.

conversion must be purified of corpse impurity.

The Yerushalmi does not explain the Shammaite position. In A-B the Shammaites simply say that the Hillelites are wrong. Scripture requires purification from corpse impurity only of converts (= slaves) who, after their conversion (= enslavement), have actually contacted a corpse. Contact with a corpse before conversion does not entail purification after conversion.[4] Why then do the Shammaites require immersion? The Yerushalmi has not a word. Similarly, the Bavli on our Mishnah (*b. Pes.* 92a) advances an explanation for the House of Hillel (an explanation that virtually ignores the Mishnah's own explanation[5]) but for the House of Shammai the Bavli can do no better than to say that the Shammaites simply reject the reasoning of the Hillelites. Why then do the Shammaites require immersion? The Bavli has not a word.

Four Possibilities

What is the unstated reason behind the Shammaites' ruling 'he immerses and eats his Paschal sacrifice in the evening'? I shall assess four possibilities: (1) the immersion is 'proselyte baptism'; (2) the immersion is the statutory immersion required of all those about to enter the temple; (3) the immersion is to purify the convert of impurity; (4) the immersion marks a change in the convert's status vis-à-vis the temple cult.

1. The immersion is 'proselyte baptism', that is, the immersion that is performed by all converts as part of their conversion ritual. This explanation is advanced by R. Moses Margulies (d. 1780/1) in the *Pnei Moshe* on the Yerushalmi (63a), by R. Yom Tov Lipmann Heller (1579–1654) in his commentary on the Mishnah (*Tosafot Yom Tov*), and by several other rabbinic commentators. They are followed unknowingly by many modern scholars who see in the statement of the House of Shammai the earliest rabbinic reference—perhaps the earliest non-Christian Jewish

---

4.   This is a common motif in tannaitic literature: acts committed by converts in their gentile state have no legal repercussions after their conversion.

5.   The Hillelites require sprinkling so that in future years, if the convert should indeed contract corpse impurity on the eve of the Paschal sacrifice, he would not erroneously think that immersion (required by the Shammaites) would suffice to remove the impurity. R. Ezekiel Landau (1713–1793) in his *Tziyun Lenefesh Hayah* (known as the *Tzlah*) on *b. Pes.* 92a suggests that the Shammaites too required immersion as the result of such a concern, but the suggestion is far-fetched.

reference—to the immersion of converts.[6] This explanation, however, is almost certainly wrong. The immersion that is required by the House of Shammai in (D) is separate from the conversion in (B). The Mishnah, neither here nor anywhere else, explains what a gentile has to do in order to convert. We may presume that male gentiles would have to undergo circumcision, but aside from the oblique hint in the statement of the House of Hillel in (E), the Mishnah contains nothing about such a requirement.[7] Nor does the Mishnah say anything about immersion as a ritual of conversion, although the Tosefta does (see below). Rather, the Mishnah says that, according to the House of Shammai, a convert *after* his conversion must immerse before being allowed to partake of the Paschal sacrifice. Similarly, *m. Ker.* 2.1 says that, according to R. Eliezer b. Jacob, a convert *after* his conversion must bring a whole burnt offering and/or a sin offering before being allowed to partake of any sacrifice. It is only post-mishnaic texts that say that a convert must immerse and bring a sacrifice as part of the act of conversion, and that the conversion is not complete if either ritual has been omitted. Perhaps the immersion that would become an essential part of the conversion process somehow derives from, or is to be connected with, the immersion mentioned here by the House of Shammai but in the Mishnah at least the immersion and the act of conversion are still distinct.[8]

2. The House of Shammai requires converts to immerse because all those who are about to approach the sancta and partake of sacrifices would routinely purify themselves through immersion. This statutory purification is mentioned in several passages in the Mishnah and Tosefta, and its reality is confirmed by the archaeological discovery of ritual

---

6.　P. Billerbeck, *Kommentar zum Neuen Testament aus Talmud und Midrasch* (4 vols.; Munich: Beck, 1924), I, pp. 102-103; E. Schürer, *The History of the Jewish People in the Age of Jesus Christ* (rev. and ed. G. Vermes, F. Millar, *et al.*; 4 vols.; Edinburgh: T. & T. Clark, 1973–87), III, pp. 173 n. 86 and 174 n. 89; L.H. Schiffman, *Who was a Jew?* (Hoboken: Ktav, 1985), pp. 27-29; M. Stern, *Greek and Latin Authors on Jews and Judaism* (Jerusalem: Israel Academy of Sciences, 1974), I, pp. 543-44 (commentary on Epictetus #254); L.H. Feldman, *Jew and Gentile in the Ancient World* (Princeton: Princeton University Press, 1993), p. 292; and many others.

7.　Similarly, the Mishnah says nothing about the circumcision of slaves, as is well observed by P. Flesher, *Oxen, Women, or Citizens?* (BJS, 143; Atlanta: Scholars Press, 1988), p. 112 n. 5.

8.　That the immersion and the conversion are distinct is well noted by R. Ezekiel Landau in his *Tziyun Lenefesh Hayah* on *b. Pes.* 92a.

baths on the steps leading to the temple mount.[9] Thus the Shammaites require the convert to immerse before eating the Paschal sacrifice just as they would require an Israelite, no matter what his or her presumed state of purity, to immerse before eating any sacrifice. This is R. Yom Tov Lipmann Heller's explanation for the ruling that an uncircumcised Jew who becomes circumcised just before Passover must immerse before eating the Paschal sacrifice (*b. Pes.* 92a; *b. Yev.* 71b; *t. Pes.*, cited below), and the same explanation can be applied to the ruling that requires a recently circumcised gentile to immerse.[10] The problem with this explanation is that the phrase 'he immerses and eats his Paschal sacrifice in the evening' seems to refer, as demonstrated by other passages where the phrase appears (see explanations 3 and 4), to an immersion that is required for a specific purpose. It is not likely that the Shammaites would have singled out the statutory immersion for mention here; they would have said simply 'he eats his Paschal sacrifice in the evening', and would not have had to mention the statutory immersion, since it would have been self-understood.

3. The purpose of the immersion is to purify the convert from an impurity akin to that of someone who has touched a 'crawling thing', a *sheretz*. This is a 'light' impurity and simple immersion is sufficient to effect purification. Whether, according to the Shammaites, gentiles in their gentile state are impure and able to transmit impurity to Israelites and Israelite property, is not clear, and whether gentiles are impure because of their very nature or only because they are presumed to have contacted a source of light impurity at some point in their lives, is also not clear, but a gentile is presumed immediately upon conversion to be in a state of light impurity and to require purification through immersion. This explanation is confirmed by use of the phrase 'he immerses and

---

9. *M. Yom.* 3.3, cf. *m. Hag.* 2.5-6; *t. Neg.* 8.9 (628 Z). All Jews purify themselves in order to partake of the festival sacrifices: *m. Sheq.* 8.1, *m. Bet.* 2.2 and *m. Hag.* 3.6. Philo too assumes that all those entering the temple would be purified first (*Spec. Leg.* 1.261); see E. Bickerman, *Studies in Jewish and Christian History* (3 vols.; Leiden: Brill, 1980), II, pp. 89-90 and E.P. Sanders, *Judaism Practice and Belief* (Philadelphia: Trinity Press International, 1992), pp. 134-35. Cf. Acts 21 (Paul).

10. I accepted this explanation in my 'Conversion Ceremony', p. 194 n. 46. A slightly different explanation is offered by R. David Pardo (1718–1790) in his commentary on the Tosefta (the *Hasdei David*): an uncircumcised Jew can be presumed not to have been careful in avoiding sources of impurity, and consequently requires purification after circumcision before partaking of the Paschal sacrifice.

eats heave-offering' in *m. Miq.* 10.8, 'they immerse and eat their
Paschal sacrifices in the evening' in *t. Oh.* 18.18 (617 Z),[11] and 'he
immerses and eats his Paschal sacrifice in the evening' in *t. Zav.* 1.1
(676 Z).[12] In these parallel passages the immersion that is mentioned is
clearly the immersion that removes a low level of impurity;[13] in *t. Zav.*
the phrase is even attributed to the Houses, as here. This explanation,
advanced by G. Alon,[14] has the further advantage of having the two
Houses share a common conceptual framework. The Houses agree that
a convert at the moment of conversion is impure, but debate the degree
of that impurity. For the Hillelites the impurity is severe, for the
Shammaites it is light. The major weakness of this explanation is that it
ignores the mishnaic context, because paragraphs A-B of the Mishnah
are not concerned (more accurately, probably are not concerned) with
purity law.

4. The House of Shammai requires immersion to mark the convert's
transition from a state of being prohibited to a state of being permitted
to partake of sacrifices. Let us return to paragraphs A-B of the Mishnah.
Lev. 10.16-20 states explicitly that a mourner on the day of bereavement (*onen*) may not eat sacrificial meats. Paragraphs A-B introduce
several important qualifications in this law. Paragraph A states that a
bereaved person on the day of bereavement immerses and eats his
Paschal sacrifice in the evening, but may not partake of other sacrificial
meats[15]—in other words, the Paschal sacrifice is an exception to the law
of Leviticus. Paragraph B states that one who learns of the death of a
close relative that had occurred some time before, as well as the one
who gathers the bones of a close relative for secondary burial—each of

---

11.   *Y. Shev.* 6.1 36c reads 'they immerse and eat their heave offerings in the
evening'.

12.   Sifra Zavim pereq 9.8 (79b Weiss) also contains the phrase and appears to be
a shorter version of the Tosefta.

13.   Similarly, in the beraita *b. Yev.* 108a concerning the minor daughter of a priest
married to an Israelite, she 'immerses and eats heave-offering in the evening', because
she must remove the impurity of sexual intercourse. In the beraita *b. Yev.* 69b ('the
daughter of a *kohen* who was married to an Israelite, and he died, she immerses and
eats heave-offering in the evening'), it is not clear whether the immersion is to remove
the impurity of sexual intercourse (so Rashi) or for some other reason; see *Tosefta
Ki-fshutah* on *t. Yev.* 6.7 (20 L).

14.   G. Alon, *Jews, Judaism and the Classical World* (Jerusalem: Magnes, 1977),
pp. 148, 150-51, and 172-77.

15.   For a somewhat different formulation of this law, see *b. Zev.* 100b.

these immerses and eats of sacrificial meats (including, of course, the Paschal sacrifice). In other words, the prohibition of partaking of sacrificial meats applies only to an *onen* on the day of bereavement. One who learns of the death of a close relative that had occurred some time before is deemed a mourner on the day of learning the sad news. One who gathers the bones of a close relative for secondary burial is deemed a mourner on the day of gathering. Nevertheless neither of these mourners is prohibited by Leviticus from eating sacrificial meats.

Why must these mourners immerse before partaking of sacrificial meats? The answer, as noted by numerous commentators, is provided by *m. Hag.* 3.3, 'a bereaved person (*onen*) and a person who lacks atonement require immersion [after completing the period of bereavement or after offering the atonement sacrifice, before being allowed to partake] of sacrificial meat'.[16] A person who lacks atonement is a person who had been impure in one of four specific categories of impurity,[17] has been purified, but still has not yet fulfilled the scriptural obligation to bring a sin offering and/or a whole burnt offering. Until the sacrifice is brought, the person 'lacks atonement' and may not partake of sacrificial meat although he (or she) is in a state of purity. After the sacrifice has been brought, the person must immerse before being allowed to partake of sacrificial meat. A beraita in *b. Pes.* 59a states explicitly, 'the person who lacks atonement on the eve of the Paschal sacrifice, [after bringing his atonement sacrifice] immerses a second time and eats his Paschal sacrifice in the evening'. The first immersion takes place on the seventh day of the purification process. It is followed by the atonement sacrifice (by which time the person is no longer impure) and by a second immersion (the subject of *m. Hag.* 3.3) which permits the person to partake of sacrificial meats, in this case the Paschal sacrifice. Neither the mourner on the day of bereavement nor the person who lacks atonement requires immersion in order to be purified, because neither is presumed to be impure; they require immersion in order to mark their transition from a state of being prohibited to a state of being permitted to partake of sacrificial meats. The Bavli correctly explains (*b. Hag.* 24b), 'What is the reason [for this ruling]? Inasmuch as they were prohibited until now [from eating sacrificial meats], our rabbis [in the Mishnah] obligated them to immerse.' Thus a beraita in *b. Eruv.* 32a

16. Sacrificial meat: literally, the sacred. See my note on the Mishnah above.
17. The woman after childbirth (Lev. 12), the leper (Lev. 13–14), the man or woman with an irregular sexual discharge (Lev. 15).

states, 'A woman who is obligated [to bring an atonement sacrifice] either for a birth or for a non-menstrual discharge, brings coins [to the temple], places [them] in the [appropriate] horn [in the temple court, the coins being used by the priests to purchase the atonement sacrifice], immerses and eats sacrificial meats in the evening.' Immersion marks transition.[18]

M. Hag. 3.3 juxtaposes the bereaved person with the person who lacks atonement; *m. Pes.* 8.8 juxtaposes the bereaved person with the convert. According to R. Eliezer b. Jacob, a convert too belongs to the category of persons who lack atonement (*m. Ker.* 2.1), a view that may be reflected here by the House of Shammai. In any event, *m. Hagigah* suggests that the immersion required of the convert by the House of Shammai in *m. Pesahim* is to mark the transition of the convert from a state in which he or she (being a gentile) had been prohibited from eating sacrificial meats to a state in which he or she (now being a convert) is permitted to do so, or, in the case of the Paschal sacrifice, obligated to do so.[19] The end of the prohibition is marked by immersion.

The Tosefta

T. Pesahim 7.14 (181-182 L)

A. R. [E]leazar b. R. Tzadoq says,

B. The House of Shammai and the House of Hillel agree in [the case of] an uncircumcised male [who contracted corpse impurity],

C. that he receives the sprinkling [of the waters of purification on the third and seventh days after contracting the impurity] and [after his circumcision] eats [his Passover sacrifice].

D. On what did they disagree?

E. On an uncircumcised gentile [who converts].

F. For the House of Shammai says, he immerses and eats his Paschal sacrifice in the evening,

G. and the House of Hillel says, he who separates himself from his foreskin is like one who separates himself from the grave.

---

18. For other possible examples of immersion to mark transition, cf. *b. Bek.* 27b and the debate between the Houses in *m. Nid.* 10.7 (adduced by the Yerushalmi in its discussion of *m. Hag.* 3.3).

19. Tosafot on *b. Hag.* 21a s.v. *ha'onen* argue that the immersion required by *m. Hag.* 3.3 does not apply to a convert. I suggest that it does apply.

H. [This rule applies equally to] a gentile who was circumcised and a female slave who immersed.

J. R. [E]liezer b. Jacob says,

K. There were soldiers and gate-keepers in Jerusalem who immersed [during the day] and ate their Passover sacrifices in the evening.

Notes: A: The Erfurt manuscript reads 'R. Yosi b. R. Judah.' The parallel in *b. Pes.* 92a reads 'R. Simeon b. Eleazar.'

B: 'The House of Shammai and the House of Hillel agree': The London manuscript reads 'The House of Shammai concedes to the House of Hillel', probably a mistake.

B: 'uncircumcised male': This is the reading of the Vienna manuscript; the Erfurt and London manuscripts, and the vulgate printed editions read 'uncircumcised stranger (or: outsider)' (*arel zar*). This reading is probably a corruption of 'uncircumcised male' (*arel zakhar*), which at first appears strange but has scriptural warrant; see Gen. 17.14. The Bavli's reading 'uncircumcised Israelite' is easier and means the same thing.

C: 'that he receives the sprinkling and eats': the Bavli reads 'that he immerses and eats his Paschal sacrifice in the evening.'

J: 'R. Eliezer b. Jacob says': omitted by the Erfurt manuscript. The vulgate printed editions, following [A], read 'b. Tzadoq' instead of 'b. Jacob.'

This Tosefta is a supplement to *m. Pes.* 8.8; paragraphs F-G of the Tosefta are identical with paragraphs D-E of the Mishnah. The sages of the mid-second century CE knew that 'the House of Shammai says that he immerses and eats his Passover sacrifice in the evening, and the House of Hillel says that he who separates himself from his foreskin is like one who separates himself from the grave', but apparently were not sure of the identity of the subject of the debate.[20] According to one version, rejected by paragraph B, the subject was an uncircumcised Jew ('an uncircumcised male'): an uncircumcised Jew contracted corpse impurity a week before the Paschal sacrifice (or, a slightly different alternative: all uncircumcised Jews are presumed to have contracted corpse impurity because all uncircumcised Jews are presumed to ignore the purity rules[21]), and, in spite of his uncircumcision, was sprinkled with the waters of purification on the third and seventh days. On the seventh day, which was the day of the Paschal sacrifice, immediately after being sprinkled for the second and final time, he could, according to the House of Shammai, be circumcised, immerse, and eat the Paschal sacrifice in the evening. According to the House of Hillel, however, 'he who separates himself from his foreskin is like one who separates himself from the grave', that is, the waters of purification cannot purify someone who is not circumcised. He remains in a state of impurity and is unable to eat

20. For a similar problem on a related issue see *t. Shab.* 15.9 (71-72L).
21. This is the suggestion of the *Hasdei David*; see above note 10.

the Paschal sacrifice. He must be circumcised before the waters of purification are efficacious. Why the Shammaites require this newly-circumcised Jew to immerse before partaking of the Paschal sacrifice, is not clear.[22] The simplest explanation, again, is that immersion marks transition: an uncircumcised Jew may not partake of the Paschal sacrifice, while a circumcised Jew is obligated to do so.[23]

This version of the debate between the Houses is rejected implicitly by our Mishnah and by R. Yosi who cites our Mishnah in *m. Ed.* 5.2, and explicitly by R. Eleazar b. R. Tzadoq (or is it R. Yosi b. R. Judah? or is it R. Simeon b. Eleazar?). Why this version was rejected, we can only speculate.[24] Perhaps because these sages (and the editor of the Mishnah) believed that uncircumcision is not a barrier to purification through sprinkling with the waters of purification, and therefore that the position ascribed to the House of Hillel is completely untenable.[25] As a result the tradition arose that the two Houses agree in the case of an uncircumcised Jew [C]. The Tosefta expresses that agreement with language that seems to reflect the position of the House of Hillel ('he receives the sprinkling and eats') while the Bavli expresses that agreement with the language of the House of Shammai ('he immerses and eats his Paschal sacrifice in the evening'). At first glance this contrast between the sources appears to be significant, but the best explanation is that the Bavli and the Tosefta mean the same thing: on the seventh day of his purification, which coincides with the day before the Paschal sacrifice, this uncircumcised Jew can be sprinkled for the second time, thereby

22. See Tosafot, *b. Pes.* 92a, s.v. *aval arel*; for further discussion see the list of works assembled by D. Halivni, *Sources and Traditions: Tractates Erubin and Pesahim* (Jerusalem: Jewish Theological Seminary, 1982; Hebrew), p. 534 n. 2. See above for the explanation of the *Tosafot Yom Tov* and the *Tzlah*.

23. In this version of the debate, what would the Houses say about the convert who was circumcised on the eve of the Passover? Perhaps both Houses would agree that 'he who separates himself from his foreskin is like one who separates himself from the grave', or perhaps the debate would extend to this case as well. See Halivni, *Sources and Traditions*, pp. 534-36.

24. The origin of the two versions of the debate is also the subject of speculation. Halivni, *Sources and Traditions*, pp. 535-36, conjectures that the 'original Mishnah' read *arel* ('an uncircumcised person') as the subject of the debate between the Houses. Later editors had to interpret: were the Houses speaking of an uncircumcised gentile, that is, a convert (the canonical answer), or an uncircumcised Jew (the non-canonical answer)?

25. See *y. Pes.* 8.6 36a, *Pes.* 8.8 36d (= *Nazir* 8.1 57a), and *b. Yev.* 71b.

removing his real or presumed corpse impurity, be circumcised, immerse, and eat the Paschal sacrifice in the evening.[26] Both Houses agree that the waters of purification are efficacious when sprinkled on an uncircumcised Jew.

What case, then, did the Houses debate [D]? According to [E], they are debating the case of 'an uncircumcised gentile'; according to the Mishnah they are debating the case of 'a convert who converted on the day before the Paschal sacrifice.' The two formulations are not precisely the same. The Mishnah's language might include female converts as well as male, while the Tosefta's language would seem to include only men; the Tosefta's language would seem to include both converts and slaves, while the Mishnah's language would seem to include only converts. These ambiguities are addressed in [H] (a continuation of the statement of R. Eleazar b. R. Tzadoq?), '[This rule applies equally to] a gentile who was circumcised and a female slave who immersed'. This clause explains that the Hillelite ruling applies not only to gentile males who have been circumcised but also to gentile female slaves who have immersed. In other words, the Hillelite maxim 'he who separates himself from his foreskin is like one who separates himself from the grave' [G] refers to women as well as men. 'Foreskin' is a metaphor for 'the gentile state'; cf. *m. Ned.* 3.11 and Eph. 2.11).[27] But clause [H] as it stands does not resolve all the ambiguities of [E], because [H] seems to exclude female converts and male slaves. That is, [H] should have read '(This rule applies equally to) a (male) gentile who was circumcised and a female gentile who immersed, to a (male) slave who was circumcised and a (female) slave who immersed'.[28] As it stands, [H] omits female converts and male slaves, and implies that immersion is a ritual of conversion only for female slaves, although elsewhere the Tosefta states explicitly that converts, presumably both men and women, must immerse (*t. Miq.* 6.11 658 Z), and that gentile male slaves must immerse in order to be regarded for ritual purposes as slaves rather than gentiles (*t. Avod. Zar.* 3.12 464 Z). I do not know how to explain the anomalies of clause [H].[29]

---

26. I follow Lieberman (who, in turn, basically follows the *Hasdei David*) in construing the Tosefta and the Bavli.

27. Medieval rabbinic Hebrew even used the term *arelah*, 'an uncircumcised woman', as a synonym for 'a gentile woman'.

28. *T. Pes.* 8.18 (188 L) pairs the circumcision of male slaves with the immersion of female slaves.

29. Lieberman *ad loc.* suggests that [H] is implicitly referring to the scriptural

In any case, if [H] is meant to explicate the position of the House of Shammai as well as that of the House of Hillel, it confirms the fact that the immersion that enables a convert to eat the Paschal sacrifice is separate from the immersion of conversion. Just as a male convert is circumcised, immerses, and eats the sacrifice, so too a female slave immerses (for conversion, that is, to attain the status of slave), immerses, and eats the sacrifice. We cannot be sure that clause [H] means to imply that the Shammaites would require double immersion of female slaves (and female converts), but [H] clearly shows that the immersion mentioned in the clause 'he immerses and eats his Paschal sacrifice in the evening' is separate from whatever ritual is implied in the phrase 'a convert who converted on the day before the Paschal sacrifice'.

The Tosefta concludes with a historical anecdote [J-K] that can be understood in two different ways: either it supports the House of Shammai against the House of Hillel, or it supports the assertion that the Houses agree in the matter of an uncircumcised Jew. According to the first interpretation, the soldiers and gate-keepers in Jerusalem were uncircumcised *gentiles* who were circumcised on the day before the Paschal sacrifice, and after immersion were able to eat the sacrifice in the evening. Thus the anecdote vindicates the position of the Shammaites. According to the second interpretation, the soldiers and gate-keepers in Jerusalem were uncircumcised *Jews* who were circumcised on the day before the Paschal sacrifice, and after immersion were able to eat the sacrifice in the evening. Thus the anecdote vindicates the position of R. Eleazar b. R. Tzadoq (or whoever the author of [B-C] is) that the Houses agree that an uncircumcised Jew can be circumcised on the fourteenth of Nisan and partake of the Paschal sacrifice in the evening. The first interpretation seems more plausible than the second, since [K] is echoing the language of the House of Shammai, and the term 'soldiers' (the Greek *stratiôtai*) is more likely to refer to gentiles

exegesis attributed by the Yerushalmi to the Houses (see above), since the verse under review refers to female war captives who have become the slaves of the Israelites. But if this is correct, the Tosefta's phraseology is still peculiar, since the point of the exegesis was to demonstrate (according to the House of Hillel) that all gentiles, not just female slaves, are susceptible to impurity. And why the selective emphasis on immersion? Perhaps [H] represents a relatively early phase in the development of the rabbinic laws governing circumcision, conversion, and immersion, but this suggestion has no literary foundation. The context of [H] seems 'early', but its language and form are unexceptional.

than to Jews. The Yerushalmi, however, cites the anecdote at the end of its discussion on the permissibility of uncircumcised Jews to be sprinkled with the waters of purification and to perform other rituals, clearly implying that the Yerushalmi understands the anecdote to refer to uncircumcised Jews (*y. Pes.* 8.8 36d; *Naz.* 8.1 57a).[30]

If R. Eliezer b. Jacob is the source of the anecdote in [K] (see the variant readings), and if this R. Eliezer b. Jacob is the same R. Eliezer b. Jacob who appears in *m. Ker.* 2.1 (as seems likely[31]), and if R. Eliezer b. Jacob is consistent in his opinions (a debatable point)—the gentile soldiers who converted on the fourteenth of Nisan must have had a busy day indeed. After circumcision, they would have immersed in order to purify themselves so they could bring the sin offering that R. Eliezer b. Jacob says was required of all converts before being allowed to partake of sacrificial meats (cf. *t. Sheq.* 3.20-22 217-218 L and *Ker.* 1.11-12 561-562 Z). After the sin offering they would have had to immerse again, in order to mark their transition from a state of being prohibited to partake of sacrifices to a state of being permitted, and then at last they would have been ready to eat the Paschal sacrifice in the evening.

Conclusion

In all likelihood when the Shammaites in *m. Pes.* 8.8 say that a convert who converted on the 14th of Nisan may immerse and eat his Paschal sacrifice in the evening, they are not referring to 'proselyte baptism'. The immersion of which they speak is separate from, and posterior to, the act of conversion, and was intended either to remove some minor impurity inhering in the convert or to mark a transition in the convert's status with respect to the temple and its cult. Perhaps the immersion that would become an integral part of the conversion ritual derives from the immersion required by the Shammaites, but *m. Pesahim* is unaware of this development.

However, even if I have explained the Mishnah incorrectly, even if the Shammaites, in fact, are referring to 'proselyte baptism', we must not exaggerate the evidenciary value of *m. Pes.* 8.8. This Mishnah hardly proves that 'proselyte baptism' was widely known, let alone widely

---

30. The implication is clear no matter what the precise language with which the Yerushalmi introduces the anecdote. See Lieberman, *Tosefta Ki-Fshutah*.

31. Although Lieberman, *Tosefta Ki-Fshutah*, p. 615, suggests that they are different.

practiced, in the first century CE, and this for three reasons. (1) Positions ascribed to the Houses do not necessarily derive from the pre-70 period;[32] (2) the Hillelites do not know, or at least do not mention, this immersion; (3) most significant, the Tosefta shows that another version of the debate between the Houses was current in the second century CE. The editor of *m. Pesahim* and R. Yosi in *m. Eduyot* have given us the 'canonical' version, but we no longer have any way of verifying that their version is more 'genuine' or 'authentic' than the non-canonical one. In the non-canonical version the Houses are not speaking of gentile converts at all, and 'proselyte baptism' is irrelevant to the discussion.

---

32. E.P. Sanders, *Jewish Law from Jesus to the Mishnah* (Philadelphia: Trinity Press International, 1990), pp. 170-172 (in debate with J. Neusner). D. Halivni, *Midrash, Mishnah, and Gemara* (Cambridge, MA: Harvard University Press, 1986), pp. 27-30 conjectures that the Shammaite view (at least the denial of the Hillelite view) was already known to Yosi b. Yoezer 'ca. 190 BCE'!

Did the Amoraim See Christianity as Something New?

Robert Goldenberg

Christianity began as an offshoot of Judaism; the first group of people who proclaimed that Jesus of Nazareth was the long-awaited divine redeemer were people of Jewish origin for whom this proclamation was the culminating expression of their Jewish religious and ethnic identity. In the course of time, however, Christianity became a gentile religion: now most people dedicated to the proposition that Jesus is Lord were not of Jewish origin and were disinclined to incorporate this proposition into a framework identifiable as Jewish.

Showering forth throughout the course of this development were all sorts of intermediate groups, sub-groups, and grouplets; each resembled Judaism in some ways, Christianity in others,[1] and each remained *sui generis* in yet others. By the end the situation was a hopeless jumble, as both ancient and modern witnesses have often testified; there was no consensus at all concerning the Jewish origins of the Christian religion.[2] Among the Christians, Marcion in the second century denied such significance altogether, while later on Chrysostom and many others felt compelled to acknowledge those origins but sought to purge them of all contemporary religious meaning. With respect to the Jews, this paper aims at shedding light on the attitude toward Christianity of one particular group of Jews, the rabbis of the third through the fifth centuries often called the Amoraim.[3]

---

1.   Of course, neither 'Judaism' nor 'Christianity' can be defined with any precision for the period under discussion. See n. 2.

2.   A useful survey of the relevant questions demanding clarification can be found in B.L. Visotzky, 'Prolegomenon to the Study of Jewish-Christianities in Rabbinic Literature', *AJS Review* 14 (1989), pp. 47-70.

3.   On the earlier Tannaim, see L.H. Schiffman, 'At the Crossroads: Tannaitic Perspectives on the Jewish-Christian Schism', in E.P. Sanders, A.I. Baumgarten and A. Mendelson (eds.), *Jewish and Christian Self-Definition*, II (Philadelphia: Fortress

The point in question here will be the quite specific matter of whether the Amoraim considered Christianity different in character from the other (illegitimate) religions of their time, and it should be noted from the outset that two other important questions do not require resolution for discussion of this question to move forward. These questions concern (1) the identity of the *minim* frequently mentioned in rabbinic texts and (2) the Jewish or gentile character of the Christianity encountered by the Amoraim. The term *min* had no single unambiguous reference. In currently available sources, it sometimes means Christians but sometimes does not and in still other cases cannot be clarified at all;[4] it usually seems to mean heterodox Jews of some kind but it occasionally seems to mean gentiles of some kind.[5] In the light of this ambiguity it becomes hazardous to cite discussions of *minim* as if they surely concern Christians; it is enough to bear in mind that the category *min* was known to the Amoraim, and that various Amoraim no doubt knew what they thought of such people, and who such people were, even if different authorities held diverse views on the subject.[6] Jewish and gentile

Press, 1981), pp. 115-56; also S.T. Katz, 'Issues in the Separation of Judaism and Christianity after 70 C.E.: A Reconsideration', *JBL* 103 (1984), pp. 43-76.

4.   See most decisively M. Simon, *Verus Israel* (trans. H. McKeating; Oxford: Oxford University Press, 1986), index. *s.v. min.*; also Katz, 'Issues', pp. 69-74. F. Millar rightly concludes that the debate over the identity of the *minim* mentioned in rabbinic literature has been 'long and fruitless' ('The Jews of the Graeco-Roman Diaspora Between Paganism and Christianity, AD 312-438', in J. Lieu, J. North and T. Rajak [eds.], *The Jews among Pagans and Christians in the Roman Empire* [London & New York: Routledge, 1992], p. 109).

5.   The rule (*b. Git.* 45b) that texts of Scripture written by *minim* must be burnt while those written by pagans may simply be put away clearly implies that *minim* are worse than pagans, hence they must be Jews who in some way have egregiously violated the basic terms of the covenant. This is also the point of a statement ascribed to R. Tarfon that he would escape a murderer into a pagan temple but not into a house of *minim* (*t. Shab.* 13.5, *b. Shab.* 116a, etc.). On the other hand the question whether a gentile can be a *min* is disputed at *b. Hul.* 13b, and is apparently resolved in the affirmative for at least some cases.

6.   Even the linkage of 'the *gilyonim* and books of the *minim*' found at *t. Shab.* 13.5 is uncertain in meaning. The original meaning of *gilyon* may well have been 'gospel' (*evangelion*), but *b. Shab.* 116a takes the word in its more literal meaning as 'margin', and there is no sound basis for determining when this (mis)interpretation arose on how widespread it became. See the comments of S. Lieberman, *Tosefta ki-Fshutah* (New York: Jewish Theological Seminary, 1955 *et seqq.*), III, pp. 206-207, esp. n. 16; also Katz, 'Issues', pp. 56-59.

Christianity for their part are notoriously hard to define,[7] and rabbinic literature nowhere inquires into what the difference between them might entail. This paper, then, will simply accept the already existing rabbinic categories of *minut* and *'avodah zarah* as intuitively meaningful though not precisely defined. The question here will be whether the Amoraim could fit Christianity in all its variety into those categories or whether they saw it as it presented itself, as something new the world had not previously seen, a *novum quid*.[8]

It will be useful to clarify ways in which early rabbis bothered at all to distinguish between one gentile cult and another. For halakhic reasons one always had to know something about particular cults and their practices: certain objects or actions became forbidden as *'avodah zarah* only if they were used or performed in the manner characteristic of a real cult, so one had to know how the followers of actual pagan cults honored the objects of their worship.[9] *M. Sanh.* 7.6 gives two examples of how this rule might work—

> One who exposes himself [or, possibly, relieves himself][10] to Baal Peor,
> that is the manner of its worship; one who throws a stone to Markulis, that
> is the manner of its worship.

In other words, people can normally perform all sorts of even distasteful acts without culpability, but when an act, however innocuous at other times, is performed out of reverence for a deity who demands precisely such behavior as his proper worship, then and only then such behavior becomes idolatry and a capital crime. It should occasion no surprise to observe that these mishnaic examples attracted later attention. 'Throwing a stone to Markulis' eventually became a standard rabbinic example of

---

7.   See Visotzky, 'Jewish-Christianities'.

8.   One might also ask more specifically whether ancient rabbis were aware of or cared about the claim of the Church to constitute such a novelty; the silence of talmudic literature suggests a negative answer to this question.

9.   See *m. 'Avod. Zar.* 3.4; *Sanh.* 7.6. A convenient summary of the relevant norms can be found in the *Code* of Maimonides, *Laws of Idolatry* 3.2. See also *b. Sanh.* 64a, *b. 'Avod. Zar.* 19b.

10.   The root *p'r* which underlies the name *Ba'al Pe'or* denotes a wide opening. The phrase in the Mishnah literally refers to 'one who opens himself wide' to Baal Peor, and this has been variously understood as meaning to stand naked or to release one's bodily waste. See *y. Sanh.* 10.2 28d, *y. 'Avod. Zar.* 3.4 42d; *b. Sanh.* 60b, 64a; Sifre Balak 131; and see Albeck's discussion of the term in his commentary on the Mishnah, p. 449.

an idolatrous act.[11] As for Baal Peor, the extravagant descriptions of the obscene ways that deity was honored[12] suggest that rabbis sometimes cultivated awareness of the particular features of various cults for purposes of gossip or slander and not just sober halakhic expertise, but this only confirms that rabbis knew perfectly well that every pagan deity had a specific cult with its own behaviors and its own conceptions; this is why each pagan cult was susceptible to parody or condemnation on its own specific terms.

On the other hand, it is a commonplace that in Talmudic literature all religious traditions other than Judaism are branded with the single label *'avodah zarah* ('alien worship'); for all their specificity, gentile cults were more or less interchangeable instances of a single phenomenon. One had to know about specific cults because one had to be able to recognize *'avodah zarah* when one saw it, but this was only technical information; the rules governing the application of this principle were themselves completely undifferentiated, because the principle itself was designed for an undifferentiated realm. Early rabbis would have been glad to do for any other deity what they did for Baal Peor; it was not that the worship of Baal Peor was in fact more disgusting than any other idolatrous cult, it was rather that in the case of Baal Peor the fundamentally vile nature of all idolatry could more plainly be demonstrated for everyone to see.

In short, the rabbis of late antiquity held the view that while each pagan cult had its own features and its own character, in the long run they were all the same. That is why the rabbinic imagination could conceive that a gentile seized with religious fervor might pledge to worship 'all the idolatries in the world';[13] it was all basically the same, and a pious gentile could not have too much of it. In that case, however, the question arises whether Christianity in its various forms was also just more of the same; at long last, was there really something new under the sun?

The argument at this point demands consideration of a point that does not always receive its due weight: so far as we now can tell, the Christianization of the Roman Empire had no halakhic consequences for hundreds of years. It provoked no new halakhic questions, it generated

---

11.   See *b. Hul.* 133a. To be sure, the rise of this expression may reflect homiletical elaboration of *m. Sanh.* 7.6 rather than everyday life.

12.   See the sources listed above, n. 10.

13.   *b. Sanh.* 64a.

no new halakhic categories, it required no adjustment of fundamental categories, norms, or attitudes. No one in the Talmud bothers to ask whether the ban on entering a pagan sanctuary[14] applies to Christian church buildings, let alone whether the same answer applies to Jewish-Christian and gentile-Christian churches; no one seems to wonder whether the ban on idolatrous cult objects[15] applies to crosses or whether Christian sacramental wine comes under the general prohibition of wine used for pagan libations. It is as though in fact nothing was new under the sun, everything was as before.[16]

This is an argument from silence, to be sure, but from the kind of silence ancient rabbis generally avoided. The Mishnah itself, for example, says almost nothing about the destruction of the Temple, treating that awful disaster as though it had occasioned nothing more than a series of technical adjustments to certain festal rituals.[17] Such technical discussions, however, added up to a profound response to a cataclysmic change; as Jacob Neusner has abundantly shown,[18] the Mishnah as a whole constitutes a response to the catastrophe precisely in its turning away from it. By saying almost nothing about the *hurban*, by silently constituting a new world that could persist without the Temple cult, the authors of the Mishnah convey the message (among others) that events in the world have no interest for Jews as long as their link to the Torah, expressed through study and fulfillment of its laws, remains unbroken.

Such a message is compatible with the attitude toward Christianity suggested here, but the talmudic silence regarding Christianity is greater in a highly suggestive way. In the case of Christianity even technical

---

14. See *m. 'Avod. Zar.* 3:7, *b. 'Avod. Zar.* 47b, *y. 'Avod. Zar.* 3:7 43b.

15. *m. 'Avod. Zar.* 3:1-3; see especially *b. 'Avod. Zar.* 42b-43a.

16. Of course there was always need to update detailed implementation of the law; see the obscure allusions to reverence for the first day of the week at *b. 'Avod. Zar.* 6a and 7b. Unfortunately the text of these passages apparently suffered from the tampering of censors; see Rabbinowicz, *Diqduqe Sofrim*, p. 15 n. 5; p. 17 n. 20.

17. The Talmud similarly says nothing whatever about the attempt in Julian's time to rebuild the Jerusalem Temple, yet this episode could still be remembered by persons alive when the *Yerushalmi* underwent its final redaction. To be sure, this episode had no halakhic consequences, and is therefore less directly germane to the present argument.

18. The classical statement of this finding appears in *Judaism: The Evidence of the Mishnah* (Chicago and London: University of Chicago Press, 1981). See also the summary statement in *Ancient Israel after Catastrophe* (Charlottesville: University Press of Virginia, 1983).

adjustments of previous rules are not considered;[19] the advent to power of a feared and hated rival arouses no halakhic discussion at all. Given the pervasive rabbinic tendency to find halakhic problems in the most far-fetched and artificial situations, the rabbinic silence about Christianity suggests that in fact the Christianization of the Empire left unchanged rabbis' perceptions of the basic reality shaping Jewish life.[20] However cataclysmic this transformation may seem today, in their view it created no fundamentally new problems and demanded no fundamental alteration in the intellectual structures their forerunners had been putting together for generations. Christians had their own peculiarities to be sure, but they were generally comparable to already familiar types.

This ability to disregard the advent of apparently epochal change apparently rested on the halakhic presumption that gentiles worship idols while Jews do not, an assumption reflected most clearly in the rule that any wine handled by any gentile must be suspected of having been used for idolatrous purposes.[21] This fundamentally national-ethnic conception of Judaism, inherited from the Bible, continued to shape the rabbinic perception that only members of the people of Israel—which in their view, needless to say, meant the Jews—can be presumed to worship the

19. One hesitates to draw conclusions from a single attribution, but the clearest halakhic reference to Christianity in the Talmud, namely the discussion at *b. 'Avod. Zar.* 6a and 7b of *Yom Nosri* is ascribed to R. Ishmael, a master who preceded by centuries the Christianization of Rome. See n. 16.

20. When the texts removed by censors are restored, they do not change the picture presented here; such texts contained purported slanders against Christianity, but not straightforward inquiries into the halakhic status of the Christian religion and its artifacts. Many of the censored talmudic passages can still conveniently be found in R.T. Herford, *Christianity in Talmud and Midrash* (London: Williams & Norgate, 1903; repr. New York: Ktav, n.d.).

Medieval texts suffered in a different pattern; many European texts of the *Code* of Maimonides simply lack the paragraph (*Laws of Idolatry* 9.4) in which he rules that 'Nazarenes' are to be considered idolators. The 'standard' Vilna edition simply moves from 9.3 to 9.5 without any indication that something is the matter (without even changing the numbering!), but the deleted paragraph has critical bearing, needless to say, on the current question. It gives an explicit ruling of the very sort that is lacking in the Talmud itself, and suggests that to Maimonides at least the matter was not obvious.

21. The rule about wine underlies most of the last third of tractate *'Avodah Zarah*. The legend that the 'evil impulse' for idolatry was successfully destroyed in the days of Ezra (*b. Yoma* 69b) seems to provide a vague rationalization for the presumption that Jews, even Jewish *minim*, no longer engage in idolatry.

one true God; all other worship is literally *'avodah zarah*, that is, alien worship, *'avodat zarim*. On this basis the overwhelmingly gentile character of fourth- and fifth-century Christendom could elicit no other rabbinic judgment: the great bulk of Christians were presumptively gentiles not loyal to the God of Israel, and the religion of such people was presumptively idolatrous whatever its apparent kinship with the Torah of Moses. As for Jews who had been infected with a Christian variety of *minut*, Israel even when it sins remains Israel,[22] and *minut* of any variety fit into an already familiar category.

The most prominent recent advocate of a differing view of these matters has been Professor Jacob Neusner.[23] His view has been that fourth-century rabbinic and Christian treatments of certain key themes show a degree of overlap, of shared agenda, that had not been seen before and was never (or at least not until our own time) seen again. In Professor Neusner's interpretation, such an overlap implies that for a brief moment Amoraic Judaism and early post-Constantinian Christianity found themselves in matching situations facing matching problems for which their respective antecedents had not prepared them. In Professor Neusner's view the symmetry of that moment led the intelligentsia of the two communities into a kind of debate on themes central to the life of both; this was 'a kind of debate' because they addressed not one another but only these common themes, each in a discourse that was isolated from the discourse of the other. The themes in question were Scripture and its interpretation, the nature of messianic redemption, and the identity of the true sacred covenant community, and in the fashion just described each community developed an understanding of these crucial issues that met its own needs while implicitly denying the claims of the other.

Now it is true that both talmudic *aggadah* and patristic discourse show great interest in the themes just mentioned, but one must never-

---

22. This widely quoted dictum (*b. Sanh.* 44a) means something different in its original context, but it has come to represent the legal principle that one possessing the status of a Jew, whether through birth or conversion, cannot lose that status through any act of renunciation or forfeiture. See J. Katz, 'Even when he sins he is Israel' (Hebrew), *Tarbiz* 27 (1958), pp. 203-17.

23. See *Judaism in the Matrix of Christianity* (Philadelphia: Fortress Press, 1986); *Judaism and Christianity in the Age of Constantine* (Chicago and London: University of Chicago Press, 1987); *Death and Birth of Judaism* (New York: Basic, 1987), pp. 3-72.

theless wonder whether this overlap by itself can bear the weight placed on it by this hypothesis. For one thing, would not rabbinic discourse[24] eventually have addressed these questions anyhow? It is true, for example, that the Mishnah and Tosefta say almost nothing about the Messiah, whereas numerous talmudic discussions evince deep concern with questions of salvation and eschatology. But the Mishnah is a kind of hothouse flower, carefully shaped—in all likelihood with great effort—to present a certain appearance and to camouflage certain realities that could not be overtly denied.[25] This effort could not easily be sustained, however, especially by a movement whose personnel were increasingly involved with more ordinary Jews in a number of everyday venues. The highly specialized diction and agenda of the Mishnah could not remain serviceable to a group attempting to guide not just a small circle of disciples and followers but an entire community through a wide range of communal needs and concerns. Rabbis had to learn to talk about more things to more people all the time. *Mutatis mutandis*, this demand still presses on them today, and the results are not altogether different.

It must also be kept in mind that the Talmuds and the later collections of Midrash are far larger books than the Mishnah and the Tosefta; they provide much wider scope for pursuing all sorts of questions. Some of the concerns of talmudic *aggadah*, for example, purported events from the lives of the patriarchs or themes pertaining to the ethics of everyday life, surely held the attention of rabbis and other thinking Jews even prior to the third century. The voluminous treatment of such themes in non-rabbinic Jewish literature from antiquity allows no other conclusion (would only the Tannaim have lacked interest in such questions?), yet these subjects too are almost entirely missing from the Mishnah-Tosefta complex, and their reappearance in Talmud and Midrash cannot plausibly be laid to the rise to power of the Christian Church.

In general, then, the evidence seems to suggest an additional hypothesis, not necessarily in place of the rise-of-the-church hypothesis but alongside it; the themes of talmudic *aggadah* reflect the natural interests of a Jewish community increasingly led by rabbis, and the scale of talmudic literature allowed for newly intensified cultivation of those interests. These interests, while not unconscious of developments in the world outside, were ultimately rooted in the unfolding exploration of the

24. I shall not presume to discuss the patristic sources.

25. See Jacob Neusner's full discussion of this matter in *Evidence of the Mishnah*, also his summary statement in *Ancient Israel after Catastrophe*.

themes of Judaism itself; they arose from the biblical foundations of Judaism and they grew with the elaboration of those foundations over centuries of Jewish inquiry. As rabbinic Judaism succeeded in making itself into a new consensus Judaism,[26] no longer the sectarian domain of a small self-declared elect but now the framework for the life-in-covenant of all Israel, it had to take account of other preoccupations and other patterns of thought than the ones cultivated by the Sages of Yavneh and Usha. None of this requires explanation by reference to the triumph of the Church, just as none of it demands that the rise of Christianity be dismissed as irrelevant. All of it, one may add, had its parallels in the developing inner life of the Christian *ecclesia.*

Two features of the situation that were noted by Neusner but left unexplained become less perplexing when seen in this light, namely the fact that neither side in this putative debate ever acknowledges the debate is underway, and the more specific puzzle that the Church Fathers seem interested in a set of biblical proof-texts that is entirely different from the set continually appearing in rabbinic literature.[27] While of course Jews were glad to deflect the pressure of Christian triumphalism—they still are—rabbinic literature is not strictly speaking engaging in a debate at all but simply (actually not so simply) pursuing its own concerns. As for Aphrahat and the rabbis of his time, they may have been different people talking about the same things, but they were not talking about the same texts, and since they were by no means talking to one another there was no reason that they should.

To conclude: the question posed in the title of this paper can be taken in a strong sense and a weak sense. In the weak sense it would simply mean to inquire whether the Amoraim knew that Christianity had its own character, more particularly that various forms of Christianity had their respective individual characters, and it should hardly be necessary to provide an answer to this weak question. Of course the Amoraim could make such distinctions; their own halakhic categories imposed such thought patterns on them. Even so, however, there is no sign that in the particular case of Christianity Amoraim put this interest into play in any special fashion. With respect to *halakhah*, both Talmuds dilate on

26. See S.J.D. Cohen, 'The Significance of Yavneh', *HUCA* 55 (1984), pp. 27-53.

27. See, for example, *Death and Birth*, pp. 41, 47; *Matrix*, p. 23; *Judaism and Christianity*, pp. 11-13, 123. The last-cited place quotes *Aphrahat and Judaism* (Leiden: Brill, 1971), p. 168.

the mishnaic ruling that any statue of a man holding a staff is presumed to be an idol,[28] but neither ever asks about a man hanging from a tree.[29] It would be perverse to doubt the Amoraim were aware that people who worshiped a man on a cross would sooner die than revere a statue of a man holding a staff, but they never took the trouble to say so. With respect to *aggadah*, there are polemics against aspects of Christian thought and practice throughout rabbinic literature, but that is no surprise; why should the Sages have done less for the Son of God than they had done for Baal Peor?

This paper, however, is chiefly concerned with the strong sense of the question: did the Amoraim judge that Christianity was not in the same category as other religions, that in precisely the sense that the others were all alike it was something new? This question, however, finds no compelling evidence in support of an affirmative answer. One is naturally tempted to assume that Jews must have reacted to the rise of the Church in such terms, but such an assumption would be entirely external to the data. Overlapping agendas of theological speculation and the sudden reversal of political relationships are important historical realities, but as already noted relevant developments within rabbinic Judaism can also be accounted for by reference to the earlier history of the Jewish religion itself, and the absence of inquiry into the halakhic implications of the rise of the Church seems decisive.

In the Middle Ages things were different; the need to confront the man on the tree became inescapable, and after many centuries of avoiding the issue rabbis could no longer suppress the question whether all the talmudic laws concerning gentiles still applied to the gentiles among whom Jews now lived.[30] Such developments, however, came long after the period under study here, and their roots must be sought in the quite different world of the Middle Ages.[31]

---

28. See *m. 'Avod. Zar.* 3.1; *b. 'Avod. Zar.* 41a; *y. 'Avod. Zar.* 3.1 42c.

29. See Gal. 3.13.

30. Many books printed in eighteenth- and nineteenth-century Eastern Europe contain explicit denials from the publisher of any implied analogy between the gentiles of the Talmud and those of later times. Of course such disclaimers can be discounted as reflecting the pressure of later oppressors, but they still reflect interest in the question whether Christians fall into previously familiar categories. See also above, n. 20.

31. An earlier version of this paper was read at the 1993 Annual Meeting of the Society for Biblical Literature.

WHAT 'THE RABBIS' THOUGHT: A METHOD AND A RESULT. ONE STATEMENT ON PROPHECY IN RABBINIC JUDAISM

Jacob Neusner

Since Professor Ben Zion Wacholder has focused his best energies in the study of Judaic sources in Greek, on the one side, and the Dead Sea Scrolls, on the other, people may lose sight of one of his important contributions to learning, which has been to the study of rabbinic literature. The best instance is his famous and influential discussion of a date for Mekhilta Attributed to R. Ishmael. But there are many others. In order to underscore his well-earned position as a scholar of rabbinic, as much as other Judaic, writings in antiquity, I offer in celebration of his seventieth birthday a discussion of a problem of method in the study of the theology and law of rabbinic Judaism, along with a single sustained example thereof. It concerns how we are to determine 'the rabbis'' opinion in a given subject of law or theology. The problem of method is simple: how do we determine what 'the rabbis'—a great many people, whose opinions are scattered through a vast literature—thought about any given topic? The topic I treat is an equally important one, the matter of how 'the rabbis' dealt with prophecy. Specifically, what did 'they' think about prophecy in their own time, and in times past? In presenting this exercise to an honored colleague in celebration of his seventieth birthday, I mean to ask as weighty a question as I can imagine and set forth an answer commensurate to what is at stake.

The problem of defining 'the rabbinic view of' one or another of the definitive topics of religion arises from the diversity of the rabbinic writings, encompassing as they do the Mishnah and the three massive exegeses thereof, the Tosefta, the Talmud of the Land of Israel, and the Talmud of Babylonia, as well as Scripture ('the written Torah'), and the compilations of Midrash-exegeses of some of the books of the Torah and the liturgical Scrolls (Lamentations, Esther, Song of Songs, Ruth). As everyone knows, in these compilations we may find attributed to one sage or another pretty much everything and its opposite. How then are we to sort matters out in such a way that we may identify a position that is authoritative and representative, if not of the whole, then at least of a significant and weighty part thereof?

What 'the Rabbis' Thought: A Method

The right answer to the question of method comes to us from the documentary organization that 'the sages' have imposed on their ideas. That is to say, we do not have writings of individual sages but only collective statements. These come to us in well-crafted documents, most of them defined by a program of editing and hermeneutics particular to itself. These documents are made up of large-scale composites, collections of completed writings on a given subject. The composites are built out of compositions, whole, complete, and coherent statements on a given subject or of a given proposition. Then the documents represent huge composites of (prior) composites, themselves comprising (prior) compositions. In the principle of selection and arrangement of compositions into composites, and composites into documents, we uncover the normative voice of the canon of this Judaism—and only there. It is in the making of connections between one thing and another, and the drawing of conclusions adumbrated by these juxtapositions or connections, that the documents' compilers speak. And it is the framers of those compilations, from the Mishnah through the Talmud of Babylonia, who have given us whatever we know of rabbinic thinking on questions of law and theology; their selections; and, more important, their arrangements of what they have selected, form the Judaism that their canon defines.

The problem of method that captures my attention therefore derives from the deeper question of how people make connections and draw conclusions. To ask about how people make connections means that we identify a problem—otherwise we should not have to ask—and what precipitated the problem here has been how a composition or a composite fits into its context, when the context is defined by the tasks of Mishnah commentary, and the composition or composite clearly does not comment on the Mishnah passage that is subjected to comment. In literary terms, we therefore ask about the purpose of introducing into the document enormous compositions and composites that clearly hold together around a shared topic or proposition.

Now to the matter at hand. We define the position of not 'the rabbis' but the definitive documents when we determine their structure and define their system. How the whole holds together at any one passage then requires explanation. Questions of structure pertain to how the document is put together and is so framed as to convey its framers' messages in consistent forms. The coherent formal program contains ample indication of the character and purpose of any given detailed analytical discussion. Questions of system concern the points of emphasis and current stress, the agenda that comes to expression in whatever topic is subject to analysis. The framers of the composites that comprise the document pursue a uniform analytical program throughout. Here too, they never leave us in doubt as to what they wish to discover or demonstrate. In the concluding chapter, therefore, through the familiar procedure of an analytical outline of the whole, this commentary aims at exposing in rich, complete and accurate detail precisely how the compositors of the document make connections and draw conclusions. By explaining the coherence of the whole through the identification of the parts and the systematic specification of what links one part to another, I mean to show the Talmud for what it is. And that is, a document that—like all enduring works of intellect—in a monotonous voice says the same thing about many things.

This documentary approach to theological and legal study is not only authentic to the character of the sources. It also addresses a problem in the prior method of dealing with the same issues of definition. Once we recognize the diversity of opinion that characterizes the various rabbinic compilations and further give full weight to the cogency of the several documents, we realize a simple fact. It is that we can no longer collect and arrange all sayings on a given topic and set forth the result as 'the rabbinic view of...' The reasons are, first, as noted, sayings prove not only diverse but contradictory; secondly, documents impose traits of thought as well as of form on their contents, with the result that statements on a given topic that occur in one document may prove important in the context of that document in particular. The result is that we may finish by reading out of all context a statement assigned to a given sage on a given topic. Thirdly, the conception of a single, unitary, coherent rabbinic Judaism has yet to be validated through detailed studies, and, it must follow, we really do not know what to make of claims to set forth 'the rabbinic view of'. What draws sayings together, apart from a common topic, is often identified as the attribution of sayings to a single authority. But that method has lost all credibility, with the advent of a critical program to the study of rabbinic literature. It is now generally acknowledged that attribution of a saying to a given authority is a happenstance and cannot be taken as fact, so any notion that we may collect and arrange all the sayings assigned to Rabbi So-and-so and set forth, if not 'the rabbinic view of...', then at least, 'Rabbi So-and-so's view of...', proves hopelessly gullible.

It follows that the history of the ideas that take their place within the canonical writings of rabbinic Judaism has to be worked out from the very beginnings. I take as my case the matter of how 'the rabbis' viewed prophecy, a subject on which a considerable literature of collecting and arranging relevant sayings is now in hand. Consult any encyclopaedia article on 'prophecy' in 'Judaism' and a fairly standard set of generalizations resting on a conventional repertoire of (unanalyzed) sayings and stories will emerge. What is wrong with these articles and their counterparts in books is simple. The authors have simply collected and arranged whatever they find on the topic. They have established no context, for example, historical or literary. They have set forth a mere pastiche of sources, and their own contribution, apart from the industry of collecting and arranging, consists in their capacity to paraphrase what the sources make obvious in any event.

A contrary and fresh approach, which I am working out in my *The Talmud of Babylonia. An Academic Commentary,* requires that we address first of all the literary context in which a subject is treated. I have chosen the Talmud of Babylonia as the first study because that is the summa and authoritative document of rabbinic Judaism. Out of that document emerged both the theology and the law of Judaism from the time of redaction to nearly the present day. What I have found is that, for a given subject, the Talmud will set forth a large-scale and coherent composite, made up of a variety of compositions. In the formation of that composite, the positioning of compositions, the unfolding of components of a large idea, we find a systematic statement of a proposition concerning said topic. That is the starting point for an account of how rabbinic Judaism, represented by the Talmud, defines its position on a given subject, locating the problematic of a topic and spelling out the proposition that the compilers of the document wish to set forth in response to that problematic.

Let me explain how we shall find in the passage the particular message that concerns us: the place of prophecy in rabbinic Judaism. For, as we shall see, when we wish to investigate a problem of law or theology, the Talmud of Babylonia sets on display, in its own characteristic idiom, a systematic account of the subject. But we have to learn how to identify its messages, since they are to be located not only in what a given authority says in his own name, but how the authoritative document selects and arranges a variety of otherwise unrelated statements. We shall review most of the treatment by the Talmud of *m. Mak.* 3.15, since it is characteristic of the document to set forth a systematic presentation of a fundamental theme by presenting a composite of distinct, free-standing compositions, which, placed into relationship with one another and juxtaposed, makes a point that, on their own, the composites of which the composite is comprised do not convey. So it is the connections between one topic and another that the compiler brings to our attention through his selection and arrangement, in one order and not in some other, of a variety of distinct statements; then the compiler—that is, the anonymous voice of the Talmud—speaks through the collage that he has formulated.

The premise of this analysis should be made explicit. How the whole of a complex composite of Talmudic materials—a set of free-standing statements or compositions—holds together at any one passage requires explanation. I maintain that in the principles of compilation—juxtaposition, arrangement of propositional compositions in one order rather than some other—the framers of the document make a statement on a large-scale topic. It is through the connections that they make that they direct our minds to the conclusions that they wish us to draw.

This we uncover through the inquiry into structure and system, in a given context. Questions of structure pertain to how the document is put together and is so framed as to convey its framers' messages in consistent forms. The coherent formal program contains ample indication of the character and purpose of any given detailed analytical discussion. Questions of system concern the points of emphasis and current stress, the agenda that comes to expression in whatever topic is subject to analysis. The framers of the composites that comprise the document pursue a uniform analytical program throughout. Here too, they never leave us in doubt as to what they wish to discover or demonstrate. So it does not suffice to cite a statement we deem relevant to our topic, for example, concerning the cessation of the Holy Spirit. We have to take a close look at what else sages say in the same context, how they say it, and the order in which they make their statements. With a mastery of not only their vocabulary, but also their grammar, we find ourselves able to discern the judgments that they wished to set forth and the message that they wished to convey about a given topic.

In the case at hand, what we have is a remarkably coherent statement on the entire problem of prophecy and the Holy Spirit, then and now; on how sages themselves fit into the framework of divine revelation; and on the particular uses to which, in the age beyond the end of the Holy Spirit and prophecy, prophecy itself is to be put. We shall work our way through the bulk of the rather subtle and complex composite, noting as we proceed the messages that the compiler's juxtapositions prove to set forth. We start with the Mishnah passage that forms the provocation and pretext for the analysis of our problem, how God conveys messages to humanity.

What Some Rabbis Thought: A Result Concerning Prophecy

For rabbinic Judaism, the Judaic system portrayed for us in the Mishnah, Talmuds, and Midrash compilations of the first six centuries CE, media for direct communication with heaven did not include prophecy. That point is made in so many words on the Babylonian Talmud's commentary at *m. Sot.* 9.12A. The Mishnah's rule states, 'When the former prophets died out, the Urim and Tummim were cancelled'. In that context, the Talmud cites a Tannaite formulation that alleges that with the end of the latter prophets, Haggai, Zechariah, and Malachi, the Holy Spirit came to an end in Israel. That statement has ordinarily been understood to mean that prophecy came to an end, which the context surely sustains.

But, as to the facts of the matter—did people in general believe that the possibilities of receiving God's word through the media of human statements, 'Thus says the Lord', in so many words?—we have to find that allegation surprising. For other Judaic systems, besides that represented by the Mishnah and the Talmud, assuredly took for granted prophets did continue to grace Israel, and the Gospels attest that that conception was common in the first century, not a hundred years prior to the formation of the Mishnah. So what, precisely, is alleged in this statement must be determined from the standpoint of the system that preserved it and found it factual and authoritative, as, assuredly, from the perspective of other Judaic systems, it was not.

When the final prophets are listed, that constitutes a judgment on the canon of revealed Scripture, excluding from prophecy all candidates for inclusion in the canonical record besides the named figures. That is the force of the systemic statement at hand: no valid prophecy continued. And that judgment forms part of a larger systemic viewpoint. There were no further holy writings, beyond those of the Hebrew scriptural canon (as then understood). The allegation that prophecy or the Holy Spirit had ceased to serve, and the conviction that, from the final prophets onward, no further prophetic books were to be recognized, formed two ways of saying one thing. From the Mishnah, c. 200 CE, rabbinic Judaism took the position that from the end of the canonical writings to the Mishnah, no Israelite composition demanded consideration as a valid communication from Heaven. When sages maintain, then, that prophecy through the Holy Spirit came to an end, the sense of that statement is simple. They took the position that all claims of writings directed to Israel with the claim of heavenly authorship or sponsorship— and they were, as we know, very many indeed—were spurious.

But that position hardly provides a complete account of the view of the Judaic sages concerning divine communication with Israel. Quite to the contrary, they certainly recorded their conviction that God continued to set forth valid messages, and that Israel remained in active, day-to-day communication with heaven. If, then, prophecy and the Holy Spirit are set aside, that only calls attention to other media of communication, and these media, too, attest to the character of the rabbinic Judaic system as a whole. Let us begin with the same context as has captured our interest.

In the analysis of a Tannaite formulation of matters now found in the Tosefta (*t. Sot.* 3.13-14), hence c. 300–400 CE, that statement of matters, rejecting the claim of authenticity put forth by competing Judaisms, immediately comes under considerable revision. The purpose of the restatement of matters cannot be missed. It is to make explicit the sages' claim that their group possessed media for direct communication with heaven. These were two, one of which is not readily discerned from prophecy or the workings of the Holy Spirit, the other of which represents a distinctive and very particular means for communication with heaven, one that defines the very character and essence of this Judaism. The former—the communication via the Holy Spirit and its surrogate, the echo—is expressed in the following, in the form in which the passage occurs at *b. Sot.* 48B. Italics represent Aramaic, bold face type, the Tosefta passage, plain type, the Hebrew of the Bavli:

O.   *Rather, said R. Nahman bar Isaac, 'What is meant by "former" prophets? It is used to distinguish Haggai, Zechariah, and Malachi, who are the latter prophets.'*

P.   *For our rabbis have taught on Tannaite authority:*

Q.   **When the latter prophets died, that is, Haggai, Zechariah, and Malachi, then the Holy Spirit came to an end in Israel.**

R.   **But even so, they made use of an echo.**

S.   **Sages gathered together in the upper room of the house of Guria in Jericho, and a heavenly echo came forth and said to them, 'There is a man among you who is worthy to receive the Holy Spirit, but his generation is unworthy of such an honor.' They all set their eyes upon Hillel, the elder.**

T.   **And when he died, they said about him, 'Woe for the humble man, woe for the pious man, the disciple of Ezra'** [*t. Sot.* 13.3].

U.   **Then another time they were in session in Yabneh and heard an echo saying, 'There is among you a man who is worthy to receive the Holy Spirit, but the generation is unworthy of such an honor.'**

V.   **They all set their eyes upon Samuel the younger.**

W.   **At the time of his death what did they say? 'Woe for the humble man, woe for the pious man, the disciple of Hillel the Elder!'**

X.   **Also: he said at the time of his death, 'Simeon and Ishmael are destined to be put to death, and the rest of the associates will die by the sword, and the remainder of the people will be up for spoil. After this, the great disasters will fall.'**

Y.   **Also concerning R. Judah b. Baba they ordained that they should say about him, 'Woe for the humble man, woe for the pious man, disciple of Samuel the Small.' But the times did not allow it** [*t. Sot.* 13.4].

Z.   For they do not raise a lamentation for those who are put to death by the government.

How sages differentiated 'the Holy Spirit' from the 'echo' is not clear in the passage before us. The two serve the same purpose and with the same effect; and both are relied upon.

To be sure, they clearly are to be differentiated. The former presumably represents direct, the latter, indirect communication; the former an articulated heavenly message, the latter one given through some indirect means, as in the case at hand, where the echo announces that the heavenly spirit is available, which, in context, means that prophecy remains viable, but the generation is unworthy to receive prophecy, even though persons of sufficient standing to serve as prophets, such as

Hillel, were available. This is made explicit in the cited prophecy of Samuel, who predicts the coming events. That fact leaves no doubt that receiving the Holy Spirit and setting forth prophecy are not readily distinguished in the source before us. But it also opens the question, how else, besides prophecy or the Holy Spirit, does heaven convey its messages?

Since sages maintained, as we see, that the Holy Spirit and prophecy no longer serve to convey to Israel heaven's wishes on any given occasion, we have to ask ourselves what media did sages identify for the same purpose, that is, what served Israel in its diminished capacity—unworthy of having the Holy Spirit represented in its midst—for the delivery of heaven's views. The answer to that question is made explicit at *b. Mak.* 23A-B, in a comment on *m. Mak.* 3.15A-D, which is as follows.

> A.   'All those who are liable to extirpation who have been flogged are exempt from their liability to extirpation,
> B.   'as it is said, "And your brother seem vile to you" (Deut. 25.3)—
> C.   'once he has been flogged, lo, he is tantamount to your brother,' the words of R. Hananiah b. Gamaliel.
> D.   Said R. Hananiah b. Gamaliel, 'Now if one who does a single transgression—[Heaven] takes his soul on that account, he who performs a single religious duty—how much the more so that his soul will be saved for [handed over to] him on that account!' [*m. Mak.* 3.15A-D].

Now the statement attributed to Hananiah maintains that heaven weighs in the balance a single transgression and a single religious duty. The latter saves the soul. Others, by contrast, require repentance. The discussion unfolds in the following; I underline the passage that is critical to my argument:

> I.1. A. [Said R. Hananiah b. Gamaliel, 'Now if one who does a single transgression—Heaven takes his soul on that account, he who performs a single religious duty—how much the more so that his soul will be saved for him on that account!':] Said R. Yohanan, 'R. Hananiah b. Gamaliel's colleagues [Aqiba and Ishmael, who insist upon repentance, not punishment, as the condition of avoiding extirpation] differed from him.'
> B.   *Said R. Adda bar Ahbah, 'They say in the household of the master, "We have learned in the Mishnah:* **There is no difference between the Sabbath and the Day of Atonement except that deliberately violating this one is punishable at the hands of an earthly**

court, while deliberately violating that one is punishable through extirpation [*m. Meg.* 1.5C]. *Now if [Hananiah b. Gamaliel were right,] then both the one and the other should be punishable in the hands of an earthly court.'*

    C.   *R. Nahman bar Isaac says, 'Lo, who is the authority behind this Mishnah-passage? It is R. Isaac, who has said, 'There is no flogging of those who are subject to the penalty of extirpation. For it has been taught on Tannaite authority:*

    D.   'R. Isaac says, "All those violations of the law that are punishable by extirpation were subject to a single encompassing statement ['For whoever shall do any of these abominations—the persons that do them shall be cut off from among their people' (Lev. 18.29)], and why was the penalty of extirpation made explicit in particular in the case of his sister? It was to impose in that case the penalty of extirpation and not mere flogging."'

    E.   *R. Ashi said, 'You may even say the opinion accords with the view of rabbis.* In the case of the Sabbath, the principal penalty is inflicted by the earthly court, in the case of the Day of Atonement, the principal penalty is inflicted by the heavenly court.'

So far, the presentation represents a standard Rabbinic dispute on a point of law. The interesting initiative now takes place:

    2. A.   Said R. Adda bar Ahbah said Rab, 'The decided law is in accord with R. Hananiah b. Gamaliel.'

    B.   *Said R. Joseph, 'Well, who has gone up to heaven and 'said' [that is, returned and made this definitive statement]?!'*

    C.   *Said to him Abbayye, 'But then, in line with what* R. Joshua b. Levi said, "Three rulings were made by the earthly court, and the court on high concurred with what they had done," ask the same question—*who has gone up to heaven and returned and 'said' [made this definitive statement]?! Rather, we expound verses of Scripture [to reach dependable conclusions], and in this case, too, we expound verses of Scripture.'*

For our purpose the interesting point comes at 2.B, Joseph's (sarcastic) statement that he thinks it unlikely that sages possess direct knowledge of heaven's will in a given point of law. Abbayye's reply in the name of Joshua b. Levi provides us with the key to the way in which, in this Judaism, people know heaven's will: sages do not have to go to heaven on consultations, because they have direct access to God's will as expressed in Scripture. The Holy Spirit, or prophecy, give way to another medium for communication between heaven and earth, although, as we shall see presently, prophecy retains a critical position for itself. The issue then becomes subtle: at what point does heaven communicate for which purpose? And the first part of the answer is, when it comes to the determination of law, it is by the correct exposition of Scripture, that sages have an accurate and reliable picture of heaven's will. The upshot, in so many words, and in the exact context at hand, is then simply stated: study of the Torah for sages has now replaced prophecy. For the age at which prophecy is no longer available, Torah-learning substitutes quite nicely. But that is only for the stated purpose and takes place only in the single context: the nature of norms and how they are determined. Here, masters of Torah enter into communion with heaven through their knowledge of the Torah, its traditions but also its logic.

The passage proceeds to expand on that claim by giving three examples of occasions on which the earthly court, that is, sages, made a ruling that was then confirmed by the corresponding court in heaven. This view is expressed in the continuation of the foregoing passage; I indent secondary glosses and expansions of the primary discourse:

> 3. A.   *Reverting to the body of the foregoing:* R. Joshua b. Levi said, 'Three rulings were made by the earthly court, and the court on high concurred with what they had done', ask the same question:
>
> B.   And what were these?
>
> C.   Reciting the scroll of Esther, greeting people with the divine name, and the presentation of the Levite's tithe to the Temple chamber.
>
> D.   Reciting the scroll of Esther, as it is written, 'They confirmed, and the Jews took upon them and their descendants' (Esth. 9.27) —
>
> E.   'they confirmed' above what they had 'taken upon themselves' below.
>
> F.   greeting people with the divine name: as it is written, 'As it is said, "And behold Boaz came from Bethlehem; and he said to the reapers, 'The Lord be with you'. And they answered, 'The Lord bless you'"' (Ruth 2:4). And Scripture says, 'The Lord is with you you mighty man of valor' (Judg. 6.12).
>
>> G.   *What is the point of the addition,* 'The Lord is with you you mighty man of valor' (Judg. 6.12)?
>>
>> H.   *Lest you say that Boaz made this up on his own, and Heaven did not approve, come and note what follows:* 'The Lord is with you you mighty man of valor' (Judg. 6.12).
>
> I.   and the presentation of the Levite's tithe to the Temple chamber: as it is written, 'Bring the whole tithe to the store house that there may be food in my house and try me herewith, says the Lord of hosts, if I will not open for you the windows of heaven and pour out for you a blessing, until there be no enough' (Mal. 3.10).

> J.   *What is the meaning of the phrase,* 'until there be no enough' (Mal. 3.10)?
>
> K.   Said Rami bar Rab, 'Until your lips get tired of saying, "Enough, enough".'

What is striking in the same composite is a matching composition, inserted immediately after the allegation that sages below made decrees that heaven accepted and confirmed. We are given three examples in which, in ancient times, the Holy Spirit did operate. Here again, the context is identical: rulings on norms of conduct, which people carried out and heaven confirmed. So retrospectively, the Holy Spirit, which, as we saw, forms the counterpart to prophecy, is shown to have worked in the age of prophecy exactly as, and for the purpose for which, the heavenly court worked in the age after prophecy in confirming sages' gifts of the spirit. That is, sages through their right reasoning and exposition of the Torah now were accomplishing precisely what, in the age of prophecy, prophets did, as in the following case:

> 4. A.   Said R. Eleazar, 'In three places the Holy Spirit made an appearance: at the court of Shem, at the court of Samuel in Ramah, and at the court of Solomon.
>
> B.   'at the court of Shem: "And Judah acknowledged them and said, she is right, it is from me" (Gen. 38.26).
>
> > C.   *'And how did he know for sure? Perhaps as he had come to her, so other men had come to her?*
> >
> > D.   'But an echo came forth and said, "She is right, these things have come about by my insistence."
>
> E.   'at the court of Samuel in Ramah: "'Here I am, witness against me before the Lord and before his anointed: whose ox have I taken or whose ass?' And they said, 'You have not defrauded us nor oppressed us, nor have you taken anything from anybody.' And he said to them, 'The Lord is witness against you and his anointed is witness this day that you have found nothing against me,' and he said, 'he is witness'" (1 Sam. 12.3-5).
>
> F.   ' "And he said" should be, "and they said", But an echo came forth and said, "I am witness in this matter."
>
> G.   'and at the court of Solomon: "And the king answered and said, 'Give her the living child and in no way kill it, she is his mother'" (1 Kgs 3.27).
>
> > H.   *'So how did he know for sure? Maybe she was just crafty?* But an echo came forth and said, "She is his mother."'
>
> > 5. A.   *Said Raba, 'But maybe Judah was able to calculate the months and days and found them to coincide?*

B.   '[And the answer is:] *Where we can see evidence, we may propose a hypothesis, but where there is no evidence to be discerned, there also is no hypothesis to be proposed!*

C.   *'Maybe Samuel referred to all Israel using a collective noun and a singular verb, in line with the usage here:* "O Israel, you [sing.] are saved by the Lord with an everlasting salvation, you shall not be ashamed" (Isa. 45.17)?

D.   *'And with Solomon too, could he reach such a conclusion merely because he saw that one woman was compassionate, the other not?*

E.   *'All of these conclusions, therefore, are tradition.'*

The force of the passage should not be missed. Even here the power of prophecy is limited by the allegation that the truth was perceived by right reason, on the one side, tradition, on the other. It follows that prophets and sagacity—the particular gift of the sages through learning—form counterparts. In that very context, we have to ask ourselves, did sages concede to prophecy any gift that they themselves did not claim in their own behalf? The answer is clearly affirmative, and to understand it, we have to call to mind the sages' name for Moses: 'our rabbi', the archetypal sage and source of the Torah. When, then, sages speak of Moses, they address themselves to the figure in Scripture with which they identify. Then when they allege that Moses made rulings that prophets nullified, they are prepared to credit prophecy with gifts that transcend even those given to the masters of the Torah in the model of Moses himself. When we realize precisely what prophecy could accomplish that Moses himself could not, we realize what is at stake. Moses gave laws, and the laws of the Torah, the five books of Moses, always take priority; the prophetic writings, we recall, do not provide sufficient evidence to sustain an opinion on a legal question.

But that is not the whole story. Prophecy in its received record retains its validity for precisely the purpose for which, to begin with, the prophets set forth their divine messages, namely, to convey the meaning of historical events and to declare the future history of Israel. Now, when it comes to history, as we shall see, matters are reversed. Moses, hence the Torah, written and oral, steps aside. The prophets, and not Moses, the lawgiver and the greatest prophet of all, take priority, and sages celebrate the enduring authority of their historical predictions, which override those of Moses, the archetypal sage, himself:

2. A.   Said R. Yosé bar Hanina, 'Four decrees did our lord, Moses, make against Israel. Four prophets came along and annulled them.

B.   'Moses said, "And Israel dwells in safety alone at the fountain of Jacob" (Deut. 33.28). Amos came and annulled it: "Then I said, O Lord God, stop, I ask you, how shall Jacob stand alone, for he is small", and it goes on, "The Lord repented concerning this: This also shall not be, says the Lord God" (Amos 7.5-6).

C.   'Moses said, "And among those nations you shall have no repose" (Deut. 28.65). Jeremiah came and annulled it: "Thus says the Lord, the people that were left of the sword have found grace in the wilderness, even Israel, when I go to provide him rest" (Jer. 31.1).

D.   'Moses said, "The Lord...visits the sin of the fathers upon the children and upon the children's children to the third and to the fourth generation" (Exod. 34.7), but Ezekiel said, "the soul that sins it shall die" (Ezek. 18.3-4).

E.   'Moses said, "And you shall perish among the nations" (Lev. 26.38), but Isaiah said, "And it shall come to pass in that day that a great horn shall sound and they shall come who were lost in the land of Assyria" (Isa. 27.13).'

Now the passage in its own terms presents the striking claim that the prophets brought Israel comfort when Moses, 'our rabbi', troubled them with a fate they could not endure.

The passage just now cited does not end the discussion of the matter. It forms part of a larger composite, and only when we note the juxtapositions that are involved here, those effected by the compositor who assembled these free-standing compositions and placed them together, do we perceive the entire message at hand. For it is one that is set forth by the making of connections between one composition and another, the setting forth as a sequence of several completed thoughts, each independent, but all changed by reason of juxtaposition with other thoughts. Through the making of the connections among the compositions at hand, that is, through forming them into a continuous composite, the compiler makes a point of his own. To understand that point, let us note that, at I.2, we have had a discussion on the relationship of the decisions of the earthly court and those of the heavenly court; I.3 has expanded on that point, a secondary development of its principal, factual allegation. I.4, continuous with the foregoing, has then introduced the Holy Spirit, giving us instances in which the Holy Spirit intervened in Israel's history. No. 2 has glossed the foregoing. Then comes a passage I need not cite verbatim, an elaborate exposition of a statement in the Mishnah passage treated here, briefly given as follows:

Therefore he gave them abundant Torah and numerous commandments:

B. R. Simelai expounded, 'Six hundred and thirteen commandments were given to Moses, three hundred and sixty-five negative ones, corresponding to the number of the days of the solar year, and two hundred forty-eight positive commandments, corresponding to the parts of man's body.'

This passage is elaborately expounded. I need not reproduce the whole. Then comes the passage cited just now, II.2, the decrees by Moses that the prophets nullified. And what follows at that point is a systematic resort to prophecy, which is to say, what do the prophets reveal that study of the Torah does not reveal? The answer, we have seen, is, Israel's history and its meaning. Here is what the Holy Spirit should convey, which is what the prophets do convey. And the passage about the supersession effected by prophecy continues.

Its message is explicit. Jacob may stand alone; Israel will find grace in the wilderness; the children will not suffer for the sins of the fathers, and Israel will not perish among the nations. The apocalyptic visions of Deuteronomy 33 and Leviticus 26 are then dispatched in favor of a benign message. If that were not sufficient to show how sages affirmed the results of prophecy for the interpretation of history, the following makes that point in so many words:

4. A. Once upon a time Rabban Gamaliel, R. Eleazar b. Azariah, R. Joshua, and R. Aqiba were walking along the way and heard the roar of Rome all the way from Puteoli, at a distance of a hundred and twenty miles. They began to cry, but R. Aqiba brightened up.

B. They said to him, 'Why so cheerful?'

C. He said to them, 'Why so gloomy?'

D. They said to him, 'These Cushites worship sticks and stones and burn incense to idolatry but live in safety and comfort, while as to us, the house that was the footstool for our God is burned [24B] with fire! Why shouldn't we cry?!'

E. He said to them, 'But that's precisely why I rejoice. If those who violate his will have it so good, those who do his will all the more so!'

5. A. Once again, they were going up to Jerusalem. When they got to Mount Scopus, they tore their garments. When they reached the Temple mount, they saw a fox emerge from the house of the Holy of Holies. They began to cry, but R. Aqiba brightened up.

B. They said to him, 'Why so cheerful?'

C. He said to them, 'Why so gloomy?'

D. They said to him, 'The place of which it once was said, "And the non-priest who draws near shall be put to death" (Num. 1.51) has become a fox hole, so shouldn't we weep?'

E.   He said to them, 'But that's precisely why I rejoice. It is written, "And I will take to me faithful witnesses to record, Uriah the priest and Zechariah son of Jeberechiah" (Isa. 8.2). And what has Uriah the priest to do with Zechariah? Uriah lived during the first Temple, and Zechariah during the second, but Scripture had linked the prophecy of Zechariah to the prophecy of Uriah. In the case of Uriah: "Therefore shall Zion for your sake be ploughed as a field" (Mic. 3.12). Zechariah: "Thus says the Lord of hosts, there shall yet old men and old women sit in the broad places of Jerusalem" (Zech. 8.4). Until the prophecy of Uriah was fulfilled, I was afraid that the prophecy of Zechariah might not be fulfilled. Now that the prophecy of Uriah has come about, we may be certain that the prophecy of Zechariah will be fulfilled word for word.'

F.   They said to him, 'Aqiba, you have given us comfort, Aqiba, you have given us comfort.'

The position of Aqiba in the case at hand repeats the results of the general statement given earlier that the prophets may be relied upon for a clear picture of Israel's future history and its meaning. Not only have the prophets reshaped Moses' prophecy concerning Israel's future; they also have provided certain and reliable grounds for optimism about Israel's near-at-hand expectations.

Prophecy in Rabbinic Judaism: The Talmud's Definitive Composite

The representation of prophecy in the authoritative writings of rabbinic Judaism proves more complex than we had anticipated. Two familiar propositions turn out to require modification in context. The first, that rabbinic Judaism rejects prophecy, and the second, that it substitutes Torah-learning for prophecy, prove necessary but not sufficient. Rabbinic Judaism affirms prophecy and recognizes the presence in the midst of its Israel of the Holy Spirit. It explicitly rejects the intervention of prophecy or the Holy Spirit in matters of the determination of law, because it maintains that these matters are resolved through the interplay of practical reason and applied logic, on the one side, and accurate tradition, on the other. The often-cited story about the debate between Eliezer and Joshua about a matter of law, in which heaven intervenes through *ad hoc* miracles, only to be rebuked by Joshua with the citation of the verse, '[The Torah] is not in Heaven', tells only part of the tale.

What changes matters is the complex composite, working its way through the logical components of the topic, that we have followed here. Beginning with the well-known allegation that the Holy Spirit ended with Haggai, Zechariah, and Malachi, we found that sages take the very opposite position. If the person of the Holy Spirit is not present, still, the workings of the Holy Spirit continue, through the echo from heaven, which conveys heaven's wishes just as reliably as did the Holy Spirit. So what, precisely, came to an end is not clear. That question becomes even more urgent when we recall how Samuel the Younger found himself able to predict the future, which is the result of receiving the Holy Spirit or the message through the echo.

Not only so, but, as we saw in so many words, sages maintained that the court in heaven confirmed precisely what sages' courts on earth determined, on the basis of the correct exposition of the Torah, to be the law. Each time sages declared the decided law emerging from controversy, Joseph's remark pertains: 'Who has gone to heaven', and Abbayye's reply comes into play: the earthly court made its rulings, the heavenly court confirmed them. The Torah, then, is the medium for communication from heaven to earth, not only way back in the time of Moses, but also in the here and now of the sages' own day. It is important to note, moreover, that the interplay of heaven and earth takes place not only in matters of law, but also theology and the interpretation of events and prediction of the future, certainly critical matters in the conception of prophecy that sages set forth for themselves. When, moreover, the prophets—for so Solomon and Samuel and David are explicitly classified—made their rulings, the same media of heavenly confirmation that serves sages came into play. Since sages represent Solomon and David as sages, the point is clear: heaven has a heavy stake in sages' deliberations, follows them, responds to them. In this context we recall the story of how heaven calls up Rabbah bar Nahmani, requiring his knowledge of a matter of purity law!

In the view of rabbinic Judaism, nothing ended with the cessation of prophecy—not direct communication from heaven to earth, not prediction of the future, not divine guidance for especially favored persons concerning the affairs of the day. Canonical prophecy ended, but the works of prophecy continued in other forms, both on heaven's side with the Holy Spirit and later on with the echo, and on earth's side with sages joining in conversation with heaven through the echo, on the one side, and through Torah-learning, on the other.

This picture of matters is expressed in so many words in a striking passage, which represents the sage as a party to the discussions of not only the earthly, but also the heavenly court. The sage now participates in that process of learning and practical reason that the study of the

Torah inaugurates, and heaven—engaged in the same issues, confirming above what sages declare below—now does more than (merely) reach the same conclusions that sages have reached. It finds itself unable—so sages present matters—to conduct its affairs without the participation of sages themselves. The story that follows states in so many words that sages are required for heaven to do its work of Torah-study. I take that statement to mean, prophecy ended in one form, continued in many forms, but found its true fulfillment in the mastery of the Torah that (some) sages accomplished.

AD VERBUM OR AD SENSUM
THE CHRISTIANIZATION OF A LATIN TRANSLATION FORMULA IN THE FOURTH CENTURY

William Adler

Translation *ad sensum* had numerous ancient exponents, particularly among those Roman writers who had tried their hand at translating the Greek classics into Latin. It is the way of 'clumsy translators (*interpretes indiserti*),' Cicero says, to attempt to render every Greek word by its exact Latin counterpart.[1] 'Do not linger along the easy and open pathway,' writes Horace in his *Art of Poetry*, '...do not seek to render word for word (*verbum verbo*) as a slavish translator (*fidus interpres*).'[2] Among the Latin church fathers of late antiquity, the case for translation *ad sensum* is so well documented that its central features need hardly be restated. Around the year 373, Evagrius, in the prologue to his Latin translation of the *Life of Anthony*, states that his translation, while not at all deficient *ex sensu*, might be found to lack something *ex verbis*. 'My version always preserves the sense, although it does not invariably keep the words of the original. Leave others to chase after syllables and letters (*alii syllabas aucupentur et litteras*), do for your part seek only for the meaning.'[3] Shortly thereafter, Jerome too claimed to belong to the same school. Only in translating Scripture, Jerome says, would he depart from the rule of translating sense for sense, not word for word.[4]

---

1. Cicero, *De finibus* 3.4.15.
2. Horace, *Art of Poetry* 133 (trans. H.R. Fairclough; LCL; Cambridge, MA: Harvard University Press, 1961).
3. Evagrius, *Life of Anthony, Prologue* (PG 26, 833 = PL 73, 125). See B.R. Voss, 'Bemerkungen zu Euagrius von Antiochien Vergil und Sallust in der *Vita Antonii*', *VC* 21 (1967), pp. 93-94.
4. Jerome, *Epistle* 57.5.2. Edition of Jerome's epistles is by I. Hilberg (CSEL 54-56; Vienna: Tempsky, 1910). Where available, English translation of Jerome is by H.W. Fremantle, in *Nicene and Post-Nicene Fathers* 6 (Second Series; ed.

Such statements are responsible for the supposition that, in Latin Christianity of the late fourth century, translators like Jerome adhered to a 'systematic, disciplined...and well-conceived' method, which continued and promoted the Ciceronian approach to translation.[5] Under certain circumstances he may have contradicted his own dicta and his stated method was not always vindicated by the final product. But these deviations are normally attributed to external constraints (such as the Origenist crisis) or Jerome's own awareness of the difficulty of adhering dogmatically to one set of principles. Despite these occasional lapses, Jerome is generally understood to have expounded clearly thought out theoretical principles which served as a general guide.[6]

In this paper, I want to suggest that although Jerome appealed to Cicero and Horace to justify his methods of translating, he used the expression 'translatio ad sensum' in a radically different way. Much of the difficulty in understanding what Jerome meant when he spoke of translation 'according to the sense' can be resolved if we better understand the rhetorical context in which his discussion of the subject typically took place.

Translatio Ad Sensum and the Classical Tradition

What particularly commended translation *ad sensum* was the skill that the translator was thought to acquire in conveying the rhetorical power

---

P. Schaff and H. Wace; Grand Rapids: Eerdmans, 1983).

5.   E. Nida, *Toward a Science of Translating* (Leiden: Brill, 1964), p. 13. Bardy refers to a 'doctrine très ferme' (*Recherches sur l'histoire du texte et des versions latines du De Principiis d'Origène* [Memoires et travaux publiés par des Professeurs des Facultes Catholiques de Lille, 15; Paris: E. Champion, 1923], p. 159). H. Hagendahl (*Latin Fathers and the Classics* [Gothenburg: Almqvist and Wiksell, 1958], pp. 163-64) refers to Jerome's principles of translation as 'sound' and 'guided by the Classics'.

6.   For discussion, see F. Winkelmann, 'Einige Bermerkungen zu den Aussagen des Rufinus von Aquileia und des Hieronymus über ihre Übersetzungstheorie und -methode', in *Kyriakon: Festschrift Johannes Quasten* (ed. P. Granfield and J.A. Jungman; Münster: Aschendorf, 1970), p. 543; P. Courcelle, *Late Latin Writers and their Greek Sources* (ET; Cambridge, MA: Harvard University Press, 1969), pp. 53-58. See also H. Marti, *Übersetzer der Augustin-Zeit* (Studia et Testimonia Antiqua, 14; Munich: Fink, 1974), p. 62. Marti's study, one of the most thorough examinations of the subject, includes a valuable collection of the relevant primary sources; to it, the present study owes a debt of gratitude.

of the Greek language. In Cicero's day, many 'plain orators' were
allegedly declaiming in the Attic style. So when Cicero undertook to
render the Greek orators into Latin, he translated according to the sense
in order to educate his Latin readers about what the 'grand, ornate and
copious' Attic style of oratory really was. 'If all the words are not literal
translations of the Greek, we have at least tried to keep them within the
same class or type (and) there will be a norm by which to measure the
speeches of those who wish to speak in the Attic manner.'[7] Translations
executed according to these prescriptions were thought to sharpen the
mind and enrich the Latin language with a new force and elegance. 'I
not only found myself using the best words,' Cicero says, '...but also
coining by analogy certain words such as would be new to our people.'[8]
Understood in this way, translation was more than simple imitation. It
was a form of cultural enrichment. 'This kind of exercise,' Pliny writes,
'develops in one a precision and richness of vocabulary, a wide range of
metaphors, and moreover imitation of the best models leads to a like
aptitude for original composition.'[9]

In the above statements, neither Pliny nor Cicero exhibit any real
doubt either about their own capacities or the inherent frailties of the art
of translation. To the contrary, Cicero was satisfied that his rhetorical
translations could stand on their own as works of fine literature. To
those critics who might say, 'It is better in the original Greek,' Cicero
replies, 'can they themselves produce anything better in Latin?'[10] A
translator might even enter into a rivalry with the text. There is no
harm, Pliny states, in competing with, even surpassing, the original text.
'You may well congratulate yourself if yours is sometimes better and
feel much ashamed if the other is always superior to yours.'[11]

This robust confidence that a well-executed translation could stand in
as a fully adequate surrogate for the original text contrasts markedly
with the professions of uncertainty that one finds elsewhere among

---

7. Cicero, *De optimo genere oratorum* 7.23 (trans. H.M. Hubbell; LCL;
Cambridge, MA: Harvard University Press, 1976).

8. Cicero, *De Oratore* 1.34.155 (trans. H. Rackham; LCL; Cambridge, MA:
Harvard University Press, 1988); see also Quintilian, *Institutio Oratoria* 10.5.2-3.

9 Pliny, *Ep.* 7.9.2-3, to Fuscus Salinator (trans. B. Radice; LCL; Cambridge,
MA: Harvard University Press, 1969).

10. Cicero, *De optimo genere oratorum* 6.18.

11. Pliny, *Ep.* 7.9.3.

ancient translators.[12] It also differs from the stereotyped expressions of self-doubt that are commonplace in literary prologues of Latin and Greek writers of the fourth century. If Libanius is correct, abasement of one's own literary skills was by his time *de rigueur*. In his 11th oration, he observes that it was 'a common custom (κοινὸν ἔθος) for encomiasts to assert that their own inadequacy (ἀσθένειαν) falls short of the task to which they addressed their discourse.'[13] Astute readers were able to identify this practice for what it really was: literary artifice. A certain Gallus, writes Sulpicius Severus (4th century), had asked to be forgiven for the fact that his 'rather coarse speech (*sermo rusticior*) might offend your refined ears.' Postumianus, who knew Gallus's literary skills, could hardly take the disclaimer seriously: 'you're doing this as an affectation (*artificiose*), like a rhetor (*scholasticus*).'[14] The τόπος of 'affected modesty' was so customary in Latin literature of late antiquity that very little can be inferred from it about the actual literary deficiencies of the author's writing. Far from being honest appraisals of the writer's own Latinity, these disingenuous affirmations of *rusticitas* were, as Norden observed, typically intended to excite admiration for the literary qualities of the work.[15]

---

12. Translators of religious works from Egypt and the Near East were especially anxious that texts which they hoped to commend to a Greek or Latin audience were being slighted by efforts that failed to convey the force and clarity of the original. See, for example, the grandson's prologue to his translation of Sirach (22-23), in *Septuaginta* 12.2 (ed. J. Ziegler; Göttingen: Vandenhoeck & Ruprecht, 1965). Rendered into Greek or any other langauge, writes the grandson of Ben Sira, the Bible 'does not have a power equal to (οὐ...ἰσοδυναμεῖ)' the original. One translator, in the name of Hermes Trismegistus, laments that sacred books composed in Egyptian inevitably suffered a loss of vitality when translated into another language. He thinks the reason has something to do with the inherent properties of Egyptian. Egyptian words have an intrinsic energy (τὴν ἐνέργειαν) that gets dissipated in translation. When the Greeks undertook to render Hermetic books into Greek, what they produced was completely obscure, the 'greatest perversion and obfuscation of his writings'. So make sure, he warns, that wherever possible, Hermetic books remain 'untranslated (ἀνερμήνευτον)' (*Corpus Hermeticum* 16.1-2 [ed. A.D. Nock and A.-J. Festugière; Paris: 'Les Belles Lettres', 1945]).

13. Libanius, *Oration* 11.6 (Vol. 1; ed. R. Foerster; Leipzig: Teubner, 1903).

14. Sulpicius Severus, *Dialogue* 1.27.2-5 (ed. C. Halm; CSEL, 1; Vienna, 1866).

15. 'Beispiele lassen sich, wie jeder weiss, Hunderte anführen aus allen Zeiten und Sphären der Literatur, und zwar kann man sicher sein, dass unter 100 Fällen 99mal daraus genau das gerade Gegenteil für den Stil des betr. Autors folgt; er will damit nur sagen: passt einmal, wie ausgezeichnet ich meine Sache mache' (E. Norden,

Variants on the same theme appear with equal frequency among those writers who had been commissioned to render a popular or highly regarded work into another form. Latin epitomists of late antiquity, for example, often make a point of stressing that the limitations of the genre required them to sacrifice both literalness and the stylistic elegance of the original. Thus, in the proem to his epitome of Cassiodorus's *Getica*, Jordanes enjoins his readers to treat his work with leniency. He entered into the project reluctantly, and his spirit lacked the fortitude to do justice to the magnificent eloquence of the work he was condensing. Above all, the task of compressing a very long work into 'one little book' was a difficult one. For that reason, he says, one should not expect or demand the strictest exactitude. 'Although I do not rehearse the words (*verba non recolo*) of the books, nevertheless I believe that I adequately retain the sense and the deeds (*sensus tamen et res actas credo me integre retinere*), mixing my own wording into the beginning and the end and much in between.'[16]

Like Cicero, Jordanes draws a distinction here between *ad verbum* and *ad sensum*. But he does so for a quite different purpose, namely to prepare his readers for a work that he fears might disappoint their expectations. It should not be surprising that translators in the late fourth century should have seized on the same tactic. But rather than calling attention to the weakness of the author's knowledge or skill with language, the translator would offer a general lament about the overall inadequacies of one language to capture a work composed in another. The epilogue to an early translation of the *Life of Antony* offers an illustration. Here the translator implores his readers to 'pardon us, if, in translating into the Latin language, we were unable to express the same force of the Greek words...knowing how great are the infirmities that the Greek language undergoes when translated into Latin style.'[17] The question that now must be posed is this: Does Jerome's appeal to

---

Die antike Kunstprosa [Teubner: Leipzig, 1923], II, p. 595 n. 1).

16. Jordanes, *De origine actibusque Getarum* 1 (ed. F. Giunta and A. Grillone; Rome: Istituto Storico Italiano, 1991). For another example see the *proem* to the breviarium of Rufus Festus (ed. J.W. Eadie; London: Athlone Press, 1967). There he tries to engage the sympathies of the readers by describing himself as one 'cui desit facultas latius eloquendi'.

17. Text in H.W.F.M. Hoppenbrouwers, *La plus ancienne version latine de la vie de S. Antoine par S. Athanase* (Utrecht: Dekker & van de Vegt, 1960), p. 194.

translation *ad sensum* come closer to Cicero's (as is often assumed) or to the 'Bescheidenheitsformel' of the fourth century?[18]

Jerome and Translation Ad Sensum

Jerome's first extended discussion of the perils of translation appears in the prologue to his translation of Eusebius's chronicle (c. 380). In his catalogue of the customary grievances against literal translation, Jerome laments the difficulties of following

> another man's lines and everywhere keep(ing) within bounds...Some word has forcibly expressed a given thought; I have no word of my own to convey the meaning. And we have to take into account the variations in cases, the diversity in figures, and lastly the peculiar, and so to speak, the native idiom of the language.[19]

It has been wrongly assumed from this, however, that what Jerome meant to do here was to prove that because of the difficulties with literal translation, idiomatic literary translations were the only desirable goal. This is not so. Unlike Cicero, Jerome does not commend translation *ad sensum* as the only way to preserve the literary excellence of the original language; nor does he claim that only this approach could reproduce a work in keeping with the standards of the Latin language. Literal translation, Jerome writes, would be the desirable goal, if it were attainable. But this is not to suggest that translation *ad sensum* is necessarily any better, or more desirable. *Any* kind of translation, he insists, will always seem to fall short of the original.

Jerome pursues this line of argument in describing the many translators that preceded him. When he invokes their names, it is not to extol any particular theoretical approach to translation. Rather, it is simply to demonstrate that the great names of the past fell short of perfection and that, for this reason, Jerome himself deserved to be excused for his own failings. Even Cicero, he says, produced atrocities when he tried his hand at literal translation. The results were so badly flawed that those who read them were hardly able to believe that a master of the Latin language could have composed them.[20] Jerome rightly takes note of the

18. This is the term used by I. Opelt in his article on the 'Epitome', in *RAC* (Stuttgart: Hiersemann, 1962), col. 959.

19. Jerome, *Chronicle of Eusebius, Praef.* (ed. R. Helm; GCS Eusebius Werke, 7; Berlin: Akademie-Verlag, 3rd edn, 1984), p. 2 ll. 2-12.

20. *Praef.-Chron.* 1.7–2.2.

fact that each one of the Greek translations of the Hebrew Bible bore its own distinctive character. Symmachus tried to capture the sense; Theodotion 'deviated not much from the elders'; and Aquila 'excelled in word for word' translation.[21] From this, Jerome might be expected to praise Symmachus and take Aquila most to task, since, according to the traditional view, word for word translation was the least desirable. But he does not. All of them, he writes, were overshadowed by the elegance of the original. 'As a result, some go so far as to consider the sacred writings somewhat harsh and grating to the ear...The persons of whom I speak are not aware that the writings in question are a translation from the Hebrew, and therefore, looking at the surface and not at the substance (*dum superficiem, non medullam inspiciunt*), they shudder at the squalid dress.'[22]

As we have seen, earlier exponents of translation *ad sensum* were confident that what they had produced rivalled, perhaps even exceeded, the original. But Jerome nowhere speaks this way on behalf of his own translation. Presenting a theoretical case for the advantages of one style of translation over another was not what was at stake. All that he seeks to do is plead with his readers to overlook whatever deficiencies they might discern, and not to judge him by any fixed principle. 'I am well aware,' Jerome says, 'that there will be many who, with their customary fondness for universal detraction (from which the only escape is by writing nothing at all) will drive their fangs into this volume...'[23] But let these hypercritical readers exercise a little forebearance, once they comprehend the magnitude of the task. 'A literal (*ad verbum*) translation sounds absurd,' he writes. 'If, on the other hand, I am obliged to change either the order or the words themselves, I shall appear to have forsaken the duty of a translator.'[24]

Indeed, it would have been passing strange had Jerome held up his translation of Eusebius's chronicle as an example of translation *ad sensum* in the Ciceronian style, that is, as one that sought to preserve the literary excellence of the original. No one ever praised Eusebius's chronicle as a work of surpassing literary qualities. This was not why Eusebius composed it. Arranged in the form of running lists of kings synchronized in tabular order, the only thing that even approximated

21. *Praef.-Chron.* 3.4-9.
22. *Praef.-Chron.* 3.14-18.
23. *Praef.-Chron.* 5.16-19.
24. *Praef.-Chron.* 2.12-15.

narrative was the historical notices embedded in these tables. In this format, there would have been little opportunity for Jerome to display the literary virtuosity of a Cicero. And his translation did not aim to do so. To the contrary, Jerome identifies the complexity of Eusebius's chronicle as one more reason why readers should overlook inaccuracy or inelegance in his translation. Even apart from the intrinsic difficulties of translation of any kind, Jerome writes, the particular circumstances attending the translation of Eusebius precluded the possibility of a fully polished and accurate outcome. This was so because the work that he undertook to render into Latin was 'full of barbarous names, circumstances of which the Latins know nothing, dates which are tangled knots...so that it is almost harder to discern the sequence for reading than to come to a knowledge of what is related.'[25] His translation, he admits, will occasionally offend the senses. If the work is 'cumbersome, or heavy with consonants, or cleft with vowels,' he writes, readers should excuse this, recognizing how difficult the whole task is.

When Jerome hoped to head off potential critics, he quite often blamed insufficient time, dictation, disease and other exigencies for the avowedly poor quality of his writing. 'Swift dictation has taken the place of careful writing,' he says in a letter to Julian. The result 'is an impromptu letter without logical order or charm of style, dashed off in the spur of the moment.'[26] The rhetorical gambit seems to have paid off. Jerome's stated habit of dictating rapidly to stenographers, writes Hagendahl, 'erhöht die Bewunderung für diesen geborenen Stilisten, dessen leichter und eleganter Stil meines Erachtens in der spätlateinischen Literatur ohnegleichen ist'.[27] In the prologue to his translation of the *Chronicle*, Jerome makes it serve this same end. The accuracy of his translation of Eusebius, he writes, was further imperilled by hurried dictation. 'My dear Vicentius and you Gallienus...I beseech you, whatever may be the value of this hurried piece of work (*tumultuarii operis*),

25. *Praef.-Chron.* 5.1-6.
26. *Ep.* 118.1.9-11; see also *Ep.* 21.42: 'itaque ignosce dolentibus oculis, id est ignosce dictanti, maxime cum in ecclesiasticis rebus non quaerantur verba'; *Ep.* 74.6.2: 'nos enim et haec ipsa in lectulo decumbentes longaque aegrotatione confecti vix notario celeriter scribenda dictavimus...; et ignosce, si scatens oratio solito cursu non fluat'; *Ep* 11.2.1: '...effutire compellar et tumultario respondere sermone non maturitate scribentis, sed dictantis temeritate...'
27. H. Hagendahl, 'Die Bedeutung der Stenographie für die spätlateinische christliche Literatur', *Jahrbuch für Antike und Christentum* 14 (1971), p. 32.

to read it with the feelings of a friend rather than those of a critic. And I ask this all the more earnestly because, as you know, I dictated with great rapidity (*velocissime dictaverim*) to my amanuensis.'[28] 'Coquetterie litté raire,' writes Cavallera of Jerome's claim; for it is virtually inconceivable that Jerome could have hastily dictated so complex a work.[29] Nor does the appeal to haste square with the Ciceronian tradition of translation according to the sense. None of the classical predecessors whom Jerome cites offered 'haste' as justification for translation *ad sensum*. To the contrary, success in this venture was supposed to require the utmost care and labor. But in his prologue to his translation of Eusebius, Jerome had other interests in mind.

Jerome 'On the Best Method of Translating'

Admittedly, the above analysis of Jerome's prologue to his translation of Eusebius's chronicle contradicts Jerome's own subsequent assessment of it. When, in his well-known letter to Pammachius (395), Jerome later has occasion to comment again upon his theory of translation, he quotes the prologue as proof that 'from my youth up, I at least have always aimed at rendering sense not words'.[30] Indeed, this letter, bearing the grandiose subtitle 'On the Best Method of Translating (*De optimo genere interpretandi*)', presents what would on its face seem to be the 'well-defined' principles of translation to which Nida refers. 'I myself,' he writes, 'not only admit, but freely proclaim that in translating from the Greek, except in the case of the Holy Scriptures...I render sense for sense and not word for word (*non verbum e verbo, sed sensum...de sensu*).'[31]

The erudition of the letter to Pammachius cannot be challenged. Jerome rehearses all the right clichés. Precise verbal equivalents, he says, do not always exist and the preservation of the order of words makes translations sound ridiculous. Words in Greek have a particular meaning

---

28. *Praef.-Chron.* 2.16-20.

29. F. Cavallera, *Saint Jérôme: sa vie et son oeuvre* (Spicilegium Sacrum Lovaniense, Études et Documents, Fasc. 1; Paris: E. Champion, 1922), I, p. 63. For an opposing view, see A. Wikenhauser, 'Der heilige Hieronymus und die Kurzschrift', *Theologische Quartalschrift* 92 (1910), pp. 61-62.

30. *Ep.* 57.6.8. For discussion of this letter, see G.J.M. Bartelink, *Liber de optimo genere interpretandi: Ein Kommentar* (Mnemosyne, 61; Leiden: Brill, 1980).

31. *Ep.* 57.5.2.

which can rarely be conveyed by a one word synonym in Latin. 'How many are the phrases charming in Greek which if rendered word for word, do not sound well in Latin, and again, how many there are pleasing to us in Latin, but which—assuming the order of the words not to be altered—would not please in Greek?'[32] And he names all the right authorities, both classical and ecclesiastical. 'Do they ever stick at words? Do they not rather in their versions think first of preserving the beauty and charm of the originals?'[33] Translation *ad sensum* was, moreover, the norm for the translators of the Septuagint, the evangelists, the apostles and the church fathers.

> Time would fail me were I to unfold the testimonies of all who have translated only according to the sense…(Hilary) has not bound himself to the drowsiness of the letter or bound himself by a stale and boorish literalism (*putida rusticorum interpretatione*). Like a conqueror, he has led away captive into his own tongue the meaning of his originals.[34]

Yet in spite of all the learning that Jerome parades, the theoretical foundation is actually very meagre. Far more than the prologue to his translation of Eusebius's chronicle, the tone of this letter is inflammatory and defensive; this was so because the damage to Jerome's reputation had already been done. At the insistence of a certain Eusebius of Cremona, Jerome had earlier undertaken to translate into Latin a letter composed by Epiphanius. Epiphanius sent this letter to John, the Bishop of Jerusalem, in order to remonstrate with him on his Origenist leanings. The letter was praised by many for both 'its teaching and the purity of its style' and Jerome agreed to translate it into Latin—only on condition, however, that Eusebius read it privately and not circulate it 'too readily'.[35] By some sort of stratagem (Jerome suggests bribery), however, a monk purloined the letter and passed it on to one of Jerome's many enemies. After studying the translation, an unnamed adversary, probably Rufinus, was able to identify many imperfections.

In his letter, Jerome characterizes these criticisms as mostly carping. What you call truth in translation, he says to his 11 critics, learned men call 'bad taste (κακοζηλία)'.[36] But from Jerome's own response, we can conclude that Jerome's adversaries, whatever were their motives,

32. *Ep.* 57.11.4.
33. *Ep.* 57.5.5.
34. *Ep.* 57.6.3.
35. *Ep.* 57.2.2.
36. *Ep.* 57.5.5.

had some grounds for their criticisms. When the letter was composed, Jerome, hoping to purify himself of the stain of Origenism, was eager to prove his orthodoxy by volunteering his own efforts at extirpating the remnants of the heresy from the Church. One of the suspected Origenists was John of Jerusalem, the addressee of Epiphanius's letter. Like others of John's opponents, Jerome had advised the monks of Bethlehem not to subject themselves to John's authority. Indeed, this was the reason why Jerome agreed to translate Epiphanius's letter in the first place—namely to show that Epiphanius, a revered defender of orthodoxy, suspected John of heresy.

The letter that Epiphanius wrote to John was, at least for Epiphanius, uncharacteristically mild, even conciliatory. In the introduction to the letter, Epiphanius addressed John as 'αἰδεσιμώτατον (most reverend)'. Jerome acknowledges that he omitted this title and substituted 'dear friend' for 'honorable sir'. In this context, it is perfectly understandable that Jerome's critics, who were probably themselves Origenists, should have accused him of deliberately trying to suppress the fact that Epiphanius was deferring to John's episcopal authority.[37] They also charged Jerome with simply misinterpreting a Greek sentence in the opening of the letter. The sentence in question reads: ἔδει ἡμᾶς, ἀγαπητέ, μή τῇ οἰήσει τῶν κλήρων φέρεσθαι ('Beloved, we ought not to be carried away by the opinion of clerics'). Now Jerome miscontrued the sentence to mean: 'we ought not to misuse our position as ministers to gratify our pride'.[38]

While dismissing such errors as 'trifles', Jerome acknowledges that there were other faults that had been detected. 'A simple translation may contain errors', he admits, 'though not willful ones.' [39] Given the polemical and defensive tone of Jerome's letter, we should not be surprised if many of them were not trivial, and that Jerome therefore

---

37. *Ep.* 57.2.3. See M. Villain, 'Rufin d'Aquilée, la querelle autour d'Origine', *RSR* 27 (1937), pp. 12-14.

38. *Ep.* 57.12.1-2. According to Jerome, one of the objections to his translation was that he should have translated οἴησις as 'judgment (*aestimatio*)' instead of 'pride (*superbia*)'. His critics attributed the error to the confusion of οἴημα with οἴησις. Jerome could have defended his translation of οἴησις as *superbia*, since the Greek word can certainly accept that sense. It is possible, however, that the Greek word which his critics claimed Jerome confused with οἴησις was not οἴημα, but rather οἴδημα. Indeed, the latter more closely approximates the Latin word 'tumor' (swelling), which they said Jerome confused with οἴησις.

39. *Ep.* 57.5.1.

decided not to call attention to them in his own response. Most of the letter is not a line-by-line defense of his translation, but rather a reitera-tion of the conventional arguments that he had made earlier in the prologue to his translation of Eusebius. Here again he contrives to make haste the culprit. 'Calling to my aid a secretary', Jerome writes, '(I) speedily dictated (*celeriterque dictavi*) my version', inserting the trans-lation into the margin of the Greek exemplar.[40] His explanation, as Cavallera has noted, is unsatisfactory. The translation reflects more care than a first draft; and if, as Jerome implies, Eusebius had only been interested in the mere contents of the letter, it would have sufficed to have translated the letter orally.[41]

Jerome then embarks upon his case for translation *ad sensum* with the standard citations from classical and ecclesiastical authorities. All of his predecessors agree, he writes, that the charm and grace of the original can be preserved only by translation according to the sense. What is notable, however, is that Jerome gives no examples of translation *ad sensum* from Cicero and Horace, the leading expositors of this approach. It is not difficult to understand why not. As Jerome knew, he was defending himself against the charge of failing to make an accurate, not a rhetorical or idiomatic translation. The translation, he confesses, was an untutored and (so he claims) a hastily composed work. It would hardly have boosted his case, therefore, if he had cited examples in which his illustrious predecessors had, by his own words, brilliantly 'led away captive into his tongue the meaning of his originals'.[42]

Instead, the illustrations that he does adduce are entirely taken from the Septuagint and from the New Testament. Their avowed purpose was to show that, in occasionally deviating from the original, Jerome was in good company. After all, the highly esteemed Septuagint and the New Testament were not always strictly literal in rendering material from the Hebrew Bible. It is well-known, he says, that the Septuagint was not unfailingly faithful to the Hebrew; but was it not still far superior to Aquila's foolish literalism? And if his critics were to indict him for imprecision, would they not then have to accuse the evangelists of the same thing? 'It is clear,' he writes, 'that the apostles and the evangelists have sought to give the meaning rather than the words, and...they have not greatly cared to preserve forms or constructions, so long as they

40. *Ep*. 57.2.2.
41. Cavallera, *Saint Jérôme*, I, p. 217 n. 1.
42. *Ep*. 57.6.3.

could make clear the subject to the understanding.'[43]

When he wrote the letter to Pammachius, Jerome was in the midst of preparing his new 'Vulgate' translation. So he, perhaps more than anyone else, would have known about the relationship of the Septuagint and the New Testament to the Hebrew Bible. Here again, however, we should not confuse learning with theory. If Jerome were serious in this letter about presenting the case for 'the best mode of translation', one might have expected him to present examples from the Septuagint in which the translation *ad sensum* better conveyed the sense than the slavish literalism of Aquila. But this is not what he does. The many examples of apparent error in the Gospels and the Septuagint which he does offer range over a wide area, most having little to do with translation.[44] Here, Jerome's only intent is to show that he was not alone in committing the occasional error. Detractors of his translation will surely agree that the Septuagint and the evangelists did no 'harm to the sense (*nihil in sensu damni*) by the addition of a few words'. Jerome's translation of Epiphanius was no worse than these earlier efforts. Even if 'in the haste of dictation, I have omitted a few words,' he says, 'I have not by doing so endangered the position of the churches.'[45]

For the limited polemical purpose of the letter, these examples from Scripture no doubt served him well. No pious person, he says, would have the effrontery to accuse the evangelists of falsification; 'far be it from us to speak thus of a follower of Christ, who made it his care to formulate dogmas rather than to hunt for words and syllables (*verba et syllabas aucupari*)'.[46] So if his literalist critics accused him of falsification, then they would be compelled to make the same charge against the Septuagint and the writers of the New Testament. In so doing, they would end up in the company of the likes of men such as Celsus, Porphyry and Julian, or Aquila, the pedant and Judaizer.[47] This was a clever forensic maneuver; those patrons of literal translation who carped at his translation now found themselves in the camp of the infidel. But it falls far short of enunciating a theoretical case for translation *ad sensum*.

---

43. *Ep*. 57.9.8.

44. *Ep*. 57.7-9. Among other things, they include Matthew's misattribution of a citation to Jeremiah (Mt. 27.9), Mark's attribution to Isaiah of material from Malachi (Mk 1.2-3), and his confusion of Abiathar and Ahimelech (Mk 2.25-26).

45. *Ep*. 57.10.4.

46. *Ep*. 57.7.4.

47. *Ep*. 57.9.1; 11.2.

High sounding principles notwithstanding, what we have in this letter is not a theoretical or programmatic statement 'about the best mode of translation'. It is one thing to say, as Cicero did, that translating according to the sense is the only way to capture the style and grace of the original in the idiom of another language. But despite naming Cicero as one of his forebears, Jerome never defends his own translation in this way. His *ad sensum* translation of Epiphanius, he writes, was 'artless (*simplex*)' and hastily wrought. In the process, certain standards of accuracy were suspended, but none of these mistakes was serious (*crimen*), and nothing had been done that would have 'affected the sense (*nihil mutatrum esse de sensu*)' of the original or 'foisted upon it a new doctrine'.[48] The meaning of the expression *translatio ad sensum* should thus be sought in the rhetoric of Jerome's dispute with his critics. What it means is this: 'Please don't judge the work too harshly. Translation is a very difficult undertaking. And besides, I did the translation rapidly and for private circulation only.'

In my judgment, a similar motive lies at the root of the other half of Jerome's formula—namely, that he abrogates the rule of translation *ad sensum* only when translating Scripture. Since even the order of the words is a mystery (*verborum ordo mysterium est*), he translates Scripture word for word, even to the extent of retaining the same order.[49]

But Jerome hardly bound himself to this canon. When it proved expedient, Jerome elsewhere did in fact claim to be translating secular works literally. Thus, in the controversy with Rufinus over Origen's Περὶ ἀρχῶν, Jerome represented his translation as an *ad verbum* correction of his adversary's work.[50] Earlier in his career, Marcellus had asked him to clarify the meaning of the Hebrew word 'Selah'. Many false interpretations of the word had been preferred by ignorant people, Jerome wrote in response (384), so it is best to go back to Origen, a real authority. I will translate Origen's views on this subject, he writes, 'word for word (*verbum... ad verbum*), so that you, because you scorn new vintages, might avail yourself of the power of old wine'.[51]

Nor did Jerome's 'Vulgate' adhere unfailingly to the rule of slavish literalism. Assuredly, Jerome strove for precision in translation of

48. *Ep.* 57.5.1.
49. *Ep.* 57.5.2.
50. See below, p. 345.
51. *Ep.* 28.5.1.

Scripture, often preserving Greek or Hebrew syntax.[52] But as Jerome knew full well, practical considerations sometimes hindered word for word fidelity, even where the Hebrew and Greek Bibles were concerned. On numerous occasions he inveighs against Aquila for his clumsy and meaningless literalism, and his corruption by 'the perverse exegesis of the Pharisees'.[53] The Vulgate itself reverses word order, replaces participial constructions with subordinate clauses and ablative absolutes, and translates a single Greek word with two Latin words.[54]

This was something that Jerome himself elsewhere did not deny. In the prologue to his translation of Job and after the customary attacks upon his detractors, Jerome says of his own translation: 'it follows none of the earlier authorities', but

> will be found to reproduce now the exact words, now the meaning, and now both together (*nunc verba, nunc sensus, nunc simul utrumque resonabit*)...For an indirectness and a slipperiness attaches to the whole book, even in the Hebrew, and as orators say, it is tricked out with figures of speech, and while it says one thing, it does another; just as if you close your hand to hold an eel or a little fish, the more you squeeze it, the sooner it escapes.[55]

When questioned by Sunnias and Fratela about his translation of the Psalms, Jerome even harks back to the Ciceronian ideal. 'If we follow the words, we destroy the arrangement of the sense...The same rules of translation should be followed, which we have often stated, that where no damage in meaning occurs (*ubi non fit damnum in sensu*), the εὐφωνία and idiom (*proprietas*) of the language into which we have translated is to be preserved.'[56] In the same letter, Jerome tellingly uses the same word to describe literal translation that he had earlier applied to

52. See F. Blatt, 'Remarques sur l'histoire des traductions latines', *Classica et Mediaevalia* 1 (1938), pp. 220-21.

53. Jerome, *Commentary on Isaiah 13*, on Isa. 49.5 (PL 24, 483CD). But even in his views on Aquila's literalism, he is far from consistent; for Jerome's positive assessments of Aquila, see, for example, *Ep.* 28.2, where he refers to Aquila as the 'most diligent expositor of Hebrew words'; also *Ep.* 36.12, where he praises Aquila for 'more conscientiously (*studiosius*) translating word for word'.

54. For the evidence, see G. Cuendet, 'Cicéron et Saint Jérome Traducteurs', *Revue des études latines* 11 (1933), pp. 389ff.; see also Courcelle, *Late Latin Writers*, pp. 54-57.

55. In *Biblia Sacra Iuxta Vulgatam Versionem* (ed. R. Weber; Stuttgart: Württembergische Bibelanstalt, 1975), I, p. 731 ll.15-20.

56. *Ep.* 106.55.1.

the detractors of his translation of Epiphanius's letter; translation *ad verbum*, he writes, produces κακοζηλία and absurdity.[57]

Jerome's failure fully to adhere to his own stated principles did not go unnoticed by his contemporaries. Indeed, Augustine shrewdly seized upon it as a way of undermining Jerome's whole translation project.[58] Why, then, would Jerome have insisted in his letter to Pammachius that in translating Scripture he pursued a technique which he in a more candid moment disowns as sometimes unattainable and 'pedantic'?

Part of the explanation has to do with Jerome's use of the expression *ad sensum* in this letter. Jerome often made a point of stressing the fact that in translating Scripture, he worked with painstaking care and accuracy. Only in the case of translating apocrypha was this practice not observed. It is especially noteworthy that when Jerome speaks of his translation of an apocryphal book, he not only confesses that it was translated rapidly; it was also translated 'according to the sense'. To the book of Judith, he claims he devoted only 'one day's hasty labor', rendering it 'more sense for sense than word for word (*magis sensum e sensu quam ex verbo verbum tranferens*)'.[59] Here, translation according to the sense did not mean, as it did for Cicero, producing a translation of high literary qualities. Instead, it was used only to justify a translation which, supposedly having been done informally and in haste, failed to achieve the utmost accuracy. In the context of the letter to Pammachius, it would then only have subverted his case had he lumped his translations of Scripture into the same category as his admittedly inaccurate and 'hastily done' *ad sensum* translation of Epiphanius's letter.

The other reason has to do with a pious view of Scripture, circulating in the fourth century, that, because the linguistic properties of Scripture were somehow inherently different from those of other literature, it required different principles of translation.[60] Moreover, it was only

---

57. *Ep.* 106.17.1.

58. See S. Brock, 'The Phenomenon of the Septuagint', *Oudtestamentische Studiën* 17 (1972), pp. 21-22, 27.

59. *Biblia Sacra*, I, p. 691, ll. 6-7.

60. See, for example, John Chrysostom *Homilies on Genesis* 15.1, on Gen. 2.20 (PG 53,119): 'Why does the short passage read, τῷ δὲ Ἀδάμ? For what reason does Moses add the conjunction δέ? Is it not enough to say τῷ Ἀδάμ? Now we are not eager to interpret this simply for the sake of an exaggerated zeal, but in order that we should interpret everything accurately, and teach you that not the least phrase or even one syllable in divine Scripture should be ignored. For these are not simply words, but the words of the holy spirit, and for that reason, it is possible to find a great

through literalism that monolingual readers could gain access to the original. Those who cannot read the original languages, Augustine writes, should 'get hold of the translations of those who keep rather close to the letter of the original, not because these are sufficient, but because we may use them to correct the freedom or the error of others, who in their translations have chosen to follow the sense quite as much as the words'. As long as they avoid ambiguity, even barbarisms were acceptable ways of capturing a Greek word or expression in Latin. There may be purists, writes Augustine, who object to this counsel and insist that translators should not introduce solecisms or unconventional usage. But what is purity in speech, 'except the preserving of the custom of language established by the authority of former speakers'?[61] The same thing applied even to word order. Latin translations of the New Testament which retain Greek order may sound unharmonious and 'offend the ears'. But despite their unaesthetic qualities, this is the goal that Augustine says a 'more serious translator (*gravior interpres*)' should aspire to.[62]

Jerome certainly did not translate according to these canons of extreme literalism. Indeed, in a rather patronizing response to inquiries from Augustine about his biblical translations, Jerome points out that he will often 'preserve the truth of the sense rather than the order of words (*sensuum potius veritatem quam verborum...ordinem*)'.[63] But in the heat of the argument against his detractors, he found recitation of the

treasure even in one syllable'. For discussion, see Marti, *Übersetzer*, pp. 69-72.

61. Augustine, *On Christian Doctrine* 2.13.19 (ed. J. Martin; CCL, 32; Turnholt: Brepols, 1962).

62. Augustine, *On Christian Doctrine* 4.20.40. To illustrate the point, Augustine refers to his own literary experiments in which, for the Greek ὤν, he rendered *existens* and *essens*, instead of *cum sit* (Augustine, *Locutiones in Heptateuchum* 3.32 [ed. J. Zycha; CSEL, 28.1; Vienna: Tempsky, 1893]). Elsewhere, he refers to a Latin translation that at Ps. 50.16, rendered *ex sanguinibus* for the Greek ἐξ αἱμάτων. 'We all know,' Augustine writes, 'that in Latin you can't say *sanguis* in the plural... Nevertheless because the Greek puts it in the plural number, not without reason, since this was the way it appeared in the original Hebrew, a pious translator (*pius interpres*) preferred poor Latin to improper translation' (Augustine, *Exposition of the Psalms* 50.19 [ed. E. Dekkers and J. Fraipont; CCL, 38; Turnholt: Brepols, 1956). At Ps. 104.12, Augustine even suggests rendering the articular infinitive construction ἐν τῷ εἶναι αὐτούς with the Latin *in eo esse illos* (ed. E. Dekkers and J. Fraipont; CCL, 40; Turnholt: Brepols, 1956). For discussion, see Marti, *Übersetzer*, pp. 79-80.

63. *Ep.* 112.19.1.

same formula useful for the purpose of establishing his own credentials as a man of religion—one who appreciated the deeper mysteries of the Hebrew and Greek Bibles and who worked conscientiously to convey these mysteries in his translations.

Jerome and the Reinterpretation of the Expression Translatio Ad Sensum

For Jerome, Cicero's theoretical statements about translation *ad sensum* proved useful, but only to the extent that they helped enlist sympathy and admiration for his literary efforts. Under these rhetorical circumstances, Jerome was often required to recast the terminology of his classical forerunners in a way that might have struck them as vacillating and contradictory. As we have seen, Cicero believed that capturing the 'power' and grace of the original more than compensated the loss of strict literalness. Jerome, on the other hand, usually demurred when it came to discussing the literary merits of the final product. No matter which method of translation he preferred, Jerome typically described his own translations as 'simple, faithful and unornate'.

This characterization would doubtless have grated on the ears of Horace and Cicero. After all they defined 'artless and simple' as the mark of the literalist, the *fidus interpres*. But in Jerome's time, elegance was not something normally extolled as a virtue. Christian authors, who in general were castigated for their unadorned writing style, quite early tried to convert this perceived deficiency into a virtue. Simplicity in style was something that Christian writers were encouraged to aspire to, as a way of defining themselves against the excesses of pagan rhetoric and philosophy.[64] As Jerome knew full well, the term 'unornate and simple' would thus have struck a responsive chord in Latin Christians of the fourth century. 'You must not in my small writings,' Jerome writes to Pammachius, 'look for any such eloquence as that which for Christ's sake you disregard in Cicero. A version made for the use of the Church, even though it may possess a literary charm, ought to disguise and avoid it' as far as possible.[65]

'In ecclesiastical matters,' he says elsewhere in an epistle to Damasus, 'it is not words that are to be sought, but rather the sense (*non quaer-*

---

64. See Norden, *Kunstprosa*, II, pp. 529-32.

65. *Ep.* 48(49).4. See also *Ep.* 52.9.3: 'of two imperfect things, holy rusticity is better than sinful eloquence'.

antur verba sed sensus), that is, life should be sustained by bread not by pulse'.[66] Here the opposing terms *sensus* and *verba* have been infused with a meaning entirely alien to Cicero's. If, for Cicero, *ad sensum* implied 'polished and literary', and *ad verbum* meant in 'a clumsy and artless manner', Jerome has invested the meaning of *sensus* and *verba* with an opposite understanding. 'Sense' now connotes the simple unadorned meaning to which the Christian man of letters should aspire, in contrast to the superficial beguilement of 'words'.

With this 'Christianized' reappraisal of the two terms, Jerome found a very effective way to forestall criticisms of his translations; and he readily added the cliché 'simple, unadorned, and faithful' to his arsenal of handy slogans.[67] He exploits it to good effect in his answer to the critics of his translation of Epiphanius. The criticisms that they made of his translation had nothing to do with matters of ornateness versus simplicity; it was one of mere accuracy. So to gain the moral high ground, Jerome deftly deflects the question, implying that his critics faulted him, not for inaccuracy, but rather for lacking fine writing skills. After reporting one of their corrections, he responds by suggesting that his unadorned translation conformed better to the Christian ideal of

66. *Ep.* 21.42.3. He says this, of course, after customary apologies for unrefined speech (*inculta...oratorio*), ailing eyesight (*dolentibus oculis*) and use of dictation.

67. Thus, in translating the *Life of Pachomius*, he states that he aimed to imitate the 'simplicity of Egyptian speech' in order to avoid corrupting the words with 'the language of rhetoric' (*Rule of Pachomius Praef.* 9.6-11 in *La règle de S. Pachome* [ed. A. Boon; Bibliothèque de la Revue d'Histoire Ecclésiastique, 7; Louvain: Bureaux de la Revue, 1932]). Rufinus later praised Jerome's translation of Origen's two homilies on the Song of Songs for the liberties that Jerome took with the original and the 'vigorous eloquence (*eloquentiae viribus*)' which enabled him to 'adorn (*ornare*) the sayings of this great man' (in Jerome, *Ep.* 80.1.2). But in the prologue to his translation of these homilies (ed. W.A. Baehrens; GCS Origenes Werke, 8; Leipzig: Hinrichs, 1925), Jerome avoided naming this as one of the standards to which he aspired. Instead, he states that 'he translated faithfully rather than with elegance (*fideliter magis quam ornate*)' because Origen's own style in these homilies was unadorned. Even those translations which he characterizes as 'according to the sense' were 'simple and unornate'. In the introduction to his Latin translation of Origen's *Homilies on Ezekiel* (c. 381), and after the customary defenses of ill-health, poverty and lack of skilled assistants, he allows that his translation 'despises the brilliance of every rhetorical art (*omni rhetoricae artis splendore contempto*)'; after all, it is 'the subject, not the words' that he wants to be praised (ed. W.A. Baehrens; GCS Origenes Werke, 8; Leipzig: Hinrichs, 1925).

simplicity than their word-for-word literalism. 'Here indeed,' he retorts in mock honor of one of their corrections,

> we have eloquence worthy of Plautus, here we have Attic grace, the true style of the Muses...I do not think the worse of any Christian because he lacks the skill to express himself...I have always held in high esteem a holy simplicity (*sancta simplicitas*) but not a wordy rudeness (*verbosa rusticitas*). He who declares that he imitates the style of the apostles should first imitate the virtue of their lives; the great holiness of which made up for much plainness of speech.[68]

Jerome has phrased the description in such a way as to frustrate criticisms from any front. If someone indicts his translation as not literal, then he can respond, in the tradition of Cicero, that his intention was only to give the sense. If then someone complains that the work lacks grace and charm, he can say that rhetorical excellence is not something that Christians should seek to attain.

Jerome's pronouncements about the properties of the Latin language reveal the same intention. Well before Jerome the linguistic deficiencies of Latin as a vehicle for translating Greek were hotly disputed. Although he knew that some of his fellow Romans 'doubted the possibility of conveying in Latin the teachings they had received from the Greeks', Cicero himself did not at all feel encumbered by his own native tongue. 'In my opinion,' he writes, 'as I have often argued, the Latin language, so far from having a poor vocabulary, as is commonly supposed, is actually richer than the Greek.'[69] Jerome too could sometimes sound a note of patriotic confidence in Latin that rivaled Cicero's. The only reason, he says to Sunnias and Fratela, why some doubt the capacity of the Latin language to translate Greek is because they endeavor to translate word for word. For if you translate in this way,

> you destroy εὐφωνία and in the course of pursuing κακοζηλία we lose all the charm of translation. And this is the rule of the good translator, to express the ἰδιώματα of another language with the proper signification (*proprietate*) of his own language. And we are convinced that Tully did this in the *Protagoras* of Plato and in the Οἰκονομικός of Xenophon and the oration of Demosthenes against Aischines...Nor should anyone think that the Latin language is extremely restricted (*angustissimam*), because he is not able to translate word for word. Even the Greeks translate many of our words through circumlocution and in translating Hebrew words they

68. *Ep.* 57.12.3-4.
69. Cicero, *De finibus* 1.3.10; see also 3.2.5; also *De natura deorum* 1.4.8.

are not strictly faithful; rather they strive to express themselves in the idioms (*proprietatibus*) of their own tongue.[70]

But this was by no means the position Jerome normally embraced in describing his translations. To the contrary, he often identified the shortcomings of the Latin language as one among many reasons why a translation might fall short of perfection. Jerome was not alone in this practice. The translator of the *Life of Antony* made the same lament, and Jerome's erstwhile friend Rufinus often complained about the deficiencies of Latin in the many prefaces to his translations.[71] So we should not be surprised to find Jerome, conforming to the same convention, deploring how, amidst so many other disabilities, he had to 'struggle with the poor resources of the Latin language (*Latinae linguae...paupertate*) to find an equivalent for the fluency (*facundiam*) of the Greek'.[72]

A particularly telling example of Jerome's shifting characterization of his translations according to circumstance appears in his descriptions of his translations of the writings of Theophilus. When it was learned that Theophilus's Paschal letter for the year 401 included an assault upon Origen, Jerome was asked to translate it into Latin. Almost as soon as the translation appeared, 'heretics' attacked it as inaccurate. Evidently stung by their criticisms, Jerome was defiant in defending his translation of Theophilus's festal letter for the following year. So sure was he about the translation's accuracy that he affixed to the letter the original Greek along with the Latin translation. This was to prove that 'nothing was added to, nothing subtracted from the original'. Not only that; it was rhetorically elegant.

> I labored hard...to preserve the charm of the diction by a like elegance in my version. I kept within fixed lines and never allowed myself to deviate from these. I did my best to maintain the smooth flow of the writer's eloquence and to render his remarks in the tone in which they are made.[73]

70. *Ep.* 106.3.2-3.
71. See, for example, Rufinus's preface to his translation of Origen's Περὶ ἀρχῶν (ed. P. Koetschau; GCS Origines Werke, 5; Leipzig: Hinrichs, 1913), where he refers to the 'inopia sermonis nostri'. For other references, see Marti, *Übersetzer*, p. 124.
72. *Ep.* 114.3.1.
73. *Ep.* 97.3.1. Notice that Jerome does not attach the Greek original of Theophilus's previous festal letter, thus leaving the validity of the 'heretics'' criticisms of his translation unresolved.

Faced with charges of inaccuracy and confident of the reliability of his work, Jerome foregoes the traditional excuses about the difficulties of translation or self-serving appeals to the literary tradition of translation 'according to the sense'. By any criteria, he says, the translation was umimpeachable. Jerome is rather more reserved, however, in the letter to Theophilus that accompanied the translation of Theophilus's Paschal letter for 404. There is first the standard recitation of the dreadful conditions under which he had to labor: sickness of mind and body and sorrow over the conditions of the church. Under these circumstances, which, he says, virtually choked off all utterance, it was only with the greatest exertion that he was able to accomplish the translation at all. In spite of this, he says, he tried hard to transfer the 'charm of diction which marked every sentence in the original and make the style of the Latin correspond at least in some degree (*aliqua ex parte*) with that of the Greek'.[74]

He is even more subdued in the letter to Theophilus accompanying his translation of a piece of invective written by the Alexandrian archbishop against Chrysostom (c. 405). The letter is composed in the customary apologetic style—that is, as a humble plea for indulgence. Theophilus's Greek original, he writes, was 'most eloquent (*disertissimum*)' and 'adorned with the Scriptures' fairest flowers'. Jerome apologizes for having not done the Greek justice. Bad weather made it hard to find sufficient time, and ill health 'dulled the edge of my intellect and obstructed the free flow of my language'.[75] Then there were the inherent difficulties of finding in the poor resources of the Latin language suitable expressions for rendering the eloquence of Greek.[76] And so in the same spirit he enlists the support of the conventional 'theory' of translation according to the sense.

> I have not indeed given a word for word rendering, as skilled translators (*diserti interpretes*) do, nor have I counted out the money you have given to me coin by coin; but I have given you full weight. Nothing is lacking in the sense (*ex sensibus*), although something might be lacking in literalness (*ex verbis*).[77]

Now the metaphor likening translation to paying out coins is Cicero's, and so it would appear that, in quoting Cicero, Jerome was placing

74. *Ep.* 99.1.2.
75. *Ep.* 114.1.2.
76. *Ep.* 114.3.1.
77. *Ep.* 114.3.1.

himself in the same literary tradition. But there is a notable difference. Cicero resorted to the image of coins in order to differentiate his fine literary productions from those 'clumsy translators (*indiserti interpretes*)' who translated according to the word.[78] In the letter to Theophilus, however, Jerome refers to these same literal translators as 'skilled'. This was no accidental lapse. In the context of the overall self-abasing tone of the letter, it would hardly have been fitting for Jerome then to contrast his translation with those of 'unskilled translators'. The abject spirit of the letter required modesty, and Jerome readily recast Cicero's maxim in order to achieve the desired result.

Jerome, Rufinus and the Translation of Origen

Rhetorical devices of the kind that we have described above work best when nobody takes them too seriously. But it was the Origenist crisis, and Jerome's own involvement with it, that forced the imprecisions in Jerome's 'theory' of translation into the open.

When he undertook to translate Origen's Περὶ ἀρχῶν for Latin readers, Rufinus, a devotee of Origen, knew that portions of the work would sound strange, even heretical, to his audience. 'I am afraid,' he writes, 'lest my deficiencies and inadequate command of Latin may detract seriously from the reputation of one whom Jerome has deservedly termed second only to the apostles as a teacher of the Church in knowledge and in wisdom'.[79] So in order to preserve and promote the reputation of Origen, and at the same time rid him of the odor of heresy, Rufinus determined to replace ambiguous or heretical sounding passages with more orthodox passages that Rufinus had culled from other places in Origen. In his view, the passages that were expurgated altogether were only later insertions into the text of Origen by heretics, bent on ruining his reputation. In so doing, Rufinus believed he was not bringing to the text a different or alien sense; he was only illuminating a dark or obscure passage. But if anything objectionable remained, the translator should suffer no recriminations. 'If there is anything in the author that displeases, why should it be hurled back at

78. See Cicero, *De optimo genere oratorum* 5.14: 'I did not hold it necessary to render word for word. I did not think I ought to count them out to the reader like coins, but to pay them by weight, as it were.'

79. The text of Rufinus is found in *Ep.* 80.1.2 in Hilberg's edition of Jerome's epistles.

the translator? I was asked to translate for the Latins, just the way it appeared in Greek. I simply applied Latin words to the Greek meanings (*Graecis sensibus verba dedi Latina tantummodo*).'[80]

For Rufinus, it was not the constraints of the Latin language that required him to take the liberties with Origen's text that he did. Rather theology and orthodoxy were the determinants.[81] But there was a kind of cruel irony in Rufinus's appeal to the authority of Jerome to sanction what Rufinus termed his own translation 'according to sense'. Jerome himself, Rufinus claimed, had taken the same liberties in his earlier translations of Origen's *Homilies*; wherever the Greek text presented stumbling-blocks, he 'smoothed them down and emended the language in such a way that a Latin writer can find no word at variance with our faith'.[82] 'Not content with rendering the words of Origen,' Rufinus writes of his soon to be former friend, 'he desires to be himself the teacher. I for my part do but follow up an enterprise which he has sanctioned and commenced.'[83]

Rufinus invoked Jerome's authority innocently and apparently with some justification. Accused by Paulinus of Nola of harboring Origenist sympathies, Jerome himself did not shrink from acknowledging to Vigilantius that he had taken over from Origen 'what is good in him and either cut away or altered or ignored what is evil'. After all, he says, translators and commentators often elected to suppress unsound portions of the original and render into Latin only that which was profitable.[84] The reason why Rufinus's appeal to Jerome's authority now offended him so was that it risked reimplicating him in a movement from which he was seeking desperately to distance himself. To undo the damage and confusion that Rufinus's translation had created, Jerome agreed to do a new translation of the Περὶ ἀρχῶν. But according to what principles should this translation be done? Jerome's sponsors demanded of him a more literal specimen in order to expose Origen and know precisely where Rufinus had misrepresented him, one that would publish in Latin the work 'exactly (*ad fidem*) as it was brought out by

80. Quoted in Jerome, *Against Rufinus* 2.11 (PL 23,453).
81. On Rufinus's 'theories' on translation, see F. Winkelmann, 'Einige Bemerkungen zu den Aussagen des Rufinus von Aquileia und des Hieronymus', pp. 534-38.
82. *Ep.* 80.2.2.
83. *Ep.* 80.1.2.
84. *Ep.* 61.2.2.

the author himself'.[85] But had Jerome himself not earlier spoken forcefully about the impossibility of translation of secular works in this way? Rufinus sensed the contradiction. 'This is the process of translating word for word, which you previously determined was objectionable, but you now in fact judge as praiseworthy (*hoc namque est verbum transferre de verbo, quod a te ante inprobabile, nunc uero laudabile iudicatum est*).'[86]

Jerome's own subsequent assessment of his translation reveals the dilemma. In his letter to Pammachius describing this same translation, he initially reverts to the niceties of convention, pleading with Pammachius not to judge his translation too harshly either by the standard of *ad sensum* or *ad verbum*.

> I leave to your judgment to discover how much labour I have expended in translating the books On First Principles; for on the one hand if one alters anything from the Greek the work becomes less a version than a perversion; and on the other hand a literal (*ad verbum*) adherence to the original by no means tends to preserve the charm of its eloquence.[87]

Elsewhere, however, he is far less diffident. To Paulinus, he represents himself as the model of the *fidus interpres*, adhering closely to the rule 'neither to add nor subtract', thereby preserving in Latin 'the true Greek (*Graecamque fidem*)'.[88] He expresses himself most forcefully on this subject in his *Apology against Rufinus*. There, in describing how his work corrected the excesses of Rufinus, he rather self-righteously characterizes himself as an apostle of sober and unadorned literalism. Rufinus had failed his duty 'to keep faithful to the original'. So to correct this translation and expose the lies of Περὶ ἀρχῶν, he writes, 'I translated simply (*simpliciter*) what was contained in the Greek.'[89] 'Compare the words of Origen that I have translated above literally (*ad verbum*) with those that were not turned, but overturned by him, and you will clearly recognize the great discrepancy that exists between them.'[90]

---

85. *Ep.* 83.1.1, from Pammachius and Oceanus.

86. Rufinus, *Apology against Jerome* 2.44 (ed. M. Simonetti; CCL, 20; Turnholt: Brepols, 1961).

87. *Ep.* 84.12.2.

88. *Ep.* 85.3.2.

89. Jerome, *Apology against Rufinus* 1.7 (PL 23,420).

90. *Apology* 2.19 (PL 23,462).

Conclusion

From as early as the first century BCE, Latin translators of the Greek classics envisaged their work as a form of cultural enrichment and an expression of national pride. By imitating and perhaps even surpassing the originals, Cicero and his successors believed they were participating in a kind of cultural transfer. An accepted canon of Greek literary models existed, and translators thought it possible to represent in the idiom of their own language what it was that made the original works acknowledged masterpieces.

By the fourth century, circumstances were quite different. The Greek language was in general decline in the West, and along with it bilingualism. Even Jerome came to the Greek language relatively late in life. And the degree of Latin chauvinism and rivalry with the Greeks that marked Roman translation of the first century was far less evident. Unlike their predecessors, Latin writers did not view the selection of texts and the translation of them as a way of enriching the Latin language in the way their predecessors had. As Winkelmann has observed, Jerome invoked the name of Cicero, but 'there were simply too few examples for good and elegant translations from the Christian environment, which corresponded to the norm of a Cicero, and on which Jerome could base himself'.[91]

Standards for selecting a work to translate into Latin and the character of these translations had thus become much more diffuse. The process by which works were selected for translation was often a very informal one. Sources chosen ranged over a wide literary field—from commentaries and histories to more popular acts of martyrs and hagiographies.[92] A work's perceived greatness certainly was no guarantee that it would be translated. To the contrary, this could sometimes act as a deterrent. In his commentaries on the Song of Songs, Jerome writes, Origen had surpassed even himself. But the work must be put aside because almost 'boundless leisure and money would be required to translate so great a work'.[93] A Greek or Syriac work might be

---

91. F. Winkelmann, 'Einige Bemerkungen zu den Aussagen des Rufinus von Aquileia und des Hieronymus', p. 540.

92. For an inventory of the works translated into Latin, see F. Winkelmann, 'Spätantike lateinische Übersetzungen christlicher griechischer Literatur', *Theologische Literaturzeitung* 92.3 (1967), pp. 229-40.

93. In Jerome's prefatory dedication to his translation of Origen's two homilies

translated at the request of an individual, for popular edification, or for the educated classes. Generally speaking, translations were undertaken by groups or individuals sympathetic to the work in question.[94] It was naturally assumed, therefore, that translation of a work implied support of its contents. But in the volatile environment of the fourth century, it was not always possible to know in advance whether a work was unobjectionable or of unimpeachable pedigree. Circumstances like these probably encouraged many translators to limit themselves to works of popular piety. Indeed, the recriminations that Jerome suffered for his early translations of Origen's commentaries must have caused him later to regret ever having undertaken this project in the first place.

More than anyone else, Jerome's variable 'theories' of translation reflect these conditions. Jerome might characterize his work as 'literal' in order to express his reverence to the original. At the same time, translation *ad verbum* could be cited as a way of distancing him from a work of doubtful orthodoxy or of correcting a previous translation. When, for example, Jerome described his translation of Περὶ ἀρχῶν as literal and simple, he did so because, in his own words, it was meant as an exposé of the original. To translate in any other way would be to risk inviting the charge that the translator was acting the part of an apologist for a now discredited thinker like Origen.[95] On the other hand, when, in his earlier days, Jerome was generally sympathetic to Origen but aware of his occasional lapses into heresy, he appealed to the theory of translation 'according to the sense' in order to justify corrections of and excisions from the original. The same theory might be defended as a way to forestall criticism or invite sympathy; his translation, he would say, was meant only to convey the sense and did not 'hunt after words and syllables'. To achieve the same end, Jerome might try another tack:

on the Song of Songs (p. 26, ll. 9-11; ed. W.A. Baehrens; GCS Origines Werke, 8; Leipzig: Hinrichs, 1925).

94. For discussion, see J. Griboment, 'The Translations. Jerome and Rufinus', in *Patrology* (ed. J. Quasten; Westminster, MD: Christian Classics, 1986), IV, pp. 195-97.

95. For the same idea, see the preface of Marius Mercator's Latin translation (5th century) of the sermons of the 'heretic' Nestorius. 'As a translator,' he says, 'I have tried to express word for word to the extent that it is possible to do this (*verbum de verbo in quantum fieri potuit conatus sum translator exprimere*)', in *Acta Conciliorum Oecumenicorum* (ed. E. Schwartz; Berlin: de Gruyter, 1930), I.5, p. 29 l. 3. For discussion, see Blatt, 'Remarques sur l'histoire des traductions latines', p. 221.

reminding his readers that, given the constraints of language, translation according to *any* method is an impossible task and that readers should forgive his lack of grace or occasional error. Not a statement of a theoretical position, *translatio ad sensum* in Jerome is only a cliché whose meaning is determined by the rhetorical situation in which it appears. What is above all clear is that only rarely did Jerome hold up his translations as models of rhetorical elegance or monuments in their own right of Latin literature. Christian simplicity was typically substituted as the literary norm.

In a study of translators of the medieval tradition in translation, W. Schwartz has noted that the dominant method of translation in the Middle Ages was word for word literalism.[96] Translators from the time of Boethius, he writes, deliberately repudiated 'stylistic elegance and rhetoric', preferring instead the style of the *fidus interpres*. For medieval translators, this method was regarded as 'the surest safeguard against any alteration of the original thought or the introduction of false or heretical views into the author's view'.[97] In Schwartz's view, this renunciation also signaled a radical departure from the approach to translation pursued by Jerome and his classical models. Boethius and his successors took the word-for-word method that Jerome had advocated only for Scripture and 'adopted the same method for other works. Therefore, a new foundation has been laid by Boethius, who, as far as can be ascertained, was the first to proclaim the principle of word-for-word translation for books which are not sacred.'[98]

But the transition may have been less extreme than first appears. Boethius, like most modern commentators, believed that Jerome's references to Cicero and Horace put him in the latter's camp. But we should not be misled by Jerome's classical citations; at heart, he would probably have had more sympathy with the attitudes and preoccupations of the *fidus interpres* who succeeded him.

---

96. W. Schwartz, 'The Meaning of *Fidus Interpres* in Medieval Translation', *JTS* 45 (1944), pp. 72-78.

97. Schwartz, '*Fidus Interpres*', p. 76.

98. Schwartz, '*Fidus Interpres*', p. 75.

DATES IN *SEPHER YOSIPPON*

Steven Bowman

It is a singular pleasure to offer the following in honor of Professor Wacholder whom I first listened to some twenty-five years ago as a visiting doctoral student in Cincinnati. Over the years I came to learn more of his interests in chronology and history through his writings and our mutual research. Shortly after I began to teach at the University of Cincinnati, I started to translate *Sepher Yosippon*. To my surprise Professor Wacholder told me that it was the first Hebrew book he began to read on his own and that experience encouraged him to pursue his later scholarly career in the problems of chronology and history. I hope the following may be a double portion for him.

Sepher Yosippon is a history of the Jews written in southern Italy by an anonymous Jewish scholar, one version of which is dated to 953.[1] It is a unique history on two accounts. First it deals with Jewish history from Davidic times with emphasis on the Second Commonwealth period and terminates with the capture of Massada. Second it interweaves Roman and Jewish history into a double helix arguing that the former were kin to the latter and that Rome and Jerusalem were locked into an immortal and tragic confrontation before even the founding of each city.[2]

The author weaves his tale using a superb Hebrew style derived from the Bible and Midrash. He writes this tale using the methodology of a critical historian, even where he relies on legendary material inherited from Latin chronicles. Since the tenth century *Sepher Yosippon* has been a basic text, considered in the *yeshivah* to be the original Hebrew text that Josephus alludes to, for Jews. It has influenced among others Rabbenu Gershom *meor ha-golah*, Rashi, the historian Joseph ha-kohen,

1. Cf. *Encyclopedia Judaica*, X, s.v. 'Josippon'.
2. Cf. my 'Sepher Yosippon: History and Midrash', in M. Fishbane (ed.), *The Midrashic Imagination. Jewish Exegesis, Thought, and History* (New York: State University of New York Press, 1993), pp. 280-94.

Micha ben Gorion, Joseph Trumpeldor, David Ben Gurion, and Shmuel
Agnon. Since the late sixteenth century it has been part of English-
speaking world and arrived in America with the Puritans who, like their
rabbinic counterparts, considered it authoritative for the events of the
first century.[3]

I have entitled this essay 'Dates in *Sepher Yosippon*', and so one
should ask what dates. Professor Wacholder's dissertation on Nicholas of
Damascus argued that it was Nicholas, not Aristotle, who was the author
of *De plantis* in which there appears the description of the famous dates
of Jericho.[4] Later we shall see that his tracing of the translation tradition
from Greek to Syriac to Arabic to Hebrew to Latin, which was the way
in which ancient wisdom and literature reached the West, will perhaps
assist us in dealing with the chronological dates in *Sepher Yosippon*. To
these other dates we may now turn.

There are several proposed dates that we shall explore in this essay.
One is the date of 953 actually mentioned in a copy of *Sepher Yosippon*.
Since however it is the crux of the scholarly controversy we shall
explore first some other dates mentioned in connection with the book.
An important date comes to us from Byzantium. In the middle of the
fourteenth century, Judah ibn Moskoni of Ohrida began to collect fragments of a history of ancient Israel which became to him 'as sweet as
honey'.[5] As he wandered through the Jewish libraries of the Byzantine
world in search of manuscripts by Abraham ibn Ezra, he kept his eye
open for more of these fragments, one of which in Latin he dates to the
sixth century. Eventually he collected a whole history which, though
never edited by a modern scholar, remains the basic text for the
yeshivah tradition.[6]

3.   D. Flusser, '*Josippon*. A Medieval Hebrew Version of Josephus', in L.H.
Feldman and G. Hata, *Josephus, Judaism, and Christianity* (Detroit: Wayne State
University Press, 1987), pp. 386-97. The influence on Ben Gurion was related to me
by Professor Flusser. The Trumpeldor reference is available in an early Zionist
biographical pamphlet (reference unavailable at time of writing). An English
translation was made in 1588 and continually reprinted through the nineteenth
century. The Puritan reference was supplied by Professor Wacholder.
4.   *Nicolaus of Damascus* (Berkeley: University of California Press, 1962).
5.   S. Bowman, *Jews in Byzantium, 1204–1453* (University of Alabama Press,
1985), pp. 133-34. For his correct name, cf. p. 133 n.; this observation has not yet
completely entered the scholarly literature on the late Byzantine period, although it has
been accepted by a number of senior scholars.
6.   The Venice 1540 edition was reprinted by Hayyim Hominer with several

For the controversial date of 953, we then move to twentieth-century Israel, and that is more complicated. Beginning in 1953 David Flusser of the Hebrew University began to publish his researches on *Sepher Yosippon* and argued that it was written in 953 based on an interesting date found in the middle of one manuscript.[7] Only with the appearance of his edited text in 1978 was it argued by reviewers that, since it contained material anterior to that date, the *terminus ab quo* of *Sepher Yosippon* should be reduced to the late ninth or early tenth century.[8] From a different perspective, a recent Tel Aviv University dissertation by Shulamit Sela has resurrected Julius Wellhausen's thesis of a century ago that the Hebrew *Yosippon* is derived from the Arabic.[9] While her analysis is more sophisticated than Wellhausen's, her argument would put the origins of the Arabic *Josippus* into the eighth or early ninth century.

Hence Flusser's date of *Sepher Yosippon* (953) has raised a whole new series of questions about the nature of the text, its date or dates of composition, and whether it is an integral or composite text. While some of these questions lie outside the parameters of this essay, we shall have to touch upon a few of the arguments where they are relevant.

Judah ibn Moskoni was not concerned with these problems. Rather to him the text he collated was important for the *contemporary* light it shed on the Temple of Jerusalem, i.e., that it was an eyewitness account that predated the material in the Mishnah. He gives us a series of important dates in his introductory letter which sheds light on his research.[10] Since it has neither been edited nor translated, the latter is offered here for the reader's reference and for its other gems:

> Behold this book [*Yosippon*] was already found among the Greeks rendered from Hebrew into Greek, and they called it *Josephus*; Strabon the author copied it for them. He too is found among the Romans and among

introductions including that of Rabbi Abraham Wertheimer who averred to me the accuracy of the attribution to Josephus; *sefer Josippon* (Jerusalem, 4th edn, 1978).

7. Cf his Hebrew article 'The Authorship of the Book of Josippon: His Personality and His Age,' *Zion* 18 (1953), pp. 109-26.

8. Review by Reuben Bonfil in the Hebrew daily newspaper *Davar*, Monday, 28 September 1981, pp. 12-14.

9. 'The Book of Josippon and Its Parallel Versions in Arabic and Judaeo-Arabic' (3 vols, PhD dissertation, Tel Aviv University, January 1991). I should like to thank Professor Ezra Fleischer for obtaining a copy of the text.

10. Reprinted by Hominer in his edition of *Yosippon* (pp. 34-40) from *Osar Tob* (ed. A. Berliner; Berlin, 1878), pp. 1-10.

all those who follow their faith. It was also rendered from Hebrew to Latin, and they called it also in their language *Hegesippus*. Indeed Joseph ha-Cohen ben Gurion ha-Cohen is also called *Yosippon*, and behold he wrote *Yosippon* in the holy tongue. He also wrote yet another book, larger than this, for the Romans in their language and in their writing in the stories of their kings and in their sources and in the stories of the universe, according to what he heard or saw, and this is the large book that is found among them to this day. And too the name of the book is *Hegesippus*; however, there is a difference among them between these two books, though both are called by them with one name. And this is because our book which was rendered for them from Hebrew to Latin by Gregory the *hegemon*, who was the greatest of the Roman *hegemon*s in the days of Emperor Sebastion, and from that day have passed about 780 years. Moreover, it is called *Hegesippus minor*, and indeed the book which Joseph ha-Cohen ben Gurion ha-Cohen wrote for them in the Latin language, and he called it *Hegesippus maior*. Know too that Gregory, who was also called Gregorius, was a great sage and complete philosopher, and he desired to contemplate in the books of the Jews, and he was a great philo-Semite and effected for them great deliverances. And in his days,[11] according to what is written in the stories of the Roman priestly books called *kanonikos*. Know too that this book, whose name among us is *Yosippon*, is the first that was written for Israel after the Prophets and Writings [of the Bible], and it precedes the writing of all the books of the Mishnah and the Talmud written for us. Also it was written prior to all the books which our ancestors (may their memories be for a blessing!) composed to explain the Torah, Prophets, and Writings by midrashic commentary.

So Judah ibn Moskoni attests to a Latin manuscript of *Yosippon* which he dates to the sixth-century Pope Gregory the Great (b. ca. 540, pope 590–604). Now the Latin *Josephus* has been securely dated to 576 by modern scholarship, a date which is within the *floruit* of Gregory.[12] Judah ibn Moskoni saw this Latin text or a copy of same with the same date. If he is accurate in his report of the figure 780 years, then we can assume he wrote his introduction in 1356, an impressive achievement since his birthdate is cited as 1328. Our Hebrew *Yosippon* then had to be composed after 576 since Flusser has shown conclusively that the texts he edited to produce his composite *Yosippon* are based on the Latin *Josephus*.

It is unlikely that *Yosippon* could have been composed in southern

---

11. Either a phrase is missing or this should continue the previous sentence.

12. Cf. Flusser's review of F. Blatt, *The Latin Josephus* (Aarhus: E. Munksgaard, 1958) in *Kiryath Sepher* 34 (1959), pp. 458-63, especially p. 459.

Italy before the ninth century, as Flusser has argued on the basis of place name spellings and events. Moreover, the renaissance of Hebrew did not occur in Baghdad much before that period. And *Yosippon* does not show any of the graecizisms that characterize the last period of Hebrew literature from Byzantine Israel.[13] Therefore it seems most likely that *Yosippon* was an independent Hebrew composition of the new period of Hebrew literature in general and parallels the rich literature that appears in southern Italy in the tenth century: piyyutim, chronicles, mystical commentaries, translations of histories, medical books, etc.[14]

The major question in dealing with Flusser's date of 953 is whether his *Yosippon* is the original *Yosippon* or whether, like that of Judah ibn Moskoni, it is a composite text created by the editor. Flusser did identify, and publish separately, an eleventh-century Romance of Alexander that had been interpolated into *Yosippon* and was accepted as an integral part of the narrative by Judah ibn Moskoni in his edition.[15] The question is whether the first two chapters that introduce *Yosippon*—the family of nations and the antiquities of Rome—were integral to the original *Yosippon* or were later added by a tenth-century editor? In other words, how much of Flusser's *Yosippon* is original and how much is anterior to his tenth-century edition which conflates several different manuscripts to produce his continuous narrative?[16]

The argument that the first chapter—the family of nations—contains material that became anachronistic at the beginning of the tenth century is not necessarily a valid critique of the date of the document.[17] True, the author knew much about his contemporary world; it is also possible that he was misinformed by his sources about other parts or mistaken in his presentation of the material. (The latter however is not a valid argument here.) That the first chapter is integral to the whole text is clear from the

13. See below n. 27 for Chwolson's argument. The renaissance of Hebrew attends the second generation of Karaite scholarship in the late eighth century; the Rabbinic response is not before the ninth. Cf. E. Fleischer, 'Hebrew Liturgical Poetry in Italy. Remarks concerning its Emergence and Characteristics', *Italia Judaica* (Roma, 1983), pp. 401-26.

14. For bibliography and discussion see R. Bonfil, 'Tra due mondi', in *Italia Judaica* (Rome, 1983), pp. 155-56.

15. D. Flusser, 'An "Alexander Geste" in a Parma MS', *Tarbiz* 26 (1956–57), pp. 165-84 (English summary V).

16. Cf. stemma of manuscript tradition in Vol II of his edition (p. 53).

17. *Pace* Bonfil in his review. Chwolson already brought up this argument for an early dating for *Yosippon*.

author's historiographical approach (based on Josephus and ultimately to Genesis, ch. 10) and the transliteration of the Germanic and Italian names throughout the text.

Another argument offered is that *Sepher Yosippon* is mentioned in a letter which has been consistantly dated to 925 by Robert Bonfil.[18] On the surface this would seem to be a strong argument; however, Jacob Mann who originally edited the letter did not accept the date of shortly after 925 for the letter but rather suggests a date sometime after 952.[19] Norman Golb has brilliantly reread the letter published by Mann and has raised the most serious opposition to Flusser's claim that the book was written in 953.[20] His thesis, tentatively and cautiously developed, argues that *Yosippon* was copied on the island of Lipara (off Sicily) circa 940–950. This thesis is based upon his understanding of the events as reflecting the persecutions of the Byzantine Emperor Romanos Lekapenos. At the end of this scholarly *tour de force*, however, Golb reverses his claim and admits there is an alternate hypothesis which he argues in several notes later. The alternate hypothesis seems to carry a better historical argument, namely that the events of the letter suggest a different set of difficulties than those presented by Romanos Lekapenos. In that case Mann's original suggestion for dating the letter after 952 is still a valid one. The arguments surrounding the dating of this particular letter have no other supporting evidence than the hazy memory of the famous south Italian hagiographer who authored the *Chronicle of Ahimaaz*. Surely a date in the text of *Sepher Yosippon* must carry greater weight, and to it we shall now turn.

The key text upon which Flusser bases his date of 953 is found at the end of chapter 40 and reads:[21]

> And many letters like this one which we found in the book of Joseph ben Gurion we did not write them here for the book is full of such letters in the copy which we found from the year 508 after the destruction of the Temple. Now we have written and copied from the book, from the book of Joseph ben Gurion the priest in the year 885 of the Destruction Era.

18. *Inter alia* cf. his 'Tra due mondi', pp. 155-56.
19. *Texts and Studies in Jewish History and Literature*, I (Cincinnati: Hebrew Union College Press, 1931; repr. New York: Ktav, 1972), p. 14.
20. N. Golb and O. Pritsak, *Khazarian Hebrew Documents of the Tenth Century* (Ithaca, NY: Cornell University Press, 1982), p. 89n. Cf. A. Scheiber and Z. Malachi, 'Letter from Sicily to Hasdai ibn Shaprut', *PAAJR* 41-42 (1975), pp. 208-18 for further notice of instabilities in Sicily.
21. All translations are from my forthcoming annotated translation of *Yosippon*.

The passage beginning with 'which we found from the year 508...' comes from the Rothschild Miscellany to which we shall turn shortly. The two dates in the passage translate as follows: (1) 508 of the Destruction Era is 576 (508 plus the medieval reckoning of the destruction of the Temple, i.e., 68); (2) 885 of the Destruction Era is 953 (885 plus 68). According to Flusser, the first date is that of the Latin Josephus which, we have seen, was mentioned by Judah ibn Moskoni in his introduction. The second date, according to Flusser, is the author's identification. Critics have preferred to argue that the latter date is not that of the author but rather that of a later copyist and hence *Yosippon* should be dated closer to the beginning of the tenth century.

The key seems to lie in the understanding of the word 'copied'. Does it refer to the Latin *Josephus* which the author used as the base text for the latter part of *Yosippon* or does it refer to the copyist who shortened even further the Hebrew *Yosippon* he was copying?[22] Now we know from the letter that Mann edited that the Hebrew *Yosippon* was being copied in the mid-tenth century. One of these copies soon even reached Rabbenu Gershom *meor ha-golah* who made his own copy for himself and his students.

The phrase 'we have written and copied from the book' appears, as mentioned, only in the Rothschild Miscellany.[23] That beautiful manuscript, now recently and handsomely reproduced, is dated between 1453 and 1479/80. It was produced in north Italy for a wealthy Ashkenazi family and contains *inter alia* a series of liturgies. Indeed *Yosippon* is preserved in the manuscript as a kind of historical commentary filling the margins surrounding the Shabbat liturgies that comprise folios 206r to 274 with the remainder of the text on folios 275r-298r. (Such a framework aptly illuminates Agnon's famous depiction of *Yosippon* as a text to be read during the Shabbat afternoon rest period.) The passage does not seem to me to indicate a shortening of the text by the fifteenth-century copyist. The question is whether it was done so by the tenth-century writer.[24] In

22. Cf A.A. Bell, Jr, 'Josephus and Pseudo-Hegesippus', in Feldman and Hata (eds.), *Josephus, Judaism and Christianity*, pp. 349-61, especially pp. 351-52 where he expounds on the difference between imitation and adaptation among ancient authors.

23. *The Rothschild Miscellany* (The Israel Museum Jerusalem & Facsimile Editions London, 1989).

24. This question was raised by Israel Ta-Shma ('The Literary Content of the Manuscript', in *The Rothschild Miscellany. A Scholarly Commentary*, pp. 39-88). There he misleadingly describes the text as 'The book of Josippon, a mediaeval Jewish chronography written in the IXth century, relating the history of the Jews from

answer to that question, no scholarly argument to date seems to have sufficient weight to challenge the interpretation that it was the Hebrew author of *Yosippon* who copied and shortened the original Latin manuscript before him.

Professor Wacholder pointed out to this author an interesting phenomenon upon which he subsequently lectured at the Eleventh Congress of Jewish Studies in Jerusalem. That is, that the appearance of a date (in the Destruction Era) in the appropriate place (usually in the middle) of a text is an important rabbinic injunction to protect the identity of a treatise whose beginning and end were subject to the vicissitudes of men, mice, and the natural elements. The phrase that usually introduces such a chronological passage is *tze ve-hashov* and is a mnemonic prescription used by scribes from early talmudic times to the fifteenth century.[25] While this information does not answer the basic question regarding authorship of the text, it does illuminate the discussion in an interesting way; that is, whoever wrote that internal chronological colophon was familiar with that scribal tradition. We might add too that the tenth-century Italian polymath Shabbetai Donnolo wrote poetic curses on those who would delete his name as author from his texts. (All this, of course, was before the Italians invented copyright law in the fifteenth century.) While the author of *Yosippon* was renamed anonymous by modern scholars, he did manage to preserve his time (directly) and place (indirectly) for modern scholars.

The most recent challenge to the authorship of *Yosippon* and its composition in 953 in southern Italy has been offered by Shulamit Sela

---

biblical times to the destruction of the Second Temple'. Further he castigates Flusser for ignoring the statement at the end of ch. 40 (cited in translation above) in order to prove his dating of the book to 953. 'It is incomprehensible to me that Flusser has relegated this most significant early document to a footnote (note 183) referring to it only EN PASSANT and without serious discussion.' Actually Flusser places this document from a fifteenth-century manuscript precisely in the middle of his edited text and has written numerous articles on this date over a period of 25 years. Whether he is right or not is another question however. Bonfil has consistently refuted this dating; see his 'Between Eretz Israel and Babylonia' (in Hebrew) *Shalem* 5 (1987), p. 28 and note, which continues the arguments expressed already in his review of Flusser's edition in *Davar*.

25. Cf. *Seder Olam* (ed. A. Neubauer, *Mediaeval Jewish Chronicles*, II [Oxford, 1895], p. 66), ch. 30 middle; *Tractate Avodah Zarah (MS J.T.S.)*, ed. Sh. Abramson (New York: Jewish Theological Seminary of America, 1957), fol 9a; and *Yalkut Shimoni* on Dan. 8. All three passages have interesting variants as well.

in her 1991 dissertation done under the direction of Moshe Gil at Tel Aviv University. In it she provides a critically edited text of the Arabic *Josephus*, all relevant Genizah documents, and the Arabic *Book of Maccabees* with accompanying Hebrew translation.[26] A full treatment of her argument is beyond the limits of this essay. A short summary, however, may encourage the reader to make use of this welcome new contribution to *Yosippon* studies.

Sela claims, following Wellhausen and Graetz, that the Arabic *Josephus* is the key to understanding the problem of composition and dating the Hebrew *Yosippon*. She argues, again following Wellhausen, that the key to the Arabic *Josephus* is the Arabic *Book of Maccabees* to which was added in Arabic and then later in Hebrew translation cycles of stories by different authors at different times in different places of different religions and in different languages, each in turn influencing the others until the Hebrew versions of *Yosippon* appeared as a new and continuing stage of expansion.[27] In other words, the attempt to find a single date and author for the Hebrew *Yosippon* leads through a labyrinth to a scholarly *cul de sac*. *Yosippon*, according to her, is a composite text from its inception in Hebrew and is based on the Arabic.

Flusser, for his part, does not deny that *Yosippon* is a composite history and identifies the Latin sources upon which the author of *Yosippon* relies from the Vulgate to the Latin *Josephus*. Insofar as the Arabic *Josephus* is concerned, to date Flusser has iterated his view that whereas it is first mentioned by the Spanish Muslim scholar Ibn Hazm (994–1064), *Yosippon* must have been translated into Arabic in the first

---

26. Sela, 'Book of Josippon', p. 36; she does not cite the medieval Hebrew translation which would have made an interesting comparison to the Arabic text she edited. Flusser suspects that the Hebrew translation was contemporary with *Yosippon*, perhaps even made by the latter's author.

27. Sela does not mention the Hebrew translation of Maccabees which was made in Italy most likely in the tenth century (correct accordingly *Encyclopedia Judaica*, *s.v.* Maccabees). David Chwolson published the fragments from an eleventh-century Paris manuscript [Berlin, 1896/7] and averred that it was translated by a contemporary of the author of *Yosippon*, whose work he dated to the ninth century. His argument assumed it would take a work written in Hebrew in Italy to reach Ibn Hazm (d. 1063) in Spain about 150 or 175 years. In a note Chwolson suggests that even an eighth-century translation for both texts was not an impossibility. Since the discovery of new material bearing on the date of *Yosippon*, he may be forgiven at least this temporal indiscretion.

half of the eleventh century.[28] Flusser, who read Wellhausen's thesis which was based on a fourteenth-century manuscript of the Arabic *Josephus*, argued that the relationship between the Hebrew *Yosippon* and the Arabic *Josephus* could only be examined after a critical edition of each was made available.[29] He provided the Hebrew edition; Sela has now provided the basis for the Arabic one. Flusser's position regarding the Arabic *Josephus* is that it was based on the version of *Yosippon* in his scholarly edition and that the Arabic translator created a new book through his free use of the Hebrew version and through his addition of other stories and sources.

A complete exposition of Flusser's position must, of course, be left to the scholar who based his life's work on establishing that position. Since the scholarly challenges to his date of 953 based on the Hebrew material have not overturned his hypothesis, the next level of *Yosippon* research will most likely be discussed on the basis of the Arabic tradition. Given the diametrically opposed views of the editors of the Hebrew and the Arabic texts, the debate should be quite lively and the results informative. But one more ingredient is lacking.

This last scholarly contribution to the debate over the dates in *Sepher Yosippon* seems to bring us full circle to Professor Wacholder's contribution mentioned at the beginning of this essay. There were apparently two major periods of translation into Arabic of Josephus's material. The first was in the eighth century by Syriac Christians who rendered Greek texts into Syriac and then into Arabic.[30] Arabic-speaking Jews and non-Jews would then have been able to make use of them in whole or in part

---

28. *Josippon*, II, pp. 10-16.

29. Wellhausen, for his part, observed that the Arabic *Josephus* was indebted to a Hebrew original: 'Der ursprüngliche Verfasser der arabischer Übersetzung war kein Christ, sondern ein Jude. Er versteht hebraisch und übersetzt aus einer hebraischen Vorlage' (J. Wellhausen, 'Der arabische Josippus', in *Abhandlungen der Akademie der Wissenschaften in Göttingen, Philologisch-Historische Klasse* [Neue Folge 1.4; Berlin, 1897], p. 43). Also he argues that the Hebrew *Vorlage* was translated from the Latin but at the same time shows Graecisms. Even his name in Arabic, *Josippus*, is indebted to the Latin (p. 44). Still he avers that the Arabic *Josippus* is closer to the Arabic *Maccabees* than to the Hebrew *Gorionides* (p. 46), and upon this point Sela structures her argument vis-à-vis Flusser's *Yosippon*.

30. Cf. entry on Syriac Literature in the *Encyclopedia Brittanica*, 11th edn. This is still the best essay on the subject and a reminder to scholars that the best work was done in the nineteenth century and that we still have not harvested its fruits by the end of the twentieth.

and add extraneous material as it pleased them to the growing corpora. This line of argument, however, ignores the continuity and independence of the Syriac tradition. Indeed the whole tradition of Syriac translation and its role in the transmission of knowledge has been absent from the scholarly discussion of *Sepher Yosippon*.[31] It has also been too muted in the discussion of midrashic studies in general. Such research is a desideratum since the Syriac tradition antedates by half a millennium that of the Arabic on the one hand and was well known to Aramaic-speaking and Aramaic-reading Jewish scholars on the other. The second period was tenth/eleventh-century Spain where Hebrew material from Iraq and southern Italy was rendered into Arabic by Jews.[32] Professor Wacholder's study of Nicholas of Damascus, then, can serve the historian well in understanding a process of translation and transmission. Hence it may suffice as a guide for further discussion of the fascinating story of the book of *Yosippon* for which no dated Hebrew material anterior to the year 953 has yet been discovered.

31. This idea receives support from the research of Steven Ballaban who informs me that a Syriac manuscript containing a copy of *Josippon* was circulating in twelfth-century western Europe. The relationship of Syriac to Aramaic would have made that text and numerous others easily accessible to Jewish scholars.

32. This material was later Latinized and so entered into Roman Catholic Europe. Greek and Slavic material represents a different line: direct transmission via Byzantine scholars of ancient Greek material and Slavic translations beginning in the ninth century and continuing through the Middle Ages. On the question of scholarly transmission and translation, the material is conveniently collected in G. Sarton, *Introduction to the History of Science* (3 vols. in 5; Baltimore: Pub. for The Carnegie Institution of Washington, by the Williams & Wilkins Company [c. 1927-1948, repr. 1962]) and M. Steinschneider, *Die hebräischer Übersetzungen der Mittelalters und die Juden als Dolmetscher*, I–II (Berlin: Kommisionsverlag der Bibliographischen Bureaus, 1893).

RESPONSA AND RHETORIC:
ON LAW, LITERATURE, AND THE RABBINIC DECISION

Mark Washofsky

In 1985, Peter Haas published an important article in which he called for a 'literary-critical' study of the rabbinic responsa (*she'elot uteshuvot*). These written rulings issued by halakhic decisors as answers to questions addressed to them are arguably the most 'rabbinic' of all genres of post-talmudic rabbinic literature. As Haas noted, this is due first and foremost to the quantity of the material. The responsa comprise 'the bulk of rabbinic writings from the early Middle Ages onward'. Since 'no other single rabbinic genre approaches the responsa literature in sheer number', since it is predominantly through this medium that the rabbis impart authoritative instruction on issues of Jewish law and observance, the responsa can well be seen as 'the literary tool-in-trade of the rabbinate', the method by which the rabbis 'seek to justify their world and exercise their influence'.[1] Haas charts the record of academic research on the responsa. For over a century, scholars have made extensive use of this vast body of writing, in particular as a major source of data for the writing of Jewish economic and social history,[2] legal

1. P.J. Haas, 'The Modern Study of Responsa', in D. Blumenthal (ed.), *Approaches to Judaism in Medieval Times* (Chico, CA: Scholars Press, 1985), II, pp. 35-71. The quotations are at p. 35. By one estimate, there are 300,000 extant responsa collected in approximately 3000 volumes; see M. Elon, *Hamishpat ha'ivri* (Jerusalem: Magnes Press, 1988), p. 1221.

2. For a summary of these researches, see Haas, 'Modern Study', pp. 38-44. Since he wrote, a number of important developments have taken place in this field. Chief among them are the various computer indices (e.g. the Bar-Ilan Responsa Project; the *Mafteah* of the Law Faculty of the Hebrew University) which enable researchers to retrieve historical data from responsa entered into the data base. The most comprehensive methodological statement concerning the use of responsa as historical sources is H. Soloveitchik, *She'elot uteshuvot kemekor histori* (Jerusalem: Merkaz Zalman Shazar, 1990).

history[3] and legal theory.[4] At the same time, he criticizes the failure of modern scholarship 'to study this corpus of Jewish material from a literary or historically critical point of view'.[5] Like traditional scholars, who read responsa in order to discover what the law is on a particular topic, the academics use these texts instrumentally, mining them for historical and legal information. They have not asked 'what *are* responsa?' and why rabbis write them; they have not investigated the role the genre plays in the religious culture of rabbinic Judaism. Put differently, modern scholars have not engaged in a *modern* study of this literature. To remedy this situation, Haas calls for a new critical approach to the responsa, aimed at discovering 'what this kind of literature has to tell us about how the rabbis attempt to organize their universe'.[6]

Haas's article helped signal what we might call a 'new direction' in responsa studies. He and the other scholars who assume this new direction read responsa not so much as storehouses of data but as the preeminent literary expression of rabbinic Judaism.[7] Given the centrality of the responsa literature to the rabbinic enterprise, they argue that these texts ought to be understood in their own right, *as* texts, as a discrete genre of literature. The significance of the responsum lies not only in what it says but in its very existence, as an artifact indicative of the nature of the religious culture which produces these texts in such great

3.   Haas, 'Modern Study', pp. 44-46. To the works he cites should be added Menachem Elon's *Hamishpat ha'ivri*, especially pp. 1213-277, and the many studies produced by the movement which bears the name of his book and of which he is the leading figure. Composed largely of scholars at Israeli law schools, *Mishpat 'Ivri* is devoted to the 'scientific' study of Jewish law. For an important theoretical debate over this movement see B.S. Jackson (ed.), *Modern Research in Jewish Law* (Leiden: Brill, 1980). See also Y.Z. Kahana, *Mehkarim besifrut hateshuvot* (Jerusalem: Merkaz Harav Kook, 1954).

4.   Haas, 'Modern Study', pp. 46-52.

5.   Haas, 'Modern Study', p. 35. There have been, to be sure, some attempts in this direction. Among those cited by Haas are Zecharias Frankel, *Entwurf einer Geschichte der Literatur der nachtalmudischen Responsen* (Breslau: Schletter'schen Buchhandlung, 1865), S.B. Freehof, *The Responsa Literature* (Philadelphia: Jewish Publication Society, 1955), and especially J.Z. Lauterbach, 'She'elot u-Teshubot', *Jewish Encyclopedia* XI, pp. 240-50. He might well have cited Elon's *Hamishpat ha'ivri*, pp. 1213 ff., who summarizes much of this pioneering scholarship. Still, his point remains that next to nothing has been done to follow up on these preliminary efforts.

6.   Haas, 'Modern Study', pp. 35, 65.

7.   Haas, 'Modern Study', pp. 35, 37.

number. Accordingly, the responsa are to be analyzed with the full range of conceptual tools which have come to define inquiry in the humanities and social sciences. Haas himself provides an example of this kind of 'new direction' study in an article, also published in 1985. Identifying the responsum form as the leading mode of rabbinic moral discourse, he considers what that kind of discourse, cast as a legal argument, tells us about rabbinic thinking, the rabbis' conception of truth and of their particular role in discerning it. The writing of a responsum, he argues, is a ritual act which demonstrates that the existing law contains the answers to all questions, no matter how controversial. It thus validates the entire received legal tradition and the foundational values of rabbinic culture.[8] Those who view the responsum from such a vantage point see it as more than a collection of historical and legal information; it is the textual arena in which a traditional religio-legal system confronts change, the nexus of the complex relationship between established law and the social, economic, and cultural forces which demand that law accommodate itself to new realities.[9] It is a text embodying the language of rabbinic legal and moral discussion, the predominant expression of what is 'rabbinic' about Jewish religious thought.

The present essay emerges from within this new direction in responsa studies. I share the view that a literature so pivotal to the historical experience of rabbinic Judaism warrants a careful and thorough literary-critical study. My goal here is to advance this scholarly agenda in some small way, to consider in some detail just what it means to study the responsa as literature. I want to argue for an approach that is, strictly speaking, 'literary', one which conceives of the responsum as a literary text, the creation of an author who employs words and literary techniques in order to achieve a desired effect. Such a method would apply to the responsum some of the canons of literary criticism heretofore reserved for the study of other genres. It would seek to understand the responsum as we understand other works of literature, as a literary

8. P. Haas, 'Toward a Semiotic Study of Jewish Moral Discourse', *Semeia* 34 (1985), pp. 59-83. See at p. 72: 'the issuance of a responsum is a kind of giving of the law at Sinai'.

9. The work of D. Ellenson is especially notable on this score. See his 'Jewish Legal Interpretation: Literary, Scriptural, Social and Ethical Perspectives', *Semeia* 34 (1985), pp. 93-114 (along with the responses by E.N. Dorff and D. Landes included in that volume), and his collected essays in *Tradition in Transition: Orthodoxy, Halakhah, and the Boundaries of Modern Jewish Identity* (Lanham, MD: University Press of America, 1989).

phenomenon, a particular experience of artistic creation, of communication between author and audience. This approach would attempt to view the responsum as it were from the inside, following the halakhic authority through the act of text-construction. It would try to explain what it means to write a responsum, so as to open new doors of understanding upon the halakhic process and the life of the rabbinic mind. While in accord with a definition of the responsum as 'legal-moral discourse', it would emphasize that this discourse must be understood in its *literary* form. The responsum, that is to say, is a *text*, and it cannot be fully understood apart from its nature as text, as a literary composition which shapes its world through the purposeful use of word, image, and authorial device.

The notion that responsa ought to be studied as literary texts will doubtless strike some readers as an odd one. They will wonder whether it makes much sense to think of responsa as 'literature' at all. And they have a point. To be sure, the responsa are halakhic 'literature', reckoned as one of the major 'literary sources' of post-talmudic Jewish law. As the 'case law' of rabbinic jurisprudence, they resemble in form and function the judicial opinion in other legal systems. Like the judicial opinion, the responsum presents the ruling of a *posek* (recognized decisor) on a particular case or question.[10] Yet do we regard judicial opinions as *literary* texts? It is, after all, customary and eminently reasonable to draw sharp distinctions between legal and literary writing. Legal texts are 'denotative' in character: they point entirely to a referent outside themselves. They are intended to provide legally relevant information to a community which accepts them as authoritative. Legal language is 'scientific', stressing content over style, accuracy and clarity of description over felicity of expression. The words of the text are irrelevant so long as they convey the specific intention of the judge or legislator. A legal text is thus more akin to the instruction manual than to the novel,

10. See Elon, *Hamishpat*, pp. 211-22, on the 'sources' of the law, a concept he borrows from English and German jurisprudence, especially the positivistic schools of legal thought (e.g., P.J. Fitzgerald, *Salmond on Jurisprudence* [London: Sweet and Maxwell, 12th edn, 1966], pp. 109-14). For the comparison of the responsa to judicial opinions see Elon, *Hamishpat*, pp. 1224-225. For a critique of this comparison, see B. Lifshitz, 'Ma'amdah hamishpati shel sifrut ha-shut', *Shenaton hamishpat ha'ivri* 9-10 (1982–1983), pp. 265-300. Lifshitz makes a good point: there is a great deal of uncertainty in the Jewish legal tradition as to whether the responsum ought to be perceived as a 'ruling' or a non-binding 'expression of opinion'. Nevertheless, from a literary standpoint, the comparison holds, as I shall attempt to explain below.

the poem, or the play. Literature by contrast is 'connotative', performative, art rather than science; literary works are those in which the aesthetic function predominates. Its language, often opaque and equivocal, does not merely point to an external reality; it *is* the reality, the constitutive element of a world constructed according to artistic conventions. Its world is 'imaginative', 'fictional', the invention of an author, entirely dependent upon the words which he or she chooses.[11] If a rabbinic responsum may be read as a source of halakhic instruction, historical information or cultural detail, its manner of discourse is that of law, a kind of writing quite different from 'literature'. Why study the one as though it were the other?

To address this question, I will rely upon the research emanating from a new and rapidly growing academic movement known as 'Law and Literature'. Many of the scholars associated with this movement declare that legal texts, including judicial opinions, can and should be read as literature as well as jurisprudence, evaluated according to aesthetic as well as 'legal' or social-scientific criteria. Examining legal materials through the lens of the literary theorist or critic, these scholars have had some interesting if controversial things to say about the commonalities shared by these kinds of writing. Some would go so far as to remove the barrier which has separated them into two distinct forms of written communication.

I believe that the insights of Law and Literature apply quite well to the understanding of the *she'elot uteshuvot*, offering a promising new understanding of the kind of literary experience these texts represent. I therefore begin my essay with a sketch of the Law and Literature movement, to be followed by a literary analysis of a responsum penned by a prominent twentieth-century halakhic authority. I think the results will show the potential of this approach as useful way to study the responsa, and I will conclude with some brief programmatic suggestions.

1. *The Law and Literature Movement*

As movements go, Law and Literature is a rather disorganized affair. That it *is* an academic movement is a measurable fact. 'Law and

11. On all this see R. Wellek and A. Warren, *Theory of Literature* (New York: Harcourt, Brace, 3rd edn, 1977), pp. 20-28. As they summarize the issue (p. 26): 'if we recognize "fictionality", "invention", or "imagination" as the distinguishing trait of literature, we think thus of literature in terms of Homer, Dante, Shakespeare, Balzac, Keats rather than of Cicero or Montaigne, Bossuet or Emerson.'

Literature' courses have become a staple of the American law school curriculum;[12] law reviews have arranged symposia on the subject;[13] and two specialized journals are now devoted to it.[14] In addition to numerous articles, book-length treatments of the theme have been published by three of the field's leading theorists—Richard Posner,[15] Richard Weisberg,[16] and James Boyd White[17]—as well as others.[18] Still, unlike other 'movements' in legal study, Law and Literature lacks a central theory and a cohesive program. Different writers holding widely varied political ideologies make their home within it and sharply criticize the most fundamental assumptions which govern the work of their colleagues. Law and Literature, in other words, is a movement without a manifesto, whose practitioners speak in 'the distinct sounds of a thousand voices'.[19]

12. For a survey of curricula and, indeed, of the Law and Literature movement in general, see E.V. Gemmette, 'Law and Literature: An Unnecessarily Suspect Class in the Liberal Arts Component of the Law School Curriculum', *Valparaiso Law Review* 23 (1989), pp. 267-340.

13. *Mercer Law Review* 39 (1988), pp. 739-935; *Texas Law Review* 60 (1982), pp. 373-586; *Rutgers Law Review* 29 (1976), pp. 223-331.

14. The *Cardozo Studies in Law and Literature* and the *Yale Journal of Law and the Humanities*.

15. R. Posner, *Law and Literature: A Misunderstood Relation* (Cambridge, MA: Harvard University Press, 1988).

16. R. Weisberg, *Poethics: And Other Strategies of Law and Literature* (New York: Columbia University Press, 1992); *The Failure of the Word: The Protagonist as Lawyer in Modern Fiction* (New Haven; Yale University Press, 1984); *When Lawyers Write* (Boston: Little, Brown, 1987).

17. J.B. White, *Justice as Translation* (Chicago: University of Chicago Press, 1990); *Heracles' Bow* (Madison: University of Wisconsin Press, 1985); *When Words Lose Their Meaning: Constitutions and Reconstitutions of Language, Character, and Community* (Chicago: University of Chicago Press, 1984). White's *The Legal Imagination* (Boston: Little, Brown, 1973) is widely regarded as a major pioneering attempt to bridge the disciplines of law and literature; see Weisberg, *Poethics*, p. 224.

18. D.R. Klinck, *The Word of the Law* (Ottawa: Carleton University Press, 1992); D. Papke, *Narrative and the Legal Discourse* (Liverpool: Deborah Charles, 1991); B.S. Jackson, *Law, Fact and Narrative Coherence* (Roby: Deborah Charles, 1988); S. Levinson and S. Mailloux, *Interpreting Law and Literature* (Evanston: Northwestern University Press, 1988).

19. See J.B. White, 'Law and Literature: No Manifesto', *Mercer Law Review* 39 (1988), p. 751. On the disunity of Law and Literature in general, see Posner, *Law and Literature*, p. 1, and Weisberg, *Poethics*, p. 3; the latter sees his work in part as the preparation of a 'unifying manifesto' for the movement.

What unites these disparate viewpoints is the conviction that the study of law can benefit from the study of literature. To say that is to define law, at least in part, as one of the humanities.[20] This definition, in turn, serves as a response to other academic trends which deny to law its own disciplinary integrity.[21] The most prominent contemporary representatives of these trends are 'Law and Economics' and 'Critical Legal Studies'. These academic legal movements are, to be sure, divided by a wide ideological gulf, in both description and prescription. The former, espoused primarily by free market conservatives, explains the history of law as a record of efforts by legal agents, judicial as well as legislative, to realize the goal of economic efficiency. The rules, procedures, and case outcomes which make up the body of the law are those which have tended to maximize the wealth of society. As a normative matter, economic analysts believe that law *ought* to be decided in this way and that judges and legislators err when they take actions that do not conform to this goal.[22] 'Critical' legal scholars, meanwhile, observe law from a decidedly leftist perspective, arguing that the rules and principles normally called 'law' are little more than the political and ideological dispositions of a society's ruling elites. Since law is simply politics in another guise, critical scholars seek to debunk the central propositions of liberal political thought, among them the notion of the rule of law, the concept that rights are somehow inherent in the legal structure, and the perception of legal reasoning as a distinct form of rationality.[23] For all

20. This theme is stressed heavily by Weisberg and by White, although Posner objects that 'law is not one of the humanities, but a branch of government'. See *Law and Literature*, pp. 11-14, and 'Law and Literature: A Relationship Reargued', *Virginia Law Review* 72 (1986), p. 1361.

21. See R. Posner, 'The Decline of Law as an Autonomous Discipline', *Harvard Law Review* 100 (1987), pp. 761-80.

22. See R. Posner, *Economic Analysis of Law* (Boston: Little, Brown, 1986); A.M. Polinsky, *An Introduction to Law and Economics* (Boston: Little, Brown, 1989); and 'Symposium: The Place of Economics in Legal Education', *Journal of Legal Education* 33 (1983), pp. 183-368. For a useful summary see R. Posner, *Problems of Jurisprudence* (Cambridge, MA: Harvard University Press, 1990), pp. 353-392. For a critique, see R. Dworkin, *A Matter of Principle* (Cambridge, MA: Harvard University Press, 1985), pp. 237-89.

23. For an overview see M. Kellman, *A Guide to Critical Legal Studies* (Cambridge, MA: Harvard University Press, 1988), and 'Symposium on Critical Legal Studies', *Stanford Law Review* 36 (1984), pp. 1ff. For a rejoinder see A. Altman, *Critical Legal Studies: A Liberal Critique* (Princeton: Princeton University Press, 1990).

their differences, these two movements are the contemporary manifestations of Legal Realism, a school of legal thought which flourished in the
United States in the early- and mid-twentieth century. Like the legal
realists, these movements share a thoroughgoing skepticism of all claims
of legal 'truth', a tendency to regard law as a body of policy choices
determined by economic or political interest rather than immanent legal
criteria. Legal language, in this view, is a snare and a delusion masking
the 'real' phenomenon of law: 'lawyers, judges, and scholars make
highly controversial political choices, but use the ideology of legal
reasoning to make our institutions appear natural and our rules appear
neutral'.[24] Law is thus better studied as though it were a branch of
economics or politics. While one need not be a 'Law and Literature'
scholar to take exception to this view,[25] literary analysis of law usually
begins with a strong assertion that law is an intellectual endeavor with its
own legitimacy and that attention must be paid to legal language on its
own terms. There is, in other words, something called 'law' which is
uniquely law, which cannot without loss be reduced or translated to the
language of the social sciences.[26]

The movement divides into two distinct trends, which can be titled
'law *in* literature' and 'law *as* literature'.[27] The first considers the representation of legal themes in fiction, studying works of literature in which

24. J.W. Singer, 'The Player and the Cards: Nihilism and Legal Theory', *Yale
Law Journal* 94 (1984), p. 5. For a similar view from a representative of Law and
Economics, see R. Posner, 'The Jurisprudence of Skepticism', *Michigan Law Review*
86 (1988), pp. 827-91, and *Problems of Jurisprudence*, pp. 454-69. On the history of
American Legal Realism see G. Aichele, *Legal Realism and Twentieth-Century
American Jurisprudence* (New York: Garland, 1990), and J.E. Herget, *American
Jurisprudence, 1870-1970* (Houston: Rice Unicersity Press, 1990).

25. See especially O. Fiss, 'The Death of the Law?', *Cornell Law Review* 72
(1986), pp. 1-16.

26. On Law and Literature as a response to Law and Economics and Critical
Legal Studies see Gemmette, 'Suspect Class', pp. 282 ff.; G.P. Miller, 'A Rhetoric of
Law', *University of Chicago Law Review* 52 (1985), pp. 247-70; P.R. Teachout,
'Worlds Beyond Theory', *Michigan Law Review* 83 (1985), pp. 849-93; and
R. West, 'Economic Man and Literary Woman: One Contrast', *Mercer Law Review*
39 (1988), pp. 867-78. For a critique see—again—Posner, *Law and Literature*,
pp. 11 ff.

27. I follow the terminology of C.R.B. Dunlop, 'Literature Studies in Law
Schools', *Cardozo Studies in Law and Literature* 3 (1991), p. 64. Regardless of
terminology, virtually all theorists in the field make a similar distinction.

law and legal proceedings play a leading role.[28] The second, which is our concern here, applies methods of literary criticism to the study of legal materials such as the judicial opinion. To justify this approach—that is, to answer the question I posed above: why study law as though it were literature?—scholars who follow it point to three major categories of literary experience which link legal texts to the more imaginative genres: interpretation, narrative, and rhetoric.

a. *Interpretation*

Interpretation, as an element of hermeneutical thought, has become a leading theme in the theory of knowledge. Philosophers who used to devote their energy to epistemology or linguistics now 'proclaim the importance of interpretation in all of inquiry'.[29] The 'interpretive turn' in the humanities and the sciences is said to herald the decline of the positivist view of knowledge which distinguished sharply between explanation and interpretation. This objectivist model, a detached approach to empirical data independent of theoretical frameworks—in other words, the scientific method—has given way to theories that question the notion that any observer, even a 'hard scientist' can explain data without interpreting it. It is, of course, Thomas Kuhn who helped pioneer the view that the observations of natural science are always grounded in a set of concepts ('paradigms') that the scientists of a particular generation inherit from their immediate predecessors.[30] When even the physical sciences can be conceived as hermeneutical disciplines, the possibility of neutral, value-free observation in the social sciences or the humanities will receive heavy criticism. If the ideal student of history or literature was once portrayed as the detached, scientific observer seeking an objective understanding of a phenomenon 'as it really was', the emphasis has shifted to the picture of scholars-as-interpreters, whose

28. Those who follow this humanistic direction argue that literature offers important perspectives on the cultural context of law as a human activity. They argue that an appreciation of literature will turn students into better lawyers, more sensitive to the nature of law as a social phenomenon and to its workings upon individuals and communities. For two points of view on this proposition, see Posner, *Law and Literature*, pp. 15-16 and 71 ff., and Weisberg, *Poethics*, pp. 188-213.

29. D.R. Hiley, J.F. Bowman and R. Shusterman (eds.), *The Interpretive Turn: Philosophy, Science, Culture* (Ithaca, NY: Cornell University Press, 1991), p. 1.

30. T.S. Kuhn, *The Structure of Scientific Revolutions* (Chicago: University of Chicago Press, 2nd edn, 1970).

understanding emerges out of a dialogical relationship between themselves and the object of their study.[31]

The most prominent voice in the new interpretive hermeneutic is that of Hans-Georg Gadamer, who teaches that all knowledge is hermeneutical and contextual. 'Understanding always involves something like the application of the text to be understood to the present situation of the interpreter'. One cannot understand a text or experience without interpreting it, reconstructing the past in light of the context of contemporary practices, interests, and problems within which the interpreter lives and works. Gadamer thus rejects the possibility of 'objective' knowledge free of prejudice and preconceptions. On the contrary: prejudice and preconceptions make understanding possible. They are part and parcel of the 'horizon' of interpretation, the framework of historical tradition which shapes our conception of reality and outside of which no understanding can take place. The way of understanding is therefore not through detached observation of a phenomenon but through engagement with it, recognizing that we cannot truly know it (or anything else) apart from our own historical situation. Gadamer notes that law, like theology, has always adhered to this hermeneutical principle. Its goal has never been an objective, value-free knowledge but one whose meaning can be incorporated into the life of a community. His point is that other disciplines share this method; law is thus of 'exemplary significance' to the humanities in general.[32]

Gadamer's philosophical hermeneutics has come to exert considerable influence over jurisprudence, accounting for what some call the 'hermeneutical turn' in current legal writing.[33] As lawyers have refocused their interest upon the interpretive process, a significant

---

31. On hermeneutics in general see note 28, *supra*, as well as D.C. Hoy, *The Critical Circle: Literature, History, and Philosophical Hermeneutics* (Berkeley: University of California Press, 1978). On hermeneutical theory in the human and physical sciences, see R.J. Bernstein, *Beyond Objectivism and Relativism* (Philadelphia: University of Pennsylvania Press, 1983); Q. Skinner (ed.), *The Return of Grand Theory in the Human Sciences* (Cambridge: Cambridge University Press, 1985); and W.J. Mitchell (ed.), *The Politics of Interpretation* (Chicago: University of Chicago Press, 1983).

32. H.G. Gadamer, *Truth and Method* (trans. J. Weinsheimer and D.G. Marshall; New York: Crossroad, rev. edn, 1989), pp. 307-308, 324.

33. T.C. Grey, 'The Constitution as Scripture', *Stanford Law Review* 37 (1984), p. 2; S. Levinson, 'On Dworkin, Kennedy, and Ely: Decoding the Legal Past', *Partisan Review* 51 (1984), p. 249.

amount of legal literature has been devoted to discussions of hermeneutical theory.[34] This interest centers upon interpretation as an antidote to
two less satisfactory explanations of the judicial process. The first of
these is objective formalism, which holds that a judge's decisions are
determined by authoritative rules and principles embodied in legal texts
and discoverable by the application of deductive reason. The second,
subjectivism or 'realism', emphasizes the role of choice in legal decision:
the judge's ruling is guided more by his personal inclination and value
preferences than by any purely 'legal' factor. Against both of these,
Gadamerian interpretivists argue that the judicial decision is the outcome
of a dialectic between the objective and the subjective, between the texts
and rules of the legal system on the one hand and the judge's own field
of vision on the other. While theoretical debates over the nature of the
judicial decision have long been a major topic of jurisprudential study,
the philosophical tone of these arguments has lately been replaced or
supplemented by the vocabulary of literary criticism. This is only to be
expected. The great issues of legal interpretation (should lawyers and
judges interpret a statute or constitution according to its 'original
intent'? are legal texts interpreted from within an ongoing tradition of
which the judge is inseparably a member? do legal texts contain any
objective meaning at all, apart from the determination of their readers?)
involve the problem of inferring meaning from any written text. They
are essentially literary questions, the same issues which have long
engaged students of literature and all those who recognize 'the ubiquity
of interpretation in the process of reading every text'.[35] Lawyers today
are therefore as likely to seek guidance on this subject from literary
scholarship as from those disciplines which have traditionally comprised
the field of legal studies. Where 'jurisprudence' was once virtually
synonymous with the philosophy or science of law, today 'the footnotes
in the kind of constitutional law articles that used to cite Rawls and
Nozick now increasingly refer to works of literary theory'.[36]

34. See Levinson and Mailloux, *Interpretation*; 'Symposium on Interpretation',
Southern California Law Review 58 (1985), pp. 1ff.; G. Leyh (ed.), *Legal
Hermeneutics* (Berkeley: University of California Press, 1991); B. Sherman,
'Hermeneutics in Law', *Modern Law Review* 51 (1988), pp. 386-402. S.C.R.
McIntosh, 'Legal Hermeneutics: A Philosophical Critique', *Oklahoma Law Review*
35 (1982), pp. 1-72.
    35. Levinson and Mailloux, *Interpretation*, p. x.
    36. Grey, 'Constitution', p. 2.

This hermeneutical—and literary—turn is illustrated in the work of Ronald Dworkin, one of the leading figures of contemporary legal philosophy. Dworkin established his reputation by arguing against legal positivism, the conception of law as a system of rules commanded by sovereign legislative authority. To the positivists, all law is instruction laid down by authoritative law-makers. In this account there is no difference between a judicial decision and the act of a legislature. In a hard case, one not determined by a clear rule of law, a judge encounters a situation in which no valid legal rule yet exists to resolve the uncertainty. His answer is therefore an exercise of discretion, the creation of new law.[37] Dworkin by contrast sees the judicial decision as an act of interpretation. The judge does not create new law in a hard case; he derives his answer by applying the principles which govern his legal system so as to create a theory of how the law ought to be decided.[38] The way in which the judge does this, Dworkin has written recently, is closely akin to literary interpretation: that is, the process by which a literary critic identifies meaning in a poem or play is virtually the same as that by which a judge imposes a structure of purpose upon the 'data' of the community's legal tradition, its statutes and precedents. Dworkin's judge, deciding a hard case, is like the latest author of a chain novel. Like that author, the judge must both interpret the existing 'chapters' of the law, to search for its developing theme and direction, and continue that theme by projecting it into the present and future, using it to derive a just resolution of the case at hand and of similar cases to come. Just as literary interpretation requires an aesthetic hypothesis, a theory of how to read a text so as to make it the best work of literature it can be, so the judge's duty is to provide what he or she believes to be the best constructive interpretation of the community's political philosophy, legal history and practice.[39] Observers have noted the obvious similarities between Dworkin and

37. This approach originated with Jeremy Bentham and John Austin in nineteenth-century Britain, and its leading modern exponent is H.L.A. Hart. See Hart, *The Concept of Law* (Oxford: Clarendon Press, 1961) and *Essays on Bentham* (Oxford: Clarendon Press, 1982). For an important statement on positivism by a sitting judge see A. Barak, *Judicial Discretion* (New Haven: Yale University Press, 1987).

38. See R. Dworkin, *Taking Rights Seriously* (Cambridge, MA: Harvard University Press, 1977).

39. R. Dworkin, *Law's Empire* (Cambridge, MA: Harvard University Press, 1986), pp. 225-38; *A Matter of Principle* (Cambridge, MA: Harvard University Press, 1985), pp. 146-66.

Gadamer. Neither regards meaning as a discrete and immutable property of a text; it is always contextual, contingent upon an interpreter who always approaches the text with a theory of what that text is and how it is best interpreted.[40] And his 'call to literary methodology' can be said to symbolize a shift away from the positivistic and idealistic approaches which had previously dominated the field of legal theory toward 'the stronger humanity of literature as the best source of law'.[41] Dworkin's critics, too, have taken the literary turn, faulting him from the vantage points of competing literary theories: those which favor authorial intent over his 'New Critical' approach;[42] those which locate textual meaning in discrete interpretive communities rather than in the texts themselves;[43] and those which see the apprehension of meaning as the act of the reader alone.[44]

I cannot in this setting enter into a detailed analysis of the debate between Dworkin and his critics, much less determine which side has the better argument. I refer to that debate merely to indicate the extent to which legal theory has become a literary discourse, wherein scholars of

---

40. G. Leyh, 'Dworkin's Hermeneutics', *Mercer Law Review* 39 (1988), pp. 851-66; J. Donato, 'Dworkin and Subjectivity', *Stanford Law Review* 40 (1988), pp. 1517-541.

41. Weisberg, *Poethics*, p. 4.

42. Posner, *Law and Literature*, pp. 220-68, portrays Dworkin as a legal 'New Critic'. New Criticism locates the meaning of a text in neither its author nor its reader but in the text itself; Dworkin argues that a legal text does bear a meaning independent of its readers but that this meaning is not identical with any so-called 'original intent'. See also J. Lane, 'The Poetics of Legal Interpretation', *Columbia Law Review* 87 (1987), pp. 197-216.

43. S. Fish, *Doing What Comes Naturally: Change, Rhetoric, and the Practice of Theory in Literary and Legal Studies* (Durham: Duke University Press, 1989), pp. 87-119 and 356-371. Fish develops his concept of 'interpretive communities' in *Is There a Text in This Class?* (Cambridge, MA: Harvard University Press, 1980).

44. This is the thrust of much of the attack mounted by deconstructionist critics against the 'hermeneutical turn' in legal (and other) theory; see C. Douzinas and R. Warrington, with S. McVeigh, *Postmodern Jurisprudence* (London: Routledge, 1991), pp. 29-73, and M. Tushnet, 'Following the Rules Laid Down: A Critique of Interpretivism and Neutral Principles', *Harvard Law Review* 96 (1983), pp. 781-827. On the affinity between deconstruction and Critical Legal Studies, see Douzines *et al.* and D.C. Hoy, 'Interpreting the Law', *Southern California Law Review* 58 (1985), p. 175. Not all 'left' critics of Dworkin are deconstructionists; see, for example, R.L. West, 'Adjudication is Not Interpretation: Some Reservations About the Law-as-Literature Movement', *Tennessee Law Review* 54 (1987), pp. 203-78.

jurisprudence resort to literary study for models with which to explain law and the judicial process. The sheer volume of writings by lawyers on the subjects of hermeneutics and literary criticism are evidence that, if law and literature are not identical fields of study, they are no longer as separate and distinct as they once were.

b. *Narrative*

The study of law and the study of literature overlap as well in the growing tendency to portray law as a kind of narrative. 'Narrative jurisprudence' observes that legal discourse seeks to recreate and structure reality in a manner quite similar to that of the storyteller.[45] This observation evokes in turn a wide range of associations between the activities of legal actors and the writings of scholars who specialize in the field of narrative or 'narratology', a theoretical approach to human thinking which seeks to explain the cognitive process in various disciplines.[46] Narrative, in this sense, denotes the means by which a series of real or fictional events are grouped together in the form of a story. A 'real-life' narrative differs from a fictional one, it is true, in that the 'narrator' does not have full creative control over the events of the tale. Still, like a fictional story, it is constructed by a narrator who perforce must choose which of an innumerable collection of facts to include and which to omit from the telling. That choice, the representation of real events, 'arises out of a desire to have real events display the coherence, integrity, fullness, and closure of an image of life that is and can only be imaginary'.[47] The point of a narrative is that it *has* a point; stories are

45. Much of this account is drawn from the excellent summary in Klinck, *Word of the Laws*, pp. 291ff. See also the works of Jackson and Papke cited in n. 18; Weisberg, *Poethics*, p. x; Legal Storytelling Symposium, *Michigan Law Review* 87 (1989), pp. 2073-494; Pedagogy of Narrative Symposium, *Journal of Legal Education* 40 (1990), pp. 1-250; J.R. Elkins, 'On the Emergence of Narrative Jurisprudence', *Legal Studies Forum* 9 (1985), pp. 123-56.

46. See W.J.T. Mitchell, *On Narrative* (Chicago: University of Chicago Press, 1981), and C. Nash (ed.), *Narrative in Culture: The Uses of Storytelling in the Sciences, Philosophy, and Literature* (London: Routledge, 1990).

47. H. White, 'The Value of Narrativity in the Representation of Reality', in Mitchell, *On Narrative*, p. 23. White is one of the foremost exponents of the idea that all historical writing and scholarship is essentially an act of narrative, an attempt to structure historical events into patterns of order and meaning. See his *Tropics of Discourse* (Baltimore: Johns Hopkins University Press, 1978) and *The Content of the Form: Narrative Discourse and Historical Representation* (Baltimore: Johns Hopkins University Press, 1987).

constructed so as to lend a meaning to affairs, to moralize about them. In this sense, much legal language can be read and understood as story-telling. The stories which clients tell their attorneys, and which their attorneys recast into the form of legal narrative, are versions of reality which make conflicting claims as to how the events occurred, their legal significance, and the way things ought to be. A judicial opinion, in turn, tells another story in its own statement of the facts of the case and its own determination of their legal significance.

In a larger sense, too, law assumes and depends upon narrative. Clifford Geertz notes that law is a discipline 'in the process of learning how to survive without the certitudes that launched it'. Legal scholars, like those in other disciplines, despair of finding an objective basis for determining the 'truth' in their specialty. More and more, they have come to realize that 'legal thought is constructive of social realities rather than merely reflective of them' and that 'law is a species of social imagination' rather than scientific description.[48] This perspective on law as a social construction of reality forms the foundation of an oft-cited article by Robert Cover, who suggests that every legal act evokes a 'master narrative' that articulates a normative understanding of social life. Narrative is the means by which society relates its positive law—its *corpus juris*—to its wider vision of justice and right.

> No set of legal institutions or prescriptions exists apart from the narratives that locate it and give it meaning...In this normative world, law and narra-tive are inseparably related. Every prescription is insistent in its demand to be located in discourse, to be supplied with history and destiny, beginning and end, explanation and purpose. And every narrative is insistent in its demand for its prescriptive point, its moral. History and literature cannot escape their location in a normative universe, nor can prescription, even when embodied in a legal text, escape its origin and its end in experi-ence...The narratives that any particular group associates with the law bespeak the range of the group's commitments. Those narratives also provide the resources for justification, condemnation, and argument by actors within the group, who must struggle to live their law.[49]

48. C. Geertz, *Local Knowledge: Further Essays in Interpretive Anthropology* (New Haven: Yale University Press, 1983), pp. 217, 232, 173.

49. R.M. Cover, '*Nomos* and Narrative', *Harvard Law Review* 97 (1984), pp. 4-5, 46. Cover's articles are collected in M. Minow, M. Ryan and A. Sarat, *Narrative, Violence, and the Law: The Essays of Robert Cover* (Ann Arbor: University of Michigan Press, 1992).

Thus, law exists within and cannot be comprehended without a narrative framework which guides the legal thinking of those within the system toward normative ends. Entire institutions of the law, for example, can be explained and accounted for by implicit narrative structures which lie at their foundation. Tort law presumes an account of the 'reasonable person' whose existence is as much fictive as it is real. Bankruptcy law relies upon the 'hard-luck story': an honest person is brought low by overwhelming economic pressure and deserves the helping hand of the law. Were we to tell a different story, for example that the bankrupt individual has received the just deserts of his or her profligacy and irresponsibility, the law would be different.[50] Narrative can also be used to explain legal philosophy itself. Every legal or jurisprudential theory, it is argued, presupposes a narrative vision of the world, and the assumptions it makes about human nature and conduct fall into recognizable literary categories.[51] Thus, to be fully understood, law must be read not only as an exercise in juristic philosophy or an act of political will, but as art, an act of 'worldmaking',[52] the creation of master storytellers.

c. *Rhetoric*
The term 'rhetoric', the third of the guiding themes of Law and Literature writing, is often used to refer to the eloquence and ornamentation with which a message is communicated. As such, it carries a faintly damning connotation: it is the art of speaking well, regardless of the truth or morality of the message spoken.[53] In its classical

50. See D.R. Papke, 'Discharge as Denouement: Appreciating the Storytelling of Appellate Opinions', *Journal of Legal Education* 40 (1990), pp. 145-59.

51. Thus R. West, 'Jurisprudence as Narrative: An Aesthetic Analysis of Modern Legal Theory', *New York University Law Review* 60 (1985), pp. 145-211, relates leading theoretical approaches to the nature of law (law as an exercise of reason or of power, law as liberal interpretivism or as an expression of statism) to Northrop Frye's 'aesthetic myths' (romantic, ironic, comic, tragic) which recur in literature as methods of storytelling and as visions of the world.

52. The term is that of A. Hutchinson, 'Part of an Essay on Power and Interpretation', *NYU Law Review* 60 (1985), p. 861.

53. This state of affairs is laid at the feet of the sixteenth-century French scholar Peter Ramus, who separated the structure of classical rhetoric. Where rhetoric had once consisted of the elements *inventio, dispositio, elocutio, memoria,* and *pronunciatio,* Ramus removed the first two (which denote the finding of arguments and the structuring of the parts of discourse, respectively), classifying them under the rubric of 'logic'. This left to 'rhetoric' the purely stylistic aspects—delivery—of discourse.

understanding, however, rhetoric pertains not merely to matters of style but with the entire realm of argumentation. In this Aristotelian usage, especially in its recent formulation in the thought of Chaim Perelman, rhetoric includes all the means by which a writer or speaker attempts to persuade an audience, to elicit its 'adherence' to the rightness of a proposition. It is a species of logic: not, to be sure, formal or analytical logic, which seeks to demonstrate the validity of conclusions, since demonstrable validity lies beyond the reach of the humanistic disciplines. It is logic nonetheless, the logic of practical reasoning and justification, the logic that forms the means of persuasive argumentation in all types of inquiry where the value of a proposition lies largely in the audience's adherence to it. It is a logic which therefore invokes such standards as shared values, custom, consequences, common sense all criteria which, though rejected as valid proof in formal syllogistic reasoning, are accepted as persuasive within a particular culture.[54]

Like hermeneutic, rhetoric has lately become its own wide-ranging intellectual movement, a leading theme in the theoretical construction of various forms of inquiry, from the humanities to the social sciences and even the 'hard' sciences. Dissatisfaction with 'objectivism' or 'foundationalism'—the positivistic outlook which holds that truth is discernible by means of rule-bound, scientific method—has led to the growing conviction that the process of inquiry is dependent upon individual and collective judgments rather than upon 'fact' and 'logic', that what constitutes 'fact' or 'logic' within a discipline is symbolically mediated and socially constructed, that 'the practice of inquiry might more usefully be understood in rhetorical terms'.[55] This 'rhetoric of inquiry' is

See C. Perelman, *The New Rhetoric and the Humanities: Essays on Rhetoric and its Applications* (Dordrecht: Reidel, 1979), p. 3.

54. C. Perelman, *The Realm of Rhetoric* (Notre Dame: University of Notre Dame Press, 1982), and C. Perelman and L. Olbrechts-Tyteca, *The New Rhetoric* (Notre Dame: University of Notre Dame Press, 1969). Perelman differs from Aristotle in his refusal to draw a sharp distinction between 'dialectic' and 'rhetoric'. Both are species of argument, albeit with different notions of what constitutes 'proof'. See H. Zyskind, introduction to Perelman, *The New Rhetoric and the Humanities*, pp. ix-x.

55. H.W. Simons (ed.), *The Rhetorical Turn* (Chicago: University of Chicago Press, 1990), p. 2. Simons, along with many other theorists, credits the pragmatist philosopher Richard Rorty with many of the creative insights of this anti-foundationalist 'movement'. See R. Rorty, *Philosophy and the Mirror of Nature* (Princeton: Princeton University Press, 1980) and *Consequences of Pragmatism* (Minneapolis: University of Minnesota Press, 1982). For examples of the rhetorical approach to the

reflected in the revival of interest in legal rhetoric, understood not as a collection of argumentative techniques and lawyers' tricks but as the central element of all legal discourse. Since law is a social practice which consists in large part of argumentation,[56] law itself, as an activity, can be understood as the most important manifestation of rhetoric. 'Legal reasoning is an elaborated case of practical reasoning', a logic which proceeds not from premises to conclusion but from a stated end or purpose to the means by which that purpose might best be achieved. It is logic that seeks to persuade an audience sharing the speaker's basic juristic assumptions that one decision, if not necessarily 'true' in the formal sense, is better than other possible decisions.[57]

The judicial opinion is thus an expression of what one observer calls 'the logic of justification', the reasoned means by which a judge seeks to persuade the legal community of the rightness of his ruling, as opposed to 'the logic of discovery', the process by which he in fact arrives at that ruling.[58] It is a carefully constructed argument as to how the members of that community ought to talk about and respond to a particular legal problem, when more than one response is possible or conceivable. Put differently, it is a literary expression of the rhetorical art as practiced within a specific legal community. Much Law and Literature research

various disciplines see the essays in Simons, as well as D.N. McCloskey, *The Rhetoric of Economics* (Madison: University of Wisconsin Press, 1985), and J. Nelson, A. Megill and D.N. McCloskey (eds.), *The Rhetoric of the Human Sciences* (Madison: University of Wisconsin Press, 1985). In general, see C. Geertz, 'Blurred Genres: The Refiguration of Social Thought', *American Scholar* 49 (1980), pp. 165-179, Fish, *Doing What Comes Naturally*, pp. 471-502, and W. Booth, *Modern Dogma and the Rhetoric of Assent* (Notre Dame: University of Notre Dame Press, 1974).

56. See Klinck, *Word of the Law*, pp. 171-207, and D.N. Haynes, 'The Language and Logic of Law: A Case Study', *University of Miami Law Review* 35 (1981), pp. 183-254.

57. See C. Perelman, *Justice, Law, and Argument* (Dordrecht: Reidel, 1980); the quotation is at p. 129. See also W. Sadurski, 'It All Comes Out in the End: Judicial Rhetoric and the Strategy of Reassurance', *Oxford Journal of Legal Studies* 7 (1987), pp. 258-78. On law as practical reasoning, see Perelman, and also S.J. Burton, *An Introduction to Law and Legal Reasoning* (Boston: Little, Brown, 1985), and *Judging in Good Faith* (Cambridge: Cambridge University Press, 1992); V.A. Wellman, 'Practical Reasoning and Judicial Justification: Toward an Adequate Theory', *Colorado Law Review* 57 (1985), pp. 45-115; and J. Dewey, 'Logical Method and Law', *Cornell Law Quarterly* 10 (1924), pp. 17-27.

58. R. Wasserstrom, *The Judicial Decision: Toward a Theory of Legal Justification* (Stanford: Stanford University Press, 1961).

concentrates upon the rhetoric of judicial opinions. As Richard Posner reminds us, the success of an opinion lies largely in its ability to persuade its readers. And since 'many legal questions cannot be resolved by logical or empirical demonstration',[59] judicial persuasion can exist in the absence of proof. Even when based upon dubious legal reasoning, an opinion may carry the day and earn a hallowed place in a legal tradition due to its forceful presentation or its aggressive assertion of one side of a balanced dispute. Through the effective use of language it sweeps its readers into assent, convincing them of the obvious correctness of what is in fact a highly debatable conclusion. Judges resort to a variety of rhetorical techniques to achieve the goal of persuasion. Common among these is the slanting of the facts of the case to fit its outcome, a tactic which seems deceitful unless we recognize that a major function of the opinion is to state a rule of law clearly and memorably. Indeed, those opinions which are arguably the greatest are not necessarily those which feature the tightest legal logic; style, metaphor, and a felicitous turn of phrase can lend a decision persuasive power even when it lacks the endorsement of right reason.[60] The famous dissent of Oliver Wendell Holmes, Jr, in *Lochner v. New York* has been criticized for its absence of close reasoning and its failure to address the major issues raised in the majority opinion. For this reason, Posner suggests, the dissent would have received a failing grade in a law school examination. Yet though not a 'good' opinion, by general reputation 'it is merely the greatest judicial opinion of the last hundred years'. Its literary power, its ability to frame subsequent legal thought make it a rhetorical masterpiece, 'and evidently rhetoric counts in law; otherwise the dissent in *Lochner* would be forgotten'.[61] The art of judging is thus inescapably rhetorical, and the

59. Posner, *Law and Literature*, p. 286.

60. See especially Posner's treatment of two of the most famous decisions of B.N. Cardozo: *Palsgraf v. Long Island Railroad Co.*, 248 N.Y. 339 (1928), and *Hynes v. New York Central Railroad Co.*, 231 N.Y. 229 (1921), in his *Cardozo: A Study in Reputation* (Chicago: University of Chicago Press, 1990), pp. 33-57. Neither opinion 'proves' its point; both 'slant' the facts, emphasizing those supportive of the decision while overlooking those which weaken it. Yet both are memorable and shaped the ongoing development of American tort law. Posner's conclusion (pp. 126-27): 'probably the most important factor (in accounting for Cardozo's eminent reputation) is the *rhetoric* of Cardozo's opinions' (emphasis in the original).

61. *Lochner v. New York*, 198 U.S. 45, 75 (1905). 'To judge (the opinion) by "scientific" standards', Posner concludes, 'is to miss the point'; *Law and Literature*, pp. 281-86.

failure to recognize this fact is a shortcoming of much legal scholarship.[62]

Posner, for all his admiration of judicial rhetoric, insists on a distinction between an opinion's legal 'correctness' and its rhetorical style.[63] Other Law and Literature writers would virtually erase that line. With a famous essay by Benjamin Cardozo as his point of departure,[64] Richard Weisberg declares that judicial opinions stand and fall on their language, 'upon the fit between the words used and the aspiration toward justice that every legal pronouncement should embody'. The articulation of the facts of the case and response to them create 'a perspective on the law that can never be identical to any earlier perspective', one which will in turn help direct the thinking of future judges. There is thus no difference between the form and the substance of the opinion.

> Rhetoric, in other words, does not assist an argument to march to its conclusion; rhetoric *is* the argument, and the perceived rightness or wrongness of the conclusion may be as much based on the style and the form of the argument as on the extrinsic application to it of the observer's notion of what the law of the case 'should have been'.[65]

Hence an opinion, if it is to produce a coherent result, must match language to outcome; 'no opinion with a misguided outcome has ever in fact been "well crafted"'.[66] In his studies of two famous decisions by Cardozo, Weisberg finds that the style with which the judge states the case and composes its facts into a narrative discourse is inseparable from the case's result and from Cardozo's conception of the 'just' decision.[67] The medium, in short, *is* the message.

James Boyd White has devoted much of his writing to the proposition that law is 'essentially literary and rhetorical in nature, a way of establishing meaning and constituting community in language'. He speaks of

---

62. Posner, *Law and Literature*, pp. 269ff.

63. Posner, *Law and Literature*, pp. 286-89.

64. B. Cardozo, 'Law and Literature', in M. Hall (ed.), *Selected Writings of Benjamin Nathan Cardozo* (New York: Matthew Bender, 1947), pp. 339-56. See especially at p. 342: 'the opinion will need persuasive force, or the impressive virtue of sincerity and fire, or the mnemonic power of alliteration and antithesis, or the terseness and tang of the proverb, and the maxim. Neglect the help of these allies, and it may never win its way.' For Weisberg on Cardozo's literary philosophy, see 'Law, Literature, and Cardozo's Judicial Poetics', *Cardozo Law Review* 1 (1979), pp. 283-342.

65. Weisberg, *Poethics*, pp. 16-17.

66. Weisberg, *Poethics*, pp. 7-8.

67. Weisberg, *Poethics*, pp. 16-34.

law as a 'constitutive rhetoric', 'the central act by which culture and community are established, maintained, and transformed'. And the culture which law creates is a culture of argument, a rhetorical community which grants its members positions from which to speak and materials and methods for discourse. Like literature, legal texts are language-centered and language-bound. Law is not mere policy-setting in another guise; it is a conversation among members of a legal community, a discourse on the meaning of texts by which they propose to define themselves and constitute their social and political reality. Like literature, therefore, law is an art, performative rather than analytical. Like the literary text and unlike scientific language, legal language creates its own world.

For White, the judicial opinion provides a powerful example of the literary and rhetorical nature of law. Through the process of 'translation'—giving life to old texts by placing them in new ways and new relations—judges create new texts which both respond to and accommodate the texts made by others. The judicial opinion is a radically literary text whose excellence, like that of other literary texts, should be measured not by its result alone but by the quality of its discourse. It is there, where the argument is developed, that the law 'lives and grows and transforms itself', that the judge, reconstituting the received texts into new patterns of meaning, displays the fullest achievement of the judicial mind. In his studies of American judicial opinions White explores the rhetorical assumptions which guide the judge's composition: the definition of intended audience, the conception of the speaker's role, the notion of the kinds of arguments which this particular audience will find persuasive.[68] It is these assumptions, he contends, rather than pure 'legal reasoning' which determine the outcome of the decision. Moreover, in their development lies the judge's unique contribution to law, the invitation to his readers to think of the law in a certain way, to perceive themselves as a certain kind of 'ideal reader' or community.[69]

Some Law and Literature writers get carried away at times by their

---

68. See especially *Justice as Translation*, pp. 123-32 and 141-59 for his analysis of *Dred Scott v. Sanford*, 60 U.S. (19 How.) 393 (1857), and *Olmstead v. U.S.*, 277 U.S. 438 (1928).

69. See White, *When Words Lose their Meaning*, pp. xi, 231; *Heracles' Bow*, pp. 28, 97-98; *Justice As Translation*, pp. 89ff; 'What Can a Lawyer Learn from Literature?', *Harvard Law Review* 102 (1989), pp. 2014-2047.

own rhetoric. White in particular has been criticized for implying that law is *nothing other than* literature, for ignoring the 'real world' factors which govern legal systems[70] and for appearing to confuse rhetoric with ethics, as though a well-written opinion is by that very fact a just one.[71] Yet they do seem to be on to something. Whatever else it may be, law is in large part a literary phenomenon which expresses its view of the world through words and texts, language and argument. This implies that law is a mode of discourse that cannot be reduced to the elements of which that discourse speaks. A judge's decision, for example, is clearly influenced by the economic, political, or social facts of the case and is therefore 'about' them, but it is more than those things. In writing an opinion, a judge does not 'do' sociology or economics. Rather, he or she creates a composition which encompasses these facts within a framework of meaning and which argues in a stylized and textual language that a particular decision best reflects the legal traditions of that community. This activity of text-creation can be said to parallel the act by which novelists and poets arrange different kinds of raw materials to create their own texts. If so, then law in a real sense *is* literature, creating its own special world through the use of words. To understand the law, it is not enough to look to the realities signified by the words of the legal text, any more than one can understand a Shakespearean drama by studying the realia included in the play while ignoring the fact that it *is* a play. Like literature, law is not simply a collection of words addressing an external reality; it *is* words, texts which must be experienced as they are. Look through its language in search of its 'substance' and you lose the interpretive, narrative, and rhetorical conversation which distinguishes law from social science as an intellectual expression.

Indeed, the category of rhetoric subsumes many of the insights of the Law and Literature movement. The most far-reaching and most enduring conclusion of this approach to legal thought is its portrayal of the legal text, in particular the judicial opinion, as literary art, as performance, as the attempt of an author or group of authors to persuade their readers of the rightness of their conclusions. And the rise of the rhetorical understanding of law challenges other, long-honored theories, threatening to

70. See G.P. Miller, 'A Rhetoric of Law', *University of Chicago Law Review* 52 (1985), pp. 247-270, and L.H. Carter's otherwise favorable review of *Heracles' Bow* in *Georgia Law Review* 20 (1986), pp. 807-808.

71. See Weisberg, *Poethics*, pp. 224-250, and J. Malhan's review of *Heracles' Bow* in *Harvard Law Review* 101 (1988), pp. 702-23.

displace them. The turn to interpretivism in many fields, including law, signifies the collapse of objective, non-interpretive standards of legal validity; this is an essential critique of the project of legal positivism, its attempt to ground the concept of law in a system of clear and verifiable rules. The stress placed upon narrative, its creative role in the structuring of legal reality and legal theory, is evidence of the waning interest in natural law speculations. In the presence of conflicting narratives which can lead to a variety of differing legal conclusions, it makes little sense to try to locate an ultimate standard of legal validity in some metalegal source. And, as indicated previously, the literary 'turn' in legal studies expresses a fundamental dissatisfaction with more 'scientific' approaches—economic, sociological, political—to law. These older theories, in other words, can no longer contend to provide an adequate account of what a judicial opinion is, of how it functions in legal history and community. What remains is rhetoric, the conception of the judicial opinion as a persuasive text, whose contribution to the development of the law rests upon the quality of its discourse and its success in influencing the discourse of contemporary and subsequent generations of lawyers.

This admittedly sketchy summary of a multi-faceted academic movement suggests the ways in which the rabbinic responsum can be perceived and studied as a literary text. Of all the halakhic genres, the responsum is in a number of ways the best suited for this kind of analysis. As the halakhic equivalent of the Dworkinian 'hard case', the responsum often addresses a question of law which has no one obviously correct answer. The role of the *meshiv* (author of the responsum) can therefore be profitably discussed within the context of interpretive theory. Some scholars have noted what we might term the hermeneutical situation of the *meshiv*. Unlike the writer of a commentary or code, who arrives at his conclusions through a process of abstract legal reasoning, the *meshiv* proceeds from the midst of a concrete halakhic problem. His answer is not a matter of theory but of *halakhah le-ma'aseh*, a concrete legal decision which disposes of a ritual or monetary case involving actual human beings. Thus, as some traditional rabbinic scholars contend, the answer derived in a responsum is superior to one reached in a more abstract code or halakhic treatise.[72] At any rate, the answer will be

---

72. Among those who make this point is R. Naftali Zvi Yehudah Berlin, *Resp. Meshiv davar* (Warsaw, 1894), I, no. 24. Since a responsum expresses a legal opinion that relates to a concrete case, some authorities hold that a decision reached in

different, because the author of a responsum works it out in the midst of a very different situation. The reader of a responsum enters what Menachem Elon calls the 'laboratory' of halakhic creativity to observe the intellectual struggles of the *posek* who confronts the needs of real individuals and communities, seeking 'a legal solution built upon the foundation of the past while serving the manifold requirements of his own contemporaries'.[73]

This recognition calls into question at least two widely accepted—and conflicting—descriptive models of the halakhic process. The first of these portrays the ideal halakhic decisor as detached and dispassionate, eschewing 'subjective considerations' and 'volitional inclinations', deriving his conclusions by deduction from fundamental principles, avoiding the ruling which is arbitrary or expedient in favor of that which is demanded by the weight of halakhic precedent or consensus.[74] The second sees the halakhist as arriving at a decision by first determining the 'best' answer in accordance with his own subjective comprehension of Jewish 'ideals' and only then searching for the halakhic rules and principles—'acceptable legal ploys'—with which to support his opinion.[75] These models closely parallel the 'formalist' and 'realist' approaches which have long dominated legal theory but which have lost ground under the strictures of current interpretive theory.[76] An acknowledgement that the *meshiv* works within a 'hermeneutical situation' would likewise require a conception of the *halakhah* which rejects

a *teshuvah* is somehow 'better' or more correct than one derived in more abstract learning. On all this see Elon, *Hamishpat ha'ivri*, pp. 1215-218, and Y.Z. Kahana, *Mehkarim besifrut hateshuvot* (Jerusalem: Mosad Harav Kook, 1973), pp. 97-107. For an opposing view see Lifschitz, 'Ma'amdah hamishpati', pp. 290-96.

73. Elon, *Hamishpat ha'ivri*, p. 1215.

74. J.D. Bleich, *Contemporary Halakhic Problems* (New York: Ktav, 1977), pp. xv ff.

75. L. Jacobs, *A Tree of Life* (Oxford: Oxford University Press, 1984), pp. 11-12.

76. See, in general, R.A. Bellioti, *Justifying Law* (Philadelphia: Temple University Press, 1992), pp. 3-14 as well as nn. 31 and 55, above. This is not to say that either of these approaches to legal thought has disappeared or does not have its contemporary adherents. On formalism, see H. Wechsler, 'Toward Neutral Principles of Constitutional Law', *Harvard Law Review* 73 (1959), pp. 1-35; F. Schauer, 'Formalism', *Yale Law Journal* 97 (1988), pp. 509-48, and E.J. Weinrib, 'Legal Formalism: On the Immanent Rationality of Law', *Yale Law Journal* 97 (1988), pp. 949-1016. On realism, see the sources on Law and Economics and Critical Legal Studies, nn. 22, 23 and 24, above.

both formalism and realism. The halakhist does not derive a rationally correct legal answer from the sources by means of a set of neutral principles applied according to some formal method, nor does he use the texts merely to supply the requisite legal window-dressing for what are essentially policy decisions. He reaches his answers through interpretation, a dialogical relationship between interpreter and text, a stance in which the texts limit the interpreter's freedom of maneuver at the same time that his understanding of them is shaped by his hermeneutical situation, the 'horizon' of perspective and practice.

If so, if the halakhic decision emerges from an interpretive process, the student of that decision ought to avoid both the formalist and the realist errors. The goal of scholarship, first of all, cannot be to critique the ruling of a responsum against some objective standard of halakhic correctness. Interpretive theory teaches that such standards do not exist. The meaning of texts will differ with the situation of the interpreter, and no calculus exists by which to determine 'objectively' which meaning is the right one. The rules and principles which are said to constrain the freedom of the legal interpreter are themselves subject to and the products of interpretation, and interpretation is always informed by the predilections—ideological, ethical, cultural—of the interpreter.[77] At the same time, it is insufficient to point to 'extralegal' factors in order to account for the rabbinic decision. Jacob Katz, in particular, has demonstrated in his own scholarly work that while halakhic rulings respond to challenges raised to Jewish law by the social environment, they are not dictated by them. Halakhists who confront these challenges must contend not only with 'the needs of the hour' but also with the demands of their legal system, its principles, precedents and traditions. Halakhic argumentation is not a smokescreen covering the 'real' motivations of the decisor; it, too, is 'real', exerting as much if not more influence upon the final ruling as do all the extralegal factors. Were this not so, Katz reminds us, the rabbis would simply have removed many of the halakhic prohibitions which impinged upon Jewish economic life during the Middle Ages. 'These barriers did not budge, despite the pressure of social reality. We must therefore inquire as to the limits of halakhic flexibility: which restrictions were easy to remove, and which remained in force in the face of the pressures of the day'.[78]

77. See Stanley Fish's critique of H.L.A. Hart's legal positivism in *Doing What Comes Naturally*, pp. 503-24.

78. J. Katz, *Halakhah vekabalah* (Jerusalem: Magnes, 1984), pp. 2-3, where he

A Law and Literature approach to the responsa would affirm Katz's prescription. Halakhic language must be taken seriously on its own terms; it cannot be reduced to a pale reflection of environmental forces. It would, however, add the proviso that even the 'limits of halakhic flexibility' cannot be sought in some objective standard that exists separately from the interpretive process itself. The halakhic responsum, like the judicial opinion, is to be read as a species of literature, a composition in which the narrative and rhetorical features predominate. The *meshiv* is a narrator, the composer of a text which constructs its own reality, arranging or shaping the facts of his *she'elah* (inquiry or case) so as to lend support to his conclusion. That conclusion may evoke a Coverian 'master narrative' which, though expressed in the form of standard halakhic discourse, is better regarded as the framework of meaning within which that discourse takes place and which largely determines the direction in which it proceeds.[79] The responsum is, as well, a discursive text: ever since the late Geonic period, authors of responsa have tended to support their decisions with accompanying argumentation.[80] This element of justification of legal rulings, so integral a part of rabbinic culture,[81] suggests that the responsum ought to be perceived as a rhetorical performance. The *meshiv* is the creator of a text whose central purpose is that of persuasion. Its language is the 'logic of justification'; its style and technique are geared toward convincing its specialized audience that the answer it reaches is the best available reading of the *halakhah* on this particular question. It is the domain of practical

summarizes the conclusions of many of the halakhic case studies collected in the volume. See especially his strictures on Heinrich Graetz and Efraim E. Urbach, two scholars whose contributions to the history of Jewish law, in Katz's view, over-emphasized the determinative power of historical and cultural influences at the expense of the *halakhah* itself.

79. This would explain the interest shown by liberal halakhic thinkers in Robert Cover's work. See G. Tucker, 'The Sayings of the Wise are Like Goads: An Appreciation of the Works of Robert Cover', *Conservative Judaism* 45 (1993), pp. 17-39; D.H. Gordis, 'Precedent, Rules, and Ethics in Halakhic Jurisprudence', *Conservative Judaism* 46 (1993), p. 88, n. 29; and D. Ellenson, 'Conservative Halakha in Israel: A Review Essay', *Modern Judaism* 13 (1993), p. 194.

80. See Elon, *Hamishpat ha'ivri*, pp. 1226-1233, and Freehof, *Responsa Literature*, pp. 30-33.

81. See, in general, D. Weiss-Halivni, *Midrash, Mishnah, and Gemara: The Jewish Predilection for Justified Law* (Cambridge, MA: Harvard University Press, 1986).

386 Pursuing the Text: Studies in Honor of Ben Zion Wacholder

reasoning, of rhetoric in its Aristotelian and Perelmanian sense. Thus, the contention of this essay is that a literary-rhetorical study offers a most valuable tool toward the proper understanding of the nature of responsa and their function in the discourse of rabbinic Judaism.

2. *Toward a Literary-Rhetorical Study of the Responsa*

The foregoing is certainly not an exhaustive (or even adequate) discussion of the literary and jurisprudential issues that inform the Law and Literature movement as they relate to the study of rabbinic responsa. That kind of discussion, which I believe is a scholarly necessity, requires a book-length treatment. Similarly, an analysis of one responsum can hardly be said to 'prove' the usefulness of a literary-rhetorical approach to this massive genre as a whole. A proper study demands a consideration of many responsa, covering a wide range of subject matter. All I can do within the framework of this essay is to exemplify this literary-rhetorical method, showing how it can aid toward the understanding of this body of literature.

To do so, I want to examine a responsum of Rabbi Benzion Meir Hai Ouziel (1880–1953), who served at the time as the chief Sefardic Rabbi of Palestine.[82] Its subject is female suffrage: does Jewish law permit women to vote in elections and to hold public office? The question became one of great public moment in 1918, when representatives of the *yishuv*, the Jewish community of Palestine, met in Jaffa to organize its institutions under the newly established British mandate. Over the bitter and vociferous objections of the *haredim*, the 'extreme' Orthodox elements of the population, the community adopted women's suffrage in 1925, a decision which spurred the secession of the *haredim* from the political institutions of the *yishuv*.[83]

---

82. Ouziel is the subject of one full-length biography: Shabbetai Don-Yehya, *Harav Benzion Meir Hai Ouziel: hayav umishnato* (Jerusalem: Hahistadrut Hatsiyonit, 1955). Also useful is the entry by Geulah Bat-Yehudah in *Encyclopaedia shel hatsiyonut hadatit*, IV (Jerusalem: Mosad Harav Kook, 1971), pp. 173-84. In the area of halakhic thought, Ouziel is a fascinating figure; his responsa await a thorough analysis. In the meantime see R. Chaim David Halevy, 'Pesikat hahalakhah ve'ahavat yisrael bemishnat R. B.Z. Ouziel', *Niv hamidrashyah* 20-21 (1978–1979), pp. 55-69, and R. Shelomo Y. Zevin, *Soferim usefarim*, I (Tel-Aviv: Avraham Tsiyoni, 1959), pp. 202-15.

83. For the history of the controversy see M. Friedman, *Chevra vedat* (Jerusalem: Yad Yitschak Ben-Tsvi, 1978), pp. 146-184.

Ouziel's published opinion on this question is an excellent model for our rhetorical method of study. It deals, first of all, with a 'hard case', one which the existing sources of the law do not answer with certainty and over which the legal authorities can reasonably disagree. More than that: his permissive ruling is clearly a minority view. The preponderance of rabbis who expressed opinions on the subject ruled that the Torah forbids women from holding positions of political authority, and most of them agreed that it denies them the vote as well.[84] The prohibitive position rests upon powerful halakhic and traditional grounds. These include the talmudic disqualification of women from serving as judges and witnesses,[85] the paradigmatic examples of the exercise of public authority and responsibility in Jewish law; the ruling of Rambam (Maimonides) that a woman may not be set upon the throne of Israel, a prohibition which he extends to all positions of authority;[86] long-standing communal practice (*minhag*) which has denied suffrage and political office to women; concern that the mingling of the sexes at campaign rallies and government meetings would threaten the accepted standards of communal morality and family harmony; and numerous talmudic and midrashic passages which declare or imply that women are deficient in rationality, mental stability, and reliability. In short, a prohibitive stance on female suffrage is not only a plausible understanding of the halakhic sources; it is, to the bulk of Orthodox authorities, the *right* understanding, or at least the most persuasive one. To support his permissive ruling, Ouziel must somehow overpower or finesse this conventional halakhic wisdom. He does so in an impressive display of interpretive skill and rhetorical power.

His responsum[87] begins, in good judicial form, with a 'statement of the facts'. Writing, he informs us, some years after the conflict (*machloket*) over women's suffrage had been settled, he briefly describes the battle 'before which the entire land of Israel quaked and trembled'. A cacophony of wall-posters, pamphlets and newspaper articles appeared

84. Friedman, *Chevra vedat*, p. 146 n. 1. That this point of view remains the rabbinic consensus is evident from the analysis by J.D. Bleich in his *Contemporary Halakhic Problems*, II (New York: Ktav, 1983), pp. 254-67.

85. *Nid.* 49b; *Shulchan Arukh, Hoshen Mishpat* 7.4; *Shev.* 30a; Rambam, *Yad, Edut* 9.1-2. On the position of the Talmud Yerushalmi on the subject, see n. 102, below.

86. *Yad, Melakhim* 1.5, drawn from *Sifre* Deuteronomy, ch. 157; see also *Pesikta Zutrati*, ch. 3.

87. *Resp. mishpetey ouziel*, 3 (Tel Aviv, 1940), no. 6.

'every day' to urge that women be denied the vote. Some based their arguments on *halakhah*, others on considerations of social morality, still others on the fear that political activity among women threatened to undermine peace and harmony between husbands and wives. 'And all of these objections', he notes, 'rest upon the familiar declaration that "everything new is forbidden by the Torah".' The section concludes with Ouziel's thanks to R. Chaim Hirschenson, whose book *Malki bakodesh*[88] collects all of this material, 'enabling me to hear the opinions of all those who forbid women's suffrage and to judge them as best I can'.

Like any 'statement of the facts', this purports to be a neutral, objective recounting of the issues before the deciding authority. In fact, it is no such thing. The reader will note how Ouziel uses this short paragraph to telegraph and to justify his ultimate decision. He accomplishes this in several ways. First, like any judge he exploits the opportunity to construct a narrative of the case. And the primary theme of this narrative is *machloket*, a raucous controversy which ultimately tore the community asunder. In his retelling, the blame for this unhappy outcome is laid squarely at the feet of the opponents of women's suffrage. It is they, rather than the secularists who in fact demanded this reform, who raised the issue to a fever pitch, who shattered what Ouziel implies were the existing peaceful intergroup relations in the *yishuv*. Thus it is they, rather than the secularists, who must justify their actions before the bar of history. Secondly, by making the opponents' views the object of his analysis, Ouziel sets himself apart from their camp. He will consider 'their' arguments; he thus implies that they are not *his* arguments. He describes their position in cool, dispassionate tones; even though the *haredim* argue for it with a great deal of passion, Ouziel evinces no sympathy for their desire to preserve what they see as the traditional Jewish way of life. His detached stance toward them invites readers to share that lack of sympathy and distance themselves from that position. Thirdly, in describing that position, he minimizes its persuasive force. He lumps those who object to women's suffrage on halakhic grounds together with those who base their opposition on concerns for morality or family harmony. This equation suggests that, as a legal question, the case against women's suffrage is weak. Since not all the opponents argue their case on halakhic grounds, those grounds must surely be unconvincing, requiring the support of other, non-legal arguments.

88.   R.C. Hirschenson, *Malki bakodesh* (Hoboken, 1921), II, pp. 171-209.

Fourthly, lest there be any doubt, Ouziel informs us that none of the specific arguments, halakhic or otherwise, is to be taken seriously. The *real* basis for the opposition is the maxim that 'everything new is forbidden by the Torah',[89] the attitude that innovation and social change somehow violate the spirit of traditional Judaism. Those familiar with Ouziel's halakhic thinking would be expected to know that he utterly rejects this maxim as a principle of Jewish law. In the introduction to his responsa, he sets down what amounts to a Coverian 'master narrative' of the halakhic process, an account of the guiding values which have shaped the history of Jewish law. The *halakhah*, he tells us, has never been frozen, wedded to a particular body of existing rulings. On the contrary: 'the way of the halakhic authority' has always been a dynamic one, in which the halakhist relies upon analysis, analogy, and logic to derive answers to new questions from the established rules and principles of Jewish law. And such must still be 'the way':

> The conditions of life, social and cultural change, and technological advancement give birth in every age to new problems which demand solution. We cannot ignore these questions by saying 'everything new is forbidden by the Torah', *i.e.*, anything not explicitly mentioned in the works of our predecessors must be forbidden. And we certainly may not issue permissive rulings on the basis of our own discretion or refrain from answering these questions at all, allowing each person to act as he sees fit. Rather, our duty is to learn the law in doubtful cases from the law in settled cases [*lilmod satum min hamefurash*].

Ouziel does not believe that 'modernity', the period of Jewish history beginning with the Enlightenment and the Emancipation, marks a fundamental break with the rabbinic tradition. Judaism remains a religion of *halakhah*; if halakhists 'in every age' have searched the texts for answers to problems to which the conditions of that time 'give birth', the same procedure suffices for this age as well. This is a rejection of the competing narrative vision, which Ouziel attributes to both conservatives and reformers, that views modernity as essentially alien to the *halakhah*.[90] To oppose an innovation merely because it is an innovation

89. This slogan, adapted from *m. Or.* 3.9, was the watchword of R. Moshe Sofer (d. 1839) in his battle against religious reform. See *Resp. hatam sofer, orah hayim* 28. On the career of Sofer see Katz, *Halakhah vekabalah*, pp. 353-86.

90. A view which leads the conservatives to reject all change and innovation while the reformers reject the *halakhah* itself. *Resp. mishpetey ouziel*, I (Tel Aviv, 1935), pp. viii-x.

is therefore the worst kind of halakhic obscurantism. And, as Ouziel describes the 'facts', such backward thinking is the sum total of the case against women's suffrage.

Law and Literature writers make much of the judicial opinion as a creative narration. The judge's response to the facts of the case, the way he describes them and places them into a narrative framework will largely determine its outcome.[91] That is certainly true here. Without announcing his ruling in favor of women's suffrage—for surely, that ruling must come at the end of his responsum, following a careful weighing of the arguments pro and con—Ouziel 'stacks the deck' in favor of his own view. Reading this 'description of the facts', one forgets that the overwhelming majority of rabbis and halakhic scholars in Palestine and elsewhere actually opposed women's suffrage. One forgets that it was the supporters of political equality for women, rather than its opponents, who 'started' the dispute by advocating a major departure from traditional halakhic practice, predictably incurring the wrath of the conservatives. Instead, one sees a narrow-minded opposition stirring up needless discord in the Jewish community on the basis of forced legal arguments and a wrong-headed conception of how *halakhah* ought to be decided. It is the opponents, rather than the supporters of women's suffrage, who deviate from the 'way of the halakhic authority' by rejecting all innovation; far from being the guardians of tradition, they are its distorters. By casting his opposition in these terms, Ouziel builds a straw man, a foil against which it is easy to mount a successful attack. His 'description of the facts' is actually the first step in achieving his rhetorical purpose: to persuade his audience that his is the correct reading of the *halakhah* on the subject.

The *meshiv* proceeds to outline his response. He will divide the question into two categories, active suffrage (the right to vote) and passive suffrage (the right to be elected or appointed to office), and he will deal with them in order. While this seems a reasonable enough procedure, the decision to begin with the right to vote is also sound argumentative strategy. The halakhic objections against 'active suffrage' were by general estimation not as weighty as those against women exercising political authority.[92] By beginning with the weaker, easily refutable part

91. See Weisberg on Cardozo, at nn. 64-65, above.
92. Some authorities who prohibited women from holding public office nonetheless ruled in favor of their right to vote. See, for example, R. David Zvi Hoffmann, 'Eine Gutachten', *Jeschurun* 6 (1919), pp. 262-66.

of the opposing case, Ouziel creates the impression that the case as a whole is similarly defective.

And, indeed, as we follow Ouziel's discussion of women's right to vote, we learn that the arguments against it are not only unsupported by *halakhah*; they transgress against reason and common sense as well. It would be grossly unfair to subject women to the political and fiscal authority of those 'whom we empower to speak in our name' without allowing them a voice in choosing those representatives. Is women's suffrage a threat to community morality, as some opponents argue? What kind of sexual misconduct can take place at a public polling station? If we fear the mingling of the sexes there, we might as well forbid men and women to visit stores at the same time or to do business with each other. Does it threaten family harmony, encouraging political disputes within the home? If so, then on the same grounds we ought to deny the vote to adult children living at home. Rather, the power of familial love will overcome this disagreement, as it overcomes others which occur naturally in the course of family life.

There is, it turns out, only one 'halakhic' argument against allowing women to vote in elections: a 'new idea' (*davar chadash*) invented by R. Jakob Ritter, who notes that women are never referred to in the biblical tradition as a political community (*kahal* or *'edah*), nor are they numbered in censuses or genealogies; for this reason, they should not take part in making political decisions. Ouziel's response is worth quoting in full:

> Let us grant that women are neither a *kahal*, nor an *'edah*, nor a census, nor a genealogy, nor anything else (*ve-lo kelum*). Yet are they not human beings created in the Divine image, endowed with reason? And do they not have an interest in the activities of the elected assembly, to whose decisions they are subject in matters relating to their property and to the education of their children?[93]

The rhetorical force of this paragraph is clear: the legal objections to 'active' suffrage are so flimsy that its opponents are forced to create

93. J. Ritter, 'Die Frauenwahlrecht nach der Halacha', *Jeschurun* 6 (1919), pp. 445-48. This is unfair to Ritter, who may well have 'invented' his argument in order to give halakhic expression to the long-standing custom under which women have *not* voted in elections and have been represented by their husbands in communal political affairs. At any rate, the same argument is offered by R. Yechiel Michael Tykocinski, *Ha'isha 'al pi torat yisrael* (Jerusalem, 1920), pp. 48-50.

new ones, which are themselves so weak that they need not be taken seriously.

Ouziel similarly rejects arguments based upon talmudic statements which denigrate women's rationality. Such passages as 'women are of unstable temperament' (*Shab.* 33b, *Kid.* 80b) and 'women's sole wisdom lies in spinning yarn' (*Yoma* 66b), he tells us, 'have a completely different meaning'. Were we to apply their literal interpretation and deny them the vote on the basis of their supposed inability to make intelligent decisions, we would have to withhold the vote from irrational or foolish males as well, yet no one is suggesting such a course. More importantly, 'reality slaps us in the face'. Both in the past and in the present, women have attained a level of education and rationality comparable to that of men, and they conduct their personal and business affairs with great acumen. Were these talmudic statements to be read literally, we would expect the opposite, that women would be incompetent to conduct their own affairs. Yet 'have we ever heard that a legal guardian should be appointed for an adult female without her consent?' Whatever their interpretation, these traditional statements offer no barrier to female suffrage.

This first section of the responsum is a prime example of literary and rhetorical values at work in halakhic writing. The language Ouziel employs—the modern Hebrew idiom of the average educated Jew rather than the traditional Hebrew-Aramaic discourse of the *yeshivah*—evokes the ethos of the modern world. The woman he describes—talented, rational, a vigorous participant in public affairs—is quite at home in that world, and her portrait would strike the citizen of that world as natural and familiar. His argument begins with an observation of the contemporary woman as she 'really' is—'are they not human beings created in the Divine image, endowed with reason?'—thus removing the ethical justification for discriminating against her in favor of the male. Indeed, it would violate natural justice and simple fairness to deny suffrage to her. Thus, when we encounter passages in traditional texts which offer a different estimation of the woman, we have no choice but to conclude that they are irrelevant to the present question.

It hardly needs pointing out that Ouziel's literary and argumentative approach is not the only one available to the halakhic authority. As anyone with a cursory knowledge of rabbinic literature knows, there are far more than two texts which touch upon the nature and the intellect of women. The traditional sources are replete with such texts, and taken together they sketch an image of the female which is anything but 'modern' and egalitarian. This fact is certainly not lost upon the *haredim*, the 'extreme' Orthodox opponents of female suffrage. A case in point is the sixty-page pamphlet authored at the height of the controversy by R. Yechiel M. Tykocinski, a noted rabbinic authority.[94] Basing himself upon ample citations from traditional sources, Tykocinski argues that, 'according to the Torah of Israel', the female does not exist in her own right but as helpmeet to the male, eternally subject to his authority. For this reason, she was created with those talents and abilities suited to her specific role. 'The nature which the Creator has bestowed upon her makes her fit for only homemaking, pregnancy, wetnursing, and childrearing',[95] while she possesses neither the intellectual capacity nor the emotional stability to engage in commerce or in legal affairs. Within the domestic sphere she exercises real authority, but her husband represents the family in all matters outside the home. Whenever the sources mention Israel in its public or communal aspects, they refer to the males. Ouziel's theory of representative government, that it is unfair to ask women to obey the laws of representatives whom they do not elect, is alien to the traditional practice in which men represent and speak for their wives in the public realm. To allow the woman to operate as a separate and independent political entity is thus to allow her to intervene in a sphere of activity which Torah denies her, to transgress a line of separation established by divine decree. With this doctrine as his premise, Tykocinski draws what appears to be the natural conclusion: female suffrage stands 'in absolute contradiction to the Torah and its spirit, to the laws and statutes of Israel'.[96]

Ouziel and Tykocinski are both 'Orthodox' rabbis, committed to deriving *halakhah* from sources whose sanctity they both recognize. How then can Ouziel virtually ignore the texts which Tykocinski cites in such abundance and still contend that his ruling is 'halakhic', based upon 'the sources'? The answer, as a rhetorician would tell us, flows from considerations of audience. The goal of any argument is to elicit the adherence of a particular audience to the speaker's conclusion; therefore, the argumentative strategy he chooses will be determined in large part by

94. See n. 93, above. Among many other works, Tykocinski is the author of *Gesher hahayim* (Jerusalem, 1947), on the laws of mourning.

95. Tykocinski, *Ha'isha*, p. 4.

96. Tykocinski, *Ha'isha*, p. 57. This attitude was not restricted to anti-Zionist Orthodox rabbis; see below at n. 110.

the values and assumptions which characterize the audience he addresses.[97] Ouziel, in this case, does not address an audience composed of all observant Jews. He speaks instead to a segment of that group, his fellow members of Mizrachi, the 'national religious' faction of the Zionist movement. Orthodox Zionists differed from their secular nationalist comrades in their loyalty to *halakhah*; nonetheless, affected as they were by the ideological currents which gave rise to Zionism in general, they held much the same modern political values and social outlook as others in the movement. Members of Mizrachi tended either to favor women's suffrage as a matter of progressive politics or to oppose it on political grounds, out of a desire to avoid a divisive split within the *yishuv* and its Orthodox community.[98] Ouziel's task in this responsum is to offer support to this political position, to give it an halakhic rationale. He therefore approaches the issue in contemporary terms, using as his point of departure an image of the contemporary woman which resonates with his modern Orthodox audience. Tykocinski, by contrast, speaks not to moderns but to his fellow *haredim*, who do not partake of the ideological world of the Zionists. Their image of the female is that which emerges from the sacred texts, an image which matches the actual role of women in haredic society today. That is the image invoked by Tykocinski, who never countenances the possibility that 'today's woman' might be different than the one described in Bible, Talmud and midrash.

We must consider this divergence as well from the perspective of narrative. As we have seen, the story Ouziel tells about the *halakhah* is that of a dynamic legal system with the capacity to respond positively to the challenges posed by changing forms of social and political life. According to that narrative, Torah does not forbid 'everything new'. It is not wed to a particular social structure; therefore, a change in that structure, with its attendant transformation of the social relationships between its various groups, does not automatically signal an abandonment of Torah. His silence in the face of the many sources marshalled by the *haredim* is not an admission that his opponents are right, but rather a function of his deeply held view that a new and transformed world requires a new set of halakhic responses. Those sources simply do not apply to the social reality of today, and they may be safely ignored.

97. See above at nn. 53-57.
98. See Friedman, *Chevra vedat*, p. 151; and G. Bat-Yehudah, *Harav maimon bedorotav* (Jerusalem: Mosad Harav Kook, 1979), pp. 232 ff.

Tykocinski, meanwhile, tells a different story about *halakhah*. In his narrative, the traditional sources provide a description of human life not merely as it was in the talmudic period but as it ought to be always, not contingent upon time and place. The fact that women seek a new definition of their social role which diverges from the toraitic ideal is evidence not of 'changing times' but of a willful rejection of divine law. Thus, it is the picture of the woman in the sacred sources, and not the 'contemporary woman' as Ouziel describes her, which serves as Tykocinski's point of argumentative departure.

The point is that considerations of rhetoric and narrative determine both the course of the argument and its conclusion. Ouziel and Tykocinski address separate audiences, each sharing the author's basic 'juristic assumptions', an ideal picture of Jewish religious life and the ultimate purposes of halakhic practice. Neither seriously addresses that segment of the observant community which rejects his 'juristic assumptions'. For this reason, it makes sense to view these responsa as rhetorical performances, essays in practical reasoning, designed to elicit the adherence of particular audiences which define their approach to *halakhah* in the same way as do the authors. Within that context of common understandings, we can say with Richard Posner that judicial persuasion can exist in the absence of proof.[99] Within that context, the responsa seek to persuade; outside of it, they cannot hope to do so.

Ouziel proceeds to consider 'passive suffrage', the right of women to be elected to public office. Here, he notes, we encounter an apparently explicit prohibition: the ruling of Rambam which forbids the appointment of women to any such office. Unlike the arguments against active suffrage, there is nothing artificial about this decision, derived directly from Deut. 17.15: *som tasim aleikha melekh*, 'you shall be free to appoint a king over you'. According to *Sifre*, the word *melekh* means 'a king, not a queen'; Rambam extends the prohibition to 'all appointments' (*kol mesimot she'atah mesim*).[100] To permit women to serve in positions of communal authority, we must somehow refute the view of Rambam, the greatest of codifiers. This is a tall order; 'these are seemingly strong and decisive proofs', writes Ouziel. And it cannot be

---

99. See above at n. 59.

100. See at n. 86, above. I render the verse here according to the latest translations; other versions read 'you shall surely appoint a king over you', *i.e.*, the verse is understood as a positive commandment. This follows *San.* 20b, and see Rambam, *Yad*, *Melakhim* 1.1.

accomplished in the way Hirschenson attempts to do so in his book, namely by suggesting that Maimonides misreads the passage in the *Sifre* upon which his ruling is based. Not only is Hirschenson's own reading of that passage faulty, but his entire approach to Rambam is unacceptable: 'even if we are entitled to disagree with (Rambam), we are not entitled to declare that he errs in the literal understanding of the words of the text'. That kind of scholarly negligence cannot be attributed to a sage of Rambam's stature.

Ouziel's detailed refutation of Hirschenson is an important step in strengthening his own case. The goal, remember, is to construct an halakhic rationale for women's suffrage that is persuasive to a particular audience of observant Jews. No such audience is likely to accept Hirschenson's theory of Rambam's mistaken reading of the *Sifre* passage. Given Rambam's towering halakhic prestige, that audience is much more likely to conclude that it is Hirschenson, writing in Hoboken, New Jersey in the twentieth century, who is mistaken. Ouziel, who like Hirschenson rules permissively, wants to escape guilt by association; he wants to remove any hint that his own decision depends upon an argumentative strategy that cannot hope to persuade even a 'modernist' halakhic audience.

'Rather', he writes, 'we will inquire whether the words of the *Sifre* and the decision of Rambam are the authoritative statement of the *halakhah*.' Is there evidence that this is but a minority or a rejected legal position? One such piece of evidence is the fact that 'this *halakhah* is not mentioned in the Talmud, neither in the Mishnah nor in the Gemara', nor is the prohibition against women holding communal office mentioned by most authorities. And while the lack of an explicit talmudic statement is not a conclusive argument, there is explicit evidence in favor of the opposing viewpoint. Commenting upon the rule in *m. Nid.* 6.4 which apparently disqualifies women from serving in the role of judge, the paradigmatic position of authority, the *Tosafot* notes that the example of Deborah and the midrash on Exod. 21.1 contradict this rule.[101] *Tosafot* offers two possible resolutions to this contradiction. According to the first, a woman is in fact permitted to serve as a judge; the rule in *m. Niddah* does not express the authoritative *halakhah*. This resolution would argue against the ruling of Rambam. According to the second, a woman may indeed not serve as a judge, and Deborah

101. *Tosafot* to *b. Nid.* 50a, *s.v. kol.* The midrash is found in *Kid.* 35a and elsewhere.

'judged' only in the sense that she instructed the actual judges in the laws they should apply. Yet even this second, more restrictive explanation, says Ouziel, allows a woman to serve as 'a legal authority (*moreh hora'ah*) and legislator (*mechokek*)'; is this not an office of authority and honor? 'Thus the position of the *Sifre* is not accepted as the absolute statement of the law (*pesak halakhah muchlat*).'

None of this, of course, proves that the law in fact permits women to hold public office. The *Tosafot* passage, as we have seen, is equivocal,[102] and as Ouziel writes, 'the mind balks' at the thought of rejecting the clear statements of *Sifre* and Rambam 'so long as we cannot find an explicit ruling that contradicts them'. Still, even these admittedly weak arguments raise the possibility that the *halakhah* does not prohibit women's suffrage. And if he has not yet 'proven' the point, by raising this possibility Ouziel achieves an important rhetorical objective: the shifting of the *burden* of proof.[103] As rhetoricians will note, it is not always necessary to 'win' an argument; one may be quite satisfied with a draw, so long as one's opponents fail to make their case. In this instance, Ouziel may not have to prove that the *halakhah* agrees with him against the rabbinic consensus. On the contrary: if another halakhic possibility exists, if Ouziel's opponents can no longer simply presume that the *halakhah* is in accordance with their view, he can argue plausibly that the burden rests upon them to prove that it does. It is

102. Indeed, Ouziel's summary of that passage is a bit too glib. He fails to mention that *Tosafot* also suggests that Deborah may have served as a judge as a result of a special divine decree; if so, her example would be a one-time exception to the rule that women do not serve as judges in any capacity. Nor does he point out that the *Tosafot* passage concludes with the remark that the Talmud Yerushalmi (*Sanh.* 18a; *Shev.* 19a) disqualifies women as judges. In addition, a related *Tosafot* passage which Ouziel does not discuss, *B. Kam.* 15a, *s.v. asher*, rules explicitly that women are ineligible to serve as judges.

103. On the role of burden of proof in legal argument see R.H. Gaskins, *Burdens of Proof in Modern Discourse* (New Haven: Yale University Press, 1992), and R. Alexy, *A Theory of Legal Argumentation* (Oxford: Clarendon Press, 1989), pp. 195-97. Perelman refers to burden of proof as 'the principle of inertia': i.e., an opinion which has been accepted in the past cannot be abandoned without sufficient reason. The theory of 'burden of proof' denotes our reliance upon presumptions and accepted norms, a reliance which makes argument—indeed, all intellectual and social life—possible. See Perelman and Olbrechts-Tyteca, *The New Rhetoric*, p. 106; C. Perelman, 'La raisonment juridique', *Archiv für Rechts- und Sozialphilosophie* 7 (1972), p. 11; and C. Perelman, 'Betrachtungen über die praktische Vernunft', *Zeitschrift für Philosophische Forschung* 20 (1966), pp. 210-21.

they, after all, who have seceded from the *yishuv* over this issue. It is they, in his recounting of the events, who have acted to shatter the political unity of the Jewish population. The legal doubts raised by Ouziel's reading of *Tosafot* suggest at the very least that there is no certain and obvious halakhic warrant for the political extremism of the *haredim*. It is therefore up to them to justify their hard stance. This shift in the burden of proof affords Ouziel a 'worst case' strategy: even if his positive argument fails, even if he does not successfully demonstrate that Jewish law permits female suffrage, he may still contend that it does not obviously deny them the right to equal participation in the political realm. On that basis, given the legal uncertainty on the question, he can successfully urge the Mizrachi position that there is no clear halakhic impediment to the observant community's continued affiliation with the *yishuv* and active involvement in its political life.

He does, of course, want to prove his case, and he bases his positive argument upon a distinction between two types of political appointment: *minu'i*, an appointment made by the Sanhedrin, the supreme legislative and judicial body which existed until the destruction of the Temple, and *kabalah*, election by the people. To Ouziel, the language of Deut. 17.15 (*som tasim*) refers to an appointment by a supreme political authority rather than popular election. According to this reading the Torah forbids the Sanhedrin, a leadership body which is *not* elected by the people, from exercising its appointive powers to set a woman in authority. It does not, however, prevent the people themselves from electing an otherwise ineligible person to office, just as litigants in a court case may agree to appoint as judge a person who is technically disqualified from serving in that position.[104] Ouziel cites several authorities who explain the case of Deborah in this way. She was a valid 'judge' because she was not appointed by the supreme legal institution (*lo minu otah*), but rather was accepted by the people (*hayu mekablim otah*), who agreed to abide by her decisions.[105] Since our system of democratic election, whether by direct plebiscite or by the people's representatives, is a form of *kabalah* and not *minu'i*, 'it is clear that even according to the view of the *Sifre* a woman may be elected as a judge or a leader'.

In this way Ouziel refutes what he sees as the one serious halakhic objection to women's suffrage. Yet the legal theory on which he bases

104. Such as a relative. See *Sanh.* 24a; *Yad, Sanh.* 7.2.
105. R. Nissim Gerondi to Alfasi, *Shevu'ot*, beginning of chapter four (fol. 13a); R. Shelomo b. Adret, *Hidushim, Shevu'ot* 30a.

his permit, that of *kabalah*, is a tenuous one. Ouziel clearly takes that theory farther than do any of his predecessors, and it is highly debatable whether the concept of public election can work as *the* mechanism by which to admit an entire excluded group to virtually all communal offices.[106] Even such a committed Zionist as R. Yitschak Halevy Herzog, who served as Chief Ashkenazic Rabbi of Palestine/Israel alongside the Sefardi Ouziel, rejects the theory. As he puts it, if the Torah expressly forbids women from holding positions of authority, then that prohibition must be addressed to whatever body selects the community's officials. In our democratic regime, that body is the people; therefore, the people may not elect women to public office. Herzog does permit women's suffrage, but he does so by way of a different legal approach. Like Ouziel, he looks to Deut. 17.15, but he focuses upon the word 'king' (*melekh*) rather than *som tasim*, 'appointment'. The word 'king' implies that the restrictions derived by *Sifre* and codified by Rambam refer only to appointments *like those of a king* and function only within *malkhut yisrael*, the monarchical system of government which the Torah had in mind for the people upon their entry into the land. Since the modern state is not a monarchy, it does not qualify as a *malkhut*; officials in a modern state are not, like a king, set in office for life. Thus, the Torah's political theory does not apply to the situation of a democratic regime, and the people are free to elect to office anyone they wish.[107]

Since both Ouziel and Herzog reach the same conclusion, is there any real significance to the fact that they do so in different ways? Law and Literature writers would answer in the affirmative. They would see the argument between the two *poskim* as more than a dispute over which word—'king' or 'appoint'—controls the legal meaning of Deut. 17.15, for that dispute itself reflects not so much a conflict in legal reasoning as a clash of variant 'master narratives', of ways of talking about Torah, and of the unstated assumptions which determine the ultimate choice between interpretive possibilities. They would note that Herzog forges his solution on the basis of a perceived lacuna in the *halakhah*: since the Torah says 'king', it refers only to a monarchical system. For Herzog, that is, the Torah has nothing to say about the constitutional structure of

106. See the critique of the theory of *kabalah* (though not of Ouziel's responsum) by R. Avraham S. Spitzer in *Sefer hayovel le-Ya'akov Rosenheim* (Frankfurt: J. Kauffmann, 1932), Hebrew section, pp. 18 ff.

107. R. Yitschak Halevy Herzog, *Techukah leyisrael al-pi hatorah* (ed. I. Warhaftig; Jerusalem: Mosad Harav Kook, 1989), I, pp. 95-113.

the democratic regime which will inevitably function as the form of government of a modern Jewish state. The permissibility of women's suffrage is derived, as indeed the very constitution of the sovereign Jewish polity is derived, from the silence of the legal sources, from their failure to express an explicit prohibition. To Ouziel, meanwhile, the language of Deut. 17.15 implicitly contains a theory of government which runs broader and deeper than the verse's specific vocabulary might indicate. For Ouziel, as for other halakhists,[108] the Torah's application to the constitution of the Jewish community does not cease with the disappearance of the Davidic dynasty. Jewish law does offer a constitutional structure for a modern state; thus, the permit for women's suffrage stems not from a lacuna in the law but from its positive grant of power to the people to elect their officials.

The dispute, in other words, involves divergent narrative accounts of how the Torah, a text whose explicit language reflects the world of antiquity, relates to the substantially different political reality of our own day. There is, of course, no systemic legal principle by which to evaluate these master narratives, to judge one legally correct and the other incorrect. Narrative, as indicated previously, is not a matter of positive law but rather the framework of history, destiny, and purpose within which all positive law exists and which gives direction to legal thinking. Rather than understand the dispute between Ouziel and Herzog as a purely 'legal' disagreement, Law and Literature would invite us to view it as a clash of two rhetorical approaches, of two ways of constituting community through text. It is in this sense that James Boyd White reads the judicial opinion as a literary text that establishes a relation with its readers by creating an ideal reader, 'the version of himself or herself that it asks each of its readers to become'.

> In every opinion a court not only resolves a particular dispute...it validates or authorizes one form of life—one kind of reasoning, one kind of response to argument, one way of looking at the world and at its own authority—or another. Whether or not the process is conscious, the judge

---

108. R. Avraham Yitschak Hakohen Kook suggested in 1916 that, in the absence of a Davidic king the power of *malkhut* reverts to the people, who may then bestow it upon whomever they choose. See *Resp. mishpat kohen* (Jerusalem, 1937), no. 144, pp. 336-38. R. Shaul Yisraeli develops this suggestion into a full constitutional theory, arguing that the modern democratic regime in Israel is the full constitutional equivalent of the biblical *malkhut*. See his articles in the journal *Hatorah vehamedinah* 1 (1949), pp. 66-78, and 2 (1950), pp. 76-88.

seeks to persuade her reader not only to the rightness of the result reached and the propriety of the analysis used, but to her understanding of what the judge—and the law, the lawyer, and the citizen—are and should be, in short, to her conception of the kind of conversation that does and should constitute us. In rhetorical terms, the court gives itself an ethos, or character, and does the same both for the parties to a case and for the larger audience it addresses...The life of the law is in large part a life of response to these judicial texts.[109]

In his narrow view of the Torah's applicability to the modern political situation, Herzog asks his readers to share his own pragmatic attitude toward our question. In his essay he displays none of Ouziel's affirmative stance toward the idea of female suffrage. He makes it abundantly clear that, in 'my personal opinion', the entry of women into the raging sea of political life is a radical and undesirable departure from Jewish tradition. It is a reform which we ought to oppose with all our strength.[110] Nonetheless, inasmuch as the secular community demands it and we observant Jews are powerless to prevent it, we have no choice but to try to find an halakhic permit for female suffrage. Otherwise, should observant Jews boycott communal elections on the grounds these elections violate Jewish law, they will lose whatever influence they might have upon the future of the new state. For the sake of statehood, a goal to which Orthodox Zionists surely aspire, we must accept constitutional arrangements that in a perfect halakhic world we would reject out of hand. The Torah therefore does not 'permit' women's suffrage; the most we can hope for is its silence, that it restrict its political doctrine to the monarchical regime so as to allow us moderns a space for pragmatic—if not halakhic—maneuver. Herzog's legal argument thus addresses an observant audience characterized by a powerful Zionist ideological commitment, a healthy dose of skepticism as to the fit between that ideology and the parameters of Torah Judaism, and a pragmatism that impels them to force the latter to fit the former. For his part, Ouziel registers no objection at all to women's suffrage; his legal stance on the subject is therefore halakhic rather than pragmatic. That is

109. J.B. White, *Justice as Translation*, pp. 100-102.

110. Herzog also accepts the traditional rabbinic picture of the female ('there are no psychologists greater than our Sages') and on that basis forbids the appointment of women to cabinet positions in the government. For another pro-Zionist rabbi who retains this traditional view—and who also opposes *all* political participation by women—see R. Ovadyah Hadayah, *Resp. yaskil avdi* 5 (Jerusalem, 1981), *hoshen mishpat* 1.

to say, the Torah speaks directly, if implicitly, to the democratic situation and permits us to take this step. It is Jewish law, and not practical necessity or *force majeure*, which warrants the inclusion of women in the political process. This more expansive presentation of the law suggests to Orthodox Zionists a different view of the *halakhah* and a more affirmative conception of their own activity than does Herzog. The *halakhah* does not merely fail to prohibit the constitutional features necessary to a modern state, it positively permits them. Orthodox Zionists need not apologize to other observant Jews for surrendering their halakhic integrity, for acquiescing in political reforms which, though inevitable, violate the letter and spirit of Torah. The acceptance of women's suffrage is no acquiescence. These reforms *are* Torah, and the Orthodox Zionists are its true expounders.

The ways in which Ouziel and Herzog talk about this halakhic issue, and the way that the *haredim* talk about it, are acts of constitutive rhetoric, the articulation of a perspective on the law that defines a particular community and its aspirations. To know what is at stake in the differences among these rhetorical approaches, one cannot be content to ask which *posek* best 'proves' his case. A standard of proof rests upon narrative, assumptions concerning the purpose of Jewish law and halakhic reasoning which these authorities do not hold in common. One must instead look to these texts as literary compositions which employ the tools of practical reasoning in order to argue, to persuade, to justify a particular course of action in the eyes of an audience that shares the writer's master narrative, and, conversely, to rehearse the narrative which helps to create and constitute that audience in the first place. This is the domain of Law and Literature, which demands that we study not solely what the law is 'about' but what it is: a discourse, a culture of argument through which communities formulate and express their deepest self-understandings.

Ouziel concludes with a treatment of the subject of *halakhah* and morality (*musari'ut*): granted that there is no legal bar against the election of women to public office, 'perhaps from the standpoint of morality and modesty there is some prohibition'. These issues, which he briefly considered in his discussion of 'active suffrage', assumed great importance in light of the prohibitive stance of R. Avraham Yitschak Hakohen Kook. The chief Ashkenazic rabbi of Jerusalem and later of Palestine, Kook was a noted writer and sage of *halakhah* and mysticism, a passionate believer in Jewish statehood and in many ways the spiritual leader of the Orthodox Zionist community. His opposition to women's suffrage, which therefore caused no little consternation to the Orthodox Zionists, was based largely on grounds of morality, especially concern over the mixing of the sexes at political meetings.[111] Ouziel confronts this opposition, without mentioning Kook by name, in an essay which occupies a full third of his responsum.

He begins by endorsing Hirschenson's view that 'morality and Torah are identical'. If the Torah does not prohibit women's suffrage in our democratic society, it follows that there can be no moral objection against the practice; 'were there any reason to forbid it on grounds of licentiousness the Torah would not have permitted it'. This statement assumes a narrative view of Torah which explains its commandments and their halakhic expansion as morally sufficient and all-inclusive. There is no ethical or moral standard aside from Torah, which provides all the instruction necessary for moral perfection; thus, there is no need for rabbinical authorities to prohibit on 'moral' grounds anything that the Torah in its wisdom has not already prohibited. This outlook is, if anything, controversial. There is ample indication in the sources of a contrary narrative, one which understands the commandments of the Torah as minimum standards or as broad principles whose precise application cannot be set down in one document. If we were to restrict Jewish observance to the letter of the law, a person could become 'a scoundrel with the Torah's permission' by steeping himself in sensory pleasures which are not expressly forbidden.[112] The authority of the *posek* is not restricted to hard, positive law; it encompasses considerations of community morality, allowing him to prohibit, should the times

---

111. See Kook, *Ma'amarey ha-rayi'ah* (Jerusalem: Mosad Harav Kook, 1984), pp. 189 ff, and Friedman, *Chevra vedat*, pp. 161-63. Kook's approach to the issue was heavily influenced by his mystical thought and by his conception of a well-ordered traditional Jewish family life; see M.T. Nehorai, 'He'arot ledarko shel harav kook bifesikah', *Tarbiz* 59 (1990), pp. 498-502. This conception, which Nehorai calls 'metahalakhic' and rightly underscores as the source of Kook's halakhic ruling, is what Cover would term a 'master narrative'.

112. The classic statement of this view is the comment of Nachmanides to Lev. 19.2. See also his note to Deut. 6.18. On the question of morality versus law in traditional Judaism, see S. Spero, *Morality, Halakha and the Jewish Tradition* (New York: Ktav, 1983), A. Lichtenstein, 'Does Jewish Tradition Recognize an Ethic Independent of Halakhah?', in M. Kellner, *Contemporary Jewish Ethics* (New York: Sanhedrin Press, 1978), pp. 102-23, and B. Herring, *Jewish Ethics and Halakhah for our Time* (New York: Ktav, 1984).

require it, that which the positive law (*din torah*) either permits or does not explicitly forbid. The Torah's 'yes', that is, does not mean that the rabbis cannot say 'no'.[113] Ouziel himself recognizes as much. Though citing Hirschenson's remarks with approbation, he adds that 'still, to render a balanced judgement, we should examine the matter to determine if the fear of licentiousness is a real one'. He realizes, in other words, that an assertion of the identity of Torah and morality is an insufficient response to Kook and his other opponents. He must demonstrate that, even if the rabbis may prohibit on moral grounds something which the law otherwise permits, women's suffrage is in fact not an occasion for immorality and licentiousness.

He begins, as he began his discussion of 'active suffrage', with notions, observations based on *sevara*, logic, empirical observation, and common sense. There is no danger of immoral conduct in public assemblies which gather for serious purposes. Men meet women every day in the marketplace, doing their business with no hint of lewd or licentious behavior; there is no reason to believe that political assemblies will be different. The presumption that there is nothing to fear from the mingling of the sexes at such meetings makes it easier for Ouziel to dismiss the various rabbinic texts which suggest an opposing view. Thus, the prohibition against 'too much conversation with women' (*m. Av.* 1.5) refers only to 'idle, unnecessary chatter' and not to serious debate over public issues. The separation of the sexes at the Temple (*Suk.* 51b) applied only to the mass public gathering of *simchat beit hasho'evah*, whose festive nature was conducive to temptation and immorality. The exclusion of women from the *zimun*, the quorum of three individuals required for the ceremonial public recitation of the grace after meals (*Ber.* 45a), is not out of fear of immodesty. After all, when three males are present women are permitted to remain in that company. And even

---

113. This power is exercised most notably by means of rabbinic *gezerot*, 'legislative' enactments; see Elon, *Hamishpat ha'ivri*, pp. 411-39. In their more 'judicial' function, as well, rabbis will often prohibit on moral grounds actions which the formal *halakhah* permits or to which it offers no clear objection. See J.D. Bleich in A. Steinberg (ed.), *The European Colloquium on Medical Ethics: Jewish Perspectives* (Jerusalem: Magnes Press, 1989), pp. 207ff., and A.T. Rabinowitz, 'He'arot lenose' medini'ut hilkhatit', *Techumin* 2 (1981), pp. 504-12. J. Katz charts the rise of the *da'at torah*, the expression of rabbinic disapproval of matters not clearly forbidden by the *halakhah*, as an important means of Orthodox response to the challenges of modernity; see *Hahalakhah bameitsar* (Jerusalem: Magnes Press, 1992), especially pp. 18-20.

if such a fear exists, it applies only to the special liturgical situation of the *zimun* and does not prevent women from joining other religious assemblies.[114] Indeed, 'with respect to a public gathering on questions of national import, we find that none of the great halakhic authorities has ever expressed' a fear of immoral behavior resulting from the mingling of the sexes.

Once more, Ouziel has mounted what Posner would call 'an aggressive assertion of one side of a balanced dispute'. The problem is not that his interpretation of the halakhic sources is 'wrong', though it may well be.[115] Even if he is right, the absence of an explicit halakhic prohibition hardly accounts for the time-honored custom of separation of the sexes in synagogue or elsewhere. For the *haredim* this separation, reflected in numerous rabbinically imposed restrictions on contact between males and females, lies at the root of the concept of modesty (*tsniyut*) which defines and distinguishes Jewish life: 'the entire history of our people is one long chapter of purity and modesty'.[116] Given this understanding of the nature and destiny of the people of Israel, the opponents of women's suffrage can argue that 'the spirit of the Torah'[117] prohibits the mingling of the sexes at public gatherings, especially political gatherings, where women are out of place. From this perspective, one would cast a jaundiced eye on attempts to find halakhic devices by which to override this prohibition, since such attempts would indicate a willingness to interpret

114. Such as the reading of the *megillah*. Ouziel cites R. Nissim Gerondi (Alfasi, *Megillah*, fol. 6b): were women to help make the quorum for a *zimun*, the resulting liturgical change would call attention to their presence 'and there would be grounds to fear licentious behavior'. In the case of the *megillah*, where women are permitted to join men, there is no liturgical change when a quorum of ten is present. Thus, no attention would be called to the women's presence and there would be no fear of licentiousness. While this explanation is patently forced, it does provide an authoritative account for the halakhic distinction, crucial for Ouziel's case, between *zimun* and *megillah*.

115. For example, Ouziel's restrictive treatment of *Suk.* 51b does not correspond with much traditional thinking. That passage, and especially its continuation in 52a, to which he does not refer, has been cited as the origin of the separation of men and women in synagogues and at other settings which are *not* mass public gatherings for festive occasions. See *Resp. hatam sofer, hoshen mishpat* 190. Herzog (p. 99), on the other hand, supports Ouziel's reading of the talmudic text.

116. Tykocinski, *Ha'isha*, p. 24. The sixth chapter of his pamphlet cites numerous sources which give backing to the concept of gender separation.

117. A term utilized by Rav Kook in his treatment of our question; see n. 111, above.

Jewish law in a way that contradicts its ultimate purpose. The *haredim* thus utilize the concept of *tsniyut* as the starting-point of their reasoning, the narrative background which lends direction to halakhic decision. Ouziel, again, begins his reasoning from a differing narrative perspective. While he certainly accepts the value of modesty in social relationships, he does not link this value to the ideal haredic picture of Jewish life. Since the Torah does not prohibit anything that is 'new', he does not presume that the changes in social relationships which have brought women into the public sphere somehow violate the Torah in letter or spirit. Thus, he assumes no prima facie prohibition against the mingling of the sexes. He begins instead from a much narrower, purely 'legal' starting point. *His* prima facie assumption is that the presence of women together with men at public meetings is permitted unless an explicit prohibition can be found in the halakhic sources. He does not find one, because the existence of such a prohibition depends upon the scholar's interpretive horizon, his master narrative, or his 'Dworkinian' theory of how the law ought to be decided. There is no legal principle inherent in the structure of the *halakhah* which can determine which interpretive approach, that of Ouziel or his opponents, is correct. Each side offers an argument which in the final analysis is convincing only to those who share its 'juristic assumptions', its understanding of the purposes and ends of Jewish law.

To summarize: R. Benzion Ouziel writes in defense of women's suffrage a text which is a thoroughly rhetorical performance. He 'proves' nothing, since at each stage of his responsum he draws conclusions that are legally contestable. Indeed, in the eyes of most halakhic authorities, who disagree with his position, the weight of the legal evidence is clearly against him. Yet for the particular audience he addresses, his performance is masterful. He composes a usable narrative of the Jewish sources on women's role in the public sphere, so that his readers can make the 'negotiated claim' that *halakhah* permits women's suffrage. More than that: his approach on this issue, governed by his 'master narrative' of the nature of halakhic decision in the face of changing times and circumstances, is the basis for a strong version of that 'negotiated claim'. Unlike Herzog, who concedes that the tradition stands in opposition to women's suffrage but who counsels on pragmatic grounds that an halakhic permit be manufactured, Ouziel sweeps away every serious legal and non-legal objection to full political equality for women. True, he does this in many cases by ignoring the multitude of traditional sources which argue against his view. And his arguments are compelling only if one shares his particular brand of *sevara* and common sense, the notion that the active participation of women in the economic and political world is a fact of history, a neutral phenomenon that does not threaten the sanctity or the moral foundations of Jewish life. The *haredim*, as we have seen, do not share these assumptions; if aimed at an haredic audience, Ouziel's responsum will fall upon deaf ears. Yet this is precisely the point made by Perelman and other rhetoricians of the law: the power of a legal argument, like that of any argument, lies in its ability to elicit the adherence of its intended audience to the conclusions it reaches. The responsa of Ouziel, Herzog, Tykocinski, and the others on this issue are inescapably audience-bound. One may call them 'law' or '*halakhah*'; they are also, perhaps primarily, exercises in rhetoric.

Legal realists, pragmatists, critical scholars and all who prefer an economic or social analysis of law would object that the rhetorical approach I have outlined is not the best way to analyze this responsum. They would point to the political context in which Ouziel worked, to his ideological commitments, and they would conclude that what we have here is a political act masquerading as halakhic discourse. Ouziel, they would note, is an Orthodox Zionist providing halakhic cover for a choice made by his Mizrachi comrades out of essentially political motivations. His ruling, in other words, provides backing for the view that legal language is transparent, that law is simply politics (or ideology, or economics) by other means, that the methodologies of the social sciences therefore offer a more fitting tool for the understanding of law than do those of literature and the humanities. I do not reject this critique out of hand. The proponent of a literary approach to the study of law would have to admit, up to a point, its validity. To perceive law as nothing other than literature, as the interpretation of texts and the construction of narrative, is to ignore the fact that 'interpretive horizons' and 'master narratives' emerge from political and ideological commitments and from the ongoing response by legal communities to changing social conditions. Too much research has been done to permit either formalists or Law and Literature scholars to pretend that law remains an autonomous discipline, flourishing in splendid isolation from the environmental influences which give direction to its development and growth.

On the other hand, few adherents of the Law and Literature 'movement' assert such a strong version of its platform. Law, they would agree, is not *only* literature, but they would add that neither is it *only* politics or ideology or economics. When social scientists study law by looking through its language for what the law is 'really' about, they overlook the element of discourse that gives law its unique character. In the case before us, Benzion Ouziel does not appoint himself as a Sanhedrin with the power to declare that women's suffrage accords with the Torah. That is a point he must argue, before both those who oppose and those who share his politics and ideology. His task is to persuade an observant audience of the cogency of his position, utilizing the texts, concepts, and modes of speaking inherent in a tradition of discourse in which both he and his audience participate. His argument is presented in the form of a text, which like all texts is an act of literary art. His use of literary device and rhetorical technique, his points of argumentative departure and assumed burdens of proof are the means by which he creates a textual world, addressing his audience by inviting them to see themselves as his 'ideal reader'. He takes the texts of the past and arranges them in new relationships so that they support new understandings of the *halakhah*. Put differently, the halakhist may derive his values and commitments from a variety of 'real' sources, but what he *does* is to compose texts, sustained arguments as to how the tradition ought to be read, texts which themselves will become part of subsequent halakhic discussion.

The message of Law and Literature is the obverse side of the realist coin: to perceive law as nothing other than politics or economics dressed in an arcane vocabulary is to condemn oneself to an impoverished view of the culture of discourse and argument which law is and has always been. To study law—or *halakhah*—solely through the methodologies of the social sciences is to ignore that culture's very existence. And given the pervasive influence of hermeneutic, narrative, and rhetorical theory over legal theory and indeed the entire range of contemporary intellectual inquiry, it is at the very least difficult to justify a study of Jewish legal texts that refuses to avail itself of the sensibilities and insights afforded by a 'Law and Literature' approach.

A more trenchant critique of the study of responsa as literature is that I have not sufficiently made my case. An analysis of one responsum does not demonstrate the value of any particular method of study toward the genre as a whole. This is especially true, it may be argued, given the politically and ideologically charged nature of this particular question. Granted that Ouziel and his opponents make liberal use of rhetorical technique to justify their positions on women's suffrage, to what extent do rhetoric and narrative play a significant role in rabbinic decisions on more 'ordinary' halakhic subject matter? My sense, the result of impressions gleaned from my own work in the literature, is that rhetoric does indeed play a large role, even the predominant role, in much halakhic decision-making. Rabbinic rulings covering a wide variety of subject matter can be usefully read as persuasive texts, as essays in practical reasoning. This is especially true, I believe, when the question at hand is a 'hard case', a matter of some controversy within the halakhic community, one which seems to allow for more than one 'right' answer, one especially which involves a new issue over which no firm consensus has yet been reached among halakhic practitioners. If so, then the literary approach I suggest here can be an enormously helpful tool in the understanding of what the responsum is and does, of the kind of culture which expresses itself predominantly through this literary form. Needed now are literary and rhetorical studies of many responsa, particularly groups of responsa dealing with similar subject matter, in order to qualify and quantify these impressions beyond the results of the study of one rabbinic decision. That may well be a long and complicated scholarly task, but I am confident it will be a fruitful one.

BIBLIOGRAPHY OF WORKS BY BEN ZION WACHOLDER

Ida Cohen Selavan and Laurel S. Wolfson

A. Books

Nicolaus of Damascus (University of California Publications in History, 75; Berkeley and Los Angeles: University of California Press, 1962).

Eupolemus: A Study of Judaeo-Greek Literature (MHUC, 3; Cincinnati: Hebrew Union College Press, 1974).

Essays on Jewish Chronology and Chronography (New York: Ktav, 1976).

Messianism and Mishnah: Time and Place in the Early Halakhah (Louis Caplan Lecture on Jewish Law; [New York]: Hebrew Union College Press, 1979).

The Dawn of Qumran: The Sectarian Torah and the Teacher of Righteousness (MHUC, 8; Cincinnati: Hebrew Union College Press, 1983).

(with Martin G. Abegg, Jr.) *A Preliminary Edition of the Unpublished Dead Sea Scrolls: The Hebrew and Aramaic Texts from Cave Four* (Washington: Biblical Archaeological Society, 1991-). Two of a projected five volumes have appeared.

B. Articles

'The Halakah and the Proselyting of Slaves during the Gaonic Era', *Historia Judaica* 18 (1956), pp. 89-106.

'Attitudes Towards Proselytizing in the Classical Halakah', *Historia Judaica* 20 (1958), pp. 77-96.

'Cases of Proselytizing in the Tosafist Responsa', *JQR* 51 (1961), pp. 288-315.

'Greek Authors in Herod's Library', *Studies in Bibliography and Booklore* 5 (1961), pp. 102-109. Reprinted in his *Nicolaus of Damascus*, pp. 81-86.

'Pseudo-Eupolemus' Two Greek Fragments on the Life of Abraham', *HUCA* 34 (1963), pp. 83-113.

'How Long Did Abram Stay in Egypt? A Study in Hellenistic, Qumran, and Rabbinic Chronography', *HUCA* 35 (1964), pp. 43-56.

'Qeta' mi-teshubat rishon be-dinei de-garmi', *Sinai* 55 (1964), pp. 323-25.

'Rabad of Posquieres', *JQR* 56 (1965), pp. 173-80.

'A Qumran Attack on the Oral Exegesis? The Phrase *'šr btlmwd šqrm* in 4Q Pesher Nahum', *RevQ* 5 (1966), pp. 575-78.

'Tosaphot yešanim we-hidušei ha-Rabad 'al pereq rišon u-pereq šeni šel Maseket Qidušin', *HUCA* 37 (1966), pp. 65-90.

'Sippurei Rabban Gamliel ba-Mišnah u-va-Tosephta', in *Papers of the Fourth World Congress of Jewish Studies* (Jerusalem: World Union of Jewish Studies, 1967), pp. 143-44.

'Biblical Chronology in the Hellenistic World Chronicles', *HTR* 61 (1968), pp. 123-33.

'The Date of the Mekilta de-Rabbi Ishmael', *HUCA* 39 (1968), pp. 117-44.

'Prolegomenon: A History of the Sabbatical Readings of Scripture for the "Triennial Cycle"', in J. Mann, *The Bible As Read and Preached in the Old Synagogue*. I. *The Palestinian Triennial Cycle: Genesis and Exodus* (New York: Ktav, 1971), pp. xi-lxxxvi.

'Visibility of the New Moon in Cuneiform and Rabbinic Sources' (with David B. Weisberg), *HUCA* 42 (1971), pp. 227-42.

Articles contributed to *Encyclopaedia Judaica* (Jerusalem, 1971): 'Aristeas', II, pp. 438-39; 'Cleodemus Malchus', V, p. 603; 'Demetrius', V, pp. 1490-91; 'Eupolemus', VI, pp. 964-65; 'Hecataeus of Abdera', VIII, pp. 236-37; 'Philo (the Elder)', XIII, pp. 407-408; 'Thallus', XV, p. 1045; 'Theodotus', XV, pp. 1102-103.

'The Calendar of Sabbatical Cycles during the Second Temple and the Early Rabbinic Period', *HUCA* 44 (1973), pp. 153-96.

'A Reply [to Morton Smith]', *JBL* 92 (1973), pp. 114-15.

'Sefirah: Yehudim', *Enṣiqlopediyah ha-'Ibrit* 26 (Jerusalem, 1974), cols. 233-36.

'Chronomessianism: The Timing of Messianic Movements and the Calendar of Sabbatical Cycles', *HUCA* 46 (1975), pp. 201-18.

'Tosaphot yešanim 'al Maseket Yebamot pereq šeliši: yoṣim la-or lephi ketab-yad Sinsinati', in *Texts and Responses: Studies Presented to Nahum N. Glatzer on the Occasion of His Seventieth Birthday by His Students* (ed. M.A. Fishbane and P.R. Flohr; Leiden: Brill, 1975), pp. 285-306.

'Sabbatical Year', *IDB*Sup, pp. 762-63.

'The Letter from Judah Maccabee to Aristobulus: Is 2 Maccabees 1:10b-2:18 Authentic?', *HUCA* 49 (1978), pp. 89-133.

'Jacob Frank and the Frankists' Hebrew Zoharic Letters', *HUCA* 53 (1982), pp. 265-93.

'The Calendar of Sabbath Years during the Second Temple Era: A Response', *HUCA* 54 (1983), pp. 123-33.

'The Beginning of the Seleucid Era and the Chronology of the Diadochoi', in F.E. Greenspahn, E. Hilgert and B.L. Mack (eds.), *Nourished With Peace: Studies in Hellenistic Judaism in Memory of Samuel Sandmel* (Chico, CA: Scholars Press, 1984), pp. 183-211.

'A Qumranic Polemic Against a Divergent Reading of Exodus 6:20?', *Journal of the Ancient Near Eastern Society of Columbia University* 16-17 (1984-85), pp. 225-28.

'The Date of the Eschaton in the Book of Jubilees: A Commentary on *Jub*. 49.22–50.5, CD 1.1-10, and 16.2-3', *HUCA* 56 (1985), pp. 87-101.

'Ezechielus the Dramatist and Ezekiel the Prophet: Is the Mysterious Zōon in the Exagōgē a Phoenix?' (with Steven Bowman), *HTR* 78 (1985), pp. 253-77.

'The Relationship Between 11Q Torah (the Temple Scroll) and the Book of Jubilees: One Single or Two Independent Compositions?', in K.H. Richards (ed.), *Society of Biblical Literature Seminar Papers* (1985), pp. 205-16.

'Josephus and Nicolaus of Damascus', *Josephan Studies* v. IV (1986), pp. 7-45 (Japanese). For English version, see below.

'The "Sealed" Torah Versus the "Revealed" Torah: An Exegesis of Damascus Covenant V, 1-6 and Jeremiah 32, 10-14', *RevQ* 12 (1986), pp. 353-67.

'David's Eschatological Psalter: 11Q Psalmsª', *HUCA* 59 (1988), pp. 23-72.
'Does Qumran Record the Death of the Moreh? The Meaning of *he'aseph* in Damascus Covenant XIX, 35, XX, 14', *RevQ* 13 (1988), pp. 323-30.
'Josephus and Nicolaus of Damascus', in L.H. Feldman and G. Hata (eds.), *Josephus, the Bible, and History* (Detroit: Wayne State University Press, 1989), pp. 147-72.
'Rules of Testimony in Qumranic Jurisprudence: CD 9 and 11Q Torah 64', *JJS* 40 (1989), pp. 53-74.
'The Ancient Judaeo-Aramaic Literature (500–164 BCE): A Classification of Pre-Qumranic Texts', in L.H. Schiffman (ed.), *Archaeology and History in the Dead Sea Scrolls: The New York University Conference in Memory of Yigael Yadin* (Sheffield: JSOT Press, 1990), pp. 257-81.
'The Fragmentary Remains of 11QTorah (Temple Scroll): 11QTorahᵇ and 11QTorahᶜ plus 4QparaTorah Integrated with 11QTorahª' (with Martin G. Abegg, Jr), *HUCA* 62 (1991), pp. 1-116.
'Ezekiel and Ezekielianism as Progenitors of Essenianism', in D. Dimant and U. Rappaport (eds.), *The Dead Sea Scrolls: Forty Years of Research* (Leiden: Brill, 1992), pp. 186-96.
'Geomessianism: Why Did the Essenes Settle at Qumran?', in S.F. Chyet and D.H. Ellenson (eds.), *Bits of Honey: Essays for Samson H. Levey* (Atlanta: Scholars Press, 1993), pp. 131-38.
'A Note on E. Tov's List of Preliminary Editions of the Unpublished Dead Sea Scrolls', *JJS* 44 (1993), pp. 129-31.

C. *Book Reviews (A Partial Listing)*

G. Aha, *The Sheeltot*, *JQR* 53 (1959), pp. 258-61.
I. Twersky, *Rabad of Posquieres: A Twelfth-Century Talmudist*, *JQR* 55 (1965), pp. 174-80.
J. Neusner, *Development of a Legend: Studies on the Traditions Concerning Yohanan ben Zakkai*, *JBL* 91 (1972), pp. 123-24.
J.P.M. van der Ploeg *et al.*, *Le targum de Job de la grotte 11 de Qumran*, *JBL* 91 (1972), pp. 414-15.
M. McNamara, *Targum and Testament: Aramaic Paraphrases of the Hebrew Bible*, *JBL* 93 (1974), pp. 132-33.
A.J. Saldarini, *The Fathers according to Rabbi Nathan (Abot de Rabbi Nathan), Version B: A Translation and Commentary*, *JBL* 96 (1977), pp. 622-23.
B.E. Thiering, *Redating the Teacher of Righteousness*, *JBL* 101 (1982), pp. 147-48.
H.W. Attridge and R.A. Oden, Jr, *Philo of Byblos: The Phoenician History*, *JBL* 102 (1983), pp. 333-34.
E.J. Bickerman, *The Jews in the Greek Age*, Hadassah (Feb. 1989), pp. 44-45.
L.H. Schiffman, *The Eschatological Community of the Dead Sea Scrolls: A Study of the Rule of the Congregation*, *JBL* 110 (1991), pp. 147-48.
M.O. Wise, *A Critical Study of the Temple Scroll from Qumran Cave 11*, *JBL* 111 (1992), pp. 329-31.

INDEXES

INDEX OF REFERENCES

OLD TESTAMENT

Genesis		9.27	131, 132,	11.8	61
1–11	52		134	11.10-18	56
1	26, 33	10–11	53	11.10	48, 56
1.1	16, 17, 68	10	47, 48, 52-	11.18-19	60
1.3-5	26, 113		55, 58-62,	11.27	48
1.3	26		66, 354	11.31	62
1.6	193	10.1	48, 51, 54	12.5	62
1.14-19	113	10.2-5	48	12.6	66
1.14	99	10.2	56	12.15	190
1.15	26	10.3	54	13.11	144
1.16-17	102	10.5	48	13.12	62
2.4	48	10.6-20	48	15	66
2.10-14	62	10.7-9	54	15.1	336
2.20	336	10.8-19	52	15.9-19	130
3.8-14	66	10.8-12	49, 53	15.9	130
4	38	10.15	54	15.17	123, 130
4.8	38, 40, 41	10.18	49	16.3	62
5.1	48	10.19	49, 125	17.8	62
5.24	275	10.20	48	17.14	287
6.9	48	10.21-31	48	17.20	123
7.11-12	66	10.21	53, 54, 60	18	122
7.12	66	10.22	56	18.20	123
7.19-24	210	10.23	50	18.31-32	122
8–10	54, 55	10.24	49, 51	22.10-12	122
8.2-4	54	10.25-30	52	25.12	48
8.2-3	54	10.25-29	49	25.18	125
8.11-12	54	10.25	49, 57	25.19	48
8.22-27	54	10.29-31	54	30.32-43	186
8.29-30	54	10.29	54	35.22	38, 40, 41
9.18-19	51	10.30	49	36.1	48
9.20-27	55	10.31	48	36.4	48
9.24	55	10.34	54	36.9	48
9.25-26	55	11	53	36.12	122
9.25	53, 55, 67	11.1-9	53	37.2	48
9.26	55	11.2	60	37.11	199

38.26	314	34	58	20.2	134, 139
43.33	219	34.2	67	20.11	124
44.11-12	199			20.14	124
49.1	127	*Deuteronomy*		20.17	123, 134
49.3-27	122	1.7	134	23.17	41
49.3	127	1.8	133	23.18	38, 40, 41
49.10	129	2.8	38, 40, 42	24.8	129
		4.25	127	25.3	311
Exodus		4.30	127	25.17-19	126
10.23	26	4.31	127	25.17-18	126
12.2	16	5.16	176	25.19	126-28
17.8-17	126	6–11	134	26.2	131
17.14	126	6.10	133	27	134
20.12	176	6.18	403	27.9	129
21.1	396	7.1	134	27.14-26	130
22.28	189	7.2	123	28	134
32.16	27	7.25-26	132	28.65	316
33.22	92	7.26	123	29.12	133
34.7	316	9.5	133	29.22	125, 127
34.10-16	132	9.27	133	30.20	133
38.21	31	12–26	128, 132, 134	31.29	127
		12.1–26.15	125	33	317
Leviticus		12.1	124	33.28	316
10.1	194	12.5	131	34.4	133
10.9	194	12.11	131		
10.16-20	284	12.14	131	*Joshua*	
12	285	13	123, 140	3.3	129
12.2-5	66	13.12-18	125	8.33	129
13–14	285	13.14-18	123	10	58
15	285	13.16-18	123	14.2	58
18.29	312	13.16	124	15.1	58
19.32	232, 234	14.23	131	17.4	58
26	317	15.12	76	18.6	58
26.10	232	16.2	131	18.8-9	58
26.38	316	16.6	131	19.51	58
		16.11	131		
Numbers		17.9	129	*Judges*	
1.51	317	17.14-20	143	3.9	181
3.1	48	17.14	143	3.11	180
11.16	232, 234	17.15	395, 398-400	3.12	190
14.30	131			3.13	192
19	279	17.18	129	3.15	180, 183, 186-88
24.14	127	18	140		
24.15-17	127	18.1-8	129	3.16	183, 194, 196
25.1-9	179	18.1	129, 130		
25.19	38, 40, 42	18.6	132	3.17	193, 256
26	42, 58	20	123, 124	3.19	194, 195
31.19	280				

3.20	182, 195, 197, 255	*Jeremiah*		19	22, 24, 26-33, 38
3.21	183, 196	7.3	131	19.2-7	22
3.22	193, 117	7.7	131	19.2-5	22
3.24	193, 195, 196, 185	7.12	131	19.2	23, 29, 30
3.25	196, 198	13.12	38	19.3	30, 32
3.26	92	31.1	316	19.4	22
3.28	185	33–34	130	19.5	21, 31
3.29	199	33	129, 135	19.8-10	22, 24, 29
3.30	181, 184	33.17	129, 130	19.8	20, 25, 30
6.12	313	33.18	129, 130	19.9	24, 31
13.8	197	34.8-9	76	19.10	32
14.1-16	179	34.17-20	130	20	38
20.18	38			69.16	183
		Ezekiel		78.60	131
1 Samuel		3.16	38	104.12	337
4.1	38	13.10	75	111	18
10.11	38	14.7	75	111.6	16, 68
10.22	38	18.3-4	316	141.10	92
12.3-5	314	43.19	129		
12.3	171	44.15	75, 129, 130	*Job*	
14.12	38	47.32	75	1.18	92
14.19	38, 92			7.19	92
16.2	38	*Hosea*		20.5	92
16.12	38	1.2	38		
				Proverbs	
2 Samuel		*Amos*		8.22	25
7.11	127	7.5-6	316	8.27	26
7.14	127	9.11	79		
19.8	38			*Ruth*	
23.10	140	*Jonah*		2.4	313
		4.2	92		
1 Kings				*Song of Songs*	
3.27	314	*Micah*		1.12	92
13.20	38	3.12	318		
17–18	206	7.11	75	*Esther*	
				2.22	197
2 Kings		*Habakkuk*		7.9	197, 199
9.22	92	1.6	140	9.27	313
10.1-3	197				
		Zechariah		*Daniel*	
Isaiah		8.4	318	2.16	199
8.2	318			3.29	190
27.13	316	*Malachi*		5.7	200
45.17	315	3.10	313, 314	5.9	200
				6.7	190
		Psalms		6.8	92
		1–59	22, 23	6.9	190
		1–50	28		

6.13	92	7	82	1.7	48
7	267	8.7-8	78	9.2	129
7.7-8	262	8.8	226	10.8	140
7.8	268	10.29	129	11.13	140
7.12	92	10.35	129	17.3	38
7.24	262, 268	11.20	129	24.7-18	145
7.25	92	11.36	146		
		12	78	*2 Chronicles*	
Ezra		13	82	5.5	129
2	78	13.16-21	249	23.18	129
9–10	82	13.23-29	249	29.12	38
10.5	129	13.28	250	29.14	38
38.12	59	13.30-31	82	30.27	129
				34.26	38
Nehemiah		*1 Chronicles*			
1.9	131	1.4-23	47		

APOCRYPHA

Ecclesiasticus		20.27-31	174	42.9-14	174
1–2	175	21.12-28	174	42.15–43.33	174
1.1-27	174	23.22-26	174	44–50	175
1.1-10	174	24.1-34	174	44.16–45.26	167
3–16	167	24.23-34	171	45.6-22	171
3.1-16	175	24.33	170	45.23-26	170
4.11-19	174	25.7-11	173	46.19	171
4.20–6.17	174	25.13–26.27	174	50.1-21	171
5.4-6	166	31.1	198	50.27-29	173
6.18-37	174	32.16	166	51	165
7.20	166	33.7-15	174	51.13-30	165, 174
7.25	166	33.14-15	174	51.13-20	165
7.27-28	176	33.16-19	172	51.30	165
7.29-31	170	34.9-13	172		
9.1-9	174	34.21–35.20	170	*1 Maccabees*	
9.17–11.28	174	36.26-31	174	1.11	255
10.19	166	37.16-26	174	1.13	255
10.31	166	38.1-15	174	1.14	255
14.20–15.10	174	38.9-11	170	1.15	255, 257
15.11–18.14	174	38.24–39.14	174		
15.11-20	173	38.24–39.11	174	*2 Maccabees*	
15.14	166	38.34–39.8	171	4.7-9	253
15.15	166	39.12-35	174	4.8	253
15.19	166	39.14-35	174	4.9	243-45, 253
15.20	166	39.27–44.17	164, 168	4.10	253, 254, 257
16.3	166	40.1-17	174		
16.24–17.14	174	40.18-27	173	4.11-15	257
18.7	176	41.1-13	174	4.11	253, 254
19.20-24	174	42–50	171	4.12	254

4.13-14	254	4.19-20	252	11.27	244
4.13	253, 254	4.19	245	11.34	244
4.14	253, 254	4.49	258	12.48	257
4.15	254	5.15	257		
4.17	254	6.8	257	*Wisdom of Soloman*	
4.18	256	11.22-26	244	13-15	149

NEW TESTAMENT

Matthew		13.20	266	*Galatians*	
24.22	266			3.13	302
27.9	333	*Acts*			
28.19	162	6.9	162	*Ephesians*	
		17.22-31	162	2.11	289
Mark		17.28	162		
1.2-3	272, 333				
2.25-26	333				

PSEUDEPIGRAPHA

1 Enoch		83.1	266	5.15	269
1.2	275			7.17	269
12.1-2	275	*2 Enoch*		7.23	269
14.8–19.3	275	3–12	275	8.18	269
19.21-36	275	10.7	260	8.26	269
19.71	275	11.36-38	275	9.12	269
73.4-8	111	13.77-78	275		
73.4	113	18.1-3	275		
80.2-8	120			*Jubilees*	
80.2	264	*4 Ezra*		1.15-17	86
87.3-4	275	4.26	266	1.17	87
89	86	4.33	266	1.26-29	86, 87
89.36	86	6.21	266	1.26	87
89.50	86			1.27	96
89.56	261	*Ascension of Isaiah*		1.29	86, 87, 96
89.61-64	263	1.4	269	4.17-24	260
89.73-74	86	1.5	269	4.21	275
90	86	1.7	269	4.23-25	275
90.17	263	1.13	269	4.23	275
90.29	86, 87	3.13	269	5.5	59
91.11-17	81	3.17	269	7	55
91.13	261	3.18	269	7.7-12	55
93.1-10	81	3.28	269	7.10-11	55
106.7	275	4.3	269	7.10	55
		4.6	269	7.11	55
2 Baruch		4.9	269	7.12	55, 131
20.1	266	4.18	269	7.13-17	55
54.1	266	4.21	269	7.13	55, 56

7.14	56	8.22	59	10.28-34	61
7.15	56	8.24	59	10.28	61
7.16	56	8.25-29	59	10.29	61
7.17	56	8.29	59	10.31	61
7.18-19	56	8.30	59	10.32	61
7.19	56	9	59	10.33	61
7.26	56	9.1	59	10.34	61, 62
8–10	47, 48, 55, 68, 69	9.9	59	10.35	62
		9.10	59	23.25	267
8–9	62	9.14-15	59		
8	58	9.14	60	*Liber Antiquitatum*	
8.1-10	56	9.15	60	*Biblicarum*	
8.5	57	10	60	4–5	47
8.7	57	10.1-14	54, 60	48.1	273
8.8	57	10.3	73		
8.9	57	10.4	60	*Letter of Aristeas*	
8.10	57	10.12-13	60	213–216	198
8.11-30	58	10.14	60		
8.11	57, 58	10.15-17	60	*Odes of Soloman*	
8.12-21	58	10.18-19	60	3.5	269
8.12	58, 59	10.18	60	3.7	269
8.17	58	10.20-26	61	7.1	269
8.18	58	10.22	61	8.21	269
8.20	58	10.25	61	38.11	269
8.21	58, 59	10.27-36	61		
8.22-24	59	10.27	61		

QUMRAN

1QH		19.2-3	140	*1QapGen*	
2.17	146			12–17	47
2.21	73	*1QS*		19.25	274
8.30	94	1–2	130		
15.11	144	1.10-15	113	*1QpHab*	
		3.13	146	2.5	127
1QM		6.16-21	94	2.11	140
1.6	134	6.16-17	94	6.6	146
2	142, 147	6.17	94	9.6	127
2.1-4	145, 147	6.21	94		
2.1	142, 143	7.19-20	94	*4Q174*	
2.2	142, 145	8.26	94	1.2	127
2.10	146	9.16	73	1.12	127
7.10	144	10.19	73	1.15	127
8.7	94			1.19	127
10.2	139	*1QSa*			
12.10	140	1.1	127	*4Q252*	
18.2	134	1.7	140, 146	1.1–2.5	135
19	140	12.9	51	2.7	131-34

2.8	131, 133	45.13	132	2.9	92
2.11-14	130	45.14	132	2.10	93
3.2-6	122	46.4	132	2.13	75
3.5-6	123	46.12	132	2.14	78
3.5	124	47.4	132	2.17	92
3.6	124	47.11	132	2.21	93
3.12-13	133	47.18	132	3.6	80
4.1-3	122, 126	51.7	132	3.13	77, 78, 80,
4.2-3	126	53.9	132		92
4.2	127	54.11	140	3.14	77
4.3–6.3	133	54.15	140	3.15-16	78
5.1-2	129	56.5	132	3.19	77, 92
5.5	130	59.9	90	3.21–4.4	75, 130
5.7	127	61.2	140	4.1	75
		61.3	140	4.3-4	77
4Q268		61.4	140	4.4	127
1.8	93	63.14-15	90	4.6	78
				4.8	92
4Q385		*11QTS*		4.12-13	79
2–3	265	15.5	146	4.12	75
		56	146	4.13	77
4Q471		56.12-21	143	4.15	80
1.1-3	141	56.12	144	4.19	75
1.3	141	56.13	143	5.5	92
1.7	141	57	146, 147	5.20	77
1.8	141	57.1-5	143	6.2	78
2.2	141	57.5-14	143	6.4	78
2.7	141	57.5-11	143	6.7	78
3.3-4	141	57.6	143	6.10	78, 92
3.3	141	57.7	143	6.11	127
3.5	141	57.8	145	6.12-13	79
		57.9	143	6.14	80
4Q507		57.10	145	6.15	73
1.3	94	57.11-15	143, 147	6.17	80
		57.11-12	143	7.6	76, 77
4QSecond Ezek.		57.11	143	7.14-20	79
4.3	265	57.12	145	7.18-20	127
		57.13	145	7.18	78
11QT		58.3	143	8.8	81
29	85-89, 95			8.11	75
29.3-10	88	*11QTorah*		8.16	81
29.7-10	132	56–59	147	8.18	75
29.8-10	85, 86			9.1	74
29.9	85, 88, 91,	*CD*		9.18	92
	95, 96	1.4	77	10.3	92
42.16	89	1.5	77	10.4	93
43.6-9	90	1.13	75	10.6	140
45.12	132	2.1	73	10.7	92

10.10	92	13.1	93	16.9	92
10.18	82	13.2	140	19.24-25	75
10.21	77	13.14	73	19.31	75
11.2	74	14.3	74	20	81
11.14-15	74	14.7	92	20.1	92
11.17	79	14.9	92	20.5	92
11.22	79	14.15	78	20.13	77
12.5	92, 93	14.16	77	20.14	92
12.6-8	76	15.5	75	20.15-16	77
12.6-7	74	15.11	92	20.17	93
12.8-10	74	15.12	78	20.20	93
12.8	77	15.15	78, 92, 93	20.23	92
12.12	92	15.26	73	20.24	81
12.15	92	16.3	146	22.7	75
12.19	77	16.4-5	79	22.29	75
12.22	77	16.5	78		
12.23	92	16.8	92		

MISHNAH

Ab.		*Ker.*		*Pes.*	
1.5	404	2.1	282, 286, 291	8.5-6	279
3.2	182			8.8	278, 279, 286, 287, 291
'Abod. Zar.		*Mak.*			
3.1-3	297	3.15	307		
3.1	302	3.15A-D	311	*Šeq.*	
3.7	297			8.1	283
		Meg.			
Bet.		1.5C	312	*Sanh.*	
2.2	283			7.2	398
		Miq.		7.6	295, 296
Ed.		10.8	284		
5.2	278, 279, 288			*Soṭ.*	
		Ned.		9.12A	308
		3.11	289		
Ḥag.				*Yom.*	
2.5-6	283	*Nid*		3.3	283
3.3	285, 286	6.4	396	7.1	31
3.6	283	10.7	286		
Kel.		*'Or.*			
1.8	251	3.9	389		

TALMUDS

b. 'Abod. Zar.		7b	297, 298	41a	302
6a	297, 298	19b	295	42b-43a	297

42c	302	*b. Mak.*		*b. Šab.*	
42d	295	23A-B	311	33b	392
43b	297			116a	294
47b	297	*b. Meg.*			
		3a	226	*b. Šeb.*	
b. Bek.				30a	387
27b	286	*b. Ned.*		36c	284
		32b	273		
b. Ber		37b	226	*b. Šeq.*	
45a	404			19a	397
		b. Nid.			
b. Erub.		49b	387	*b. Soṭ.*	
32a	285	50a	396	47b	266
				48b	309
b. Giṭ.		*b. Pes.*			
456	294	36a	288	*b. Suk.*	
		36b	280	51b	404, 405
b. Ḥag.		36d	288, 291	52a	405
21a	286	59a	285		
24b	285	63a-b	280	*b. Yeb.*	
		92a	281-83,	108a	284
b. Ḥul.			287, 288	69b	284
133a	296			71b	283, 288
13b	294	*b. Sanh.*			
		18a	397	*b. Yom.*	
b. Kam.		20b	395	66b	392
15a	397	24a	398	69b	298
		28d	295		
b. Kidd.		44a	299	*b. Zeb.*	
35a	396	60b	295	100b	284
80b	392	64a	295, 296		
		64b	295	*j. Meg.*	
		91a	67	4.1	226

TOSEFTA

t. Abod. Zar.		*t. Ohol.*		*t. Soṭ.*	
3.12	289	18.18	284	3.13-14	309
				13.4	310
t. Ker.		*t. Pes.*		14.10	266
1.11-12	291	7.14	286		
		8.18	289	*t. Yeb.*	
t. Miq.				6.7	284
6.11	289	*t. Šab.*			
		13.5	294	*t. Zab.*	
t. Neg.		15.9	287	1.1	284
8.9	283				
		t. Šeq.			
		3.20-22	291		

MIDRASH

Gen. R.		61.6	67	Ruth R.	
1.1	69	99.3	181	2.9	182
1.2	16				
1.11	69	Lev. R.		Sifre	
3.5	26	20.8-9	194	131	295
26.3	273				
36.8	226	Meg. Ta'an.			
38.13	274	3.5	67		

PHILO

De Abrahamo		De Josepho		78	229, 232, 234
2.53	222	99	222	79	233, 234
De Agricultura		Legatio ad Gaium		De Sobrietate	
18	224, 229	2.12	251	32–33	222
De Cherubim		Quod Omnis Probus Liber sit		De Somniis	
105	227-29	23	149	1.53-54	236
De Confusione Linguarum		80	236	1.205	224, 228, 229
		141	149		
14	222	De Opificio Mundi		De Specialibus Legibus	
De Congressu Eruditionis Gratia		136	222	1.8	234
		137	222	1.261	283
15	229				
53	236	Quaestiones in Genesin		De Vita Mosis	
74	224, 229	1.32	222	1.4	222, 231, 233, 234
148	224	2.79	222		
148	228, 229	4.196	222	1.13	222
148-50	230				
		De Sacrificiis Abelis et Caini			
Quod Deus sit Immutabilis		77–79	231		
133	222				

JOSEPHUS

Antiquities of the Jews		1.14	179	1.93-94	203, 205
1.5	177	1.30	193	1.94	204
1.8	177	1.58-59	206	1.94-95	206
1.9	177	1.89	210	1.95	209
1.10-12	177	1.92	210	1.107-108	205, 208
1.12	177	1.93	204, 210	1.107	203, 204

1.108	209	4.152-53	187	7.126	187
1.109-39	47	4.158	209	7.129	187
1.112	189	4.207	189	7.142	188
1.117	191	4.328-331	185	7.147	198
1.118-119	205	5.118	185	7.301	188
1.118	202-204	5.132	184	7.302	188
1.119	203, 204	5.179	184, 190	7.390-391	185
1.155	188	5.184	180	8.144-49	203, 205, 206
1.157	212	5.185-97	180	8.144	204
1.158-160	205	5.185	190	8.157	203-205, 211
1.158-59	203	5.186	180, 190, 191	8.205	191
1.158	204	5.188	183, 187, 188, 197	8.209	192
1.159-60	206	5.189	187, 197, 200	8.211	185
1.159	202, 204	5.190	196, 197, 200	8.253	204, 205
1.165	190	5.191	187, 196	8.253-62	203, 211
1.167-68	274	5.192	189, 200	8.260	204, 205
1.176	189	5.193	184, 193, 196, 198	8.262	209
1.177	199	5.194	185, 194	8.314	191
1.232	187	5.195	185, 198, 200	8.315	185, 187
1.240-41	202	5.196	198, 199	8.324	203-206
1.240	203-206	5.197	181, 184	8.356	192
1.241	189	5.198	190	8.370	192
1.256	185	5.217-18	187	8.409	192
1.269	186	5.255	191	8.415	192
1.346	185	5.257	188	9.118	187
2.12	199	5.258	189	9.126	197
2.89	190	5.260	189	9.182	185
2.94	189	5.261	189	9.283-287	205
2.133	199	5.280	197	9.283	203, 204
2.173	186	5.286-317	179	10.18-20	203, 205
2.196	185	5.298	188	10.18	204
2.198	185	5.310	197	10.19-20	211
2.201	190	5.317	185	10.20	204
2.212-216	198	6.84	191	10.34	203-205
2.237	189	6.111	188	10.36	185
2.290	185	6.177	188	10.44	192
2.348	209	6.210	188	10.45	192
3.19	185	6.292-294	185	10.76-77	187
3.23	184	6.343-350	185	10.198	199
3.49	188	7.13	187	10.217	190
3.81	209	7.16	187	10.219-228	205
3.300	185	7.101	203-206	10.219-26	203, 204
4.2	185			10.227	203, 204
4.12	191			10.227-28	203
4.105	189			10.228	203, 204
4.106	189			10.236	200
4.131-55	179				
4.140	191				

10.238	200	18.167	187	1.69-218	208
10.254	190	18.372	250	2.39	250
10.256	188	19.54	185	2.135	178, 186
11.207	197	20.262	177	2.148	178, 188
11.261	197, 199			2.190-219	175
11.266	197	*Apion*			
11.306-309	250	1.1	178	*Life*	
11.344	248	1.1-6	214	2080-10	198
12.77ff.	159	1.2-3	207	54	249
12.100	159	1.2-5	212	56	249
12.119	250	1.16	212		
12.142	253, 255	1.73	214	*War*	
12.145	251	1.74	214	1.126	187
12.240-41	255	1.130	214	2.587	192
12.258	248	1.142	214	3.351-43	198
12.260	253	1.183	202	3.358	188
14.68	184	1.218	202	5.194	251
14.115	250	1.279	183	7.43	250
15.417	251	1.309	189	7.196	188

JEWISH AUTHORS

Maimonides
Laws of Idolatry
3.2   294
9.4   295

CHRISTIAN AUTHORS

Augustine
Exposition of the Psalms
50.19   337

Locutiones in Heptateuchum
3.32   337

On Christian Doctrine
2.13.19   337
4.20.40   337

Barnabas
3.6   269
4.3   264, 265
4.3-4   265
4.4   264, 265, 267
4.1-6   262

4.3   261, 263-65, 268, 269, 272
4.3-4   265, 272, 277
4.4   262-65, 267, 268
4.5   262, 268
4.8   269
12.1   264, 265, 269
16.5   261
16.6   261

Eusebius
Praeparatio Evangelica
8.6.5   223
9.17.9   273

9.18.1   274
9.21.13   219
9.29.1   219, 220
9.29.16   220
13.12.1-2   150, 161
13.12.6   162
13.12.9-11   150
13.12.13-16   155

Hippolytus
Refutatio
9.16.4   269

Jerome
Against Rufinus
2.11   344

Apology against Rufinus
1.7   345

Epistles
11.2.1	328
21.42	328
21.42.3	339
28.2	335
28.5.1	334
36.12	335
48.4	338
52.9.3	338
57.2.2	330, 332
57.2.3	331
57.5.1	331
57.5.2	321, 329, 334
57.5.5	330
57.5.a	334
57.6.3	330, 332
57.6.8	329
57.7-9	333
57.7.4	333
57.9.1	333
57.9.8	333
57.10.4	333
57.11.2	333
57.11.4	330

57.12.1-2	331
57.12.3-4	340
61.2.2	344
74.6.2	328
80.1.2	339, 343, 344
80.2.2	344
83.1.1	345
84.12.2	345
85.3.2	345
97.3.1	340
99.1.2	342
106.17.1	336
106.3.2-3	340
112.19.1	337
114.1.2	342
114.3.1	340, 342
118.1.9-11	328

Praef.-Chron.
1.7–2.2	326
2.12-15	327
2.16-20	329
3.4-9	327
3.14-18	327

5.1-6	328
5.16-19	327

Justin Martyr
Apology
1.20	271

Lactantius
Divine Institutes
7.15.9	276
7.16.1-3	268
7.16.10	266

Origen
Apology
2.19	345

Contra Celsum
1.60	274

Pseudo-
  Clementine
Homilies
9.3-6	274

CLASSICAL

Acta Archelai
12.7-11	271

Arrian
Anabasis
2.24.5	252
2.24.6	252
3.6.1	252

Cicero
De Oratore
1.34.155	323

De finibus
1.3.10	340
3.2.5	340
3.4.15	321

De natura deorum
1.4.8	340

*De optimo
  genere oratorum*
5.14	343
6.18	323
7.23	323

Curtius
4.2.10	252
4.3.19	252

Dio Chrysostom
Orationes
36.40-41	275

Diodorus Siculus
2.6.7	213
2.8.5	213
2.17.1	213
2.21.8	213
17.46.6	252

18.7.1	257
20.14.1	252
40.3.4	189

Dionysius of Halicarnassus
1.13.1-4	213

Dionysius Thrax
Ars grammatica
1	225

Euripides
Medea
340-41	199

Herodotus
1.209-10	276
2.123	209

Horace
Art of Poetry
133   321

Juvenal
Satires
6.450-56   235
7.230-36   235
14.103-104   189

Libanius
Orationes
11.91-92   250

Livy
1.27-28   186
2.12   184

Malalas
201.12-202.6   250

Meleager
Greek Anthology
5   250
7   250
419   250

Pausanias
10.4.1   257

Pliny
Epistles
7.9.2-3   323
7.9.3   323

Natural History
11.97   275

Plutarch
De Isid. et Osir.
46   276

Porphyrius
De Antro Nympharum
6   275

Vita Plotini
16.15-20   274

Quintilian
Institutio Oratoria
1.4.2   227, 229
1.4.3   237
1.8.18-21   235
1.9.1   227
10.5.2-3   323

Rufinus
Apology against Jerome
2.44   345

Seneca
De brevitate vitae
13   235
13.9   235

Epistles
88.2-8   235
88.3   227
88.6-8   235
88.37-40   235

Sextus
Adversus Mathematicos
1   236, 238
1.49   230
1.57-58   224
1.91   226, 229
1.92-93   226
1.92   230
1.93   229, 235, 238, 339
1.96   226
1.97-99   230
1.97   226
1.131-32   230
1.175   230
1.176   230
1.206   238
1.218   238
1.247   226
1.248   226
1.252   226
1.253   239
1.269   226
1.270-320   238, 239, 241

1.270   226, 229, 238
1.280   238
1.310   238
1.313   239
1.316   238
3.64   238
5.49   238
5.73   238
7.62   238
7.78   238
7.109   238
7.260   238
7.397   238
8.56   238
8.62   238
8.99   238
8.112   238
8.118   238
8.122   238
8.139   238
8.142   238
9.2   238
9.41   238
10.111   238
11.15   238

Outlines of Pyrrhonism
1.34   238
1.113   238
1.116   238
1.124   238
2.42   238
2.101   238
2.105   238

Strabo
Geography
3.4.4-5   213
12.8.5   213
17.1.12   250
17.1.32   250

Suetonius
De grammatica
  et rhetorica
20   234

Tacitus
Histories
5.5.1   189

Thucydides
2.53.1   191
6.2.1   209

OSTRACA, PAPYRI AND TABLETS

ACh Supp   Nabnitu XXII   403.8   43
33.17   43   263   43
                          Nbk

Abegg, M.G. 93, 98, 102, 120, 136, 138, 139, 141
Abel, F.M. 244, 248
Adam, A. 270
Albani, M. 100
Aichele, G. 367
Alexandre, M. 228, 230
Alexander, P.S. 53, 63, 68
Allegro, J.M. 121, 127
Alon, G. 284
Alter, R. 193
Amir, Y. 151, 152, 233
Anderson, B.W. 15
Andreas, F.C. 271
Aptowitzer, A. 68
Attridge, H.A. 155, 203
Austin, J. 371

Bacher, W. 68, 226
Bagrow, L. 46, 47
Baillet, M. 101, 137-39, 141
Ballaban, S. 359
Bamberger, B.J. 216-18
Barak, A. 371
Bardy, G. 322
Bartelink, G.J.M. 329
Barthélemy, D. 166
Barwick, K. 224, 225, 227, 229, 230
Bat-Yehudah, G. 386, 394
Baumgarten, J.M. 83, 101, 147
Baumgartner, W. 21
Bécares Botas, V. 238
Beck, R. 274, 275
Beckson, K. 42
Beckwith, R. 120
Beentjes, P.C. 171, 172
Belkin, S. 216

Bell, A.A. 355
Bellioti, R.A. 383
Ben-David, A. 251
Bentham, J. 371
Benveniste, É. 269, 276
Berlin, N.Z.Y. 382
Bernstein, M. 122, 123, 128, 131, 147
Bernstein, R.J. 369
Betz, O. 236
Bevan, E.R. 243, 244
Bickerman, E.J. 104, 109, 151, 215, 232, 243-46, 249, 251, 252, 258, 283
Bidez, J. 265, 266, 268, 274, 276, 277
Billerbeck, P. 282
Blatt, F. 335, 347
Bleich, J.D. 383, 387, 404
Blenkinsopp, J. 51-53
Boccaccini, G. 71
Bogaert, P.-M. 180
Bohlen, R. 175
Bonfil, R. 351, 353, 354
Bonner, S.F. 227, 235, 238
Bonnet, C. 252, 255
Booth, W. 377
Borgen, P. 216
Bousset, W. 266, 273-76
Bowman, J.F. 368
Bowman, S. 350
Boyce, M. 266, 271, 272, 277
Braude, W.G. 27, 33
Bréhier, E. 218
Brichto, H.C. 41
Brock, S. 336
Brooke, G.J. 97, 121, 130
Brown, R.E. 121
Brox, N. 150
Büchler, A. 68

Burton, S.J. 377

Callaway, P. 88
Cardozo, B.N. 378, 379, 390
Carter, L.H. 381
Cavallera, F. 329, 332
Charles, R.H. 57, 59, 67, 260, 261, 267
Charlesworth, J.H. 91, 97
Childs, B.S. 15
Chwolson, D. 353, 357
Clifford, R.J. 15
Cohen, C. 183
Cohen, G.M. 249
Cohen, S.J.D. 203, 204, 209, 278, 283,
    301
Collins, J.J. 15, 151, 153
Colson, F.H. 227-30, 232, 233, 235, 237,
    238, 241
Conzelmann, H. 151, 159
Cooper, A. 25, 32, 38
Courcelle, P. 322
Cover, R.M. 374, 385
Craigie, P.C. 28
Cuendet, G. 335
Cumont, F. 265, 266, 268, 269, 274, 276,
    277

Daube, D. 184
Davidson, H.A. 19, 24, 31
Davies, P.R. 71, 79, 81, 92, 93
Deissmann, A. 232
Delcor, M. 87, 248
Delling, G. 149, 151, 157
Delorme, J. 256
Dewey, J. 377
Dewing, H.B. 68
Di Benedetto, V. 226, 237
Di Lella, A.A. 166, 168
Dimant, D. 87, 97, 138, 264, 265
Donato, J. 372
Doran, R. 219, 221
Douzinas, C. 372
Downey, G. 250
Drews, R. 211, 215
Dunlop, C.R.B. 367
Dupont-Sommer, A. 93, 94
Dworkin, R. 366, 371, 372

Eisenman, R. 98, 111, 121, 126, 136
Eissfeldt, O. 253
Elkins, J.R. 373
Ellenson, D. 362, 385
Elon, M. 360, 361, 363, 383, 385, 404
Erbse, H. 238
Eshel, E. 136, 137, 141-44
Eshel, H. 136, 141-44
Even-Shemuel, Y. 267

Feldman, L.H. 178, 182, 187, 198, 199,
    202, 282
Fish, S. 372, 377, 384
Fiss, O. 367
Fitzmyer, J.A. 121, 263, 274
Fleischer, E. 353
Flesher, P. 278, 282
Flügel, G. 270
Flusser, D. 266, 268, 272, 277, 350-58
Ford, J.M. 119
Fordyce, C.J. 184
Fortuna, S. 226
Fraenkel, J. 217, 218
Frankel, Z. 361
Fraser, P.M. 157, 221, 256
Frede, M. 230, 255
Freehof, S.B. 361, 385
Freudenthal, J. 148, 220, 222
Friedman, M. 185, 386, 387, 394
Fritz, K. von 150
Frye, N. 375
Fuks, A. 248

Gadamer, H.G. 369, 372
Ganz, A. 42
Gärtner, B. 95
Gaskins, R.H. 397
Gaster, M. 274
Gauthier, P. 256
Geertz, C. 374, 377
Gemmette, E.V. 365
Ginsburg, C.D. 37, 38, 40, 41
Ginzberg, L. 25, 180, 216, 273
Glaser, O. 195
Glessmer, U. 99, 100, 111, 121
Gnuse, R. 198
Golb, N. 354
Goldstein, J.A. 54, 257

Goodenough, E.R. 234
Gordis, D.H. 385
Gottheil, R.J.H. 274
Gowan, D.E. 52
Grabbe, L.L. 216
Graetz, H. 35, 38, 357, 385
Grainger, J.D. 247, 255
Greenfield, J.C. 47, 51
Grelot, P. 260
Gressmann, H. 266
Grey, T.C. 369, 370
Griboment, J. 347
Grinzel, F.K. 104
Gudeman, A. 219, 220, 225, 237
Gutman(n), Y.(J.) 161, 219, 221

Haas, P.J. 360, 362
Habicht, C. 255, 256, 258
Hadas, M. 220
Hadayah, O. 401
Hadot, J. 173
Hagendahl, H. 322, 328
Halevy, C.D. 386
Halivni, D. 288, 291, 385
Halpern, B. 194-96
Hanhart, R. 160
Hart, H.L.A. 371
Haspecker, J. 173, 176
Hatzopoulos, M.B. 256
Haupt, P. 34
Haynes, D.N. 377
Hayward, R. 273
Heinemann, I. 149, 159, 221, 223, 240
Hengel, M. 91, 151, 161, 247, 248, 250, 251, 257
Henning, W.B. 270, 271
Herford, R.T. 298
Herget, J.E. 367
Herring, B. 403
Herzog, Y.H. 399-402, 405-407
Hilberg, I. 343
Hiley, D.R. 368
Hilgard, A. 225
Hill, G.F. 247
Hinnells, J.R. 265
Hirschberg, H.Z. (J.W.) 68
Hirschenson, R.C. 388, 396, 403, 404
Hoffmann, D.Z. 390

Holladay, C.R. 202, 220, 221
Holmes, O.W. 378
Hölscher, G. 63
Hominer, H. 350, 351
Hood, R.T. 48, 62
Hoppenbrouwers, H.W.F.M. 325
Horowitz, G. 248
Horst, P.W. van der 149, 155, 219
Hoy, D.C. 369, 372
Hultgård, A. 275-77
Hunger, H. 44
Hunzinger, C.-H. 137
Hutchinson, A. 375

Idel, M. 18, 21
Instone Brewer, D. 216, 218
Isaac, B. 249

Jackson, A.V.W. 274, 276
Jackson, B.S. 361, 365, 373
Jacobs, L. 383
Jacobson, H. 121, 122
Jacoby, F. 211, 214
Jastrow, M. 35
Jeremias, J. 249, 251
Jouguet, P. 257
Joüon, P. 144

Kadman, L. 246
Kahana, Y.Z. 361, 383
Kamesar, A. 39, 220, 222, 231, 235, 241, 242
Kamin, S. 16
Kaminka, A. 226
Kapstein, I.J. 27, 33
Kasher, A. 247, 251, 253, 255, 257, 258
Katz, J. 299, 384, 385, 404
Katz, S.T. 294
Kaufman, S.A. 88
Kellman, M. 366
Kemp, A. 224
Kieweler, V. 172
Kippenberg, H.G. 266
Kister, M. 121, 123, 136, 141, 264, 265, 269, 272
Klinck, D.R. 365, 373, 377
Knibb, M.A. 54, 264
Knohl, I. 98, 100, 101

Koehler, L. 21
Koenen, L. 270, 271
Kook, A.Y.H. 400, 402-405
Kraabel, T.A. 159
Kraeling, E.G. 194, 195
Kraft, R.A. 263
Kraus, H.-J. 22, 23
Krauss, S. 39
Kroll, W. 241
Kuhl, C. 35
Kuhn, K.-G. 93, 159
Kuhn, T.S. 368

Laidlaw, W.A. 251
Lake, K. 261-63
Landau, E. 281, 282
Lane, J. 372
Launey, M. 249, 257
Laurence, R. 260
Lauterbach, J.Z. 361
Lawlor, H.J. 261, 264
Le Rider, G. 246
Lee, T. 175
Levenson, J.D. 15
Levinson, S. 365, 369, 370
Lewy, H. 218
Lewy, J. 68
Leyh, G. 370, 372
Licht, J. 94
Lichtenstein, A. 403
Lichtheim, M. 172
Liddell, H.G. 39
Lieberman, S. 280, 289, 291, 294
Lifshitz, B. 363
Lim, T.H. 121
Loader, J.A. 125

MacKenzie, D.N. 270
Macdonald, J. 182
Mack, B.L. 175, 216, 217
Maier, J. 87, 89
Mailloux, S. 365, 370
Malachi, Z. 354
Malhan, J. 381
Mann, J. 354, 355
Marböck, J. 173, 174
Margulies, M. 281
Marti, H. 322, 337

Mazor, L. 15
McCloskey, D.N. 377
McConville, J.G. 129
McCready, W. 83, 84
McGinn, B. 266, 268, 276
McIntosh, S.C.R. 370
McVeigh, S. 372
Méasson, A. 232
Megill, A. 377
Mendel, G. 249
Mendels, D. 91
Mendelson, A. 232, 234
Meyer, E. 243
Michelini, A. 39
Middendorp, T. 170, 172
Milgrom, J. 87, 95
Milik, J.T. 54, 99-101, 112, 113, 121, 138, 140, 264
Millar, F.G. 244, 247, 248, 250, 294
Millard, A. 42, 43
Miller, G.P. 367, 381
Minow, M. 374
Mitchell, W.J.T. 369, 373
Molé, M. 275
Momigliano, A. 151, 158, 202, 215, 248, 274
Moore, G.F. 195
Morfill, W.R. 261
Müller, B.A. 230
Murphy-O'Connor, J. 93
Mørkholm, O. 244

Nadel, B. 184
Nash, C. 373
Nehorai, M.T. 403
Nelson, J. 377
Nelson, M.D. 168
Neugebauer, O. 105, 110, 111, 120
Neuschäfer, B. 225, 226, 229, 238, 239
Neusner, J. 67, 297, 299-301
Newton, R. 105
Nickelsburg, G.W.E. 54, 87
Nicolai, R. 237
Nida, E. 322, 329
Niditch, S. 16
Niese, B. 202, 243, 244
Nikiprowetzky, V. 223
Nilsson, M.P. 103, 257

Norden, E. 338
Novak, D. 16
Oesch, J.M. 37
Ohr, A. 35, 37
Olbrechts-Tyteca, L. 376, 397
Opelt, I. 326
Oppenheim, A.L. 43
Ouziel, B.M.H. 386-402, 404-408
Oxtoby, W.G. 121

Papke, D.R. 365, 373, 375
Pardo, D. 283
Parker, R.A. 101, 109
Paschke, F. 160
Pease, A.S. 247
Penar, T. 167
Perdrizet, P. 249
Perelman, C. 376, 377, 397
Perrot, C. 180
Peters, A. 47, 248, 250
Petit, M. 223
Pfann, S.J. 111
Pilhofer, P. 158
Plassart, A. 256
Polinsky, A.M. 366
Posner, R. 365-68, 372, 378, 379, 395, 405
Powels, S. 119
Prato, G.L. 174
Prigent, P. 263
Pritsak, O. 354
Puech, H.-C. 273

Qimron, E. 47, 51, 86, 92, 265

Rabbinowicz, R.N. 297
Rabin, C. 73, 93, 267
Rabinowitz, A.T. 404
Rad, G. von 131, 134
Rahlfs, A. 41, 179
Rajak, T. 203, 204, 206, 209, 213, 221
Ramus, P. 375
Reed, S.A. 137
Reeves, J.C. 271, 274
Reiner, E. 43
Reiterer, F.V. 167, 251
Rendtorff, R. 19
Richter, H.-P. 121

Rickenbacher, O. 166, 174
Ritter, J. 391
Robert, L. 256
Robinson, J.M. 98, 111
Robinson, R.B. 51
Rokeah, D. 151
Römer, C. 271
Rorty, R. 376
Rösel, H.N. 195, 196
Rosenbaum, M. 69
Rostovtzeff, M. 247-49, 256
Rüger, H.P. 167
Runia, D.T. 233
Rutherford, W.G. 224, 237, 239
Ryan, M. 374

Sacks, O. 71
Sadurski, W. 377
Samuelson, N. 16
Sanders, E.P. 71, 283, 291
Sanders, J.A. 165
Sanders, J.T. 171, 172
Sanderson, J.E. 124
Sandler, P. 36
Sandmel, S. 216-18, 236, 240
Sarat, A. 374
Sarton, G. 359
Saulcy, L. de 246
Schalit, A. 258
Schäublin, C. 225
Schauer, F. 383
Scheiber, A. 354
Schiffman, L.H. 89, 90, 92, 97, 282, 293
Schmidt, F. 59, 63
Scholem, G. 29, 273
Schubert, K. 161
Schuller, E. 138
Schürer, E. 110, 151, 152, 203, 244, 251, 282
Schwartz, D.R. 127
Schwartz, W. 348
Scopello, M. 275
Scott, R. 39
Segal, M.Z. 36
Sela, S. 351, 356-58
Sevenster, J.N. 159
Seyrig, H. 246
Shaked, S. 266

Shaw, F. 39
Sherman, B. 370
Shusterman, R. 368
Siebenborn, E. 225, 230
Siegert, F. 159, 222
Siegfried, C. 216, 222, 231, 233
Silbermann, A.M. 69
Simon, M. 294
Simons, H.W. 376, 377
Singer, J.W. 367
Skehan, P.W. 168
Skinner, J. 50
Skinner, Q. 369
Slater, W.J. 226, 227, 229
Smith, M. 97, 137
Soloveitchik, H. 360
Speiser, E.A. 52
Spero, S. 403
Speyer, W. 150
Spitzer, A.S. 399
Sragow, H.M. 199
Stadelmann, H. 170, 171
Starcky, J. 244, 252
Stegemann, H. 91, 122, 126, 159
Stein, E. 216, 222, 231, 233
Steinschneider, M. 359
Steinthal, H. 228, 237
Stern, M. 158, 244, 251, 282
Strack, M.L. 256
Stroumsa, G.G. 270
Strugnell, J. 136, 141, 264, 265
Stückelberger, A. 241
Swete, H.B. 41

Ta-Shma, I. 355
Talmon, S. 36, 37, 98, 100, 101
Tardieu, M. 270
Tcherikover, V.A. 151, 152, 243-45, 247, 248, 251, 253, 254, 257, 258
Teachout, P.R. 367
Teixidor, J. 121
Testuz, M. 63
Thackeray, H.StJ. 177, 184, 191
Thiersch, H. 248, 250
Tov, E. 41, 141, 161
Treitel, L. 216, 217
Trenchard, W.C. 174, 175
Treu, K. 160

Tucker, G. 385
Tuckerman, B. 104
Tushnet, M. 372
Tykocinski, Y.M. 391, 393-95, 405, 407

Urbach, E.E. 385
Usener, H. 225, 227

Vaillant, A. 261
Van Seters, J. 51
Van Unnik, W.C. 149
VanderKam, J.C. 46, 54, 56, 59, 96, 97, 100, 260
Vattioni, F. 166
Vaux, R. de 101
Vermes, G. 89, 244
Villain, M. 331
Visotzky, B.L. 293, 295
Völker, W. 236
Voss, B.R. 321

Wacholder, B.Z. 34, 70, 85, 86, 88-90, 92, 93, 95-100, 102, 121, 128, 132, 136, 139, 141, 147, 149, 151, 202, 221, 245, 275, 350, 356, 358, 359
Walbank, F.W. 211, 213
Walter, N. 150-52, 154, 155, 158, 219-21, 241
Warren, A. 364
Warrington, R. 372
Wasserstrom, R. 377
Wechsler, H. 383
Weinfeld, M. 125, 126
Weinrib, E.J. 383
Weisberg, R. 365, 366, 372, 373, 379, 381, 390
Wellek, R. 364
Wellhausen, J. 351, 357, 358
Wellman, V.A. 377
Wendel, C. 225
West, R.L. 367, 372, 375
Westermann, C. 50-52
White, H. 373
White, J.B. 365, 366, 379, 380, 400, 401
Widengren, G. 265, 270, 273
Wiese, K.M. 194
Wikenhauser, A. 329
Wilensky, S.H. 29

Wills, L. 88
Wilson, A.M. 88
Wilson, B.R. 72
Wilson, R.R. 52
Windisch, H. 274, 276, 277
Winkelmann, F. 322, 346
Winston, D. 266, 274
Wintermute, O.S. 96
Wise, M.O. 87, 89, 97, 100, 121, 126, 128, 136
Wolfson, E.R. 19
Wolfson, H.A. 233

Woude, A.S. van der 139
Wright, B.G. 169

Yadin, Y. 85-87, 89, 91, 92, 95, 132, 139, 164
Yeivin, I. 34
Yisraeli, S. 400

Zevin, S.Y. 386
Ziegler, J. 165, 166
Zyskind, H. 376

JOURNAL FOR THE STUDY OF THE OLD TESTAMENT

Supplement Series

1   I, HE, WE AND THEY:
A LITERARY APPROACH TO ISAIAH 53
D.J.A. Clines
2   JEWISH EXEGESIS OF THE BOOK OF RUTH
D.R.G. Beattie
3   THE LITERARY STRUCTURE OF PSALM 2
P. Auffret
4   THANKSGIVING FOR A LIBERATED PROPHET:
AN INTERPRETATION OF ISAIAH CHAPTER 53
R.N. Whybray
5   REDATING THE EXODUS AND CONQUEST
J.J. Bimson
6   THE STORY OF KING DAVID:
GENRE AND INTERPRETATION
D.M. Gunn
7   THE SENSE OF BIBLICAL NARRATIVE I:
STRUCTURAL ANALYSES IN THE HEBREW BIBLE (2nd edition)
D. Jobling
8   GENESIS 1–11:
STUDIES IN STRUCTURE AND THEME
P.D. Miller
9   YAHWEH AS PROSECUTOR AND JUDGE:
AN INVESTIGATION OF THE PROPHETIC LAWSUIT (*RIB* PATTERN)
K. Nielsen
10   THE THEME OF THE PENTATEUCH
David J.A. Clines
11   STUDIA BIBLICA 1978 I:
PAPERS ON OLD TESTAMENT AND RELATED THEMES
Edited by E.A. Livingstone
13   ISAIAH AND THE DELIVERANCE OF JERUSALEM:
A STUDY OF THE INTERPRETATION OF PROPHECY
IN THE OLD TESTAMENT
R.E. Clements
14   THE FATE OF KING SAUL:
AN INTERPRETATION OF A BIBLICAL STORY
D.M. Gunn
15   THE DEUTERONOMISTIC HISTORY
Martin Noth
16   PROPHECY AND ETHICS:
ISAIAH AND THE ETHICAL TRADITION OF ISRAEL
Eryl W. Davies

17 THE ROLES OF ISRAEL'S PROPHETS
    David L. Petersen
18 THE DOUBLE REDACTION OF THE DEUTERONOMISTIC HISTORY
    Richard D. Nelson
19 ART AND MEANING:
    RHETORIC IN BIBLICAL LITERATURE
    Edited by David J.A. Clines, David M. Gunn & Alan J. Hauser
20 THE PSALMS OF THE SONS OF KORAH
    Michael D. Goulder
21 COLOUR TERMS IN THE OLD TESTAMENT
    Athalya Brenner
22 AT THE MOUNTAIN OF GOD:
    STORY AND THEOLOGY IN EXODUS 32–34
    R.W.L. Moberly
23 THE GLORY OF ISRAEL:
    THE THEOLOGY AND PROVENIENCE OF THE ISAIAH TARGUM
    Bruce D. Chilton
24 MIDIAN, MOAB AND EDOM:
    THE HISTORY AND ARCHAEOLOGY OF LATE BRONZE AND
    IRON AGE JORDAN AND NORTH-WEST ARABIA
    Edited by John F.A. Sawyer & David J.A. Clines
25 THE DAMASCUS COVENANT:
    AN INTERPRETATION OF THE 'DAMASCUS DOCUMENT'
    Philip R. Davies
26 CLASSICAL HEBREW POETRY:
    A GUIDE TO ITS TECHNIQUES
    Wilfred G.E. Watson
27 PSALMODY AND PROPHECY
    W.H. Bellinger, Jr
28 HOSEA:
    AN ISRAELITE PROPHET IN JUDEAN PERSPECTIVE
    Grace I. Emmerson
29 EXEGESIS AT QUMRAN:
    4QFLORILEGIUM IN ITS JEWISH CONTEXT
    George J. Brooke
30 THE ESTHER SCROLL:
    THE STORY OF THE STORY
    David J.A. Clines
31 IN THE SHELTER OF ELYON:
    ESSAYS IN HONOR OF G.W. AHLSTRÖM
    Edited by W. Boyd Barrick & John R. Spencer
32 THE PROPHETIC PERSONA:
    JEREMIAH AND THE LANGUAGE OF THE SELF
    Timothy Polk

33 LAW AND THEOLOGY IN DEUTERONOMY
J.G. McConville

34 THE TEMPLE SCROLL:
AN INTRODUCTION, TRANSLATION & COMMENTARY
Johann Maier

35 SAGA, LEGEND, TALE, NOVELLA, FABLE:
NARRATIVE FORMS IN OLD TESTAMENT LITERATURE
Edited by George W. Coats

36 THE SONG OF FOURTEEN SONGS
Michael D. Goulder

37 UNDERSTANDING THE WORD:
ESSAYS IN HONOR OF BERNHARD W. ANDERSON
Edited by James T. Butler, Edgar W. Conrad & Ben C. Ollenburger

38 SLEEP, DIVINE AND HUMAN, IN THE OLD TESTAMENT
Thomas H. McAlpine

39 THE SENSE OF BIBLICAL NARRATIVE II:
STRUCTURAL ANALYSES IN THE HEBREW BIBLE
David Jobling

40 DIRECTIONS IN BIBLICAL HEBREW POETRY
Edited by Elaine R. Follis

41 ZION, THE CITY OF THE GREAT KING:
A THEOLOGICAL SYMBOL OF THE JERUSALEM CULT
Ben C. Ollenburger

42 A WORD IN SEASON:
ESSAYS IN HONOUR OF WILLIAM MCKANE
Edited by James D. Martin & Philip R. Davies

43 THE CULT OF MOLEK:
A REASSESSMENT
G.C. Heider

44 THE IDENTITY OF THE INDIVIDUAL IN THE PSALMS
Steven J.L. Croft

45 THE CONFESSIONS OF JEREMIAH IN CONTEXT:
SCENES OF PROPHETIC DRAMA
A.R. Diamond

46 THE BOOK OF JUDGES:
AN INTEGRATED READING
Barry G. Webb

47 THE GREEK TEXT OF JEREMIAH:
A REVISED HYPOTHESIS
Sven Soderlund

48 TEXT AND CONTEXT:
OLD TESTAMENT AND SEMITIC STUDIES FOR F.C. FENSHAM
Edited by W. Claassen

49   THEOPHORIC PERSONAL NAMES IN ANCIENT HEBREW:
      A COMPARATIVE STUDY
      Jeaneane D. Fowler
50   THE CHRONICLER'S HISTORY
      Martin Noth
      Translated by H.G.M. Williamson with an Introduction
51   DIVINE INITIATIVE AND HUMAN RESPONSE IN EZEKIEL
      Paul Joyce
52   THE CONFLICT OF FAITH AND EXPERIENCE IN THE PSALMS:
      A FORM-CRITICAL AND THEOLOGICAL STUDY
      Craig C. Broyles
53   THE MAKING OF THE PENTATEUCH:
      A METHODOLOGICAL STUDY
      R.N. Whybray
54   FROM REPENTANCE TO REDEMPTION:
      JEREMIAH'S THOUGHT IN TRANSITION
      Jeremiah Unterman
55   THE ORIGIN TRADITION OF ANCIENT ISRAEL:
      1. THE LITERARY FORMATION OF GENESIS AND EXODUS 1–23
      T.L. Thompson
56   THE PURIFICATION OFFERING IN THE PRIESTLY LITERATURE:
      ITS MEANING AND FUNCTION
      N. Kiuchi
57   MOSES:
      HEROIC MAN, MAN OF GOD
      George W. Coats
58   THE LISTENING HEART:
      ESSAYS IN WISDOM AND THE PSALMS
      IN HONOR OF ROLAND E. MURPHY, O. CARM.
      Edited by Kenneth G. Hoglund, Elizabeth F. Huwiler, Jonathan T. Glass
      & Roger W. Lee
59   CREATIVE BIBLICAL EXEGESIS:
      CHRISTIAN AND JEWISH HERMENEUTICS THROUGH THE CENTURIES
      Edited by Benjamin Uffenheimer & Henning Graf Reventlow
60   HER PRICE IS BEYOND RUBIES:
      THE JEWISH WOMAN IN GRAECO-ROMAN PALESTINE
      Léonie J. Archer
61   FROM CHAOS TO RESTORATION:
      AN INTEGRATIVE READING OF ISAIAH 24–27
      Dan G. Johnson
62   THE OLD TESTAMENT AND FOLKLORE STUDY
      Patricia G. Kirkpatrick
63   SHILOH:
      A BIBLICAL CITY IN TRADITION AND HISTORY
      Donald G. Schley

64 TO SEE AND NOT PERCEIVE:
    ISAIAH 6.9-10 IN EARLY JEWISH AND CHRISTIAN INTERPRETATION
    Craig A. Evans
65 THERE IS HOPE FOR A TREE: THE TREE AS METAPHOR IN ISAIAH
    Kirsten Nielsen
66 SECRETS OF THE TIMES:
    MYTH AND HISTORY IN BIBLICAL CHRONOLOGY
    Jeremy Hughes
67 ASCRIBE TO THE LORD:
    BIBLICAL AND OTHER STUDIES IN MEMORY OF PETER C. CRAIGIE
    Edited by Lyle Eslinger & Glen Taylor
68 THE TRIUMPH OF IRONY IN THE BOOK OF JUDGES
    Lillian R. Klein
69 ZEPHANIAH, A PROPHETIC DRAMA
    Paul R. House
70 NARRATIVE ART IN THE BIBLE
    Shimon Bar-Efrat
71 QOHELET AND HIS CONTRADICTIONS
    Michael V. Fox
72 CIRCLE OF SOVEREIGNTY:
    A STORY OF STORIES IN DANIEL 1–6
    Danna Nolan Fewell
73 DAVID'S SOCIAL DRAMA:
    A HOLOGRAM OF THE EARLY IRON AGE
    James W. Flanagan
74 THE STRUCTURAL ANALYSIS OF BIBLICAL AND CANAANITE POETRY
    Edited by Willem van der Meer & Johannes C. de Moor
75 DAVID IN LOVE AND WAR:
    THE PURSUIT OF POWER IN 2 SAMUEL 10–12
    Randall C. Bailey
76 GOD IS KING:
    UNDERSTANDING AN ISRAELITE METAPHOR
    Marc Zvi Brettler
77 EDOM AND THE EDOMITES
    John R. Bartlett
78 SWALLOWING THE SCROLL:
    TEXTUALITY AND THE DYNAMICS OF DISCOURSE
    IN EZEKIEL'S PROPHECY
    Ellen F. Davies
79 GIBEAH:
    THE SEARCH FOR A BIBLICAL CITY
    Patrick M. Arnold, S.J.
80 THE NATHAN NARRATIVES
    Gwilym H. Jones

81   ANTI-COVENANT:
       COUNTER-READING WOMEN'S LIVES IN THE HEBREW BIBLE
       Edited by Mieke Bal

82   RHETORIC AND BIBLICAL INTERPRETATION
       Dale Patrick & Allen Scult

83   THE EARTH AND THE WATERS IN GENESIS 1 AND 2:
       A LINGUISTIC INVESTIGATION
       David Toshio Tsumura

84   INTO THE HANDS OF THE LIVING GOD
       Lyle Eslinger

85   FROM CARMEL TO HOREB:
       ELIJAH IN CRISIS
       Alan J. Hauser & Russell Gregory

86   THE SYNTAX OF THE VERB IN CLASSICAL HEBREW PROSE
       Alviero Niccacci
       Translated by W.G.E. Watson

87   THE BIBLE IN THREE DIMENSIONS:
       ESSAYS IN CELEBRATION OF FORTY YEARS OF BIBLICAL STUDIES
       IN THE UNIVERSITY OF SHEFFIELD
       Edited by David J.A. Clines, Stephen E. Fowl & Stanley E. Porter

88   THE PERSUASIVE APPEAL OF THE CHRONICLER:
       A RHETORICAL ANALYSIS
       Rodney K. Duke

89   THE PROBLEM OF THE PROCESS OF TRANSMISSION
       IN THE PENTATEUCH
       Rolf Rendtorff
       Translated by John J. Scullion

90   BIBLICAL HEBREW IN TRANSITION:
       THE LANGUAGE OF THE BOOK OF EZEKIEL
       Mark F. Rooker

91   THE IDEOLOGY OF RITUAL:
       SPACE, TIME AND STATUS IN THE PRIESTLY THEOLOGY
       Frank H. Gorman, Jr

92   ON HUMOUR AND THE COMIC IN THE HEBREW BIBLE
       Edited by Yehuda T. Radday & Athalya Brenner

93   JOSHUA 24 AS POETIC NARRATIVE
       William T. Koopmans

94   WHAT DOES EVE DO TO HELP? AND OTHER READERLY QUESTIONS
       TO THE OLD TESTAMENT
       David J.A. Clines

95   GOD SAVES:
       LESSONS FROM THE ELISHA STORIES
       Rick Dale Moore

96   ANNOUNCEMENTS OF PLOT IN GENESIS
       Laurence A. Turner

97 THE UNITY OF THE TWELVE
    Paul R. House
98 ANCIENT CONQUEST ACCOUNTS:
    A STUDY IN ANCIENT NEAR EASTERN AND BIBLICAL HISTORY WRITING
    K. Lawson Younger, Jr
99 WEALTH AND POVERTY IN THE BOOK OF PROVERBS
    R.N. Whybray
100 A TRIBUTE TO GEZA VERMES:
    ESSAYS ON JEWISH AND CHRISTIAN
    LITERATURE AND HISTORY
    Edited by Philip R. Davies & Richard T. White
101 THE CHRONICLER IN HIS AGE
    Peter R. Ackroyd
102 THE PRAYERS OF DAVID (PSALMS 51–72):
    STUDIES IN THE PSALTER, II
    Michael Goulder
103 THE SOCIOLOGY OF POTTERY IN ANCIENT PALESTINE:
    THE CERAMIC INDUSTRY AND THE DIFFUSION OF CERAMIC STYLE
    IN THE BRONZE AND IRON AGES
    Bryant G. Wood
104 PSALM STRUCTURES:
    A STUDY OF PSALMS WITH REFRAINS
    Paul R. Raabe
105 RE-ESTABLISHING JUSTICE
    Pietro Bovati
106 GRADED HOLINESS:
    A KEY TO THE PRIESTLY CONCEPTION OF THE WORLD
    Philip Jenson
107 THE ALIEN IN ISRAELITE LAW
    Christiana van Houten
108 THE FORGING OF ISRAEL:
    IRON TECHNOLOGY, SYMBOLISM AND TRADITION IN ANCIENT SOCIETY
    Paula M. McNutt
109 SCRIBES AND SCHOOLS IN MONARCHIC JUDAH:
    A SOCIO-ARCHAEOLOGICAL APPROACH
    David Jamieson-Drake
110 THE CANAANITES AND THEIR LAND:
    THE TRADITION OF THE CANAANITES
    Niels Peter Lemche
111 YAHWEH AND THE SUN:
    THE BIBLICAL AND ARCHAEOLOGICAL EVIDENCE
    J. Glen Taylor
112 WISDOM IN REVOLT:
    METAPHORICAL THEOLOGY IN THE BOOK OF JOB
    Leo G. Perdue

113 PROPERTY AND THE FAMILY IN BIBLICAL LAW
Raymond Westbrook

114 A TRADITIONAL QUEST:
ESSAYS IN HONOUR OF LOUIS JACOBS
Edited by Dan Cohn-Sherbok

115 I HAVE BUILT YOU AN EXALTED HOUSE:
TEMPLE BUILDING IN THE BIBLE IN LIGHT OF MESOPOTAMIAN
AND NORTHWEST SEMITIC WRITINGS
Victor Hurowitz

116 NARRATIVE AND NOVELLA IN SAMUEL:
STUDIES BY HUGO GRESSMANN AND OTHER SCHOLARS 1906–1923
Translated by David E. Orton
Edited by David M. Gunn

117 SECOND TEMPLE STUDIES:
1. PERSIAN PERIOD
Edited by Philip R. Davies

118 SEEING AND HEARING GOD WITH THE PSALMS:
THE PROPHETIC LITURGY FROM THE SECOND TEMPLE IN JERUSALEM
Raymond Jacques Tournay
Translated by J. Edward Crowley

119 TELLING QUEEN MICHAL'S STORY:
AN EXPERIMENT IN COMPARATIVE INTERPRETATION
Edited by David J.A. Clines & Tamara C. Eskenazi

120 THE REFORMING KINGS:
CULT AND SOCIETY IN FIRST TEMPLE JUDAH
Richard H. Lowery

121 KING SAUL IN THE HISTORIOGRAPHY OF JUDAH
Diana Vikander Edelman

122 IMAGES OF EMPIRE
Edited by Loveday Alexander

123 JUDAHITE BURIAL PRACTICES AND BELIEFS ABOUT THE DEAD
Elizabeth Bloch-Smith

124 LAW AND IDEOLOGY IN MONARCHIC ISRAEL
Edited by Baruch Halpern & Deborah W. Hobson

125 PRIESTHOOD AND CULT IN ANCIENT ISRAEL
Edited by Gary A. Anderson & Saul M. Olyan

126 W.M.L. DE WETTE, FOUNDER OF MODERN BIBLICAL CRITICISM:
AN INTELLECTUAL BIOGRAPHY
John W. Rogerson

127 THE FABRIC OF HISTORY:
TEXT, ARTIFACT AND ISRAEL'S PAST
Edited by Diana Vikander Edelman

128 BIBLICAL SOUND AND SENSE:
POETIC SOUND PATTERNS IN PROVERBS 10–29
Thomas P. McCreesh

129   THE ARAMAIC OF DANIEL IN THE LIGHT OF OLD ARAMAIC
Zdravko Stefanovic

130   STRUCTURE AND THE BOOK OF ZECHARIAH
Michael Butterworth

131   FORMS OF DEFORMITY:
A MOTIF-INDEX OF ABNORMALITIES, DEFORMITIES AND DISABILITIES
IN TRADITIONAL JEWISH LITERATURE
Lynn Holden

132   CONTEXTS FOR AMOS:
PROPHETIC POETICS IN LATIN AMERICAN PERSPECTIVE
Mark Daniel Carroll R.

133   THE FORSAKEN FIRSTBORN:
A STUDY OF A RECURRENT MOTIF IN THE PATRIARCHAL NARRATIVES
Roger Syrén

135   ISRAEL IN EGYPT:
A READING OF EXODUS 1–2
G.F. Davies

136   A WALK THROUGH THE GARDEN:
BIBLICAL, ICONOGRAPHICAL AND LITERARY IMAGES OF EDEN
Edited by P. Morris & D. Sawyer

137   JUSTICE AND RIGHTEOUSNESS:
BIBLICAL THEMES AND THEIR INFLUENCE
Edited by H. Graf Reventlow & Y. Hoffman

138   TEXT AS PRETEXT:
ESSAYS IN HONOUR OF ROBERT DAVIDSON
Edited by R.P. Carroll

139   PSALM AND STORY:
INSET HYMNS IN HEBREW NARRATIVE
J.W. Watts

140   PURITY AND MONOTHEISM:
CLEAN AND UNCLEAN ANIMALS IN BIBLICAL LAW
Walter Houston

141   DEBT SLAVERY IN ISRAEL AND THE ANCIENT NEAR EAST
Gregory C. Chirichigno

142   DIVINATION IN ANCIENT ISRAEL AND ITS NEAR EASTERN ENVIRONMENT:
A SOCIO-HISTORICAL INVESTIGATION
Frederick H. Cryer

143   THE NEW LITERARY CRITICISM AND THE HEBREW BIBLE
David J.A. Clines & J. Cheryl Exum

144   LANGUAGE, IMAGERY AND STRUCTURE IN THE PROPHETIC WRITINGS
Philip R. Davies & David J.A. Clines

145   THE SPEECHES OF MICAH:
A RHETORICAL-HISTORICAL ANALYSIS
Charles S. Shaw

146 THE HISTORY OF ANCIENT PALESTINE FROM THE PALAEOLITHIC PERIOD
TO ALEXANDER'S CONQUEST
Gösta W. Ahlström

147 VOWS IN THE HEBREW BIBLE AND THE ANCIENT NEAR EAST
Tony W. Cartledge

148 IN SEARCH OF 'ANCIENT ISRAEL'
Philip R. Davies

149 PRIESTS, PROPHETS AND SCRIBES: ESSAYS ON THE FORMATION
AND HERITAGE OF SECOND TEMPLE JUDAISM IN HONOUR OF
JOSEPH BLENKINSOPP
Eugene Ulrich, John W. Wright, Robert P. Carroll & Philip R. Davies (eds)

150 TRADITION AND INNOVATION IN HAGGAI AND ZECHARIAH 1–8
Janet A. Tollington

151 THE CITIZEN-TEMPLE COMMUNITY
J.P. Weinberg

152 UNDERSTANDING POETS AND PROPHETS: ESSAYS IN HONOUR OF
GEORGE WISHART ANDERSON
A.G. Auld

153 THE PSALMS AND THEIR READERS: INTERPRETIVE STRATEGIES
FOR PSALM 18
D.K. Berry

154 MINḤAH LE-NAḤUM: BIBLICAL AND OTHER STUDIES PRESENTED TO
NAHUM M. SARNA IN HONOUR OF HIS 70TH BIRTHDAY
M. Brettler and M. Fishbane (eds)

155 LAND TENURE AND THE BIBLICAL JUBILEE: DISCOVERING
A MORAL WORLD-VIEW THROUGH THE SOCIOLOGY OF KNOWLEDGE
Jeffrey A. Fager

156 THE LORD'S SONG: THE BASIS, FUNCTION AND SIGNIFICANCE OF
CHORAL MUSIC IN CHRONICLES
J.E. Kleinig

157 THE WORD HESED IN THE HEBREW BIBLE
G.R. Clark

158 IN THE WILDERNESS
Mary Douglas

159 THE SHAPE AND SHAPING OF THE PSALTER
J. Clinton McCann

160 KING AND CULTUS IN CHRONICLES:
WORSHIP AND THE REINTERPRETATION OF HISTORY
William Riley

161 THE MOSES TRADITION
George W. Coats

162 OF PROPHET'S VISIONS AND THE WISDOM OF SAGES: ESSAYS IN
HONOUR OF R. NORMAN WHYBRAY ON HIS SEVENTIETH BIRTHDAY
Heather A. McKay and David J.A. Clines

163   FRAGMENTED WOMEN:
       FEMINIST (SUB)VERSIONS OF BIBLICAL NARRATIVES
       J. Cheryl Exum
164   HOUSE OF GOD OR HOUSE OF DAVID:
       THE RHETORIC OF 2 SAMUEL 7
       Lyle Eslinger
166   THE ARAMAIC BIBLE: TARGUMS IN THEIR HISTORICAL CONTEXT
       Edited by D.R.G. Beattie & M.J. McNamara
167   SECOND ZECHARIAH AND THE DEUTERONOMIC SCHOOL
       Raymond F. Person
168   THE COMPOSITION OF THE BOOK OF PROVERBS
       R.N. Whybray
169   EDOM, ISRAEL'S BROTHER AND ANTAGONIST:
       THE ROLE OF EDOM IN BIBLICAL PROPHECY AND STORY
       Bert Dicou
170   TRADITIONAL TECHNIQUES IN CLASSICAL HEBREW VERSE
       Wilfred G.E. Watson
171   POLITICS AND THEOPOLITICS IN THE BIBLE AND POSTBIBLICAL
       LITERATURE
       Edited by Y. Hoffman & H. Graf Reventlow
172   AN INTRODUCTION TO BIBLICAL ARCHAEOLOGY
       Volkmar Fritz
173   HISTORY AND INTERPRETATION:
       ESSAYS IN HONOUR OF JOHN H. HAYES
       Edited by M. Patrick Graham, William P. Brown & Jeffrey K. Kuan
174   'THE BOOK OF THE COVENANT':
       A LITERARY APPROACH
       Joe M. Sprinkle
175   SECOND TEMPLE STUDIES:
       2. TEMPLE AND COMMUNITY IN THE PERSIAN PERIOD
       Edited by Tamara C. Eskenazi & Kent H. Richards
176   STUDIES IN BIBLICAL LAW:
       FROM THE HEBREW BIBLE TO THE DEAD SEA SCROLLS
       Gershon Brin
177   TEXT-LINGUISTICS AND BIBLICAL HEBREW:
       AN EXAMINATION OF METHODOLOGIES
       David Allan Dawson
178   BETWEEN SHEOL AND TEMPLE:
       A STUDY OF THE MOTIF STRUCTURE AND FUNCTION OF THE I-PSALMS
       Martin R. Hauge
179   TIME AND PLACE IN DEUTERONOMY
       James G. McConville and John G. Millar
180   THE SEARCH FOR QUOTATION:
       VERBAL PARALLELS IN THE PROPHETS
       Richard Schultz

181 THEORY AND METHOD IN BIBLICAL AND CUNEIFORM LAW
    Edited by Bernard M. Levinson
182 STUDIES IN THE HISTORY OF TRADITION:
    MARTIN NOTH'S UBERLIEFERUNGSGESCHICHTLICHE STUDIEN
    AFTER FIFTY YEARS
    Edited by Steven L. McKenzie & M. Patrick Graham
183 RELIGION OF SEMITES-LECTURES ON THE RELIGION OF THE SEMITES
    (SECOND AND THIRD SERIES)
    Edited by John Day
184 PURSUING THE TEXT:
    STUDIES IN HONOUR OF BEN ZION WACHOLDER
    Edited by John C. Reeves & John Kampen

GENERAL THEOLOGICAL SEMINARY
NEW YORK